Theatre Lethbridge

A History of Theatrical Production in Lethbridge, Alberta (1885-1988)

George Mann

Detselig Enterprises Ltd.
Calgary, Alberta

© 1993 **George Mann**
    Lethbridge, Alberta

Canadian Cataloguing in Publication Data

Mann, George Adolf, 1931-
  Theatre Lethbridge

  Includes bibliographical references.
  ISBN 1-55059-055-3

  1. Theater – Alberta – Lethbridge – History.   I. Title.
PN2306.L4M36   1993   792'.097123'45   C93-091508-9

Detselig Enterprises Ltd.
210, 1220 Kensington Road N.W.
Calgary, Alberta T2N 3P5

Printed in Canada   SAN 115-0324   ISBN 1-55059-055-3

To the Memory of

Alex Johnston

Cathy Evins

William Andrew (W.A.) Rea

and

Alfred William (A.W.) Shackleford

This book is also dedicated to the
many theatre practitioners included herein
To Them
Many Grateful Thanks

Contents

Tables

Preface

In 1978-79, my interests in history and drama were combined formally when I had the opportunity to spend the academic year studying theatre history under the tutelage of Alan Hughes and Linda Hardy at the University of Victoria. Upon my return to Lethbridge, I assumed the maintenance of the scrapbooks for the Playgoers Club, of which I had been a member since 1963. After becoming aware of the fact that the scrapbooks were incomplete and that considerable data, particularly from some of the early years of the club, was missing, I decided to fill the gaps as much as possible and to document completely all of the scrapbook entries dating from 1923 to the present. As I did so, I became intrigued with other artistic endeavors within the city of Lethbridge, and subsequently, resolved to extend my research and to publish a book on the history of the arts in Lethbridge. An integrated study seemed ideal because of the considerable interdependence that existed between the various arts and artists. When the data collection process was half completed, I realized that my ideal topic was too extensive for a single volume; therefore, I decided to focus on theatrical production since it is in such production that the various arts are most obviously interrelated. I also chose to concentrate on those productions which were produced primarily by and for adults. In addition, my interest turned to how theatre in Lethbridge was influenced by broader regional, national and international forces in the theatre and how local theatrical persons and activities affected the broader scene.

With regard to sources of information about local productions, I relied heavily upon newspaper reports, organizational documents and personal interviews. To document theatrical activities external to Lethbridge, I referred more specifically to published materials. I am pleased to report that the publication of Canadian data has increased tremendously during the past few years — stimulated to a large extent by the efforts of the Association for Canadian Theatre History — now the Association for Canadian Theatre Research. Wherever possible, I verified information from one source by seeking supporting reference elsewhere. For information appearing in the Lethbridge newspapers, I sought verification in other newspapers such as the *Macleod Gazette*, the *Saskatchewan Herald*, the *Calgary Herald* or the *Medicine Hat Daily News*. Later news reports were verified through perusal of theatrical programs or by personal interviews.

With regard to the time frame of this study, it was my original intention to cover the 100 year period from 1885-1985. Unfortunately, theatrical productions, whether amateur or professional were rare in the early pioneer days in Lethbridge. However, a tradition of production was firmly established in the summer of 1888, when Captain Burton Deane of the North West Mounted Police (NWMP) presented the first of many subsequent productions under his direction. Accordingly, I decided to extend my research through the summer of 1988. It is recognized, of course, that these dates are quite arbitrary; however, one has to establish limits and in this instance, 1988 was a practical limit as far as organizing and developing the content of this book was concerned.

George Mann
Lethbridge, Alberta. September, 1993

Acknowledgements

I would like to express my sincere appreciation to all those people and groups who provided me with resource materials and/or information. The University of Lethbridge library and its personnel were extraordinarily helpful; members of the Sterndale Bennett family: Muriel Ritchie, Michael Sterndale Bennett, Paddy Jury and John Sterndale Bennett have been very kind in providing information and contacts for me. The following people also supplied me with significant information: Bernadette Carpenter, Eildon Kondaks, A.W. Shackleford, Kaye and Murray Robison, Joy Pritchard, Muriel Jolliffe, Joan Waterfield, Marie Louise Loescher, Brian Parkinson, Richard Epp, Lawrence Adams, Dean Goodman and numerous members of the Lethbridge artistic community. Specialized advice and assistance, provided by Dr. William Baker, Professor, Department of History, University of Lethbridge; Dr. Alex Johnston, local historian (and recipient, Honorary Doctor of Laws Degree, University of Lethbridge); Greg Ellis, City of Lethbridge Archivist, and his staff; Marlene Menard, Technical Writer and Instructor, University of Lethbridge; Robert Thomsen, Computing Services, University of Lethbridge; and Craig Bullock, Computing Services, University of Lethbridge, were most beneficial. I acknowledge the support of the Playgoers Club of Lethbridge which encouraged the early stages of my study by providing me with a research grant which, in conjunction with a Federal STEP grant, enabled me to hire a student assistant, Lawrence Kopp, whose help and advice were invaluable. I also acknowledge the assistance of the University of Lethbridge Research Fund insupporting two other excellent research assistants, Jim Nikkel and Hillary Tarleck. My deepest gratitude is reserved for my secretary, Carol Tomomitsu and for my wife, Nellie. Both have shown remarkable patience and understanding. Carol typed numerous drafts of the manuscript and provided valuable advice and information about the potential of the word processor. Her constant good humor was also very much appreciated. Nellie has been my greatest source of encouragement. I am most grateful to her for her critical advice as well as her editorial and proofreading assistance. Nellie's extensive knowledge of dramatic literature and theatre history has proved to be particularly beneficial.

Additional Credits

The author would like to thank the following organizations, whose financial assistance has helped to make the publication of this text possible:

The Lethbridge Foundation

Lethbridge Musical Theatre

Also, I would like to acknowledge the sources of the photographs contained in this book and to thank the individuals and institutions which gave me permission to use them:

City of Lethbridge Archives
A.W. Shackleford
Glenbow Museum (Calgary)
The Playgoers Club of Lethbridge
The Sterndale Bennett Family
Doris Balcovske
University of Lethbridge Archives
The Lethbridge Herald
Jean Warburton

In addition, I would like to express my gratitude to the past and present publishers of the various newspapers cited within this text. Their generally excellent coverage of local theatrical activities has contributed immeasurably to the authenticity of this work. Special permission to cite works has been received from the publishers of the following newspapers:

The Calgary Herald, The Edmonton Journal, The Lethbridge Herald, The Macleod Gazette, Medicine Hat News, The Leader-Post (Regina)*, The Globe and Mail* (Toronto), *Moose Jaw Times.*

A special thank you is extended to Don Doram, publisher, *The Lethbridge Herald*, for allowing me to quote so liberally from the *Herald*.

The kindness of the following copyright holders is acknowledged: The Tyrone Guthrie Centre; Curtis Brown Ltd.; City of Lethbridge Archives and Records Management; Dean Goodman; Glenbow Museum; Lethbridge Historical Society; Maclean Hunter; Pat Pettigrew; Russell and Volkering Inc., Literary Agents; University of Alberta Alumni Association; University of Lethbridge. (For additional acknowledgements, see the Bibliography.)

Permission to cite from or to refer to information in numerous books and journals has been granted by the publishers whose works have been essential to this publication. Care has been taken to trace the ownership of copyright material used in the text. The author and publisher welcome any information enabling them to rectify any reference or credit in subsequent editions.

Detselig Enterprises Ltd. appreciates the financial support received for its 1993 publishing program from Canada Council, Department of Communications, and the Alberta Foundation for the Arts, a beneficiary of the Lottery Fund of the Government of Alberta.

1

The Pioneer Era (1885 - 1905)

Community Setting

In 1985 the City of Lethbridge, Alberta, celebrated its one hundredth birthday. This centennial anniversary date for the founding of Lethbridge is based on the argument that, although the nomadic Blackfoot Indians had previously occupied the area, and although recent non-indigenous entrepreneurs had coal mined the banks of the adjacent Oldman River (then referred to as the Belly River), a permanent settlement was not assured until the summer of 1885.[1] It was then that the North-Western Coal and Navigation Company, Ltd. (NWC&NCo) completed the construction of a narrow gauge railway line to Coalbanks (Lethbridge) from the CPR junction at Dunmore, just east of Medicine Hat. This company began its mining operations at Coalbanks in 1882; however, its economic prospects floundered considerably during the initial years because of the lack of adequate transportation access to potential markets. Then, Alexander Galt, the major promoter of the company, was able to arrange financing for the proposed railway line; subsequently, the first train arrived on August 25, 1885.[2] Shortly thereafter (on October 15, 1885), the community was officially named Lethbridge after the first president of the NWC&NCo, Mr. William Lethbridge, an associate of the English publishing and distributing firm, W.H. Smith and Co.[3]

Once reliable delivery of coal from Lethbridge was assured, the demand for the local product increased dramatically, resulting in rapid demographic and socio-economic changes for the community. To accommodate the increasing population (by 1891 the population of Lethbridge had passed the 2 000 mark), construction of homes and businesses began in earnest, complemented by the emergence of significant social institutions. A detachment of the NWMP was established; a weekly newspaper, (the *Lethbridge News*) was founded; churches, schools, and medical facilities were planned. Nevertheless, Lethbridge was basically a company town during those first few years. The local coal industry experienced remarkable growth and the town's economic future looked promising; Lethbridge was touted as the emerging industrial centre of western Canada. However, a severe depression in the early 1890s temporarily halted this growth and dampened the promotional enthusiasm. Immediate effects of the depression were manifest in the closing of businesses and the abandonment of residences as net migration to the community declined considerably.[4] It was not until Lethbridge began to evolve as an agricultural centre near the turn of the century that its economic outlook began to brighten again. The catalyst for this economic diversification was the development of irrigation, which was achieved through the cooperative efforts of Alexander Galt's son, Elliott Torrance Galt (the first resident manager of the NWC&NCo), Charles A. Magrath (the company's land commissioner), and recent Mormon immigrants who began, under the leadership of Charles Ora Card, to settle southwestern Alberta in 1887.[5] These first Mormon settlers became relatively prosperous; therefore, many other members of the Church of Jesus Christ of Latter Day

1

Saints (LDS) were enticed to move to the area. Based upon their farming experience in Utah, these new residents quickly demonstrated the advantages of irrigating southern Alberta farmland. By September 1899 irrigation was extended to the environs of Lethbridge by the Canadian North-West Irrigation Company.[6] The promise of good irrigated land, at reasonable prices, attracted many additional settlers to the neighboring rural areas, for which Lethbridge was viewed as the major trading centre. Fortunately, too, the depression had abated; consequently, the local population growth rate increased somewhat, commercial and residential construction picked up considerably, and all signs pointed to "economic prosperity" again.[7]

During much of the frontier era under discussion, the town remained a fairly isolated community. Since Lethbridge was not located on the major western Canadian transportation routes, travel to and from the town was difficult. Although travellers could proceed from Medicine Hat to Lethbridge via the narrow gauge railway (replaced by CPR regular gauge in 1893),[8] connections were neither timely nor convenient. In addition, the railway line terminated at Lethbridge; travel beyond Lethbridge was limited to horseback, horse and carriage, or stagecoach. The latter conveyance travelled to Macleod via ferry over the Belly River three days per week (Sunday, Tuesday, and Thursday).[9] Unfortunately, the weather often wreaked havoc with the ferry and it was put out of commission on numerous occasions. A bridge across the river at Lethbridge was completed in September 1890; however, for some time after this, the approaches to the bridge were considered inadequate, so most people continued to use the ferry.[10] Unquestionably, travel to the west and north of Lethbridge continued to be rather difficult until the CPR completed the Lethbridge section of the Crowsnest Extension in April 1898. In the meantime, rail service to the south was provided in 1890 when the Galts completed the Great Falls and Canada railway line to the Montana city.[11]

Certainly, the difficulties encountered in travelling to and from Lethbridge, especially until the completion of rail service west to Macleod, did little to entice the professional performers and theatrical companies that had begun to tour western Canada following completion of the trans-continental railway. Nevertheless, a few companies did manage to reach Lethbridge by other transportation means. However, the number of touring companies which visited Lethbridge multiplied considerably after the Crowsnest Extension was completed. In the meantime, the community had to rely heavily upon its local talent for most of its early theatrical and musical entertainment. In addition, local performers were more willing to use the rather inadequate facilities which were available for theatrical performances.

Local Theatrical Facilities

Edwards reports that, in Canada, "most early theatres were, in fact, extensions of drinking parlors" or saloons.[12] Lethbridge was no exception. In December 1885 the *Lethbridge News* carried an announcement by Bourgoin and Boiteau, proprietors of Bourgoin's Saloon, that they had just added a "large theatre hall" to their premises, and that the hall would be available for public use every night of the week except Saturday when weekly concerts would be scheduled.[13] Bourgoin's Lethbridge Hall, was also the scene of various ladies' assemblies, balls, variety programs, and even roller skating.[14] The first entertainer to appear at the hall was Tim H. Dunne, whose press notices for his performance on December 22, 1885, advertised him as, "Professor T.H. Dunne, Late of the Egyptian Hall, Piccadilly, London, England."[15] Stuart informs us that Dunne was also an active Dramatic Club member in Calgary in early September 1884.[16] More information about Dunne's theatrical career will be presented later in this chapter.

Bourgoin's Lethbridge Hall did not appear to be completely adequate for entertainment purposes. The editor of the *Lethbridge News,* on numerous occasions, appealed for the construction of a "suitable building" for public meetings and entertainments.[17] Obviously, the proprietors also began to feel that their facility could be used more profitably, so in December 1888 the hall was converted into a restaurant.[18] Fortunately, by this time, some optional facilities were available. Four church halls were constructed in the town during 1886 and 1887, and these buildings, though relatively small, could accommodate musical concerts and other small entertainments. Although there is little evidence that St. Patrick's Roman Catholic Church was used for such programs, St. Augustine's Anglican Church, Knox Presbyterian Church, and Wesley Methodist Church were frequently put to this purpose.

It was the dining room (mess hall) of the local North-West Mounted Police (NWMP) barracks that replaced the Lethbridge Hall as the major theatrical venue. In the summer of 1885 Lethbridge became the home of a small detachment of the NWMP. Soon thereafter, the force decided to establish a major post in the town. A building contract for the necessary barracks to house a division was awarded in October 1886,[19] and construction was completed by early 1887, at which time the non-commissioned officers and men of D Division, NWMP, sponsored the first annual Police Ball in the new dining room. The ball was attended by 200 guests who danced to the music of a local seven piece orchestra.[20] Shortly thereafter, K Division, under the command of Superintendent A.R. Macdonnell, replaced D Division. For many years, members of K Division were instrumental in stimulating both theatrical and musical entertainment in the community. Their commanders were also responsive to the need for more adequate performing space, so they made the mess hall available for such artistic productions. The first documented entertainments of this kind to take place at the "Barracks Hall" occurred on December 16 and 20, 1887. The evenings' programs included vocal and instrumental music as well as some short dramatic works.[21]

Shortly after these programs, it was rumored that a dramatic club was being formed in K Division and that the members, together with some ladies from the community, were planning to give a performance.[22] There is no evidence, however, that such a performance did occur in the winter or spring of 1888. However, a very important development, destined to affect the role of the NWMP in the local theatre scene, took place in May 1888. Captain R. Burton Deane took over command of K Division after being transferred from Regina where he had been stationed for a number of years in various responsible positions – most recently as commander of "the Depot Division to which all recruits were posted. . . . ."[23] He was also responsible for the secure detention of Louis Riel. While in Regina, Deane organized a theatrical troupe composed primarily of police personnel and their wives.

Deane's interest in theatre was soon demonstrated in Lethbridge by his willingness to direct and to act in many local productions and to encourage touring professionals and theatre companies to use the Barracks Hall, even though it was generally recognized that this space was not entirely functional for such activities. In support of this latter contention is the following statement which appeared in a special railway edition of the *Lethbridge News* published in September 1890 on the occasion of the opening of the Great Falls and Canada Railway:

> The kindness of the Commandant of the Northwest Mounted Police force here has enabled the use of the Barracks' mess room to be had whenever occasion requires, but having been built for military rather than operatic purposes, the hall is somewhat unsuitable.

Deane was considerably more optimistic about the facility. In his reminiscences, he writes:[24]

The Division messroom was a fine big room opening through double doors into a spacious kitchen. It was easy to construct proscenium and stage fittings in a more or less permanent form and to leave a passageway about eight feet wide through the stage without in the least interfering with the ordinary purposes of the room.

More adequate facilities were, however, being planned for the community. The railway edition, referred to above, reported that a building company comprised of various respected members of the business and professional community had been formed "with the object of erecting substantial buildings for public and private purposes." Actually, provisional directors were named for the Lethbridge Building Company (Limited) as early as September 1887.[25] One of the Company's major building enterprises was to construct an $18 000 building, referred to as the Building Company's Hall, located opposite the city square (Galt Gardens) on Glyn Street (7th St.). The main floor of this building was to be used for entertainments, public meetings, theatrical productions, and similar activities. The *Lethbridge News,* Railway Edition, described the prospective hall in the following way:

> It will be a two-storey brick with 75 feet of a theatre pit, but 43 feet in width. The stage will be 33 feet in depth, with dressing rooms in the rear and at the sides of the stage. A gallery will also be put in. This will probably be the finest building of its kind in the Territories.

Later editions of the paper described the theatre further by indicating that the stage, which was twenty feet wide, was provided with professional scenery, and that the theatre was outfitted with 400 seats manufactured by the Bennett Furnishing Company of London, Ontario.[26]

The hall took approximately a year to build, primarily because of a shortage of materials, especially bricks.[27] A touring magician, Signor Bosco, performed at the Building Company's Hall in October 1891; however, the official opening function was a grand Masonic Ball held on Wednesday, November 25. The first actual theatrical performance to be given at the Building Company's Hall was produced by Captain Deane and his local players who, on December 23, 1891 (the second official opening), presented *The Porter's Knot* (a one act play) and *Illustrious Stranger* (four acts).

The Building Company's Hall was the community's first real "Opera House," and it became the venue for many succeeding amateur productions. However, it was still very difficult for touring professionals to include Lethbridge in their itinerary. The ensuing economic depression contributed to the fact that little artistic use was made of the hall during its first five or so years. This fact brought into question its economic viability as a theatre space. As the economy was later spurred on by the development of irrigation, the building's potential as an office complex became apparent; therefore, the building was sold in 1899 to the Alberta Railway and Irrigation Company and was, henceforth, referred to as the A R & I Building. In this regard, the *Lethbridge News* reported:[28]

> The Building Company's Hall as a place of amusement will be a thing of the past in the course of a few days. The carpenters are now tearing out the stage and fittings preparatory to partitioning it off into offices for the Irrigation Company.

Fortuitously, a new hall for public gatherings, concerts, and theatrical performances was about to open its doors. In the spring of 1899, Mr. William Oliver, a local contractor and entrepreneur (and mayor of Lethbridge from 1901 through 1904), moved his Round Street blacksmith shop to some buildings at the rear of his property, and then proceeded to convert the lower level of his existing 47' x 72' two storey building into a hall.[29] This new "Opera House" or Oliver's Hall was opened in late August 1899 with the usual ball (under the auspices of the local bicycle club). The November 23, 1899, edition of the *Lethbridge News* reported that Oliver's Hall, which was fitted with stage, scenery, piano, electric lights, and seating for an audience of 350, could be rented for the following rates:[30]

1. $15 per night for touring groups or $10 per night if rented for more than one night

2. $10 per night for local entertainments and balls

3. $7.50 per night for social activities

Oliver's Hall was then, the only "theatre facility" in Lethbridge and basically remained so until the Lyceum Theatre was opened in 1908.[31]

Building Company' Hall (Opera House); later referred to as the AR&I Building.
Photo: City of Lethbridge Archives and Records Management.

Amateur Theatrical Activities

It was the two major institutions of social control, the Church and the NWMP, which provided the community with its first local musical and dramatic entertainment. Most of the "leading citizens" in the community were major participants in the local churches, especially the Protestant churches. In addition, the NWMP officers were regular church attenders and Captain R. Burton Deane was a valuable member of St. Augustine's Anglican Church. Together, these two institutions provided the personnel for most of the local theatrical and musical activities.

Since one of the major functions of these amateur activities was to provide charitable support for worthy causes, concert evenings were presented in aid of the community's churches, libraries, and recreation halls. The first documented evidence of local dramatic activity in Lethbridge was a "Social and Concert" held at Knox Presbyterian Church in August 1886.[32] In addition to musical selections, a number of recitations were offered. Later that same year, another concert at the Presbyterian Church also included recitations as well as readings.

Various entertainments were held in 1887 in order to raise funds for furnishings for the Presbyterian Church and for St. Augustine's Anglican Church. The Presbyterian Christmas entertainment on December 16 included a scene from *School for Scandal.*[33] The December 20th program, held at the NWMP Barracks under the auspices of St. Augustine's Ladies Aid Society, was unusual for Lethbridge in the sense that the evening concert concluded with possibly the first amateur production of a complete, albeit a short play, *Martyr to Science.*[34] Unfortunately, although the soloists and instrumentalists who participated that evening are listed in the *Lethbridge News* write-up, the cast of the farce are not. Additional concert evenings were held in the spring of 1888 but the programs were generally restricted to tableaus, shadow pantomimes, recitations, and of course, musical numbers. An exception to this practice occurred in April when scenes from *Bluebeard* and *The Bohemian Girl* were included in the program.

Captain Deane Provides the Impetus for Community Theatre

Once Captain Deane took over command of K Division, he encouraged his associates and a few others in the community to combine their talents both for the benefit of the community and for the creative fulfillment of the individual participants. A portent of future developments was contained in a *Lethbridge News* article in the summer of 1888 when it was reported that a forthcoming dramatic and musical entertainment in aid of St. Augustine's Anglican Church was put in charge of Captain Deane who, according to the *Lethbridge News,* "so successfully managed the amateur theatricals in Regina last year." The success of Dean's theatrical endeavors in Regina is verified by the *Regina Leader* whose reviews of the original farcical comedy, *Engaged* (January 1888), and of the two act W.S. Gilbert comedy, *Sweethearts* (February 1888), state, respectively, that:[35]

> Captain Deane had the leading role in "Cheviot Hill," a young man of property with a soft head, close fisted as a miser and with a peculiar mania for proposing to every female that crossed his path. As is always the case, Captain Deane made his part a splendid success. . . . In Captain Deane's hands, supported by the talent of Regina and the Barracks, an entertainment will always be anticipated with pleasure.

> The second entertainment of the series under the direction of Captain Deane was given on Wednesday evening the 22nd inst. in the concert hall, at the Barracks to a fairly large audience. . . . Captain Deane as Mr. Harry Spreadbow and Mr. White-Fraser as Wilcox filled their respective parts satisfactorily and well.

During his positing in Regina, Deane produced, directed, and acted in at least seven plays, four of which were presented in the first two months of 1888.[36] Notable among the casts of some of the later productions were Sergeant and Mrs. Tim Dunne as well as Inspector and Mrs. White-Fraser, all of whom, subsequently, appeared in Lethbridge productions.

R. Burton Deane was a former British military officer who had distinguished himself in military activity in Africa before coming to Canada and enlisting in the NWMP. He was appointed an Inspector in the North-West Mounted Police on July 1, 1883, and was promoted to Superintendent the following year. Although he was born in India (April 30, 1848), he was educated in England where he completed his formal education at the Royal Military College in Sandhurst. His British schooling undoubtedly included some dramatic instruction and experience. It is certainly clear that his interest and involvement in the theatre developed long before his coming to Lethbridge.

Undoubtedly, Captain Deane was the major catalyst for community theatre in Lethbridge until the mid-1890s.

On August 16, 1888, the long promised evening of entertainment under the direction of Captain Deane took place in the dining room of the NWMP Barracks. Deane relates the circumstances leading up to the program in the following way:[37]

> We had not been there [Lethbridge] very long when my friend Mr. C.F.P. Conybeare, K.C., presented himself one morning "as a deputation of one" to say that the newly built church was badly in need of pews and to ask if it would be possible to get up a theatrical entertainment in aid of funds on that behalf. I replied that it would be quite easy if the townspeople would lend a hand.

Musical entertainment that evening was provided by the Anglican Church Choir and its soloists as well as by guest musicians from Macleod: Mrs. P.R. Neale (wife of Superintendent Neale of the NWMP detachment in Macleod), Miss Harwood (the future Lady Steele), Mr. F.W.G. Haultain, Dr. L.G. DeVeber, and Staff Sergeant Bagley. The evening's entertainment was capped off with a short comedy, *Cut Off With a Shilling*, directed by Captain Deane who also performed in the playlet. Dean reports that the profits for the program amounted to about one hundred dollars. Although this money was donated to St. Augustine's Church, other evidence suggests that it did not aid the pew fund. Rather, the program in December 1889 contributed to that need. The review for *Cut Off With A Shilling* in the *Lethbridge News* stated that the acting of Captain Deane and Mr. and Mrs. White-Fraser was "equal to many professionals."[38] Before being transferred to Lethbridge, Inspector White-Fraser had completed postings in Regina and Battleford where Mrs. White-Fraser had garnered considerable praise for her acting and singing; the *Regina Leader,* commenting about her portrayal of Jenny Northcott in the February 28, 1888, production of *Sweethearts*, stated, "Mrs. White-Fraser's impersonation . . . was one that will add fresh laurels to the reputation of a very clever amateur actress."[39] While in Lethbridge, her talents as both a singer and actor were recognized. But the White-Fraser's stay in Lethbridge was short lived. Inspector White-Fraser was soon stationed in Pincher Creek for a short period, then in Maple Creek. While living in Maple Creek, Mrs. White-Fraser occasionally returned to Lethbridge for concert engagements. White-Fraser retired to Wardner, British Columbia, in early 1898.[40]

Three months after his first local success, Captain Deane presented two more plays at the Barracks to raise money for reading materials for the Barracks' recreation room. The program on November 20-21, 1888, was an "original domestic drama" entitled *The Chimney Corner* plus a comedy, *Ici on parle français.* The *Lethbridge News* commented that a large and appreciative audience attended both evenings and that "the acting throughout was very good"; the cast sustained their parts "to perfection." This was particularly true of Captain Deane and Mrs. White-Fraser who, in both plays, acted "as though to the manor [sic] born." Receipts amounted to $225.[41]

Approximately one year later, the Barracks was the scene of the musical and dramatic evening in support of new seats and choir stalls for St. Augustine's Church. Mrs. R.F. (Anna) Godwin (wife of the manager of the Union Bank and sister of C.A. Magrath) supervised the musical portion; Captain Deane directed the play, *Dearest Mama.* The *Lethbridge News,* again, reported that a large and appreciative audience was in attendance, and that it was treated to acting that "could scarcely have been improved upon." Captain Deane, as Browser, was described as "simply splendid"; Mr. Charles McCaul, Q.C., was "admirable as Croker." Others in the cast such as Norris T. Macleod were termed "excellent." Young Miss Dolly Jardine as Edith was "quite well possessed." A newcomer to Lethbridge theatricals, Mrs. P.R. Neale, "acquitted herself well in a difficult part."[42] Superintendent and Mrs. Neale had stimulated the development of the performing arts while Neale was Commander of H Division in Macleod. Superintendent Neale organized theatricals in Macleod and Mrs. Neale performed in a number of the productions there. Mrs. Neale was also an accomplished singer and pianist. In February 1889 the Neales moved to Lethbridge where Mrs. Neale contributed immeasurably to the musical and theatrical life of the community for many succeeding years.[43]

These early amateur productions were short one act plays, but in 1890 Captain Deane undertook something more demanding. On March 17 and 18, he presented a bill of two plays which included a major production, *The Wonderful Woman* (described as the first dress play in the Territories), and a somewhat less ambitious offering, *Betsy Baker*. With respect to costuming *The Wonderful Woman*, Deane reports:[44]

> To me, one very interesting feature of this venture was the facility with which we were able to dress the characters. I procured the necessary wigs in Chicago, and, for the rest, J.G. Baker & Co., of St. Louis, had had in the town since its inception a general store which was able to supply us with velveteens and such other finery as was needed to make our costumes.

By this time, Tim (T.H.) Dunne had become involved with Captain Deane's company of local amateurs. Dunne, who had taken up employment in the Alberta Railway and Coal Company's (AR&CCo's) machine shop, had previously made quite a name for himself in various western Canadian communities as an entertainer, actor, and scenic designer. In addition to taking the role of Crepin (a cobbler) in *The Wonderful Woman*, he also provided new scenery for the evening's production – scenery which was roundly applauded.

In a 1935 interview, Mrs. H. (Margaret) Bentley recalls that Dunne was the "clever comedian" of the group. She also reports that: Captain Deane not only directed but also played the leading male roles, Mrs. Neale portrayed the leading ladies, Dolly Jardine was a delightful comedienne, and she (Mrs. Bentley) took the ingenue parts.[45] Mrs. Bentley was another member of the Anglican elite whose husband, Harry, a very successful local entrepreneur, was mayor of Lethbridge during the years 1892-93 and 1896-98.

Captain Deane's portrayal of the Marquis de Frontenac in *The Wonderful Woman* was described as admirable; in addition, the local critic commented, "Encomiums have long since been exhausted in describing that gentleman's excellence as an actor."[46] On March 20, the Lethbridge troupe travelled to Macleod to perform *The Wonderful Woman* and *Cut Off With a Shilling* in support of the Presbyterian Church. The White-Frasers, who were now living in Pincher Creek, joined Captain Deane in the cast of the latter play. In the reminiscent interview referred to earlier, Mrs. Bentley reports that the troupe almost lost all their scenery and props when they broke through the ice as they were fording the river near Kipp (a few miles west of Lethbridge).

The year 1891 was a very active one for amateur dramatics in Lethbridge. Anna Godwin produced an operetta, *The Pedlar,* in January; Tim Dunne organized a Literary Society among the employees of the Alberta Railway and Coal Company, which produced an evening of plays near the end of the year, and Captain Deane presented plays in September and December. In the September program, Deane combined his talents again with those of Mrs. Godwin who resurrected *The Pedlar;* Captain Deane relied on the old standby, *Ici on parle français*. This interesting season of amateur theatre was concluded on December 23, with Captain Deane's offering of a major four act play, *Illustrious Stranger*, in conjunction with a one acter, *The Porter's Knot.* As mentioned earlier, these productions were mounted to commemorate the opening of the Building Company's Hall. Captain Deane, in the role of Sampson Burr, was described as "a natural"; Mrs. Bentley was"great"; and Mrs. Neale was "an excellent, proficient amateur." Mr. Clarke, on the other hand, was described as "lacking the freedom and grace of a good actor."[47]

A THEATRICAL

ENTERTAINMENT

Will be given at the

Mounted Police Barracks,

LETHBRIDGE,

Monday AND Tuesday,

March 17th and 18th, 1890,

AT 8 O'CLOCK.

To commence with a Comic Drama, in Two Acts, entitled

"The Wonderful Woman."

CHARACTERS:

The Marquis de Frontignac	CAPTAIN DEANE.
The Viscount de Millefleurs	MR. H. F. GREENWOOD.
Rodolphe, (a young artist)	MR. C. C. McCAUL.
Crepin, (a cobbler)	MR. T. DUNNE.
Madame Hortense Bertrand, (a rich widow)	MRS. NEALE.
Cecile	MRS. H. BENTLEY.
Maid,	MRS. DEANE.

Tailor, Servants, etc.

SCENE I.—Tapestry Chamber in Madame Bertrand's House in Paris.

SCENE II.—The Cobbler's shop near Paris, opposite the entrance gate and Chateau of the Marchioness de Frontignac.

A lapse of Ten Months between the Acts.

To conclude with a Farce, in one Act, entitled,

"BETSY BAKER."

CHARACTERS:

Mr. Marmaduke Mouser,	MR. H. MARTIN.
Mr. Crummy,	MR. N. T. MACLEOD.
Mrs. Mouser,	MISS DUFF.
Betsy Baker,	MISS JARDINE.

SCENE.—Room in Mr. Mouser's House.

Entire New Costumes & Scenery.

Admission, 50cts.; Reserved Seats, 75cts.

Tickets can be procured at the Post Office, where plan of Hall may be seen.

A Theatrical Entertainment (March 17 and 18, 1890)
Photo: City of Lethbridge Archives and Records Management

The success of the December play productions and of a subsequent musical concert (February 16, 1892) stimulated the call for the creation of a more formalized choral and drama society. In February 1892 an organizational meeting was chaired by H. Bentley; Captain Deane consented to take charge of the dramatic activities, Mrs. Godwin agreed to direct the choral work, and W.G. Cleveland, whose conducting and instrumental talent had recently been displayed at the aforementioned concert, undertook to oversee the orchestra. The following officers were elected to the executive of the new Lethbridge Choral and Dramatic Society:[48]

President: C.A. Magrath

Vice-President: H. Bentley

Secretary Treasurer: J.E. Lethbridge

Executive Committee: Captain R.B. Deane, N. T. Macleod,
                          W.G. Cleveland, Dr. L.G. DeVeber

Musical and Dramatic

ENTERTAINMENT

——AT THE——

BARRACKS MESSROOM,

On Thursday, September 10th, 1891,

Under the Auspices of the Lethbridge Building Company.

Programme.

OPERETTA :

"THE ● PEDLAR."

Characters.

PETER	- - -	MR. N. McLEOD.
REUBEN	- - -	MR. W. G. CLEVELAND.
DOLLY	- - -	MRS. GODWIN.
CHERRY	- - -	MRS. DEACON.
PEDLAR	- - -	MISS ENID MARTIN.

Song . . . . "A che la morte" . . . . Verdi.
Dr. DE VEBER.

Piano Solo . . . . "Marche du Concert" . . . . Wollenhaupt.
Miss M. SHERLOCK.

Song . . . . "The Boys of England" . . . .
Mr. MATHEWS.

. . . . "Three Little Maids" . . . . .The Mikado.
(By special request.)

Song . . . . "The Skipper of St. Ives" . . . .
Mr. N. T. McLEOD.

Vocal Duett . . . . "Army and Navy" . . . .
Dr. DeVeber and Mr. MATHEWS.

Chorus . . . . "Come where my Love lies Dreaming" . . . .

To conclude with the Farce,

"ICI ON PARLE FRANCAIS."

Characters.

MAJOR REGULUS RATTAN	- -	MR. DUNNE.
VICTOR DUBOIS	- - -	CAPTAIN DEANE.
MR. SPRIGGINS	- - -	MR. MARTIN.
MRS. SPRIGGINS	- - -	MRS. NEALE.
ANGELINA (their Daughter)	-	MRS. BENTLEY.
JULIA (wife of Major Rattan)	-	MRS. GODWIN.
ANNA MARIA (a Maid of All Work)	-	MISS JARDINE.

Scene.—A Fashionable Watering Place.

Doors open at 8 o'clock, to commence at 8.30, sharp.

ADMISSION, 50c.   RESERVED SEATS, 75c.

Musical and Dramatic Entertainment (September 10, 1891).
Photo: City of Lethbridge Arvhices and Records Management

This executive further illustrates the close relationship which the performing arts in Lethbridge had with the prominent citizenry of the town. H. Bentley took over the mayor's office in 1892. He succeeded Charles A. Magrath who was, in fact, the first mayor of Lethbridge (1891). Magrath relinquished that position when he took a seat on the NWT Legislative Assembly. He later represented the Lethbridge-Medicine Hat riding in the Federal Parliament (1908-1911). Dr. DeVeber set up his medical practice in Macleod after receiving his discharge (in Calgary) from the NWMP; however, he had since moved to Lethbridge.[49] DeVeber replaced Magrath as MLA for Lethbridge in 1898 and held the seat through 1905, after which he was elevated to the Canadian Senate. Norrie T. Macleod was a nephew of Colonel James F. Macleod of the NWMP. It is certainly true that these and other leading citizens in the community organized many cultural and recreational associations in order to make Lethbridge a more attractive and "civilized" place in which to live. Another feature of these pioneer artistic societies that becomes apparent when perusing lists of executives is the fact that, although women participated in many of the programs, even as accompanists and directors, it was the "gentlemen" who functioned in the major organizational roles.

Decisions arrived at during the initial meeting of the choral and drama society included: 1) the assessment of a monthly membership fee of fifty cents; 2) the drawing up of a constitution and bylaws by the executive; and 3) the provision of some type of entertainment every two weeks. As it turned out, it was impossible to live up to the latter intention, and, in fact, only two artistic activities were generated by the organization: a major theatrical production and a choral concert, both of which were scheduled for May of that year. The dramatic presentation of this new society was a three act comedy by W.J. Byron, *Not Such a Fool as He Looks,* directed by Captain Deane. The play was staged at the Building Company's Hall on May 4; unfortunately, the weather was so miserable that very few people turned out to see what was described by the local critic as "one of the best performances it has been the privilege of a Lethbridge audience to witness." Again, Captain Deane and T.H. Dunne, were described as "excellent"; Miss Jardine, Mrs. Neale, and Mrs. Conybeare acted, according to one of the critic's favorite expressions, "as to the manor [sic] born."50

Mrs. Ida Conybeare was a relative newcomer to Lethbridge. Her marriage to the local lawyer and crown prosecutor, Charles Frederick Pringle (C.F.P.) Conybeare, took place in St. Paul, Minnesota, in the summer of 1890.[51] Shortly thereafter, the former Ida Letitia Atwood made her debut on the Lethbridge stage when she performed the role of Cherry in Anna Godwin's production of the operetta, *The Pedlar.* Henceforth, the Conybeares gave considerable support and status to community theatre as did two of their children (Elaine and Ethel) and their grandchildren, especially, Bernadette Fisher and Eildon Brander.

Over two and a half years passed before another production was mounted by the Captain. Possibly, Deane was discouraged by the lack of response to his hard work in the spring of 1892. But a number of other circumstances probably contributed to this theatrical hiatus. For example, Captain Deane lost some of the mainstays of his acting contingent. The transfer from Lethbridge of the White-Frasers was a severe enough blow, but Tim Dunne's subsequent move to Butte, Montana, in July 1892 left a decided void in the local company of thespians. To complicate matters more, Captain Deane fell ill for a couple of months in the early part of 1893. In addition, inspections among the detachments of his district (including the Canadian-American border) were beginning to require more and more of his time.

Nevertheless, another evening of musical and dramatic entertainment at the Building Company's Hall, under the supervision of Mrs. Godwin and Captain Deane, was organized on December 3, 1894. The evening's entertainment included a two act farce, *Who Killed Cock Robin,* which played to a well filled house. First United Church benefitted by the amount of $80. This presentation concluded Captain Deane's major theatrical efforts in Lethbridge except for a reprise of one of his earliest productions, *Dearest Mama,* in 1901. In the interim, his official police duties multiplied considerably. In 1897 he was assigned, in addition to his supervisory responsibilities in Lethbridge, the task of commanding the Macleod NWMP post.[52] For a rather extended period of time, he was required to spend three days per week at each post. Inspector Morris took charge at Lethbridge during the Captain's semi-weekly absences. The conscientious manner in which Captain Deane performed his duties was rewarded in September 1898 when he and Mrs. Deane were able to take their first holiday in fifteen years. They spent about a month at the West Coast. Approximately a year after his return, it was announced that the Superintendent would be transferred to Macleod and that his position in Lethbridge would be filled by Inspector Cuthbert.[53] Just prior to this move, the Deanes were occupied with arrangements for the marriage of their eldest daughter, Jessie, to W.G. Dickinson of Victoria (formerly with the AR&CCo. in Lethbridge).

The Deanes had just barely settled in Macleod when the Captain's responsibilities were extended again to include command of the posts at Macleod and Lethbridge. Consequently, in 1900 Captain and Mrs. Deane moved back to Lethbridge, and Captain Deane had the opportunity to display his directing and acting talents, locally, one more time. It was in April 1901 that he gave his farewell performance and once again regaled the audience with his portrayal of Browser in the comedy, *Dearest Mama*; Ida Conybeare portrayed the title role. Mrs. Bentley played a designing flirt who was attracted to the cynical and circumspect Nettle Croker, played by W.C. Ives. W.H. Macdonald, who frequently entertained Lethbridge audiences with his comic dance routines, portrayed Harry Clinton, the "too happy newly married man." On this occasion, St. Augustine's Rectory fund benefited from the evening's activities. Captain Deane undoubtedly experienced extra pleasure from this production since his youngest daughter, Lily, joined him in the cast, taking the role of the ingenue, Edith Clinton.[54] Miss Deane had gained some previous acting experience performing in a number of productions while attending the local St. Aloysius Convent School.

Captain Deane left Lethbridge permanently when he was transferred to Maple Creek (1902). In 1906 he was moved to Calgary, where he served as Commanding Officer of the Calgary detachment until his retirement in 1914. After his move from Lethbridge, Deane maintained close ties with friends in Lethbridge as evidenced by the fact that, upon the death of his dear wife, Martha, in late 1906 he called entirely upon old Lethbridge friends to act as pallbearers.[55] In addition, his oldest son, Dr. Reginald Deane, joined Dr. Frank H. Mewburn's Lethbridge practice from 1908-1910, after which he practiced in Calgary.[56] Close contact was also maintained with Macleod since Deane's daughter, Lily, had recently married Superintendent Primrose of the Macleod detachment of the NWMP.

Deane's move from Lethbridge brought an end to the close and direct relationship which had existed between the NWMP force and local dramatic activities. Further separation between the community and the NWMP occurred in 1902 when Lethbridge hired its own police constable.[57] On the other hand, the religious institution maintained its close ties with the artistic community. This latter relationship was preserved both indirectly and directly. Many participants in community arts organizations were active church members; in addition, the churches continued to sponsor many musical and dramatic activities.

T.H. Dunne Organizes the Employees' Literary Society

Although Captain Deane was the major driving force behind local theatre during the period under discussion, the work of a few other individuals such as the acting and the scenic designing of T.H. Dunne is certainly noteworthy. Although some of the details of Dunne's life are unknown, what appears in various documents suggests a rather checkered but extraordinarily interesting career. Skinner informs us that:[58]

> Dunne was from London, England, and it was there that he received his training in stagecraft, in particular at the Prince of Wales Theatre. He came to Canada in 1870 and was for awhile stationed with the School for Gunnery at Quebec before joining the NWMP in 1876. (While in Quebec he was called upon to perform for the Governor General and Lady Dufferin.)

We are also informed that, as mentioned earlier, Dunne was active in a Calgary Dramatic Club more than a year before his Lethbridge appearance on December 22, 1885 (as a professional magician). We later note that both he and his wife participated in Deane's productions at the Regina Barracks in the winter of 1888 and in other Regina presentations during the spring of that year. The *Regina Leader* was always very complementary about the various theatrical activities of Dunne and about the acting of his wife:[59]

> It is scarcely necessary to say that Sergt. Dunne as "Major McGillicudy" was perfection itself.

> Sergt. Dunne . . . was as mirth provoking as ever.

> Sergt. Dunne excelled himself with the scenery and artistic mounting of the pieces. . . .

> . . . Sergt. Dunne impersonated "Mr. Wigfall" the weak-minded, disheartened and woman-ruled "man" with his well-known ability.

> The "Steeplechase". . . was put on the boards with the following strong cast: . . .and a "Chambermaid" in which Mrs. Dunne appeared with excellent effort.

> Mrs. Dunne made a charming "Ruth" and we are looking forward to seeing her in the important roles.

At that time, Dunne was listed as a Sergeant with the NWMP. After leaving the NWMP, and subsequently, moving to Lethbridge, Dunne appeared in the March 1890 production of The *Wonderful Woman*. When the play toured to Macleod, the local *Gazette* made the following comment: "Mr. T. Dunne is pretty generally known throughout the territories as a clever and amusing actor." *The Lethbridge News* also complimented Dunne on the "fine scenic designs" which he created for T*he Wonderful Woman* and *Betsy Baker*.[60] Following *The Wonderful Woman,* Dunne took a number of other roles in Deane's productions: Major Regulus in *Ici on parle français* (September 10, 1891), Alebayon in *Illustrious Stranger* (December 11, 1891), and Mr. Mould in *Not Such a Fool as He Looks* (May 14, 1892). In this latter production, he was responsible again for newly painted scenery. It should be kept in mind that it was not uncommon at that time for local theatres or opera houses to use standard scenery; accordingly, it was reported that additional scenery for this latter production was by "Cosman and Landis of Chicago."[61]

Besides participating in some of Deane's productions, Dunne also took it upon himself to organize a Literary society among the employees of the Alberta Railway and Coal Company and to direct its first production on November 30, 1891, at the Employees' Library Hall.[62] Presentations that evening included a farce, *Turn Him Out*, and a burlesque, *Bombastes Furioso*.[63] Mr. and Mrs. Dunne acted in both productions.

Luke the Laborer, presented in February 1892 was the second production of this group. T.H. Dunne, who played the title role, also directed the play. The local critic commented, "Mr. Dunne . . . is a well proved actor as is his wife." Mrs. Dunne played the leading female role. The local critic commended the group for its marvelous costumes and scenery, but showed some concern about the forgetting of lines. Additionally, the critic reported that H. Gregory excelled in the part of the cowardly Crasher in the second offering of the evening, "a laughable farce, *Slasher and Crasher.*" All in all, the evening, capped off with a dance, was declared a "pronounced success."64

Unfortunately for the local theatre scene, Dunne decided to leave Lethbridge in July 1892. The *Lethbridge News* of July 27, 1892, carried the following item:[65]

> Mr. T.H. Dunne who for the past three years has been in the employ of the A. R. and C. Company in the machine shops left on Sunday for Butte, Montana. We understand he has secured an engagement in the McGuire Opera House there.

Dunne later moved to Medicine Hat to manage the American Hotel and appeared again on a Lethbridge stage in 1896 when he performed with the Columbia Minstrels from Medicine Hat.[66] Later, we are told, "Tim Dunne left the CPR shops in Golden to join the Harry Lindley Company who will stock the Rossland Theatre next season."[67] Nevertheless, Dunne was not with the Lindley Company when it played Lethbridge a year later.

It was quite a few years before the theatrical void created by the leaving of Tim Dunne and Captain Deane would be filled. The dramatic expertise required to direct plays was lacking, and this situation lasted until 1909 when Richard Hincks emerged as the next major stimulant of local acting talent. In the meantime, musical productions in the form of operettas, as well as minstrel and variety shows, became the mainstay of community theatre in Lethbridge.

Locally Produced Operettas

Mrs. Godwin's production of *The Pedlar* was the first community operetta to be performed in Lethbridge. The operetta was offered at the Barracks on January 13, 1891, as part of a concert arranged in aid of the fencing fund for the Protestant Cemetery.[68] The operetta featured Mrs. Conybeare (Cherry), Mrs. Godwin (Dolly), Miss Jardine (the Pedlar), N.T. Macleod (Reuben), Sergeant Cleveland (Peter), and Mrs. Neale as accompanist. The concert netted receipts of one hundred and eighteen dollars and seventy-five cents. In a repeat performance on September 10, 1891, the cast was changed considerably although Mrs. Godwin maintained her role. The two male performers exchanged their roles; Miss Enid Martin replaced Miss Jardine; Mrs. Deacon took the role of Cherry.[69] A decade later, Miss Martin performed professionally at a musical concert held at Oliver's Hall on March 13, 1902. By this time, she had formed the Enid Martin Concert Company composed of herself, Fellowes Hanson (vocalist), and Edgar Baylis, LRAM (organist and pianist). The local Methodist Church sponsored the tour to Lethbridge. Prior to the concert, the *Lethbridge News* reported that, "The Western Press speaks very highly of the Company." Following the concert, the local reviewer stated that the Lethbridge audience acclaimed the artistic trio, and that Miss Martin, a former Lethbridge resident, displayed a "clear sweet voice" and sang "without effort."[70] Later that year, Miss Martin sang before Governor General and Mrs. Minto at Rideau Hall.[71] Possibly, Enid Martin was the first Lethbridge resident to become a professional concert singer. Others, such as Jessie Glover and William MacKenzie, were professionals before settling in Lethbridge.

During Captain Deane's holiday absence in 1898, the *Lethbridge News* reported that William MacKenzie (professional Scottish baritone and humorist) and his wife, Jessie Glover (soprano), who had been giving a series of entertainments in Lethbridge, had decided to stay in the town for three months; MacKenzie would give lessons in "voice culture and elocution" and would conduct the Methodist Church Choir. During the fall, the MacKenzies offered additional Sunday night sacred concerts as well as other evenings of concert, comedy, and drama to the delight of local audiences.[72]

Shortly after deciding to stay in Lethbridge for the fall, MacKenzie announced auditions for the Gilbert and Sullivan operetta, *The Pirates of Penzance*. The show, which ran for four nights in mid-December, was double cast except for the two leads, Frederic, played by Jessie Glover, and Mabel, portrayed by Mrs. A. Southard. The *Lethbridge News* reported that Miss Glover's work was the "most perfect piece of acting we've seen in Lethbridge." Also, the critic commented that Miss Glover was a professional, and that the addition of this lady was an excellent choice: "She was the only person who could handle the songs – certainly no local males could." Mrs. Southard, whose husband operated a men's clothing store on Redpath (3rd Avenue So.), was called "excellent in every respect."[73]

Following the success of this production, the MacKenzies decided to stay in Lethbridge for awhile longer. MacKenzie continued to lead the choir at Wesley Methodist Church and to give entertainments in aid of the church. In fact, the couple remained in Lethbridge until early fall 1899 when the local arts community tendered them, at Oliver's Hall, a grand farewell benefit concert of music, comedy, and drama. Then, the MacKenzies left for Chicago where Mr. MacKenzie report-edly joined the Castle Square Opera Company.[74] Just before they left for Chicago, an intriguing story about the MacKenzies appeared in the *Lethbridge News*.[75] The article quoted the Auckland, *New Zealand Star,* as reporting that Mr. W. MacKenzie and wife, (nee) Miss Jessie Glover, who recently had toured New Zealand with a concert company, had disappeared on a trip to the Klondike in Canada. It was feared that the pair had been swept away and drowned in the MacKenzie River when a ferry broke loose. The *Lethbridge News* was happy to report that the MacKenzies had planned such a trip, but that their sojourn in Lethbridge had kept them from following through with these plans.

It was more than two years before Lethbridge amateurs were to display their talents in another operetta. On January 24, 25, 1901, Miss Haas presented her production of *Gypsy Queen*. In addition to directing the show, Miss Haas, who had previously performed in a local concert in conjunction with a touring "Scottish entertainer" (Mr. T.J. Scott), portrayed the leading female role – Rosalie.[76] The *Lethbridge News* critic commented that these amateurs of Lethbridge scored a "surprising success" and that the audience displayed great interest in the production from start to finish. The title role was played by a prominent member of Lethbridge society, Mrs. Fred W. Downer; her portrayal was described as "resplendent."[77] Also included in the cast were Ethel and Elaine Conybeare, who as young fairies, were probably making their debuts on the Lethbridge stage; nevertheless, they were to grace that stage quite often, thereafter. In conclusion, it is interesting to note that a significant technical innovation was added to this production. H. Chase, who frequently worked the lights for local productions, apparently manufactured and operated an arc light chaser, which was described as "strictly up to date," and which "illuminated the stage in first class style."

Local Minstrel Productions

One of the most popular forms of American entertainment prior to the turn of the twentieth century was the minstrel show. The minstrel show was a kind of vaudeville in which the performers blackened their faces with burnt cork to appear on the stage as stylized Negroes. Even Black performers playing minstrels had to make up, accordingly. The minstrels sat in a semicircle, usually with a band behind them. An interlocutor or "straight man" acted as the master of ceremonies; he was assisted by a number of performers including the two end men, Mr. Bones and Mr. Tambo, who were usually played by the stars of the company. These minstrel shows featured comedy routines, singing, variety acts, and dancing. In those days, the minstrel show was considered to be an ideal type of program for amateur productions, especially when performed in aid of some worthy charity. The charitable nature of local minstrel productions encouraged support from leading professional and business members of the community, whose presence in the cast tended to attract even greater audiences. Such shows did not require the training and acting expertise necessary to produce a play, nor the time and effort to produce an operetta. Towns like Lethbridge and Macleod had residents with considerable musical training and ability. The churches attracted choir masters, whereas the NWMP and the colliery maintained excellent bands. Teaching opportunities opened up for private music instructors such as Mrs. Neale and Messrs. Wasterlain and Malacord, the latter two of whom, in the winter of 1889, opened a school of vocal and instrumental music.[78] Malacord also directed the colliery band. Balls and dances provided instrumental musicians with considerable opportunity to participate in dance bands and to practice their musical skills.

After witnessing the successful presentation of a minstrel show staged in Macleod (in early 1888 by members of H Troop, NWMP), potential Lethbridge participants were stimulated to produce minstrel shows as well. The Sunflower Minstrels were organized with John Gamble as Secretary Treasurer and C.W. Heller as Business Manager. This group performed at the Barracks in Lethbridge on February 18-19, 1889. Admission for the evening's entertainment was seventy-five cents for reserved seats and fifty cents for rush seats. The Sunflower Minstrels also toured to Macleod where the performance of Mr. Dougherty was particularly noted. A quick perusal of the cast list will verify that the participants were not the usual thespians and musicians who performed in the many evenings of musical and dramatic activities in Lethbridge; nevertheless, their presentation was very well received. The local newspaper reviewer commented, ". . . as amateurs, it can be said that the troupe exceeded the most sanguine expectations." Mr. John Gamble was singled out for his performance as a circus tight rope walker – a performance which apparently "took down the house."[79]

Other local theatrical activities temporarily eclipsed the Lethbridge minstrelsy interest, so the experience wasn't repeated until 1901. In the interim, however, Lethbridge audiences witnessed at least two such productions by Medicine Hat groups and a number of presentations by professional touring minstrel companies. Local interest was reawakened in February 1901 when the "Dark Town Swells" were organized. Their production, *The White Eyed Coterie,* was presented to large audiences on April 23-25, under the direction of E.A. Cunningham, stage manager and musical director. In those day, directors were usually referred to as stage managers. Cunningham had arrived in Lethbridge in August 1900 and was employed as storekeeper for the AR&ICo.[80] He was also appointed the choir director at St. Augustine's Anglican Church. From the point of view of audience appreciation and critical comment, the production was an extraordinary success. The local critic commented that it was the "most conspicuously successful local event in the history of our town."[81] Such success led to the formal organization of the Lethbridge Amateur Minstrel Club in September 1901 at a meeting called under the chairmanship of Mayor W. Oliver. The following executive (again, comprised of professional and business men) was elected, and plans were laid for another production in early 1902:[82]

Honorary President	– P.L. Naismith
Honorary Vice-President	– Dr. Mewburn
President	– Mayor W. Oliver
Vice-President	– T. McNabb
Secretary	– D.W. Kain
Treasurer	– G.W. Robinson
Musical Director	– E.A. Cunningham

```
Committee Members          - A.E. Humphries, A.G. Nedham,
                             G.H. Johnson, T. Burnett,
                             H. Chase
```

The sole production under the auspices of this organization took place on May 27-29, with the proceeds of the final show being designated for local flood relief and for victims of a recent explosion in Fernie, British Columbia. Although the local newspaper's review was again quite ecstatic, it was, nevertheless, a fairly well balanced review in that it praised some performances and criticized others. The review also noted that the production may have erred somewhat by being too long, and that the second part fell somewhat flat; nevertheless, the review complimented improvements shown in the second evening's performance. The orchestra was awarded "unstinting praise."[83]

A.E. Cunningham was now ensconced as the artistic director of such productions. With the help of Reverend J.S. Chivers (Rector, St. Augustine's Church) as assistant vocal director and Mrs. Neale as accompanist, another minstrel show was presented on April 20, 1904, under the auspices of the Ladies of St. Monica's Guild. This minstrel show was unique in the sense that it was made up of an all female cast. The effort was a great success. In the meantime, the gentlemen entertainers of the town had just completed an "hilarious" show for the local order of the IOOF. This show, referred to as *High Illustrious Grand Hiankidink: the Supreme Head of the Ancient Order of Hercules,* was advertised as an amusing takeoff on initiations into such secret societies. The aim to amuse was obviously fulfilled since it was reported that there was "scarcely a break in the laughter provoking situations."[84] Additional entertainment during the evening included a boxing match between the "Medicine Hat Murderer" and the "Lethbridge Kid".

Neighboring Theatrical Societies

The town of Macleod had a very active dramatic and musical environment, which was also stimulated by members of the NWMP. After Superintendent Neale and his wife moved to Lethbridge, Staff-Sergeant Heap took on the leadership role. Lethbridge residents often travelled to Macleod to see productions. Neighboring Mormon communities also showed an early interest in dramatic activities. There is evidence that Cardston drama associations were active within their own community well before they brought their production *Time and the Hour* to Lethbridge. This play was presented by the Cardston Mutual Improvement Association Drama Company in the Building Company's Hall on June 21, 1897.

In March 1900 the Magrath Amateur Comedy Company rented Oliver's Hall for two evenings and presented a drama, *Dutch Jake,* and a farce, *The Yankee Pedlar,* on the first evening and two other plays, *The Toodles* and *The Spectre Bridegroom,* on the second evening. Proceeds were to aid in the purchase of a new organ for their community's church. Within a month following this performance, the same Magrath group purchased the scenery created for the stage of the AR&C Company's reading room and gym by T.H. Dunne.[85]

Five years later, the Brigham Young Drama Society of Raymond, under the direction of Brigham S. Young, performed a four act comedy, *The Merry Cobbler,* on the evenings of February 6 and 7, 1905. Major roles were taken by Young, David Horton Elton, and Miss Sloan, the latter two of whom resided in Cardston. It was reported that "the piece was most creditably presented and that it offered much pleasure to those in attendance."[86] After the turn of the century, Brigham S. Young left his position with the Raymond newspaper and moved to Lethbridge. Then, in his leisure time, he became involved in musical theatre and dramatic activities, there. His co-actor, D.H. Elton, an exceptional person, was also associated with the development of southern Alberta community newspapers. He later established a very successful law practice in Lethbridge where he also became noted for his oratory. In addition, Elton was a highly respected mayor of Lethbridge during the years 1935-43.[87]

Medicine Hat theatre groups were probably more active than any others in southern Alberta. This contention is supported by the number of times groups from Medicine Hat toured their productions to Lethbridge. For example, the Georgia Minstrels, an amateur group from Medicine Hat, played a benefit at the Building Company's Hall on March 20-21, 1899, in aid of a Medicine Hat widow whose engineer husband had recently been killed in a bridge accident. The troupe also travelled to Fernie and Cranbrook for benefit performances. Medicine Hat minstrels (Columbia Minstrels) returned to Lethbridge on April 10-11, 1896, under the auspices of the Lethbridge Galt Hospital. Performing with this group was the former Lethbridge actor, T.H. Dunne. Orrell reports that these same Columbia Minstrels also played in Edmonton.[88] Three years later, the Medicine Hat Drama Club performed (under the auspices of the Medicine Hat Hospital) a comedy drama at Oliver's Hall, *For a Brother's Sin.*

Professional Theatre

Professional theatrical groups that toured to Lethbridge from 1885-1905 can be classified into six categories: 1) theatre stock companies; 2) single production or road show companies; 3) vaudeville or speciality companies; 4) minstrel organizations; 5) Uncle Tom companies; and 6) musical theatre (operetta) companies.

The touring theatre stock companies include those aggregations that presented plays, exclusively, whether farce, comedy, melodrama, or tragedy. Like resident stock companies, they presented a number of plays in repertoire; the genre of the programs tended to vary, although there seemed to be a preference for popular melodramas such as *East Lynne, The Two Orphans,* or *The Black Flag.* Many of these companies maintained residence in various communities for part of the year and then toured during the remainder of the year.

The Keene Theatre Company had the distinction of being the first theatre stock company to perform in Lethbridge. Their first engagement (in 1889) was in the Barracks Hall, and the leading lady, Caroline Gage, was destined to become a favorite with the local audiences. Gage returned as head of the company in 1890; at that time, her troupe was reported as being superior to the only other company to perform at the Barracks, the Star Theatre Company. In May 1892 The Caroline Gage Company also had the honor of being the first organized theatre company to perform in the Building Company's Hall – a performance which was, however, the company's last one in Lethbridge. The Carolyn Gage Company did play *A Double Wrong* in Macleod on June 24, 1893, on their way from Calgary to Great Falls. After leaving Macleod, the driver of the team carrying the troupe's equipment misjudged the water level in the river at Kipp, and again, the river took its toll. The water was higher than expected and the costume boxes were saturated. Consequently, J.B. Smith, who had been contracted to transport the outfit, lost about eighty dollars on the deal.[89] The Carolyn Gage Company never returned to southern Alberta. Such transportation difficulties, coupled with the economic depression, discouraged the touring of similar stock companies until January 1896, after which audiences at the Building Company's Hall witnessed the performances of an increasing number of theatrical companies. Companies bearing the names: Wilbur, Katie Putnam, Orris-Ober, Clara Hanmer, Aaron Johnson, Lyceum, Shirley and Russell, Buchanan, Stultz, and Cornyn toured to Lethbridge once, only. The Fraser Company appeared twice; however, the bookings occurred within a month in early 1896; thus, these two presentations could be considered part of the same tour. The Sherman and Platt Company also appeared twice (in June and November 1905); whereas, the Andrew McPhee Company and the French Theatre Company performed on three separate occasions.

The most consistent visitors to Lethbridge after the Carolyn Gage Company stopped touring to southern Alberta were the Harry Lindley - Clara Mathes Companies. The Harry Lindley Company was a Canadian stock company which played throughout Canada. Lindley preferred to spend as much time in British Columbia as possible; therefore, his company established residence in various B.C. communities for extended periods. But he toured Alberta from 1897-1902, and his company was always popularly received, even though, as Edwards maintains, he tended to pirate many of his plays.[90] The company was particularly honored whenever it visited Macleod; for example, following a full week run in August 1898, the entire company was feted to a banquet at the NWMP Barracks.[91] After this engagement, the company cancelled its promised tour to Lethbridge and headed back to British Columbia.[92] At the end of this tour, Clara Mathes, Lindley's leading lady, organized her own troupe which, after the turn of the century, performed in Lethbridge on six separate occasions. The Lindley Company returned on two other occasions with Miss Adelaide Flint as leading lady.

Two other Canadian actors and their companies, Harold Nelson and George Summers, became perennial favorites in the later years of this period as well as during the succeeding period. Edwards states that Harold Nelson was "apparently, an intelligent actor,"[93] and Stuart contends that Nelson should be remembered as a true theatrical pioneer "who was sincerely concerned with raising standards."[94] It is Douglas Arrell who provides us with the most complete analysis of Nelson's theatrical activities, his personal characteristics, and his talents. Arrell presents considerable evidence that, although Nelson was generally considered a fairly competent actor, a number of critics found fault with his acting style and elocutionary speech patterns.[95] Unlike most of his contemporaries, Nelson presented plays from the classical repertoire including many Shakespearian productions. Nelson was booked into Oliver's Hall on at least seven separate occasions from 1903-1905, and his performances there were invariably described as excellent. George Summers, known on the road as "the Canadian Comedian,"[96] made his Lethbridge debut in January 1905 and returned on numerous occasions, thereafter.

The Canadian theatre historian, Murray Edwards, has ranked various theatre companies which toured eastern Canada from 1880-1914 as follows: 1) The Touring Stars, 2) Some Lesser Known companies, and 3) The Rank and File of the Road.[97] Many of the companies which toured to Lethbridge are not included in any of these categories. This fact suggests that these latter companies either did not include eastern Canada in their tours or that they were insignificant or "fly-by-night" outfits. In addition, none of the companies which toured Lethbridge before 1906 are included in Edwards's two top categories; however, the following companies are included among the "Rank and File of the Road": Harry Lindley Company, Lyceum Dramatic Company, Harold Nelson and Company, Katie Putnam and Company, and George H. Summers Stock Company. Nevertheless, these were probably some of the better companies to tour western Canada in this early historical period. Theatre historians such as Evans, Orrell, and Stuart discuss the professional groups which toured to Edmonton and other western towns and cities in these early years. It seems that they were basically the same companies that appeared in Lethbridge. Certainly, C.P. Walker, from Winnipeg, who managed Harold Nelson, and also toured other productions to Lethbridge, was destined, shortly, to become western Canada's foremost theatre manager, agent, and tour promoter.

Before long, a number of touring productions were presented by C.P. Walker or other managers or producers such as Edward R. Salter or Arthur Aylesworth. Generally, these producers would tour the entire country or continent with the same play which would be presented over and over again.

Some independent companies such as The Too Rich to Marry Company and A Wise Member Comedy Company followed this same practice – a practice that became fairly standard when a growing number of Broadway productions toured the country. These troupes represented the second category listed earlier – the single production or road show companies.

Vaudeville, a form of entertainment made up of music, singing, dancing, skits, and other specialty performances began to play North American theatres around 1870. Shortly thereafter, theatres were built particularly for vaudeville; for example, the Gaiety Museum constructed in Boston by Benjamin Keith in 1883, Tony Pastor's Theatre in New York (1891), and later, the Palace, which opened in New York in the fall of 1913.[98] Vaudeville gradually became one of the most popular forms of theatrical entertainment, with its foremost period stretching from the early 1890s to the mid-1920s.

Vaudeville troupes which arrived in Lethbridge during the city's formative decade included: Dolan Comedy Co., Silver Speciality Co., Campbell and Seaches Pavilion Co., and the Oliver Comedy Co. Although these companies were given a good reception in Lethbridge, they did not make return engagements. Neither did the following troupes which played Lethbridge between 1897 and 1905, inclusive: Royal Specialty Co., R.H. Hardie's Ideals, Columbia Comedy Co., Miner East Comedy Co., Kelly Merry Makers, Otto Frechtl's Co., Clipper Novelty Co., The Strollers, Firth-Eaton Concert Co., Maridor-Goulding Co., Jolly Entertainers, Shipman Comedians, The Peerless Entertainers, Arnold Shows, and Patten and Perry Co.

It was not until the late 1890s that tours of vaudeville or comedy companies to Lethbridge became more regular and frequent. It was the Bittner Theatre Company (May 1899) which was credited with being the best drama and vaudeville company to come to Lethbridge up to that time. The Boston Comedy Company helped Lethbridge celebrate Canada's birthday (July 1, 1899). This company was one of the few specialty groups to play a return engagement. It is reported that, on this latter occasion, a very large audience was "kept in a continuous state of hilarity."[99] The Scottish Concert Co. also played Lethbridge on two occasions.

Lethbridge audiences had even less opportunity to develop a following or appreciation for any particular vaudeville or specialty organizations than they did for the touring theatre companies. The one early exception to this was the Cosgrove Family which toured to Lethbridge in 1898, 1902, and 1903. Later, Jimmy Fax and his Fax Concert Company became favorite entertainers in Lethbridge after their introduction in October 1903. Although the Fax Concert Company did not return until April 1906, the company made many succeeding Lethbridge appearances which the local audiences anticipated with pleasure because the company's first appearance "convulsed them with laughter."[100]

Lethbridge audiences did not witness professional minstrel shows until the genre was in its decline. Although a few amateur productions were mounted prior to 1900, the first professional troupe to come to town was the Willis Coontown 400 Company. Unlike most minstrel companies, this group, headed by Charlie Arnold, was made up of Black entertainers. They packed Oliver's Hall on a January evening in the year 1900, and the audience thoroughly enjoyed this performance.[101] The Willis Minstrels played two additional engagements in 1905. Richard and Pringle's Georgia Minstrels, who appeared in Lethbridge on three occasions (July 1901, July 1904, October 1905) were, according to the local critic, not of the same calibre. The Richest Coon in Georgia Company, which was the third minstrel company to play Lethbridge in 1905, was subsequently described by the local critic as the best of the three companies. Probably because its performance followed the other two companies, this latter troupe attracted very small houses.

Undoubtedly, the most popular play presented on American stages during the late 1800s was Uncle Tom's Cabin. In this regard, Blum states that:[102]

> Another '70's phenomenon was the explosion of Uncle Tom's Cabin dubbed "Tom Shows." By 1879 at least 50 productions were on the road. . . . By the 1890's almost 500 of the shows were reported in operation.

Gerould, who claims that *Uncle Tom's Cabin* was the "greatest success" in the history of the American theatre, explains the popularity of the "Tom Shows" in the following way:[103]

> Those two special melodramatic pleasures – excitation at flight and pursuit, and moral outrage at the victimization of innocence – find their highest expression in *Uncle Tom's Cabin.*

Again, Lethbridge lagged behind in theatrical experiences. The first such production staged there was in January 1903 when Wilson's Mammoth Uncle Tom's Cabin Company came to town. Surprisingly, the number of such companies touring to Lethbridge increased during the next historical period to be reviewed.

In addition to the vaudeville and minstrel shows, which contained a great deal of musical entertainment, musical comedy was brought to Lethbridge in the form of operetta – the standard form of musical theatre around the turn of the century. Possibly the most significant night of theatre in the history of the Building Company's Hall was the night of Friday, May 12, 1899, when the Metropolitan Opera Company's touring members supposedly made a special trip from Calgary to perform Gilbert and Sullivan's *The Mikado.* The *Lethbridge News* reports that this company was enticed to Lethbridge by a number of local backers who, stimulated by the largest advanced sale of tickets for any production in Lethbridge, convinced the company to make a detour to Lethbridge prior to their engagement in Calgary. Among the thirty members with the company were Will Rising (tenor), Blanche Aldrach (prima donna), Jeannette Lincoln, Agnes Millard, Alice James, Lillian Kemble, Charles Walters, Maurice Hageman (stage director), Eddie Smith, and Sidney Rhorer. Reserved tickets sold for $1.50; rush tickets were $1.00. This company also planned to stop at the Macleod rink on May 11, to perform *La Mascotte.*[104] Since no review appeared in either the *Lethbridge Herald* or the *Macleod Gazette,* the performances are problematic.[105]

Five years passed before C.P. Walker of Winnipeg brought operetta back to Lethbridge. He presented *La Mascotte,* which was performed by the Beggar Prince Opera Company (June 24, 1904). This company returned in November of the same year to perform *Fra Diaviolo* by Daniel F.E. Auber and *Girofle-Girofla* by Charles Lecocq. Both performances of this company were apparently very well received by the local audiences. But the *Lethbridge News* critic was much more impressed with the production of John Philip Sousa's opera, *El Capitan,* by The Roscian Comic Opera Company in December 1905. This company was described as, unquestionably, the best comic opera company to ever tour western Canada. Much to the pleasure of Lethbridge audiences, the company returned many times, thereafter.

Other Professional Entertainment

In addition to theatrical organizations and their productions, individual entertainers and small ensembles also visited Lethbridge. Among this group were a number of non-musical entertainers such as magicians, hypnotists, ventriloquists, impersonators, stand up comics (humorists), and elocutionists. Most of the early independent entertainers were magicians and hypnotists. Such entertainers were also commonly found among the vaudeville or speciality acts. Humorists were frequent visitors as well. Two of Lethbridge's favorites, Owen A. Smily and Walter McRaye, accompanied Pauline Johnson (Canadian poet) on her tours. Smily, who later toured with his own concert company, was once described by the local critic as "a prince of an entertainer." On the other hand, a recent analysis by Chad Evans reports that Smily had "slight but diverse talents," ("ventriloquism, musical mimicry, piano playing and jocosity").[106] Walt McRaye, former member of the Harry Lindley Company, and author of the book, *Town Hall Tonight*, enriched his reputation with his humorous readings from the works of Drummond.[107] Another well liked humorist was J.W. Bengough who illustrated his act with crayon sketches, particularly of prominent local citizens. Bengough, who was billed as Canada's most popular entertainer, played Lethbridge on at least four occasions from 1889-1912. Although Bengough generally lived up to his billing, the local critic commented on his second appearance, that some of his selections were "not up to standard."[108]

Beginning in 1890, elocutionists, as well as readers of drama and poetry, started to appear in Lethbridge. Occasionally, these entertainers were truly appreciated, for example, Agnes Knox (1890), Effie Elaine Hext (1894), Marietta La Dell (1897), Morrielle Patton (1903), and members of the Maridor-Goulding Company (1903). At other times, planned performances had to be cancelled because of lack of audience interest: Rube Allyn (1893), Marietta La Dell's second engagement (1903). Other performances simply were not well attended (Professor Rae, 1893). The Canadian poet, Pauline Johnson, was always a favorite, especially when she read her native poetry while dressed in full Mohawk regalia, which she did at some point in each of the four appearances she made in Lethbridge between September 1894 and June 1904.

Mass Entertainment

The circus has always been a favorite form of mass entertainment. In August 1898 the Lemen Brothers Circus advertised themselves as the first circus to visit Lethbridge. Apparently, the three major attractions were the bare back riding of Little Edna; Tom, the boxing Kangaroo; and Rajah, the elephant, which was advertised as the "largest elephant ever captured; he stands two inches taller than Barnum's Jumbo and weighs 2000 pounds more."[109] The *Lethbridge News* reported that while the circus was in town, a shell game was kept going nearly all afternoon even though the police closed it down a number of times. The *Macleod Gazette* stated that this circus was just like any other – no better, no worse. Nevertheless, Lemen Brothers reported that they took in more money in Macleod (where the circus played on August 24) than anywhere else in Canada.[110]

The Walter L. Main Circus set up its tent in Lethbridge on August 4 of the following year. Evans reports that this circus was a relatively large one, and that, unlike many other circuses of that day (especially Lemen Brothers), it "maintained a semblance of respectability." According to Evans, it was Main's ambition to be the best and cleanest circus on the road.[111] Nevertheless, about two weeks after the Lethbridge engagement, the following item appeared in the *Lethbridge News:*[112]

> The side show in connection with Main's Circus has been unfortunate on its tour in the west. A few days ago the "human skeleton" died in the hospital at Medicine Hat, and last week the giant died at Calgary.

Neither of these circus companies returned to Lethbridge, nor did any other circus pitch its tent until the Great Floto Show came to town in August 1905. Henceforth, the circus became a fairly regular annual visitor to Lethbridge.

Animal acts were always an important ingredient of the circus; they were also included in various vaudeville and specialty programs. In addition, independent animal shows occasionally appeared [Gentry Brothers (July 2, 1902) and Cozack's Famous California Show (August 14, 1905), which advertised itself as a dog and pony show].

A final form of entertainment to be introduced to Lethbridge was the motion picture. Of course, illustrated entertainment was not new. As mentioned earlier, the Canadian humorist and social critic, Bengough, mastered the art of cartooning and regularly illustrated his program with crayon sketches of local and other noted personalities. The projection of pictures was, however, a relatively recent form of entertainment. Reference to a "stereopticon entertainment" at Knox Presbyterian Church to illustrate *Pilgrim's Progress* was contained in an 1894 edition of the *Lethbridge News*.[113] A stereopticon was a projector for transparent slides. Later that year, a magic lantern show and musical entertainment was held at the Oddfellow's Hall.[114]

The exhibition of moving pictures occurred rarely during the period of history under discussion, but these infrequent showings, nevertheless, whetted the appetite for a form of entertainment that would very shortly become extremely popular. It was the Royal Animatograph and Specialty Company which, in August 1897 introduced moving pictures to Lethbridge. The animatograph (from the root word animate) was an early moving picture projector invented by Edison. Later that same year, the Cosgrove Family brought a kinetoscope with them. The kinetoscope, as defined by *Webster's Ninth New Collegiate Dictionary*, was a "device for viewing through a magnifying lens a sequence of pictures on an endless band of film moved continuously over a light source and a rapidly rotating shutter that creates an illusion of motion."[115] The film and its associated apparatus were housed in a large black box which, in turn, was commonly located in a penny, peepshow, or kinetoscope arcade. Ackery points out that only one person at a time could view the moving pictures through the eyepiece of the kinetoscope; Griffith, Mayer and Bowser comment that:[116]

> To see these scraps of film, you dropped a penny in a slot, looked into an aperture like that of a stereoscope, and ground a crank. A light flashed on, and for a minute you watched Fatima wiggle her torso or a small boy squirt the garden hose on a well-dressed gentleman.

In September 1900 the Emerald Duett Temperance Evangelists included moving pictures about the Boer War in their programs when they played to a full house at Oliver's Hall.[117] In late 1901, the *Lethbridge News* reported that local musicians had to help out with the program at Oliver's Hall when the cinematograph (another movie projector) began to give trouble. In July 1902 Professor Parke's Exhibition Company showed moving pictures of the Dawson mining scene and of the "mighty" Yukon River.[118] On October 2, 3, 1905, the London Bioscope Company presented moving pictures depicting an English stag hunt and the Making of a Great Newspaper.[119] It is quite conceivable that other such showings occurred during the period under discussion; however, no additional documented evidence could be located. It is certainly true, that the public was becoming intrigued by this new form of entertainment, and local entrepreneurs were becoming exhibitors throughout western Canada. Shortly (August 15, 1907), the Bijou Theatre was opened in the Hill Block of Lethbridge, and within a few months, manager G.A. Stevens, was regularly exhibiting films in other southern Alberta communities, as well.

2

The Touring Era (1906 - 1922)

Community Setting

On September 1, 1905, the provinces of Alberta and Saskatchewan were created. Shortly thereafter, on November 9, 1905, Alberta provincial elections were held, and A.C. Rutherford's Liberal Party took the reins of power. Lethbridge was represented by Liberal MLAs in the Alberta Legislature from 1905-1911 except for a short period in 1909.[1] By 1906 economic and political developments in Lethbridge were beginning to reflect the increased prosperity which southern Alberta had experienced for the past few years, especially since irrigation technology brought needed moisture to the parched farmlands in the southwest corner of the province. Transportation routes to the city had improved considerably, business and residential construction had accelerated somewhat, and the population had passed the 3 000 mark. In response to some of these developments, the Provincial Legislature granted the community a city charter on May 9, 1906, just as the city was to embark on the most dramatic period of demographic growth in its history. It was during the years 1906 - 1911 that Lethbridge experienced its most rapid rate of population increase ever; the city practically tripled in size during those five years.[2]

This urban growth was generally a by-product of the overall influx of immigrant farmers to southern Alberta in order to obtain farms in the dryland areas surrounding the city. Johnston and den Otter inform us that the first major rush of settlers in 1908 was subsequently followed by other rushes in 1910 and 1912.[3] As the major trading centre in the area, Lethbridge grew as well. By 1912 Lethbridge emerged as an important urban centre in western Canada which, nevertheless, remained closely integrated with its agricultural hinterland. This symbiosis was acknowledged by the Federal Government in 1906 when it selected Lethbridge as the site for one of the country's largest experimental farms (to be headed by Dr. W.H. Fairfield), and by the International Dry Farming Congress when it chose to hold its 1912 conference in the city.

In addition to these agriculturally related developments, many other socio-economic changes accompanied the rapid population growth. Commercial and residential real estate boomed; old industries such as the Lethbridge Iron Works (Foundry), and the Lethbridge Brewery and Malting Company became entrenched, whereas many new industries and businesses were established. The completion in 1909 of the new CPR viaduct (high level bridge) over the wide valley of the Belly (Oldman) River, helped to establish Lethbridge as a major railway centre, and also helped to reduce further the city's isolated status. This viaduct, which is over one mile long, is considered by many observers to be the city's most impressive, man made landmark.[4] The introduction in 1905 of a second newspaper, The *Lethbridge Herald,* and its conversion in 1907 to a daily paper, simultaneously reflected and fostered a more urban outlook.

The business community was ecstatic about the growth; the political leaders were convinced that the city was destined to continue its development for years to come. Optimism reigned supreme. Unfortunately, such rapid urban growth does not occur without some negative consequences. Modern sociologists consider an urban growth rate of about 3-4% per year to be about the maximum for which most North American communities can provide adequate municipal services at a manageable cost. The average annual growth rate in Lethbridge during the 1906 - 1911 period exceeded this optimum rate considerably, and thus, it created havoc with municipal planning and financing. City officials naturally anticipated that the growth would continue indefinitely; therefore, they planned numerous new subdivisions,[5] and they provided services for a much larger city. But the growth ground to a virtual halt with the economic downturn in 1913, followed by the declaration of World War I in 1914, after which the population of Lethbridge remained fairly stable until the late 1920s. In addition, the ecological pattern of the city changed very little until the 1950s. Although some growth was associated with the expansion of irrigation to the north, south, and east of Lethbridge, which began in 1917, this growth was rather short lived because the city suffered from the effects of another economic recession in the early 1920s, which resulted in the only population decline recorded within any census period in the city's history.[6]

Possibly the most significant general consequence of the expansive economic and demographic developments from 1906-1913 in Lethbridge was the fact that the community became more directly involved and thus, more clearly identified with western Canadian society and its political and social institutions. Consequently, Canada's participation in World War I was deeply felt by the citizens of Lethbridge. Extensive economic and military contributions to, and sacrifices for, the war effort stretched the boundaries of identification even further as Lethbridge residents became more acutely aware of the fact that their social structure and culture were seriously effected by external forces – some emanating from very distance sources.

A number of theatrical events characterized the first two decades of the twentieth century in western Canada. One such event was the growing influence of the motion picture industry, which stimulated the construction of local theatres to exhibit its ever increasing product. Another development was the increasingly dominant role which touring American and English road show companies played in providing theatrical entertainment for the masses in the "hinterland." Local demand for this type of theatrical entertainment was complemented by a demand for more adequate facilities to stage these productions; therefore, theatres like the Majestic (in Lethbridge) and the Sherman Grand (in Calgary) were designed primarily for the presentation of live theatre including the increasingly popular musical revues. Vaudeville also became a regular feature on the stages of both the movie houses and the legitimate theatres; soon Lethbridge was included in the circuits of the major western vaudeville exchanges (Pantages, Orpheum, Hippodrome). Then, there was the introduction of the annual Chautauqua which, according to Johnston and den Otter, first came to Canada to present its program of lectures, concerts, and plays in 1917.[7] Finally, there were the various touring military based shows which usually had their origins in the concert parties organized to entertain the troops overseas. But except for these latter two developments, the touring of professional theatre to Lethbridge had almost ceased by the early 1920s. In 1923 local amateur theatre became more prominent as the Little Theatre movement began to take hold in the city.

Local Theatre Facilities

During the economic boom years of the early twentieth century, most of the communities on the Canadian prairies witnessed considerable construction related to both legitimate theatre and the

TABLE 2-1

Theatres and Opera Houses by Location
Lethbridge, Alberta (1885 - 1989)

Map*	Location	Hall or Theatre	Operating Dates
1	1st Avenue & 4th Street South	Burgoin's Lethbridge Hall	1885 - 1888
2	NWMP Barracks (Civic Centre)	NWMP mess hall	1887 - 1891
3	207 - 7th Street South	Building Company's Hall	1891 - 1898
4	316 - 5th Street South	Oliver's Hall	1899 - 1908
5	Hill's Hall (4th Avenue South)	Bijou	Aug 15/07-Nov 7/08
6	410 - 5th Street South	Eureka	Oct 12/08-Nov 1911
7	330 - 5th Street South	Lyceum Starland Phoenix King's Kings	Oct 12/08-Sept 1910 Jan 28/11 Jun 21/20 Jan 1921 Feb 1922-Jul 1925
8	428 - 5th Street South	Bijou/Variety	Nov 20/11- 1917
9	512 - 5th Avenue South	Majestic	Jan 21/10-Nov 1942
10	5th Street South [opposite Eureka]	Grand Electric	Spring 1910
11	414-416 - 5th Street South	Morris Sherman Orpheum Colonial Palace Capitol	Nov 16/11-Aug 1913 Sept 1913-Feb 1915 Feb 10/15-Oct 1918 Oct 18/18-Dec 1924 Dec 6/24-Feb 1929 Feb 1929-1969
12	250 - 13th Street North (13th Street North)	Monarch Lealta	Dec 25/11-1918 Jan 5/38-Dec/40
13	258 - 13 Street North	Lealta	Dec 31/40-1963
14	328 - 5th Street South	Empress Roxy	Jan 7, 1913-Mar 1933 Oct 4/34-1959
15	246 - 13 Street North	Regent	1915
16	723 - 4th Avenue South	Paramount Paramount II	1950- 1967-
-	Mayor Magrath & Scenic Drive	Green Acres Drive-In	1951-1986
17	10th Street & 4th Avenue South	Yates Memorial Centre	May 1, 1966-
-	College Mall (Mayor Magrath Drive)	College Cinema	1969-
-	4401 University Drive (U of L)	U of L Drama Studio	1972-1977
-	4401 University Drive (U of L)	U of L Theatre Lab	1977-1981
8	418 - 5th Street South	Lethbridge Centre Cinemas I & II	1975-

Map*	Location	Hall or Theatre	Operating Dates
	4401 University Drive (University of Lethbridge)	U of L Theatre U of L Experimental Theatre	Mar 18, 1981- Apr 7, 1981-
18	Park Place Mall 501 - 1st Avenue South	Cineplex Odeon (6 cinemas)	Aug 1988-
17	Yates Memorial Centre	Sterndale Bennett	1990-

Sources: Lethbridge News, Lethbridge Herald,
Alex Johnston, A.W. Shacklford
*See Map: Theatre Locations, Downtown Lethbridge

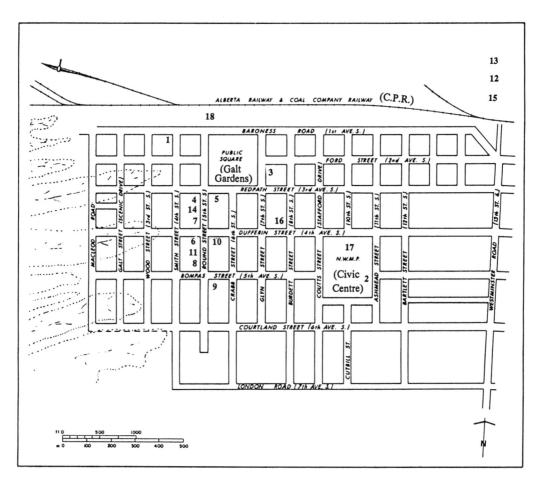

Theatre Locations Downtown, Lethbridge (see table 2-1)
Map: City of Lethbridge Archives (modified)

exhibition of movies. Lethbridge was certainly no exception. From 1907-1913 eight different theatre halls opened in the city. Because some of these halls subsequently closed during this time, the number which operated in any one year varied considerably. However, by 1913 six fairly permanent theatres were established: four movies houses (Bijou, Starland, Empress, and Monarch); one movie and vaudeville theatre (Morris); and one theatre designed primarily for live productions of plays and musicals (Majestic). For the following four to five years, Lethbridge patrons had a choice of more theatre venues than they were to enjoy for the next fifty years. It is true, however, that external forces such as the economic downturn of 1913, World War I (1914-1918), and the Spanish Flu (fall 1918) took their toll on these theatres. The following discussion will analyze the growth and decline of Lethbridge theatre facilities during this era, (1906-1922). Table 2-1, nevertheless, illustrates the life span of Lethbridge theatres through 1990.

Oliver's Hall

As this era began, Oliver's Hall was still the major venue for theatrical productions, lantern slide shows, and the occasional moving picture, but its future as a performance and exhibition facility was in jeopardy. William Oliver's various business enterprises, as well as his political career (mayor of Lethbridge, 1901 - 1904), demanded his attention. He advertised the building (valued at $4 900) for sale in March 1902 but apparently received no serious offers.[8] Then in August 1904 he considered leasing the building to Mrs. Hoaglin of Raymond, but again these plans did not materialize.[9] On March 1, 1907, the *Lethbridge Herald* reported that Oliver was planning to convert his building into a block of retail stores, and on April 11, 1907, the Herald carried the following news item:[10]

> The Labor Temple is to be used as an opera house for small companies after Oliver's Hall is no longer available. The bigger companies are to be cancelled until the new opera house is built.

At the same time, rumors were being spread that C.J. Eckstorm was considering building a new "up-to-date opera house"; however, neither this project nor a later proposal (spring 1908), whether seriously considered or not, ever came to fruition.[11] It is nevertheless true, that the Labor Union Hall and similar spaces around the city such as Hill's Hall and the Knights of Pythias Hall were called into temporary use as theatre spaces during 1907. In addition, some touring theatre companies pitched their own tents. Nevertheless, Oliver's Hall was employed for theatrical purposes until the 1908 Halloween performance of the Tom Marks Company.

Bijou (Variety) Theatre

By this time, additional theatre facilities had come into being. On August 15, 1907, the first regular movie house, the Bijou Theatre, began operating in Hill's Hall on Dufferin Street (Fourth Avenue South between 5th and 6th Streets) under proprietor and manager, G.A. Stevens.[12] The first moving picture to be offered at the Bijou was *The Bell Ringer's Daughter;* admission was $0.15 (adults) and $0.10 (children). Occasional vaudeville acts and fighting matches were presented as added attractions; admission under these latter circumstances was $0.25 and $0.15. Before long, Stevens also made weekly trips to Okotoks, High River, and Macleod to exhibit motion pictures one night per week in each town.[13] The competition of two somewhat more commodious theatres, the Lyceum and the Eureka, both of which opened on October 12, 1908, probably contributed to the closing of the Bijou Theatre on November 7 of that year.[14] At that time, manager Stevens advertised that the Bijou Hall would still be available for dances and other social gatherings. A farewell dance was held on November 25, after which G.A. Stevens left Lethbridge because he had purchased the Regina Bijou Theatre.[15] Shortly thereafter, the Hill Brothers built a more modern building on this site.[16] A new Bijou theatre on 5th Street South, managed by L. Huhl, opened on November 20, 1911.[17] In September 1912 a $10 000 addition to the Bijou Theatre was undertaken in order to double the seating capacity as described in the following excerpt from the Lethbridge Herald:[18]

> While the front of the new structure will become a 25 by 25 foot store, the bulk of the building will serve to double the movie house's seating capacity to more than 500.

Although the theatre was renamed the Variety for a few months in mid-1915, it returned to the original name in November of that year. For a short period, thereafter, it exhibited movies on Friday and Saturday nights, only, but eventually succumbed to competition from newer and more popular movie theatres. In 1917 the premises was converted into a garage and show room for the local Elgin automobile dealer; the establishment was referred to as the Bijou Motor Parlor.[19]

Lyceum (Starland, Phoenix, King's, Kings) Theatre

In addition to exhibiting films, the Lyceum became the major performing facility for live presentations until the Majestic usurped this function in early 1910. Vaudeville acts and movies were booked by Fred Brown, proprietor and manager, for the opening of the Lyceum; similar fare played throughout the fall 1908. The first major theatre company to perform there was the National Opera Company which staged the comic opera, *His Highness the Bey,* by Joe Howard, on November 30, 1908. This company was followed by the Tom Marks Stock Company which appeared in early January 1909. Soon, a number of touring companies were attracted to Lethbridge by this new facility, even though it had its shortcomings. Some of the weaknesses were pointed out in the following comments made by the *Lethbridge Herald* reviewer in his conclusion of the review for *His Highness the Bey*:[20]

> Say Manager Brown, why don't you enlarge that stage, raise the top, arrange for a scenery shifting device overhead and put on this kind of show often? The people like it.

Apparently, Brown responded immediately. By mid-January 1909 the *Lethbridge Herald* announced that Brown:[21]

> . . . has raised the stage, both floor and top fixture with a fine curtain and scenery shifting device above. A sectional extension which may be used for extraordinarily large or special productions has been built and was used last night on account of the boxing contest. It makes an exceedingly large stage with this addition. Commodious dressing rooms are provided beneath the stage where performers may find comfort between acts . . . so many western theatres are lacking in this respect. Electric bells are arranged to warn the players of the time of their acts.

But on July 12, 1909, shortly after Dawson May leased the theatre, its walls collapsed. Proprietor Brown quickly put up an alternate Lyceum Tent Theatre while reconstructing and enlarging the theatre building, which reopened on November 15, 1909.[22] During the renovation, a new and larger stage was added to the back of the old building. The larger premises provided for improved dressing rooms and an increased seating capacity of 350 patrons compared to the original 200. Incidently, May, a former agent of the Dominion Express Company, had previous theatrical experience as a road manager for a large eastern Canadian and U.S. touring company.

While the construction was proceeding, Brown and some business associates organized the Brown Amusement Company, of which Fred Brown was president and general manager. Then, the Brown Amusement Company built the Arcade across the street from the Lyceum. The Arcade provided bowling alleys on the ground floor and billiards upstairs.[23] During the week of July 17, 1909, Brown also organized the Lethbridge Free Carnival which took place in the city square.[24] The following year, his Amusement Company arranged for the appearance of the Al Barnes 3 ring Wild

Animal Circus.[25] Before another year passed, however, Brown divested himself of all his Lethbridge property, whereupon he left the city.

Lyceum Theatre
Photo: City of Lethbridge Archives and Records Management

After February 1910 the Lyceum was relegated to presenting vaudeville and movies. This circumstance was brought about by the opening of the Majestic Theatre where facilities were much more appropriate for touring productions. In the early part of that year, the Lyceum Theatre introduced the Pantages Vaudeville Circuit to Lethbridge; then, in September 1910 the Lyceum was sold to the Starland Theatre Company of Winnipeg which remodeled the building again and reopened it on January 28, 1911, as the Starland Movie Theatre.[26] The Starland was strictly a movie theatre and remained one of the major cinemas in Lethbridge for many years. Beginning in 1919, however, this theatre witnessed a succession of owners and name changes. On June 21, 1920, it was renamed the Phoenix Theatre under manager Ken Bishop.[27] Six months later it changed hands again; it was renamed the King's Theatre and was placed under the management of twenty-one year old, A.W. Shackleford, whom the new owners had enticed from his job with the Fox Film Exchange in Calgary. By this time, Shackleford had already spent a number of years in the theatre business – as an usher (beginning at the age of 14) at the Regent Theatre in Calgary, and as an employee with the Pathe and Fox Film Exchanges.[28] Fortunately, Shackleford also encouraged George and Katherine Brown to move to Lethbridge where these superlative musicians (violinist and pianist, respectively) made extraordinary contributions to the music scene for many years, thereafter. The Browns also established Brown's Music Store in 1928 which they operated for many years before selling it to Fred and Mary Leister.

Starland Theatre
Photo: City of Lethbridge Archives and Record Management; © Glenbow Archives (NC2-407)

In January 1922, Rogers and Company purchased the King's Theatre which they renamed the Kings (no apostrophe). A.W. Shackleford was retained as manager. Rogers and Company, which was comprised of a group of local and district business and professional men presided over by Mark C. Rogers, also bought the Colonial Theatre at that time and shortly thereafter, leased the Majestic Theatre.[29] A.W. Shackleford was also hired to manage these latter two theatres.

Eureka Theatre and Grand Electric Theatre

The Eureka Theatre, which was located next door to the 1908 offices of the *Lethbridge Herald*, had a much less auspicious history than did the Lyceum/Starland Theatre.[30] From the time of its opening on October 12, 1908, until its closing in November 1911, its owners and managers, Morris and Thaten, advertised moving pictures and advanced vaudeville. In fact, the acts presented at the Eureka were very small time vaudeville; nevertheless, they were enjoyed daily by many patrons as evidenced by the attendance which, as Al Morris claimed in 1910, averaged 3 000 per week.[31] The Thatens often performed vaudeville acts at the Eureka; for example, in December 1908 Mr. and Mrs. Thaten presented "the great comedy sketch," *Under the Truthful Tree*, and in August 1909 the Thaten duo, assisted by Jack Waters, presented the sketch *A Woman's Wit*.[32]

An addition to the rear of the original theatre was constructed in the summer of 1909, new equipment was installed, and much effort was expended in making the building fireproof. The proprietors took particular pride in their new folding opera chairs and the water curtain which surrounded the proscenium. In case the movie screen caught fire, a spray of water would descend from a perforated pipe above the proscenium in order to prevent fire and smoke from entering the auditorium.[33] Shortly, however, even the new Eureka proved to be inadequate and, therefore, Al

Morris planned to build the Morris Theatre, adjacent to the Eureka. Once the new theatre opened, Morris closed the Eureka. In the interim, the Grand Electric Theatre also exhibited movies for a short period of time in 1910. This theatre, which operated across from the Eureka Theatre, showed moving pictures every afternoon at 2:30 and every evening at 7:30. It often advertised special matinees for ladies. Charges at the Grand Electric Theatre were $0.10 during the day $0.15 at night.[34]

Morris (Sherman, Orpheum, Colonial) Theatre

The Morris Theatre opened on November 16, 1911, featuring the movie, *Brewster's Millions*.[35] Morris's new theatre had a seating capacity of 550 patrons and was provided with a 450 square foot stage, an orchestra pit, and four dressing rooms. This theatre was designed to accommodate smaller stage productions as well as movies.[36] Although the stage facilities of Morris's new theatre were not equal to the standards of the Majestic, they were sufficient to provide some competition for the Majestic; for example, the former theatre featured vaudeville which was always very popular with Lethbridge audiences. When the fortunes of the Majestic floundered at various times in its history, the Morris was called upon to book both touring and local productions. Such a circumstance occurred in the fall of 1912 through the winter of 1913, at which time companies like the Allen Players and the Juvenile Bostonians booked the Morris. Although this arrangement was not entirely satisfactory to the performers, the audiences appreciated it because the Morris was considered to be more comfortable and possibly even more attractive than the Majestic. The *Lethbridge Herald* referred to the Morris as the "prettiest theatre west of Winnipeg."[37]

But apparently, Morris overextended himself financially. In the fall of 1913, a Bailiff's sale was declared for Saturday, August 30, at which time all equipment and furnishings of the Morris Theatre were sold by public auction. The theatre was taken over by W.B. Sherman of Calgary, manager of Calgary's magnificent new Sherman Grand, owned by Senator Lougheed.[38] The Morris was subsequently renamed the Sherman and Mr. Wilson was hired as the local manager.[39] Since Sherman had recently leased the local Majestic Theatre, and since he booked many of the theatrical companies that played western Canada, he presented some companies at the Majestic and others at the Sherman, depending upon booking dates and the needs of the companies. Thus, in addition to exhibiting movies and presenting vaudeville, the Sherman became a second facility for the presentation of legitimate theatre. Such a mandate continued throughout the long history of this theatre, even though its ownership, management, and name changed on numerous occasions. For example, the Orpheum replaced the Sherman on February 10, 1915, under the management of Mr. Light, who was succeeded by Roy Moulton in July and Charles Hansen in October.[40] On October 18, 1918, Len S. Brown took over the theatre and renamed it the Colonial.[41] It was during his tenure as manager of the Colonial Theatre, that Brown was elected the first president of the Alberta Motion Picture Association, which was organized on May 16, 1921. According to the *Lethbridge Herald,* the association was organized in order to improve motion picture entertainment and to protect exhibitors from unfair "legislation, agitation or censorship."[42] As mentioned earlier, Rogers and Company gained control of the Colonial Theatre in January 1922 and employed A.W. Shackleford as manager.

Monarch Theatre

The Monarch Theatre opened on Christmas Day, 1911, in the old Burgmann's Hall which was located on the west side of 13th Street North, just south of 3rd Avenue.[43] The Monarch closed in 1918 and North Lethbridge was left without a movie theatre until January 5, 1938, when the Lealta Theatre opened in the same building.[44] An alternative North Lethbridge theatre, the Regent, operated for a short period of time in 1915.[45]

Morris Theatre
Photo: City of Lethbridge Archives and Records Managment. © Glenbow Archives (NA-3267-22)

Empress Theatre

Grace McCurdy opened the Empress Theatre on January 7, 1913. The first manager of the Empress, Frank Evans, advertised the theatre as "Canada's Finest Photo Play House" and "the most luxurious and comfortable theatre in the city."[46] The *Lethbridge Herald* write-up was somewhat less exuberant – describing it as one of the most attractive movie houses in the city. The Empress was certainly one of the most stable theatre operations in Lethbridge. The second manager, Charles Hansen, was associated with the Empress for about fifteen years, during which time he occasionally booked vaudeville acts.

Majestic Theatre

It was the Majestic Theatre which made Lethbridge attractive to road shows and touring companies after its opening in 1910. In the fall of 1909, Sam Griffith, an enterprising entrepreneur from Sweet Grass, Montana, decided to construct the city's largest theatre on the south side of Bompas Street between Round and Crabb Street.[47] This new "Griffith" Theatre was designed especially to house live stage presentations including large touring road shows. On January 21, 1910, even though the theatre seats had not arrived, E. Willis, temporary manager, arranged for the John P. Slocum Company to perform the comic opera, *The Gay Musician,* by Julien Edwards. Shortly thereafter, the Jeanne Russell Stock Company was booked for the "official" opening of the new facility. Fred Brown and the Brown Amusement Company leased the theatre as of February 9, 1910, and contracted the Summers Stock Company for the "Real Final Completion, Christening and Opening" of what was, henceforth, to be called the Majestic Theatre.[48] Admission to the various opening performances ranged from twenty-five cents to one dollar.

Empress Theatre: Note also the Starland Theatre and the Oliver Building (The Florsheim Shop)
Photo: City of Lethbridge Archives and Records Management

On February 7, 1910, the *Lethbridge Herald* described some aspects of the new theatre in the following way:[49]

> Mr. Griffith . . . has without doubt given to the public the most beautifully appointed theatre west of Winnipeg. The rotunda is tastefully decorated. The walls are tinted in the palest shades of green, the raised work being tinted in gold. The foyer is tinted in light brown, shading into a rich cream, the raised work on the balcony and boxes being gold, a very pretty effect being secured. The beautiful oil painted curtain which Mr. Griffith had painted in New York by Lee Lasch, the world's greatest scenic artist, is a real treat for the lovers of art . . . . it blends beautifully with the decorations throughout. The subdued electrical effects are exceedingly pretty, transforming the theatre into a veritable dreamland.

Other descriptions of the Majestic tell us that the main floor, balcony, and boxes seated in excess of 800 patrons and that the stage accommodated more than 75 cast members.[50] Unlike all other theatres in the city, the Majestic also boasted of an extensive fly gallery.

The Brown Amusement Company retained the lease through 1910, although one of Brown's associates, H. Cleveland, took over the managerial duties in October.[51] At the end of that year, Griffith transferred the lease to W.B. Sherman of Calgary. Much to the chagrin of Cleveland, Sherman hired Harry Turner as local manager.[52] When Turner left for Brandon at the end of 1911, he was replaced by Len S. Brown who remained through 1912, even though the future of the Majestic became somewhat uncertain in the late months of that latter year.[53]

During the first two years of its existence, the Majestic Theatre presented live theatrical performances almost every night of the week except for short periods during the summer months. Nevertheless, the fortunes of the Majestic Theatre varied. Lethbridge patrons were not always generous with the support they gave the touring companies. During 1911 and 1912, a number of explanations were provided for this lack of support: competition from the much cheaper and increasingly available motion pictures and vaudeville; limited variety and poor quality of the visiting companies; and economic problems associated with an extensive miners' strike. Obviously, all of these factors played a role; however, it is likely that these and other concerns combined to make going to the legitimate theatre somewhat unattractive at that time. Even though the cheaper seats at the Majestic Theatre were not that much more expensive than movie-vaudeville admission, such differentials could become increasingly important, especially for salaried employees who were more likely to opt for the lower priced programs in times of economic insecurity. With respect to the quality argument, it appears that poor quality itself was not a deterrent. The music and drama critic of the *Lethbridge Herald* stated on numerous occasions that high class entertainment was not properly patronized in Lethbridge and that improvements in quality were not reflected in increased audiences. "People in Lethbridge have not yet acquired the habit of patronizing high class theatrical attractions."[54] It is true that the quality of most touring shows was rather uncertain; therefore, patrons may not have been willing to risk their limited entertainment funds on such chancy circumstances. It is also possible that the local theatre managers overextended themselves and that a city of 9 000 simply could not adequately support the large number of performers and companies that were booked into the Majestic. Other concerns were voiced about the physical comfort of the theatre. When the Majestic ceased operation for several months in late 1912 and early 1913, it was rumored that the theatre might, in fact, be closed permanently.[55] The *Herald* reporter suggested that the theatre should certainly be shut down for general repairs, painting, and for renovation of the heating system – ". . . the place cannot be heated properly."[56]

Only three years after the momentous opening celebrations in the winter of 1910, the Majestic was put "on the block" to satisfy Griffith's creditors, particularly the Northern Trust Company to whom $16 645 was owing. K.D. Johnston, manager of the local Molson's Bank purchased the theatre for $34 145,[57] and then leased it to C.P. Walker of Winnipeg who hired a succession of local managers before installing Len Brown in the position, again. By this time (October 1918), Brown was also an associate in the management of the Colonial Theatre.

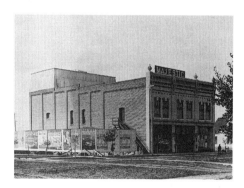 

Majestic Theatre – Exterior and Interior
Photos: City of Lethbridge Archives and Records Management (photographer: A. Rafton-Canning)

Walker brought the Orpheum vaudeville circuit to Lethbridge, but his more impressive contribution to the local theatre scene came about because of his affiliation with the British-Canadian Theatrical Organization Society, which enticed a number of English performers and companies to Canada. Outstanding among these was Sir John Martin-Harvey and Company, who performed *The Only Way* and *The Breed of the Tresham* at the Majestic on March 17 and 18, 1914, respectively. Unfortunately, World War I brought the English booking arrangement of these organizations to a sudden halt. The war years also slowed down the general flow of touring companies from the United States and eastern Canada.

In May 1921 the Majestic was sold to the owners of the local Commercial Cafe, George and Steve Hyt, who placed the theatre under the management of A.H. Dettlar.[58] Before the year passed, however, Len S. Brown returned to the Majestic by taking on the lease. He immediately announced that the Majestic would combine exclusive photo play attractions with stage presentations including all the Trans-Canada Road Shows. The first troupe which Brown booked at the Majestic was the Maple Leafs, a group of former "fighting men" from the 4th Canadian Division, under the direction of Captain Merton W. Plunkett.[59] This show had originally been scheduled to play the Colonial Theatre, but since Brown now managed both theatres, he was able to switch the booking. However, Brown soon divested all of his interests in Lethbridge theatres. He then left Lethbridge for Hollywood where he planned to engage in movie production; however, he apparently did not enjoy that aspect of the movie industry. He then moved to Racine, Wisconsin, and gradually developed a chain of theatres in Wisconsin.[60]

In the winter of 1922, Rogers and Company leased the Majestic and named A.W. Shackleford as manager.[61] Shackleford reopened the Majestic on May 1, 1922, and shortly thereafter, booked a local production of *His Excellency the Governor* under the direction of Richard Hincks. Movies and the Pantages Vaudeville Circuit dominated the fare at the Majestic throughout the remainder of 1922.

Amateur Theatrical Activities

Plays, operettas, minstrel shows, and patriotic concerts characterized amateur theatre in Lethbridge from 1906-1922. Theatrical activities were rather sparse during the first few years of this era since the local artistic community was passing through a period of transition, in which many of the "old guard" had retired or had moved away from the city. Certainly, there was a dire need for new leadership for the production of plays. In the musical theatre realm, the presence of Reverend J.S. Chivers provided some stability, and soon, the talents of J. George Harper gave the necessary expertise and leadership. Gradually, other musicians such as George Mitford, T. Roberts, Leo Coombs, E.F. Layton, and the Frank Waddington Family joined Harper in sharing their various musical talents and leadership abilities. The production of plays generally depended upon the leadership of one man, Richard Hincks, who dominated the local drama scene throughout the period under discussion, following the success of his first production in January 1909.

Unlike the previous period when it was common to organize evenings of combined musical and dramatic activities, the present period was characterized by a greater separation of these artistic activities, except, of course, in musical theatrical productions such as operettas and minstrel shows. The tendency toward specialization was also frequently set aside during the World War I years when patriotic concerts of greater variety were organized. These latter concerts also tended to break down the age grading that seemed inherent in the performing arts. Generally, adult community activities were quite distinct from children's school and church productions; however, the patriotic concerts encouraged performances by all age groups. Following the war, the traditional age graded activities resumed.

Some new dimensions were added to the amateur theatrical scene in Lethbridge prior to the 1920s. One of these was the contribution made by a number of the local theatre managers: Al Morris and Len Brown both directed and participated in local productions; G.E. Fleming was considered one of the finest vocalists in the city, so he took a number of starring roles in musical theatre; Roy Moulton performed on his violin in various pit bands and during many concert evenings. While performing in pit orchestras, Moulton referred to himself as Mr. Rubelitzsky. The theatres themselves provided exceptional opportunities for the honing of musical talents. Individual and ensemble musical accompaniments were provided for the silent films, and vocal and instrumental performances were commonly presented before and between movies or as the movie reels were being changed.

Another new development was the introduction of formal dance instruction. As early as 1909, Miss ("Madam") Norman advertised tuition in ballroom and stage dancing at the Caledonian Hall on Glyn Street. It could not be ascertained how long Miss Norman operated her school; however, her ads were still carried in the 1911 editions of the paper. In addition to dance instruction, she advertised for students of pianoforte and voice culture, and she stated that she had 25 years experience in operatic, dramatic, and vaudeville activities.[62] On the other hand, it is quite clear that Gladys Attree and her associate, Lola Strand, offered instruction in Lethbridge for about ten years, beginning in 1917. Attree was born and raised in England. Her parents, Mr. & Mrs. George Frederick Attree, and her two brothers moved to western Canada in 1908 settling near Nelson, British Columbia. Whether or not Gladys moved to Canada at that time or whether she was still studying dance in Russia is uncertain. Johnston and den Otter assure us that Attree had received dance instruction with the Russian ballet, but because of her exceptional height, she was forced to dance male roles.[63] It is clearly documented, however, through articles and the classified ads in Calgary, Lethbridge, and Medicine Hat newspapers during the fall 1917, that Attree had just returned from Los Angeles, California where she had been studying with the famous American dancer, Ruth St. Denis.[64] Miss Denis and her husband, Ted Shawn, who operated the renowned Denishawn Studio,[65] offered to hire Miss Attree in 1918; however, it seems that Attree preferred to maintain her independence. It is also possible that she preferred to remain in Canada to be near her mother, who had recently been widowed. Nevertheless, one of Attree's former students, Edna Malone, of Nelson, B.C., completed some advanced studies at Denishawn and was then invited to tour the U.S. and Canada with Miss St. Denis during the 1918 season. In the meantime, Attree established her main studio on 8th Avenue West in Calgary. She also commuted weekly to Medicine Hat and Lethbridge where she offered instruction in the Becker Block and the YMCA, respectively. In addition to formal teaching, it was customary for Attree to present her students in recitals, dance reviews, and evenings of classical dance – often as added attractions at the local movie theatres. Some of her Lethbridge students were even invited to join her Calgary students in a performance at the Grand Theatre in Calgary on April 5 and 6, 1918.[66] Incidently, her instruction brought greater finesse to the dancing components of various musical shows and nurtured young dancers who later made immeasurable contributions to the dance elements and choreography of future shows. One of Miss Attree's more accomplished Lethbridge students was Hilda Church, who assisted in choreographing a number of productions for the Playgoers of Lethbridge in the 1920s-1930s, and who became an important teacher of stage movement in Toronto in the 1950s. Attree's career in Calgary and later in Vancouver extended over many years. Ackery informs us that Miss Attree performed at the opening of

Calgary's Capitol Theatre in 1921, whereas programs from the Vancouver *Sun's Sun-Ray Revues* of 1935 and 1937 list her dancers as participants.[67]

Amateur Musical Theatre

In 1909 C.F.P. and Mrs. Conybeare collaborated with Reverend Chivers and E.Allan Allen on the operetta *The Darling of the Geishas* for the Lethbridge Opera and Dramatic Club. Conybeare wrote the book and lyrics; Mrs. Conybeare took on the task of organizing the production; Reverend Chivers was composer and musical director; Allen directed the actors.[68] Some of the old stalwarts like G.W. Robinson (a stationer), Mrs. A. Southard, Mrs. A. Jackson, and Mrs. Conybeare, herself, joined the cast; newcomers like G.E. Fleming, Harold (Al) Cooper, D. May, Mrs. G. Rogers, and Miss Bawden made their local debuts. Sixteen year old Elaine Conybeare was also a featured performer. As usual, Mrs. P.R. Neale provided piano accompaniment. Mesdames Conybeare and Southard were the hit of the evening in their duet, "Kiss by Wire." A year later, the operetta was also produced in Moose Jaw where Reverend Chivers had ministered before coming to Lethbridge. The Moose Jaw critic commented that, "Both author and composer . . . are to be sincerely congratulated."[69]

During the period 1910-1914, it was the Musical Drama Club of the Lethbridge Conservatory of Music which dominated the operetta scene in the city. On June 26, 1906, the *Lethbridge News* reported that J. George Harper, director of a musical conservatory in Pembroke, Ontario, was considering the possibility of opening a similar school in Lethbridge. The news article speculated that Harper would shortly visit Lethbridge to assess the instructional potential. In fact, Harper quickly decided to move to Lethbridge where he established the Lethbridge Conservatory of Music. Once settled in Lethbridge, Harper also agreed to become choir master at Knox Presbyterian Church. Although the Conservatory was temporarily located on the second floor of the Tuff Block (present site of Southminster Church), it was soon moved to permanent facilities on the southeast corner of 11th Street and 5th Avenue South.[70] Harper's Conservatory of Music operated out of the two-storey building on that site well into the 1950s.

Before long, the Conservatory became the major musical training centre within the city. In addition, the Conservatory maintained a retail business for the sale of instruments and music. This business also operated an instrument repair section. Harper, who gave instruction on the violin, hired additional faculty so that vocal, instrumental, dramatic, and art instruction could be covered. To provide opportunities for ensemble playing, Harper also organized a conservatory orchestra, which was touted as the largest such group in the province.[71] Vocal music, too, was encouraged, and soon, the Conservatory prided itself in the organization of the Lethbridge Choral Club composed of approximately one hundred members.[72] Both of these ensembles prepared a number of recitals which were enthusiastically received by local music lovers. But Harper's interests extended beyond the recital format; consequently, he took on the task of organizing and directing minstrel shows and operettas. Within five months after moving to Lethbridge, he directed his first Lethbridge production – a minstrel show which played Oliver's Hall on December 6, 1906. The cast of this production represented a complete turnover from previous minstrel shows. Although the effort was a rousing success, Harper decided to concentrate, for the next few years, on the prime function of the Conservatory, and to assure the establishment of the school as a strong training ground for musical development. However, his interest in musical theatre remained strong and manifested itself some years later when he organized a Conservatory Musical Drama Club which presented Edward Solomon's *Billee Taylor,* a nautical comic opera, on February 1 and 2, 1911. This operetta was a major undertaking involving a cast of 75 participants. Of course, no other stage in town but the Majestic could accommodate such a cast. Among the leading actors, dancers, and singers in *Billee*

Taylor, who performed in many subsequent local productions, were Elaine Conybeare, Bessie Hazell, Richard Hincks, and Frank Waddington. The many theatrical activities of Hincks and Waddington will be analyzed in detail, later. Elaine Conybeare was described as an "enchanting danseuse"; whereas, Bessie Hazell, as Phoebe, "used her bright voice with skill."[73] Some years later, Hazell's father, Edward G. Hazell (owner of the Summit Lime Works, Ltd.), became a regular participant in the early Rotary shows.

NWMP Barracks with Lethbridge Conservatory of Music building in right centre
Photo: City of Lethbridge Archives and Records Management

Chorus members associated with *Billee Taylor*, whose later contribution to local theatre was also notable, included Chris Gibson, Al Morris, Alan McAlpine, Charles Sydal, James Aird, and J.T. Vallance. More will be said about these participants later. *Billee Taylor* was revived in October 1912 as part of the festivities associated with the International Dry Farming Congress. This revival witnessed the introduction to musical theatre of a new accompanist, Mrs. Frank (Elizabeth) Waddington, who had replaced Mrs. Neale as the foremost accompanist in the city. In the meantime, the Conservatory Drama Club produced a western comedy drama, *Nevada or The Lost Mine*, which opened at the Eureka Theatre on April 27, 1911. Al Cooper, who was noted as a fine vocalist, took the leading role. The following excerpt from the Lethbridge Herald critique of the revival gives us some insight into the process of local criticism at that time:[74]

> One must keep in mind that this was a purely amateur production and for that reason, criticism would be ungallant. But I would say that the manner in which the performance was carried out impressed me very favorably.

Nevertheless, the critic did make the following negative comment about the singing of the chorus whose '"good voices . . . would have been heard to better advantage had it not been for a spasm of the "shakes." This however, one is glad to say, wore off as the week progressed."'

Male Chorus from Billee Taylor *produced by Lethbridge Conservatory of Music, 1911*
Photo: Doris Balcovske

Following the 1912 revival of *Billee Taylor,* it was decided to broaden the executive base of these theatrical activities. Public meetings were held in the Conservatory with the intention of forming a community operatic and dramatic society.[75] George Harper agreed to direct the productions; George Mitford (local realtor and Wesley Church Choir director) volunteered to supervise the choral work. Shortly thereafter, the newly formed Lethbridge Operatic and Dramatic Society began rehearsals for the operetta *The Country Girl* by Lionel Monckton to be presented in May 1913. The theatre was originally booked for May 12 and 13, only; however, these nights were quickly sold out, so the executive decided to extend the run another night. Since this extra performance still did not satisfy the demand, the show was revived on June 25 and 26. The extensive cast included many members of the city's leading professional and business community such as Fred Rose, G.W. Robinson, Frank Waddington, E.L. Jarvis, Dorothy and Brigham S. Young. Music was provided by a twelve piece orchestra.

Shortly after the May performances, members of the Lethbridge Operatic and Dramatic Society held a social gathering at the Conservatory to celebrate the forthcoming marriage of George Harper to Florence H. Day, and to express their appreciation for his work with the Society. On behalf of the club, George W. Robinson (a local merchant), presented the prospective couple with a case of silverware. In recognition of Harper's marriage, the Society relieved him of stage managing (directing) the revival. Following his marriage, Harper basically retired from theatrical activities, although he continued to provide musical instruction for many succeeding years. Brigham S. Young (former director of the Brigham Young Drama Society of Raymond) was recruited to replace Harper as director[76] – a role which Young also performed for the second major production of the Society, *San Toy,* composed by Sidney Jones.

Cast of The Country Girl *produced by Lethbridge Musical and Dramatic Society, 1913*
Photo: City of Lethbridge Archives and Records Management

San Toy, which was described as a "charming Chinese opera," was presented on December 10-13, 1913, and January 1, 1914. Many of the performers who had participated in *The Country Girl,* took leading roles, again. A complete newcomer to local musical theatre was T. Roberts who replaced George Mitford as musical director when Mitford moved to Winnipeg in October of that year. T. Roberts was later responsible for organizing the local Excelsior [Male] Choir which put on a number of choral concerts in the city during 1913 and 1914. The *Lethbridge Herald* critic was enthusiastic about the stage sets and the costumes of San Toy but not about the show itself. Although he extended congratulations to many of the actors, the critic felt that the show was not as good as its predecessor, *The Country Girl.* However, his review of the second night's performance of *San Toy* was much more enthusiastic. Elaborate compliments were accorded Dorothy Young, Fred Rose, B.S. Young and Richard Hincks as follows:[77]

> Miss Dorothy Young . . . who took the name part, with her brilliant voice, natural acting and graceful movement well sustained the reputation she has made.

Mr. Fred Rose invested Li with every bit of the vivacity and the humor which tended to make the character the element of fun in the play.

Mr. B.S. Young rendered the part of Yen How with all the characteristics belonging to a high Chinese dignitary.

Mr. Richard Hincks had not very much to do as Emperor of China but he did it to the manner born and showed himself an actor of much capacity.

San Toy was the last theatrical production to be associated with the Conservatory. Other community based musical theatre productions included the operetta, *The Wild Rose,* presented on December 4, 1922, by the St. Patrick's Drama Society, and two productions not associated with organized theatrical societies. Henry Viney, the lone male cast member in *The Wild Rose*, eventually became one of the most respected sports announcers and commentators in Alberta. The other two musical shows were organized and directed by visiting professionals. The first of these was the operetta *Queen Zephra* which played the Majestic Theatre, May 10-13, 1911. On this occasion, the manager and director of the Queen Zephra Company, Harry J. Booth, organized a group of about 150 local singers and actors. The company provided the sets and dressing which apparently were very impressive. The production was a great artistic and financial success. Unfortunately, the same could not be said for *Scandals of 21*, a revue which was organized under the auspices of the Army and Navy Veterans' Association. A couple of "big time" promoters, Messrs. Jordan and MacDonald, "breezed" into the city and volunteered to direct the show. But after the show, they "skipped out of town" with the receipts.[78]

Amateur Dramatic Entertainment

Most of the local dramatic productions in this period owe their debt to the energies and talents of Richard Hincks, a local representative for a major hardware distributor, who had recently immigrated to Canada from England. From 1909 through 1923, Hincks participated in approximately one theatrical presentation per year. He directed and acted in seven productions of three major plays and in fourteen short plays or sketches. In addition, he portrayed roles in two operettas and in a one act play which was produced by the Playgoers Club of Lethbridge after the club was organized in 1923. Although Hincks was the major catalyst for amateur legitimate theatre during this era, the rather narrow range of the productions which he directed suggests that his knowledge of theatrical literature was, perhaps, limited. His interest in performance was passed on to his son, Richard Hincks, Jr. (Dick), who participated fairly extensively in his father's productions from 1917-1922. Neither Hincks's wife, Cora, nor his other son, Phillip, engaged in these activities.

Hincks first gathered together a group of local actors to present the three act comedy *Sweet Lavender* at the Eureka Theatre on January 25 and 26, 1909. *Sweet Lavender* had a long and successful run on Broadway in 1888 plus at least one major revival in 1893.[79] Hincks's production was the first play presented by Lethbridge amateurs since *Dearest Mama* in 1901. Although the local critic was enthusiastic about the production, in general, and the acting of Hincks, J. Eakin, and Mary Hings, in particular, his criticism of much of the projection of many of the other players was quite harsh. But Hincks was obviously encouraged by the experience; so three months later, he presented *Sweet Lavender*, again, together with the farce, *Dandy Dick*. Local reviews of these plays were very positive with respect to the acting and direction; Hincks received particular commendation. On December 13, 1910, Hincks's core of loyal actors put together a series of short comedies for presentation at the Majestic. Mr. Hincks was again singled out for praise because of "his very humorous portrayals." Judging by the audience's reaction, as reported in the *Lethbridge Herald*, the evening was a great success.[80] As illustrated earlier, the next three years of local theatre were filled with the activities of the Conservatory's Musical Drama Society and the Lethbridge Musical and Dramatic Society; therefore, Hincks temporarily hung up his director's cap. He seemed to be particularly interested in ensemble directing and acting, although he did participate in the Conservatory productions of *Billee Taylor* and *San Toy*.

During the four years of World War I, a number of evenings of entertainment were produced under the auspices of various war time charities and patriotic societies. Hincks, and various actors with whom he had become associated, participated in many of these concerts. For example, on December 4, 1914, the IODE sponsored a patriotic entertainment with children's presentations of various kinds. A comic sketch, *A Sister to Assist 'Er* (starring Messrs. L. Asquith and F. Waddington) was included in the program. According to the local critic, these gentlemen "convulsed the audience with laughter."[81] On August 16, 1915, at the Orpheum Theatre, the three gentlemen, Hincks, Asquith (realtor), and Waddington (auctioneer), were joined by Mrs. Lionel Asquith in presenting "three screamingly funny sketches" for the benefit of the IODE and the Nursing Mission. The four performers took various parts in the three sketches: *Packing Up, A Sister to Assist 'Er*, and *That Brute Simmons*. On April 27, 1916, the Alexander Galt Chapter of the IODE presented another evening of variety with a comic sketch by Messrs. Hincks, Waddington, and Guilbault. A year later, Hincks revived an old favorite of his, *Dandy Dick*, in which he also played the leading role of the Dean. This three act production at the Majestic Theatre was given in aid of the Red Cross, the European War Veteran's Association, and the Nursing Mission. Among those supporting Mr. Hincks, were F. Waddington, Mr. and Mrs. G. Fleming, together with some new talent including Charles R. Matthews, who made many valuable contributions to future amateur theatre in the city, especially as a very active member of the Lethbridge Playgoers.

His Excellency the Governor was the April 1918 production of Richard Hincks and Company, with Hincks in the leading role of Sir Montague Martin. The supporting cast included Mrs. J.N. (Louie) Ritchie, the wife of a very prominent Lethbridge lawyer.[82] Ritchie soon became one of the community theatre's leading ladies; in addition, she and her husband, Norman, were founding members and active participants in the Playgoers Club of Lethbridge. Postwar charitable needs, such as the Nursing Mission and "Tobacco for the Boys", were causes for Hincks to produce another evening of short plays in December 1918: *The Changeling* by W.W. Jacobs, *The Collaborators* by Daisy McGeoch, *Cinders* by Lily Tinsley, and *The Playgoers* by A.W. Pinero. Comic relief between plays was provided by Alan McAlpine, who became the major technical designer for the Lethbridge Playgoers in its formative years. The Waddington three piece orchestra was augmented with the talents of George Kemm and George Porter. The local critic commented that this was "one of the best nights of amateur entertainment for some considerable time."[83]

Several years passed before Hincks directed another play. On May 8,9, 1922, Lethbridge audiences witnessed Hincks's final directorial offerings in Lethbridge, a short curtain raiser, *The Bathroom Door*, followed by a revival of *His Excellency the Governor*. In the latter play, Mrs. J.N. Ritchie again portrayed Mlle. Stella De Gex and Hincks recreated his role as the Governor. [Later, Hincks appeared in the Playgoers' one act play, *The Man in the Stalls* (September, 1923), before moving to Calgary.] New faces in the revival of *His Excellency the Governor* included Rose Pomeroy, Ernest Gaskell Sterndale Bennett, and Elizabeth Belle Sterndale Bennett. Alan McAlpine looked after the business arrangements and stage management. The local critic, W.A.R. Cocq, noted that the acting of Miss Pomeroy was "great," and that Mrs. Sterndale Bennett "made the most of her part and was altogether pleasing." But the major accolades were reserved for the acting of E.G. Sterndale Bennett who was described as:[84]

... an amateur of undoubted merit . . . who gave a very fine interpretation of Mr. John Baverstock, the private secretary. The part was very convincingly played, with all the "stage tricks" which would have done credit to many a seasoned actor. The actor was decidedly in his groove and gave a finished performance."

The Sterndale Bennetts had moved to Lethbridge in 1921 and their talents were immediately recognized when they participated in the 1921 Rotary Minstrel Show. On that occasion, their special talents were utilized in the one act farce, *The Village Fire Brigade*, in which they were assisted by George Dixon. The critic commented, "Mr. and Mrs. Sterndale Bennett obviously have both had acting experience before."[85] For more than a decade, thereafter, the Sterndale Bennetts' contribution to theatre in Lethbridge was such that amateur theatre in Lethbridge became viable enough to fill much of the theatrical void which was created when the touring of professional companies began to diminish. An analysis of this contribution is reserved for Chapter Three. In the meantime, it should be pointed out that plays produced by groups or individuals other than Richard Hincks were extremely rare during this era. In fact, only two such plays, both of which were presented in 1915, have been documented: *Sunbonnets,* produced by the St. Augustine's W.A. on April 30 and May 11, and *Fabiola,* organized by St. Patrick's Drama Society for May 13, 14, and June 3.[86]

Amateur Specialty and Variety Entertainment

The theatrical activities of one of Hincks's associates, Frank Waddington, need also to be recognized. The Frank Waddington family had moved to Lethbridge from Leicester, England, in 1907.[87] While living in England, Frank Waddington had participated in light opera, so it is not surprising that after settling in Lethbridge, Waddington not only performed in most of Hincks's productions but also contributed to productions of the local operatic and dramatic societies and to concerts and entertainments sponsored by various church and charitable societies. Then, in February 1921 Waddington organized an evening primarily of musical entertainment, which he advertised as Frank Waddington's "Black and White Pierrots." The original performances (February 3,4) were given in St. Augustine's Hall, with proceeds in aid of the Fourth Troop, Boy Scouts. Musical numbers were provided by Frank, Eileen, and Geoffrey Waddington; Frank Colpman; James Cranney; Alan McAlpine; and Miss Paterson. Accompanists for the production were Mrs. Waddington, Eileen Waddington, and Mrs. Frank Colpman.[88] The packed houses enjoyed the entertainment so much that Waddington was encouraged to repeat the show on February 21, and again on June 8. Then, an entirely new Pierrot program was offered as a farewell performance on September 2, 1921, after which the Frank Waddington family moved to Toronto.[89] This was a sad time for Lethbridge's patrons of the arts who had enjoyed the many talents of the Waddington family over a period of about fourteen years. But the Waddingtons felt a need to reside in Toronto so that Eileen (pianist) and Geoffrey (violinist) could continue their musical education at the Toronto Conservatory of Music, which had recently awarded Geoffrey a scholarship. Both of them excelled there and later developed professional careers in music. In the meantime, their father, Frank Waddington continued his auctioneering career in Toronto (specializing in antiques). He was also appointed official auctioneer for the CNR and for the Canadian Customs Department.

Other directorial contributors to variety theatre in Lethbridge included two of the local theatre managers, Al Morris and Len S. Brown. In 1913 the owner and manager of the new Morris Theatre, Al Morris, organized the Al Morris Minstrels, a group that performed on the stage of the Morris Theatre, February 16, 17. Morris, who took on the responsibility of Interlocutor, was assisted by the Chapman Brothers [Thomas, James, and Harry (CPR employees)], G.E. Fleming, Mr. Jarvis, and R. Barrowman (future mayor of Lethbridge). This production, which was the first local minstrel show since the one sponsored by the Knights of Pythias in December 1910, was described as being much better than one presented by West's touring professional minstrels.[90] Incidently, William H. West was a former member of the Primrose Minstrels which played Broadway in 1875.[91] Although Morris disposed of his interest in the Morris Theatre in September 1913, he nevertheless organized another minstrel show for presentation at the Sherman (former Morris) Theatre on April 24, 25, 1914. He then took over the operation of a theatre in Trail, B.C. Two succeeding minstrel shows (December 25, 26, 1914; September 27, 28, 1915) were organized by Len S. Brown. His group, which was referred to as the Columbia Minstrels, was basically composed of the same core of players who had participated in Morris's productions.

When Brown became manager of the Majestic Theatre in January 1912, he proposed that a new community drama club be formed; however, the vissisitudes of his own managerial career did not allow him immediately to pursue this interest. But when things began to settle a bit, he did participate a little more actively. In addition to his minstrel activities, Brown directed and acted in a major production sponsored by the local IODE, *Are You a Mason?*, which played at the Majestic Theatre February 15, 16, 1915.

In the latter days of the war, a number of additional concerts and evenings of variety were arranged under the auspices of the Great War Veterans' Association (GWVA). Most elaborate among these productions was the *Veterans' Vaudeville Show,* under the direction of Mrs. Jessie Bond Pawson. At that time, Pawson, who resided in the neighboring town of Coaldale, was in charge of the oratory, physical culture, literature, and dramatic art classes at the Lethbridge Conservatory of Music. This show, which took place at the Majestic Theatre on June 10, 1918, included: comedy skits, cartooning acts by Robert Barrowman, a patriotic tableau, vocals, dramatic readings, classical dances featuring Hilda Church, band selections by the Lethbridge Band under the direction of George Harper, and a two act original play, *The Parlor Snake.* The cast of *The Parlor Snake* included L.S. Brown and Leo Coombs (one of the most reputed music teachers in the city). A one act comedy, *The Rehearsal,* featuring Brown was also presented. In addition, Brown participated in a short black-face sketch.

A few years after the war, the IODE again sponsored an evening of entertainment at the Majestic Theatre. On this occasion (January 21, 1921), local theatre patrons witnessed the second local revival of *Dearest Mama.* Mrs. C.F.P. Conybeare played Mama. Remember that Mrs. Conybeare had joined Captain Deane in his 1901 revival of that same play. Notable also in the 1921 cast were Roy Keivill, Eric Ings, and Minnie Hazell (Thrall) who became founding members of the Playgoers of Lethbridge. Minnie Hazell and Eric Ings also contributed a musical sketch, *Any Old Time, Any Old Place.*

But it was the Rotary Club of Lethbridge which helped to cap off the theatrical activities of the community in the period under discussion. The stimulant for this theatrical interest probably resulted from the success achieved by the Calgary Rotary Club, which toured its minstrel show to Lethbridge in the spring of 1919. Not to be outdone, the Lethbridge Club began to lay plans for what was referred to as the first Annual Rotary Club Show, and which materialized in December 1921. This first production (a minstrel show) had tremendous community support, especially since the cast included about fifty local business and professional men, their wives, and their children. Directors for the show included Robert Barrowman (stage director) and C.J. Ferguson (musical director). Dance routines were choreographed by Hilda Church. Members of the crew included Bob Winters (props) and Guy Roy (lights). It was in this Rotary show that E.G. and E.B. Sterndale Bennett made their Lethbridge theatrical debuts.

The second "Annual Rotary Show", which played December 11-13, 1922, included an original musical comedy, *The Czar of Zanzibar*, which had been conceived by Robert Barrowman. This production was a huge critical and financial success. The club cleared $1 500 and the local *Herald* critic claimed that patrons "can't afford not to go."[92] E.G. Sterndale Bennett headed the cast in the title role; he was supported by Ed. G. Hazell (Czar's Chamberlain), Tom and Harry Chapman, and many other well known members of the community. The second half of the show included a variety of acts and a skit *A Southern Flirtation* which starred Thomas Chapman. The local critic was particularly captivated by the dancing performances of Hilda Church, her sister Betty, Flossie Workman, Grace McNulty, Margaret Dunning, and "little Ella MacIntosh." Also singled out for praise were Rose Pomeroy, Avril Little, and Ernest Sterndale Bennett: the ladies were "clear and sparkling" in their successive versions of "What Us Poor Girls Go Through" and "Gee, I Certainly Must Be In Love." A short second act sketch, *Admiral Peters*, gave "Mr. Bennett an excellent opportunity of bringing into play that histrionic talent which he has in good store. He was well supported by Mrs. Bennett and Mr. H. Norman Davis."[93] Norman Davis was an important force in the growth of amateur dramatics in Medicine Hat as well as a very close friend of the Sterndale Bennetts.

Neighboring Theatrical Societies

Recognition should be accorded the amateur productions which were toured to Lethbridge by neighboring community groups. Outstanding in this regard were the productions which came from Medicine Hat beginning with the St. Patrick's Minstrels in October 1913. This show was very well received. In addition, lavish praise was recorded by the *Lethbridge Herald* critic for the various operettas which were performed at the Majestic Theatre by the Medicine Hat Opera Society: *Tom Jones* (Jan. 1, 1917), *Erminie* (Jan. 1, 1918), *San Toy* (Jan. 1, 1920). These operettas were under the direction of either G.W.H. Simpson or Percy Schutte. George Stewart directed the music and conducted the orchestra; Mrs. Simpson was usually responsible for the choreography. In the technical realm, Mr. G.A. Caldwell produced the scenery; Malabar Limited provided the costumes.[94] Onstage favorites were Norman Davis, C.S. Blanchard, Mrs. G.W.H. Simpson, Olive Fossum, and Mary Holt (dancer). Of particular interest to Lethbridge readers is the fact that, included in the various cast names, was Percy Gaynor, a "versatile comedian" and a future Lethbridge Playgoer.[95] Active theatre performers from Raymond also provided Lethbridge audiences with two evenings of solid entertainment: *The Stubborn Motor Car* (January 1, 1919) and *The Squire's Daughter* (January 15, 1920).

Professional Touring Companies

Stuart informs us that in the theatrical history of western Canada, the years 1907-1925 were dominated by professional touring companies.[96] From the perspective of theatre in Lethbridge, this generalization basically applies. The years 1906-1908, which were somewhat transitional, were characterized by touring patterns similar to those of former years, although some limited changes were evident. Certainly, there was still considerable variety in the kinds of productions offered: drama, comedy, melodrama, operetta, vaudeville, minstrel, and Uncle Tom shows. Most of the former stock, speciality, and musical companies were now defunct, but some of the traditional performers and companies such as Harold Nelson, Andrew McPhee, Roscian Opera Company, and the Beggar Prince Company continued to appear. Nevertheless, even these groups basically completed their touring during this period. On the other hand, some more recent organizations such as Jimmy Fax, George Summers, and the Juvenile Bostonians established themselves as regular visitors to the city.

Certain vestiges of the past still plagued the theatrical scene in Lethbridge through 1908; for example, Oliver's Hall, although generally recognized as being an inadequate theatre facility, was the only sizable hall available for stage productions. In addition, transportation through Lethbridge was still cumbersome. Consequently, theatre groups continued to view Lethbridge as a "one-night stand" town. Yet, the number of companies appearing each year began to increase somewhat as the city's growing population became an attractive force. Slight changes were also evident in the type of shows being booked; a few musical revues and road shows were included. Theatre construction during this period was also a harbinger of change. The Bijou Theatre, which opened on August 15, 1907, accelerated the exhibition of motion pictures. But it was October 1908 (with the simultaneous opening of the Eureka and Lyceum theatres), which marked the beginning of the new era in the theatrical life of Lethbridge. As indicated earlier, the Eureka Theatre presented moving pictures in combination with touring vaudeville acts throughout its short three year history. This was the beginning of regular, more formally organized vaudeville in the city. The Lyceum also opened with vaudeville, which was, however, considerably higher class vaudeville than that which played the Eureka. But touring stock companies like the Tom Marks Company soon became aware of the potential of the Lyceum Theatre, which during 1909 became a major factor in attracting a growing number of such stock companies. But before reviewing this and other major developments, it might be useful to consider some of the theatrical activities that remained fairly consistent during the entire period under discussion: opera and operetta, production by children, minstrel, and Uncle Tom shows.

The presentation of grand opera in Lethbridge was rare, and its reception by local audiences varied considerably. In June 1909 the Boston Grand Opera Company presented *Lucia di Lammermoor* and *Faust* at the Lyceum Theatre to enthusiastic audiences. Nevertheless, serious opera did not return until October 1912 when the Sheehen English Opera Company toured with *Il Trovatore* and Robert Planquette's *The Chimes of Normandy*. Shortly thereafter, on November 6, 1912, Alice Nielsen and Company gave an opera concert including an abridged version of *The Barber of Seville*. This organization reported suffering a loss of $1 100 from their venture to Lethbridge. *Lucia di Lammermoor* returned to Lethbridge in January 1918 when it was offered by the San Carlo Grand Opera Company. A year later, the same company played *Cavalleria Rusticana*, and *Pagliacci*.

Comic opera or operetta appeared more frequently during this period, although there were short hiatal periods such as 1910-1912, 1914, 1916-1917, and 1922. Otherwise, such productions appeared at least once and occasionally twice per year. Companies such as the Roscian Opera, Amsden Musical Company, Beggar Prince Opera, San Francisco Opera, Boston Opera, Whitney Opera, and the Royal English Opera Company presented the occasional Gilbert and Sullivan production and other operettas such as *The Chocolate Soldier* (by Oscar Straus), *Said Pasha*, and *Olivette* (English version by H.B. Farnie).

Three additional companies, composed of juvenile artists, also performed in the operetta vein: the Royal Lilliputian Opera Company, Pollard's Juvenile Opera Company (from Australia), and the Juvenile Bostonians. Although the former two organizations appeared two or three times only, the Juvenile Bostonians appeared almost yearly from 1906 to 1918 with frequent return engagements per year.

Professional minstrel shows continued to appear occasionally, averaging about one show every two years. Nevertheless, such productions spanned the entire period (Mahara's Mammoth Minstrels in June 1906 to Herbert's Greater Minstrels in June 1921). The Richard and Pringle's Georgia Minstrels was the only minstrel aggregation to play the city more than once. In fact, from 1901 through 1914 the group entertained Lethbridge audiences on five separate occasions. Uncle Tom Shows pretty well withered away during the era, although a few companies, including the most famous company to tour western Canada, Stetson's, played Lethbridge now and then.

Other common forms of entertainment throughout the period 1906-1922 included ensemble jubilee concert groups, circuses, and the Lethbridge Fair which began in the fall 1897, and to which the Rodeo was added in 1904. Of course, fairs and circuses were generally suspended for most of the war years. The Norris and Rowe Circus appeared from 1906-1908, but later the Sells Floto and the Al G. Barnes circuses were more common. Probably the most exciting circus to visit Lethbridge during this era was in 1914 when the Sells Floto Circus, which had combined with the Buffalo Bill aggregation, came to town, and Buffalo Bill, himself, led the big circus parade.

With regard to professional theatre in 1909 and a number of years thereafter, three developments are particularly noteworthy: the frequent and extended bookings of a number of stock companies, many of which maintained residence in western Canada; the developing dominance of road show companies playing the latest hits from Broadway and other major theatrical centres in North America and England; and the introduction of circuit vaudeville through arrangements particularly with Alexander Pantages of Seattle, and Martin Beck of Chicago and New York.

Many of the new theatres across western Canada prided themselves in attracting resident stock companies. Edmonton, for example, was home to the Dominion Stock Company (with Jeanne Russell) and the Empress/Lyceum Company. Saskatoon provided a base for the Eckhardt Players while Kamloops, as well as other communities, hosted the Ray Brandon Players.[97] Other cities and towns maintained similar stock companies for various periods of time. Lethbridge theatres experimented with this phenomenon on two occasions during these years but both attempts were rather short lived. In the spring of 1909 the owner and manager of the Lyceum Theatre, Fred Brown, announced that he had arranged with Ray Brandon for the establishment of a resident company. At that time, Brandon was referred to as the manager of the Jeanne Russell Company, which was presently booked into the Lyceum Theatre. Brandon proceeded to augment the existing Russell Company until the emerging company was composed of sixteen members.[98] Combining the successive engagements of the Jeanne Russell Company and the new Brandon Players, the resident relationship lasted about three weeks, after which it was reported that the Jeanne Russell Company planned to reside in Calgary for the rest of the season. Nevertheless, Jeanne Russell and her company returned for a two week stint in the Lyceum Tent Theatre during the late summer 1909. No further mention is made of Brandon's appearances in Lethbridge.

Many years later, Len S. Brown, manager of the Colonial Theatre, enticed Cecille Elliott to gather together a small troupe, the Colonial Players, and to operate out of the Colonial Theatre. This arrangement lasted for about a month beginning on November 29, 1918. Of course, the severe Spanish flu epidemic, which claimed 129 lives in Lethbridge[99] and closed many public facilities, including the theatres, for about six weeks just prior to this engagement, did not help this company "get off the ground." Similar attempts at establishing local resident companies occurred in later eras, but these efforts will be discussed at the appropriate time.

Regardless of these rather aborted attempts at residential theatre, Lethbridge audiences had vast opportunities to witness professional theatre during this era. Canadian stock companies were eminent during the years immediately succeeding 1908. Although the Tom Marks Company was the first such stock company to play the Lyceum Theatre, similar companies began to book one and two week engagements. Tom Marks was one of the several Marks brothers from Christie Lake in northern Ontario. Edwards tells us that the Marks brothers organized three touring companies prior to 1900. These companies were managed by three of the brothers, Bob, Ernie, and Tom. The brothers met together each summer to plan their next season's tours and to organize their repertoires, which were basically composed of the popular melodramas of the day. As Edwards points out, "The people wanted melodrama as far as R.W. Marks and his brothers could ascertain and working on that assumption, they never varied their bill."[100]

Besides the Tom Marks Company and the Jeanne Russell Company, other stock companies, which made a number of appearances and were generally appreciated by Lethbridge audiences, included the following: Stoddard Company, Oliver Eckhardt and Company, George Summers Company, the Partello Company, the Sanford Dodge Company, and the Allen Players. The latter group was one of the city's favorites, and Lethbridge audiences always anticipated with pleasure the performances of Mrs. Allen, her daughter, Verna Felton, and Verna's husband, Lee Millar. The company made its first appearance in Lethbridge at the Lyceum Theatre in the fall of 1909, after which it played Lethbridge on numerous occasions for many succeeding years, until its final appearance at the Majestic Theatre on February 19, 1927. The manager, P.R. Allen, usually did not perform when the company toured to Lethbridge; however, on November 19, 1910, the *Lethbridge Herald* stated, "Mr. Allen himself will perform tonight" in the *Heir to the Hoorah*.[101] His stepdaughter, Miss Felton, was undoubtedly the most popular leading lady among the various stock companies to play Lethbridge. Born in Salinas, California, in 1890, Felton spent most of her seventy-six years in the theatre. After many years with the stock company, she settled in Hollywood and extended her career into radio, movies, and television. She performed on the Jack Benny Show as Dennis Day's mother;[102] she did voice over work for Disney animated films *(Cinderella, The Jungle Book, and Alice in Wonderland)*,[103] and in the 1950s she appeared in a popular television situation-comedy, *December Bride*, where she played the humorous "side kick," Hilda, to Spring Byington's Lily.[104] Miss Felton returned to Alberta in the summer of 1946 when she holidayed in Edmonton. At that time, she expressed fond memories for Lethbridge, Calgary, and Edmonton. She also disclosed that her favorite stage part was Madame X. The news article which covered her visit confirmed the tremendous popularity of Miss Felton and pointed out that:[105]

> Local theatre fans recall that with equal ease she could bring tears to the eyes of all while playing Camille. Then she would bring forth gales of laughter with her homely lines in Sis Hopkins.

Other popular leading ladies were Belle Stevenson (Summers Company), Adelle Nickerson (Sanford Dodge Company), and Leah Stoddard (Stoddard Company). A number of other stock companies played Lethbridge on one or two occasions, only. A rather unique and exciting experience was accorded one of Lethbridge's young aspiring actresses in January 1914 when Eugene West and Catharine Henry brought their company to town to perform a number of one act plays. Miss Dorothy Young, who had appeared previously in local productions of *The Country Girl* and *San Toy*, was incorporated into the professional cast during their three day stand at the Sherman Theatre.

The year 1912 brought to an end the "golden age" of the Canadian stock companies. Actually, the transition was becoming apparent in Lethbridge in the spring of 1911 when road show plays and musicals began to compete for eminence with the stock companies' productions. Most of these road shows were presented by a company composed of a star performer, surrounded by a number of actors who were hired for that particular tour. These companies generally presented one play, only. They were booked for one or two nights, after which they moved on to the next city in their

TABLE 2-2
Broadway Actors in Lethbridge and Selected New York Productions*

Actor	Productions Staged in N.Y.	Year	Road Shows: Lethbridge
Zoe Barnett		1912	Red Roses
	All Aboard	13	
	The Tenderfoot	1904	
	The Mayor of Tokyo	05	
	The Spring Chicken	06	
	Mary's Lamb	08	
	Jumping Jupiter	11	
Richard Carle	The Girl From Monte Carlo	12	
	The Doll Girl	13	
	Ninety in the Shade	15	
	The Cohan Revue of 1916	16	
		19	Fur and Frills
	The New Yorkers	30	
Charles Coburn	The Yellow Jacket	1916	
	The Better 'Ole	18	
		21	French Leave (director)
		23/24	So This is London
	Diplomacy	28	
	The First Legion	34	
	The Country Chairman	36	
Mrs. Charles	The Yellow Jacket	16	
Coburn	The Better 'Ole	18	
(Ivah Wells)		23/24	So This is London
Jefferson De	All Aboard	1913	
Angelis		20	The Mikado
Max Dill	Lonesome Town	1908	
		11	Lonesome Town
Lawrence D'Orsay**	A Royal Family	1900	
	The Earl of Pawtucket	03	
	Trelawney of the Wells	11	
	The Lights 'O London	11	
	Whirl of Society	12	
	All Aboard	13	
		21	Tootlums
	Trelawney of the Wells (revival)	27	

Actor	Productions Staged in N.Y.	Year	Road Shows: Lethbridge
Max Figman	Fine Feathers	1913	
		18	Nothing But the Truth
Charlotte	The Passing Show of 1912	1912	
Greenwood	Ziegfeld Follies	13	
	So Long Lettie	16	
	Linger Longer Lettie	19	So Long Lettie
	Music Box Revue	22	
	Out of the World	50	
Margaret Illington	The Two Orphans	1904	
	Mrs. Leffingwell's Boots	05	
	His House in Order	06	
	The Thief	07	
	The Kindling	11	
		12	The Kindling
	The Lie	14	Within the Law
	Our Little Wife	16	Within the Law
Charles McNaughton		1916	Nobody Home
	The Better 'Ole	18	
Olga Nethersole**	Carmen; Denise; Frou-Frou;	1895	
	Camille		
	Sappho	1900	
	The Labyrinth; Carmen; Sappho	05	
	Carmen; Sappho; Magda; Camille; The Second Mrs Tanqueray; Adrienne Lecouvreur (in repertoire)	08	
	The Writing on the Wall	09	
		11	The Redemption of Evelyn Vaudray
	Mary Magdalene	13	
Phyllis Nielson	Twelfth Night	1914	
Terry**	Trilby	15	
		18	Maggy
	Separate Tables	56	
Alice Nielsen	The Singing Girl	1900	
		12	Barber of Seville (abridged)
Paul Nicholson	The Summer Widowers	1910	She Walked in Her Sleep
Guy Bates Post	The Bridge	1909	
	The Nigger	09	
	The Bird of Paradise	12	
	Omar the Tent Maker	14	

Actor	Productions Staged in N.Y.	Year	Road Shows: Lethbridge
	The Masquerader	17	
		20	The Masquerader
Tyrone Power**	Mary of Magdalla	1902	
	Ulysses	03	
	Servant in the House	08	
	Thais	11	
	Julius Caesar	12	
	Chu Chin Chow	17	
		20	Servant in the House
		20	The Little Brother
	Hamlet	22	
	The Rivals	22	
	Diplomacy	28	
May Robson	Liberty Hall	1892	
	The Importance of Being Ernest	95	
	Lord and Lady Algy	99	
	The Messenger Boy	1901	
	The Billionaire	02	
	Dorothy Vernon of Haddon Hall	03	
	It Happened in Nordland	04	
	Cousin Billy	05	
	The Rejuvenation of Aunt Mary	07	
		17	The Making Over of Mrs. Matt
		18	A Little Bit Old Fashioned
		20	Tish
		21	Nobody's Fool
Elsa Ryan	The Kiss Waltz	1911	
		18	Out There
		19	Tea for Three
Marie Tempest**	The Red Hussar (American debut)	1890	
	Nanon; The Fencing Master	92	
	Vanity Fair	1911	
	The Marriage of Kitty	03	
	Penelope	09	
	Caste	10	
	The Marriage of Kitty (revived)	14	
	The Duke of Killicrankie	15	The Marriage of Kitty
	Rosalind (1 act)	15	Nearly Married
	A Lady's Name	16	

Actor	Productions Staged in N.Y.	Year	Road Shows: Lethbridge
	Her Husband's Wife	17	
Lewis Waller**	The Garden of Allah	1911	
	Monsieur Beaucaire; The Explorer; Discovering America	12	
	Henry V	13	A Marriage of Convenience
Gus Weinburger		1910	The Burgomaster
		11	The Burgomaster
	A Tailor Made Man	17	
Thomas Whiffen**	HMS Pinafore	1879	
	Hazel Kirke	80	
		1913	The Time, The Place, The Girl

*Major source of N.Y. data: Blum, Daniel, A Pictorial History of the American Theatre (1860-1970), N.Y.: Crown Publishers, Inc. 1969
**Also established stars of the British Theatre

itinerary to repeat the show. One of the first of such road show productions to captivate Lethbridge audiences was *The Burgomaster* by Gustav Luders (starring Gus Weinburger), which played the Majestic Theatre in August 1910 and January 1911. Some years later (1917), Weinburger took a leading role in New York's Broadway production of *A Tailor Made Man* (see Table 2-2). Of course, the road companies had a number of advantages: they were backed by aggressive and frequently wealthy producers; they advertised that their productions were the original or associated road shows of the latest Broadway hits; they exploited the star system by touring well known actors, often, however, surrounded by less competent companies. In addition, many of the road companies presented musical revues, which became the most popular form of theatrical entertainment during this era. Unfortunately, the standards of these musical productions varied more than any other form of theatre. But, because of the manner in which these shows were toured, it was impossible to predict the quality of forthcoming productions. Naturally, press releases were always glowing, and the limited engagements provided little opportunity for reputations to develop.

Besides Gus Weinburger, some of the other musical theatre stars who accompanied productions to Lethbridge were Max Dill, who recreated his 1908 Broadway hit, *Lonesome Town*, at the Majestic Theatre in May 1911; Jefferson De Angelis, who starred in *The Mikado* (September 1920); and Zoe Barnett, who performed in the very popular musical, *Red Roses* (November 1912), which had recently completed its Broadway run starring Valeska Suratt. Zoe Barnett and Jefferson De Angelis later appeared together on Broadway in the 1913 musical, *All Aboard.*

Generally, musicals relied more on the reputation of the musical, the writer, or the producer than they did on specific performers. Therefore, advertisements for musicals often stated that the show was presented by producers such as Klaw and Erlanger, Selwyn, or Brady, or were written by popular playwrights such as George M. Cohan. On the other hand, road productions of plays relied much more on the reputation of the leading actor(s), or in the case of Annie Adams, the reputation of her daughter, Maude. Annie Adams spent most of her acting career in the western United States, especially in Utah, Nevada, and California.[106] She gave birth to Maude in 1872. Throughout most of her childhood, Maude toured with her mother. At a relatively young age, Maude, herself, began to perform, and by 1889 she was ready to take a featured role in the Broadway production of *A Midnight Bell*. Soon, Maude was an established star, and in 1905 her name became synonymous with Peter Pan. Jackson claims that by 1915 when Maude recreated the role of Peter Pan, she was "probably the most popular actress in America."[107] It was just two years prior to this revival that her mother toured western Canada and performed in *The Butler's Secret*, in Lethbridge. Unfortunately, Annie was nearing the end of her theatrical career. When she performed the same play in Edmonton, such a small house greeted her that she decided to disband her company, which she did shortly thereafter.[108] Barely three years passed before Annie Adams died in March 1916.

Actors who played Lethbridge prior to 1923, and who also starred on Broadway are listed together with their Lethbridge presentations and selected Broadway productions in Table 2-2. This list includes actors who also established their reputations on the London stage.

Some of these actors are familiar to us because of the reputation they later established as movie stars, for example, Charlotte Greenwood, May Robson and Charles Coburn. Greenwood was a tall, slim, comedic dancer with a characteristic high kick, who started her career as an acrobatic dancer in vaudeville, but who was soon starring in comedy and musical theatre. Besides being a star of live theatre, she was involved in silent films as of 1918, and later, talkies. She will be remembered as Aunt Eller in the movie version of the musical *Oklahoma*.[109] May Robson, the Australian born comedienne and musical theatre star, also acted in movies (both silent and sound). She received an Oscar nomination for her portrayal of Apple Annie in *Lady for a Day*, directed by Frank Capra.[110] Robson began her American acting career prior to the twentieth century, when she appeared in New York with a repertory company, which also included Henry Miller, William Faversham, and Viola Allen. Charles Coburn became a well known movie actor after establishing himself on the Broadway stage in a number of productions over a span of many years. One of his first major stage roles was Old Bill in *The Better 'Ole* which played Broadway in 1918. Also included in the cast were Mrs. Charles Coburn and Charles McNaughton.[111] All three of these actors graced the stage of the Majestic Theatre: McNaughton starred in the musical Nobody Home in 1916; Mr. & Mrs. Charles Coburn took the leading roles in So This is London on New Year's Eve and Day, 1923-24. Charles Coburn also directed French Leave which played the Colonial Theatre in 1921.

It is easy to become confused when discussing the theatrical career of Tyrone Power because there were actually three well known actors bearing that name; as of the 1980s, a fourth joined the acting fraternity. The "first Tyrone Power was," according to his great grandson, Tyrone Guthrie, "the leading exponent in his day of Irish comedy."[112] Although Power regularly played the Haymarket Theatre in London, he also acted on the American stage during two separate visits to the U.S.A. in the 1830s. Unfortunately, he drowned on his return trip to England when the steamship on which he was travelling was sunk by an Atlantic gale. Two of his sons, Harold and Maurice, rather unsuccessfully carried on the theatrical tradition. Of his other sons, Frederick was an engineer, and his namesake, Tyrone, was a professional soldier (and incidently, Tyrone Guthrie's grandfather). It is Harold's son, (Frederick) Tyrone Power (Sr.), who is referred to in Table 2-2. Guthrie comments that this grandson of the great Irish actor "went early to America where he did well as an actor mostly in Shakespeare and costume plays."[113] In turn, his son, Tyrone Power, Jr., began his acting career in 1931 when he appeared in a crowd scene in Fritz Lieber's Chicago production of *The Merchant of Venice* which starred Tyrone Power, Sr., as Shylock. After this production closed, father and son moved to Hollywood where Power Sr., took the title role in the Paramount movie, *The Miracle Man*. Shortly thereafter, Power Sr., died.[114]

John Kellerd, who helped keep the love for Shakespeare alive on his two appearances in Lethbridge, was probably best known for his Broadway production of *Hamlet* (1912) whose 102 successive performances broke the Broadway record previously established by Edwin Booth.[115]

Margaret Illington was possibly the best known Broadway star to play a number of engagements in Lethbridge. She vaulted to prominence after her New York performance in the 1904 revival of the famous melodrama, *The Two Orphans*. Acting with her on that occasion were Kyrle Bellew, Grace George, and James O'Neill.[116]

Most of these performers had very interesting biographies, but circumstances surrounding the rise to fame, in America, of Olga Nethersole are particularly fascinating. Miss Nethersole brought her repertory company to New York in 1895. She soared to stardom following the aborted production of *Sappho*, which opened at Wallace's Theatre on 30th Street, New York, in 1900. The run of *Sappho* was cut off abruptly when the New York police closed it because the ending of the second act implied that the leading man (Hamilton Revelle) "carried the voluptuous Olga Nethersole upstairs to an unseen bedroom where, many thought a terrible sin occurred at every performance."[117] Mordden claims that the show was closed after four weeks, but once the actors were acquitted, the play ran for eight more weeks, and on many occasions, thereafter.[118] Miss Nethersole revived Sappho a number of times for presentation on New York stages as well as for road shows. The closing of the show certainly did not hurt Olga's reputation; in fact, most scholars agree with Spitzer who maintains that, following the trial and acquittal, Miss Nethersole's reputation was made.[119]

Other lesser known but competent actors who visited Lethbridge fairly regularly were the comedians, Billy Oswald (Scottish comedian), Billy "Single" Clifford, and Max Bloom, as well as the dramatic actors, Albert Brown and Frank Ireson. Brown originally toured to Lethbridge (January 1916) with a William A. Brady production; whereas, Ireson was introduced to Lethbridge by the New York producer, Klaw and Erlanger. Brady as well as Klaw and Erlanger were among the ten major producers in New York around the turn of the century.[120] Brady also produced the musical *Ready Money* for the road show company which played the Majestic in November 1913. Previously, he made his name on Broadway for producing the following hit shows: *Under Southern Skies* (1901), *Frou-Frou* (1902), *A Gentleman From Mississippi* (1908). He then added to his laurels with revivals of Gilbert and Sullivan operettas (1915).[121] Klaw and Erlanger were noted for initiating the Theatre Syndicate in 1896 which, for many years, maintained firm control over many American and Canadian theatres. Another influential New York producer, Liebler, sent his very successful, *The Deep Purple* (1911), on tour after it completed 150 performances on Broadway;[122] it reached the Lethbridge Majestic Theatre on January 12, 1914. Less prominent but still well known Broadway producers such as William Elliott, Oliver Morosco, Henry Savage, Ray Comstock (with Morris Best), and Gus Hill also handled shows which Lethbridge audiences enjoyed. Elliott, who had established his Broadway reputation as an actor in *Charley's Aunt* (1906), and *Madame X* (1910), produced two New York shows in 1914, *Kitty MacKay*, by Catherine Chisholm Cushing, and *Experience*. He then sent the former production on tour.[123] Morosco, whose hit play, *The Unchastened Woman*, played Broadway in 1915, toured Madam G. Johnstone-Bishop in *Peg 'O My Heart*.[124] *The Devil* (1908) was a big New York hit for Henry Savage, completing 87 performances with Edwin Stevens in the leading role. Theodosia de Cappet, who was to become the film star, Theda Bara, was also in this production.[125] One of Savage's touring companies performed *Every Woman* at the Majestic on November 20, 1916. Many years after Comstock and Best first produced road shows which toured to Lethbridge, they provided New York audiences with one of the theatrical events of the year 1924 when they presented *The Miracle* staged by Max Reinhardt.[126] Gus Hill presented some of the most popular productions to visit Lethbridge. He practically became a household name in Lethbridge by entertaining local audiences for many years with musicals based on Mutt and Jeff as well as Maggie and Jiggs, the leading characters in two popular comic strips of that time.

During the first two decades of the twentieth century, two other producers achieved prominence on Broadway: Charles Dillingham and George M. Cohan. In 1904 Dillingham presented (in New York) a musical version of *She Stoops to Conquer* called, *The Two Roses*. The next year, he followed this up with Shaw's *Man* and *Superman*. In 1916 he produced a magnificent entertainment at New York's Hippodrome called *The Big Show* which featured Anna Pavlova.[127] He also toured the popular musical *Chin-Chin* which played the Majestic on January 7, 1920. George M. Cohan established himself as a writer, actor, singer, dancer, composer, and producer. Actually, few of his shows played Lethbridge, although a number of companies presented *Forty-Five Minutes From Broadway* which Cohan wrote and first staged at the New Amsterdam Theatre in New York on January 1, 1906.[128] In 1913 Cohan and his major collaborator, Sam Harris, sent their production of *Officer 666*, written by Augustin MacHugh, on tour after completing 192 performances at New York's Gaiety Theatre.[129] The production played the Majestic on September 6, of that year.

In concluding this discussion on American producers, we should also mention a truly unique organization, The Theatre Guild, which grew out of an amateur and semi professional company known as the Washington Square Players.[130] The Guild brought their first commercially successful play, *John Ferguson*, to Lethbridge in 1919. The American Theatre Guild quickly became a very influential force in American theatre.

Many Canadian booking agents decried the stranglehold which American companies and producers had over Canadian theatres. Some of these agents looked to England to provide some competition for the Americans. In 1913 the Anglo-Canadian Booking Office was created, and then, in association with English dramatists, who formed The British-Canadian Theatrical Organization Society, tours of British companies were planned.[131] Unfortunately, as stated earlier, World War I quickly brought this experiment to an end. Following the war, however, the Trans-Canada Theatres Ltd., as well as other organizations, took over this role. It was at this time, that Lethbridge audiences were introduced to English actors like Lawrence D'Orsay, Edward Lewers, Walter Edwin, Lewis Waller, Tyrone Power, Phyllis Neilson-Terry (Ellen Terry's niece), Muriel Martin-Harvey (Sir Martin-Harvey's daughter), Percy Hutchison, and the great English Music Hall performer, Sir Harry Lauder.

Three other theatrical developments generally coincided with the post-World War I period: the introduction of English pantomime, the establishment of the Western Canadian Chautauqua circuit, and the development of Canadian Army shows. Actually, F. Stuart Whyte began his touring of English pantomime during the war when he presented *Aladdin and His Wonderful Lamp* in 1916. The next five or six years witnessed annual tours of such pantomimes presented by Stuart Whyte. Long before he got involved with English pantomime, however, Whyte had been engaged in booking musical entertainers such as the Old Country Pierrots and The Versatiles. His theatrical activities in Canada extended well into the 1920s.

E. Ross Stuart informs us that the Chautauqua was brought to Canada in 1917 when Mr. & Mrs. John M. Erickson obtained the Canadian rights to the American Ellison and White Chautauquas.[132] Chautauquas presented a series of musical entertainments, plays, and lectures; occasional musical theatre was also provided. Chautauqua bookings were made only after a community signed a rigid contract guaranteeing a certain fee. Profits beyond this minimum fee were divided among the local sponsors and the Chautauqua organization. Johnston and den Otter claim that Lethbridge was the first Canadian community to sponsor the Chautauqua, and this claim is verified by Sheilagh Jameson. According to Jameson, it was in the fall of 1916 that J.M. Erickson met with the local lawyer, Samuel S. Dunham, who became very enthusiastic about Lethbridge hosting a Chautauqua. Dunham convinced other prominent business and professional men to meet with Erickson, after which Dunham and 29 others signed the contract. Soon, other western towns and cities followed suit. In June 1917 the Chautauqua entered Canada and pitched its tent in Mission, B.C. During the summer, it travelled throughout western Canada and visited Lethbridge for the week of August 7-13.[133] Following this initial experiment, Mr. Lyle Armel of the Chautauqua Circuit (Salmon, Idaho), wrote a letter to the local committee commending them and the citizens of Lethbridge. Armel declared that all hopes and expectations in pioneering the Dominion Chautauqua Circuit in Lethbridge had been realized; the executive was very proud of Lethbridge, especially since it had provided the biggest crowds on the circuit.[134] From 1917 to 1922 the Chautauqua became an annual affair, although the specific dates varied. From 1917-1920 August bookings were retained, but in 1921 and 1922 the Chautauqua occurred in the spring or early winter. Indoor Chautauqua festivals were held in Lethbridge during one season only (the winter and spring of 1919 when a series of musical concerts were presented at the Majestic Theatre). Although the Chautauqua set up its tent in neighboring towns during some of the years after 1922, it did not return to Lethbridge until August 1929, after which it became an annual event, again, until June 17-30, 1933, when the Chautauqua made its final appearance in Lethbridge.

A more truly Canadian by-product of World War I was the production of plays, revues, and vaudeville by military and ex-military groups. Sergeant Gittus brought his productions of army life to Lethbridge in March and December 1918. Captain Fred Fisher and his Canadian Army Players provided plenty of humor with *Madamoiselle From Armentieres* in October 1921. But it was Captain M.W. Plunkett who really captivated Canadian audiences with his overseas revues, *Camouflage* (presented by the Fourth Canadian Army Division, Maple Leafs) and *Biff, Bing, Bang* (by the Dumbells). Because the success of these revues stretched through the next historical period to be covered, it seems reasonable to discuss their place in Canadian theatre history in Chapter Three. However, at this point, it should be mentioned that these army revues basically developed out of the vaudeville tradition. Vaudeville, itself, had experienced considerable change during the second decade of the century. Most of this change was organizational in nature, whereas the content of the vaudeville shows remained fairly stable. By 1909 independent vaudeville companies had been pretty well squeezed out by movies and circuit vaudeville. Nevertheless, a few troupes such as the Fax Fun Company, Kenny-Harvey, and the Musical Eckhardts functioned throughout most of this time. In fact, the late war years saw a slight resurgence of the independents – and this development continued somewhat in the post war years with the emergence of Canadian groups such as the Winnipeg Kiddies, the Calgary Kiddies, and the ex-army units.

But the most significant development which characterized vaudeville in the early 1900s was the movement toward centralized control of the touring process, which, in turn, facilitated local scheduling of various vaudeville acts. Most vaudeville touring in western Canada was controlled by major American vaudeville circuits, through affiliation with some of the most influential theatre managers in western Canada such as W.B. Sherman and C.P. Walker. The Western Vaudeville Association, of which the Orpheum Circuit, ruled by General Manager, Martin Beck, was an important part, controlled most of the vaudeville in the United States from Chicago west to the coast and in parts of Canada.[135] Beck immigrated to the United States around 1893 as a juvenile member of a small troupe of German actors. After a few years of various ventures in the American theatre (including theatre management), Beck became associated with Martin Lehman, a partner in the

Orpheum Theatre, San Francisco.[136] Then, Lehman started up the Orpheum Circuit and quickly acknowledged Beck's talent for selecting profitable existing theatres and recognizing appropriate potential theatre sites. In the late 1890s, the operation was moved to Chicago, and by 1905 Martin Beck was in control. Since the Orpheum Circuit acts were booked through the Keith-Albee United Booking office in New York, eventually Beck moved there to oversee operations.[137] Around 1912 Beck decided to compete more directly with B.F. Keith in New York and proceeded to build the Palace Theatre on 47th Street. But Beck experienced trouble with financing the project, and when the theatre was completed, B.F. Keith actually controlled 75% of the stock of what was, consequently, referred to as Keith's Palace.[138] With Keith's death in 1914, and that of his son, Paul, in 1918, Keith's associate, E.F. Albee, ruled over much of the vaudeville in North America. Later, Albee added to his empire by acquiring the New York Hippodrome as well as the Canadian United Theatres. In 1927 his circuit was merged with the Orpheum Circuit. But shortly thereafter, Albee was, in turn, dethroned by Joseph Kennedy.[139]

In the meantime, some equally interesting developments were happening on the west coast, which would have important ramifications for circuit vaudeville in western Canada. Alexander Pantages, a Greek immigrant, who had participated in the Klondike Gold Rush, attempted to combine vaudeville with movies while resident in Victoria, British Columbia.[140] Unfortunately, the venture there was not very fruitful; however, a second attempt at his Crystal Palace in Seattle was so successful that he soon spread his Pantages operations along the coast and into the western interior of the United States and Canada. Before long, the Pantages vaudeville circuit became a major competitor to the Orpheum circuit in the west. The only other serious competition on the west coast came from the Sullivan-Considine Circuit. Pantages and Considine were apparently bitter enemies; however, when their children (Carmen Pantages and John Considine, Jr.) married each other, the rivalry was resolved. Considine, Jr., went on to become a Hollywood producer. During the 1920s, Pantages overextended his operations somewhat and was severely hurt by the 1929 stock market crash, after which he was forced to sell most of his theatres.[141]

Although theatres were frequently constructed throughout the United States and Canada to accommodate the burgeoning circuit vaudeville, many of the acts were booked into existing theatres through an arrangement whereby exclusive contracts were signed by local theatre owners, leasers, or managers. This latter arrangement prevailed in Lethbridge, and as mentioned earlier, the Eureka Theatre was the first local theatre to engage in regular circuit vaudeville, although the character of that early vaudeville was pretty small time. This fact does not necessarily imply, however, that the performers were incompetent; rather, they were often beginners who were in the process of developing their routines.

In 1909 the Empire Agency Vaudeville circuit provided Oliver's Hall and the Lyceum Theatre with a number of acts. This agency sent acts directly from Chicago to Calgary, then to Edmonton and Lethbridge and back to the United States by way of Spokane, Washington. Participants in the Empire Vaudeville presented at Oliver's Hall on January 21, 1909, included: YBUR (the Handcuff Queen); Billionaire Trio (comedy sketch artists); Signor Joseph St. Claire (European harpist); The DeComas (sensational novelty acrobats); Weaver and Williams ("Refined Entertainers"); Dave Gaston (Australian comedian).[142] The Webster Circuit also provided acts during the summer of 1913. But it was the two major circuits (referred to above) plus the Hippodrome circuit that dominated the local vaudeville scene from 1910 through the period under discussion. Pantages was the first of the major impresarios to invade Lethbridge when he assigned acts such as the Tyrell Children to the Lyceum in 1910. Through the succeeding years, acts from the Pantages Circuit were presented sporadically at the various Lethbridge theatres that featured vaudeville. The Orpheum

Vaudeville circuit, which was generally considered to be more staid and conservative than the Pantages Circuit, was most aggressively pursued during 1915 and 1916 by both the local Orpheum and Majestic theatres. An earlier Orpheum Circuit act, which stopped in Lethbridge on its tour from Calgary to Spokane, was the Marx Brothers. Their show, *Mr. Green's Reception* (hardly a staid act), was presented at the Majestic Theatre, August 25-27, 1913, by their mother, Minnie Palmer. The show, an updated version of their earlier sketch, *Fun in Hi Skule*, was about the antics of students under the tutelage of an eccentric teacher. When *Mr. Green's Reception* grew stale, the boys' uncle, Al Shean, of the comedy team, Gallagher and Shean, wrote them a new sketch, *Home Again*, which they presented throughout the years 1914-1919.[143] The Lethbridge show was advertised as the Four Marx Brothers with a company of twenty including George Lee ("formerly principal comedian with the Arlington Four"), Mr. Paul Yale (bass singer), and the Harris Brothers (dancers). In the *Lethbridge Herald* write up, only Arthur (Harpo) and Leo (Chico) are identified as performing on their respective instruments of the harp and the piano. Undoubtedly Julius (Groucho) and Milton (Gummo) were also involved since Groucho always played the teacher and Gummo customarily took various parts in these early routines. The *Lethbridge Herald* commented that, when the curtains went up, there was bedlam on the stage; the antics of the students and the eccentricity of the teacher were exhilaratingly funny, and, "as a company of vaudeville artists, they excel anything that has been seen here."[144] Obviously, the critic recognized talent; two years later, the Marx Brothers were playing the Palace in New York, and by 1917 they were headliners there. Prior to their performance on August 27, the company challenged the "pick of Lethbridge" to a ball game.

Sullivan and Considine advertised that they, in association with Edwin J. Fisher, would provide the Variety Theatre in Lethbridge with unequalled vaudeville as of August 30, 1915. This arrangement lasted only a couple of weeks because the Variety closed; however, some of the acts were then booked into the Orpheum Theatre. Few circuit vaudeville acts toured to Lethbridge during the last two years of World War I. This fact may have contributed to the increased number of specialty or vaudeville companies that played the city during those years. Finally, acts from the Hippodrome Circuit were first seen in Lethbridge in May 1917. From October 1919 through May 1921, this circuit became the only consistent circuit vaudeville in the city. The "Country Store Vodvil Nite" was also quite common during these later years. The Country Store idea was a means of attracting larger crowds to small time vaudeville by awarding a number of prizes to patrons during the evening's entertainment. The Pantages Circuit returned to the Majestic Theatre in late 1922 after an extended absence of many years. Henceforth, the Pantages Circuit dominated circuit vaudeville in Lethbridge during the succeeding years. It should be noted that vaudeville was frequently offered in combination with moving pictures; some theatres featured vaudeville on specific nights of the week such as Monday and Tuesday, or Friday and Saturday and exhibited films on the remaining nights.

Moving Pictures

Early vaudeville and motion picture houses such as the Bijou and the Eureka advertised motion pictures according to their length (3 000 feet of moving pictures) or according to the subject matter ("Forty dollar CPR trip from Calgary to Vancouver" or the "Grand National Steeple Chase"). When the Starland Movie Theatre opened in early 1911, it became more common to advertise movies by their titles. By this time, attending movies had become a common pastime in western Canada as well as elsewhere. On January 13, 1912, the *Lethbridge Herald* reported that 130 movie houses involving 500 employees were operating in the prairie provinces; $4 500 was paid out each week to various exchanges for the rental of films.[145] Shortly thereafter, the star system began to be felt, and theatre ads more frequently bore the name of the leading actor, for example, Sarah Bernhardt in *Queen Elizabeth* at the Starland Theatre in October 1913, Mary Pickford in *The Bishop's Carriage*, or James O'Neill in *The Count of Monte Cristo* at the Bijou in February and March 1914, respectively. Lethbridge audiences looked forward to seeing some of these famous stars on screen since they had little opportunity to see them in person. Although Sarah Bernhardt had toured to some of the larger centres in western Canada, she did not come to Lethbridge. To see James O'Neill (Eugene O'Neill's father) portray the role with which he had become so closely associated, was a thrill, even though viewing a silent screen version was hardly equivalent to witnessing a live performance. Before long, Lethbridge movie audiences were treated to movies starring all the major silent screen actors of that time. Patrons also began to look forward to the latest films of producers and directors such as D.W. Griffith and Cecil B. DeMille. On at least one occasion in this era, Lethbridge audiences were treated to sound films. Gaumont, a French film company with a subsidiary operation in Great Britain,[146] exhibited three short "Talkies" during the week of January 12, 1914, at the Empress Theatre. These short sound films included: *Beautiful Isle of Somewhere*, *Bedouin Love Song*, and a presentation of the great English music hall entertainer, Harvey Lauder. With regard to these "Talkies," the *Lethbridge Herald* commented as follows:[147]

> The house of Gaumont are the original and only successful manufacturer of this, the greatest innovation in the field of entertainment in the moving picture world of modern days. . . .

> The marvelous manner in which the reproduction of the human voice synchronizes with the action of the characters on the screen is perfect, the motion of the lips seeming to actually speak the words.

> . . . absolutely realistic reproduction of voice, action and other peculiarities of the greatest vaudeville artist of modern days.

By 1922 going to the theatre, whether to enjoy road shows, vaudeville, or movies was a very common nightly occurrence. Provincial statistics quoted in the *Lethbridge Herald* reported that Lethbridge theatres had experienced an average daily attendance during the past year of 997 patrons,[148] which represents about 9 percent of the population of the city at that time. It should be remembered, however, that the city served a large rural area. Such figures were available from the provincial government because of a provincial entertainment tax which had been introduced on June 1, 1916, and which was assessed each patron who attended the theatre.[149]

In July 1920 the Starland Theatre exhibited a locally produced film, *The Romance of Lethbridge*, with a cast "composed entirely of Lethbridge people."[150] This film obviously received limited distribution. However, *Cameron of the Royal Mounted*, which starred established movie actors, Gaston Glass, Vivienne Osborne, and Irving Cummings received broad distribution throughout North America. The movie was based on Ralph Connor's story of pioneer days in Alberta and was filmed in and around Calgary, Macleod, and Banff. In addition, an entire squadron of officers and men from the Royal Canadian Mounted Police including men from the Macleod detachment, were involved in the picture. Both the Macleod Barracks and the local commander, Inspector Townsend, were conspicuous in the film. The *Lethbridge Herald* and the *Calgary Herald* gave the film enthusiastic reviews.[151]

3

The Little Theatre Era
A Time Of Growth And Development (1923 - 1932)

Community Setting

As the year 1923 began, Lethbridge was still reeling from the economic recession which had affected western Canada since 1921. Although the recession had peaked prior to the onset of 1923, its negative socioeconomic consequences continued to be evident throughout most of that year, and later in some instances. The local unemployment rate, which had risen from 2 1/2% of the labor force in 1921 to 5% in 1922,[1] remained relatively high until bumper crops in the fall of 1923 opened opportunities for farm labor. After that, with minor fluctuations, unemployment remained low in Lethbridge through the rest of the 1920s; however, unrest among Alberta's coal miners aggravated the employment situation in 1923-24.

Some positive forces were at work during and immediately after the recession to maintain faith in southern Alberta's ability to weather periodic economic setbacks. Thanks to the provincial government, which guaranteed loans in 1921 to the Lethbridge Northern Irrigation District (LNID), the latest irrigation project in the Lethbridge area was able to proceed during the recession. This development was accompanied by an influx of settlers, primarily from the Netherlands and Switzerland. Besides increasing the yields of traditional grain crops, irrigation provided opportunities for agricultural diversification which, in turn, provided greater economic stability in the Lethbridge area.[2] The fall of 1923 also ushered in an era of prosperity for dryland farmers as wheat prices began to rise. In addition, 1923 was a bumper year for crop yields and each succeeding year until 1928 witnessed increased production throughout most of the province. In 1927 the per bushel price of No. 1 wheat stood at $1.64 compared to the price of $0.77 per bushel in 1922.[3]

Within the City of Lethbridge, some signs of economic recovery were evident as early as 1922. The opening of the new library in Galt Gardens on January 23, 1922, seemed to introduce a degree of optimism, reflected, shortly thereafter, in the report of the *Lethbridge Herald* that building in the city "was brisk."[4] In July it was reported that the city fathers had recently unveiled a concentrated city planning proposal to accommodate an anticipated population of 40 000[5] – a figure which, in fact, was not achieved until about fifty years later. But there is evidence that their faith in economic recovery was somewhat warranted. The value of building permits began to rise slowly in 1923 and reached in 1925 their highest level since 1914. After remaining fairly steady through 1926, permit values soared during the next five years. In 1927 a $170 000 permit for the new community owned Marquis Hotel provided a major boost that year. About 400 Lethbridge investors purchased shares in this 78 room hotel.[6] An interesting development in 1928 was a roof-top addition to the Marquis Hotel to house radio station CJOC. The exuberance felt by the Lethbridge business community was well expressed by John I. McFarland, a well known Calgary financier and president of Imperial Motors in Lethbridge, who said, "Lethbridge shows every indication of wide-awakeness and progress, and the optimism I find among the citizens here is fully justified. Lethbridge is bound to grow."[7] Shortly thereafter, the *Lethbridge Herald* carried the following statement which underlines McFarland's argument:[8]

> Lethbridge is experiencing a building boom the equal of which has not been seen in the city for some years. Big changes have taken place in the city's business blocks, with old landmarks torn down or remodeled, new business blocks being built and other business centres changing hands.

This kind of commercial activity continued throughout the next two years, and in 1930 and 1931 residential construction contributed significantly to the value of building permits. In fact, the year 1930 was the best year for house construction in Lethbridge for some time.[9] Then, as the depression settled in, construction declined considerably.

The economic boom associated with the late 1920s drew people to Lethbridge, again. The overall population growth of about 21.6% for the decade (1921-1931) exceeded the provincial growth rate for that period by over 2 1/2%.[10] This growth rate differential was consistent with the demographic trend toward urbanization which was occurring, albeit slowly throughout most of Canada. Other socioeconomic trends in Canada during the 1920s which influenced behavior in Lethbridge included mechanization and the consequent growth of oil and gas industries, electrification and the concomitant spread of the broadcasting industry, recreational development and the evolution of the tourist industry, religious diversification represented by the cultivation of fundamentalism (a trend countered somewhat by unification of the United Church of Canada), and women's liberation with the recognition of women as "persons"[11] when the English Privy Council decided that women could be named to the Canadian Senate.

Unfortunately, the exuberance created by these developments was dashed considerably in early 1929 when the New York Stock Market experienced its first major slump in many years.[12] Locally, economic consequences were somewhat mixed. Wheat prices fell almost immediately, but they soon began to rise again; in the summer of 1929 prices reached their highest level since World War I.[13] September wheat deliveries for the CPR's Lethbridge division set a new record.[14] Prospects for local farmers looked very promising. In addition, as illustrated earlier, business and institutional construction continued unabated. Then, in October 1929 the major stock market crash occurred. The New York market experienced panic selling; the Toronto and Montreal exchanges witnessed the most spectacular price drops in their history. Thus, the economic depression of the 1930s was ushered in. The devastating effects of the crash were tempered somewhat in Lethbridge for the first year or so because of a number of on-going and planned construction projects. One hundred and fifty thousand dollars in contracts were let in early 1930 for extensions to the Galt Hospital and the Marquis Hotel. Later that summer, the Sisters of St. Martha awarded the contract for construction of St. Michael's Hospital. The hospital opened in September 1931. These building activities encouraged belief that Lethbridge would be spared this latest economic upheaval. Lethbridge city council also demonstrated their faith by approving a major street paving program and a $100 000 storm sewer project.[15] This optimistic feeling was buoyed further by the establishment of a commercial air schedule between Lethbridge and Edmonton originating from the new airport in North Lethbridge. Shortly thereafter, air mail service to the city was inaugurated.[16] All this activity stimulated the *Lethbridge Herald* to report on numerous occasions in 1930 that Lethbridge was the "bright spot" in western Canada.[17]

Certain negative consequences of the broader economic situation could not, however, be escaped. After rebounding to a high of $1.70 a bushel in the fall of 1929, wheat prices tumbled continuously during the next few years reaching a price of $0.38 at Winnipeg by December 1932. MacGregor informs us that this would translate to about $0.20 to the farmer.[18] A number of businesses closed, including the Hudson's Bay Store which had served the community for many years.[19] Soon, unemployment and associated problems increased.[20] Both civic workers and teachers took pay cuts of about 15% in 1932. Also that year, the recently introduced air mail service to Lethbridge was discontinued. Another area of life, which was seriously affected in Lethbridge as it was elsewhere in Canada, was the arts, and in particular, the professional theatre arts. This, of course, was due to the heavy reliance on external resources. It is true, however, that the demise of touring professional theatre had been anticipated for many years. Fortunately, the Little Theatre movement was prepared to "take up the slack."

The Little Theatre Movement

By 1924 Broadway producers had determined that it was no longer economical for them to send their shows on the road; in addition, the vaudeville era had reached its peak and was in decline. Nevertheless, a number of English companies managed to tour the country. Also, the Chautauqua continued to visit southern Alberta, but it tended to concentrate on smaller communities such as Cardston, Pincher Creek, and Coaldale during the years 1923 - 1928. The most successful Canadian contribution to professional theatre during the 1920s was the ex-army group known as the Dumbells which successfully toured Canada annually for fourteen years. However, regardless of the excellent quality of these shows, the one or two productions toured per year, could not satisfy the demand for live theatre.

The need to fill the void created by the severe reduction of touring professional companies provided the ideal stimulus for the growth of local theatre. Since there was very little foundation in western Canada for the establishment of local professional theatre, concerned amateurs took up the challenge. Fortunately for Lethbridge, Ernest Gaskell Sterndale Bennett was willing and able to provide the necessary artistic leadership so that Lethbridge was able to secure an honorable place in the Little Theatre movement as it began to sweep through the prairie provinces. Brockett informs us that the Little Theatre movement was America's response to the development of independent theatre in Europe.[21] Gardner, in turn, points out that, "Although enlightened Canadians absorbed developments in Europe, more direct influence came from the U.S."[22] With regard to the characteristics of American "little theatres" Brockett states:[23]

> For the most part they depended upon unpaid volunteers for personnel and upon subscribers for financial support; most produced a series of plays each year. . . . After 1920, the little theatres began to be indistinguishable from community theatres.

As for the development of the Little Theatre movement in Canada, Gardner maintains that:[24]

> When Toronto's Hart House Theatre was opened in 1919, Vincent Massey invited [Roy] Mitchell to be its first stage director and together they turned Hart House into the flagship of Canada's Little Theatre movement.

During the next two decades, a large number of these amateur indigenous companies emerged throughout Canada. The Playgoers Club of Lethbridge, established by E.G. Sterndale Bennett and H.W. Church in the spring of 1923, was truly representative of the Canadian Little Theatre. But before reviewing the activities of Sterndale Bennett and other local amateurs, an analysis of the ever changing fortunes of the local performing facilities would be in order.

Local Theatres

By 1923 three of Lethbridge's remaining four theatres were controlled by Rogers and Company with A.W. Shackleford as manager: the Colonial, Kings, and Majestic. The Kings, together with its somewhat larger and more attractive neighbor, the Empress, were primarily movie houses, although the Empress did occasionally present vaudeville and other live performances. The Colonial and the Majestic exhibited movies and presented live performances.

Following a disagreement with Mark Rogers over a lease agreement for the Kings Theatre, Shackleford resigned and returned to Calgary. Within a few months, however, Shackleford was contacted by Henry Granger, secretary- treasurer for Rogers and Company and associated businesses, to see if he would consider managing the Lethbridge Arena. Shackleford agreed, on the condition that he be allowed to lease the Kings Theatre. A lease agreement, setting an annual rental fee of $3 000, was arranged. Shackleford borrowed one-half of that amount from his father; the other half was provided by a silent partner, J.B. De Guerre (commonly known as "D the Tailor"), local agent for Leishman Clothes.[25] Shackleford, who would also manage the theatre, was now on the threshold of becoming one of the must successful local entrepreneurs and civic minded individuals in the history of Lethbridge.[26] Even though the Kings Theatre was closed permanently in the summer of 1925, Shackleford had taken steps to consolidate his position in the local theatre business.

Following the tragic death of Mark C. Rogers in his home on September 30, 1924, Henry Granger took over the operation of the Colonial Theatre which he renamed the Palace Theatre in December 1924.[27] By this time, A.W. Shackleford had formed the Lethbridge Amusement Company which managed the Henderson Lake Dance Pavilion and the Lethbridge Arena and now assumed management of the Palace Theatre.[28] Under the new management, the Palace began to book a few more vaudeville acts.

In 1928 Shackleford became associated with Famous Players Corporation. In October it was announced that a new theatre would shortly replace the Palace and that this new theatre, which would be called the Capitol Theatre, would be an exclusive theatre for road shows and movies booked by Famous Players Theatres.[29] The following May, a contract was let for $140 000 in order to restructure the old Palace Theatre. The costs were to be shared by Famous Players Corporation and by Lethbridge Theatres Ltd., which had recently been organized with a capitalization of $100 000. Considerable stock in Lethbridge Theatres Ltd. was held by the Lethbridge Amusement Company. J.B. De Guerre became the first president of Lethbridge Theatres Limited while A.W. Shackleford was named managing director. In addition, Shackleford retained the management of the theatre.[30] Since Shackleford's dividends were rolled over into equity in the company, while other investors received cash, he gradually assumed complete control of Lethbridge Theatres Ltd.

The new Capitol Theatre, designed by the local architect, Harry Meech, was truly a magnificent structure. From the audience's perspective, it was luxurious. The painted ceiling and centre chandelier were exquisite. The enlarged foyer opened up into a 60 foot by 72 foot auditorium which accommodated approximately 700 patrons. Because the ceiling had been raised in order to incorporate a new balcony seating about 200 additional people, a definite feeling of spaciousness existed.[31] As a movie house, the new Capitol was, indeed, a splendid facility. With this updated facility, Shackleford planned to attract more road shows. Unfortunately, most good sized companies found the stage facilities to be somewhat inadequate. Although the proscenium opening was a fair size (34 feet wide by 18 feet high), the depth of the stage was quite limited. In addition, the wings were almost non-existent, and the basement dressing rooms were designed for fairly small groups. Nevertheless, for some years the Capitol vied with the Majestic for live performances.

In the meantime, the fortunes of the Majestic Theatre "hung in the balance." When Rogers and Company relinquished its lease of the Majestic in the fall of 1924, concern was voiced among members of the local amateur theatre society that the Majestic would be taken over by movie interests or closed. This concern led Ernest Sterndale Bennett to write an open letter to the *Lethbridge Herald* stressing the need to keep the Majestic available for legitimate theatre.[32] Shortly after this, through the cooperation of the Lethbridge Playgoers and the theatre operators, A.W. Shackleford and H.H. Granger, the Community Theatres Limited was formed to lease the Majestic Theatre. Sterndale Bennett, who joined these two theatre managers to form the executive committee, was generally the spokesman, and he tended to represent the theatre at meetings of associated groups such as the Western Canadian Theatre Managers Association.[33] But even Sterndale Bennett's avid commitment to live theatre could not counteract the forces of change which were affecting the theatres at that time. Efforts to attract some of the few larger touring companies to Lethbridge often went for naught as is illustrated by the following comment in the *Lethbridge Herald* in the spring of 1926:[34]

Certificate: Community Theatres Ltd. dated March, 1925
Photo: Al Greenway

The theatre-going public will learn with regret that, in spite of the efforts made by E.G. Sterndale-Bennett [sic] to secure the engagement of the company, "No, No, Nanette" will not come to Lethbridge. . . . The fact that Lethbridge cannot support a three days' show militates against companies such as "No, No, Nanette" coming here, . . . Some of the better companies who have come here have not been supported as they should have been, and this, no doubt, has had its effect in Lethbridge being omitted when it comes to arranging the schedule of tours.

In order to keep afloat, the management of the Majestic was forced into booking movies to fill in the long periods between touring and amateur shows. Nevertheless, the operation was not a financial success and Playgoers was forced to withdraw from the arrangement. The Lethbridge Community Theatre Ltd. reluctantly relinquished the lease in the spring of 1929 to G.W. Peacock who owned a number of movie theatres south of Calgary.[35] On May 9, 1929, Peacock exhibited the first talky at the Majestic, *The Younger Generation,* starring Jean Hersholt and Ricardo Cortez.[36] Al Jolson in *The Jazz Singer* ran from June 13-15, 1929. Two years later, C.D. Dowsley (Calgary theatre owner) leased the Majestic which then opened under manager William Cole, Jr., on April 20, 1931.[37] In July Dowsley closed the theatre for about three weeks in order to carry out some structural changes, after which it reopened with a new manager, T.D. Cooke, who announced a new price schedule: $0.25 (adults), $0.15 (children) at all times. The next spring, the Capitol followed this pricing policy except for loge seats. Less than a year later, the Majestic Theatre was sold to Famous Players Corporation and Lethbridge associate A.W. Shackleford.[38] Although Shackleford hoped to book more road shows for Lethbridge and for the Majestic Theatre, specifically, times were against him, so the Majestic essentially became another movie house. At this time, only it and the Capitol were operating.

The Empress had recently been closed and was, subsequently, put up for auction on Saturday, October 29, 1932, to satisfy claims against the property amounting to $30 000. Charles Hansen had previously purchased the Empress Theatre, and as of March 1933 the following monies were owed: taxes [$7 032], first mortgage [$2 500 (A.M. Grace, former Lethbridge Commissioner of Public Works)], second mortgage [$10 000 (Mrs. Grace McCurdy)] and third mortgage [$12 000 (Royal Bank)]. A reserve price of $60 000 was placed on the property; because the top bid was only $35 000, no sale was completed.[39] Then, McCurdy, through her lawyer, A.B. Hogg, sued Hansen for the money owed her. The trial division of the Supreme Court of Alberta ordered that McCurdy be paid, and that, if necessary, the theatre be sold to raise the money. A second auction was held in early March 1933, at which time a bid of $21 000 was accepted from R.V. Gibbons on behalf of A.W. Shackleford and associates who remodeled the building at considerable expense and reopened it as the Roxy Theatre on October 4, 1934.[40] In the interim, goods and chattels were also sold at a public auction on March 28, 1933. Hansen appealed the sale of the theatre; however, the sale was upheld by the Appellate Court.[41]

Considering the fact that the period from the late 1920s through the 1930s was a golden age for movies, the City of Lethbridge now had surprisingly few movie theatres. Some proposals for new theatres in Lethbridge were rumored, but none of these ever reached fruition. In 1928 the Empire Theatre of Winnipeg announced the purchase of property on the west side of the 300 block of 6th Street South in order to develop a new theatre to be called the Garrick Theatre.[42] Plans had proceeded sufficiently by October so that a $40 000 pipe organ had been ordered from Wick's Organ Company of Chicago. In addition, the *Lethbridge Herald* announced on November 9 that all the necessary furnishings and equipment had been ordered, and that the new theatre would officially open on February 15, 1929.[43] Naturally, interest in the venture was high throughout the next few months, but the theatre never materialized. In April 1929 the Winnipeg associate of the company created to build the theatre, D.E.L. Fisher, reported that he had recently sold the site to the Lethbridge Amusement Company.[44] Of course, this was just at the time when the Lethbridge Amusement Company, through its affiliation with Lethbridge Theatres Ltd. and Famous Players Corporation, was investing considerable funds in the development of the Capitol Theatre, which, although it was a restructured theatre, was also in a sense, a new theatre. It was certainly able to accommodate many more theatre patrons than the old Palace Theatre since its seating capacity was about double that of its forerunner. Another new theatre proposal was mooted in 1932. After Dowsley disposed of his interest in the Majestic Theatre, he spoke about the possibility of developing a new theatre on the site of the old Bijou Theatre. However, 1932 and subsequent years were not conducive for construction, so nothing more was heard of this proposal.[45]

Amateur Theatrical Activities

The interesting thing about this period is that it was a time when amateur theatre in western Canada gained prominence over professional theatre. This fact was particularly true in Lethbridge, as will be demonstrated in the following discussion.

The Playgoers Club of Lethbridge: The Sterndale Bennett Era

Theatre has always performed a number of important functions, for example, to entertain, to enlighten, to facilitate emotional release, and to express one's creativity. But another major purpose of amateur theatre was to serve the community's charitable needs. According to Sterndale Bennett, this charitable purpose frequently became the *raison d'être* for amateur productions, and thus, artistic excellence was often sacrificed, if not neglected completely. Accordingly, amateur theatre was considered to be synonymous with incompetent, though occasionally entertaining theatre. Although the charitable function continued to be served in the 1920s and 1930s by church and youth oriented drama societies, and by entertainments sponsored by community service or fraternal organizations such as the Rotary, Gyro, or Elks clubs, 1923 witnessed the dawning of a new era in which the production of community drama could be viewed as primarily serving an artistic or expressive function; the belief was voiced that drama had an intrinsic purpose and a value in and of itself – "theatre for the sake of theatre." Ernest Gaskell Sterndale Bennett was the local spokesman for this belief.

The Sterndale Bennetts moved to Lethbridge in 1921, and both of them very quickly were recognized as possessing considerable dramatic talent. Because they made such a lasting impression on community theatre in Lethbridge, it seems reasonable to probe a little more thoroughly into their personal backgrounds. Ernest Gaskell Sterndale Bennett was born to James Robert and Mabel Agnes (nee Gaskell) Sterndale Bennett in London, England, on May 30, 1884. After preparatory school, he completed his elementary and secondary education at Derby School where he apparently displayed little talent for the theatre. A perusal of the records of the school in 1986 by the then headmaster, B.D. Seager, indicates that Ernest took part in only one school production (*Twelfth Night*), in which he played "one of the animals!" Nevertheless, it is interesting to note that the play was produced by his father who also played Sir Andrew Aguecheek. His brother, Thomas (Tom), was cupbearer.[46] Although Ernest Gaskell was not very actively involved in dramatics in his early years, his interest in the arts was thoroughly stimulated by members of his family and by the legacy of his famous grandfather, Sir William Sterndale Bennett, the noted nineteenth century English composer. The family certainly encouraged theatre attendance, and because of his grandfather's earlier social position, his family was occasionally extended the privilege of taking the Royal Box at Drury Lane.[47]

At the age of sixteen, Ernest Sterndale Bennett entered the Central Technical College of the City and Guilds of London Institute where he qualified as a Civil and Mechanical Engineer with first class standing. In later years, Ernest Sterndale Bennett frequently referred to himself as: "engineer by training; actor and singer by avocation." Shortly after leaving the Institute, he married Sarah O'Donnell, and then in 1905 he and his wife emigrated to Canada. The Sterndale Bennetts settled in Montreal where Ernest worked in the draughting department of the Montreal Locomotive Company, Structural Steel Department. After a very short period of time in this department, Sterndale Bennett was named Assistant Superintendent in the shop. Sterndale Bennett's reminiscences tell us that his interest in theatre remained keen. Upon landing in Montreal, he attended a production of the musical *Tom Jones* which he felt was equally as good as he would expect to see in London. Then it was revealed to him that this was the London production, and that most Canadian professional theatre was imported either from the United States or England. One year after settling in Montreal, Ernest and Sarah Sterndale Bennett celebrated the birth of their son, Michael (May 1, 1906). Shortly thereafter, however, Sarah died; consequently, Michael was sent home to England to be cared for by his paternal grandparents.

Because of the recession in 1907-08, work at the Montreal Locomotive Company slowed down considerably, so Sterndale Bennett decided to move to western Canada where he obtained employment with the Moose Jaw, Saskatchewan, Machine Works. Later, through his efforts, a newly organized company, The Saskatchewan Bridge and Iron Co. Ltd., was established; Sterndale Bennett fulfilled the position of Secretary Treasurer and Mechanical Superintendent. Soon, this new company was making bridges for the Alberta and Saskatchewan governments and contracting steel work for many new buildings throughout western Canada.

In late 1910 Bennett and five or six former professional actors, then living in Moose Jaw, organized themselves into a cooperative professional theatre company called The Green Room Club, in which the members shared the profits. John Backus was their president and director, and the company initially staged its productions at the 350 seat City Hall Theatre where they paid a nightly rental of $25. When Backus left for England in the fall of 1912, the company voted that Sterndale Bennett should succeed as president and director. Although Sterndale Bennett appreciated his own lack of experience, he was encouraged to take on the responsibility by the company who promised to "correct him", when necessary.[48] Actually, the directorial experiences of the next few years undoubtedly helped to develop in Sterndale Bennett, the great self-confidence which was characteristic of his later theatrical career.

Because of his love for singing and his interest in church music, Ernest joined St. John's Church Choir where he met Elizabeth Wallace Belle Seater (usually referred to as Belle) whom he married on May 30, 1911. Belle, who was small, pretty, and very charming, was born in Detroit, Michigan, in 1891 to James and Mary Seater (nee Little). After James drowned, when the boat on which he was employed capsized while making its regular run between Owen Sound, Ontario, and Detroit, Mary moved her family to Lyle, Saskatchewan, and then to Moose Jaw.

After their marriage, Ernest and Belle travelled to England so that Belle could meet the Sterndale Bennett family and so that the newly married couple could accompany young Michael back to Canada. A few years later, Ernest and Belle gave birth to a daughter, Muriel (May 27, 1915). Both Belle and Muriel proved to be invaluable supporters of Ernest's avocational interests. In fact, Belle was just as interested in the theatre as her husband. Apparently, right from her early school days,

Belle took an intense interest in drama. Then, she became involved in the activities of the Green Room Club. Henceforth, the couple enjoyed about twenty-five years of cooperative work in the theatre. As Muriel grew up, she participated in many of her parent's theatrical activities. Michael, on the other hand, was much more interested in technological pursuits which led him to a career in the mining industry.

When World War I broke out, the Saskatchewan Bridge and Iron Co. Ltd. was converted to the manufacture of various munitions for the British, and later, the American armed forces. Sterndale Bennett received numerous formal commendations by inspectors for his organizational and supervisory achievements associated with this work, for example, "The execution of their work was greatly facilitated by the skill and ingenuity displayed by Mr. Bennett in various machines and mechanisms designed and built by him with a view to the more efficient production of these shell [sic]."[49] As the war slowed down, operations were transferred to Medicine Hat, and Sterndale Bennett followed the company to the Alberta city where he assumed the position of manager. With the cessation of war contracts, the company began providing telephone pole hardware for Alberta Government Telephones.

While in Medicine Hat, the Sterndale Bennetts were active members of St. Barnabas Anglican Church and its choir, as well as major participants in the 1921 Rotary Club show and significant contributors to the 1921 production of *Raffles* produced by the Medicine Hat Stroller's Dramatic Society. Reports from the *Medicine Hat Daily News* indicate the important role which Ernest and Belle played in these various organizations.[50] The following compliment was tendered Ernest for his performances in the Rotary minstrel show, *The Jollies of 1920*, which played the Empress Theatre on January 21 and 22, 1921:

> The fun is fast and furious in the second part of this unique entertainment. Norman Davis and E.G.S. Bennett start it with a song and a stunt that sets a great pace.

Bennett's direction of, and acting in, *Raffles* elicited the following accolades:

> The production and stage management will be under the direction of Mr. E.G. Sterndale Bennett who brings to the task a large and varied experience in Canada and England. Success from an artistic standpoint is already assured.

> It is not necessary here to eulogize Mr. Bennett – the theatre going public of Medicine Hat is fully aware of the excellent work in this line that he has done in the past and can rest assured that in the production of "Raffles" he will worthily maintain the high standard achieved by other organizations here.

> Presentation of 'Raffles' won new laurels for Medicine Hat amateurs – better than average road show.

> After seeing Sterndale Bennett in his masterly "Fragments From France", one expected him to give a good performance . . . ; nor was one disappointed, Mr. Bennett endowing the character with just the right shade of realism, a master in his line.

Complimentary references relating to Belle's acting included:

> Mrs. Sterndale Bennett has won distinction at Moose Jaw and other cities by her clever delineation of important and difficult roles.

> Mrs. Bennett has a decided stage personality, and made a big hit with the audience by her charm and sweetness as well as by her histrionic gifts in emotional scenes with Raffles.

After fire destroyed the Medicine Hat plant of the Saskatchewan Bridge and Iron Co. Ltd., the Sterndale Bennetts decided to return to England. On the eve of their leaving Medicine Hat (February

20, 1921), they were tendered a farewell reception at St. Barnabas Church where their contributions to all branches of the church were acknowledged. Ernest was thanked particularly for his participation in the choir and for his fine solo presentations at numerous church services. The minister, Reverend E.A. Davis, expressed his sincere appreciation for Belle's assistance to the Women's Auxiliary, the Sunday School and other auxiliaries, and her direction of "a most successful Cantata." When the Sterndale Bennetts arrived in England, they discovered that employment opportunities there were limited. One day while in the Strand, Ernest happened to meet George Davies who had been associated with the Alberta Foundry and Machine Co. Ltd. in Medicine Hat, but who since 1920 had operated the Lethbridge Iron Works. Davies convinced Sterndale Bennett to join him as Secretary-Treasurer of the Lethbridge Iron Works in Lethbridge. Thus, the Sterndale Bennetts moved back to Canada in September 1921 where they settled in Lethbridge until their move to Toronto in late 1932.

Belle and Ernest Sterndale Bennett
Photo: The Sterndale Bennett Family

It was not very long before the Sterndale Bennetts were deeply involved with amateur theatre in Lethbridge. Their participation in local theatricals produced by Richard Hincks and the Rotary Club, which was discussed in Chapter Two, was merely a prelude to the extraordinary effort expended during the following decade by both Ernest and Belle Sterndale Bennett to further the development and appreciation of theatre in Lethbridge and throughout the province of Alberta. They continued to contribute to theatrical productions sponsored by various service clubs, for example, they directed and acted in special sketches presented as components of the Rotary Shows of 1923, 1924, and 1929 as well as in the *Gyro Cheerio Revue of 1926*. E.G. Sterndale Bennett also took over the reins as musical director for the 1930 minstrel show presented by St. Augustine's Men's Society. But most of their effort was funnelled through the activities of the Playgoers Club of Lethbridge, an amateur theatre society which was conceived by Sterndale Bennett and then fostered by an article entitled "The Amateur Stage," which he submitted to the *Lethbridge Herald* for publication on January 13,

1923.[51] In this article, Sterndale Bennett outlined his conception of the important community role which should be performed by what he referred to as a playgoers' club. In addition, he stressed the benefits that accrue to a community where such a society exists. Although he wrote in rather general terms, it seems apparent that he was, in fact, laying the groundwork for the organization of a Lethbridge "Playgoers' Club," which would, hopefully, live up to his strong beliefs. According to Sterndale Bennett, this club should have a large membership "composed of all lovers of the theatre." In addition, it should be divided into separate operatic and dramatic sections with members belonging to the particular section which interested them, and the club should be formally organized with officers and committees elected according to recognized procedures.

Sterndale Bennett also suggested that the aims of such a playgoers' club should be (as paraphrased):

1. To attract, to disseminate information about, to attend, and to endorse worthy professional shows. E.G. Sterndale Bennett argued that the club should "use its influence to bring the very best of the travelling companies to the city, to obtain reliable advanced information regarding these shows, and to encourage all of the club's membership to attend such performances."

2. To produce quality shows for the love of art. Sterndale Bennett was adamant that every effort should be expended to pursue the perfection of the art; a task which should not be diluted by overriding aims such as raising money for charity.

3. To train and develop local dramatic and musical talent. Because communities such as Lethbridge lacked formal opportunities and facilities for the development of dramatic talent, Sterndale Bennett considered it essential that the experienced members of the club provide guidance to the inexperienced, and that the club encourage participation by these beginners in "simple one act plays and operettas" presented to an audience of their own club members "until they became sufficiently trained" to participate effectively "in the larger productions of the society."

In his personal reminiscences, Sterndale Bennett reports that he received only one response to his letter, "but it was an important one for it was from a prominent local lawyer, Henry Warrington Church," who gave him the encouragement to pursue the matter further. H.W. Church was born in Cardiff, Wales, but the family later moved to Chicago and then to Toronto where Henry received his law degree. Church married Gertrude Pemberton who bore him four children, Dorothy, Hilda, John, and Betty. In 1909, the Churches moved to Macleod and, subsequently, to Lethbridge where Henry joined the law firm of C.F.P. Conybeare. In his association with Conybeare, Church was encouraged to express his interest in the arts. (A rather interesting coincidence which involved these two families is the fact that the Conybeares' granddaughters, Bernadette Fisher and Eildon Brander, as well as the Churchs' daughter, Hilda, made major contributions to the Lethbridge and Canadian dance communities.) After careful discussions relating to Sterndale Bennett's proposals, the two gentlemen decided that they should test the idea. An informal meeting of interested associates was called for January 20, 1923, in St. Augustine's Hall. Temporary executive officers who were elected included H.W. Church as President, and E.G. Sterndale Bennett as General Director. It was also decided to begin a membership drive and to call a formal organizational meeting for February 15.[52] Fifty-seven prospective members attended this latter meeting, at which time: a constitution was approved which explicitly reflected the principles outlined by Sterndale Bennett, the prior elections were ratified, and additional officers were elected; in fact, the Playgoers Club of Lethbridge was established.[53] The evening's business was capped off with a chorus rehearsal for Playgoers' initial production, the musical comedy *Going Up* to be staged at the Majestic Theatre on April 9 and 10, under the direction of Ernest Sterndale Bennett. In a January 31, 1964, letter addressed to the president of Playgoers, Mary Heinitz, Sterndale Bennett recalls the reasons for choosing to produce *Going Up*:

> Realizing that musical shows were, generally, more consistently popular than plays, I felt the opening performance of a new group named 'The Playgoers' Club' should be a musical show, to take advantage of this wide appeal and thus get the Club off to a good start.
>
> Naturally, the first choice turned to Gilbert and Sullivan but any ardour on my part in that direction was immediately blunted by thought of the excellent work being done at that time by our close neighbour, The Medicine Hat Operatic Society, which organization had attained an almost professional standard of perfection. We could not attempt to compare with the high standard already set by Medicine Hat.
>
> What we needed most of all was a show which would have the greatest appeal to the largest number of people. My experience told me that the only sensible decision would be towards a light, very up-to-date musical comedy and GOING UP had recently enjoyed a highly popular run in New York.

Sterndale Bennett was right; the production was a great audience pleaser. Over 1 000 patrons attended the performance making it a financial success; after meeting expenses of $786, the club realized a profit of $370.[54] But Sterndale Bennett was interested in more than satisfying popular tastes or turning a good profit. As the program for *Going Up* stated, "This community club has been organized with a view to improving the quality of theatrical performances in the city." Sterndale Bennett was committed to excellence and to maintaining a standard of performance of which conscientious actors (amateur or professional) could be proud. The accomplishment of this aim was verified from the beginning as the critic of the *Lethbridge Herald* W.A.R. Cocq stated:[55]

> Splendid! The Playgoers Club in presenting its first venture . . . to the public, captivated the audience with *Going Up* and set up a standard as to how a play should be turned out when it comes to amateur acting in the city. Congratulations are due to Mr. Sterndale Bennett, as general manager and to one and all who helped to make *Going Up* the decided success it was. It was a performance of which any amateur company could be justly proud.

This commitment was manifest throughout the ten years in which Ernest and his constant companion and helpmate, Belle, were associated with Playgoers. They left a legacy which has sustained community support for the Lethbridge Playgoers Club for almost seventy years with no foreseeable end in sight. The following analysis of the Club's activities from 1923-1932 will illustrate quite clearly the significant role which the Sterndale Bennetts played in institutionalizing the organization.

With regard to formal leadership of the Playgoers Club of Lethbridge, the original constitution provided for a governing body made up of the following officers: President, Vice-President, Secretary, Treasurer, General Director, Musical Director, Technical Director, Business Manager, and three other executive members, all of whom were to be elected at the annual general meeting of the club. Although most of the executive offices were rotated among various members of the club during the 1920s, the general director's position fell to E.G. Sterndale Bennett throughout his tenure with the club. In 1925 the constitution was amended to provide for a Director of Little Theatre. This title was rather unfortunate since the club was basically a Little Theatre organization. However, in this unusual situation, Playgoers envisioned that the specific role of this director was to provide training and experience for novice members. In order to accomplish this aim, Playgoers followed Ernest Sterndale Bennett's suggestions that inexperienced members be channeled into short plays which would then be performed during evenings of one act plays reserved for members, only. The presentations were referred to as "Evenings of Little Theatre." The new position was admirably filled by Mrs. Sterndale Bennett, who, regardless of this formal appointment, had unofficially performed this task from the first Little Theatre presentation staged on June 5, 1923.[56] Consequently, Ernest and Belle Sterndale Bennett shared the club's artistic direction, and as such, provided the incentive for a very active period of amateur theatricals.

In addition to being the director of most of the major productions which the Playgoers produced during this era, E.G. Sterndale Bennett performed in many of these same productions as well as in many of the Little Theatre one act plays and festival productions. It was not uncommon for him to direct a major production such as *Raffles* (1923) and also to play a major role. Comments about his acting and directing were always very complimentary. Some selected comments are quoted below:[57]

> The part of Raffles was an outstanding one, and was played with consummate skill by E.G. Sterndale Bennett. It was Raffles to the life, sincere and without a suspicion of over-acting. It would have done credit to an actor of the professional type.

> E.G. Sterndale Bennett added distinction to the play . . .

> As the Raja of Rukh E.G. Sterndale Bennett added fresh laurels to his reputation as an amateur actor. It was an impressive and imposing presentation, cool and calculating with what the role called for and highly polished.

> The general director is Mr. Sterndale Bennett, who has put every ounce of energy in striving to make "Going Up" serve as a hallmark of what the local players are capable.

> Now then, "Cock Robin", is really a play within a play and calls for careful coaching. This the company clearly has had from Mr. E.G. Sterndale Bennett, director of the more extended productions of the Playgoers' Club.

Reviewers from other Alberta cities had various opportunities to witness Sterndale Bennett's work in the Alberta Drama League festivals. Comments such as the following give considerable credence to the opinions expressed locally:[58]

> It would be hard to find better acting than that of Sterndal [sic] Bennett as the priest . . . (*Edmonton Journal*)

> . . . one of the most interested supporters and talented directors of drama in the province. (*Calgary Herald*)

> Mr. Sterndale Bennett is always excellent . . . (*Calgary Herald*)

> Mr. E.G. Sterndale Bennett . . . took the honors of the festival . . . in his fine and subtle portrayal. (*Edmonton Bulletin*)

During his association with the Lethbridge Playgoers, Ernest G. Sterndale Bennett directed six major musicals, four major plays, and one festival production (screen scene from *The School for Scandal*). In addition, he performed in three musicals, three major plays, eleven one act plays (including three festival plays), and other variety or novelty presentations. Also, Sterndale Bennett became the spokesman for the Playgoers as well as for drama in Alberta, generally. Newspaper reports indicate that he was called upon to speak on behalf of Playgoers on numerous occasions. For example, during an interval in the Little Theatre program in February 1924 he "gave an enlightening discourse on the past, present, and future of the Playgoers' Club and the Little Theatre and Big Theatre undertakings of the amateurs."[59] Another example of this activity is reported in the review of the Lethbridge Playgoers' production of October 9, 1928. On this occasion, Sterndale Bennett encouraged members to attend two major road shows booked for Lethbridge.[60]

Mr. Sterndale Bennett spoke briefly after the first sketch explaining the aims and hopes of the Playgoers' Club and making a strong appeal for generous support of the shows coming through the winter particularly the elaborate musical shows, Rose Marie and Hit the Deck which are coming at great cost.

In 1929 Sterndale Bennett initiated meetings which resulted in the formation of the Alberta Dramatic League, to which he was the elected president for the first two terms and vice president for the succeeding term.[61] Speaking of festivals, E.G. Sterndale Bennett was chosen as the Alberta delegate to attend the organizational meeting of the Dominion Drama Festival which was hosted by Governor General Bessborough, in Ottawa, and held on October 29, 1932. An Ottawa wire story in the *Lethbridge Herald* illustrates that Sterndale Bennett also played an active role in fostering the national festival movement.[62] "On motion of Colonel D.M. Biggar, Ottawa, seconded by Sterndale Bennett, Lethbridge, a general committee was appointed . . . " – a committee to which Sterndale Bennett was named a member.

Alberta Dramatic League: Festival Covers (1930-1932)
Photo: Lethbridge Playgoers' Archives; City of Lethbridge Archives and Records Management

Although many of the theatrical activities of E.G. Sterndale Bennett are fairly generally recognized, those of E. Belle Sterndale Bennett are not as well documented. Nevertheless, her contribution was very extensive, although it was confined more completely to the local scene. She, too, performed in many of the major musical and dramatic productions of the Lethbridge Playgoers, but her greatest contribution was to the "Little Theatre" movement, the aims of which were clearly outlined in the program for *Going Up:*

> Hope for the future of the drama on this continent lies largely with the Little Theatre movement . . . . Earnestly endeavoring to develop the dramatic talent latent in their communities, studying the art of dramatic presentation, presenting good plays in an efficient manner . . . educating the public to appreciate the good things and to discriminate against the poor or offensive plays.

> The Playgoers' Club aims to make Lethbridge a factor in this movement; and, as soon as work is completed on "Going Up" the study and preparation of small works by members of the club will be taken up, with a view to training material for the larger productions.

Mrs. Sterndale Bennett immediately took on the responsibility of organizing and directing the Little Theatre activities. By maintaining this role until leaving Lethbridge, Mrs. Bennett was responsible for supervising approximately thirty-six one act plays including two festival productions.

A review of the contributions of the Sterndale Bennetts makes it obvious that they often worked together as a team by assisting each other wherever possible. This cooperation, although not always formally acknowledged in the assignment of a specific position such as assistant director, was, nevertheless, informally recognized by the club and the local press. For example, Belle Sterndale Bennett's name does not appear on the program for the 1924 production of *Oh, Lady! Lady!!,* but both she and E.G. were presented with a gift from the Playgoers' Club "in appreciation of the trouble taken in preparing the production."[63]

Similar circumstances surrounded the staging of the musical comedy *The Toreador* in 1928. The *Lethbridge Herald* review stated:[64]

> "The Toreador" undoubtedly marked a high water performance in local stage renderings. Mr. and Mrs. Sterndale Bennett are to be highly congratulated on the marked success which their efforts gained.

On reflection, it is apparent that the Sterndale Bennetts were prepared to make enormous personal sacrifices in order to further the cause of the arts in Lethbridge. As though their efforts on behalf of Playgoers were not more than anyone could expect, they also contributed to many other organizations and activities. Both were concerned citizens who readily volunteered for community service and participated in charitable and church activities. They continued to add a special dimension to the annual Rotary shows. Further community service was provided by E.G. Sterndale Bennett through his active participation in the Gyro Club, and his efforts on behalf of the local music festival committee, not to mention Ernest's struggle to maintain the Majestic Theatre's role in facilitating legitimate theatre. Belle, on the other hand, volunteered to direct plays for the Lethbridge high school and for the Lethbridge Anglican Mission. St. Augustine's Anglican Church also benefited from their strong religious commitment. In addition, Ernest directed St. Augustine's Choir for several years. What a tremendous loss the City of Lethbridge suffered when the Sterndale Bennetts moved to Toronto. Playgoers acknowledged its debt to the Sterndale Bennetts by honoring them with life memberships.[65]

The old adage, "our loss was their gain," could not possibly have been truer. Toronto theatre owes a tremendous debt to the Sterndale Bennetts. It seems appropriate to diverge from the discussion of the Lethbridge Playgoers a bit to briefly sketch the Sterndale Bennett's theatrical activities after leaving Lethbridge. What specifically was it that attracted the Sterndale Bennetts to Toronto? Actually, there were a number of good reasons for the move. Muriel was a promising young piano student and so direct contact with the Toronto Conservatory was considered to be beneficial. Belle suffered from rather acute diabetes; therefore, Toronto, the home of Drs. Banting and Best, gave promise of superior medical treatment. But probably the most compelling reason was the employment offer extended to Ernest and Belle by the T. Eaton Company. The Eaton Recreation Department, under the supervision of Frank Rostance (R.Y. Eaton's personal secretary and, incidentally, a very fine actor), had recently organized the Eaton Dramatic Club for company employees. When the group began to search for a director, the name of Sterndale Bennett came to mind since he came highly recommended by Vincent Massey who had developed great respect for Sterndale Bennett in the deliberations relating to the establishment of the DDF. Consequently, Sterndale Bennett was hired as director; Belle Sterndale Bennett was named co-director. The first formal presentation of the club (four one act plays) took place in the Margaret Eaton Hall (McGill Street) on October 10, 1933. Shortly thereafter, the club was renamed The Toronto Masquers.[66]

Under the Sterndale Bennetts' direction, the Toronto Masquers' Club was extraordinarily successful in regional and dominion drama festivals. Unfortunately, Belle was able to enjoy this success for just a few years. She died on May 22, 1936, from a brain hemorrhage which may have been related to the diabetes from which she had suffered most of her life, although she had also been stricken by rheumatic fever at the age of seventeen. Her passing was a terrible blow; however, Ernest managed to maintain his directorial responsibilities. Fortunately, he benefitted from the close companionship of his daughter, Muriel, who gradually became more involved with the Masquers' Club. Among many awards, which the club garnered over the years, was the Bessborough Trophy won in 1937 for the best play in the Dominion Drama Festival.

In addition to his work with the Masquers, Sterndale Bennett cooperated with Edgar Stone, artistic director of Hart House Theatre, in organizing a 1933 summer school for instruction in aspects of the theatre. In subsequent years, Sterndale Bennett conducted summer schools in the Old Conservatory Building on Spadina and at Centre Island, Toronto. Notable among the students who attended these summer classes was Robert Christie. In later years, Robert Christie was recognized as one of Canada's finest professional actors. Belle had added to her credentials by teaching drama at both the Margaret Eaton School and the Central Technical School.

With the outbreak of World War II, Sterndale Bennett organized the Masquers into a Concert Party which performed at various Canadian military bases. This task was not taken lightly as can be determined from the following contents of the plaque which was presented to the Toronto Masquers by the Armed Forces of Military District No. 2, and the Toronto Citizens' Committee for Troops in Training. This recognition took place on the occasion of the Masquers' one hundredth performance for members of the armed forces:

> The Citizens' Committee for Troops in Training together with the Royal Canadian Navy, the Canadian Army and the Royal Canadian Air Force in this district desire to express their deep sense of gratitude for your meritorious contribution to the war effort.

> From October Nineteen Hundred and Thirty-Nine to October Nineteen Hundred and Forty-One, you have voluntarily given generously of your time and abilities, travelling over ten thousand miles in order to bring entertainment to eighty-five thousand sailors, soldiers and airmen.

> This splendid achievement has won for you our sincere admiration and affection.

Shortly before this honor was bestowed on Sterndale Bennett and the Masquers, Ernest married Hilda Church at St. Michael's Anglican Church, Toronto (August 5, 1941). Marie Loescher, of Lethbridge, was their attendant. Although the Masquers' Concert Party continued to perform throughout the war – travelling over 60 000 miles and playing about 280 times to a total audience of 300 000 in Canada – and then, touring overseas from June 24, 1945, to December 8, 1945, where they played to an additional 90 000 troops, the Sterndale Bennetts spent the remainder of the war in Boston where Ernest was contracted by the British Admiralty Technical Division to inspect munitions being produced by the Hesse Machine Co. for the British Navy (reminiscent of his work activities during World War I). In addition, Sterndale Bennett took on the responsibility of "Personnel Officer for a staff of inspectors comprised of British, Canadian, and American employees, and ... earned the complete confidence and respect of both his subordinates and his superiors."[67]

After the war, Sterndale Bennett returned to Canada to become "Director of Plays" at the Royal Conservatory of Music. Together with the help of his wife, Hilda, he organized his senior classes into a touring company known as the People's Repertory Company. Among the students participating in this company were Barbara Hamilton, Kate Reid, and George Luscombe.

Following this venture, the Sterndale Bennetts decided to open the Canadian Theatre School at 123 Church Street, Toronto. Bennett taught directing and playwriting, whereas Hilda, and Jack Medhurst apparently taught "everything from mask-making to modelling." Later, the school was moved to 55 College Street; in addition, Medhurst left the school to enrich his career. Some of the students who attended this school were Hugh Webster, Pamela Beckwith, Donald Jack, Irena Mayeska, and William Fruet.

The Canadian Theatre School was the first full time school devoted to the development of professional theatre practitioners in Canada. Certainly, dramatic training had been provided previously in various other institutions throughout Canada. Many Canadian universities offered a wide range of drama courses and theatrical experiences. In addition, the Canadian theatre historian, James Hoffman, informs us that L. Bullock-Webster operated the B.C. Drama School from 1921-1932 and taught dramatic techniques to about 800 students.[68] Although some of these students developed careers in the theatre, the school was not founded specifically for that purpose; rather, the goal was to provide dramatic training and experiences for people from various "walks of life."

The Canadian Theatre School operated from 1949 until 1956 when failing health and the decision to demolish the building in which the school was housed, forced Sterndale Bennett to retire from regular teaching. Nevertheless, he continued to engage in part time professional coaching. Hilda, on the other hand, continued her professional career through association with the National Ballet as assistant to the General Manager.[69] Ernest Sterndale Bennett formally retired at the age of 77. He and Hilda continued to live in Toronto for a number of years; however, they eventually moved to Vancouver. In August 1980 Hilda predeceased Ernest, who died on April 9, 1982, just prior to his 98th birthday. The family requested that in lieu of flowers, donations to the National Theatre School would be appreciated. What a full and rewarding life the Sterndale Bennetts enjoyed. Although their life work did not reap great monetary benefits, it provided many personal satisfactions in both family and professional relationships. Their personal talents, coupled with their devotion to excellence, brought them accolades from critics, respect from colleagues, and, in the case of Ernest, formal awards from honorary societies. His early theatrical career was capped off with the receipt of the prestigious Canadian Drama Award (CDA) in 1935. Forty years later, he was invested into the Order of Canada. Regardless of all of this formal recognition, Sterndale Bennett reported that, "my greatest satisfaction has come from watching my students forge ahead – many of them already at the top – as actor, actress, playwright, technician, director."[70] In addition, he would be the first to admit that he owed much of his success to his two close companions, Belle and Hilda.

The following discussion will concentrate more specifically on the activities of the Lethbridge Playgoers, and it will analyze how the aims, set out by E.G. Sterndale Bennett and endorsed by Playgoers' constitution, were put into practice by the club.

1. To Attract Quality Professional Companies and to Endorse Their Activities

On May 25, 1923, a printed notice was distributed to all members of the Playgoers Club which announced the forthcoming performance of the Dumbells, (Thursday, May 31). The notice read:[71] As you probably know the "Dumbells" have divided into two independent companies, one of which is playing "Carry On" at present in Eastern Canada, the other is coming to Lethbridge as above in "Full of Pep." Both of these companies are playing very good shows and there is very little to choose between them. Naturally, neither is as good as the original company, but they are well worth attending, and as we get so few good companies visiting our City, we certainly believe we should give them our hearty support. The Box Office is now open at the King's Theatre.

Playgoers' Club
Ralph A. Thrall, Secretary

Similar notices included comments such as:

GRAND PLAYERS - This company recently appeared in Lethbridge playing in "Adam and Eva." This is a Stock Company from Calgary giving a splendid performance at reasonable prices. They will appear in either "Cappy Ricks" or "Nothing But The Truth." Both very good plays.

MR. BRANSBY WILLIAMS . . . is the world's greatest portrayer of Dickens' characters . . . The Playgoers' Club has been largely instrumental in having Mr. Williams' schedule changed to include Lethbridge and every member of the club is urged to attend and influence all friends so the house may be filled to capacity.

"So This Is London," a musical comedy of the typical Cohan modern type will be played by a George M. Cohan Company. This comedy had long runs in New York and other eastern cities, and the company is understood to be up to standard.

SIR JOHN MARTIN-HARVEY - It is scarcely necessary to make any comments in this case . . . .

The distribution of these printed announcements was abandoned around the mid-1920s, probably because of the fact that the local *Lethbridge Herald* presented rather extensive publicity and general coverage of theatrical activities. In addition, announcements of forthcoming productions, both Playgoers and non-Playgoers, were generally made at Playgoers' productions.

2. To Produce Dramatic and Musical Productions of High Standards

A resume of Playgoers' productions during the years 1921-1932 lists seven musicals, five major plays, approximately forty short plays (spread over fourteen Little Theatre presentations), plus variety, minstrel, and novelty acts. As has been stressed earlier in this chapter, it was always the aim of the Playgoers Club to achieve and maintain rather high standards in their productions – a fact which is attested to in the majority of reviews relating to their productions. However, one justifiably might be suspect of local reviews, especially by a home town newspaper in a community of 10 000-11 000 population. The *Lethbridge Herald,* and before it, the *Lethbridge News,* had always provided excellent coverage of theatrical presentations (both live and film). At various times, the pre-presentation coverage was very extensive: daily columns bearing titles such as, "What the Press Agents Say," were common during the early years of the *Lethbridge Herald.* Reviews, too were commonplace; however, professional shows which played for one night, only, were frequently not reviewed. Possibly the publishers felt that there was little percentage in providing a review for patrons whose presence or interest was not influenced by the critical comments. It seems that many of the bigger Broadway shows also were not reviewed locally. In this instance, local reviewers might not have considered themselves competent enough to review major touring shows. Nevertheless, many of the touring shows, as well as most of the local productions, received some critical comment which tended to be fairly positive, generally; however, there were some interesting exceptions:[72]

... above average company is wasting its time with this production. [New York touring production of *The Girl From Rectors*]

... there was a lack of "ginger" in the production. [Local production of *San Toy*]

On the whole, however, the critical reader is forced to read between the lines and to distinguish degrees of positiveness. Also, upon reading the reviews thoroughly, it becomes apparent that specific comments relating to the performers tended to be more balanced. The attempt to be more objective was particularly evident in the criticisms presented by the first local reviewer to be identified by his byline, W.A.R. Cocq, who was the *Lethbridge Herald* drama critic throughout most of the 1920s. The following comments from several of Cocq's reviews of various Playgoers' productions are presented below to illustrate his objectivity:[73]

Miss Hilda Church showed herself possessed of a sweet voice though lacking in volume . . . Her performance was enriched with the dancing she showed she was capable of.

A trifle studied in the opening, the performance gained strength as it proceeded.

"The Prince of Pilsen" was crowned midst popular acclamation. . . . At no time within recollection has an amateur performance of this character been seen locally, and the way in which the play was staged and the manner in which it was presented by the players marked a distinct evolution in the activities of the Playgoers' Club in bringing amateur theatricals to the verge of the best in professionalism . . . To be thoroughly important it is true that at odd moments there was just the suspicion of a drag, of not being "quick in the uptake" . . .

In addition, the high quality of Playgoers' productions is attested to by external reviewers who witnessed Lethbridge presentations at the provincial festivals of 1930 to 1932. For example:[74]

May I say in conclusion that Medicine Hat and, in a lesser degree, Lethbridge have set an excellent example. Calgary and Edmonton have begun well (*Calgary Herald*).

. . . "And So To Bed" (Act III), the choice of the Playgoers' Club of Lethbridge, . . . was the most elaborate, the most entertaining and at least in the front rank for honors, if not the finest, of the plays shown (*Edmonton Bulletin*).

In conclusion, all available evidence seems to support the contention that the Lethbridge Playgoers, during the Sterndale Bennett era, lived up to their goal of achieving and maintaining a quality product.

3. To Develop Artistic Talent

All members of the community who were interested in theatrical activities were encouraged to join the Playgoers Club. A major incentive was the fact that all productions of the Little Theatre organization were open to admission by membership card, only. Also, the membership fee of fifty cents was appealing. Over 300 memberships had been sold by April 1923, and this number generally grew steadily until reaching a peak of 800 members in 1932.[75] Obviously, all of these members were not active participants in the club's productions. Purchasing a membership was equivalent to subscribing to the club's season of Little Theatre presentations. Nevertheless, it must be stressed that many members made extremely valuable contributions to the group's activities.

In the early days of the Playgoers' Club, artistic and design matters were left in the hands of members with such inclinations, but executive and business affairs were frequently turned over to members of the business and professional community who had particular affinity for these practical matters. Thus, early executives of the Playgoers' Club included many prominent "leading citizens" who preferred not to become directly involved in the stage-related business of the club. For example, H.W. Church was president of the club for about six years but rarely, if ever, appeared on stage. Others who performed primarily executive roles, included: Ralph Thrall, George Davies, E.A. Sharman, and W.E. Huckvale. Important members of the business community, who complemented their executive skills with artistic interests included: Fred Rose, R.M. Hume, Arnold Raworth, and Alan McAlpin.

A fairly large number of people were involved in onstage activities, especially during those years when the club produced musicals. (The club never did divide into the two separate sections which Sterndale Bennett originally conceived – operatic and dramatic.) Speaking about overall involvement in Playgoers' productions, in 1932 the *Lethbridge Herald* reported that, "More than 305 have taken part in the shows, and of this number 150 have [had] speaking parts."[76] It is nevertheless true, that the majority of the speaking roles were performed by a relatively small core of very active members. When speaking and chorus roles are combined, about 18 percent of the participants performed in four or more productions. A more careful perusal of the data provides evidence that a core of approximately thirty members (about ten percent of the participants) portrayed over 50% of the major parts in both the larger productions and the Little Theatre productions. Obviously these people gained remarkable experience and undoubtedly had tremendous opportunities to develop their talents. Members comprising the core of onstage participants are listed in Table 3-1.

Chris Gibson as the Rajah of Bhong in Playgoers' The Country Girl *(1932)*
Photo: Doris Balcovske

During this era, the onstage activities of Blanche Roy (wife of Dr. Louis Arthur Roy), noted local vocalist, were centered almost exclusively on musical theatre. Other members who were frequent participants in the "operetta" productions of the club, included: Hilda Church, Minnie (Hazell) Thrall, Percy Gaynor, Eric Ings, Roy Keivill, Fred Rose, and Fred Teague. However, most of the individuals listed in Table 3-1 engaged in all of the forms of theatrical production presented by the club.

TABLE 3-1

Onstage Participants
Lethbridge Playgoers (1923-1932)

Extraordinarily Active	Ernest G. Sterndale Bennett C.R. Matthews	Fred Teague	Fred Rose
Very Active	Hilda Church Tom Feguson Ronald Hick	George Holman Eric Ings Aileen Jones	Roy Keivill Vinnie Martin
Active	Kathleen (Lindsay) Barnhill Echo Becker Maybelle Bryans P.J. Collins Dave Elton Lyn Fairbairn Nancy Farris Ted Faunch George Frost	Percy Gaynor Chris Gibson Edith Gibson Ian Hendry Chas. F. Hiscocks Robert Hume Ethel Jones Lyn Jordan Kathleen Martin	Haze C. Moore Blanche Roy Louie Ritchie* Carl Sandquist Phil Sangster Muriel Sterndale Bennett Isobel Teague Nan Thomas Minnie Thrall
*Mrs. Norman Ritchie's given name was Louie; however programs regularly referred to her as Louise.			

Rarely, did initial participation in the Little Theatre activities lead to involvement in major productions since only about 8% of those members who initiated their participation in the Little Theatre, followed this up with more extensive involvement in the organization. Nevertheless, the Little Theatre provided an entree for a few members who became very influential members of the club, for example, Maybelle Bryans, Charlie Matthews, Tom Ferguson, Arnold Raworth, James Rosewarn, Mary Sydal, Ted Faunch, and Lena Connor.

Unfortunately, there is very little documented reference to matters associated with design and technical activities. What evidence there is, suggests that these matters were basically left in the hands of a small core of individuals who showed special skills or particular interests in these areas. Alan McAlpin, who designed and built most of the sets for Playgoers' major productions until 1929, provided both stability and competence to the position of Technical Director during the early years of the club's existence. McAlpin performed that role for all eight major productions from *Going Up* in 1923 to *The Toreador* in 1928. During most of this time, he was able to count on the artistic skills of Phil Sangster, the window dresser for the Hudson's Bay Co., who routinely took on the task of scene painter. Following the 1928 season, McAlpin was forced to give up much of this work for health reasons. Two of his assistants, Alastair Ian (A.I.) Brander and William Watson, took on the task of Technical Director in 1929 and 1930, successively; Charles R. (C.R.) Matthews contributed as scenic designer and master carpenter. In 1929, Percy Morris (nephew of Al Morris), who was employed by the CPR, handled the duties of stage manager, which he performed, on occasion, during the the next couple of years; for the production of *The Country Girl* (December 1932), Morris acted as Technical Director. The director of *The Country Girl,* Lyn Jordan, had recently moved to Lethbridge from Edmonton. According to the *Lethbridge Herald,* Jordan had many previous years' experience in musical comedy work. Apparently, he was also an accomplished scenic designer as the following quotation from the *Lethbridge Herald* points out:[77]

Another interesting feature of this production will be the scenery which is being specially built and is being painted by Lyn Jordan, who has had considerable experience in this work at Edmonton and in other cities.

Jordan lent his technical and directorial talents to various major and Little Theatre productions through 1934. Shortly thereafter, he ended his association with Playgoers. Unquestionably, set design was an important feature of Playgoers' major productions as is illustrated in the following *Lethbridge Herald* report:[78]

When the theatre-going public view the "Green Goddess" show . . . , not the least impressive feature will be the scenic effects. One is safe in making such a forecast after visiting the improvised studio of the clever scenic artist of the Playgoers' Club, Phil Sangster, in the Hull Block. Here all the paraphernalia of that important department of play production may be found, including a remarkable working model of the first scene.

Costuming for major plays and musicals requiring elaborate costumes was usually left to the professional experts – Malabar's costume rentals.

Playgoers' Set: H.M.S. Pinafore *(1926)*
Photo: Playgoers' Archives and the City of Lethbridge Archives and Records Management

The responsibility for directing was customarily taken by the Sterndale Bennetts; Ernest, for major productions, Belle, for Little Theatre productions. Nevertheless, as time passed, other members of the club were initiated into the directorial circle. This was particularly true in the Little Theatre. During the last two years in which Mrs. Sterndale Bennett was associated with Playgoers, she encouraged some other members to try directing – Maybelle Bryans, Percy Gaynor, and Norman

D. Smith. Eventually, Maybelle Bryans became heir to the position of General Director. Undoubtedly, other members learned much about directing from observing both Ernest and Belle, who were excellent models. Hilda Church, Charlie Matthews, and James Rosewarn served this apprenticeship, though in a very informal way. Lyn Jordan, who had directing experience before coming to Lethbridge, probably improved his technique by association.

Because the Playgoers presented a number of major musicals and operettas, other directorial opportunities were afforded. Maisie Vyvyan contributed to the choreography of a number of shows. Also, a talented young dancer, Hilda Church, was provided with ample opportunity to hone her artistic skills. Hilda's dancing potential began to show itself at a rather young age. While she was still in her teens, she became a noted dancer in the numerous classical dance recitals offered by the dance students of Gladys Attree. At that time, she also began, personally, to offer dance instruction. After graduating from high school, Church enrolled for two years in the Chicago Ballet School. For personal and family reasons, she returned home to Lethbridge where she was employed by the telephone company. She became a founding member of the Playgoers Club, and from the first Playgoers' production through 1937, Miss Church's theatrical contributions in Lethbridge included choreography, dancing, directing, acting, and backstage participation. Obviously, her later association with the Canadian Theatre School and the National Ballet School benefited from these extensive and varied experiences. Musicals also provided opportunities for local musicians, orchestra leaders, and choir masters to broaden their musical interests, as well as increase their competence. Because formal musical training was much more common than formal dramatic training, numerous musicians, choral leaders, and music teachers were available for directing the music, accompanying, and playing in the pit orchestra. The following musicians generally handled the musical direction and accompaniment:

Musical Direction: C.J. Ferguson, Charles H. Whitfield, G.E. Bower, Percy T. Moseley, George Brown, Ernest F. Layton, Aileen Jones, Mrs. A.I. (Ethel) Brander.

Musical Accompaniment: C. Whitfield; Mrs. Matheson, Mrs. K.G. McKillop, Katherine Brown, Ethel Brander.

Hilda Church
Photo: The Sterndale Bennett Family

Another dimension was added to Playgoers' developmental projects in 1931 when the annual meeting of the club endorsed the suggestion by E.G. Sterndale Bennett that the club sponsor a one act playwriting contest to be open to any amateur writer in Lethbridge.[79] Later, L.W. Brockington, Calgary city solicitor and "an authority on plays and players," was chosen to judge the seven entries.[80] Brockington also agreed to act as official critic for the first three Alberta Dramatic League festivals (1930, '31, and '32). Playgoers' members E.G. Sterndale Bennett and Charlie Matthews submitted *Second Fiddle* and *The Perfect Crime*, respectively; the latter play was selected as the best entry.[81] Three of the seven plays were produced for the Little Theatre evening of February 17, 1932. In the following year, a provincial playwriting contest was sponsored by the Carnegie Trust Fund for Promoting the Arts in Alberta. The adjudicator, Professor E.A. Corbett of the University of Alberta, was faced with the task of choosing the best from among forty-nine plays. The entry by Playgoers' members E.G. Sterndale Bennett and H.W. Church, a three act play entitled *The Devil of New France,* was awarded third prize.[82]

In conclusion, although Playgoers may not have achieved all of its aims to the extent it may have wished, in reality, its accomplishments were so sufficient that the organization basically became a major institution in Lethbridge. Its long history attests to the solid foundation which was laid during the first decade of its existence. The following factors seem to have been prominent in structuring that foundation:

1. The charismatic leadership of the Sterndale Bennetts coupled with their enthusiasm, hard work, and determination to achieve perfection.

2. A solid core of about forty talented and hard-working members.

3. A formal, constitutionally based social structure founded on democratic principles ensuring extensive involvement in the decision-making processes.

4. A very full schedule of activities contributing to a high level of commitment by the active members.

5. The nurturing of a small, but dedicated group of members who could give later leadership in various areas of production, but especially in directing.

6. Enthusiastic support from the community.

Although the Lethbridge Playgoers was an extremely active group, its numerous activities did not seem to deter other organizations from producing theatrical entertainments as well. In fact, some degree of complementarity developed between Playgoers and other groups, most of whom continued to produce for charitable purposes. For example, the Playgoers' Club, in conjunction with the Kiwanis Club, presented the three act mystery drama, *Cock Robin,* in May 1930 with proceeds in aid of the Kiwanis Mothers' Vacation Camp at Waterton National Park. In addition, active members of Playgoers also contributed immeasurably to the production, direction, and presentation of many other shows. Let us now examine the activities of these other societies more thoroughly.

Other Local Theatre

The other groups that sponsored theatricals represent basically four types of organizations: service clubs (Rotary, Elks, Gyro), social and athletic clubs (C.P.R., Y.M.C.A.), church dramatic and choral groups, and high school dramatic or literary societies. Participants in the service club productions were primarily adult members of the community, whereas the participants in the athletic clubs and church groups were adults and youths in various combinations; the adults usually functioned in production roles, or, as in the case of the Y.M.C.A. Minstrel Show (March 1925), took the leading parts. High school productions were, of course, performed by students although direction and other production activities were conducted by teachers and other adults from the community such as E.F. Layton and Belle Sterndale Bennett.

"Can Pac" Minstrels *produced by the C.P.R. Social and Athletic Club, 1923.*
Photo: Doris Balcovske

Because the adult shows were produced primarily for charitable purposes, they tended to be big cast and popular fare productions such as minstrel shows, revues, or musicals. The minstrel shows continued to feature members of the community who had carved out this particular entertainment niche for themselves. Many local singers were also important contributors to these productions.[83] Musical direction and accompaniment were shared by musicians who also performed these tasks for the musical productions of the Playgoers. Stage directors for some of the major productions sponsored by the Elks and Gyro clubs were professionals who provided this service for local service clubs throughout the United States and Canada. Local musical directors such as C.J. Ferguson and George E. Bower, also acted as stage directors. In addition, the Sterndale Bennetts directed numerous sketches that were incorporated into the minstrel and variety programs.

Professional Theatre

During the years 1923-1932, professional theatre in Lethbridge continued to be the prerogative of touring companies and performers. However, in early 1932 the manager of the Majestic Theatre, C.L. Dowsley, renewed prospects of establishing a resident company. The Majestic Players, headed by George A. Secord, were given a mandate to perform abridged versions of the latest New York and London hits. These productions were presented in combination with movies. The arrangement, however, lasted a couple of weeks, only. Unfortunately, 1932 was not a good year for establishing long term theatrical projects. Cheap, but extremely popular movies had long since challenged live theatre (especially road shows, and particularly musicals with their large casts and extensive production personnel). Fewer and fewer such productions made their way to Lethbridge as the 1920s progressed. Finally, the poor economic conditions of the 1930s helped seal the fate of the touring companies.

Vaudeville continued to enjoy popularity and was, undoubtedly, the most common form of professional entertainment provided in Lethbridge during this era. As mentioned previously, circuit vaudeville had pretty well "run its course" although acts from the Pantages Circuit appeared, off and on, through 1926. Revival of the Western Canada Vaudeville Circuit as an extension of touring through Minneapolis was mooted in 1928, but nothing along these lines materialized locally.[84] Then, in 1931 it was announced that Calgary would be included in the Radio-Keith-Orpheum (RKO) Circuit; Lethbridge, however, would be excluded.[85] In the meantime, independent vaudeville performers like Harry C. Willis, and small comedy companies appeared more often as added attractions with movies, particularly at the Palace and Empress Theatres.[86] Another trend was an increasing number of Canadian vaudevillians – a fact that seems especially true of the ever popular child performers, for example, the Winnipeg Kiddies, the Calgary Kiddies, the Totten Children, and Jimmie Fisher.

Few stars of the Broadway stage were seen in Lethbridge during this time. As mentioned earlier, George M. Cohan presented Mr. and Mrs. Charles Coburn in the comedy *So This Is London* in 1923-24. The Coburns were trained as classical actors, but according to Brooks Atkinson, they broke out of this mold when they appeared on Broadway in *The Better 'Ole*, in which they portrayed "the most winning parts they ever had."[87] The couple continued to appear on Broadway for many years after coming to Lethbridge; however, Mrs. Coburn died at a relatively young age in 1937. Coburn, who appeared in about seventy movies, was nominated for the Best Supporting Actor Academy Award on three occasions; he took home the Oscar for his performance of Benjamin Dingle in the 1943 movie *The More the Merrier*.[88]

Although most of the major New York producers had pretty well discontinued touring their shows by 1924, there were a few exceptions to this policy. In the mid-1920s, two very successful operettas, *Blossom Time* and *Rose Marie*, were toured to Lethbridge by the most outstanding producers of that time, the Shuberts and Oscar Hammerstein, respectively. Alan J. Lerner tells us that a rumor was fairly widespread in those days that Lee and J.J. Shubert had so many road companies playing the "popular *Blossom Time*" that they actually lost one of them; "They knew it was out there somewhere but somehow they just could not find it."[89] Nevertheless, the production found its way to Lethbridge on two occasions: once in 1925, and again in 1927; *Rose Marie* appeared in 1928. Both productions attracted capacity houses and drew rave reviews.

In 1929 the producer (and former actor), Gilbert Miller (Henry Miller's son), brought *Journey's End* to the local Majestic Theatre. Atkinson informs us that Miller began producing on Broadway in 1919 with a rather light weight show called *Daddy-Long-Legs*.[90] Later, his 1926 production, *The Captive* (Arthur Hornblow, Jr.'s adaptation of *Bourdet's La Prisonniere*), played 160 performances at New York's Empire Theatre before being closed for being morally unacceptable. Miller was also associated with other Broadway productions such as *The Petrified Forest* (1935), and Laurence Housman's *Victoria Regina* (1936).[91]

Most of the major road shows to play Lethbridge in the period under discussion were from England. On three separate occasions (1924, 1926, 1932), Lethbridge audiences had the distinct pleasure of experiencing the magnificent acting style of Sir John Martin-Harvey in company with his wife, Miss N. de Silva. The special effort which English companies such as the Martin-Harvey Company made in order to tour Canada during this time exacted commendations such as the following:[92]

> In these days when the constant cry of New York theatrical managers is that they cannot afford to send the "number one" casts and complete productions of their larger plays upon the road, it should be a matter of pride to all Britishers to note that it has remained for Sir John Martin-Harvey to bring his entire London Company and no less than five of his largest productions across the Atlantic for a coast to coast tour of Canada and the United States . . .

Other stars of the English stage to grace the Majestic Theatre were Percy Hutchison, Cameron Matthews, Seymour Hicks, Brandsby Williams, and "wee" Georgie Wood (of pantomime fame). Speaking of English pantomime, the year 1929 concluded the visits of such groups. During the decade under discussion, only three touring pantomimes played Lethbridge: *Aladdin* in 1927, *Dick Whittington and His Cat* (booked by Stuart Whyte) in 1928, and *Humpty Dumpty* in 1929.

A few Canadian stock companies continued to perform, some of which closed their books during the 1920s. Arlie Marks (Tom's daughter) and Company made their last tour to Lethbridge in 1926. In addition, Lethbridge patrons had their final opportunities to enjoy a live performance of one of their long time favorite actresses, Verna Felton, who appeared at the Majestic Theatre on November 1926 and February 1927 in George M. Cohan's *So This is London* and Anita Loos's *The Whole Town's Talking,* respectively. Miss Felton's mother (Mrs. P.R. Allen) and husband (Lee Millar) were appreciated, as usual.[93] Although this was a difficult time for stock companies, some new western Canadian ones arose during this period. Ensembles such as the Grand Players of Calgary achieved considerable success, but the activities of such companies generally did not extend beyond 1927. Goffin illustrates the short life span of some of these resident stock companies as follows:[94]

> For almost two years, the Grand employed resident companies to play in repertory. From August, 1922 to May, 1923 the Royal-Collins Players from Vancouver presented a different play each week. When their engagement ended five of the actors remained in Calgary to form the core of another company, the Grand Players. This company followed the Royal-Collins model offering Calgarians a wide variety of plays. . . . This experiment with repertory ended as suddenly as it began in March, 1924 when the Grand returned to a weekly bill featuring touring performers.

Companies which were associated with the Chautauqua were a little more long lived. One company which visited Lethbridge on several occasions with the Chautauqua, the Erwin Players, provided an interesting experience for one Lethbridge actress, Mrs. Minnie Thrall. She joined the company in Coaldale to play the part of Florence Ricks in the July 27, 1926, performance of *Cappy Ricks,* and "gave her friends reason for pride in her fine sustaining of the role."[95]

The most significant venture in Canadian theatre during this era was the touring of professional plays and revues by ex-military personnel. Lethbridge audiences were treated to this experience initially when Sergeant George D. Gittus presented his military comedy dramas, *The Volunteer* in early 1918 and *Private Murphy, C.B. (Confined to Barracks),* in late 1918. Press releases for these productions promised large casts of "talented bona fide war veterans" who would depict real army life "from the recruiting office until the armistice . . ." In *The Volunteer,* Gittus appeared as Sergeant Matt Murphy, whereas Gerald Mclean, of the 13th CMR, formerly stationed in Medicine Hat, played the lead role, Private Fish. Mclean was originally from England where he was professionally known as Gerald F. Maitland. *Private Murphy, CB,* was replete with songs, jokes, and speciality acts; however, the production also had its serious moments, especially during the climax when Private Murphy (the most incompetent soldier in the Canadian Army) and a cowardly associate changed their colors and displayed true bravery. The *Lethbridge Herald* critic reported that the local audience enjoyed every line, every scene, every song; indeed, the whole play. Sergeant Gittus, as Private Murphy received high praise.[96]

In October 1921 Lethbridge audiences were treated to the variety production, *Mademoiselle From Armentieres,* which was written, produced, and acted by "soldier players" under the direction of Captain Fred M. Fisher. The plot of this show revolves around the adventures of Lieutenant Edward Brock Green, "a bumptious young sub," who decides to teach some experienced soldiers the proper way to fight. Again, the show combined "realism" and touches of "pathos" with "rollicking, roaring comedy" interspersed with musical numbers.[97]

But the most successful of all of these military troupes were the Dumbells and the Maple Leafs, respectively. The genesis of these groups was the military concert party which was created by various military units during the later years of World War I to entertain fellow soldiers on the fighting lines – soldiers who could not be relieved for long periods of time in order to return to bases where regular theatrical companies, primarily from England, gave performances. Apparently, one of the most popular of these entertainment units was the Princess Patricia Canadian Light Infantry Comedy Company. Modelled after this group was the Y Emmas directed by Merton W. Plunkett, a captain with the YMCA and former secretary of Toronto's Central "Y." The YMCA had taken on much of the responsibility for providing front line entertainment. Plunkett, himself, was a noted stand-up comic, singer, and an effective organizer. In addition to the Y Emmas, Plunkett helped organize a number of concert parties whose members were required to excel in acting, singing, dancing, or playing musical instruments.[98] Since the casts were composed strictly of males, the performing of female roles fell to these men, as well. A story has it, that when the Dumbells was first organized, the performers drew numbers out of a hat, and those who got odd numbers were required to take the female roles.[99] Some of these "female impersonators" became better known by their stage names than by their own names. "To any returned soldier, the most famous girl in France was 'Marjorie'" (Ross Hamilton).[100]

Following World War I, both the Maple Leafs and the Dumbells were reorganized as cooperative theatrical companies by Captain M.W. Plunkett.[101] Since the new version of the Maple Leafs existed for a couple of years, only, its Lethbridge visits will be analyzed first. Prior to the postwar reorganization, many performers from the 4th Division theatrical unit had been absorbed into ongoing London musicals. Similarly, Harry Ashton, "the Queen of the impersonators," had been enticed into a Broadway production. But then, Captain Plunkett brought many of these performers back together again in order to tour Canada with the wartime revue, *Camouflage.* The first performance of *Camouflage* in Lethbridge (October 1920) came about eight months after local audiences had been introduced to the Dumbells (see Table 3-2). *Camouflage* was thoroughly enjoyed locally and it was described by the *Lethbridge Herald* as being "just as enjoyable a show as the Dumbells." In fact, some performers such as Bert Wilkinson (baritone) and Bobby Scott (tenor) were singled out as outdoing the Dumbells. Further accolades went to the female impersonators (Harry Ashton, Leslie Benson, Jack Kelly, Ormund Perley, and Hughie Williamson) for presenting what was referred to as an excellent camouflage of feminine grace. The production was described locally as glorious fun, animated nonsense, and full of vim; the singing was praised as being particularly melodious.[102]

Following this tour, some of the fellows signed up for an engagement as headliners on the Shubert Vaudeville Circuit in the United States.[103] However, since their sister group, the Dumbells, had been so popularly received on their tour to New York and other American cities, Plunkett decided to schedule a second but final tour of the Maple Leafs in 1921, during which the company played two weeks in each of Toronto, Winnipeg, and Vancouver followed by four weeks at the Majesty's Theatre in Montreal. They appeared at the Majestic Theatre in Lethbridge on December 16 and 17, 1921, with their new version of *Camouflage*. Although members of the Maple Leafs participated in various skits, musical numbers, monologues, and dances, in which they displayed numerous talents, they each became identified with some particular type of character or performance – Table 3-2 illustrates this fact. After this final tour, some of these performers were absorbed by the Dumbells.

TABLE 3-2

Typical Characterizations: The Maple Leafs (1920-21)

CAST MEMBER	CHARACTERIZATION	CAST MEMBER	CHARACTERIZATION
Ben Allen	Black Faced Comedian	Bill Morrison	chorus
Bob Anderson	Light comedy	Morley Plunkett	Dancer & Juvenile
Harry Ashton	Leading Lady	Ben Petch	Ethnic Characters
Leslie Benson	Female Impersonator	Ormund Perley	Vamp; female impersonator
Sammy Birch	the "General"	Pat Rafferty	Eccentric Irishman
Jack Challes	chorus	Bob Scott	Tenor vocals
Sergeant Evans	Comic singer	Arthur Sorenson	chorus
James Farley	chorus	Syd Walsh	Opera selections
Jimmy Graham	Dancer & Irish characters	Bert Wilkinson	Baritone vocals
Jack Kelly	ingenue; Leading lady	Hughie Williamson	Vamp & dancer
Howard Large	chorus		

The original Dumbells Concert Party was founded in 1917 by Captain M.W. Plunkett. It apparently took on its unusual name in token of the field markings of the 3rd Canadian Division which was under the command of Major General L.J. Lipsett, C.B., C.M.G., who had authorized its creation.[104] According to O'Neill, the Dumbells was initially comprised of eight entertainers; however, they were soon augmented by performers from other units.[105] With the cessation of fighting, a reorganized Dumbells' group remained in France for awhile playing for the occupation troops. This interlude was followed by a season of light opera and musical comedy revue in Belgium under the patronage of King Albert, after which the company proceeded to London where it presented about sixty performances before audiences estimated to number anywhere from 90 000 - 133 000.[106] After returning to Canada, the Dumbells toured the country with the revue *Biff, Bing, Bang,* which literally started a love affair with their countrymen which lasted throughout their subsequent thirteen annual tours. O'Neill points out that only three of the original Dumbells were part of the first Canadian tour; however, the group generally contained the "cream of the concert parties."[107] Table 3-3 summarizes the various productions which the Dumbells and other military troupes presented to Lethbridge audiences.

Although, as Table 3-3 illustrates, the Dumbells's shows through 1922 carried the title of their famous wartime revue, *Biff, Bing, Bang,* the material was revised annually. Many of the routines

TABLE 3-3

Professional Stage Productions: The Dumbells and Other Military Based Touring Companies

Lethbridge, Alberta (1918-1945)

WINTER TOURS				FALL TOURS			
YEAR	Date	Troupe	Production	YEAR	Date	Troupe	Production
1918	Mar 4,5;Apr 8	Sgt. Gittus & Co.	*The Volunteer*	1918	Dec 25,26	Sgt. Gittus & Co.	*Private Murphy, C.B.*
1920	Feb 25 Apr 6	Dumbells Dumbells	*Biff, Bing, Bang* *Biff, Bing, Bang*	1920	Oct 11,12 Nov 15	Maple Leafs Maple Leafs	*Camouflage* *Camouflage*
1921	Jan 14,15 Feb 19	Dumbells Dumbells	*Biff, Bing, Bang* *Biff, Bing, Bang*	1921	Oct 7,8 - Dec 16,16	Capt. Fisher's Army Players - Maple Leafs	*Mademoiselle From Armentieres* *Camouflage*
1922	Feb 3,4	Dumbells	*Biff, Bing, Bang*	1922			
1923	May 31	Old Dumbells	*Full of Pep*	1923	Nov 26,27	Originals (Old Dumbells)	*Rapid Fire*
1924	Jan 29,30	Dumbells	*Cheerio*	1924	Dec 10	Originals	*Stepping Out*
1925	Jan 19 Feb 4 Mar 9,10	Originals Dumbells Dumbells	*Stepping Out* *Ace High* *Oh, Yes*	1925	Oct 19,20	Originals	*Thumbs Up*
1926	Feb 8,9 Mar 8,9	Dumbells Dumbells	*Lucky 7* *Three Bags Full*	1926	Dec 27,28	Dumbells Sister Show	*Revue of 1926*
1927	Jan 21 Feb 7,8 Mar 7,8	Dumbells' Sister Show Dumbells Dumbells	*Revue of 1926* *Joy Bombs* *That's That*	1927			
1928	Feb 10,11	Dumbells	*Oh! La! La!*	1928			
1929	Jan 18,19 Feb 22,23	Dumbells Dumbells	*Why Worry* *Here Tis*	1929			
1930				1930	Nov 25,28	Dumbells	*Come Eleven*
1931				1931	Nov 16,17	Dumbells	*As You Were*
1933	Feb 14	Dumbells	*Here We Are Again*	1933			
1940	Mar 4 Apr 19-20	Stars of the Dumbells Stars of the Dumbells		1940			
1945	Jan	Stars of the Dumbells	*Lifebuoy Follies* (selected audiences)	1945			

were similar, of course, because the members of the troupe had developed certain stock characters or types of characterization. Core members of the company during these early years were:[108]

1. *Captain M.W. Plunkett* - producer, orchestra leader, song writer.

2. *Al Plunkett* - comedian and singer of outrageous and sentimental songs such as "Since Ma's Gone Crazy Over Crossword Puzzles," "Do Shrimps Make Good Mothers?", or "I Know Where The Flies Go!"

3. *Al G. Murray* - dancer and noted female impersonator, the "dainty soubrette Marie."

4. *Ross Hamilton* - famous for female impersonation of "Marjorie." Even New York critics commonly referred to Hamilton as the finest female impersonator in the world. Singer of seductive songs like, ""I'll Make You Love Me."

5. *Arthur "Jock" Holland* - female impersonator who, prior to joining the Dumbells, was with a famous Imperial concert troupe known as the Bow Bells.

6. *"Red" Newman* - comedian who was associated with songs like, "Oh, Oh, Oh, It's a Lovely War," "Let's Keep the Money in the Country," and "How Does the Milk Get Into Coconuts?"

7. *Jimmy Goode* - black faced comedian whom critics often placed in a class with Al Jolson. He was famous for never telling the same joke twice.

8. *Jack McLaren* - noted for writing the comedy sketch, "The Duchess Entertains" which often starred "Red" Newman and "Jock" Holland. McLaren also was very entertaining as the inebriated Sergeant in one of the Dumbells' lengthy Bistro scenes (former member of the Princess Patricia Comedy Company).

9. *Ted Charter* - starred in riotously funny and satirical "kit inspection" sketch; Chaplinesque comedian.

10. *Bill Tennant* - singer and member of female "beauty chorus."

11. *Jerry Brayford* - singer and female chorus member.

12. *Tom Young* - baritone vocalist and Juvenile player.

13. *Bert Wilkinson* - bass baritone who joined the Dumbells after the Maple Leafs disbanded.

14. *Leonard Young* - costume designer and writer.

15. *Jack Ayres* - musical director and piano accompanist.

In 1923 Captain Plunkett sent two companies on the road again: the Dumbells and the Old Dumbells, but only the Old Dumbells played Lethbridge. Appearing with the Old Dumbells in their May 31st performance were former members of the Maple Leafs like Bob Anderson and Jack Challes as well as newcomers, Art and Fraser Allan, Stan Bennett, Gordon Calder, Jimmy Devon, T.J. Lilly, Dick Kimberley, Bertram Langley, and Bert Mason. In the return performance of the of the Old Dumbells, then referred to as the Originals, Gene Pearson was introduced as the lead female. Pearson was noted for his "wonderful soprano voice with not a tinge of falsetto."[109] He thrilled the audience with his rendition of "The Last Rose of Summer." The *Herald* critic also singled out the former Dumbell, "Red" Newman, and his performance in *The Stoker* "for special commendation." Ted Charter rendered the music hall favorite, "Burlington Bertie", whereas "Jock" Holland performed the amusing skit *The Duchess Entertains*. Leonard Young (also a former Dumbell), director, wrote the selection, "My Dear Old Mother's Songbook," which was sung by the juvenile lead and baritone vocalist, Tom Young. As can be seen from Table 3-3, the Originals returned to the Majestic Theatre in 1924 and 1925 to present *Stepping Out* and *Thumbs Up*, respectively. Most of the cast remained throughout this period, although the occasional new face was added, for example, Thomas Dunn (baritone), Gus McKinnon (tenor), Norman Blume (English musical comedy performer),

Jimmy MacDonald (comedian), Lionel Broadway (vocalist), Stuart Callaghan (female impersonator and dancer), and Percy Campbell (director).

Following the 1925 tour, the Originals was discontinued, and for 1926 only, a female counterpart of the Dumbells was formed which presented *The Revue of 1926.* Captain Plunkett wanted to try something new on the Canadian theatre public, so he introduced an authentic "girlie" show which featured both Miss Toronto (Jean Fara Tolmie) and Miss Winnipeg (Patricia O'Shea). The cast included 25 performers, most of whom were female. According to the *Lethbridge Herald,* the scenery was elaborate, the dancing was predominant, but the show lacked originality and was not particularly outstanding.[110] Although the concept of a predominantly female cast was subsequently dropped, Captain Plunkett obviously saw merit in using some female performers in his succeeding Dumbells' casts. The year 1926 was noted for another innovation in the producing activities of Captain Plunkett when he booked a tour of the musical *Three Little Maids* starring the "celebrated" English comedian, G.P. Huntley. Huntley's "quaint and quiet humor" was well received in Lethbridge. The *Lethbridge Herald* reported, "seldom has a performance been so completely good by a particularly well balanced cast."[111] Less than two years later, the local paper announced the death of G.P. Huntley.[112]

With regard to the Dumbells, it is noted that, although the Old Dumbells/Originals toured to Lethbridge twice in 1923, the Dumbells, themselves, did not appear that year because they were kept busy playing eastern Canada and parts of the United States. They, nevertheless, returned to the Majestic Theatre in 1924, and from then through 1931 they appeared in Lethbridge at least once per year. Then, following a break of one year, the Dumbells made their final tour to Lethbridge in 1933.

When the Dumbells appeared in 1924, Lethbridge audiences were pleased to see former members of the Maple Leafs such as Pat Rafferty, Ben Allen, and Morley Plunkett. Additional members included Lethbridge's favorite Dumbell, "Marjorie" (Ross Hamilton), Stan Bennett, Jim Foley, Jack Grace, John Hagen, Bert Thomas, and Jimmy Devon (dancer) as well as Gordon Calder and T.L. Lilly, both of whom appeared in a "riotous sketch," *O'Brien Entertains.* According to news reports, a major innovation introduced into the second half of the program for *Cheerio* was an extensive orchestral presentation by Captain Plunkett's ten piece orchestra.[113]

By 1925 "Jock" Holland, "Red" Newman, and Al Plunkett rejoined the Dumbells. When the Dumbells performed *Lucky 7* in February 1926, the core players included the three Plunketts, Ross Hamilton, "Red" Newman, "Jock" Holland, Stan Bennett, Pat Rafferty, Glen Allen, and Jimmy Devon. Although Stan Bennett left the company after the 1926 tour, the Dumbells remained fairly intact through 1927. With respect to the 1927 shows, *Joy Bombs* and *That's That,* the *Lethbridge Herald* critic praised Rafferty's comic dive from the deck of the S.S. Canada, Newman's comic portrayal of "The Stoker," Hamilton's gorgeous gowns and wonderful figure, Holland's marvelous impersonation of Beatrice Lillie, as well as Morley Plunkett and Glen Allen's acrobatic dancing. In *Joy Bombs,* the skit, *Tea for Three,* in which the women were portrayed as earning the living and the men as staying home to mind the babies, was proclaimed "a scream!"[114]

Among the newcomers who joined the company in 1928 were Harry Binns (tenor), Cameron Geddes (bass), Charlie Jeeves (comedian), and Fred Emney, an established London stage star whose family was associated with English pantomime and music hall productions.[115] Emney was described as the subtle comedian "par excellence" who "does everything." But Lethbridge audiences missed his performance in *Why Worry* (January, 1929) because he had come down with the flu; Scotty Morrison filled in. Yet, a month later, Emney thoroughly entertained the local audiences in *Here 'Tis* some years later, Lethbridge movie audiences were able to enjoy Emney in one of the many film versions of *Brewster's Millions* (starring Jack Buchanan).[116] *Why Worry* was notable for introducing female entertainers into the regular Dumbells' cast. Aileen Parker (dancer) and Jessie Butt (contralto) contributed to both shows that year. A chorus of female "Dumbellettes" was added for the eleventh annual revue, *Come Eleven*. The Corrigan Sisters, Jessie Butt, and the dainty comedienne, Audrey Corline, also contributed their talents. The usual female impersonators were no longer with the show, so the chorus line in *Come Eleven* was performed by the real female members of the cast. *Come Eleven* appeared in Lethbridge on November 25 and 26, 1930, following an absence of the Dumbells of approximately twenty-one months. Apparently, the company had remained in the east where it had established attendance records in Ontario at a time when most road companies had been forced out of business. When the Dumbells returned to western Canada, the *Lethbridge Herald* stated that, "we had just about given up hope of seeing another road show in Lethbridge."[117] The *Herald* also speculated that *Come Eleven* would be a test for road shows – "Does the public just want a steady fare of pictures . . . or is this talk of the demise of the drama and the strangulation of the stage just so much talk?"[118] Well, the overflowing Lethbridge audience was most appreciative and the local paper's criticism was filled with superlatives: "a very delectable show," "supremely enjoyable evening," "all that could be desired in a performance of this nature."[119]

In 1931 Captain Plunkett returned to the old format of the all-male show when he presented *As You Were*. Lethbridge audiences were ecstatic about "Marjorie's" return after an absence of more than three years, especially, since it had been mistakenly reported in 1930 that Ross Hamilton had died in Kalamazoo, Michigan.[120] Glen Allen returned too, after a two year's stint with the Folies-Bergere in Paris. Captain Plunkett replaced the girls' chorus with his ten piece orchestra. Regulars such as Al Plunkett, "Red" Newman, and Scotty Morrison were supported by Curly Nixon (who joined the 1930 cast of *Come Eleven*), Don Romaine (a former headliner on the Keith Vaudeville Circuit where his impersonation of the Black "Madam Queen" was considered to be one of the great comedy sensations of that time), Joe Carr (a former Broadway dialect comedian), Bill Handorf (violinist), and former radio stars, Gene Fritzley and Laurie Thompson. *As You Were* was reported to have much more vigor than the last couple of shows because the all-male cast tended to present a peppier, more lilting show than those in which female performers were involved.[121]

The thirteenth annual tour bypassed Lethbridge; rather, it was February 1933 when the Dumbells returned in *Here We Are Again*. Audrey Carline rejoined the company; she and Irene Fox (dancer) added the feminine touch, again. Unfortunately, this was the final tour of the Dumbells – a group which had become a most welcome Canadian institution.

As a postscript to the discussion about the touring Dumbells, it is noted that a few of the old regulars were brought together in 1940 to help raise morale among Canadians and their fighting forces during the early years of World War II. The stars of the Dumbells, together with an acrobatic troupe called the Lowells, came to Lethbridge and presented about an hour of entertainment at the Capitol Theatre. George Hamilton proudly presented Ross Hamilton, "Red" Newman, and Pat Rafferty in songs and comic routines reminiscent of the "good old days." Jack Ayre (original musical director of the Dumbells) provided piano accompaniment. Apparently, these performers had lost little of their sparkle. "Red" and Pat convulsed the audience with their "riotous songs and comedy"; whereas, Ross, described as a "little heavier," still cut a fetching figure in the stately gowns that had always been so much a part of "Marjorie's" charm.[122] Following this Canadian tour, the company, which was hailed by press and public alike, prepared to venture overseas to entertain the troops. Some years later, as the war was beginning to "run its course," former Dumbells, Pat Rafferty, Jimmy Devon, and Jack Ayres, and a number of other entertainers appeared in *Lifebuoy Follies* sponsored by Lever Brothers for the local Veterans' Guards. While in Lethbridge, the group also presented a short performance for the Kinsmen Club.[123] Unquestionably, the Dumbells and its associated organizations will be remembered as one of Canada's foremost cultural institutions. Besides providing outstanding entertainment, these groups also contributed to the Canadian sense of identity and pride. Each tour reminded Canadians of the gallant effort made by their troops in the fierce hand-to-hand combat of World War I. In addition, the international acclaim which followed these groups wherever they performed was viewed by Canadians as proof of the fact that their entertainers had reached, if not surpassed, the standards of Broadway and London. This glorious achievement was fittingly celebrated in the summer of 1977 when the Charlottetown Festival presented the musical comedy *The Legend of the Dumbells* conceived, directed, and choreographed by Alan Lund. According to reports, two former members of the Dumbells, Jack McLaren and Bill Redpath, were in the audience for the opening night performance.[124]

Mass Entertainment

Throughout the history of the Dumbells, they, like so many of the popular vaudeville performers, came about as close to providing mass entertainment and becoming "pop" stars as one can possibly imagine among live entertainers of their day. Other entertainment which continued to be enjoyed by large numbers of people of various social backgrounds, included the circus (represented in Lethbridge primarily by the Sells Floto, Al G. Barnes, and Barnum and Bailey aggregations); the annual Lethbridge Exhibition and Fair; and the movies. "By the 1920s the American film industry was big business."[125] According to Hiebert, et al., three kinds of film dominated the final decade of silent film: the feature-length comedy, the western, and the comedy of manners such as Cecil B. DeMille's *Male and Female* and *Why Change Your Wife*. In addition to these three major genres, there were also the occasional epics like *Ben Hur* and social dramas such as *The Man They Could Not Hang*, based upon the life of John Lee. Many movie critics believe that in this era, "film comedy reached its zenith."[126] While enjoying the films' comic stars like Charlie Chaplin, Buster Keaton, and Harold Lloyd, Lethbridge audiences also appreciated the antics and predicaments of Larry Semon whose life and career are much less documented than these other silent film comedians – possibly because his film career was cut short when he died from pneumonia at the age of 39 in October 1928.[127] The better class of westerns such as *Covered Wagon*, *Iron Horse*, and *Tumbleweeds* played the Majestic or the Palace Theatres, whereas patrons at the Kings or the Empress followed the many exploits of romantic cowboy heros, Tom Mix and Kit Carson. A.W. Shackleford recalls that the Tom Mix westerns were his means of bringing the Kings Theatre "out of the red."

Although background sound had been associated with movies for many years, the late 1920s witnessed various attempts at coordinating sound with the singing and speaking of the film actors. Opera film introduced the concept of touring opera singers with the movie so that the singers could present the arias live as the film of the opera was projected on the screen. Opera films of *The Bohemian Girl* and *William Tell* were presented in this manner in November 1927 and April 1928, respectively. Mechanical means of synchronizing sound with the movie pictures were also being introduced about this time. Lethbridge movie theatres began to vie with each other in their efforts to be the first to install the latest sound equipment. As early as August 1926, the Empress Theatre installed a Victor Orthophonic Victrola which synchronized background music. Soon, Warner Brothers' Vitaphone System was bringing Al Jolson's voice to millions of movie goers throughout the United States and Canada, and before long "talkies" had pretty well superseded silent films. "By 1930 some 95 percent of Hollywood films were talkies. . . . "[128] As mentioned previously, the first major talkies were exhibited locally at the Majestic Theatre in the spring of 1929. The Empress followed suit in September, and when the Capitol opened in the fall of that year, it showed the talking movie, *Close Harmony*, starring Charles "Buddy" Rogers and Nancy Carol.[129] Color technology was also advancing. Movies with some color had been exhibited off and on. By 1930 short subjects such as the *King of Jazz,* featuring Paul Whiteman and his orchestra, were filmed entirely in technicolor. Black and Whitney inform us that colored features made their debut in 1935 with *Becky Sharp*, starring Miriam Hopkins.[130]

Some other local developments related to the movies were the introduction of special midnight shows associated with holidays such as Thanksgiving and New Years and the acceptance of agricultural products like potatoes or grain for admission.[131] An additional local venture was another filming of a home town movie. With the encouragement of A.W. Shackleford, a number of local actors were enticed into performing for the cameras on the stage of the Palace Theatre in 1927. [132]

But from the point of view of southern Albertans, possibly the most exciting happening related to the movies was the rise to stardom of "their own Fay Wray" who is probably best remembered for her role in the David Selznick version of *King Kong* produced in 1933. Fay Wray was born on September 15, 1907, near Mountain View, Alberta (between Cardston and Waterton National Park).[133] Although she moved to the United States as a relatively young child, Albertans still prided themselves on her achievements. Local ads for Wray's early movies certainly capitalized on this sentiment, for example:[134]

> Fay Wray is our Sweetheart, coming right from the picturesque Cardston District. You will see your own star from Cardston, Alberta, in one of this year's finest pictures.

This publicity accompanied the Lethbridge showing of *The Legion of the Condemned* (May 1928), which provided Gary Cooper with his first leading role. Shortly thereafter, Wray and Cooper were touted as "Paramount's glorious young lovers."[135] Similar publicity was evident when local theatres exhibited other Fay Wray movies such as *The First Kiss,* which also co-starred Gary Cooper (Palace Theatre, January 1929), and *The Wedding March* (March 1929). Strangely, no such local publicity accompanied the showing of *King Kong* at the Capitol Theatre on May 15-17, 1933.

Before completing high school, Fay Wray began her full time career with the Hal Roach studios and then with Universal where she played leading ladies in two-reel westerns. In early 1928 her contract was picked up by Paramount when she was chosen by director, Eric Von Stroheim, as the romantic interest in *The Wedding March*. Haver comments about Paramount's acquisition of Fay Wray as follows:[136]

> The film had been in production for so long that Pat Powers, its principal backer had sold out his share to Paramount; the deal included Fay Wray's contract. The young actress had come to the States from Canada when she was three years old and arrived in Los Angeles at fourteen. School was the first consideration, but during vacations she got some bit parts and even one or two leads in short films at the Fox and Century Comedy studios.

The *Lethbridge Herald* kept fairly close tabs on Miss Wray, and on September 28, 1931, the paper announced that Wray was to begin her legitimate acting career by starring in Harrison Hall's musical production, *Nikki* (written by her husband, John Monk Saunders), at the Longacre Theatre in New York.[137]

A supporting actor in this production was a young man named Archie Leach (Cary Grant) who had just completed a number of shows for the Shuberts.[138] The staging of *Nikki* coincided with a significant decision made at Paramount as outlined by Haver: "In late 1931, in an unprecedented move for a movie studio, the entire list of featured players were released from their contracts."[139]

This development also paved the way for Miss Wray to star in *King Kong* which was produced by RKO studios. Throughout the 1930s and early 1940s, Miss Wray performed in numerous movies and in the occasional stage play. Then, after a hiatus in her career beginning in 1942, she returned to the movies from 1953 - 1958.[140] Later in life, Miss Wray took up writing. A play of hers, *The Meadowlark,* was produced in 1985; in 1989, her autobiography (which opened with her memories of returning to Cardston to celebrate the 75th anniversary of the town's settlement) was published.[141]

In concluding this discussion on developments in the movie industry, it is interesting to note one technological development which was displayed in Lethbridge in late 1931 but which was not adopted until many years later. The reference in the *Lethbridge Herald* to a demonstration of the "visionola" at the local Teco store is so intriguing that it has been quoted verbatim in order to substantiate its authenticity:[142]

> The visionola is a radio combined with equipment for the showing of moving pictures and talkies. The views are projected on a mirror and reflected from there to a silver screen above the machine. Recording of voice and music are perfect and the small machine turns out talkies as fine as any in any theatre.

> The visionola is not a television machine, but is a combined phonograph and movie which, from the record, produces the sound and projects moving pictures on a screen at the top of the machine, depicting singing and action at the same time.

Although the visionola stimulated a great deal of interest, it obviously was not considered very practical, especially in the early days of the Depression. It was destined to be "put on the shelf" together with television, the latter of which had actually been around in one form or another for some years. Early patents for sending pictures by wire were issued in some European countries prior to the year 1900. Experimental T.V. broadcasting occurred in the United States in 1927-28. Pember tells us that in 1930 an Englishman, J.L. Baird, was selling television sets to the public for about $130 and was broadcasting video signals via the BBC.[143] However, in North America, the large broadcasting networks were much more interested in developing radio, so North Americans had to wait until the late 1940s and early 1950s to enjoy regular television broadcasting, and later still, to enjoy the "talkies" in the comfort of their own home.

4

The Little Theatre Era
A Time Of Crisis And Change (1933 - 1945)

Community Setting

The era under discussion in this chapter can be divided into two broad but rather distinct politico-economic periods, the Depression (1933 - 1939) and World War II (1939 - 1945). Since these events were fairly global in nature, significant social consequences resulting from them affected societies and communities throughout the world. Lethbridge and district were not spared from these forces; therefore, economic, political, and social developments in southern Alberta were determined to a great extent by forces external to the community.

By 1933 the Depression was well entrenched across Canada as evidenced by high unemployment, low wages, increased relief bills, and reduced trade. Compounding the economic concerns of the average consumer was growing inflation related to commodity prices.[1] The apparent inability of the Federal and Provincial governments to deal effectively with these economic woes led to considerable political unrest in western Canada, with the consequent rise of new political parties promising economic reform, for example, the Cooperative Commonwealth Federation (CCF) and the Social Credit.[2] In 1935 the new Social Credit Party headed by William Aberhart swept into power in Alberta.[3]

Regardless of considerable controversy generated by Aberhart and his government, they did manage to survive the troublesome years of the late 1930s. When Albertans returned to the polls in 1940, economic and political conditions had changed considerably, and as MacGregor suggests:[4]

> ... by 1940 the depression and drought were over and a second world war had come. Fewer people had time for politicking [sic]. When the election results were tallied up, Aberhart and his government were returned to power with a substantially reduced, but nevertheless, working majority of thirty-six seats out of fifty-seven.

During the 1940s the Social Credit Party was able to consolidate its position – a process which was made even more certain by the selection of Ernest Manning as head of the party and Premier of Alberta following William Aberhart's death in May 1943.[5] Economic prosperity experienced throughout the province in the 1940s assured the government of stable support for many future years. Even Lethbridge voters, who had abandoned the Social Credit Party in a 1937 by-election when they elected the unity candidate, Dr. Peter Campbell, to the Alberta legislature, returned to the fold in 1944 by electing John Landeryou (S.C.) as MLA. Henceforth, the Social Credit Party maintained a stranglehold on Lethbridge until 1975 when Lethbridge belatedly joined the swing to the Progressive Conservatives,[6] who had taken over the reins of provincial power from the Social Credit party in 1971.

But the basis for most of the political upheaval in western Canada during the 1930s was economic insecurity. At that time, the prairie economy was still dependent primarily on agriculture, specifically, the production and sale of wheat. Both production and prices fluctuated considerably during the 1930s; however, the general economic outcome was rather bleak since increased production tended to coincide with falling prices and vice versa. Generally speaking, however, economic conditions did improve somewhat during the latter half of the 1930s, and then the rate of improvement accelerated during the war and postwar period.

The manner in which these general economic trends effected Lethbridge is shown in various demographic and economic indices. For example, population figures for the City of Lethbridge clearly illustrate that the population growth rate in the early 1930s was negligible, whereas the growth rate increased steadily through the next decade and one-half, reaching in 1946-51, the second highest five year rate of increase in the city's history.[7] Construction in Lethbridge reached an all time low in 1933, and it remained relatively depressed during the succeeding few years. Surprisingly, the number of building permits jumped considerably in 1936 at a time when the Lethbridge district experienced its smallest agricultural crop since 1919 as a consequence of two successive dry years. Higher wheat prices in 1937 and near record agricultural production in 1938 and 1939 helped to maintain this economic recovery as did a number of local public works projects.[8] Another interesting economic development which occurred in 1939 was the city's acquisition of the Mounted Police property and barracks for a sum of $6 841.[9] After the war, this property became the site of a new city hall, other civic and provincial buildings, and various recreational facilities; the site was then referred to as the Civic Centre.

Following Canada's declaration of war on Germany in September 1939, an increasing amount of the economic activity in Canada was devoted to the war effort. In Lethbridge, during the first few years of the war, municipal, commercial, and local institutional construction continued at the fairly high pace set in the late 1930s.[10] Most of the construction during 1940-42 was concentrated on military units, on the one hand, and residential construction, on the other. Nevertheless, the growing demand for housing apparently could not be satisfied. The Lethbridge population had increased by more than 8 percent between 1931 and 1941 when little residential construction took place. Later, the influx of construction workers involved in building military establishments, and the subsequent growth in the number of military personnel, placed tremendous pressure on existing housing.

Shortly after Canada entered the war, the local RCMP Barracks were quickly converted to the Lethbridge Military Garrison.[11] Then, southern Alberta was selected as a prime site for the training of air force personnel. In association with the British Commonwealth Air Training Program, flying schools were established in Lethbridge, Pearce, Macleod, Claresholm, and Vulcan.[12] Because of the prevailing winds in Lethbridge, the #5 Elementary Flying Training School was moved in June 1941 to High River.[13] However, the RCAF operated the No. 8 Bombing and Gunnery School at the Kenyon Airport from November 1941 to December 1944.[14]

The Japanese bombing of Pearl Harbor on December 7, 1941, and the subsequent hostilities in the Pacific resulted in one of the most questionable decisions made by the Canadian Government during the war: the invoking of authority, under the War Measures Act, to move Japanese Canadians from their homes on the West Coast. This decision was to have an enormous impact upon Lethbridge and district because it was decided that about five hundred of these families should be moved to the environs of Lethbridge where they would be put to work in the sugar beet fields.[15] They, and other concerned citizens who witnessed the deprivations which these Japanese Canadians suffered and the deplorable conditions under which they were forced to live, found it difficult to excuse the Canadian Government for this ruthless action. Finally, in 1988 the Federal Government apologized to the Japanese Canadian community and agreed to a compensation package.[16]

The severity of the war in 1942 prompted Canadian politicians to consider the possibility of military conscription; a possibility which, when put to Canadian voters in April was approved by a 2:1 margin. Lethbridge voters gave an overwhelming 5:1 approval.[17] A draft for nineteen year olds was announced on September 30, 1942, while Canadians were still reeling from the news of the abortive attack on Dieppe (August 19), where almost 3 000 Canadian troops were either killed or taken prisoner.[18]

Although the Dieppe invasion was a military fiasco, the war against Germany was gradually turning in favor of the Allied forces.[19] On the home front, Lethbridge residents could look back on 1942 as a year of rather favorable economic circumstances, at least. The district experienced the largest grain crop in its history even though dust bowl conditions had prevailed for a while during the spring.[20] Although commercial construction in the city was at a standstill, a federal building priority system encouraged residential building. Military construction in the region amounted to about $2 000 000 (not included in local building permits). Among these projects was the building of a POW camp in Lethbridge large enough to house 15 000 German prisoners of war. Economic optimism was further stimulated by the Federal Government's announcement of a $15 million postwar St. Mary's Irrigation project.

By 1943 the tide of the war had definitely turned.[21] At home, building and labor shortages continued to stall commercial building, but housing remained constant. To aid in the general labor shortage, local POW's were provided for work in the sugar beets.[22] Restrictions were also loosened on the local Japanese evacuees who were given permission to work in selected industries in the city such as Broder's Canning Company.[23]

Although the year 1944 witnessed considerable success by the Allies in the European offensives, the joy was interrupted by the mysterious attack on Great Britain of robot or buzz bombs.[24] With the coming of fall, Canada hosted the Quebec Conference.[25] On the local home front, building materials were becoming more readily available, and although tradesmen were still scarce, permits increased about 75 percent over the previous year. Still, reports indicated that the housing shortage remained rather acute. The major event directly affecting the city in 1944 was the announcement in October that #8 B. & G. School would be closed (which it was on December 1, 1944).[26] Shortly thereafter, plans were announced to close the Pearce #2 FTS in January 1945 and the Claresholm Air School as of April 1945. On May 4, the Nazis surrendered. Negotiations proceeded for unconditional surrender which was finally achieved; May 8, 1945, was declared VE Day (Victory in Europe).

Now, attention was focussed on the Pacific where the Americans continued their fight in the Philippines as well as in the islands of Iwo Jima and Okinawa; Russian troops invaded Manchuria. As summer set in, a major decision was made to drop atomic bombs on the cities of Hiroshima (August 6) and Nagasaki (August 8). Almost immediately after these bombings, the Japanese capitulated; August 14, 1945 was declared VJ Day.[27]

During 1945 Canada Victory Loan drives were successfully completed in April and October. The citizens of Lethbridge and district had conscientiously supported all of the War and Victory Loan drives from their inception in 1941.[28] Lethbridge prided itself in being one of the first, if not the first, Canadian city to achieve its quota in all of the campaigns. This fact underscored the economic conditions of the time: incomes increased considerably but few opportunities to spend that income on consumer goods existed. The amount of new wealth generated in the Lethbridge area increased yearly throughout most of the 1940s, reaching a peak of $152 000 000 in 1948 (almost two times the 1945 figure and three times the 1942 figure).[29] House construction was the other major form of investment, and in the year 1945 permits were issued for 246 residential units which helped to raise the value of building permits above the previous Lethbridge high figure set in 1912.

Disruption of Theatrical Activities

The Depression, followed by World War II, had a distinct influence on the growth and development of the arts in Canada and in specific communities such as Lethbridge. During the Depression, most of the existing artistic social structure was greatly weakened, if not destroyed. Certainly, professional touring was basically terminated. Many of the large producers and theatre managers lost their holdings with the stock market crash. Those who did survive, quickly realized that depressed communities could not support the costs incurred by touring companies. Also, movies had achieved tremendous popularity, and with the perfection of sound, patrons in even the most remote communities could more fully witness the popular stars of Hollywood. How could a stage show priced at $2.00 - $2.50 possibly compete with the latest Busby Berkeley movie extravaganza which could be seen for an admission price of fifteen to twenty-five cents?

One might suspect that the lack of professional competition would give added impetus to the development of local amateur theatre. Unfortunately, the Depression also adversely affected the amateur companies. Many of the legitimate theatres across western Canada were closed or converted into movie houses; therefore, local companies were relegated to inferior performing facilities. In addition, patron support also declined. Local amateur companies were forced to cut back on expensive productions such as musicals which usually demanded higher royalties and incurred more costs for extensive costume rentals and scenic designs than did plays. Admission prices tumbled in order to compete with the movies, and consequently, the resulting limited income prohibited the rental of theatre space even if such space were available. Festival competition was also adversely affected. Although the Alberta Drama festivals had experienced an auspicious debut in 1930 and considerable success in the first few years of the Depression, and although the Dominion Drama Festival was introduced in the depths of the Depression (1933), it soon became apparent that costs associated with travelling to festivals greatly restricted the ability of some groups to participate. The outbreak of World War II resulted in further disruption. In late 1939 the DDF announced the cancellation of its 1940 festival. In addition, most of the provincial festivals were cancelled for the duration of the war years.[30] Groups became depopulated as various members left their community to become involved in military service. Other members felt that their efforts were needed in more "serious" service. When the need was felt to entertain, programs requiring relatively short term rehearsal periods (variety shows) became the dominant form of entertainment. These shows were often cooperative ventures, for example, local participants combined their talents with itinerant military personnel. Of course, increased military activity stimulated the greater development of military entertainment: military bands, army show units, the navy show, and so forth. Many of these groups also entertained at public gatherings and concerts. Rallies intended to engender patriotism and raise funds for the war effort relied extensively on the popular appeal of military bands, variety entertainers, and movie stars such as George Murphy. Orchestras, such as Mart Kenney and his Western Gentlemen, also attracted mass crowds. At the same time, some traditional forms of popular entertainment such as circuses were generally suspended throughout most of the war years; however,

I personally recall attending a circus in Winnipeg during the earlier war years, for which the price of admission was a kitchen pot or pan (to be converted for military purposes). Of course, the circus returned with all its glitter after the war to compete with other mass forms of entertainment.

Local Theatre Facilities

By 1934 A.W. Shackleford and Famous Players Corporation controlled all of the theatres in the city (Majestic, Capitol, and Roxy). The Capitol Theatre was the most modern and comfortable of the three theatres; it was, therefore, the hub of the corporation's business in Lethbridge. First run, highly rated movies were featured at the Capitol; whereas, the Roxy specialized in Westerns. The occasional movie was shown at the Majestic, but throughout most of the 1930s, it remained dark. Legitimate theatre was rare now; touring shows were scarce and local business provided by schools, festivals, and groups like the Playgoers of Lethbridge could hardly sustain the operation of the Majestic or provide incentive for upgrading the facility. On the other hand, the Capitol Theatre experienced a major face lift in 1936 when the 1898 front of the building was replaced with a "modern fireproof facade."[31]

Roxy Theatre
Photo: City of Lethbridge Archives and Records Management

In the case of the Majestic Theatre, A.W. Shackleford and his associates found that the building was too inefficient to operate. Also, renovating the structure would not be cost effective. But the popularity of movies certainly warranted additional theatre space in Lethbridge; therefore, in March 1938 Shackleford purchased a building site on the corner of 4th Avenue and 8th Street South with the intention of constructing a modern movie theatre.[32] However, before construction plans were arranged, the outbreak of war forced postponement of the development until 1950 when the project eventually materialized with the completion of the 1 000 seat Paramount Theatre, designed strictly for movies.[33]

In the interim, Famous Players Corporation disposed of the Majestic Theatre in November 1942 when the local businessmen, Stan and Romeo Fabbi, purchased the building and moved their Purity Dairy operations there.[34] Some retail space was maintained at the front of the building on the ground level; also, office space was rented in the front upper level. Unfortunately, there was no such organization as a Heritage Committee in those days to protect and preserve such important landmarks. Thus, this particular performing facility was lost forever.

Some other developments relating to the extension of the theatre business in Lethbridge during the 1930s are worthy of note. On January 5, 1938, Cameron F. Doughty and his wife, Emily, opened the Lealta Theatre in the old Monarch Theatre Building.[35] The opening day program was a double feature: *Green Light* with Errol Flynn and Anita Louise, and *Down the Stretch* with Mickey Rooney and Pat Ellis. Approximately three years later, Doughty opened his new Lealta Theatre (immediately north of the former facility) in the renovated Canadian Bank of Commerce building (the former Standard Bank).[36] Its opening night showing (New Year's Eve, 1940) featured Jack Benny in *Buck Benny Rides Again*. The Lealta was a minor cinema which generally exhibited second run movies but occasionally brought in specialized features such as filmed operas. A little more than a year later, the *Lethbridge Herald* reported that a new Odeon Theatre was being planned for a location on 5th Street South – across the street from the Capitol Theatre;[37] nevertheless, these plans did not materialize.

So by 1942 legitimate theatre in Lethbridge had been relegated to the Capitol Theatre and various inadequate halls throughout the city. As mentioned earlier, the stage of the Capitol Theatre was basically inadequate for large stage shows. Nevertheless, this facility was used for plays and musicals until the mid-1960s. Throughout these years, Shackleford was prepared to spend the necessary funds to enlarge the Capitol's stage; however, city ordinances would not allow him to encroach upon the alley behind the theatre. Other venues such as St. Augustine's Hall and other church and school halls were used, but they had all the usual disadvantages of meeting spaces not designed for theatrical presentations. Some auditoriums such as that at the Lethbridge Collegiate Institute had unique problems. This auditorium basically had no stage; folding doors merely opened up into the front hallway which could then be converted into a temporary stage. The YMCA had a relatively small gymnasium which was occasionally used for gymnastic displays and various youth programs. Following the war, active YMCA theatre groups presented many of their dramatic and musical productions in this very inappropriate facility.

During the war, various military establishments in and around Lethbridge provided additional performance space; however, performances in these facilities were almost exclusively reserved for the personnel of the garrison or flying school. Fortunately, a new LDS Stake House was constructed during the early war years; it contained one of the largest auditoriums in the city. This facility quickly became a popular place for plays and concerts by LDS church groups as well as other community and touring groups and performers.

Amateur Theatrical Activities

As explained earlier, it was in the period prior to the Depression that the amateur regained prominence in the performing arts throughout western Canada. During the Depression, itself, the work of these amateurs was enhanced in Alberta by two significant forces: leadership in dramatic training provided by the University of Alberta's Department of Extension and standards of performance excellence emphasized by the adjudicating process adopted and maintained by the various festivals which spread throughout the province.

The Department of Extension (University of Alberta)

The Department of Extension, formed in 1912, had always displayed a commitment to cultural education. But this commitment revealed itself most evidently in 1932 when Edward A. (Ned) Corbett, director of the Department, submitted an application to the Carnegie Corporation of New York for special funding in order to hire a provincial drama supervisor. According to Day and Potts:[38]

> In May 1932, the University of Alberta received a promise of a $10 000 yearly grant for three years. The funding would provide for a full-time drama instructor who would give direction to drama groups throughout Alberta and who could help teachers establish drama programs. The grant also supplied finances to secure competent adjudicators for school festivals . . . .and to increase the morale of rural people by sponsoring art shows, school fairs and Extension lectures in the Fine Arts.

Almost immediately, Corbett hired Elizabeth Sterling Haynes as extension drama instructor – a position which she retained until 1937. One of Haynes's early concerns centered around the need for intensive instruction in theatre arts, especially for people involved in community theatre. Haynes had offered summer courses in Edmonton for teachers of drama, but both she and Corbett recognized the need for a more substantial program. In November 1932, following consultation with Dr. Wallace, President of the University of Alberta, Corbett announced that a summer school of drama, conducted by Haynes, would be offered at Banff during the summer of 1933. The summer school would function under the auspices of the Carnegie grant and would provide participants with the opportunity to experience all of the elements of play production. Proof of the need for such a program was evidenced by the fact that 190 students enrolled in the first program, which operated August 7-25.[39] The students were charged a registration fee of one dollar, and they had to provide their own lodging; there was no tuition fee.[40] The program was well received, and the demand for subsequent summer schools remained high. In fact, it soon became apparent that instruction relating to the other arts was also necessary; Banff was envisioned as an ideal location for a major school of the fine arts. In March 1936 the *Lethbridge Herald* reported that the first School of Fine Arts was to be held in Banff from August 3-29, 1936, under the direction of the Extension Department of the University of Alberta.[41] According to this newspaper article, art classes would be under the supervision of Mr. Leighton of the Calgary Institute of Technology; drama classes would be supervised by Dr. Joseph Smith, University of Utah and President of the International Council of Speech; music classes would be conducted by "the best possible teachers." Within a year, a scholarship program was announced, and soon, Lethbridge performers and artists were benefiting from this program.[42] Since its inception, the Banff School of Fine Arts (BSFA) has grown to become one of the finest institutions of its type in the world. Reflecting other developments in society, its purpose gradually changed over the years; its programs became geared more and more to the training and encouragement of professionals.

During her five years as Drama Extension Specialist, Elizabeth Sterling Haynes worked unceasingly at: organizing drama courses (workshops, short courses, summer courses); adjudicating various festival productions; advising drama societies throughout the province; developing school curricula; establishing and expanding the extension drama library; and stimulating an interest in drama everywhere she went. When an associate and former student of Haynes's, Gwen Pharis Ringwood, was interviewed by Day and Potts, she referred to Haynes as, "One of the truly seminal forces in the establishment of the Western Canadian Theatre." Day and Potts add their own comment: "A whole generation of Western Canadian theatre practitioners were trained either by Haynes personally or through teaching institutions or methods she helped to establish or pioneer."[43]

Gwen Pharis Ringwood was also associated with the Department of Extension for a few years, but her national reputation was achieved through her playwriting. Southern Albertans proudly recall that Miss Pharis spent her formative years in Magrath.[44] Later, she enrolled at the University of Alberta where she received her B.A. degree in 1934 (English). In the interim, she attended the first summer program at Banff. In addition, she worked as secretary to Haynes until becoming Registrar of the Banff School of Fine Arts in 1936. It was during the summer of 1933, that her first play, *The Dragons of Kent,* was debuted simultaneously by the Junior Division of the Banff School and the Edmonton Summer School.[45] During these early years in Edmonton, Pharis also gained some valuable experience in writing radio drama since she collaborated with another Edmonton playwright, Elsie Park Gowan, on a ten-play series entitled *New Lamps for Old*, which was aired on the University of Alberta's radio station, CKUA.

In order to enrich her playwriting abilities, Pharis enrolled in 1937 in the Carolina Playmakers School at the University of North Carolina (Chapel Hill) under the tutelage of Dr. Frederick Koch, Chairman of the drama department and a frequent summer instructor at the Banff School.[46] Pharis proved to be an outstanding student and a worthy recipient of a Rockefeller Foundation Fellowship. During her two years at the University of North Carolina, she wrote the following plays which the school produced: "*Chris Axelson, Blacksmith; Still Stands the House; Pasque Flower; Dark Harvest; One Man's House*."[47] In 1939 a number of laurels were heaped upon Pharis Ringwood for the excellence of her various folk plays. In April the DDF honored Ringwood with an award of one hundred dollars in recognition of the best Canadian play *(Still Stands the House)* presented at any of the regional festivals.[48] This play became a perennial favorite at one act play festivals throughout the country. Almost half a century later, Richard Plant (editor of a major anthology of Canadian plays), referred to *Still Stands the House* as a "Canadian classic" in realistic one act plays.[49] Later that spring (1939), Pharis graduated with an M.A. in drama and was awarded the Roland Holt Playwriting Cup for the school's outstanding playwright of the year. Also, during that year, *Chris Axelson, Blacksmith*, was awarded the Gwillym Edwards prize in the Alberta playwriting competition.[50]

Following graduation, Pharis returned to Edmonton where she assumed the post of Director of Dramatics for the Department of Extension (University of Alberta). She also married Dr. John Brian Ringwood, M.D., on September 16, 1939.[51] The following year, the couple moved to Saskatchewan to accommodate Dr. Ringwood's career. However, her productivity and consequent honors continued unabated. In 1941 Ringwood's entry in the three act section of the fifth annual playwriting competition held by the Ottawa Little Theatre, *Dark Harvest*, was chosen winner.[52] In addition, *The Courtship of Marie Jenvrin* was selected to be included in *The Best One Act Plays of 1942*, published by Dodd, Mead and Company of New York.[53] The year's honors were capped by the reception of the Governor General's medal for outstanding service in the development of Canadian drama.[54] Throughout the remaining years of the 1940s, Ringwood divided her time between her responsibilities as a mother and those of her writing and teaching. While bearing and raising four children, she continued to write stage plays and radio plays, as well as to teach at Banff where she instructed students like George Ryga. In the early 1950s, the Ringwoods moved to Williams Lake, British Columbia, where they continued to live for many years. There, Ringwood revived the Players' Club and initiated "coffeehouses" or evenings of short plays.

In her later years, Ringwood extended her accomplishments by writing lyrics for musicals (*The Wall; Look Behind You Neighbor*), by penning a novel, (*Pascal*), and by adjudicating drama festivals in British Columbia and Alberta. Various additional awards bestowed upon Gwen Pharis Ringwood included: Williams Lake named its new 1971 theatre after her, she was made honorary president of the B.C. Drama Association for Amateur Theatre,[55] and two of her plays were selected to be featured at meetings of the Learned Societies of Canada: *Mirage* (at the 1979 meetings in Saskatoon) and *Garage Sale* (at the 1984 meetings in Guelph). Unfortunately, Ringwood was too ill to attend the Guelph meetings; she died shortly thereafter. Both the University of Victoria and the University of Lethbridge had recently (1981 and 1982, respectively) recognized Ringwood's significant contribution to the performing arts in Canada by awarding her honorary doctorate degrees.

Alberta Dramatic League and Regional Festivals

Although amateur drama festivals had operated in Canada in the early 1900s, it is generally conceded that Alberta was the first province to organize a provincial dramatic league, which, according to Gardner, sponsored in 1930 the first provincial festival in the country.[56] As mentioned in Chapter Three, the idea of a provincial festival was actually the brainchild of Ernest G. Sterndale Bennett of Lethbridge. In his personal notes, he reminisces:

> In the spring of 1929, I was in my garden in Lethbridge, Alberta, when suddenly I became aware of a very obvious fact, "If you want to grow a plant, you must start with a seed!" This had a surprising turn of events for it gave me an idea which I immediately put to use. For many years I had attended and taken part in very large and very well organized musical festivals in Alberta and had always wished that the same could be done for drama.

Sterndale Bennett then proceeded to manifest his dream. He wrote to Norman Davis (Medicine Hat), E.J. Thorlakson (Calgary), and Elizabeth S. Haynes (Edmonton) suggesting that they meet together in Calgary in order to discuss the possibility of organizing a provincial drama festival. Sterndale Bennett continues:

> The meeting was arranged and I remember travelling to Calgary, full of excitement, full of trepidation and full of determination coupled by a queer mixture of anxiety and hope – but to my tremendous satisfaction, I found that the Calgary Little Theatre had arranged for the meeting to be held in the Oval Room of the Palliser Hotel. This was a stroke of genius for it immediately gave to the meeting a feeling of importance which I believe, in turn, gave us a new feeling of gravity and responsibility.

The four representatives and an associate of Thorlakson's, Gwillym Edwards, met at the Palliser Hotel on August 4, 1929, and agreed to organize themselves formally as the Alberta Dramatic League (ADL). Sterndale Bennett was named President; Davis and Edwards were selected as Vice President and Secretary-Treasurer, respectively; Haynes and Thorlakson were referred to as advisory members. The addition of Mr. Edwards proved to be very worthwhile as he very effectively fulfilled the role as Secretary-Treasurer until the festival activity was suspended during the war. At this inaugural meeting, it was also agreed that each of the four groups represented would prepare a one act play to be performed at the first Alberta Dramatic Festival to be held in Calgary on February 15, 1930. The festival was so successful that it became an annual affair. For the initial festival, the dramatic societies from Edmonton, Medicine Hat, and Lethbridge were responsible for covering their own travel expenses; since the Calgary club incurred no such expenses, it took on the responsibility for "on the spot expenses and advertising." Publicity was handled by Nola B. Erickson (Chautauqua operator) with the assistance of Elfie Brown. The delegates pooled their resources in order to book the Grand Theatre. The festival was not to be competitive; rather Leonard W. Brockington, K.C., of Calgary was approached to act as an official critic rather than an adjudicator. His criticisms were to be printed in the two Calgary newspapers. This policy was adhered to through the 1932 festival, although, during the latter festival, Brockington's professional responsibilities kept him from arriving at the Edmonton festival in time to view the plays and to comment upon them. The ADL was, in fact, so opposed to the idea of a competitive festival that it refused an offer of a cup for competition made by Mrs. C.B. Freeland of Calgary because, as the League argued, "competition would introduce a spirit of jealousy that might easily mar the future." Sterndale Bennett and L.W. Brockington both voiced adamant opposition to competition as is illustrated in the following statement by Brockington:[57]

> There is some talk of an annual competition and the awarding of prizes. Enough promising musicians have already been ruined in these parts by medals and adulation to find an echo to the wish so admirably voiced by Mr. Sterndale Bennett on the opening night, that friendly cooperation may be allowed to continue without the injection of apples of discord to start another Trojan war.

However, the introduction of the Dominion Drama Festival (DDF) initiated a competitive ranking system.

The possibility of a Dominion Drama Festival (DDF) was investigated at a meeting of interested parties held in Ottawa in 1932 under the auspices of his excellency, Governor General Bessborough, who, upon arriving in Canada in the spring of 1931, perceived a need for more and better theatre in Canada.[58] As mentioned in Chapter 3, Sterndale Bennett was the one representative from Alberta invited to the meeting, at which agreement was reached to establish the Dominion Drama Festival which would operate in the following way: various regions in the country (mostly coterminous with the provinces) would hold preliminary provincial or regional festivals; each of these festivals was to be adjudicated by a highly experienced and respected professional dramaturge; and on the basis of these adjudications, a number of representative winning productions would compete in the final competition of the Dominion Drama Festival. Plays to be presented were selected from a list distributed by the Dominion Drama League; interested dramatic societies were to indicate their first and second choices, and then, the League would inform the society which play it should produce. Adjudicators were to evaluate a number of components of acting, production, and stage management; then, the production was awarded an aggregate score. With the introduction of the DDF in 1933, the Alberta Dramatic Festival became the Alberta Regional Drama Festival. The first Alberta Regional Festival was held at the Majestic Theatre in Lethbridge on March 10 and 11, 1933, and was hosted by the Lethbridge Playgoers. Admission prices were $.50 and $0.75 for the evening presentations and $0.35 for matinees; children were charged $0.15.

The executive structure and membership of the provincial drama association remained fairly consistent throughout the decade of the 1930s. Sterndale Bennett continued as President of the ADL through 1931 and assumed the office of vice-president for most of the year preceding his move to Toronto. Elizabeth Sterling Haynes retained her position as advisor to the executive of the ADL for a number of years, even though her work with the University of Alberta and the Banff School, as well as her responsibilities as artistic director of the "newly formed Edmonton Little Theatre (1929-1932),"[59] kept her very busy. Her supervisor at the Extension Department, E.A. Corbett, also became a major participant in the early 1930s. He took over the presidency from Sterndale Bennett in 1932 and retained the position through 1934. His successor as Director of the Extension Department, Donald Cameron, acted as Vice-President during 1937 and 1938. Like Gwillym Edwards, H. Norman Davis (Medicine Hat) was a fairly permanent member of the executive. Although Davis temporarily left the executive following the initial festival, he returned as Vice-President in 1933 – a position which he retained in 1934. The following four years he held the position of president. Others who sat on the provincial executive during the 1930s included: D.W. Clapperton (Calgary Little Theatre), Dr. W.G. Hardy (U of A), Alex Mitchell, Robert Muir (Edmonton), A. Paice (Calgary), S.J. Shepherd, K.C., (Lethbridge), F.R. Duncanson (Lethbridge),

A.J. Round (Lethbridge), A.B. Hogg, K.C., (Lethbridge), G. Dover (Calgary), Sidney G. Martin (Edmonton), Mrs. Stanley D. Skene (Calgary) and Mrs. E.J. Thorlakson (Calgary). Table 4-1 illustrates the role played by these executive members.

TABLE 4-1

Alberta Dramatic League Executive (1929-1939)

POSITION	1929	1930	1931	1932	1933	1934	1935	1936	1937	1938	1939
President	S.B.	S.B.	S.B.	Corbett	Corbett	Corbett	Davis	Davis	Davis	Davis	Martin
Vice President	Davis	Thorlakson	Hardy	S.B./ Shepherd	Davis	Davis	Hogg	Dover	Cameron	Cameron	Skene
Secretary	Edwards	Edwards	Edwards	Edwards	Edwards	Edwards	Edwards	Edwards	Edwards	Edwards	Edwards
Treasurer	Edwards	Clapperton	Mitchell/ Muir	Paice/Round/ Duncanson	Edwards	Edwards	Edwards	Edwards	Edwards	Edwards	Edwards
Advisory Member(s)	Haynes Thorlakson	Haynes Thorlakson	Haynes Thorlakson	Haynes	Haynes	Haynes	Haynes				
Assistants							Mrs. E.J. Thorlakson	Mrs. E.J. Thorlakson	Mrs. S. Skene	Mrs. S. Skene	
Festival Stage Mgr.								Rob't Hume	Rob't Hume	Rob't Hume	Rob't Hume
Sources: L.H. Feb 19/30/11; Feb 23/31/7; Feb 22/32/6; Mar 13/33/7; Feb 27/34/7; Feb 11/35/9; Feb 10/36/9; Mar 22/37/9; Feb 21/38/8; Feb 27/39/8 Alberta Dramatic League Festival programs											

At the 1935 meeting of the ADL executive, a resolution was passed providing for an honorarium of $200 per year to Mr. Edwards who, in addition to his duties as secretary-treasurer, was selected as the League's representative to the DDF succeeding E.A. Corbett. The meeting also extended authority to the executive to appoint a stage manager for future festivals. Robert Marshall Hume, a former member of the Lethbridge Playgoers, then residing in Calgary, was named to this position for the years 1936-1939. Some years later, his son, Robert M. Hume, a professional sculptor designer, was named Acting Director of the National Design Centre in Ottawa and Supervisor of Installations for the National Gallery of Canada.[60]

Beginning in the mid-1930s, the executive also named some honorary members who, incidently, lent greater dignity to the organization and to the festival movement. Dr. R.C. Wallace and Dr. W.A.R. Kerr, Presidents, University of Alberta, were recognized as Honorary Presidents. Both of these nominations recognized the tremendous assistance given to the development of drama in the province by the University of Alberta. Canadian Senator, W.A. Buchanan, publisher, *Lethbridge Herald*, was named an Honorary Vice-President from 1935 through 1939. Both Mr. & Mrs. Buchanan were staunch supporters of the arts; in recognition of this fact, Senator Buchanan was installed as Honorary President of Playgoers in the 1930s; whereas, Mrs. Buchanan became Honorary President of the Lethbridge Women's Musical Club. Other Honorary Vice Presidents of the Alberta Dramatic League included E.A. Corbett, H. Milton Martin (Edmonton), and W.H. Greenham (Banff).

As the 1930s progressed, many theatre groups began to develop throughout the province and to enter the annual competition. The stimulation for this growth of community theatre came primarily from Elizabeth Sterling Haynes through her work with the Department of Extension, University of Alberta (1932-1937). By 1937 the number of competing groups was so overwhelming (fifteen) that the executive decided to introduce preliminary sub-regional festivals the following year in order to reduce the number of competitors in the Alberta Regional Festival. Societies chosen to represent Alberta at the DDF from 1933 - 1939 include:

YEAR	SOCIETY	YEAR	SOCIETY
1933	Medicine Hat Little Theatre (1st) Edmonton Little Theatre (2nd)	1937	Medicine Hat Little Theatre Assoc.
1934	U ofA Dramatic Club	1938	U of A Drama Society
1935	Joachim Drama Club (Edm.)	1939	Clive Dramatic Club
1936	Edmonton Little Theatre		

It was in 1937 that individual awards for most outstanding actor and actress were introduced at the Alberta Regional Festival. The festival was suspended until after World War II following the 1939 competition; however, the prewar recipients of these awards were:

YEAR	ACTRESS	ACTOR
1937	Muriel Langfield (Calgary Theatre Guild)	Robert H. Haskins (Clive)
1938	Sheila Morrison (U of A)	Wesley Oke (Red Deer)
1939	Ethel Finley (Medicine Hat)	R.H. Haskins (Clive)

Robert Haskins and the Clive Dramatic Club gained considerable attention because of the unlikely nature of dramatic activity among farmers from a relatively isolated rural community. At that time, Clive (located northeast of Red Deer) was a relatively small hamlet of 240 people. The fifty-six year old director, V.G. Duffy, was a district farmer as was Robert Haskins, who was obviously possessed of a fine natural talent. In the 1937 festival, adjudicator George de Warfaz commented that Haskins, "was not only a clever comedian . . . but could undoubtedly handle any role, including tragedy."[61] Not only did Haskins receive the award for best actor on both of the occasions when he participated in the Alberta Regional Festival, but he was also awarded the best actor award at the DDF finals in 1939.[62]

Apparently, the Clive Dramatic Club maintained its high standards for a number of years. In April 1942, Barclay Leathem, the Executive Director of the American National Theatre Conference and Head of the theatre and drama division of Western Reserve University in Cleveland, Ohio, visited Clive as an official observer sponsored by the Rockefeller Foundation. After viewing the following three one act plays: *Walk Into Our Parlor* by Josephine Boyarchuck of Edmonton, *Final Edition* by John McNaughton (Halifax), and *The Bear* by Anton Chekhov, Leathem remarked that the evening's entertainment was more "fresh, alive and vigorous" than many New York professional shows.[63] Robert Haskins appeared in two of these plays.

The Playgoers Club of Lethbridge participated in most of the Regional festivals. The club's first competitive festival entry, *Becky Sharpe* (1933), was directed by Maybelle Bryans, a relative novice at directing. She also directed the festival productions in 1934 (*The Road of Poplars*), 1936 (*Recoil*), and 1937 (*Four Into Seven Won't Go*). Adjudications relating to these plays varied considerably. In reference to *Becky Sharpe*, Mr. Brockington commented, "The presentation was well staged but the real atmosphere of 'Vanity Fair' was missing."[64] Rupert Harvey praised the production of *The Road of Poplars* when he stated, "I have seen many performances of this play, both here and in England and this was the best production of it I have yet seen."[65] Allan Wade felt that *The Recoil* "was not realistically convincing . . . The main fault was lack of proper atmosphere."[66] Of the 1937 entry, adjudicator George de Warfaz claimed, "Well done and well directed.[67] The 1935 and 1938 festival presentations (*Good Theatre* and *She Was No Lady*) were directed by Florence Mackenzie and Eric Johnson, respectively. Both of these members also had little training or experience in this role. This lack of directorial experience undoubtedly affected Playgoers' competitive abilities throughout the 1930s. At no time during this decade was their entry selected for presentation at the final competition of the DDF, nor were their productions singled out for second or third rankings. Undoubtedly, the club suffered tremendously from the loss of the Sterndale Bennetts and a number of other core members. Fortunately, Lethbridge Playgoers could bask somewhat in the success achieved by the Sterndale Bennetts and the Toronto Masquers. An early example of this adulation is illustrated by the *Lethbridge Herald* report of the 1934 DDF written by the local correspondent, Donald Buchanan:[68]

> Mr. and Mrs. Sterndale Bennett's production of "The Devil Among the Skins," by the way was the most delightful comic offering of the week.

Then, in 1935 the Lethbridge Playgoers pointed with pride to the fact that their mentor, Ernest Gaskell Sterndale Bennett, was among the initial recipients of the Canadian Drama Award (CDA), which was instituted in 1934 by the British Columbia Drama Festival Association, Inc. under the chairmanship of Mr. Justice A.E. McPhillips of the B.C. Court of Appeals. The CDA quickly became the most prestigious honor bestowed upon Canadian theatre practitioners for their contribution to the advancement of the art.

Others receiving the C.D.A. in 1935 included: The Earl of Bessborough, Honorable Vincent Massey, C.S. Blanchard (Medicine Hat), Gwillym Edwards (Calgary), Mrs. C.P. Walker (Winnipeg), and Harold Nelson Shaw [(Hollywood), the actor, Harold Nelson, referred to in Chapter Two]. The following year, members of Playgoers were greatly saddened by the news of Belle Sterndale Bennett's death on May 22, 1936. In her honor, the club commissioned an Elizabeth Sterndale Bennett Trophy to be awarded to the best individual performance by a student in the provincial high school drama festival.[69] Even though Belle was deeply mourned by the club, members were pleased to hear that Ernest was determined to continue his association with the Toronto Masquers, and when the Masquers won the Bessborough Trophy (for best play) in the 1937 DDF for their production of John Coulter's *The House in the Quiet Glen*, Lethbridge Playgoers were understandably ecstatic. When the Toronto Masquers walked away with the 1938 trophy for the best production of a play in English, *The Guardsman* by Ferenc Molnar, Playgoers' pride swelled even further.

The year 1937 brought further joy to local drama circles when another former Playgoer, Roy Keivill, was praised by the DDF adjudicator for his fine portrayal of the soldier in *The Last War* by Neil Grant, which was presented by the Vancouver Little Theatre.[70] Lethbridge Playgoers were also happy to share the joy when accolades were bestowed upon their "sister" group, the Medicine Hat Little Theatre. The Medicine Hat Little Theatre topped the Regional competition in 1933 and 1937; the group came second in 1934 as well as in 1935 and third in 1939. As illustrated on numerous

> *E.G. Sterndale Bennett Esq.*   *August 23rd*
> *1935.*
> *Toronto*
>
> *Dear Sir:*
>
> *I have the honour to inform you that the Canadian Drama Award has been conferred upon you in recognition of your splendid work and leadership in the cause of Canadian Drama.*
>
> *The parchment Diploma will follow in due course. The award confers the right to place the letters C.D.A. after the name in matters referring to Drama.*
>
> *May I mention that the Committee in making this award has in mind also the fine support you have had from Mrs. Sterndale Bennett in the many pioneer movements you have launched along these lines.*
>
> *Believe me.*
>
> *Yours very truly,*
> *L. Bullock Webster*
> *Honorary Organizing Secretary*

occasions in this publication, Lethbridge audiences had thoroughly enjoyed the various Medicine Hat productions that had toured to Lethbridge, starting as early as the late 1890s. But in the 1920s a particularly close bond developed between the Playgoers and the Medicine Hat Little Theatre probably because of the fact that the Sterndale Bennetts had participated in theatrical activities in Medicine Hat and had developed a respect for the extraordinary talent of such people as Mr. and Mrs. George W. Simpson, C.S. (Stewart) Blanchard, and Norman Davis. This respect was complemented by true friendship. In fact, the Sterndale Bennetts and the Davises became life long friends. Undoubtedly, Lethbridge Playgoers also cheered the Medicine Hat recipients of the CDA: C.S. Blanchard (1935), N. Davis (1936) and Mrs. W.D. (Joan) Hays (1937).

On the individual level, some members of the Playgoers Club received considerable recognition in festival productions. Ernest Gaskell Sterndale Bennett was always singled out for special commendation in the productions in which he performed before L.W. Brockington. Another Lethbridge participant who received especially high praise from Brockington was Ian Hendry, who played a young lad in Playgoers' 1931 festival production, *Back of the Yards*. Of Mr. Hendry, Brockington stated, "I consider him the find of the festival and the most promising amateur juvenile I have yet seen in Alberta."[71] Another young Lethbridge man, Eric Johnson, was praised by adjudicator, Rupert Harvey, for his performance as Mr. Arlington in the U of A's 1934 production of *Derelict* by E.J. Thorlakson (Calgary). In his turn, Harvey referred to Johnson as the "find" of this festival and commended Johnson for his "excellent study of a man with over-wrought nerves," and his "notable handling of long lines."[72] Although Johnson was not, at that time, a member of Playgoers, he later became a staunch member after graduating from the University of Alberta, returning to his hometown, and taking on teaching duties at the L.C.I. where he also assisted W.A. Rea in supervising the high school dramatic offerings. In 1940 Johnson left Lethbridge in order to engage in advanced speech arts courses at Columbia University in New York.[73] After completing his course work, Johnson accepted a position with the Toronto public school system. Later, after spending considerable time in Europe studying languages, he capped off his teaching career at Saint Michael's Boys School (Toronto).[74]

Playgoers of Lethbridge: The Bryans-Matthews Era

The year 1933 was a year of "ups and downs" for the Playgoers Club. Not only had it lost its two invaluable artistic directors, Ernest and Belle Sterndale Bennett, but the following active participants had recently moved from Lethbridge or retired from the club: Eric Ings, George Holman, Robert Hume, Roy Keivill, Alan McAlpin, and H.C. Moore. Then, in January 1933 the club received word that another stalwart member, Fred Teague, chief accountant with the CPR in Lethbridge, was being transferred to Calgary. Later that year, McAlpin, Teague, and the Sterndale Bennetts were honored to receive Honorary Life Memberships in Playgoers. Although McAlpin continued to live in Lethbridge and to work for the city as paymaster until his death in 1944, he suffered from ill health for many years.[75]

Fortunately, the club did not have much time to dwell upon these losses because it quickly had to rally its resources in order to host the first competitive Alberta Regional Drama Festival. As a prelude to the festival, Playgoers also organized a formal dinner at the Marquis Hotel. Speakers for the evening were Ned Corbett and L.W. Brockington.[76] Incidently, social and educational gatherings at the Marquis Hotel were popular activities for the club. These evenings were complemented with theatrical activities such as make-up demonstrations or variety entertainment (skits, juvenile orchestral programs under the direction of Mrs. George Brown, plays, and informative talks). On March 28, 1935, J. Rosewarn presented the one act play, *Banquo's Chair;* on October 25, 1935, G.W.G. O'Meara spoke on the playwriting of Felix Lope de Vega and then presented his play, *Pastry Baker.*[77] On September 9, 1936, Professor Joseph Smith, head of the Drama department at the University of Utah and a popular teacher at the Banff School of Fine Arts, delivered a talk entitled "From Tobacco Road to Winterset."[78]

In one sense, the 1933 festival was a respite for the club because it provided an alternative to the evenings of Little Theatre one act plays which the club traditionally presented at that time of year. The club had difficulty mounting a full season of productions in 1933; the only other Playgoers' presentation that year was the three act farce *A Little Bit of Fluff* directed by James Rosewarn, which played in November. Undoubtedly, that year was a period of transition – a year in which the club had to adjust to the severe wrenching of its internal structure as well as to the dire external economic circumstances. This need for adjustment is reflected in concerns which were voiced at the rather reflective annual meeting held in June 1933 – concerns about membership, finances, and artistic leadership. As the ensuing discussion will show, these concerns continued to haunt Playgoers throughout the 1930s.[79]

The 1933-34 membership fee, which was set at one dollar, was to include admission to four or five Little Theatre evenings, but unfortunately, the club offered no such programs that season. In fact, Playgoers managed to live up to the minimum commitment of four evenings of Little Theatre during the 1934-35 and 1938-39 seasons, only. In 1933 the club boasted that its membership of 600-700 was the largest of any similar organization in Alberta.[80] It is apparent, however, that the members gradually became discouraged with the club's inability to meet its production commitments, and therefore, the membership began to decline. By September 1936 membership stood at 400. Although the next few years witnessed aggressive membership drives, headed by respected community leaders such as Roy Davidson, K.C., Max Hoffman, and Doug Sutherland, the membership remained stable at about 400.[81] The club reported that public and individual support was not encouraging during the 1938-39 season.[82]

But, membership was not necessarily the main concern aired at the 1933 meeting; rather, active participation of members was considered more urgent. As a result of these discussions, the club began a serious campaign to solicit members who could make an administrative or artistic contribution to the club's activities. These efforts, which were complemented by the establishment of a play reading group under the direction of Mrs. J.N. (Louie) Ritchie, classes in pantomime under Maybelle Bryans, and workshops in scenic design and set construction by Lyn Jordan soon began to "pay off" as a number of new fully participating members gradually joined the ranks of the few remaining old guard. By the mid-1930s, the club could again rely seriously on quite active involvement by a core of about thirty-five members, not unlike the situation in the 1920s. The executive was strengthened by the addition of A.B. Hogg, a local lawyer, and Mrs. C.A. (Hazel) Long, wife of a local furniture dealer. With regard to backstage activities, it was fortunate that, by this time, the technical skills and leadership ability of Tom Ferguson (future city manager) were apparent. In 1935, when Lyn Jordan left Lethbridge, Ferguson assumed the position of Technical Director and retained that position until the temporary demise of the club during World War II. His most consistent backstage assistants included Hector Frey, Cliff Humphries, Don Carpenter, Tom Middleton, Louie Ritchie, Elaine Fisher, and Hilda Church. Most of the back stage construction work took place in the "dug-out" – a small area in the basement of the Majestic Theatre.[83]

Over two hundred and fifty individuals were involved onstage during the decade, 1933-1942. However, most of these participants took part in one production, only. Those participants who performed most regularly in Playgoers' productions during this time are listed in Table 4-2.

The club was aware of the fact that it could not sustain the active involvement of most of the members; perennial discussions centered around means of involving more members since one of the main objectives of the club remained the development of new talent. The club took considerable pride on occasions such as the Little Theatre night of November 15, 1937, when it announced that "eighteen out of the twenty-two aspiring actors on the stage" had not appeared in previous Playgoers' productions and three of the four directors were novices.[84] Still, the general mood throughout this decade seemed to reflect despair arising from a fear of a lack of interest in the club's activities on the part of the public and prospective members. This lack of interest was seen as manifesting itself both in "difficulties in casting plays and in the smallness of houses for productions."[85] Even major productions such as the 1938 three act comedy, *Squaring the Circle*, played to a "small house."[86] Overall concern about the club's future seems, best, to be shown in the following comment contained within the news article announcing the 1937 meeting:[87]

> Members of the executive say this meeting will be one of special importance. The club has reached a stage that is critical, not financially, but socially, and there is some misgiving about the club's continuing its activities on the present scale in the light of other attractions in the form of entertainment which threaten its continued success.

With regard to the financial situation of the club, the treasurer's report presented in June 1933 showed a deficit of thirteen dollars. Although the economic fortunes of the club fluctuated somewhat, the overall financial picture during the 1930s was rather bleak. During most of these years, the club barely managed to break even. The exceptional year was 1936-37 when the club ended the year with a balance of one hundred sixty-two dollars and sixty-five cents ($162.65).[88] However, that surplus quickly disappeared, and in 1939 the club decided it could not compete in the Regional Festival (in Edmonton) because of a lack of funds.[89] It is true, however, that the club

TABLE 4-2

Onstage Participants
Playgoers of Lethbridge (1933-1942)

Most Active Participants (5 or more roles)	Lena Connor Margaret Davidson Ted Faunch Tom Feguson George Frayne Harvey Greenway	Fred Holmes Allan Lewis C.R. Matthews Helen Maynard Olive Pauling Blanche Roy	Mary Sydal J.T. Vallance Syd Vallance Jim Worthington
Moderately Active Participants (3-4 roles)	Harry Baalim Reg Bailey Eildon Brander Ethel Brander Hilda Church Mary Clarke Jean Galbraith Camille (Connor) Hay Josephine Hughes	Kay Jenks F. Nowell Johnson Lyn Jordan Carl Lambert Ted Lawrence Eveline Meech Alathea Mellor Langdale W.P. Pineau Horace Poole	A.C. Raworth Robin Ritchie James Rosewarn Jean Scott Frank Steele Herbert Stretton Minnie Thrall

operated on a budget in excess of five hundred dollars that year, and within that budget was able to organize three local evenings of Little Theatre in the spring, and to travel to Macleod on March 29 where it joined together with little theatre groups from Macleod and Granum to present an evening of one act plays.[90] In May 1939 the club reported a surplus of $28.97.[91]

The tight money situation during the 1930s affected the club's operations in other ways: publicity associated with coming productions was curtailed considerably; more expensive shows such as musicals became scarce. In fact, Playgoers mounted only two musical shows in the period under discussion, a locally written revue, *Musical Pie,* in 1934 and *The Gingham Girl* in 1935. It was not until the 1970s that the club again produced the occasional musical. Unfortunately, the suspension of musicals probably contributed to the lagging interest in the club's activities since musicals had always attracted the majority of the participants and the audiences. In addition, musicals provided numerous outlets for people to express their various artistic talents. Musical talent was always abundant in Lethbridge, but the demise of silent movies resulted in an even further decline of opportunities for instrumental ensemble work. The occasional Rotary, YMCA, and LDS variety shows, plus the two Playgoers' musicals did, however, encourage some orchestral work under the baton of directors such as George Brown, George Etherington, K.A. Maclure, Francis "Morse" Stevenson, George Laycock, and Aileen Jones.

Musicals and variety shows provided for the development of artistic talents such as choreography. When the club's original choreographer, Hilda Church, became more involved in directing and acting, her choreographic responsibilities were assumed by Bernadette Fisher, who had established her dance academy in Lethbridge in 1930. Bernadette, the daughter of Fred and Elaine Fisher, was born in Lethbridge in 1914, and she was introduced to dance instruction at the age of three by the youthful Hilda Church. Shortly thereafter, her father, who was employed with the Bank of Montreal, was transferred from Lethbridge. After several rapid moves, the family settled in Toronto; Bernadette was enrolled in Havergal College, and she continued her dance instruction under teachers such as May March, Adele Sternberg, Dimitri Vladimiroff, Boris Volkoff, Leon Leonidoff, and Florence Rogge. Unfortunately, the stock market crash of 1929 had a devastating effect on the family's finances; the family was required to separate temporarily. Bernadette and her mother moved back to Lethbridge where they shared the Conybeare family home, "Riverview," with Mrs. Conybeare and the Branders. (Dr. Conybeare had died in July 1928.) Bernadette's father, Fred, and her brother, Crawford, joined other members of the Fisher family in Baltimore, Maryland.

Although the youthful Bernadette did not yet feel truly competent to instruct in dance, the family realized that her teaching was their only hope of income. So the Bernadette Fisher School of Dance was established. At first, instruction was given in the drawing room of "Riverview," but as the number of students increased dramatically, the school was moved to the Knights of Pythias Building on 5th Street South and to the Lethbridge Conservatory of Music building. Her mother provided the musical accompaniment. Within a very few years, the school had an enrolment of about 500 students including students from neighboring towns and farms where Fisher would commute to teach. Fees for instruction were $0.75 for a one hour group lesson and $1.25 for a private session. Gradually, her younger cousin, Eildon ("Penny") Brander, was called upon to assist in the instruction. Mrs. Ethel Brander provided additional accompaniment. During these years, Fisher furthered her own technique by enrolling in summer classes with Adolph Bolm (ballet) and Reid McLean (tap) in San Francisco. In 1937 Fisher turned the school over to Eildon Brander and, subsequently, moved back to Toronto where the Fisher family was reunited. Shortly thereafter, Bernadette married her former Lethbridge suitor, Donald Carpenter. Carpenter had been a very helpful backstage worker for various amateur productions in Lethbridge, including numerous shows which Bernadette had directed or choreographed. Although Carpenter had recently moved to Vancouver, he soon followed Bernadette to Toronto. For a number of years, thereafter, Bernadette Carpenter combined marriage and motherhood with personal dance instruction. She, again, took dance classes with Boris Volkoff and also performed in many of the productions with which Volkoff was associated at Varsity Arena, the Royal Alexandra Theatre, Massey Hall, Eaton Auditorium, and Hart House Theatre.

Following the war, Bernadette's frustration in not being able to purchase appropriate ballet shoes in Canada led to her becoming the country's first distributor of lightweight European pointe shoes (Freed's of England). Before long, she opened the Bernadette Carpenter Shop, "the Shop for Dancers," and business began to boom. In 1954 she began to manufacture leotards and tights under her own label. Carpenter states that by 1966 when she sold her business to Malabar's, her shop supplied over 40 companies and about 75 percent of the dance schools across Canada.

In addition to her business enterprises, Carpenter made other substantial contributions to the development of dance in Canada. Her efforts helped to create the Canadian Dance Teachers' Association (CDTA), whose basic aim was to promote dance training in Canada. She became a founding member of the Standards Committee of the CDTA. Carpenter was also very supportive of the establishment of the National Ballet, and she strenuously maintained that Celia Franca could make it a success. In addition, Carpenter published, from 1955-1960, a dual advertising and dance news bulletin, *The Spotlight,* which kept teachers, dancers, and students informed of dance activities across the nation. In the late 1950s, this activity reached its peak when 1 500 monthly copies were being mailed throughout Canada for each of ten months of the year. Eventually, the economic burden associated with the publication, which the Carpenter Shop bore entirely, became too great, so the publication was suspended in 1960.[92] Although Carpenter basically retired in 1966, she continued to be considered a very respected member of Canada's dance community.

Returning to our discussion of Playgoers' activities, the club's mandate to encourage new directors seemed to be succeeding quite well. Even in 1931 and 1932, while Ernest and Belle Sterndale Bennett were still officially fulfilling the roles of General Director and Director of the Little Theatre, respectively, directorial duties were shared by a number of members. In order to maintain this greater division of labor, Playgoers decided not to elect general directors in 1933 and for a number of years, thereafter. Rather, numerous individuals were encouraged to "try their hand" at directing. Six individuals were responsible for taking on the directorial tasks involved in the eleven major productions offered by Playgoers between 1931 and 1939, inclusive; over 25 members took on directorial duties for the Little Theatre. James Rosewarn and Lyn Jordan, who had previous directing experience before becoming involved with Playgoers, each directed two major productions in the early 1930s. After 1934 the major productions were directed by Hilda Church, C.R. Matthews, Maybelle Bryans, and W.P. Pineau, manager of the Standard Bank in North Lethbridge. The outbreak of World War II ended Pineau's short relationship with the club.

Church, Matthews, and Bryans were long time members of Playgoers who had many opportunities to act under the careful direction of Ernest and Belle Sterndale Bennett. Since Church was also an accomplished dancer and choreographer, she had a special interest in musical productions. She took on the task of directing *The Gingham Girl* in the fall of 1935 with the assistance of Aileen Jones as musical director and George Brown as orchestra leader. The local reviewer remarked that the dancing numbers were the highlight of the show. The fact that Bernadette Fisher was one of the featured dancers and that she performed a "German burlesque dance" did a great deal to give the dancing that special appeal.[93] The *Herald* reviewer also commented that the musical numbers "were catchy," but that there was not enough "body to the show." Yet, *The Gingham Girl* had just played for over a year at the Earl Carroll Theatre in New York and was generally acknowledged to be a big hit in New York.[94] During the next two years, Church participated in a number of Little Theatre productions, both as director and actor. She took the leading female role in Playgoers' 1937 festival entry, *Four Into Seven Won't Go*. Shortly thereafter, Hilda Church left the city to take up employment in Toronto.

Charles ("Charlie") R. Matthews, a man of many talents, was born the same month and year as E.G. Sterndale Bennett (May 1884) in South Hackney, London. He was educated at Tillington Park College and King's College, London. After moving to Lethbridge in November 1907, he worked for various lumber companies including the Rogers Cunningham Lumber Company before joining the *Lethbridge Herald* staff in 1917 as an accountant. In subsequent years with the *Herald*, he was named a Director (1927), Secretary (1937), and Secretary Treasurer (1947) – a position which he maintained until he retired in 1957.[95]

Within the Playgoers' organization, Matthews could be counted upon to do whatever had to be done and to do it well. He contributed immeasurably to the backstage work of the club where he engaged in activities as diverse as set construction and make-up. But Matthews was also a competent actor; he was, therefore, cast in numerous productions during the 1930s including four of the nine festival plays produced by Playgoers from 1930-1938. Directing chores began for Matthews in 1928 when he assisted the Sterndale Bennetts in their direction of *The Toreador*. In the mid-1930s, he assumed the direction of two major productions, *The Thirteenth Chair* (1934) and *Ruth Ripley or The Orphan's Sacrifice* (1936). Both of these productions were apparently well received, and Matthews's directing was commended by the local critic.[96] In *The Thirteenth Chair*, Matthews also portrayed one of the leading roles, Inspector Donahue, which incidently, was always his favorite role.[97] In reference to this performance, the *Lethbridge Herald* critic commented, "He was thoroughly at home in the part and did much to sustain the action of the show." The year 1932 revealed another aspect of Matthews's artistic talents when one of his plays, *The Perfect Crime*, was selected as the best one act play in the provincial playwriting competition.[98] That same year, he also authored the one act play, *Dad, Meet My Girl*. In addition, Matthews lent organizational strength to the Playgoers Club. He became a very active member of the Playgoers' executives following his initial election to the position of Secretary in 1925.[99] In the subsequent fifteen years, he fulfilled a number of positions including president for three separate terms (1929-30; 1933-34; 1937-38). Symbolic of the high esteem in which Charlie Matthews was seen in dramatic circles in 1938, was his appointment as an Honorary Governor of the DDF for the forthcoming season.[100] Matthews was not an active participant in Playgoers' functions during the war years, but he took over the presidency when the club was revived in 1951.

Charles R. Matthews
Photo: Playgoers of Lethbridge Archives and Gainsborough Galleries, Lethbridge

As the 1930s progressed, Maybelle Bryans unquestionably emerged as the most willing and capable director in the Playgoers' organization. In addition to the apprenticeship which Bryans completed under the Sterndale Bennetts in Lethbridge, she enrolled in the 1933 Hart House Theatre's Summer Drama course (in Toronto) taught by Ernest and Belle Sterndale Bennett, Edgar Stone, and other experienced instructors. Playgoers' Little Theatre was definitely Bryans's first love, so she became the most active and consistent director of one act plays for evenings of Little Theatre. Of course, the Little Theatre encouraged all members to try their hand at directing. In response, a number of members took up the challenge, but for many of these people, once was enough. Of the sixty or so one act plays presented by Playgoers between 1930 and 1942, the following individuals directed more than one such play: Maybelle Bryans (9), Louie Ritchie (4), Florence Mackenzie (4), Hilda Church (4), Betty (Natalie) Bletcher (3), Harvey Greenway (3), Norman D. Smith (3), Echo Becker (2), Elizabeth Crowe (2), Agnes Davidson (2), Eric Johnson (2), Robin Ritchie (2), and James Rosewarn (2). Unfortunately, some prospective talented directors such as Robin Ritchie and Eric Johnson left Lethbridge, permanently, just as their dramatic talents were beginning to blossom. Ritchie, the son of Mr. and Mrs. Norman Ritchie, returned to Lethbridge for a short while after graduating in psychology from the University of Alberta. He became involved with Playgoers by acting in three Little Theatre productions as well as by directing. Ritchie then spent some time working in Winnipeg and then in Toronto, where he married Muriel Sterndale Bennett.[101]

Of the five major productions presented by Playgoers from 1936 to 1938, Bryans was responsible for directing three of them; in addition, she was called upon as assistant director for a fourth. Bryans also began to display other theatrical talents, for example, she showed a considerable interest in pantomime; consequently, she offered various workshops in the art. On two separate occasions, Bryans directed a religious play, *The Miracle*, presented in pantomime. As the *Lethbridge Herald* reporter commented after the first presentation, "Too much praise cannot be given the setting and atmosphere created in the religious production *The Miracle* directed by Maybelle Bryans."[102] Following the 1937 revival, the local critic's comments were:[103]

> . . . Monday night perhaps reached heights of beauty and dramatic power not attained in the first presentation. It is experimental theatre and the director, Maybelle Bryans, is deserving of commendation for striking out into a new field and emerging so successfully in her venture. The deeply spiritual theme was brought out with a conviction that carried through to a moving climax. It was reverential, poetic, clothed with a simple grandeur that touched the heart.

Another new venture for Bryans was adjudicating, which she did increasingly for school, church, and district drama organizations. As a consequence of all of these experiences, Bryans became one of the city's most accomplished theatre practitioners; this fact was formally recognized by the following honors which were bestowed upon her: in October 1937 she, together with Joan Hays of Medicine Hat, were the Southern Alberta recipients of the CDA;[104] in 1938 the position of General Director was reinstituted by the Playgoers Club, and Bryans was installed into the position which had been filled by only one other person, E.G. Sterndale Bennett. Henceforth, Bryans functioned in that position until Playgoers suspended activity during the later war years.

With the onset of World War II, the club's activities were directed to slightly more select audiences. In the fall of 1939, Playgoers decided to prepare variety programs to be presented for members of the local military garrison in their recreation hut. These programs, which began on December 20, 1939, usually included one or more one act plays together with variety entertainment. On January 28, 1940, vocal duets by Blanche Roy and Ethel Brander were interspersed between two short plays directed by Doris Hester and Maybelle Bryans, the latter of whom continued to be active in Playgoers for many subsequent years even though her husband, Dr. W.E. Bryans, announced his retirement as Medical Superintendent of Galt Hospital early in 1940.[105] Tom Ferguson generally acted as Master of Ceremonies for these programs. As the early years of the war progressed, Playgoers began to join together with other associations interested in providing entertainment, the aims of which were to boost morale, to encourage local war efforts, and to stimulate the purchase of war bonds. In each of the years 1940-1942, Playgoers prepared one act plays and skits to be incorporated into programs arranged by groups such as the YMCA War Services Committee or the IODE. The 1941 program was organized for presentation at the Royal Air Force School in Medicine Hat. After 1942 the club could no longer sustain itself as an organization; therefore, its participation in these wartime programs ceased to exist. Doris Hester directed skits for some of these programs. Members who took the most active parts in these war time productions included: Maybelle Bryans, Ted Faunch, Tom Ferguson, George Frayne, Doris Hester, Sydney Vallance, and Jim Worthington. George Brown, Jr. (accompanied by his mother, Katherine Brown) was a frequent contributor to the musical elements of these programs until military service required him to leave Lethbridge. Brown, a highly accomplished baritone who had been trained by his mother and by Terry Horne (a professional tenor and local voice teacher),[106] was an extraordinarily successful competitor in the local and provincial music festivals. In 1939 Brown began his broadcasting career as an announcer for radio station, CJOC. During his tour of military duty, Brown served his country in various ways including involvement in a daily radio show produced by the

Winnipeg station, CJRC, to attract recruits to the armed forces. He also participated for a short period of time in the Army Show before being stationed in Australia where his vocal abilities continued to be recognized; his singing voice was heard on broadcasts from radio stations in Melbourne, Sydney, and Brisbane. In 1945 Brown formed a male quartette which sang for the Duke of Gloucester, Governor General of Australia. Following their return to Canada, the quartette was featured on the CBC national network. At this time, Brown assumed the position of production manager for the Lethbridge radio station, CJOC. In 1952 he moved to Calgary to become production manager of CFAC. He then held a number of management positions in Calgary radio and T.V. before returning to Lethbridge to administer CJOC radio and CFAC (Lethbridge) T.V. While living in Calgary, Brown became a member of the Excelsior Glee Party; he was also a soloist at Central United Church. He did concert engagements, and in December 1954 he was guest soloist with the Calgary Symphony under the direction of Clayton Hare. He toured to Lethbridge on a number of occasions: in early 1955, he, together with the Coste House Chamber Music Group, appeared at Southminster Church under the auspices of the Lethbridge Women's Musical Club; in 1962, he appeared at the Lethbridge Collegiate Institute with the Mount Royal Opera Workshop.[107] Brown's musical career was so very extensive that it cannot be covered adequately in this discussion, but readers should be aware of the fact that wherever this gentleman resided, the musical life of that community was enriched immeasurably. Brown also devoted an extraordinary amount of time and effort to community service.[108]

Other Community or Local Theatre

Pre-World War II Activities

Numerous church and service organizations provided opportunities for members to participate in local theatrical productions. In reality, most of these groups sponsored what might be referred to as quasi community theatre societies since membership or participation in them required membership in the parent organization, club, or church. Some of these organizations also sponsored shows and concerts which involved a number of invited guest artists or societies.

During the early 1930s, church dramatic groups dominated the quasi community theatre scene. The most active groups came from the United churches, the Anglican churches, St. Patrick's Roman Catholic Church, and the LDS Church. Many of these societies were young people's groups who were primarily interested in drama festivals. St. Augustine's Men's Club also organized various minstrel shows, whereas St. Andrews Presbyterian Church Choir presented the operetta *Miss Polly's Patchwork Quilt* (April 30, 1931). Greater variety was seen in the theatrical presentations of the Mutual Improvement Association of the LDS Church since they offered a number of three and one act plays as well as the operetta *Where There's a Will* (March 1935). In the latter half of the 1930s, the Southminster Players directed by Agnes Davidson, who had achieved considerable success with her dramas and operettas at Central School as well as with her work with Playgoers, began to produce annual religious plays.

Theatrical productions participated in by a broader segment of the community were offered by the Rotary Club and the YMCA. The Rotary Club presented one minstrel show and numerous musical revues during the 1930s. The three local dance schools were major contributors to these productions. The Bernadette Fisher School was the most active participant, but dancers from the Alice Murdock School and the Mrs. Fred Humby School also cooperated. Alice Murdock was a Calgary teacher of dance who began to commute weekly to Lethbridge after Gladys Attree discontinued her local activities. One of Attree's former students, Lola Strand, assisted Miss Murdock at the Lethbridge school. In the fall of 1937, Strand took over the Alice Murdock School in Lethbridge. Miss Strand was a featured dancer in many of the Rotary revues. Although Alice Murdock withdrew from teaching in Lethbridge, she continued to be a very active teacher in Calgary for many more years, and during the war, her revues were important components in at least 236 concerts for the armed forces.[109] Mrs. Fred Humby, whose husband was an RCMP Inspector,[110] operated a dance school in Lethbridge for a few years in the mid-1930s. Her dancers participated particularly in the *Rotary Sunshine Revues* of 1934 and 1936. So popular was this type of fare, that the YMCA decided to combine musical revues with their regular gymnastic displays or circuses.[111] In the summer of 1935, the Lethbridge Exhibition Board also relied on the musical extravaganza (a *Golden Jubilee Pageant*) to help Lethbridge celebrate its 50th anniversary. Eildon Brander and students from the Bernadette Fisher School of Dance were the featured performers.

War Time Activities

Agnes Davidson's Southminster Players continued to produce religious plays through the spring of 1942. But it was the LDS drama societies, stimulated particularly by Maydell Palmer, Marian Brandley, Jessie Ursenbach, and Milton Strong which became the dominant church related theatrical groups in the city. Mrs. Palmer, wife of A.E. Palmer, Superintendent of the Lethbridge Agricultural Research Centre (Experimental Farm), was a keen supporter of the arts who furthered her dramatic skills by enrolling in courses at the Banff School of Fine Arts.[112] Brandley's interest in drama and music was very serious as is evident by the fact that she completed a B.A. degree program in speech (1948) as well as a Master's degree in Musicology and Applied Music (1956).[113] Ursenbach was primarily an artist of considerable distinction, and Strong made a tremendous contribution to the Lethbridge musical scene.

During these years, various military and civilian groups combined their talents to provide entertainment. Shortly after Canada declared war on Germany, the Canadian YMCA organized its war services activities throughout the country. The main purpose of the War Services was to provide a "home away from home" for the military personnel stationed in or near communities served by the YMCA. Lounges and recreational rooms were thrown open for the use of the "boys in uniform." In April 1940 the *Lethbridge Herald* carried a report that the YMCA War Services across Canada had already been used by over one million service men.[114] Besides the usual recreational activities available at the YMCA, many entertainments (concerts, sing-songs, and movies) were provided. The Lethbridge YMCA very quickly established a local War Services Committee which, in cooperation with Lethbridge Playgoers and other local and military dramatists and musicians, set about to provide a variety of entertainment. Ralph Johnson, a well known local musician, and Mrs. C.A. Long, President of Lethbridge Playgoers, were among the entertainment conveners who arranged entertainment at the YMCA and in the various garrisons and air force training schools throughout southern Alberta.[115] Other groups such as the IODE also organized programs to raise funds for the war work of the local chapters. A 1940 example of these patriotic programs is illustrated below:[116]

> At the Boxing Day Concert in the Majestic Theatre on December 26th, the following program will be presented . . . Proceeds of the concert will be donated to the war work of Sir Alexander Galt Chapter, I.O.D.E. All artists taking part in this concert have donated their services, including a five piece orchestra in the pit, under the leadership of George Brown [Sr.].

Program

"O Canada"

Play	"The Pirate King", Central School
Dances	(a) Highland Fling
	(b) Highland Laddie, Miss Janet McGregor
Selection	Marquis Quartet
Vocal Solo	George Brown, Jr.
Dances	(a) Sean Truibhas
	(b) Sword Dance, Miss Janet McGregor
Play	"Happy Journey", Playgoers Club
Dances	(a) Sailors' Hornpipe
	(b) Irish Jig, Miss Janet McGregor
Selection	Marquis Quartet

"GOD SAVE THE KING"

Cast of Operetta Erminie, *produced by the MIA of the LDS Church, 1943*
Photo: City of Lethbridge Archives and Records Management.

Approximately one year later, the following article appeared in the *Lethbridge Herald*:[117]

Members of the Lethbridge YMCA War Services entertainment committee, convened by Mrs. C.A. Long, motored to Medicine Hat Monday where they provided a program for between three and four hundred boys in the Royal Airforce school in that city. A warm reception was accorded the visitors with the contributing artists including George Brown, Jr., soloist; Mrs. George Brown, accompanist; LAC Fey, R.C.A.F. soloist; Evelyn Nelson of the Lethbridge C.A.T.S., singer of cowboy songs; Tom Ferguson and Sydney Vallance in a comedy skit directed by Doris Hester.

In the spring of 1942, talented performers from Air Force Schools at Pearce, Lethbridge, Macleod, and Claresholm joined local performers and members of the Playgoers Club in producing the *Spring Wartime Revue* convened by Ken Howard and sponsored by the YMCA War Services Committee. Many of the RAF participants were professional entertainers: PO. Ronald Morton (saxophonist), Cpl. Charles Homer (popular pianist), and Cpl. Norman Chapman (concert pianist).[118] The opening number featured George Brown, Jr., singing "Deep in the Heart of Texas" while being assisted by a bevy of local "cowgirls." Also included in the program was a one act play, *Goodnight Please*, presented by Playgoers under the direction of Maybelle Bryans. Among the cast was Margaret Brenton, who had established herself as a fine comedienne and character actor. She was particularly well known for her Lancashire dialects (wee Albert) and her impersonations of Gracie Fields.[119] Two years after this *Spring Time Revue*, the *Lethbridge Herald* reported that Private Margaret Brenton Cross had been selected to participate in the new Canadian Army show produced by the #6 Canadian Army Entertainment Unit. The show, referred to as *About Faces of '44,* toured to Lethbridge and performed for personnel at the local POW camp in July 1944.[120] Brenton played the lead role – a gypsy fortune teller who conjured up dance numbers which were then performed by the eleven CWACs in the show. Brenton, a graduate of the Lethbridge Collegiate Institute, had worked locally for a few years before leaving Lethbridge for Halifax with her husband, William Cross, who was serving with the Royal Canadian Corps of Signals. After joining the CWAC, her comedic talent was discovered by an army show talent scout at an amateur contest at basic training camp in Kitchener, Ontario. This 23 year old lass quickly became a favorite entertainer with the show.[121] After the war (in 1947), Lethbridge audiences were excited to hear that she was to be an assisting artist at the local Jr. Band Concert together with youthful Lethbridge performers: Dale Bartlett (piano), Juanita Irving (violin), and Bill Primachuck (accordion).[122] In 1952 Brenton appeared in the Army, Navy and Air Force Veterans' *1952 Varieties* at Massey Hall, Toronto, where she had become a regular floor show entertainer and a performer in promotional films.[123] In June 1952 Margaret (now Mrs. Jack McLean) again assisted the Lethbridge Junior Band (under the direction of Frank Hosek); her comedic singing "brought down the house." On this occasion, she added Betty Hutton to her repertoire of impersonations as she offered a number of selections from *Annie Get Your Gun.*[124]

In the *Spring Wartime Revue* (of 1942), other musical numbers were provided by vocal and instrumental soloists from the RCAF #15 SFTS (Claresholm), #8 Bombing and Gunnery School (Lethbridge), and the RAF Flying Training School at Pearce. Members of the RCAF Women's Division, FTS (Macleod), formed a chorus to present *Songs of the Air Force.* The entire show was supported by an orchestra under the direction of George Brown, Sr. Proceeds from the concert were earmarked to help furnish the YMCA lounge, "now used extensively by his Majesty's forces".[125] This revue was the last major live production staged in the Majestic Theatre because, as mentioned earlier, the theatre was sold to the owners of the Purity Dairy. Subsequently, later revues were held in military facilities or in the LDS auditorium.

The 1944 *Victory Revue* featured Cliff Palmer and his local Kinsmen Orchestra; the Jean Gauld dancers; other local artists such as Elsie Persson (violin), Helen McKenzie (piano), Dixie Botterill (piano); and various military entertainers such as L.A.W. Leona Marshall who, prior to joining the armed forces, appeared as a vocalist on a weekly CBC radio show. A year later, Palmer's Kinsmen Orchestra and Jean Gauld's dancers joined together with various other local and military performers to present the *Springtime Revue of 1945* under the auspices of the YMCA.[126] Cliff Palmer, a local optometrist, was a very competent violinist who, many years later, became the concert master for the Lethbridge Symphony. The dancer, Jean Gauld, had a varied professional career. She first appeared on a Lethbridge stage in March 1928 when she played the Palace Theatre in vaudeville during her tour of the U.S.A. and Canada. At that time, she was billed as, "The Versatile Scot, Canada's champion dancer."[127] She was, in fact, the Canadian champion in Scottish, Irish, and Hornpipe dancing.[128] During the war, she operated the Jean Gauld School of Dance in Lethbridge.

The cast of the *Springtime Revue of 1945* also included a local brother and sister team, DaNaze and Bryce Spencer, whose cousin, Haila Stoddard, a professional actress, starred in the *Voice of the Turtle* at the Biltmore Theatre in Los Angeles and in the Broadway production of *Springtime for Henry* [with Edward Everett Horton (1954)]. Among Stoddard's many other credits were roles in the Broadway productions of *Yes, My Darling Daughter* and *Blithe Spirit,* as well as in the touring production of *Tobacco Road.* Bryce Spencer furthered his interest in drama by taking summer courses in Banff and by enrolling in a drama program at Brigham Young University in Provo, Utah. While at Banff in the summer of 1946, he was elected to the executive board at the Western Canada Theatre Conference presided over by Dorothy Somerset of Vancouver, an associate director of the Everyman Theatre Company.[129]

Military Productions

Regardless of these cooperative revues, it is true that as military establishments became entrenched, they were more and more capable of providing much of their own entertainment. For example, in March 1942 a troupe of military entertainers from the Lethbridge #8 Bombing and Gunnery School staged a concert evening for American military personnel at Cut Bank, Montana, where the Lethbridge group was "royally received."[130] Civilians, too, began to rely upon military personnel to provide them with most of their live entertainment. A different type of entertainment was provided for Lethbridge and district residents by the personnel of #8 Bombing and Gunnery School on October 9, 1943. With the permission of Group Captain Murray D. Lister, Commanding Officer, the officers and men of the school decided to celebrate their second anniversary with a jubilee open house. Activities for the day included a parade (downtown), air show, carnival, and dance; the #7 SFTS Band, Macleod was in attendance. The *Lethbridge Herald* reports that over 11 500 civilian and military guests attended the function and that many of these guests enjoyed dancing to the music of two local dance bands, the Royal Albertans and the Alberta Ranch Boys.[131]

Throughout 1943, numerous Canadian military show units were organized to entertain the troops overseas as well as those stationed throughout Canada. Many of these units staged their productions for the general public as well. For example, *The Army Show,* starring Sergeants Johnny Wayne and Frank Shuster, premiered in Toronto in April 2, 1943, and following a week of performances there, proceeded to tour across the country. By August 1943 the navy show, *Meet the Navy,* was also in rehearsal and planning a trans-Canada tour. Although neither of these shows played Lethbridge, local residents were particularly interested in the *Army Show* because of the involvement in it by Eileen and Geoffrey Waddington. Eileen was the accompanist for the show, whereas Geoffrey was the original musical director who had traversed the country recruiting musicians and artists for the show. Unfortunately, by the time the show reached Calgary, Geoffrey Waddington was no longer associated with it. Lethbridge patrons of the arts had followed the young Waddingtons' careers quite closely and these patrons were cognizant of the fact that both young artists had excelled at the

Toronto Conservatory and had developed into fine professional musicians. It is true, however, that Geoffrey's activities were more apparent, not only because he had appeared in local recitals, but also because of his work with national radio. In 1922 he became associated with radio station, CKNC, Toronto.[132] He was later named music director of that station, and he conducted orchestras for various sponsored programs such as the *Neilson Hour.* During the years 1925-28, he played for the Toronto Symphony,[133] and from 1933-35, he served as music director for the Canadian Radio Broadcasting Commission (CRBC), which had taken over CKNC. In 1934 the CRBC broadcast a series called *Forgotten Footsteps,* hour long dramatic presentations accompanied by Geoffrey Waddington's orchestra.[134] Following a period of freelance conducting, Waddington took on the position of Music Director for CBC Winnipeg (1938-1943) and was responsible for *Geoffrey Waddington Conducts.*[135] Then, he received considerable publicity because of his work with the *Army Show.* After the war, Waddington helped to establish the CBC opera company; he founded and conducted the CBC Symphony Orchestra and became director of CBC music. In 1956 he was awarded an honorary Doctor of Law's degree from Dalhousie University.[136]

In late 1943 news was received that Eildon C. Brander had joined one of the five units of the *Army Show* before it sailed to entertain the Canadian troops overseas.[137] As noted earlier, Miss Brander had assumed control of the Bernadette Fisher School of Dance in 1937, after which she became the major dance teacher and choreographer in Lethbridge; the Eildon Brander School of Dance, which operated out of the YMCA, was the leading academy. How did Miss Brander become such an accomplished dancer and choreographer? She received her basic training from her cousin, Bernadette Fisher, who also encouraged her to master various kinds of dance so that when she began to assist in the academy, she could instruct in whatever kind of dance was in demand by the students. She learned Scottish dancing in Calgary; she, like Bernadette Fisher, studied extensively in San Francisco with the great Russian ballet master, Adolph Bolm, under whose tutelage, and as a member of the San Francisco Opera ballet, she danced in a number of productions: *The Bartered Bride, Scheherazade,* and *Carmen.* In addition, Brander was a member of the Golden Gate Theatre chorus line and performed with various other professional organizations throughout the time she spent in San Francisco. Actually, during the years 1936-1938, Brander studied in San Francisco for three summers plus an extended six month period. Then, she resided in the California city from 1940-1943, after which she returned to Canada to join the Canadian Women's Army Corps (CWAC). Brander's move from Lethbridge brought to a conclusion the lengthy direct relationship between the Conybeare family and the arts in Lethbridge. While performing in the Army show, she met and married a young musician, Stephen Kondaks. Following the war, the Kondaks settled in Montreal where Stephen joined the Montreal Symphony, assisted with the Canadian Youth Orchestra, and then became a Professor of Music at McGill University. Eildon continued her dance studies with Elizabeth Leese and Françoise Sullivan; she also completed her B.A. degree in Psychology as well as her M.A. degree in English at Sir George Williams University.[138]

About the same time that the *Army Show* played Calgary, a concert party of 32 performers plus an orchestra from a Calgary RCAF flying school entertained personnel at #8 Bombing and Gunnery School with their production, *Blackout of 1943,* under the direction of F.O. Wishart Campbell, formerly of the the C.B.C.[139] Shortly thereafter, residents of Claresholm were entertained by members of No. 15 SFTS who staged a revue entitled, *Foothills Follies.* The show featured LAW Leona Marshall who, at that time, was attached to an RCAF entertainment unit in Calgary.[140]

An early army unit, which produced the *Tin Hat Revue* (often referred to as the successor to the Dumbells), also toured the country after returning from the war front.[141] *Tin Hat Revue* was performed for the staff of the Lethbridge POW camp in February 1945.[142] Although Lethbridge and district citizens did not have the opportunity to see this and many of the other major military shows on local stages, they, nevertheless, were treated to some fine military band concerts, variety shows, revues, and other types of entertainment. Reserve Army Week, March 21-28, 1943, provided the impetus for demonstrating various aspects of military activities and careers. The Macleod Air Force Band helped in opening and closing the festivities by presenting concerts at the Capitol Theatre.[143] During the Fifth Victory Loan Drive held in October 1943, the #7 SFTS Band from Macleod, together with a number of other military entertainers (Flt. Lt. A. Clifford, DFC, AW1 June Tipping, Corp. Lew Ingham, LAW Dorothea Simpson, and Supt. John Blair) toured fourteen southern Alberta towns with the revue, *Speed the Victory*, in order to stimulate bond sales.[144] E.R. McFarland, a local businessman and Chairman of Public Relations for the loan drive, was Master of Ceremonies. The Currie Barracks band (from Calgary) provided concerts at the Capitol Theatre in aid of the spring victory loan drives in April 1944 and 1945. At the latter concert, the Currie Band was joined by the CWAC Concert Band which included three Lethbridge women in its complement, Ernestine Stafford, Anne and Ricky Linders. The Royal Canadian Air Force Band performed in support of the ninth Victory Loan Drive on October 5, 1945.

Professional Entertainment

Touring dramatic companies rarely played Lethbridge between 1933 and 1945. In fact, most of the few professionals who appeared on Lethbridge stages during this time were novelty or musical entertainers. Few impressarios and booking agents still considered the Canadian prairies a viable market. However, there were a few exceptions. Next to the Dumbells, probably the most entertaining stage shows to appear in Lethbridge during the 1930s were the Wilbur Cushman units, which booked the Capitol Theatre throughout most of the fall of 1935. Generally, the Cushman units were composed of a touring band accompanied by a group of performers who staged a musical revue based on a theme such as "Mardi Gras." The management of the Capitol Theatre presented these shows as added attractions in conjunction with the ongoing movie. During the years 1935-1938, similar entertainments were provided by Irvin C. Miller (Miller's Brown Skin Models), by Frederic Shipman (Tipica Mexican Orchestra), and by Robert Bell (Hawaiian Follies).

The growing importance of mass media (radio, movies, records) during the 1930s, contributed to changing patterns of entertainment experienced by Lethbridge patrons. As early as 1934 audiences at the Capitol Theatre were thrilled to witness a live performance by "the famous radio artists, Ken Hacklay and his Oklahoma Cowboys."[145] Shortly thereafter, similar fare was presented by the Crockett Family, the stars of the radio show, *Hollywood Barn Dance*. By 1936 radio was firmly entrenched as a means of entertainment in North America, and one of the most popular variety shows was the *Major Bowes Amateur Hour*. Selected competitors from this show were toured throughout the United States and Canada and occasionally appeared at the local Capitol Theatre (June 1936; September 1937). Later (1940), this type of entertainment featured: "youngsters from screen and radio" in the *Paramount Starlet's Revue;* Lethbridge's (and Calgary's) own Henry Viney and company in *The Big Radio Jamboree;* and a stage performance by local radio artists, The Alberta Ranch Boys. In the postwar era, local audiences turned out by the thousands to hear the "Happy Gang" and to participate in Roy Ward Dickson's *Fun Parade* – both, famous Canadian radio programs.

Radio and the phonograph also popularized the swing music of the Big Bands in the 1930s. Lethbridge citizens were personally introduced to one of Canada's major professional orchestras as early as 1932 when A.W. Shackleford invited Mart Kenney and His Western Gentlemen to play at the Henderson Lake Pavilion before the band settled in for the summer season at Waterton Lakes. For many years thereafter, the Mart Kenney orchestra played at numerous local dances at various Lethbridge dance halls such as the Trianon, Henderson Lake Pavilion, and the Marquis Hotel.[146] Then, in the spring of 1938, Mart Kenney and His Western Gentlemen began a series of biannual concerts and dances held in the local arena where large numbers of patrons could listen and dance to the music of one of their favorite orchestras. This tradition continued until 1943 when the band also entertained the troops in training at the #8 Bombing and Gunnery School. Undoubtedly, the orchestra helped to strengthen morale during the darker days of the war. The long association between Mart Kenney and Lethbridge was formally recognized in the spring of 1985 when the University of Lethbridge awarded Kenney an honorary Doctor of Laws degree. On this occasion, Lethbridge citizens were pleased to see Mart Kenney, accompanied by many members of his family including his very gracious wife, Norma Locke, who had also brought so much joy to the city with her delightful song stylings as lead female singer with the Kenney band.

Immediately following the war, other professional dance bands which toured to Lethbridge were Bert Niosi, Spike Jones and His City Slickers, and Gene Krupa. Because most of the bands performed in the Lethbridge arena, they entertained rather large crowds and therefore might be considered a form of large scale entertainment, other forms of which are discussed in the remainder of this chapter.

Large Scale and Mass Entertainment

As was pointed out earlier, the last Chautauqua to play Lethbridge pulled up its stakes on June 30, 1933. Other forms of large scale entertainment such as the circus and the local exhibition continued to be annual events except during the war years. Prior to the war, various circuses such as the Polock, Baddeley, Ringling Brothers/Barnum and Bailey appeared once, only. The most consistent organization was the Al G. Barnes Circus, which visited Lethbridge on three occasions between 1933-1939, inclusive. The Lethbridge exhibition combined a number of activities to provide competition and entertainment of various kinds in order to meet the interests of all segments the society. In addition to the traditional fair, special features such as rodeos, midways, and grandstand shows were offered. The 1934 exhibition featured the RCMP Musical Ride, whereas the 1935 program was designed to celebrate Lethbridge's Golden Jubilee. An elaborate pageant was produced under the auspices of the Lethbridge Exhibition Board. Frank Hemingway, from Toronto, was contracted to direct the extravaganza, and, as mentioned earlier, Eildon Brander of the local Bernadette Fisher School of Dance provided the choreography. In the following years, professional grandstand shows became the norm. No exhibition was held in 1940[147] or in the successive years of World War II.

Ice shows were a very popular form of entertainment in the late 1930s and throughout much of the 1940s. Actually, it was in 1937 that the Glencoe Club of Calgary introduced fairly regular ice shows to Lethbridge. Two additional Glencoe ice carnivals were staged in the city during 1938; however, World War II brought this activity to a halt for a number of years. Then, in the mid-1940s the Lethbridge Figure Skating Club (under manager Ralph Potts), either independently or in cooperation with the Glencoe Club of Calgary, produced a series of very popular ice carnivals. The Lethbridge Figure Skating Club took the initiative in 1944 by hiring Ian Mackie (a well known comic skater) to produce *Ice Cabaret*. Mackie gathered together skating talent from Calgary, (Muffy McHugh Mackenzie), Regina (Don and Ethel Higgins), Seattle (Carol Lynn), and about fifty members of the local club. In the succeeding three years, the Glencoe Club of Calgary was featured in the local ice carnivals. In the meantime, two professional ice shows played the Lethbridge arena. On February 28, 1940, the *Cracked Ice Follies of 1940,* starring the world's male figure skating champion, Hope Braine (from Australia), supported by Margaret Manahan (England) and a cast of forty skaters, was presented to a crowd of 2 500. The show was touted as the "most ambitious ice project ever booked for the city."[148] In addition, the *Stars of the Winterland Ice Revue* included Lethbridge on their itinerary on February 8, 9, 1943. This professional show, which was brought to the city under the auspices of the local Kinsmen Club, featured Megan Taylor, world champion skater from Britain, and former member of the *Ice Capades.* Taylor, and other members of her company had also performed in the Bud Abbot and Lou Costello movie, *Oh, Doctor.*[149]

The 1930s and '40s are often referred to as the golden age of the movies and therefore one would suspect that some local movie aspirants would be attracted to Hollywood. There is little evidence, however, to indicate that this was a common phenomenon. Nevertheless, one young Lethbridge girl, Audrey Leonard, did gain the experience of acting in at least one major studio movie when she was cast by Warner Brothers to play the part of Barbara (as a child) in the 1938 movie, *Love, Honor and Behave.* Leonard appeared opposite the well known child actor, Dickie Moore. Priscilla Lane played Barbara as an adult. The *Lethbridge Herald* envisioned Miss Leonard achieving fame similar to that accorded Dickie Moore, and thus, suggested that, "Audrey is also well away on her climb to motion picture success."[150] The *Herald* went on to comment that Lethbridge people would remember Audrey as a "clever stage performer." As a very young girl, Miss Leonard had appeared in some local LDS productions in the mid-1930s as well as in Playgoers' *Musical Pie* (1934). Then, the family moved to California for a number of years. Miss Leonard returned to Lethbridge to complete her high school shortly after World War II.

In the realm of commercial movie production, Lethbridge was selected in 1940 to be one of the sites for the filming of the British movie, *49th Parallel*, which starred Leslie Howard, Elisabeth Bergner, and Raymond Massey. Producer, Roland Gillett, of London, received permission from the Canadian and British governments to film RAF planes operating out of the Lethbridge airport. Actually, the film crew spent only about three or four days in Lethbridge, and the featured "stars" were not involved in these scenes. British and Canadian actors who were here for the filming included Eric Portman, Peter Moore, John Chandos, Forbes Rankin, Ian St. Clair, and Carla Lehmann, who began her theatrical career at the age of fifteen when she performed in *Peter Pan* for the Winnipeg Little Theatre. Miss Lehmann later moved to England where she studied drama, and then, she began a professional stage career which provided her with the opportunity to appear with experienced performers such as Marie Tempest.[151] Readers are reminded that Marie Tempest was one of the British stage actresses who appeared at the Majestic Theatre prior to 1920. Some members of the local Playgoers Club also had the opportunity to appear in *49th Parallel* as extras.

About two months later, Lethbridge movie patrons were excited to read that the local theatre manager, A.W. Shackleford, had been responsible for making arrangements to host the stars of the forthcoming movie, *North West Mounted Police* (Madeline Carroll, Preston Foster, and Robert Preston), as they passed through Banff on their way to Regina to attend the world premiere.[152]

Because of the tremendous popularity of the movies during the 1940s, Hollywood visitors to the city received considerable press coverage. George Murphy, Ian Hunter, and Claire Trevor came to the city on contract to boost the sale of War Savings and Victory Loan Bonds.[153] Gale Storm and some professional associates passed through the city in June 1941 on a photographic location story for *Look Magazine.*[154] Part of the assignment included filming graduation exercises at the Service Flying Training School in Macleod. Much more publicity accompanied the visit to the city, in August of that same year, by Mary Astor who had just finished filming *The Maltese Falcon* with

Humphrey Bogart. She flew to Lethbridge from Los Angeles to spend a weekend with her husband, AC2 Manuel Del Campo. Del Campo had recently joined the RCAF in Vancouver, and after a short training stint at Penhold, Alberta, had been transferred to #8 B & G School.[155] Shortly after this visit, Del Campo was sent to #4 Initial Training School, RCAF, Edmonton. Some years later, a USO troupe stopped at Lethbridge (in early 1944) to perform for personnel at #8 Bombing and Gunnery School. This troupe included screen stars Kay Francis, Reginald Gardiner, Marsha Hunt, Patty Thomas, Teddi Sherman, and Nancy Barnes.[156]

5

The Festival Era (1946-1970)

Community Setting

The postwar years opened up an era of sustained growth which was unprecedented for Lethbridge. The growth was evident in demographic trends as well as in general economic developments. Much of this growth was attributable to broader forces, which affected all of Canada in many ways, and the Alberta region in particular ways. The most obvious forces included the following: postwar reconstruction, the baby boom movement, burgeoning oil exploration, accelerated urbanization, and internal migration to Alberta. The Alberta Government profited from development related to the oil industry because of massive public revenues generated through provincially held mineral rights.

MacGregor reports that during the period 1947-1971, Canada's population grew by about 74 percent. Both increased fertility rates (reaching a high of about 30 births per 1000 population in 1950) and positive net migration contributed to this rapid rise. MacGregor also notes that during this same time, Alberta's population increased by approximately 100 percent. Evidence of rapid urbanization within the province was also evident, particularly in the larger cities of Calgary and Edmonton (and in the smaller urban centres located where oil exploration was most active). Nevertheless, the population of Lethbridge grew rather remarkably, too; though not at a rate comparable to the oil dominated communities. From 1946-1971 Lethbridge's population increased by almost 140 percent, whereas both Calgary and Edmonton increased their populations by more than double that rate.[1]

Increased population necessitated the growth of housing, public institutions, and commercial facilities. Each successive year of the immediate postwar period saw the building permit records of the previous year exceeded until 1950 when a small decline was witnessed. The generally expanding Canadian economy, coupled with increases in materials and consumer goods, and the removal of price ceilings in January 1946 helped to inflate these figures somewhat, so their effect is not quite as great as it seems at first glance. Nevertheless, the amount and type of construction suggests a very active local economy. In addition, two major developments associated with the district's agricultural industry were begun: the St. Mary's Dam Project and a $2.5 million sugar beet factory in Taber.[2] Extension of irrigation in the Lethbridge area was especially welcome following severe dust storms in 1945 and 1946 which reminded local residents how vulnerable the shallow topsoil was. The postwar years were also characterized by considerable expenditures for upgrading and extending utilities as well as communication and transportation facilities.

After February 13, 1947, when a major oil reserve in Leduc, Alberta, had been confirmed, Lethbridge benefited greatly from the prosperity which the provincial coffers began to experience.

Provincial grants in aid of public construction projects were extraordinarily generous. Commercial development in the city also began to accelerate, and soon the downtown business district was greatly transformed.[3] Commercial development was also attracted to outlying residential areas.[4] The first suburban supermarket development, Shoppers' World, opened on Mayor Magrath Drive, a major highway artery on the eastern outskirts of the city. During the next few years, Mayor Magrath Drive developed into a major commercial area devoted primarily to motels, hotels, restaurants, supermarkets, and commercial malls.[5]

As Alberta's economic condition became more and more closely tied to the oil industry, the central Alberta area became the prime destination of migrant populations. Even Lethbridge residents felt the attraction as young and old, alike, compared opportunities available in Lethbridge with those of their "more fortunate" northern neighbors. Certainly, in economic terms, Lethbridge residents experienced relative deprivation. Young people were forced to leave the city in order to obtain post secondary education (whether technical, vocational, or university instruction), and upon graduation, most of these young people became employed in the larger centres. Young people not inclined to further their education were attracted to the oil exploration areas where well paying jobs were plentiful. Even the opening of Alberta's first junior college, the Lethbridge Junior College (LJC), in 1957 did very little to stem this movement.[6]

By this time, a depressed attitude had settled on the community. This attitude was fueled throughout 1956 and 1957 by tight money circumstances and a consequent reduction in funds for new home mortgages which, in turn, severely curtailed the major building industry in the city – residential construction.[7] Although the easing of mortgage funds in the latter part of 1957 contributed to a surge of house construction in the late 1950s, most of this was "catch up" construction. During the mid-1960s, residential construction sank to the lowest levels since the Depression. On October 16, 1965, the *Lethbridge Herald* referred to Lethbridge as a "sick city."[8] Fortunately, before the lapse of another year (on July 28, 1966), the province's Minister of Education, R.H. McKinnon, announced that Lethbridge had been chosen as the site for Alberta's third provincial university – the University of Lethbridge. The plan was that the university would develop out of the university transfer section of the LJC; it was incorporated as an autonomous institution on January 1, 1967 – Canada's Centennial university.[9] The college, which was later renamed the Lethbridge Community College (LCC), retained the technical-vocational studies. Now, the city could boast of three major educational and research centres: the University of Lethbridge, the Lethbridge Community College, and the Federal Agricultural Research Centre. In addition to stimulating intellectual development, these institutions were major forces in helping to diversify the economic base of the city. The most important consequence of the establishment of the former two institutions was that they undoubtedly provided the most exciting economic prospects the city had ever enjoyed. In 1968 the two institutions' payrolls amounted to almost three million dollars;[10] in succeeding years, these payrolls increased dramatically as the two institutions grew in student numbers and expanded their program offerings. Associated with these developments, were a number of important consequences which helped renew the local residents' faith in their community. Capital construction on both campuses helped reduce the unemployment rate; new teaching personnel were attracted to the city; many ancillary employment opportunities opened up; young people had more reason to remain in Lethbridge. The population trends of the early and mid-1960s did a turnabout; Lethbridge was again seen as an economically and socially attractive city. This renewed viability was reflected almost immediately in increased commercial development: two major malls were constructed during the period 1967-1970.[11]

Lethbridge continued its reliance on agriculture. Although new industries began to settle in Lethbridge's new Industrial Park in North Lethbridge, much of the local industrial growth was associated with agricultural production, especially the burgeoning live stock business. Grain production and sales varied considerably throughout this era, but livestock production, sales, and prices remained consistently high. Associated with this increased production was the growth of livestock processing facilities within the city.

On the world political scene, two major conflicts disrupted the political balance of power: the Korean War (in the early 1950s) and the Vietnam War (in the late 1960s). But, on the whole, the local political scene was reasonably stable through the 1950s and 1960s. The Social Credit MLA, John Landeryou, represented the Lethbridge constituency throughout this period. In fact, Lethbridge was represented in the Alberta Legislature by Social Credit candidates for thirty consecutive years, 1944-1975. In the Federal Parliament, local conservative politicians from either the Social Credit or the Progressive Conservative party represented the Lethbridge area riding from 1930 through to the present.

Theatrical Awakening

Diversity was also apparent in the city's cultural activities which, to a large extent, reflected the increasingly important role that indigenous artistic concerns began to play in Canada. Canada's contribution to World War II brought considerable pride to its citizens. There was a feeling that Canadian institutions were equal to, or better than, any others in the world. Surely then, the country was capable of creating a respectable art community as well. This attitude stimulated an outpouring of Canadian theatrical activity among amateurs and professionals, alike. Amateur theatre was greatly stimulated by the festival movement which began to stir again in 1946 under the auspices of the Alberta Drama League, and which resulted in the reestablishment of the DDF in 1947. As the DDF moved toward an exclusive three act festival, various regional groups began to sponsor one act festivals. In the early 1950s, the Alberta Drama League divided the province into 6-7 regions for preliminary competitions, and then hosted a culminating Alberta One Act Festival which took place in Red Deer from 1953-1963, after which it was moved to Banff until the Alberta Drama League was disbanded in 1968.

Professional theatre also blossomed in various parts of Canada. This development was aided by the growth of professional training centres. Ernest Sterndale Bennett was at the forefront of these developments, first through his involvement with the Speech Department of the Toronto Conservatory where he not only taught classes, but where he also organized a touring company of young actors. Then, in 1949 he and his wife, Hilda, opened the Canadian Theatre School in Toronto. A number of Sterndale Bennett's students later became associated with the Stratford Company, the touring Canadian Players, and other professional organizations; others, like George Luscombe, operated successful playhouses such as Toronto Workshop Productions.[12] Toronto and area quickly became the centre of English Canadian professional theatre. Much of the success of the Stratford Festival, founded in 1953, is due to the fact that most of Canada's trained professional actors were close at hand and were eager to be involved in repertory theatre, even if for part of the year, only.[13] Some of this partial employment problem was resolved in 1954 when The Canadian Players was organized with the purpose of touring during the winter months with quality classical productions.[14] The idea of the Canadian Players was conceived by Tom Patterson, founder of the Stratford Festival, who approached Douglas Campbell, a veteran of the Old Vic in London and of the Edinburgh Festival, to help establish a winter touring company of Stratford players. Campbell enjoyed the challenge, and together, Patterson and Campbell forged the company (with Lady Eaton as patron); Campbell took on the directorial responsibilities. The company's first tour was conducted through southern Ontario in the fall of 1954.[15] The following year, the company engaged in a trans-Canada tour which virtually became an annual event through 1964. As the years passed, the personnel of the company changed somewhat. Patterson reports that, "I, personally, remained with the company for only about a year and a half, and was replaced by my first wife, Robin, and Laurel Crosby."[16] Directorial duties were shared by a number of directors, notably Tony Van Bridge. In addition, company members began to be selected from a variety of sources – not exclusively from the ranks of the Stratford players.

As the 1950s progressed, Toronto and vicinity tightened its grip on the professional theatre community as major television production facilities were located there. With the addition of the Shaw Festival in 1962, southern Ontario was established as English Canada's theatre centre.[17] But other areas of Canada were undaunted in their quest to provide professional theatre. The west coast had always been an important theatre centre. The very popular summer showcase, Theatre Under the Stars, was established in Vancouver in 1940. Shortly after World War II, the Everyman Theatre Company was founded in Vancouver by Sidney Risk.[18] Winnipeg took pride in its outdoor facility, the Rainbow Stage (1954), which had the distinction of providing Jon Vickers, Len Cariou, and Gordon Pinsent with some of their earliest professional experiences.

Educational institutions in western Canada gradually began to put more emphasis on the needs of the theatre profession. At the university level, this movement was particularly noticeable at the University of Alberta (Studio Theatre) and at the University of British Columbia (Frederic Wood Theatre). In addition, the Banff School of Fine Arts emerged from the doldrums of World War II and gradually began to take its place as a major centre for the study of the arts, albeit during the summer months, only. Besides its traditional programs, the school established divisions of opera and musical theatre during the 1950s.[19]

As the 1950s were drawing to a close, another major development occurred in Canadian professional theatre – the establishment of "regional theatres" throughout the country. The Manitoba Theatre Centre in Winnipeg, established in 1958 by John Hirsch and Tom Hendry, is generally considered to be the prototype of the regional theatres in Canada.[20] The 1960s and early 1970s saw the establishment of similar theatres throughout the country in most major urban centres (see Table 5-1).[21]

Although Prince Edward Island did not develop a regional theatre, it, nevertheless, played a significant role in the furtherance of professional theatre in Canada through the operations of the Charlottetown Festival which began in 1965 under artistic director, Mavor Moore. From the beginning, it was decided that the Charlottetown Festival would showcase Canadian productions, only. The first summer witnessed the staging of *Spring Thaw* (a musical revue), *Laugh With Leacock* (a play), and *Anne of Green Gables* (a musical, which became the regular ingredient of every successive festival). In 1968 the festival committee instituted an "all musical policy."[22]

Some other notable developments associated with the growth of professional theatre in Canada were the establishment of two major ballet companies [The Winnipeg Ballet (later, the Royal Winnipeg Ballet) and the National Ballet Company of Canada] and the founding of the Canadian Opera Company. All three of these organizations helped to bring musical theatre to the hinterland; certainly, Lethbridge audiences were generally ecstatic about their various appearances.

A major problem that had to be confronted in almost every Canadian community during this period of time was the lack of adequate performing facilities. As explained earlier in this text, most of the country's legitimate theatres had been destroyed or converted for other purposes. No wonder that outdoor theatres were often the first ones to develop in many communities. Of course, this practice did have the effect of reducing, tremendously, the theatre season. Summer weather conditions are very difficult to predict in most areas of Canada. Stratford achieved a compromise by operating out of a tent facility for the first four years. This compromise was not entirely satisfactory since the shows were frequently disturbed by external noises such as train whistles and shouting from nearby baseball games. In addition, the interior temperature of the tent became quite unbearable. Patterson relates some very amusing anecdotes in his reminiscences about the early days at Stratford, and some of the most outrageous stories recall how many of these problems were gradually resolved through various kinds of compromise.[23] However, the ultimate solution occurred in 1957 when a permanent theatre, seating 2 258 patrons, was constructed.

TABLE 5-1

Founding Dates:
Canada's Regional Theatres

YEAR	THEATRE	YEAR	THEATRE
1952	Théâtre du Nouveau Monde, Montreal	1967	Theatre Calgary, Calgary
1958	Manitoba Theatre Centre, Winnipeg	1968	Theatre New Brunswick, Fredericton
1962	Vancouver Playhouse, Vancouver	1969	National Arts Centre Theatre, Ottawa
1963	Neptune Theatre, Halifax	1969	Centaur Theatre Co., Montreal
1964	Bastion Theatre Co., Victoria	1970	Toronto Arts Productions (CentreStage, 1983)
1965	Citadel Theatre, Edmonton	1970	Théâtre du Trident, Quebec City
1966	Globe Theatre, Regina	1971	Theatre London/The Grand Theatre, London, Ont.

As regional theatres began to spring up around the country, they searched for any kind of facility that could serve as (hopefully) a temporary home. Some companies became ensconced in old warehouses, former churches, and school buildings. Other companies, like Mac 14 (Calgary), were fortunate enough to inherit existing facilities such as the Allied Arts Council Theatre.[24] Of course, former members of that company relate how hopelessly inadequate those facilities were, too. Gradually, however, most of the regional theatres upgraded their facilities, either through renovation or through construction of new buildings, supported by public subscription, private donation, and government grants.

During the 1950s, various provincial governments began to take a greater interest in the arts. In Alberta, for example, the debt free Social Credit government announced plans to build two large performing halls: the Northern Alberta Jubilee Auditorium (Edmonton) and the Southern Alberta Jubilee Auditorium (Calgary). Of course, these auditoriums were magnificent, but they were also very large. The auditoriums, with two large balconies, each accommodated over 2 500 patrons; the stages were immense and were furnished with the latest staging facilities. These jubilee auditoriums were ideal facilities for large musical and visual productions; however, they were completely inappropriate for most dramatic productions.

The question now arises, "How did Lethbridge fit into this theatrical scene?" As far as amateur theatre is concerned, the answer is clear: Lethbridge and district amateur theatrical societies were extraordinarily active participants in the festival movement. With regard to professional theatre, the answer is less clear. Resident professional theatre finally came to Lethbridge for an extended stay in the mid-1950s; however, it seems that Lethbridge had not yet reached the critical size needed to support such an endeavor even for just the summer months. On the other hand, Lethbridge audiences generously supported the touring companies, almost all of which were now Canadian. Both local and touring theatre benefitted greatly from the founding of the Lethbridge Allied Arts Council which was conceived of in late 1957 and established in March 1958. The council was patterned after the Calgary Allied Arts Council, with similar aims: to coordinate local arts' activities, to develop a greater interest about the arts among members of the community, and to publish a yearly calendar of arts' activities. Local arts' organizations were invited to become members and name representatives to the Board which was initially presided over by President - Van Christou; Vice-President - Ted Godwin; Secretary - Jessie Baalim, and Treasurer - David Howell. Eighteen local arts' organizations, including the Playgoers Club, the Lethbridge Sketch Club, the Jolliffe Academy of Dancing, and the Lethbridge Women's Musical Club were charter members. The Council's first sponsored tour was the National Ballet which appeared at the Capitol Theatre on May 3. Thereafter, the Council became a very active sponsor of touring individuals and groups. In 1964 the Council fostered a summer arts educational program and shortly thereafter, lent its support to numerous local productions.[25] Much of this activity will become apparent in later sections of this book.

Local Theatrical Facilities

With regard to theatre facilities, Lethbridge was very much in the same unfortunate position as most other Canadian communities when this era began, and facilities remained fairly inadequate throughout the 1950s and most of the 1960s. As the 1940s came to a close, the city opened the Civic Sports Centre which was basically composed of the Fritz Sick swimming pool and two auditoriums. The large auditorium was built particularly to provide a venue for basketball. Tiered seats lined the side walls. The smaller auditorium could be used for practice or for children's basketball games. The building was designed, however, so that the small auditorium could open up into the large auditorium and thus function as a stage. The stage was therefore quite large but it had limited wing space. The main disadvantage of the centre was the flat floor of the auditorium. In the early 1950s, a summer professional theatre company, which took up temporary residence in the city, preferred to act on the floor of the main auditorium and seat the audience around them in the tiered seats on the side. The year 1950 saw the completion of another large auditorium designed particularly for basketball, the gymnasium of the new Lethbridge Collegiate Institute. Also, as mentioned earlier, the Paramount (movie) theatre opened that year.

During the 1950s and '60s, a large number of school, church, and civic auditoriums were constructed in the city. Although most of these auditoriums had stage areas, they were generally not too suitable for theatrical productions. In addition, all of the local theatre houses (Capitol, Roxy, Lealta, and the new Paramount) were primarily designed for movies. The former three theatres were all closed during the decade 1959-1969.[26] Two modern movie theatres were constructed by the Shackleford family and their associates to fill the void created by the aforementioned closings; however, neither of them (College Cinema nor Paramount II) had stage facilities.[27] This era also witnessed the usual promise of another new theatre – to be located on 9th Avenue South, east of St. Michael's Hospital; the promise never materialized.[28]

From the mid-1950s, Lethbridge residents anticipated the construction of a cultural centre with an appropriate live theatre facility. It was felt that the Alberta government should construct a Jubilee Auditorium in Lethbridge, the third largest city in the province. No one really anticipated as large an auditorium as the ones in Calgary and Edmonton, but many people envisioned one with a seating capacity of at least 1 500. It soon became apparent, however, that the Alberta government had no intention of extending such cultural facilities. Then, in 1957 an announcement was made that Deane R. Yates, a former lumber dealer, had left the city a bequest of $200 347 in the name of his wife, Genevieve, which was to be used for the construction of a cultural facility within the city.[29] Unfortunately, once the estate was settled, it became apparent that the available funds were not sufficient to construct a theatre facility, let alone a multipurpose cultural centre; therefore, additional funds were required from the public purse. Then, various interest groups became concerned about matters such as location, size, and cost of the facility. A number of locations were suggested, among them, Galt Gardens and the Civic Centre. In late 1964 city council eventually settled on a 500 seat theatre to be located in the Civic Centre property just east of the City Hall.[30] Sam Lurie, a local architect, was given authorization in December 1964 to proceed with plans.[31] In the interim, the concept of a multipurpose cultural centre was scrapped, so various arts organizations and activities had to be housed elsewhere.[32]

About 800 people attended the official opening of the Genevieve Yates Memorial Centre on May 1, 1966. Costs for the building and furnishings amounted to $547 000.[33] Citizens were pleased with the expansive foyer and the tastefully decorated auditorium, in which all of the seats had a clear view of the stage. Prospective users of the theatre were also ecstatic about the stage dimensions, the sight lines, the wing space, and the dressing rooms. They were less happy about the absence of rehearsal space, the lack of a fly gallery, and the shortage of backstage storage and workspace. Almost twenty-four years passed before many of these deficiencies were corrected. Regardless of these inadequacies, the centre proved to be an excellent facility for many productions and entertainments. The lights were rarely turned off. Of course, the critics were partially vindicated in 1969 when the Royal Winnipeg Ballet passed up Lethbridge because their usual performance facility, the Capitol Theatre, had been closed and the Yates's seating capacity was considered to be inadequate.

Amateur Theatre

Following World War II, dramatic activity in the city began to pick up; it was the YMCA theatre groups and the Mutual Improvement Association (MIA) of the LDS Church which were the initial centres of that activity. The local and district MIA's of the LDS church were the first groups to represent Lethbridge in the reorganized provincial festival movement. Unfortunately, the local MIA did not maintain its participation in the Alberta festivals beyond 1947. Nevertheless, local audiences continued to enjoy various LDS productions presented under the direction of Maydel Palmer, Ila Green, Eleanor Matkin, and her multi-talented husband Dr. B. Wayne Matkin, the latter two of whom became the most prominent directors in the church. Wayne Matkin reports that he gained all of his dramatic and musical education through the auspices of the MIA, the church Sunday School, and the LDS festival activities. He had also participated in Playgoers prior to W.W. II. A native of Magrath, Alberta, Matkin obtained his DDS degree at the University of Alberta, and during World War II, he practiced his profession at the Prisoner of War Camp in Lethbridge. After the war, he returned to Magrath for a short period of time, and then in 1947 he took up permanent residence in Lethbridge.[34] Shortly thereafter, both he and his wife, Eleanor (who had majored in speech and drama at the University of Utah), began to direct for the local LDS Theatre group. In 1948 Eleanor directed *What Doth it Profit*, and the following year, Dr. Matkin was both musical director and stage director for the LDS production of the operetta *Belle of Barcelona*. Throughout the next few years, the Matkins made extraordinary contributions to local theatre (through the Playgoers, the LDS dramatic societies, and various community projects) and to the local musical scene. Wayne Matkin organized an extremely successful LDS choral group, the Choralaires, who excelled in festival competition, performed in local concerts, contributed to church services, and formed the core for musical productions such as *Amahl and the Night Visitors*, which was presented at the Yates Memorial Centre during the Christmas season of both 1967 and 1968. The following year, Matkin was named a Bishop of the LDS church, and therefore, he had much less time to devote to local artistic endeavors. In 1974 his beloved wife, Eleanor, died.

Minstrel Show Band (YMCA's So-Ed Club)
Photo: City of Lethbridge Archives and Records Management

The YMCA's So-Ed (Social-Education) Club resurrected the annual minstrel and variety shows, whereas the YMCA Little Theatre specialized in evenings of one act plays. Although there was some overlapping in the membership of these two organizations, they did operate somewhat independently; the directors' tasks were usually taken by different people. The first So-Ed Minstrel Show (May 1946) was produced by Morton Brown in collaboration with Mrs. Percy (Annie) Cull (musical director), and it featured George Brown, Jr., who had just returned from service in the armed forces.[35] Subsequent minstrel and variety shows under the auspices of the So-Ed Club were frequently written by Ab Chervinski or Bill Rasmussen with the directorial and production chores being shared by Bill Cross, Bill Rasmussen, Joe Montgomery, and Alex Harper. Musical direction was handled by Remo Baceda, Effie Reid, and Lois Donnat. Choreography was frequently performed by Joyce (Bateman) Hill, whose dancers contributed greatly to the productions; Phyl Trca also provided some choreography. Over forty individuals supplied their talents to these annual shows between 1946 and 1950.

Mrs. Chester (Helen) Robbins presided over the Little Theatre Group in its formative years. One of this group's initial public performances was an evening of one act plays presented at the "Y" on March 24, 1947; Maybelle Bryans directed one of the plays. Bryans encouraged others to try their hand at directing, and before long, the group had developed a dedicated core of directors. Bryans maintained her association with the organization in an advisory capacity (honorary chairman) and also took responsibility for directing *The Happy Journey* in February 1949. This play was privately adjudicated by Robert Stuart, visiting professor of dramatics at the University of Alberta, and adjudicator of the 1948 Alberta Drama Festival, in order to determine whether it should be entered in the Alberta Regional Festival. Other YMCA plays receiving adjudication at that time were *The Black Sheep* directed by P.H. Henson, and *The Gallant Lady* directed by Helen Robbins. The fact that the Regional Festival had primarily become a festival of three act plays probably contributed to the fact that none of these YMCA offerings was advanced to the Calgary festival.

These YMCA groups played an important role in socially integrating young people from various religious and social backgrounds. Although the school system in Lethbridge separated Roman Catholic students from Protestant students through grade twelve, the YMCA helped to bring these diverse religious groups together. In addition, participants in both the So-Ed Club and the Little Theatre group came from widely dispersed residential areas of the city. As the 1940s drew to a close, the very active dramatic interests of the YMCA dropped away. Fortunately, other groups helped fill the void.

During the early 1950s, Southminster United Church became active as a centre of theatrical production again. A.K. Putland, choir leader at Southminster Church, was fortunate in having a number of extremely competent and experienced singers among his choir, for example, Mary (Needs) Thomson, a former Stuchbury Cup winner in provincial music festival competition. The choir presented numerous operettas (primarily Gilbert and Sullivan), much to the pleasure of Lethbridge music and theatre patrons. Other groups within the church presented the occasional variety show or short play.

Minstrel and similar shows were generally passé, but since the Rotary Minstrels were such a local tradition, they "hung on" a little longer. It is true, however, that the final Rotary shows (1952-55) tended to take on the form of general variety shows. In the early 1960s, the organization of the local chapter of the Society for the Preservation and Encouragement of Barber Shop Quartet Singing in America (SPEBSQSA) organized annual "Harmoni Nights" which occasionally included minstrel acts. Wayne Matkin and V.M. "Buck" Rogers were leaders in organizing the local chapter and directing the singers.

Historical pageants became quite popular during this era. The city's Department of Recreation organized a number of these pageants in the early 1950s to coincide with Recreation Week. Most of these pageants displayed aspects of local history, and were brought together under the supervision of the local recreational director, Ralph "Lefty" Eshpeter. Then, in 1955 (Alberta's Golden Jubilee year) a special Lethbridge Jubilee committee commissioned Harry Baalim to write a major historical pageant, *Saga of a Prairie Town*, which was presented in early September. A professional director,

Dean Goodman, agreed to direct the pageant; Wayne Matkin supervised the music. Additional pageants were presented by various church groups; for example, local and district congregations of the United Church produced *Triumphs of Faith* in October 1953, and the Lethbridge Stake MIA staged the pageant *Preludes to Eternity*, written locally by Eva Ellison and directed by Wayne Matkin. Serving somewhat the same purpose was the Lethbridge Stake MIA production of the LDS musical and historical play, *Promised Valley*, at the LDS auditorium in October 1961. In this instance, Eleanor Matkin and Marie Smith handled the stage direction; whereas, a local junior high school teacher and band leader, Grant Erickson, acted as musical director.[36]

A popular theatrical event that continued throughout the late 1940s and early 1950s was the annual ice show or carnival. Skating professionals from Calgary's Glencoe Club such as Edward and Gladys Rushka and Betty Cornwall directed the shows in the immediate postwar years. These ice carnivals featured well known North American skaters such as Betty Atkinson and Charles Hain (formerly of Hollywood and the *Ice Follies*), Ralph and Beth Fogal (former Kitchener, Ontario, professionals), Ian Mackie (skating comedian), Muffy McHugh Mackenzie (formerly of Calgary and participant in numerous North American ice shows), Doreen Sutton (Canadian Junior Champion from Drumheller), Shirley Martin, Ron Kinney, and Don and Ethel Higgins, who by 1947 had moved to Lethbridge. Shortly thereafter, the Lethbridge Figure Skating Club (LFSC) contracted Ralph and Beth Fogal as club professionals, who then took on the responsibility of directing *Ice Fantasy* which was presented at the Lethbridge Arena on April 2, 3, 1948. Fifty junior members of the local club joined thirty members of the Glencoe Club and various Canadian Figure Skating Champions such as Wally Diestelmeyer and Suzanne Morrow (pairs champions), Pierette Paquin (Gold Medalist from Ottawa's Mente Club), and Donald Tobin (Canadian Junior Junior Champion – also from the Mente Club). For a number of years, thereafter, the LFSC maintained a very active program. When Fay Morris left her position with the Lethbridge Figure Skating Club after the 1954 production, the club disbanded operations for a number of years. This lengthy hiatus in the activities of the LFSC came at a rather inopportune time for devotees of figure skating because, after November 1954, Lethbridge audiences were deprived of professional ice shows for a period of twenty years. Sonja Currie Jacobson was hired in the early 1960s to be the club's professional. Slowly, with the help of her mother and sister, she began the process of rebuilding the club. Excellence of performance was aided by the introduction in the latter half of 1960s of a summer skating school.[37]

But the most significant development to occur in the field of local amateur theatre was the organization of numerous societies devoted exclusively to the production of plays or musicals: Playgoers of Lethbridge, Coaldale Little Theatre, Our Town Workshop, and Lethbridge Musical Theatre. Each of these groups will be analyzed thoroughly in the succeeding discussion.

Playgoers of Lethbridge

In February 1950 the *Lethbridge Herald* reported the following:[38]

A few former members of the Lethbridge Playgoers Club met Tuesday evening at the home of Mrs. C.A. Long to discuss the feasibility of renewing activities of the club which has been dormant for some years.

Although this meeting resulted in no immediate action, additional open meetings arranged by the YMCA and other interested parties generated greater interest, which eventually resulted in the naming of a committee to re-establish the Playgoers.[39] This committee, composed of Maybelle Bryans (Chairman), Mrs. Jack Malbert, Dr. Wayne Matkin, Hugh Buchanan, Lena Connor, Don Oates, Tom Ferguson, and Don Frey, was to prepare a new constitution and call an organization meeting for the new year so that officers of the club could be formally elected. Such a meeting was held on January 9, 1951, and C.R. Matthews was elected president. Mrs. W.E. Bryans was named general director, and she promised to direct whatever play the club selected for entry in the Alberta Regional Drama Festival which was to be held in Calgary on April, 2-4.[40] The entry date for the Regional Festival was just a few days hence; nevertheless, the play *Mr. Pim Passes By* was cast and some early rehearsals were carried out. Then, the club realized that it was not capable of mounting a major three act play so quickly; therefore, *Mr. Pim Passes By* was withdrawn and the members put their full efforts into producing *Arsenic and Old Lace* for presentation in the Civic Centre on November 26 and 27.[41] This was undoubtedly an excellent decision; the comedy, ably directed by Wayne Matkin, was joyously received by about 1 000 patrons, and therefore, Playgoers was on its way to becoming a local institution once again.

Arsenic and Old Lace was remarkable in that it brought together an abundance of dramatic talent. A perennial Playgoer and participant in most of the operettas produced by the Southminster United Church Choir, Ted Faunch, made his final appearance for Playgoers in the role of Mr. Gibbs, a prospective roomer. Wayne Matkin, the director, presented a number of new faces to Lethbridge audiences. Elsie Biddell and Denise Black were destined to become major contributors to local theatricals. Biddell and her engineer husband, Cecil, had recently moved to Lethbridge from Regina where she had been very active in theatre as director, playwright, adjudicator (Saskatchewan Drama League), and actress.[42] Within the next six years, Elsie Biddell directed two major productions for Playgoers as well as a winning entry in the Lethbridge and District One Act Festival. She also appeared in two major productions and a one act festival entry. She quickly developed a reputation as one of the leading actors and directors in the city. Her charisma attracted a number of people to her, and when she decided to establish an alternate theatrical society, the Chinook Theatre Guild, a number of former Playgoers joined with her. The year 1957 was the most active one for the Chinook Theatre Guild. In April the Chinook Theatre Guild entered three plays in the Lethbridge and District One Act Festival and captured a number of individual awards. However, the adjudicator, Walter Kaasa, selected Playgoers' production of *From Paradise to Butte* as the winning play. It was then that Elsie Biddell lost much of the honor she had gained locally as she proceeded to berate the adjudicator publicly through "Letters to the Editor" in the *Lethbridge Herald* and the *Calgary Albertan*. Eventually, she publicly apologized; shortly thereafter, the Biddells left Lethbridge and the Chinook Theatre Guild disbanded.[43]

Black had recently moved to the city (from Victoria) with her husband, Brian, a radiologist, who had been appointed to the medical staff of St. Michael's Hospital.[44] Although Brian occasionally helped out backstage, it was Denise who became a stalwart with the Playgoers Club and who gave so much to the club over a period of about 20 years. Her talent for portraying very strong characters was immediately apparent. Dean Goodman, director of the Great Plays Company, recognized that talent and incorporated Black into a number of his professional summer productions. Her crowning glory came in 1960-61 when she portrayed the Dowager Empress in Playgoers' *Anastasia* and copped the award for Best Character Actress in the Alberta Regional Festival. Following this production, Black turned her talents more to directing, and during the 1960s she directed four major productions, one Little Theatre production (*Red Peppers*), and assisted in the direction of *Rebecca*. Black will be particularly remembered for her direction of the 1962 Alberta Regional Festival entry, *The Dark at the Top of the Stairs*, for which she was awarded Best Director by adjudicator David Gardner. The production also garnered five other awards including Best Play; it was selected to represent Alberta at the DDF in Winnipeg.

Technical direction and stage management for *Arsenic and Old Lace* were in the capable hands of Harry Baalim who had been associated with the club since the mid-1930s. It was during the 1950s, however, that Baalim became an indispensible member of the club through his overall contribution to all facets of the club's activities as well as to other community theatrical presentations. Baalim also sat on the executive of the Alberta Drama League, was selected as a Governor of the DDF in 1953, and presided over the Alberta Drama Festival Committee in 1953 and 1957, when the Alberta Regional festivals were held in Lethbridge.[45] Baalim's very active involvement in the Lethbridge Theatre scene came to an end in 1958.

Costume mistress for *Arsenic and Old Lace* was Joan Waterfield, who, since moving to Lethbridge from Scotland as a war bride, had been seeking to recapture some of the artistic culture she had left behind her. Waterfield's contributions to Lethbridge culture were so extensive over the following forty years that they cannot be easily summed up here. Therefore, additional reference will be made to her work, where appropriate, throughout the remainder of this book.

Less than one and one half months after the opening of *Arsenic and Old Lace*, Playgoers presented their 1952 Alberta Regional Festival entry, *Angel Street*, directed by the club's General Director, Maybelle Bryans. This production was the first festival entry of Playgoers since 1938, and also the first three act play to be entered in competition by the club. Featured in the cast were three long time members of the club, Harry Baalim, Lena Connor, and C.R. Matthews. Making their Playgoers debuts were Hugh Buchanan, Eric Hohm, Eleanor Matkin, and Yvonne Turner.[46] Turner (who had been active in the YMCA theatre groups) and Eric Hohm were married shortly thereafter, and moved to Spring Coulee where Eric was Superintendent of the St. Mary Dam and Irrigation project. Yvonne (Turner) Hohm became one of southern Alberta's most prominent speech teachers. Hohm's interest in speech was stimulated early in her life, and she had the good fortune in 1944 to receive instruction from Dr. Leona Patterson at Mount Royal College, Calgary. She later enrolled in the Drama program at the BSFA. Following her marriage and her move to Spring Coulee, Hohm maintained her dramatic interests by entertaining church and other groups with monologues. When her children were a little older, she resumed her speech training and became formally recognized as an Associate of the Royal Conservatory as well as of Mount Royal College; she also obtained a Licentiate in Speech and Drama from Trinity College, London. In addition to teaching and administrating speech programs at the Lethbridge Community College, she engaged in the adjudication of speech art festivals, public speaking, and debating. She also acted as a speech consultant to the Faculty of Education, University of Lethbridge, and functioned as a Lay Minister with the United Church of Canada.[47]

Although Hugh Buchanan never appeared on stage in another Playgoers' production, he was a very influential contributor to the club during the years 1950-1957 through his generous contribution to the executive and through his directing. His position as Managing Editor of the *Lethbridge Herald* gave him considerable autonomy and also provided the club with a certain degree of status. But in the late 1950s, when Buchanan took over the position as publisher of the family newspaper, he had to forego his dramatic interests. In mid-1959 he relinquished his position with the *Lethbridge Herald* and moved to California. He later joined the staff of the Hamilton (Ontario) *Spectator*. Hugh's brother, Donald Buchanan, was a staff member at the National Gallery of Canada who rose to the position of Associate Director.[48]

Following the successful run of *Angel Street*, Hugh Buchanan took on the responsibility of directing *Fumed Oak*, which was presented at an Evening of Little Theatre in cooperation with the Coaldale Players' *Eldorado* and the LDS Players' *Grandma Pulls the Strings*. By now, Playgoers felt sufficiently well established to host the 1953 Alberta Regional Festival to be housed in the relatively new LCI auditorium. Playgoers' entry, *Night Must Fall*, was directed by Hugh Buchanan.

Behind the scenes, Harry Knowles took over the responsibility of technical director and stage manager; he continued to provide this service to the club for a number of years, thereafter. In addition, Knowles performed in about five productions and was an important member of the executive. Two members of the cast received commendation by the Regional Festival adjudicator, John Allen. Mary Waters, who had previously appeared in *Fumed Oak*, was awarded the Best Character Actress trophy for her portrayal of Mrs. Terrence; Bill Fruet, Jr., as Danny, was singled out for special praise. At that time, Waters was a teacher of commercial subjects at the LCI, but her interest in drama was furthered by summer courses at the Banff School of Fine Arts. She also completed a Master's Degree in Drama at the University of Washington (Seattle), and therefore, became one of the few local thespians with considerable training in theatre arts. Later in her teaching career, she offered instruction in high school drama courses at the LCI. Waters was a very active member of Playgoers for about fifteen years, during which time she participated on the executive, she directed, she acted, and she worked backstage. As a member of the executive, she functioned as president for two seasons and also acted as business manager and member at large. Following her marriage to Jack Heinitz, a local businessman, she convinced him to sit on the executive in the capacity of treasurer. Her directing activities during the 1950s centered on Little Theatre presentations (both for Playgoers and for Southminster United Church Young Peoples). In 1954 her Playgoers' production, *Lonesome Like*, was selected to represent Lethbridge and District at the Alberta One Act Festival. In 1963 she turned her directing talents to a major production, *Dark of the Moon*, and in the following year, she organized and directed an extensive program designed to commemorate the fortieth anniversary of Playgoers. This program was made up of excerpts from former Playgoers' productions, including its initial show, *Going Up.* Original cast members were involved, wherever possible. Waters was a very fine actress, and in addition to the award which she received for her acting in *Night Must Fall*, she was accorded the Best Actress Award in 1954 for her portrayal of Mrs. Phelps in *The Silver Cord.* This award was followed by the announcement that Waters had been selected as the recipient of the Burton W. James Memorial Scholarship for study in dramatics at the Banff School of Fine Arts in the summer 1954.[49] Later (1955), she won a $75 scholarship to Banff based on her directing of *Lonesome Like.*[50] Other very memorable performances were Mrs. Danvers in the 1963 production of *Rebecca*, Lavinia in *The Heiress*, and Mrs. McCutcheon in *The Man Who Came to Dinner.* In backstage activities, Waters (Heinitz) brought her expertise to the position of make-up artist. In the mid-sixties, Heinitz resigned from her teaching position and basically retired from Playgoers. Some years later, she organized a drama group among the Lethbridge Senior Citizens which presented productions on a few occasions, including the 1982 Lethbridge and District One Act Festival.

Bill Fruet, Jr. received a scholarship to the BSFA (for the summer of 1953) for his acting in *Night Must Fall.* Also, Dean Goodman gave Fruet an opportunity to participate with his professional company when it first visited Lethbridge in the spring of 1953. Following the summer in Banff, Fruet, together with Bill Lazaruk (another cast member of *Night Must Fall*), left Lethbridge to attend Sterndale Bennett's Canadian Theatre School.[51] Sterndale Bennett, who had attended the Alberta Regional festival as a specially invited guest, issued a tuition bursary to the Playgoers Club and suggested that Fruet be the specific recipient. In 1961 Fruet was cast in the *Drylanders*, which starred Frances Hyland and Don Francks.[52] Later, Fruet became one of Canada's foremost playwrights, screen writers, and directors. Most Canadians probably remember him best because of his association with the Canadian films, *Going Down the Road* and *Wedding in White.* Fruet was honored with the Canadian Film Award for Best Screenplay of 1969, *Going Down the Road*, which also won the Etrog for the best Canadian made Feature Film of the year.[53] Just slightly more than two years later, the movie, *Wedding in White*, written by Fruet, was selected as the best picture in the 1972

Canadian Film Awards.[54] Fruet also wrote the screenplay for the movies *Rip-Off* and *Slip Stream*, the latter of which was filmed in and around Lethbridge.[55] Among his many other creative activities, Fruet directed a segment of the 1988 CBC production, *Chasing Rainbows*.

Following a term at the Canadian Theatre School, Lazaruk spent part of the summer of 1954 acting and working as a scenic artist with the Mountain Playhouse (in Montreal), whose producer was Norma Springford. Later that summer, he participated both on and backstage in the western comedy, *They Went Thataway*, produced by the Little Theatre Group of Toronto. Lazaruk then accepted a one year contract with the Crest Theatre in Toronto as an assistant stage manager,[56] after which employment with Peoples' Credit Jewellers brought Lazaruk back to Lethbridge where he became fully involved with all of Playgoers' activities until he was transferred to the jewellery company's Grande Prairie branch.

So by 1953 a significant core of Lethbridge executive, onstage, backstage, and production personnel had set a pattern for Playgoers to follow throughout the next few years. When the club was regenerated in 1951, its main purpose was to produce plays primarily for festival competition; therefore, its original mandate, which included the production of musical theatre, was narrowed considerably. With regard to the club's executive, a characteristic that developed following the reorganization of the club was the tendency for a greater number of the executive to be selected from members who were also active in production activities; nevertheless, treasurers such as Jack Heinitz and Bill Baird participated almost exclusively in executive capacities. The necessity to conscript competent treasurers with accounting or business experience was recognized by the club because it constantly operated on a very limited budget. In fact, during most of the 1950s, the club ran a deficit of about $300. This deficit was incurred when the club borrowed $400 from the bank in order to send the production of *Angel Street* to the Alberta Regional Festival in Edmonton in 1952. Three years later, president Mary Waters reported that, even though the club had paid back some of the principal, the club still owed $300 because of accumulated interest. Certain members of the 1954 executive felt that the small profit of $200 generated that year should be used to pay off the debt, but the majority agreed that the sum should be used to support the club's forthcoming festival entry, *The Silver Cord*. Therefore, even though the director as well as some cast and crew members of *Angel Street* returned their expense money, and three of them took out life time memberships for twenty-five dollars (annual dues were $1 at that time), the debt continued.[57] Subsequent executives wished to eradicate the debt, so "belt tightening" and money raising schemes were introduced. The club declined entering the 1955 and 1956 festivals, and, in fact, never again appeared in a Regional Festival in Edmonton.

Hoping to raise additional funds, the club sponsored the appearance of Eric Christmas in his one man show, *Christmas Party*, on November 28, 1955. Christmas, an honor graduate of the Royal Academy of Dramatic Arts in London, England, had come to Canada around 1947 and had become a popular actor on numerous CBC productions. He captured the attention of large numbers of Canadian radio and T.V. patrons with the character of Madame Hooperdinck, whom he had created for the Wayne and Shuster Show. Unfortunately, Playgoers sold only 175 tickets (at $1 per adult; $0.50 per child) to the performance.[58]

Slightly more than a year later, the club was more successful in raising funds by sponsoring the local appearance of the Medicine Hat Civic Theatre's Regional Festival winner, *Stalag 17*. By the annual meeting of 1956, Playgoers had liquidated its debt.[59] Nevertheless, the club operated under considerable financial restraint throughout the entire era under discussion. Following fairly active seasons in 1953 and 1954, the club did not prepare any new productions in 1955, and only three major plays were presented by Playgoers during the last five years of the 1950s [*Harvey* (1956),

The Heiress (1957), and *White Sheep of the Family* (1958)]. On the other hand, a fair amount of effort was expended on mounting one act plays, many of which were entered in festival competition. However, the production of one act plays practically ceased after the evening of one act plays presented on November 28, 29, 1960. The production pattern throughout the first half of the 1960s was for the club to prepare two major presentations, one of which was the annual festival entry. Of course, this pattern was disrupted after 1967 when the Alberta Drama League disbanded and regional competition for the DDF was placed in jeopardy. Generally, the latter half of the 1960s saw the presentation of one production only, per year. It is true, however, that beginning in 1964, most of the Playgoers' members also participated in the musicals and plays produced by Lethbridge Musical Theatre. Now that the general developments of the Playgoers Club during the period 1951-1970 have been outlined, some of the more specific aspects of its activities will be reviewed.

Production Personnel

a) Directors

During this twenty year period, no fewer than fourteen directors handled the task for twenty-five major productions, whereas about sixteen directors supervised twenty-seven one act plays. Of course, there was considerable overlapping of directorial duties from major productions to one act productions as can be seen from Table 5-2.

The work of the most prolific directors listed in Table 5-2 has been discussed elsewhere in this chapter; therefore the following analysis will concentrate on the directorial contributions of Phil Ellerbeck and Daphne Manson, only. Ellerbeck and Manson, who had joined the club in the mid-1950s after moving to Lethbridge from Winnipeg and Edmonton, respectively, had previous theatre experience: Ellerbeck with the Winnipeg Little Theatre and Manson with The Studio Theatre, University of Alberta.[60] Manson was also incorporated into the casts of *Laura* and *Personal Appearance* for the Great Plays Company in the summer of 1954. For Playgoers, Manson directed two major festival entries, *The Heiress* (1957) and *Anastasia* (1961); whereas, Ellerbeck directed two three act comedies, *The Curious Savage* (1960) and *Blithe Spirit* (1961), which were non-festival productions. Ellerbeck was also a tireless worker behind the scenes through her involvement primarily with wardrobe, props, and stage management.

b) Set Designers

Fortunately, some of the city's best visual artists shared their talent with the Playgoers Club: Mike Pisko, Cathy Evins, and Cornelius (Corne) Martens. In his youth, Pisko enrolled in spring art classes sponsored by the local sketch club in association with the Extension Department, University of Alberta, and taught by Mr. G.H. Glyde. Through his achievement in this course, Pisko was awarded a tuition scholarship to the BSFA. He then became a stalwart member of the Lethbridge Sketch Club where he served on the executive in a number of capacities and also instructed classes for the club. As a commercial artist, he developed a very successful local art business, City Sign Company.[61] In 1953 he contributed his artistic talents to the design and painting of the set for *Night Must Fall*.

Evins, who received her early training in England, practically took up residence in the local theatre. Settling in Lethbridge in the early 1960s, she associated herself with the Lethbridge Sketch Club and the Allied Arts Council; both organizations employed her as an instructor for their various art courses and workshops.[62] Evins became active in the Lethbridge theatre scene in 1966 when she volunteered to design the sets for *Teahouse of the August Moon*. Later that year, she joined the painting crew for Lethbridge Musical Theatre's production of *South Pacific*. Costume designing was added in 1967 when Evins took on this task for LMT's *Show Boat*. In 1968 she designed her

TABLE 5-2

Directors: Playgoers' Productions* (1951-1970)

DIRECTOR	M	O	TOTAL	DIRECTOR	M	O	TOTAL	DIRECTOR	M	O	TOTAL
Harry Baalim	-	2	2	Phyl Ellerbeck	2	2	4	Wayne Matkin	2	-	2
Elsie Biddell	2	1	3	Ron Hartmann	1	-	1	Dick Mells	2	-	2
Cliff Black	1	-	1	Cam Hay	-	1	1	Lee Mells	1	-	1
Denise Black	4	3	7	Connie Ingoldsby	-	1	1	Joan Perkinson	-	1	1
Maybell Bryans	1	-	1	Ron Johnson	-	1	1	Babs Pitt	-	1	1
Hugh Buchanan	3	1	4	G.H. Knowles	-	1	1	Sam Pitt	1	-	1
Bruce Busby	-	1	1	Bill Lazaruk	-	2	2	Mary Waters (Heinitz)	2	4	6
Agnes Davidson	-	1	1	Phyllis Lilly	1	-	1	Kaye Watson	-	1	1
Jean Ede	-	2	2	Daphne Manson	2	1	3	**TOTAL**	25	27	52

*M = major productions; O = one act productions

first major set for Playgoers (*The Madwoman of Chaillot*). Following this, she designed numerous sets for Playgoers and Lethbridge Musical Theatre and contributed in immeasurable ways to both organizations.

Martens, a district artist, who also designed sets for Coaldale Little Theatre and Lethbridge Musical Theatre, designed the Regional Festival award winning set for *Gently Does It* (1960). Martens had an extraordinarily interesting artistic career. He was born in the Ukraine of Dutch Mennonite parents. The family emigrated to Saskatchewan when Corne was still a boy; subsequently, they settled in Coaldale, Alberta. Although Martens had no formal training in art, his natural talent enabled him to obtain a position as design and promotion director with the Lethbridge television station, CJLH-TV.[63] Although his early artistic interest focussed on sketching, he progressed to clay sculpture in the mid-1960s, and then, developed the skill for which he is best known – bronze casting. As his bronze castings became internationally recognized, Martens was able to participate in this activity full time. He was commissioned to cast some of the medals for the 1988 Winter Olympics held in Calgary.

Many other individuals, including David Thomson, designed sets for Playgoers. Thomson's setting for *Therese* (1964) was awarded the Best Visual Presentation at the Alberta Regional Festival. Thompson also designed the *Oklahoma!* set for Lethbridge Musical Theatre.

c) Technical Personnel

In many amateur productions, technical roles are not very clearly defined. When members of Playgoers took on the task of technical director in the 1950s and 1960s, it usually meant organizing and supervising set construction. Frequently, the role of technical director also involved set design, set building, set painting, stage management, and numerous other backstage chores. Norville Getty achieved a unique honor among his peers in the Lethbridge Playgoers; he received the only Regional Festival award given to Playgoers for Best Stage Management (for the 1962 production of *Dark at the Top of the Stairs*). Also that year, he and his assistants, Bill Ede, Jack Rallison, Frank Bennett and Kaz Ayukawa (lights) garnered the award for Best Visual Presentation.

TABLE 5-3

Playgoers of Lethbridge: Technical Directors*
Stage & Assistant Stage Managers (1951-1970)

Kaz Ayukawa	Howard Ellison	Kay Haworth	Corne Martens
Harry Baalim*	Hazel Evans (Skaronski)	Bill Hay	Percy Morris*
Ed Bayly*	Norville Getty*	Ray Jolliffe	Joy Pritchard
Cecil Biddell*	Frank Gostola	Harry Knowles*	Doryanne Robertson
Phyl Ellerbeck	Al Greenway	Bill Lazaruk*	Margaret Willis

Generally speaking, the technical aspects of lighting tended to attract people to the theatre who had special or unique talents or interests, and who specialized in the task. As technical director of the Yates, (as of March 1966) Ed Bayly quickly honed his skill as lighting designer and operator; his considerable artistic talent facilitated this process. Other members who developed a particularly keen interest in lighting included Bruce McKenzie, Bob Johnson, W. Royer, Al Candy, and Bob Reed. MacKenzie, an employee with Alberta Government Telephones, worked on the occasional Playgoers' production, but carved out a specific niche for himself as lighting specialist for Our Town Workshop. Royer, together with Hector Frey, had been involved in lighting shows for various local groups such as Playgoers and the YMCA since the mid-1930s; their involvement abated during the 1950s. An early interest in lighting and special effects was shown by Bob Reed who became intrigued by the theatre, in general, when he was exposed to productions at the Majestic Theatre in the 1920s. Trained as a radio technician in his youth, his avocational interests in theatrical lighting began in 1932 when he lit up the stage for a production by the First United Church.[64] His interest quickly blossomed, and before long, he was called upon to design and work lights and provide special effects for all kinds of community and district organizations (schools, churches, YMCA) and activities [plays, musicals, dance revues, ice shows (in Calgary as well), and sportsmen's dinners]. Reed purchased and maintained his own equipment, and he became a local specialist in the art of black light affects. Following the war, he interested Al Candy, a local junior high school teacher, in joining him in his lighting ventures. For many years, thereafter, groups like Playgoers could count on Reed and Candy to design, provide, set, and operate lights both cheerfully and free of charge.

Sound is a technical area that tends to be neglected by amateur theatre groups to a large extent, and therefore, they do not always appreciate what contribution an appropriate sound program can make to a production. Few amateurs make a career of sound; each production tends to be served by a willing worker who, nevertheless, has had very little experience in designing and offering a complete sound package. An exception to this in Lethbridge was Doug Card who was a professional radio and T.V. sound technician. In addition, Garry Kohn had an avid interest in sound, as was manifest in the various musical ensembles with which he worked and the stereo and T.V. outlet which he later opened. Other contributors to the task of producing sound are listed in Table 5-4.

d) Costume Personnel

When the club was reorganized, all of the costumes had to be made from "scratch," but the wardrobe soon began to grow and had to be stored wherever the club could find room. Eventually, a room was made available to them in the Bowman Arts Centre. The Bowman Arts Centre was established in the former Bowman School in January 1965; its operation was turned over to the

TABLE 5-4

Playgoers of Lethbridge:
Sound Personnel (1951-1970)

Linda Bayly	Muriel Jolliffe	Tony Pydee
Doug Card	Garry Kohn	Joe Shannon
Wendy Carson	Brian Manson	Kaye Watson (Robison)
Sharon Gostola	Wayne Matkin	
Marvin Haynes	George Nuttall	

Lethbridge Allied Arts Council. Classrooms were rented to various arts and craft groups such as the Lethbridge Sketch Club, Playgoers, Jolliffe Academy of Dancing.[65] Later, a good storage space was reserved for Playgoers in the Yates Memorial Centre because the original Yates bequest made special reference to the needs of Playgoers.

In the 1950s and 1960s, costuming was definitely considered "women's work" among local amateurs, so assistance from Bill Ede and Peter Hornsby was exceptional (see Table 5-5). Although most of the costumers were also enthusiastic actors, Winona Anderson and Fran Bayly tended to concentrate on backstage activities. Besides costuming, Anderson spent many hours creating, building, and handling properties and set pieces. Bayly, her husband, Ern, and son, Ed, moved to Lethbridge from England in 1952. Shortly thereafter, the entire family became deeply involved with the Our Town Workshop. Later, Fran Bayly became costume mistress for Playgoers and for Lethbridge Musical Theatre.

Waterfield, Watson (Robison), Ellerbeck, and Evans (Skaronski) were multi-talented members and total participants in all aspects of theatre. Evans, a professional home economics teacher, brought the greatest formal expertise to the task of costuming. Watson took the task so seriously that she later entered the business of costume rentals. Because of the club's fragile financial situation, such a luxury as renting costumes was inappropriate, but most of the wardrobe mistresses were ingenious and developed excellent scrounging abilities and skills at creating a "silk purse"; therefore, costume budgets were usually kept relatively low (yet costumes were often praised by festival adjudicators).

TABLE 5-5

Playgoers of Lethbridge:
Wardrobe Personnel (1951-1970)

Winona Anderson*	Phyl Ellerbeck*	Doreen Morita
Fran Bayly*	Hazel Evans (Skaronski)*	Betty Old
Denise Black	Sharon Gostola	Fay Olsen
Bill Ede	Peter Hornsby	Joan Waterfield*
Jean Ede	Connie Ingoldsby	Kaye Watson (Robison)*
*most active		

e) Props Personnel

 Property management was another female dominated activity of Playgoers, and with the odd exception, the work was usually performed by members who enjoyed being associated with drama organizations but did not necessarily want to appear on stage. Consequently, most of the participants listed in Table 5-6 either did not appear on stage for Playgoers or performed in only one or two productions. Exceptions to this generalization are noted. Many of the props personnel also contributed to other technical tasks.

 Doris Balcovske (nee Gibson) could usually be called upon to do all of those kinds of tasks which have to be done but for which there is very little, if any, glory. But then, Balcovske was raised in a family where volunteer service to the community and to its organizations was an accepted way of life. As a Playgoer, she participated in the executive, she performed many tasks backstage, she maintained the scrapbooks for many years, and she appeared onstage, occasionally. She even agreed to perform as Sergeant Presson's trusty dog, Rex, in Ed Bayly's melodrama, *Priscilla Pringle's Predicament.* Representative of Balcovske's local volunteer activity was her work with the Lethbridge Allied Arts Council, and many years later, with Centre Stage Productions as a director on the Board. Both Doris Balcovske and her father, Chris Gibson, sat on the original Allied Arts Council as representatives. Within the next few years, Balcovske performed every major role on the executive including president (1962-63). In November 1968 she was awarded a life membership by the Council, as was her father, who, because of ill health at that time, was forced to retire from the Council and from his executive position as treasurer.[66] It seems appropriate to digress here in order to discuss the theatrical contributions of Chris Gibson and of Balcovske's daughter, Sandra.

TABLE 5-6

Playgoers of Lethbridge:
Properties Personnel (1951-1970)

Joan Abbott	Doris Colpitts**	Joy Meek
Winona Anderson	Lena Connor*	Martha Rae
Jessie Baalim	Jean Ede*	Jan Redfern
Truus Baird	Phyl Ellerbeck*	Mette Vaselenak
Doris Balcovske	Hazel Evans (Skaronski)*	Joan Waterfield*
Frank Bennett*	Kay Haworth	Kaye Watson (Robison)*
Chris Burgess	Lois Head	Leslee Watson (Nuttall)
		Judy White

*active onstage participants
**very active contributor to Our Town Workshop

 Chris Gibson, who retired from his post as Inspector for the Lethbridge office of the Weights and Measures Department in 1948, made a substantial contribution to Playgoers as well as to various other community organizations. Actually, his local dramatic activities preceded the establishment of Playgoers by many years, since he had been in the chorus of the nautical musical comedy, *Billee Taylor*, in 1911 and 1912. Gibson was also in the cast of Playgoers' initial production, *Going Up* (1923). From then through the 1950s, Gibson was a loyal member and active participant in all aspects of the club's organization, including president (1954-55). In addition to being named an honorary lifetime member of both Playgoers (1964) and the Allied Arts Council, Gibson received numerous other awards for lengthy and valuable community service as did his wife, Linda.[67]

A third generation of the Gibson family, Sandi Balcovske, provided the Playgoers Club considerable mirth and merriment when she participated in the club's activities for a short while in the mid-1970s. Her term as social and program convener (1974-75) is particularly memorable because she organized many unique activities for the non-business part of the club's regular meetings. Unfortunately for local theatre, but luckily for a number of Canadian alternate theatres, Sandi moved on to devote her theatrical talents to Catalyst Theatre and Second City in Edmonton and later, to the Second City organization in Toronto where her direction of plays at the Old Firehall theatre on Lombard Street was particularly notable.[68]

f) Make Up Artists

Generally speaking, members of Playgoers' productions were encouraged to do their own makeup. However, since novice members required advice and help, makeup specialists were assigned to give this help and to plan and apply special makeup effects such as beards, hair stylings, and aging. Most of the Playgoers' makeup personnel during this period were seasoned performers such as Albina Barry, Helen (James) Bennett, Elsie Biddell, C.R. Matthews, Lee Mells, Babs Pitt, and Mary Waters. In addition, the club often called upon the expertise of professional hair stylists such as Freda Walton.

Onstage Participants

TABLE 5-7

Playgoers of Lethbridge:
Onstage Participants (1951-1970)

I. Three Roles	Harry Baalim Ed Bayly Bob Befus Cecil Biddell Elsie Biddell	Syd Clarke Brenda Cordwell Bill Ede Phyl Ellerbeck Connie Ingoldsby	Leo Lancaster Phyllis Lilly Jack Maynard Joe Shannon Jack Warburton
II. Four Roles	Jean Block Bruce Busby Paul Ciesla Ella Findlay Jack Gibson	Frank Gostola Al Greenway Peter Hornsby Bill Lazaruk Lee Mells	Stan Sawicki Ted Scheurkogel Anita Susman
III. Five Roles	Frank Bennett Sharon Bolen (Magee)	Harry Knowles	Hazel Evans (Skaronski)
IV. Six or Seven Roles	George Mann (6) Sandy McCallum (6)	Bill Matheson (7)	Mary (Waters) Heinitz (7)
V. Eight or Nine Roles	Cliff Black (8) Daphne Manson (8)	Joan Perkinson (9) C.R. Matthews (9)	Joan Waterfield (9)
VI. Ten or More Roles	Helen James (Bennett) (10) Kaye Watson (Robison) (11)	Colin Turner (11) Jean Ede (12)	Denise Black (13)

Approximately two hundred different people were involved in the fifty-two productions mounted by Playgoers in the period 1951-1970, inclusive. Of these, one hundred and fifty acted in one or two productions, only. Like previous periods discussed earlier in this book, the majority of the multiple roles were filled by a group of about 45-50 core members. The onstage participation of members taking three or more roles is illustrated in Table 5-7.

Although Denise Black was the most prolific actor during this era, her involvement with Playgoers has already been discussed; therefore, this analysis will begin with the performances of Jean Ede (nee Peachy), a Lethbridge native who, after graduating from the University of Alberta in Education, married Bill Ede, a fellow teacher. Jean Ede was a tall, strikingly beautiful woman who could play comedy and drama equally well. She frequently played very strong minded individuals; yet, she was equally capable of portraying warm and sympathetic characters. Illustrative of the variety of roles she portrayed are Myrtle Mae Simmons in *Harvey*; Mrs. Bradman in *Blithe Spirit*; Sister Joanna in *The Cradle Song*; Varya in *Anastasia*; and Karen Wright in *The Children's Hour*. Adjudicator, David Gardner awarded Ede the Best Actress trophy for her portrayal of Cora Flood in *Dark at the Top of the Stairs*; in addition, adjudicator, Herbert Whittaker selected Ede for Best Character Actress for Madame Raquin in *Therese* (1964).[69] Ede was truly a consummate performer; her move from Lethbridge in the late 1960s left an extraordinarily large void in Playgoers' human resources.

Kaye Watson (nee O'Mara) was born in Seattle, Washington, and was raised in Medicine Hat; she later moved to Fort Macleod, and then, to Lethbridge where she and her husband, Fred, settled. Unfortunately, Kaye was widowed within a few years; therefore, she went to work with Roy Electric in order to support herself and her two children. Many years later (on October 5, 1966), she married Murray Robison. Watson joined Playgoers in the mid-1950s and quickly became one of its most valuable members. Watson was a tireless worker with tremendous energy and enthusiasm. She functioned well in almost every capacity of the club's executive, backstage, and onstage activities. As mentioned earlier, she was an extremely creative costumer. Onstage, she exuded a wealth of talent; she is probably best remembered for her broad comedic parts such as Madam Arcati in *Blithe Spirit*, but she was equally capable of portraying a stately lady. Watson (Robison) brought much pleasure and many laughs to Lethbridge audiences; her work on the stage was always appreciated and her talent was formally recognized by adjudicator Robert Gill who awarded her Best Supporting Actress for her portrayal of Emmy (the housekeeper) in Playgoers' 1960 Alberta Regional Festival presentation of *Gently Does It*.[70] She also received accolades for various portrayals in numerous one act festivals.

Helen James (Bennett) was born in Taber, Alberta, but she received her high school education in Lethbridge. After receiving her teacher's certificate, James taught in rural schools for a while, and then in 1929 took a position with the Lethbridge school district.[71] Just a few years prior to her retirement in 1969, James married a former city fireman, Frank Bennett, who also acted in a few Playgoers' productions and was very helpful backstage. Although James was primarily a mathematics teacher, she took on the responsibility of teaching the Grade 10 drama option at the LCI in 1959. Fortunately, James had considerable experience in drama, and was, herself, a fine character actress. She had, in fact, been a member of Playgoers in the 1930s and then rejoined the club around 1954 as a member of the cast of *The Man Who Came to Dinner*. During the 1957-58 season, she took on the responsibilities of Vice President. For a number of succeeding years, James graced the Lethbridge stage with her portrayal of strong female characters. The excellence of her acting was formally recognized by adjudicator David Gardner in 1962 when he awarded James, Best Character Actress, for her portrayal of Lottie Lacey in *The Dark at the Top of the Stairs*. When she retired from active participation following her portrayal of Mrs. Hedges in *Born Yesterday* (1965), the club lost another very valuable member.

After joining Playgoers in 1951, Joan Waterfield spent almost ten years behind the scenes contributing to all facets of the club's backstage needs. Her reputation as a responsible and knowledgeable theatre person was recognized quickly, and in the spring of 1955, she was asked to act as one of the adjudicators for the Lethbridge and District One Act Festival.[72] In 1957 her costumes for *The Heiress* received praise from adjudicator, Cecil Bellamy.[73] During the next year, she assumed the position of business manager for the Allied Arts Council – a position which she maintained until her retirement in early 1988.[74] In 1960 Waterfield made her local stage debut as Freda Jeffries in *Gently Does It*. Again, she was an instant success and garnered the Best Character Actress Award as determined by adjudicator, Robert Gill.[75] Two additional Alberta Regional Festival awards (as Best Actress) confirmed the fact that Waterfield was undoubtedly one of the finest actresses in the Province of Alberta. In fact, she was the only actress to capture the Best Actress Award on two or more occasions; the first of which was presented to her in 1965 for her role of Argia, the prostitute, in *The Queen and the Rebels* produced by Our Town Workshop; the second was for Mrs. Malabone in the Playgoers' production of *Chinook* (1967). Interestingly enough, she previously had been awarded the Best Actress Award for Mrs. Malabone in the original one act version of *Chinook*, presented by Our Town Workshop in the 1963 Lethbridge and District One Act Festival.[76] Because of her extraordinary talent, Waterfield was cast for a role in at least one major Playgoers' production per year in the 1960s (except in 1965). Vital, elegant, and endowed with a beautifully cultured voice, Waterfield was ideally suited for distinguished roles such as the Vicaress in *Cradle Song* or Amelia Tilford in *The Children's Hour*. With regard to her performance in *The Cradle Song*, the *Lethbridge Herald* reviewer said:[77]

> Star of the play for my money was the superbly polished actress, Joan Waterfield, whose every word, mannerism and movement was a delight. Her final speech . . . was a masterpiece of restraint. . . . It was not only her social inflexions that won praise, but the utter concentration which she gave to the role.

Waterfield's commitment to the total needs of local theatre was exemplified by her readiness to accept roles as needed, for example, the Charwoman in *Anastasia* and Madame Louise in *Therese*, both of which are rather small supporting parts. In addition, Waterfield's ability to tackle successfully a great variety of roles is exemplified by her excellent portrayals of the decidedly unattractive Mrs. Malabone (*Chinook*) and the sharp tongued Lily Peppers in *Red Peppers* (1960). The breadth of her stage talent is further illustrated by the resounding success which she (and George Mann) achieved in presenting the musical sketch, "Mad Dogs and Englishman," as Playgoers' presentation in the Lethbridge Symphony's production of *Southern Showcase* (1964). By the end of the 1960s, Waterfield had shown that she could easily handle almost every aspect of the thespian's trade, except directing. Although she had assisted Daphne Manson with the direction of *Anastasia* (1961), she actually did not take full rein of a production until after 1970. Then, however, she took up the challenge of directing most sincerely, and by doing so, she proved her total commitment to the following belief which she espoused consistently: "It's not sufficient to just act - my idea of amateur theatre is doing everything."[78]

Joan Perkinson, another (English) war bride, made her Playgoers' debut in the 1954 production of the one acter, *The Stepmother*. For about ten years, Perkinson contributed greatly to the success of the club through her fine acting; she also directed the one act play *The Monkey's Paw* in 1958. Tall, slim, and seductively attractive, Perkinson, like Phyl Ellerbeck, was the perfect "other woman." She is probably best remembered for Nurse Kelly in *Harvey*, Catherine Sloper in *The Heiress*,

Charlotte Young in *Gently Does It*, and Beatrice Lacy in *Rebecca*, for which she was awarded Best Supporting Actress by adjudicator, Esse Ljungh.[79]

Joan Waterfield and George Mann – "Mad Dogs and Englishmen"
from Southern Showcase *produced by Lethbridge Symphony Association, 1964*
Photo: *Lethbridge Herald*

Sharon (Bolen) Magee was the ideal engenue such as Mrs. DeWinter in *Rebecca* and Suzanne in *Therese* (1963). For the latter role, she received the Best Supporting Actress Award from Herbert Whittaker. But her greatest triumph probably came in 1962 when she was in contention for a $2 000 scholarship to the National Theatre School. This possibility developed out of her portrayal of the ten year old boy, Sonny Flood, in Playgoers' DDF entry, *Dark at the Top of the Stairs*, for which Bolen received Honorable Mention at both the regional and final festivals. Honorable Mention at the DDF was accompanied by a $300 scholarship to the Banff School of Fine Arts and a nomination for the National Theatre School Award. In order to be judged for this latter award, Bolen and four other young Canadian actresses were required to complete a film test which, in Bolen's case, was made possible through the auspices of CFCN-T.V., Calgary. Helen Bennett appeared with Bolen in a scene from *The Heiress*, and also assisted Bolen in preparing two improvisations and a scene from *Romeo and Juliet*. In September 1962 Bolen received word that she had been selected as one of the two finalists; in October, she was informed that the award was to be given to Eva Marie of Trois Rivieres, Quebec.[80]

Hazel (Evans) Skaronski's contribution to backstage work for Playgoers has already been discussed; however, her onstage participation is also rather remarkable. Evans moved to Lethbridge from England in the mid-1950s, and in 1959 she took a position with the local school district as a

Home Economics teacher specializing in Fabrics and Dress. After a few years, she retired from teaching; later, she took up a position as Assistant Director of the Bowman Arts Centre for the Allied Arts Council. Because Evans had been actively involved in theatre in her native England, she was encouraged by her housemate, Kaye Watson, to join Playgoers. She immediately became involved backstage, and in the fall of 1959, she made her local debut as Mrs. Paddy in *The Curious Savage.* She was a scream. Playgoers could now count on another great character actress and comedienne. Skaronski brought these talents to other roles such as Edith in *Blithe Spirit*, Agatha (the maid) in *The Children's Hour,* and Old Ropeen in *The Hostage.* Her superlative characterizations achieved recognition in various festivals. At the Alberta Regional Festival in 1970, her portrayal of Old Ropeen was accorded Best Character Actress.[81] In the succeeding Dominion Drama Festival, this portrayal was mentioned as runner up for the Best Supporting Actress Award.[82]

Males who made a significant contribution to the acting component of Playgoers' productions were not as evident as the female members. The contributions of Harry Knowles and Frank Bennett have been discussed previously, so the following discussion will concentrate on the actors who performed six or more roles. Colin Turner was raised in Lethbridge and participated in dramatic activities at the LCI. He completed his teacher education at the University of Alberta, specializing in Social Studies and French. He returned to Lethbridge and carved out a lifetime career of junior and senior high school teaching. His first role for Playgoers was Bert Jefferson in the 1954 production of *The Man Who Came to Dinner.* Of this performance, the *Lethbridge Herald* critic stated, "Colin Turner was admirable, clean cut and straight forward as a young newspaper reporter and turned up in the last act with one of the show's best comedy sequences."[83] Henceforth, Turner was a fairly consistent performer for the club through 1968, at which time he basically retired from the local theatre scene. He did, however, return to Playgoers in 1974 when he gave a brilliant portrayal of the role of Dr. Einstein in the club's revival of *Arsenic and Old Lace.*

The Man Who Came to Dinner also introduced Cliff Black to the Lethbridge stage although he had joined the executive the preceding year. Black also appeared in the 1956 production of *Harvey,* but it was not until the 1960s that he became a major force, both onstage and behind the scenes, for the club. From 1962 until 1968, inclusive, Black appeared in almost all of the club's major productions. Black was a forceful character actor whose portrayal of the lead character, Harry Brock, in *Born Yesterday* was superb. In addition, he directed the festival entry, *Rebecca,* in 1963 and acted as Technical Director for the following year's production of *Therese,* in which he portrayed the Inspector. During the period from November 1963 until January 1972, he presided over the club's activities for three consecutive terms and he took the position of Vice President for more than two years. As a popular city alderman and member of a number of significant commissions, Black brought considerable status to the Playgoers Club.

Throughout the history of Playgoers (1923-1990), no member other than Ed Bayly, approached the extent of C.R. Matthews's onstage performances for the club. Like the other elder statesmen and honorary lifetime members of the club (Gibson, Connor, Bryans), Matthews was looked to for wise council and early leadership in the period of reorganization and for many years, thereafter. Matthews participated in most of the executive committees; as well, he took the chair, again, in 1957 and 1958. He fulfilled his final official post with the club during the 1960-61 season when he held the position of treasurer. The Alberta Drama League also sought his expertise, so they elected him treasurer of the League in 1952 – a position which he retained until 1957, at which time he was succeeded by Murray Robison. Matthews's outstanding contribution to Playgoers, to the Alberta Drama League, and to the development of theatre, in general, was recognized by the awarding of the CDA in 1952-53. Although Matthews gradually weaned himself away from executive responsibilities, he continued his association with the club as make-up assistant and actor until officially retiring in the spring of 1965 (after his portrayal of the hotel manager in *Born Yesterday*). Matthews died the following January at the age of eighty-one, just three days after Lethbridge residents were also shocked to hear of the death of Geoffrey Waddington.[84] The memory of C.R. Matthews's contribution to amateur theatre was maintained through the annual presentation of the Matthews Trophy for best director in the Alberta Drama League One-Act Festival.[85]

A Lethbridge product, Bill Matheson, was undoubtedly one of the greatest talents to tread the Lethbridge boards. Matheson was an extremely articulate man whose World War II army training in meteorology opened up opportunities in the Lethbridge broadcast media as the local weatherman. In addition, Matheson was a reporter (for the *Lethbridge Herald*) who specialized in the city hall beat. Matheson's literary ability led to his writing the one act play, *Chinook*, which was based on the ancient legend of Aphrodite, and whose plot revolved around the southern Alberta chinook winds. The play was produced for stage and television by the Our Town Workshop.[86] In 1967 an expanded three act version of *Chinook* was produced by Playgoers, and garnered for Matheson, the centennial Alberta Regional Festival Award for Best Canadian play.[87] It should be remembered that all plays presented in the 1967 festival had to be penned by Canadians. Matheson's acting talent was so exceptional that he was sought out by all local groups; during the period 1957-1970, Matheson appeared in seven productions for Playgoers, three for Coaldale Little Theatre, four for Our Town Workshop, three for Lethbridge Musical Theatre, and a number of other local shows for various community organizations. His popularity and overall knowledgeability led to his being named the first moderator for a local radio phone-in show.

Matheson's debut performances for Playgoers were prophetic. In the 1957 Lethbridge and District One Act Festival, Matheson appeared in two productions for Playgoers, *Hello Out There* and *From Paradise to Butte*, both directed by Harry Baalim. The latter production was selected to represent the Lethbridge and district zone at the Alberta One Act Festival. At both festivals, Matheson was honored with the Best Actor Award.[88] In addition, both of the above mentioned plays were invited to participate in the official opening of the Southern Alberta Jubilee Auditorium.[89] Speaking of festival awards, it should be mentioned here that Matheson won three awards at the Alberta Region Three Act festivals: Best Actor for Amos, the Commissar, in *The Queen and the Rebels* (Our Town Workshop, 1965); Best Character Actor for Davies in *The Caretaker* (Our Town Workshop, 1966); and Best Character Actor for Monsewer, the owner of the house, in The *Hostage* (Playgoers of Lethbridge, 1970).

Another Lethbridge weatherman and extraordinarily talented actor was Sandy McCallum who won more three act festival acting awards than any other participant in Alberta festivals [Best Supporting Actor in *All Summer Long* (Coaldale Little Theatre, 1958) and *The Beautiful People* (Coaldale Little Theatre, 1961); and Best Actor for roles in *Gently Does It* (Playgoers of Lethbridge, 1960) and *The Well of the Saints* (Coaldale Little Theatre, 1963)]. For the latter production, his portrayal of Martin Dhoul was selected as runner up for the Best Actor Award at the DDF finals in Kitchener, Ontario.[90] Adjudicator Pierre Lefevre praised McCallum's portrayal as follows: "In the case of Mr. McCallum when the script called him a shabby little man, he seemed to become a shabby little man. This was the real magic of acting. . . . Here was really fine acting."[91]

McCallum was born and raised in Hanley, Saskatchewan. Employment as a meteorologist took him to Watson Lake, Yukon, where he worked for about seven years. In 1954 he moved to Lethbridge where he assumed a position of copy editor and announcer with radio station CJOC. When Lethbridge's first T.V. station, CJLH-T.V., came on air in October 1955, McCallum joined the staff as weatherman. In 1957 he resigned this position in order to take up a life insurance career;

he nevertheless continued to work in radio and T.V. for various community projects.[92] McCallum began his local amateur theatrical career with Playgoers of Lethbridge when he took the part of William R. Chumley, M.D., in *Harvey* (1956). During 1956 and 1957 McCallum appeared in four Playgoers' productions: *Harvey, Bathsheba of Saaremaa, Hello Out There*, and *From Paradise to Butte*. By this time, McCallum's acting potential was recognized by Murray Robison, Director of the Coaldale Little Theatre, who asked him to join the cast of *All Summer Long*. Although McCallum appeared twice more for Playgoers [in a variety musical sketch, *With Her Head Tucked Underneath Her Arm* (1959) and in *Gently Does It* (1960)], most of his acting in Lethbridge from 1958-1964 was with the Coaldale Little Theatre. He also appeared in two, one act productions with Our Town Workshop, for whom he directed the 1963 production of *Romanoff and Juliet*, which was presented shortly after he had been named a governor of the DDF.[93] During the summer of 1963, McCallum attended an Alberta Summer Theatre Workshop under the direction of Tyrone Guthrie. Guthrie was so impressed with McCallum that he invited him to join his professional company in Minneapolis. McCallum took up the challenge in February 1964, and consequently, he became a professional actor like his younger brother, Neil.[94] Neil is probably better known in Canada because of his movie and television work as well as numerous Canadian stage appearances; nevertheless, Sandy McCallum has had an extraordinarily successful stage career in the U.S.A. He remained with the Guthrie Theatre for a number of years; his characterization of Firs in the Guthrie production of Chekov's *The Cherry Orchard* starring Jessica Tandy and the Minnesota Theatre Company is recorded for posterity on the Theatre Recording Society's album of the complete production.[95] After leaving the Guthrie Theatre, McCallum appeared on numerous stages throughout the U.S.A., but in the 1970s he became associated primarily with the Globe Theatre in San Diego and with the College of the Pacific Northwest in Santa Maria, California. In the late 1980s he joined the Oregon Shakespeare Festival in Ashland as an actor and director. His son, Kim, operates two professional theatres in the southwestern United States.

George Mann, graduate of the Lethbridge Collegiate Institute, and participant in high school productions under the direction of Bill Rea and Enid Parsons, completed his Bachelor and Master of Education degrees at the University of Alberta where he enrolled in a few drama courses and participated in Studio Theatre productions under the direction of Robert Orchard, Irene Powlan (Prothroe), and Elizabeth Sterling Haynes. During his early teaching career, he directed junior and senior high school productions. In 1960 he joined the staff of the Lethbridge Junior College, where in 1966 he organized a College Drama Club and entered the Noel Coward play, *Ways and Means,* in the Alberta College's Drama Festival held in Red Deer.[96] During the years 1967-1970, Mann's energies were directed primarily to furthering his education. Mann's first appearance on a Lethbridge stage since high school days was in March 1963 when he took the role of Jack Favell in the Playgoers' production of *Rebecca*. Then, in the fall 1963 he hit the boards with vengeance taking leading roles of the General in the Our Town Workshop production of *Romanoff and Juliet* and Preacher Hagler in Playgoers' production of *Dark of the Moon*. Altogether, from March 1963 to November 1970, Mann performed in six major productions for Playgoers, in one for Our Town Workshop, in three for Lethbridge Musical Theatre, and in two *Southern Showcase* productions for the Lethbridge Symphony. Mann was also President of Playgoers during the 1966 season. In festival competition, Mann was relatively successful, being awarded three trophies: Best Character Actor for Jack Favell (*Rebecca*) and Best Supporting Actor for his roles as Grivet and Barton Connor, (an exuberant professor) in the Playgoers' productions of *Therese* and *Chinook*, respectively.[97]

A number of actors who also displayed considerable potential when participating in Playgoers' festival productions during this era but whose theatrical careers in Lethbridge were rather short lived because of their geographic mobility, were George Hall [Best Actor (1958)], Brenda Cordwell [Best Character Actress (1958)], Derek Charnley [Best Supporting Actor (1963)], Syd Clarke [Best Actor (1964)], Lois Dongworth [Best Actress (1970)], and Sheila (Hawn) Pisko [Best Actress (1970)], the latter two of whom appeared in numerous local productions during the succeeding years. Dongworth had recently moved to Lethbridge from Medicine Hat where she had been very active in little theatre and musical theatre. While participating with the Medicine Hat Little Theatre, Dongworth displayed her mettle by capturing the Best Character Actress Award for her portrayal in the Medicine Hat production, *Summer of the Seventeenth Doll*.[98] Pisko was a young Lethbridge actress who, at the time of her appearance in Playgoer's production of *The Hostage*, was best known for her outstanding vocal talent, for which she had won numerous musical festival awards. At the 1970 DDF finals in Winnipeg, Pisko was awarded a special scholarship for the Best Actor or Actress under the age of 26.[99] Later that year, Pisko thrilled Lethbridge audiences with her superlative portrayal of Eliza Doolittle in the Lethbridge Musical Theatre's production of *My Fair Lady*.

Mention should also be made of another young actor, Ed Bayly, who developed very quickly under the careful direction of Murray Robison and the Coaldale Little Theatre, with whom he first participated in a Shakespearean Workshop in 1962. The following year, Bayly made his initial stage appearances in two local productions under directors Murray Robison and Sandy McCallum, respectively: *The Well of the Saints* (Coaldale Little Theatre) and *Romanoff and Juliet* (Our Town Workshop). From 1963-1970, inclusive, Bayly appeared in approximately eighteen local productions: seven for Coaldale Little Theatre, three for Our Town Workshop, four for Lethbridge Musical Theatre, and four for Playgoers of Lethbridge. By the time Bayly joined Playgoers for the 1966 production of *You Can't Take It With You*, he had gained considerable stage experience. In addition, he had just been hired by the city as building supervisor and technical director of the Yates Memorial Centre,[100] and therefore, he was launched on a lifelong career of theatre maintenance, supervision, and management. Bayly's early work experiences in a number of the building trades, his summer employment with the city, and his obvious theatrical interest and talent made him an ideal candidate for this new employment opportunity. Besides his acting potential, Bayly's innate artistic talents were soon directed to stage and lighting design.

Some of the activities of the Playgoers Club which were not directly related to production included the arranging of courses and workshops for the study of different components of production. Some of these programs were organized and taught by members of the club; others were arranged by the club in association with groups or agencies such as the Extension Department, University of Alberta, or the various departments of government which had an interest in the arts. Harry Baalim and Elsie Biddell were particularly interested in youth theatre, so they agreed to teach courses and conduct "study groups" for young people and teens. For example, in the summer of 1955, Biddell, through the auspices of the Lethbridge Recreation Department, conducted meetings on Monday nights in the Civic Centre with the aim of assisting teenagers who wanted to act and study the "general principles of stage composition."[101] In the spring of the following two years, Harry Baalim supervised twelve weekly creative drama classes.[102]

In late 1955 the Alberta Department of Economic Affairs, under Honorable Russell Patrick, appointed Jack McCreath as Provincial Drama Supervisor.[103] McCreath immediately set about to visit and talk with representatives of various theatrical societies throughout the province in order to determine their needs. Based upon these discussions, arrangements were made to conduct both local workshops and provincial summer programs. Over the next many years, numerous members of Playgoers and other local amateur theatre groups learned a great deal about the theatre arts at the community theatre programs sponsored by the Department and held in provincial institutions such as the Olds Agricultural College. In addition, McCreath contracted various drama specialists such as Esther Nelson, Director of Drama for the University of Alberta's Extension Department and the Banff School of Fine Arts, to conduct local short workshops and extension evening classes in areas such as makeup, acting, speech, directing, and stage craft.[104] Even though these provincially sponsored workshops were offered fairly regularly in Lethbridge and district, especially during the decade beginning in 1956, Playgoers continued to encourage its own members to provide similar instruction to novice or prospective members. In November 1963 Mary Heinitz gave a number of Tuesday evening workshops on acting and voice projection.[105]

Finally, mention should be made of two presentations made by the club in memory of C.R. Matthews. The first was in November 1963 when the club donated a trophy to the One Act Festival Committee in honor of C.R. Matthews; the trophy, as mentioned earlier, was to be awarded to the Best Director.[106] The second major presentation was a portrait of Matthews which was donated to the Yates Centre in March 1967. For a number of years, this portrait hung beside the original costume sketch for the dwarf played by Sandy McCallum in the Guthrie Theatre production of *Volpone*. McCallum had sent the sketch, which was created by the internationally renowned designer, Tanya Moiseiwitsch, to the Yates Memorial Centre with the request that it be dedicated to the memory of Yvonne Robison. Some years later, the sketch was returned to McCallum to be included in his professional portfolio.[107]

The Coaldale Little Theatre (CLT)

Although the town of Coaldale is a separate municipality, its close proximity to Lethbridge warrants that the theatrical activities of the Coaldale Little Theatre be reviewed in this book. Coaldale is located approximately six miles (9.6 km) east of Lethbridge on the main highway to Medicine Hat. As such, the Coaldale Little Theatre was generally considered to be part of the Lethbridge theatrical milieu, and certainly, Lethbridge thespians and patrons of the theatre revelled in the many successes which the Coaldale Little Theatre achieved. Of all Lethbridge and District amateur theatre groups, the Coaldale Little Theatre must be acknowledged as the most successful festival competitor; it won just about every one act festival in which it competed, and with the exception of Calgary's Workshop 14, it represented Alberta at the DDF more often than any other Alberta amateur theatre group. CLT accomplished these honors even though it did not enter the Three Act Festival until 1956.

The Coaldale Little Theatre was distinctly a creation of Murray Robison, a local public school teacher. Robison's interest in the theatre dates back as far as he can remember; it was primarily stimulated by his mother who took him, as a child, to live shows at the Empress Theatre in Medicine Hat. Robison also recalls his mother taking him to a Pantages vaudeville program in Calgary. Throughout elementary school, Robison put on shows at home for his friends and the neighbourhood children; he also loved to make "peep shows" with shoe boxes and cardboard characters. His dramatic interests were furthered by the high school dramatic society in Medicine Hat and by the shows which students were encouraged to produce at the Calgary Normal School. After receiving his teaching certificate in 1934, Robison taught in country schools for four years. He thoroughly enjoyed organizing and directing Christmas and similar concerts. From 1938 to 1942 Robison was appointed to various school staffs in southern Alberta. Then, he joined the Canadian Air Force, and following his basic training as a radar operator, he served overseas. While stationed in England, he married Yvonne Allen. After returning to Canada, Robison was assigned to teach at a country school west of Lethbridge (McLean School) from January - June 1946. He then took on a position in the town of Coaldale where he taught until he retired in 1974.[108]

During Robison's early years at Coaldale, the local teachers generally organized yearly productions; he directed two of these productions: a one act play, *Eldorado*, which was invited by Playgoers of Lethbridge to be included in one of their evenings of plays, and a longer play, *Pink String* and *Ceiling Wax*, in which Robison also performed. Robison then took the leading role in *The Dover Road*, which was directed by Elizabeth Brauer. An additional Coaldale teachers' production, *The Family Upstairs*, was directed by Donald (Don) Baldwin.[109] It then occurred to Robison that these productions should be "opened up to the community" by forming a community little theatre society, so he called a meeting of interested citizens to determine the level of support for such a group. The interest was evident; the Coaldale Little Theatre was formed and the following positions were filled: Director, Murray Robison; Recording Secretary, Peggy Mallalieu; Business Manager, Peggy McCann. These were the only officers the club ever elected, and the incumbents remained in their respective positions throughout the history of the society; the club disbanded in the early 1970s. In its organizational structure, the club was very unlike the Playgoers of Lethbridge which had always operated in a much more democratic manner. However, it was undoubtedly this very stable non-democratic structure which gave the Coaldale Little Theatre much of its strength. Also contributing to the club's success, was the fact that Robison took his role of director very seriously, and he became one of the very few directors of little theatre productions who actually had some formal training in the techniques of directing. In the summer of 1951, Robison attended summer school at the University of Alberta where he enrolled in drama courses under Robert Orchard. During the following three summers, he attended the Banff School of Fine Arts. For the first summer, he paid his own tuition, but during the succeeding two summers, his tuition was covered – first, by the Burton W. James Memorial Scholarship in Theatre, and second, by an assistantship in set construction. The Burton W. James Scholarship of $250 was the top scholarship awarded at the school at that time.[110] It was presented to Robison primarily in recognition of the success which his production, *The Case of the Crushed Petunias*, achieved at both the Lethbridge and District and the Alberta One Act festivals. Although Robison's 1954 assistantship required that he assist in set construction, he was also allowed to enroll in a directing course.

As a result of his experiences in Banff, Robison absorbed the basic principles of directing as well as set design, set construction, set decorating, and set dressing, all of which he personally applied in the many years in which he was associated with community theatre. In addition, he freely passed on his knowledge to others through cooperative colleagueship, apprenticeship, workshops, and personal example. His meticulous attention to detail brought out the best in people's talents, both onstage and backstage. His careful and insightful analysis of the text, combined with a skillful means of nondirective directing, greatly aided his actors in defining their characters and developing their roles. Careful study of the times and setting of the play contributed to the appropriate visual presentation of settings and costumes. Adjudicators constantly remarked on the detailed work manifest in both settings and characterization.

Robison was definitely committed to excellence, and his productions regularly reflected that commitment. This contention is clearly supported by the fact that Robison was selected as a recipient in 1963 of the Canadian Drama Award (CDA), and in 1977 of the Province of Alberta Achievement Award for Outstanding Service in Drama. Robison was basically, however, an educator, and as such, he was probably more concerned with the careful nurturing of talent. Little wonder that so many of his company captured numerous festival awards, and little wonder, too, that many years later, actors and directors with extensive theatrical experience such as Sandy McCallum, Ed Bayly, and Joy Pritchard considered Robison to be their mentor and credited him with helping them to develop and appreciate their own potential. Of course, the success which one achieved working with Murray Robison and the Coaldale Little Theatre helped to build confidence. Robison admits that his rehearsal process was unique among little theatre groups. To some extent, that uniqueness resulted from his position as Vice-Principal and drama teacher at the R.I. Baker School in Coaldale and from the understanding which he was able to obtain from local school officials. It was agreed that the stage of the R.I. Baker School auditorium should be under the sole jurisdiction of Robison and that his drama classes and the Coaldale Little Theatre had first priority on the space. The need for adequate time for dramatic rehearsals was recognized and was built into the scheduled use of the auditorium. Robison and his technical crew constructed the set during the early rehearsal period – a time which was also devoted to careful readings of the script and thorough discussion of plot, sub plots, and characterization. By the time the cast was ready to block the show, the set was in place. In addition, hand props and important elements of costuming were also available.[111] The other important element that gave strength to the organization was the fact that Robison was able to attract and hold a number of highly committed and responsible citizens who devoted their talents and energies to the overall betterment of the community and the Coaldale Little Theatre.

The Coaldale Little Theatre: Productions

The first official production of the Coaldale Little Theatre was Noel Coward's comedy, *Blithe Spirit*, which was presented on February 4 and 6, 1953. Later that year, CLT offered the one act play, *The Case of the Crushed Petunias*, by Tennessee Williams. Twenty-two years later, the club closed its books after reviving *The Case of the Crushed Petunias*. During the history of the club, it produced twelve full length plays, ten one acters, and one Christmas pantomime, *Mother Goose*. Of the twelve full length plays, eight were prepared for festival competition; one of these, *Liliom*, was eliminated by the pre-festival adjudicator, Betty Mitchell. In addition, *The Red Shoes* was judged ineligible for the Best Play Award at the 1965 Alberta Regional Festival because it was categorized as a children's play; nevertheless, the adjudicator, Walter Massey, remarked that the Coaldale production had provided the best entertainment of the entire festival week, and he awarded *The Red Shoes* best visual presentation and best stage management. Robison's fifteen year old daughter, Wendy, was singled out for "a spiritual award" for her unique portrayal of the clown.[112] Coaldale Little Theatre entered its first Alberta Regional Three Act Festival in 1956 with Patterson Greene's drama about a family of Old Order Mennonites, *Papa Is All*. In a sense, this was a very appropriate play for a group from Coaldale to present because the Coaldale agricultural area had been homesteaded primarily by immigrant Mennonites, and the community still contained a large proportion of Mennonite residents – although, not Old Order adherents. The second major festival entry for Coaldale Little Theatre was *Ladies in Retirement* which the club had presented for local audiences two years earlier. The revival had basically the same cast as the original production with the exception of two roles. This production was probably the least successful of Coaldale's official festival entries. The next few years witnessed extraordinary success for the group as its entrants in 1958, 1961, 1963, and 1967 were all winners of the Alberta Regional Festival. The first three productions, *All Summer Long*, *The Beautiful People*, and *The Well of the Saints*, were selected to represent the Alberta region at the DDF. In 1967, *Teach Me How to Cry* did not participate in the DDF because the rules then declared that only one play from the four western provinces could be selected. On that occasion, the Vernon Little Theatre's production of *The Firebugs*, directed by Paddy Malcolm, was chosen.[113] Graciously, Coaldale Little Theatre sent a cheque to the Vernon group to help defray expenses associated with the trip to St. John's, Newfoundland.

After the 1967 festival, the Alberta Drama League was disbanded and Regional Festivals associated with the DDF became problematic; however, a number of interested individuals and organizations decided to sponsor a Western Canada Arts Festival in Lethbridge on April 17-22,

1968. Coaldale Little Theatre prepared *Playboy of the Western World,* which adjudicator Firman Brown, professor of drama, University of Montana, described as "rich, lively and attractive." Later that year, CLT produced a Christmas pantomime, *Mother Goose.*[114] Following *Mother Goose,* the club became inactive for a few years, but before it closed its books, CLT prepared two final productions, the three act play, *Butterflies are Free* (in 1973), and the one act play, *The Case of the Crushed Petunias (in 1975).*

Of the ten short or one act productions presented by Coaldale Little Theatre, all but two were associated with various festivals. The two exceptions were *The Unseen* and *To What Purpose,* directed by Betty Smith and Yvonne Robison, respectively. *The Unseen* was first entered in an Evening of One Act Plays (in November 1953) arranged by Ralph Robinson of the Lethbridge Playgoers Club. Lethbridge audiences were treated to an experience which they would rarely ever witness again – Murray Robison in an acting role. He never again performed for Coaldale Little Theatre, but he did appear on the Lethbridge stage once more in a small role (the conductor) for the Lethbridge Musical Theatre production of *The Music Man.* About one and a half weeks after the Lethbridge evening of one acters, *The Unseen* joined together with *To What Purpose* in an evening of Little Theatre presented to a Coaldale audience at the R.I. Baker School auditorium.

When Coaldale Little Theatre presented their first one act production, *The Case of the Crushed Petunias,* in the Lethbridge and District One Act Festival, it captured the top honors. Two more best play awards (for *Riders to the Sea* and *Catherine Parr*) followed in the succeeding years, 1954 and 1955. Each of these awards granted inclusion in the Alberta One Act Drama Festival. In 1955 Robison and the Coaldale Little Theatre declined the invitation to the provincial festival arguing that the experience of participating in a provincial festival should be given to another southern Alberta group; Playgoers was, subsequently, asked to enter the production, *Lonesome Like.*[115] For the next few years, Coaldale Little Theatre concentrated on producing the following plays for the Alberta Regional Drama Festival: *Papa is All* (1956), *Ladies in Retirement* (1957), and *All Summer Long* (1958), the latter of which was invited to the DDF at Halifax. CLT did not produce another one act play until 1959 when they again captured the Best Play Award for their production of Gwen Pharis Ringwood's *The Jack and the Joker.* In 1960 the club was invited to participate in the Alberta One Act Festival even though there was no preliminary Lethbridge and District Festival that year; their entry was *The Devil Among the Skins.* In that production, a relatively new theatrical personality, Joy Pritchard, gained some prominence by achieving the Best Actress Award.[116] Gradually, Joy Pritchard and her husband, Fred, became more deeply involved in community theatre, and when they moved to Lethbridge, they established their own little theatre group, Our Town Workshop.

Two more trips to the DDF (Montreal and Kitchener) and an extensive workshop program occupied the energies of the Coaldale Little Theatre from 1961 - 1963, inclusive. However, the club again participated in one act festivals in 1964 and 1965. In 1964 *The Tinker's Wedding* brought additional honors to the group as it was selected to represent Lethbridge and District at the Alberta One Act Festival. The following year, Coaldale Little Theatre was requested by Jack McCreath to present the premier performance of Joyce Doolittle's award winning play, *The Golden Goose,* during the Alberta One Act Festival.[117] It was shortly after this performance that Yvonne Robison passed away. The activities of the club were put "on hold" for over a year. On October 5, 1966, Murray Robison married a staunch member of Playgoers and Lethbridge Musical Theatre, Kaye Watson. Appropriately, their wedding reception was held in the foyer of the Yates Memorial Centre. Kaye immediately became an important member of Coaldale Little Theatre where she brought the same energy and enthusiasm she had always displayed in the Playgoers Club. During the next few years, she worked diligently on costumes and also appeared in the last three major productions of the club.

However, the future years of the club were definitely numbered. Robison suffered from some nagging health problems and decided to opt for early retirement from his teaching post in June 1974 and to move to Lethbridge, shortly thereafter. Since he was no longer formally associated with R.I. Baker School, he and the members of the Coaldale Little Theatre decided to disband the group. Many of the core members were also close to retirement age; younger members such as Ed Bayly turned their talents to Playgoers and Lethbridge Musical Theatre. Nevertheless, the Robisons were not ready to retire from the theatre. Upon moving to Lethbridge, they purchased a large three storey house where they established the Attic Theatre, which will be discussed in Chapter Six.

Personnel of the Coaldale Little Theatre

Over the twenty-three year history of the Coaldale Little Theatre, about 100 people were involved in the twenty-two productions (excluding the pantomime, *Mother Goose*) presented by the society. However, as was the case with the Playgoers of Lethbridge, the group achieved its cohesion from the very active participation of a core of about thirty-five actors and backstage participants. Generally speaking, this core of participants formed a close primary group who worked smoothly together to complete whatever tasks had to be done. Nevertheless, although it was true that onstage participants usually worked backstage as well, the reverse was not quite so common. It is also true, that certain backstage tasks became particularly associated with individuals who excelled in that area. For example, Ivan Meyers became the club's regular stage manager after he illustrated how effectively he could handle the role. Other examples of specialized role playing include properties by Audrey Davidson; costuming and makeup by Yvonne Robison and Kaye Robison; publicity by Betty Meyers and Jintie Graham; fund raising, ticket sales, and other economic matters by Peggy McCann; set design by Murray Robison; set construction by Ivan Meyers, Ray Jolliffe, and Fred Pritchard; and directing by Murray Robison. Although Robison directed most of the productions of the Coaldale Little Theatre, he did encourage others to learn the art of directing. He usually engaged an assistant director in an apprenticeship relationship. Unfortunately, the master was so successful that few of his assistants ever felt equal to the challenge. The major exception to this was Joy Pritchard whose apprenticeship really inspired her to become deeply committed to directing – a commitment which she was able to manifest, later, with the Our Town Workshop. With regard to the core members of the club, Tables 5-8 and 5-9 clearly illustrate the level of activity engaged in by these members.

Jennie Emery was a teacher, mother, and homemaker who had grown up in Coleman, Alberta, and then taught in rural schools in southwestern Alberta for a number of years before joining the Coaldale teaching staff in 1944 where she gained a reputation as an outstanding Grade I teacher. She retired in 1976, and later, moved to Lethbridge. Throughout her teaching career, Emery devoted much time and energy to educational committees associated with the ATA and the Department of Education. Following her retirement, she became highly involved in the Coaldale Arts and Crafts Association, for which she was president for several years. Her association with the CLT proved her to be an excellent character actress who is probably best remembered for her role as Mama in the 1956 production *Papa is All,* for which she won the Best Actress Award at the Alberta Regional Festival.[118] This was just one of numerous awards which Emery garnered. Always helpful and reliable, Emery could be counted upon to assist wherever she was needed. This characteristic was particularly appreciated during the rehearsals of *Liliom*; when Murray Robison became ill, Emery volunteered to take over the direction of this major production.

TABLE 5-8

Coaldale Little Theatre:
Backstage Participants (1953-1975)

I. Very Active Participants	Audrey Davidson Ed Davidson Jennie Emery Russell Fairhurst Jintie Graham Dorothy Hughes	Peggy Mallalieu Peggy McCann Gwen Meroniuk Betty Meyers Ivan Meyers Ray Jolliffe	Ern Bayly Fran Bayly Kaye Robison Murray Robison Yvonne Robison
II. Moderately Active Participants	Pauline Archer Ed Bayly Charles Connor	Lorene Harrison Betty McLennan Elizabeth MacIntyre	Fred Pritchard

TABLE 5-9

Coaldale Little Theatre:
Onstage Participants (1953-1975)

I. Six - Ten Roles	Ed Bayly (6) Ed Davidson (6) Jennie Emery (10)	Russell Fairhurst (8) Theresa King (6) Peggy Mallalieu (8)	Peggy McCann (7) Yvonne Robison (6) Phil Story (8)
II. Three - Five Roles	Dorothy Hughes (3) Jean Mannington (5) Bill Matheson (4)	Sandy McCallum (5) Fred Pritchard (3) Frank Huszar (3)	Kaye Robison (4) Wendy Robison (4) Betty Smith (3)
III. Two Roles	Fred Bodie Tom Hughes	Lorene Harrison Gwen Meroniuk	Joy Pritchard

Peggy Mallalieu, a Scottish war bride, was another excellent character actress who also, on one occasion, tried her skills at directing. Her production of *The Jack and the Joker* topped the local festival and was judged very favorably in the provincial one.[119] Mallalieu garnered the following acting awards: Best Actress Award in the Alberta Regional Three Act Festival production of *The Well of the Saints*, and Best Character Actress Awards for her characterizations in *Papa is All* and *Teach Me How to Cry*.[120]

An English war bride, Jean Mannington, whose husband worked at the Lethbridge Agricultural Research Centre, also showed considerable promise. Unfortunately, her participation was limited to the few years from 1955 to about 1959, after which her husband retired and the family moved to Victoria. The Mannington's twelve year old son, David, received particular commendation from adjudicator, Richard West, for his role in *All Summer Long* at the Alberta Regional Festival.[121]Two other English war brides added to the store of Coaldale's marvelous female actresses: Theresa King and Yvonne Robison. King, primarily a homemaker and the mother of four children, captured a number of festival honors, for example, Best Supporting Actress in *Papa is All* (1956) and in *The Beautiful People* (1961).[122] In addition, she was recognized as the Best Actress in the Playgoers' One Act Festival production, *Hello Out There* (1957).[123] Yvonne Robison combined homemaking with her career as public librarian in Coaldale. Wife of Murray and mother of three children, Yvonne Robison was also the backbone of the makeup and costuming department of Coaldale Little Theatre. In addition, she was a very sensitive actress whose ability was recognized when awarded Best Actress for her role in the One Act Festival production of *The Tinker's Wedding* (1964).[124] She will also be remembered for her superb work in *The Well of the Saints* (1963). Unfortunately, tragedy struck in 1965 when Yvonne contacted a rare disease, scleraderma, and she died in December of that year. This was a loss from which Coaldale Little Theatre never really recovered.

Peggy Dick was born in Scotland in 1908 but moved to Lethbridge as a young girl. After her marriage to Mel McCann, Peggy moved to Coaldale where she raised her three children. Her sports announcer son, Alan, is well known to CTV sports viewers. Although widowed fairly early in her marriage, McCann managed to provide for herself and family by opening and operating the first drug store in the community. She was an excellent business woman, and this characteristic made her an ideal person to perform the function of business manager for Coaldale Little Theatre. Through her careful management, the group was always solvent even though it travelled to the DDF on three different occasions and provided financial assistance to various workshops, scholarships, and other DDF participants. McCann was a very active member of the community, devoting herself to the Women's Institute and the United Farm Women's Association. Besides keeping Coaldale Little Theatre financially afloat, McCann made other important contributions to both backstage and onstage. Festival honors were bestowed upon her for her acting in the one act plays, *The Case of the Crushed Petunias* (1953) and *The Jack and the Joker* (1959). Although individual awards were not given out at the early one act festivals, McCann received honorable mention in the 1953 production; in the latter festival production, she was awarded Best Supporting Actress.[125]

Young male leads were portrayed by Russell Fairhurst, Russell Wiber, and Ed Bayly, each of whom was honored at various provincial festivals. Following the 1956 festival production of *Papa Is All*, Russell Fairhurst received a one hundred and fifty dollar scholarship in recognition of his excellent portrayal of Jake (the son).[126] At that time, Fairhurst had just resigned his employment in his father's men's wear store in Coaldale to join the staff of Canada Trust in Lethbridge where he specialized in estate and trust administration. For his portrayal of a crippled young basketball player, Don, in *All Summer Long* (1958), Fairhurst received honorable mention at the Alberta Regional Festival, and he was also singled out at the DDF as runner-up for the Best Acting Award; the adjudicator praised him for his "extremely sensitive interpretation."[127] Russell Wiber was selected for Best Acting honors for his festival role in *The Beautiful People*.[128] Unfortunately, Wiber moved from southern Alberta, shortly thereafter. But soon, another youthful actor, Ed Bayly, was to have his talents carefully honed by director Murray Robison. Bayly made his acting debut for Coaldale Little Theatre in the 1963 festival production, *The Well of the Saints*. About a year and a half later, Bayly accepted the Best Actor Award for his portrayal in the one act festival entry, *The Tinker's Wedding*. Another Best Actor award was bestowed upon him following the Three Act Festival production of *Teach Me How to Cry* (1967).[129] Unfortunately for Ed, this was one of the occasions when the winning Alberta entry was not invited to participate in the DDF.

Somewhat more mature male roles were fairly regularly assigned to Phil Story, Sandy McCallum, Bill Matheson, and Edwin "Red" Davidson. Story, a lab assistant at the Lethbridge Research Station, was one of the most cooperative, dependable, hard working, congenial, and good natured members of the organization. From 1958 to 1975, he appeared consistently in CLT productions where he specialized in character roles. Following the demise of the Coaldale Little Theatre, he lent his special charm and dedicated effort to almost every community theatre association in Lethbridge. Although the theatrical career of Sandy McCallum was discussed quite thoroughly in the section on the

Playgoers Club, it must be emphasized that his acting talent was carefully nurtured by Murray Robison. From 1958 through 1963, McCallum developed into one of the most outstanding actors to enhance the stages of southern Alberta.[130] By the following February, McCallum was ensconced in the Guthrie Theatre in Minneapolis where, as stated earlier, he began an extremely successful professional acting career. He, nevertheless, maintained a very close relationship with his mentor, Murray Robison, with whom he corresponded regularly. Bill Matheson joined forces with the Coaldale Little Theatre on five different occasions between 1961 and 1975: *The Beautiful People* (1961); *The Well of the Saints* (1963); *Playboy of the Western World* (1968); *Mother Goose* (1968); and *The Case of the Crushed Petunias* (1975). In these various theatrical activities, Matheson proved himself capable of playing every kind of role from leading man to the most outrageous character parts. Ed Davidson was one of the most unlikely people to appear on stage. He was born in April 1913 and was raised on a farm near Coaldale. After finishing high school at the Provincial Agriculture School in Raymond, Alberta, he proceeded to the University of Alberta where he completed a bachelor's degree in Agriculture and an M.A. in Economics. While there, he met Audrey Dean, whom he married in 1939, and with whom he had five children. Davidson maintained a 640 acre farm at Coaldale and an extensive sheep ranch in southwestern Alberta. In addition to being a board member of the Alberta Wheat Pool, he was a very active and useful member of his community where he held numerous civic positions. Frequently, he was also called upon to teach various extension courses related to agriculture. As Chairman of the Coaldale School Board, he developed a great respect for Murray Robison who convinced Davidson that his strength and talents could be put to good use by the local theatre group.[131] Davidson was a tall and powerful man; at the same time he was a gentle man in every sense of the word. He was intelligent, curious, and mechanically skillful. For Coaldale Little Theatre, he was a "Jack of all trades" and an extremely hard worker. Unquestionably, he was an ideal backstage man who was ready to contribute wherever his services were required. In 1960 his contribution was extended to onstage participation when he joined the cast of the one act festival production, *The Devil Among the Skins*. For the next decade, "Red" Davidson appeared in most of the productions presented by the Coaldale Little Theatre. In addition, he turned in a particularly hilarious portrayal as one of the wicked stepsisters in the 1967 English pantomime, *Cinderella*, directed by Muriel Jolliffe and sponsored by the Lethbridge Allied Arts Council. Davidson's theatrical career ended with the demise of Coaldale Little Theatre, and unfortunately, for the community of Coaldale, he died in 1980. Red's wife, Audrey, devoted herself almost exclusively to backstage activities, particularly as property mistress. She, too, was a very industrious worker, and Coaldale Little Theatre was fortunate to involve such a dedicated couple as the Davidsons. Following Ed's death, Audrey moved from the farm and settled in Lethbridge.

The phenomenon of married couples working together for the benefit of Coaldale Little Theatre was fairly common. It has been mentioned that Yvonne Robison was an indefatigable aid to her husband, Murray. Murray's second wife, Kaye (Watson), was equally active both onstage and backstage, where her creative skills were manifest primarily in the costuming department. Of course, her lengthy theatrical experience with Playgoers of Lethbridge, the Chinook Guild, and the Lethbridge Musical Theatre prepared her well for all facets of community theatre. It was not uncommon for Kaye to be organizing and creating costumes while at the same time performing a leading role. Other active couples associated with Coaldale Little Theatre were Fred and Joy Pritchard, Tom and Dorothy Hughes, Ern and Fran Bayly, and Betty and Ivan Meyers. The theatrical activities of the Pritchards will be analysed in the discussion of the Our Town Workshop. The Hugheses were both local teachers; Dorothy was also a piano teacher. They were active participants with Coaldale Little Theatre both on and offstage until they moved to British Columbia in 1960. Ern and Fran Bayly were recognized as highly dependable and competent workers. Ern's assistance on set construction was greatly appreciated, and Fran's skill as a seamstress solicited many requests for her participation in costuming. Both Fran and Ern made valuable contributions to various other theatrical groups in Lethbridge. Ivan and Betty Meyers, who made their presence felt behind the scenes, owned a two section dryland farm plus a quarter acre of irrigated land. In addition to raising four children, Betty and Ivan were extraordinarily involved in the community, the United Church, and educational service organizations. Their contribution to the welfare of the community was deeply appreciated and recognized in various ways. On July 6, 1988, Ivan Meyers received the Paul Harris Fellowship Award from the Coaldale Rotary Club for long, effective, and loyal service.[132] Shortly thereafter, on January 30, 1989, Ivan Meyers died from complications associated with cancer. Three of the most highly revered ministers of the United Church in southern Alberta participated in the memorial service. Within the Coaldale Little Theatre, Betty Meyers was primarily responsible for publicity and public relations, whereas in 1958 Ivan took on the position of stage manager which he retained throughout the history of the club. Like Ed Davidson, Ivan maintained a formidable external presence, but he was one of the finest gentlemen one would ever hope to meet. Ivan's subtle good humor, his cooperative spirit, his warm but efficient manner, and his attention to detail made him the ideal stage manager. In recognition of these attributes, he was presented with the Best Stage Manager Award on four different occasions at the Alberta Three Act Festival: *The Beautiful People* (1961), *The Well of the Saints* (1963), *The Red Shoes* (1965) and *Teach Me How to Cry* (1967).[133]

Set for The Well of the Saints, *Coaldale Little Theatre, 1963 Regional Three Act Festival Production*
Photo: Coaldale Public Library

If awards had been given out for hard and conscientious backstage activities, Jintie Graham would possess a shelf full of them for her work on properties and sound. Like so many of the members of the Coaldale Little Theatre, Jintie and her husband, Alan, were extraordinarily active members of their community. Alan was a honey producer, an elder of the Coaldale United Church, and a perennial mayor of the town. Jintie was a teacher, homemaker, active church and choir member, leader in the Home and School Association, and board member of the Coaldale Centennial Library. The Grahams also raised three children, two of whom, Jean and Margot, became very active in theatre circles in various Alberta communities.

Set painting and decoration received considerable attention from Murray Robison; therefore, he frequently supervised or did much of the set painting himself. On other occasions, he sought out artistic members of the community such as Corne Martens, the Brauer sisters, and Ed Bayly. Martens built and painted the set for *The Jack and the Joker*, after which he began to concentrate on his personal artistic career.[134] Katherine and Elizabeth Brauer captured the Best Visual Award for their set design and decorating for *The Well of the Saints*, whereas Bayly received the same award for *The Red Shoes*. Katherine Brauer's natural talent won her two scholarships to the Banff School of Fine Arts. She also majored in art at the University of Alberta and then took on a teaching position at the R.I. Baker School in Coaldale.[135] Over the twenty year history of the Coaldale Little Theatre, many other people participated in the activities of the club for varying periods of time and in different capacities.

In concluding this discussion of the Coaldale Little Theatre, it should be reiterated that Murray Robison and his company were imbued with the spirit of development; their aims were to encourage, to nurture, and to challenge the theatrical skills of all members of the community who wished to partake in the group activities. These goals were accomplished not only because of the careful production process that characterized each of the plays presented by the Coaldale Little Theatre, but also because the club exuded a spirit of cooperative altruism – a spirit which is exemplified in the following comments quoted from published reports in the *Lethbridge Herald*[136] and a local history book, *Coaldale, Gem of the West*, respectively:[137]

> He [Murray Robison] likes to think his cast acts for the love of it – that Little Theatre is an instrument to encourage better theatre through participation, sponsoring workshops, granting scholarships, encouraging and cooperating with other groups, providing better theatrical facilities in schools, assisting the school drama program and supporting the allied arts. . . .

> Coaldale Little Theatre provided seven scholarships to the Olds and Drumheller Schools, two scholarships to the Banff School of Fine Arts, and one scholarship to the Shakespearean seminar at Stratford, Ontario. We also gave: several travel assistance grants to groups going to the final DDF festival; two substantial donations to the National Theatre School in Montreal; a donation to the library fund of the Lethbridge Community College; and financial assistance to one of our members, Sandy McCallum, who decided to go professional . . . Our Coaldale Little Theatre sponsored three one act festivals, two short courses in make-up, a twenty week workshop in Shakespearean theatre, a one week speech workshop and several short acting workshops.

This cooperative spirit is also shown in the fact that Robison encouraged two of his most promising members, Joy and Fred Pritchard, to found their own theatre group, the Our Town Workshop, which could count continuously on the support of Robison and the Coaldale Little Theatre. In this regard, Joy was quoted by the *Lethbridge Herald* staff writer, Lorraine Moore, as saying:[138]

> Working with Murray Robison as my instructor, mentor and coach, all through these years has been more valuable to me in the field of drama than I can ever hope to express...his presence and guiding hand with his invaluable advice has helped [my] flagging spirits on many occasions, and encouraged [me] on when the going was tough.

Our Town Workshop

The Our Town Workshop community theatre group was organized in Lethbridge by Joy and Fred Pritchard in the latter part of 1962. The Pritchards had moved to Lethbridge in 1958 from Taber, Alberta, where Fred had established his law practice in 1949. Both Joy and Fred had been involved in dramatic productions in their high school years – Joy in Stettler High School under the supervision of Miss Jennyjohn and Fred at the Lethbridge Collegiate Institute under Bill Rea. Upon graduating from high school, Fred completed his LLB at the University of Alberta. During the latter years of World War II, Fred and Joy were located in Calgary – Fred had joined the army and was stationed with the Pay Corps at Curry Barracks; Joy was working in a nearby bank. Their paths crossed, they met, they fell in love, and they were married in 1944. Following the war, Fred was sent overseas to help maintain the peace. On his return, the Pritchards moved to Taber.[139] Some years passed before Fred and Joy were able to express their theatrical interests, again, but in the mid-1950s they became involved with some local musical and minstrel shows as well as with the Taber Little Theatre under the direction of Winnifred Bar. Fred took the leading part in the 1956 one act festival entry, *Ali, the Cobbler*, produced by the Taber Little Theatre. He also portrayed a tanner in the group's 1957 entry, *The Devil Among the Skins*.[140] Although Joy took the part of the Woodsman's wife in this latter production, she tended to work backstage or to opt for small acting parts such as a chorus member in the local minstrel show. Much of Joy's reluctance to become too involved in theatrical activities, at that time, was the fact that she had taken her role as mother very seriously.

Just prior to moving to Lethbridge, Fred Pritchard assisted backstage for the Coaldale Little Theatre production of *All Summer Long* (1958). By the next year, both Fred and Joy were active participants in the Coaldale Little Theatre; they each took parts in the three act play, *Liliom*, and Fred, additionally, helped with set construction. Later that year, Fred acted in the one act festival play, *The Jack and the Joker*. The couple appeared together in *The Devil Among the Skins* (1960), for which Joy was selected as the Best Actress in the provincial festival. Then, Joy had her appetite whetted for directing when Murray Robison asked her to assist him in the direction of the 1961 Alberta Regional Festival entry, *The Beautiful People* – the play for which Fred Pritchard received his first major award when he was selected as the recipient of the Best Character Actor Award. [141]

In the spring of the following year, Joy Pritchard "went solo" when she took on the task of directing the religious drama, *Christ in the Concrete City*, for McKillop United Church, Lethbridge.[142] The following August, she, with the assistance of the Lethbridge Parks and Recreation Department, attended a week long directing and acting seminar in Olds. Upon completing this seminar, Joy requested that the Lethbridge Parks and Recreation Department sponsor a local workshop in basic acting and makeup in conjunction with the provincial recreational and cultural development branch. The ultimate aim of the workshop was to uncover and help develop new acting talent in the city. From this workshop, Pritchard gathered together the founding members of a new community theatre group to be known as the Our Town Workshop since the workshop centered around the Thornton Wilder play, *Our Town*, and since the new group chose to produce *Our Town* as its initial stage offering. *Our Town* opened at the W.R. Meyers High School in Taber on March 9, 1963, for a two night stand, and then played at Hamilton Junior High School in Lethbridge March 11 and 12.[143] Except for Fred Pritchard, Cliff Black, and Ed Sloboda, the remainder of the large cast were new to the boards in Lethbridge. A local hospital administrator, Stu Chapman, formerly of Lacombe, Alberta, played the stage manager and stole the show with his superb timing and exceptional performance. Unfortunately for Lethbridge, Chapman moved to Langley, British Columbia, shortly thereafter.

During its short six year existence (1963-68), Our Town Workshop was extraordinarily active; it produced eleven major productions, three of which were entered into festival competition: *The Queen and the Rebels* (1965), *The Caretaker* (1966), and *The Wheel* (1967). In addition, the club presented twelve short plays and a sketch, *Here We Are*, which was offered in conjunction with a variety program sponsored by the Bridge City Chorus. Seven of these one act plays were entered in festival competition. In many ways, the Our Town Workshop patterned itself after the Coaldale

Little Theatre: no elected executive, no membership list or fees, and substantial dependence on the artistic director. In this latter regard, it is significant to note that Joy Pritchard was responsible for directing seven of the main productions and eleven of the shorter plays. Fred Pritchard took the responsibility for directing one major festival production, *The Caretaker* (for which he received the Best Director Award at the Alberta 1966 Regional Festival), and one one act festival production, *The Dumb Waiter*; both of these plays were penned by Harold Pinter. Sandy McCallum directed *Romanoff and Juliet* in 1963, and it is conceivable that, had McCallum not moved from Lethbridge, his directorial skills might have been called upon again. Dick Mells agreed (with the assistance of Muriel Jolliffe) to direct *Teahouse of the August Moon* in 1966 when the Our Town Workshop was contracted to produce two shows for the official opening week of the Yates Memorial Centre in May. In order to produce this play adequately, Mells sought and received support from the Lethbridge Japanese Canadian Citizens' Association. Joy Pritchard was responsible for directing the second show for the opening, a children's production, *The Three Little Pigs*. The final alternate director associated with Our Town productions was the professional director, Ron Hartmann, who had been contracted by the Canada Council and the DDF to direct *The Madwoman of Chaillot* as a learning experience for local theatre participants associated with the Our Town Workshop and the Lethbridge Playgoers. In this case, Joy Pritchard and a Playgoers' member, Lee Mells, acted as assistant directors.

Fred Pritchard and Bill Matheson from the Our Town Workshop Production, The Queen and the Rebels *(1965)*
Photo: Our Town Workshop Archives

Scene from The Madwoman of Chaillot – *Joan Waterfield, Joy Pritchard, Norma MacInnes, Claudia Peterson.*
Joint production of Playgoers of Lethbridge and Our Town Workshop
Photo: Our Town Workshop Archives

Sheila Hawn (Pisko), Ed Bayly and Earl Colpitts – from Our Town
Workshop production of Rominoff and Juliet *by Peter Ustinoff (1963)*
Photo: Our Town Workshop Archives

An interest in children's theatre was another characteristic which Our Town Workshop shared with the Coaldale Little Theatre. Following The *Three Little Pigs*, which was produced in association with Muriel Jolliffe and the Jolliffe Academy of Dancing, as well as with Effie (Reid) Langmead (musical director) and the McKillop AOTS Boys Choir, the Our Town Workshop closed off its 1966 season with a production of *Little Red Riding Hood*. A function which was quite unique to the Our Town Workshop was its manifest concern for social issues. This concern undoubtedly reflected the social conscience of its founders, the Pritchards. You will recall that the Pritchards and some of their associates at McKillop United Church had presented the religious drama, *Christ in the Concrete City*, in the spring 1962. Later, in January 1968 the McKillop Players again staged a play, *It Should Happen to a Dog*, which aimed at provoking serious discussion about man's contemporary condition. More specifically under the auspices of the Our Town Workshop, Joy Pritchard toured her 1966 production of the social drama, *The Coffee House*, to various churches in southern Alberta. During the next two years, the club, in association with the National Council of Jewish Women and the Mental Health Association of Canada, produced plays aimed at increasing the public's knowledge of mental health problems. For her contribution to this worthy cause, Pritchard was honored as Council Woman of the Year in 1968 by the National Council of Jewish Women, Lethbridge section. This was the first time that the annual award had been presented to a woman who was not a member of the Council.[144]

Our Town Workshop also prepared seven of its dozen or so little theatre productions for presentation at festivals; five of these plays were invited to the Alberta One Act festivals. Then, in the fall of 1968, the Pritchards decided to close the books of the Our Town Workshop. Three factors undoubtedly contributed to the discontinuation of their activities: (1) the disbanding of the Alberta Drama League and the withdrawal of the competitive festivals; (2) the growth of theatrical activity among other local groups, such as Lethbridge Musical Theatre, Jolliffe Academy (Christmas pantomimes), and the Allied Arts Council (summer musicals); (3) other community, professional, and family demands placed upon the Pritchards. By 1968 the Pritchard legal firm had become one of the most successful law offices in southern Alberta, and Fred was no longer able to devote the extraordinary amount of time he had given previously to theatrical activities. In addition, Joy, the mother of five children, began to turn her talents more and more to the needs of her family and various social causes. Following Fred's relatively early and completely unexpected death in 1985, Joy devoted herself to the Lethbridge Handicapped Riding Association.[145]

Personnel of the Our Town Workshop

Although about one hundred people participated in the various activities of the Our Town Workshop during its six year existence, the group depended primarily upon the extraordinary efforts of about thirty core members. With rare exceptions, these core members contributed to both onstage and backstage needs. Of course, the extent of participation in the various facets of production varied. Resumes of onstage and backstage participation by core members of the Our Town Workshop are presented in Tables 5-10 and 5-11.

Upon perusing Tables 5-10 and 5-11, one becomes aware of the fact that some of the participants in the Our Town Workshop were also associated with the Playgoers Club of Lethbridge and the Coaldale Little Theatre. However, the backbone of the organization was provided by the Pritchards, Earl and Doris Colpitts, and Joan Haig. As mentioned earlier, Joy Pritchard was basically the artistic director of the organization and she personally directed over three-quarters of the club's productions. Joy contended, however, that she relied on Fred, a prolific reader, to select many of the plays. In addition, Fred, together with Earl Colpitts, created most of the organizations' stage sets and supervised the production crews. Fred also dominated the acting component of the productions by appearing in one-half of the club's productions. The excellence of his acting is attested to by the fact that he captured acting awards at every level of festival competition in which he was involved. In addition, his direction of *The Caretaker* was roundly applauded by adjudicator, Peter Boretski, at the 1966 Alberta Regional Festival.

TABLE 5-10

Our Town Workshop:
Onstage Participants (1963-1968)

I. Eight - Twelve Roles	Fred Pritchard (12)	Bud Iverson (8)
II. Six - Seven Roles	Dianna Turner	
III. Four - Five Roles	Ed Bayly Doris Colpitts Earl Colpitts Jim Elliott Bruce Haig	Joan Haig Bill Matheson Muriel Matheson Glen Seeman Joan Waterfield
IV. Two - Three Roles	Frances Anderson Bill Berg Bruce Branston Esther Goorevitch Angela Gunstone Jack Horn Sheila (Hawn) Pisko Connie Ingoldsby Leslie Ker Velma Litchfield	Diane Matisz Sandy McCallum Garry McNair Helen McKenzie Jay Pritchard Martha Rae Nina Sejerson Ed Sloboda Phil Story

TABLE 5-11

Our Town Workshop:
Backstage Participants (1963-1968)

Very Active	Fran Bayly (costumes) Doris Colpitts Earl Colpitts (set construction) Joan Haig Leslie Ker	Bruce McKenzie (lights) Fred Pritchard Marie Rokas Ed Sloboda Judy White
Moderately Active	Gloria Albritton Betty Chapman Elaine Liebelt Helen McKenzie	Camillia Pilling Phil Story Pheona Sloboda

Earl Colpitts and his wife, Doris, were extraordinarily hard workers for Our Town Workshop. Earl, who was the Service Manager for the Beny Chevrolet Oldsmobile Car dealership in Lethbridge, was one of those multi-skilled "gems" who occasionally get involved in community theatre. In addition, he was extremely reliable and highly committed to the welfare of the club. Besides providing considerable stability backstage, Earl also performed well in a number of acting roles. He is particularly remembered for his portrayal of Papa in *I Remember Mama*. Doris Colpitts, a legal secretary with the Pritchard firm, was somewhat more active onstage than her husband, but she, too, was a stalwart contributor to all aspects of production for the Our Town Workshop. Devotion to the club and considerable acting talent were also exemplified by Joan Haig, who, although she was a qualified teacher, preferred, during the 1960s, to remain at home and nurture her children. Haig not only assisted in all aspects of the club's production activities but also provided excellent advice to the organization, both formally, in her position as the club's perennial secretary-treasurer, and informally, as a loyal and concerned member.

Our Town Workshop was shaken considerably when the Colpitts's family left Lethbridge in 1965. The void was not easily filled, but fortunately, other members such as Bruce and Helen McKenzie, Ed Sloboda, Leslie Ker, Marie Rokas, and Judy White took on more responsibilities backstage. Bruce McKenzie had supervised the lighting for the odd Playgoers production; however, by 1963, he was entrenched as the "resident" lighting expert with the Our Town Workshop. His wife, Helen, also assisted backstage and portrayed a few minor roles. Sloboda, a young farmer and CPR employee, was a very handy person, so his skills were directed toward set construction and painting; nevertheless, he, too, was cajoled into taking on the occasional acting role. About the mid-point in the club's existence, Sloboda married Pheona Kuehn and then convinced her to lend a helping hand backstage.[146] Leslie Ker, a bookkeeper with Kitson Wholesale Company, participated in whatever activity she was most needed. Ker also contributed in this unselfish manner to various other local groups before she retired and moved to Medicine Hat. Marie Rokas had an extremely interesting background. She was raised in Estonia and was forced to work in Germany during the war. After the war, she moved to the Crowsnest Pass where she married a miner; later, they moved to Lethbridge. Her excellent European education provided her with the background to join the library staff at the Lethbridge Junior College, and subsequently, the University of Lethbridge. She was also a very helpful person in the costume department for Our Town Workshop, as was Judy White, a local bank employee. Another bank employee, Dianna Turner, made her theatrical mark primarily onstage where she played a number of secondary roles in addition to the occasional leading role; probably her most demanding portrayal was Flo in the 1967 festival production, *The Wheel*. Turner was also a frequent contributor to other amateur theatre companies.

The following discussion will analyze the activities of the remaining members who functioned more regularly as actors for the Our Town Workshop. Jim Elliott, a local radio announcer, had made an impressive local debut portraying Maximilian de Winter in Playgoers' 1963 production of *Rebecca*. Following this, he was attracted to the Our Town Workshop where he continued to perform successfully. In the fall of 1964, he was awarded the Best Actor trophy for his portrayal of Tegeus Chromis in the one act festival production, *A Phoenix Too Frequent*. His presentation of Tom in *The Glass Menagerie* (1965) was well received, and his acting in the 1966 production of *The Caretaker*, where he played Mick, was memorable. Shortly thereafter, Elliott, left the city for a number of years.

Bruce Haig, a local junior high school social studies, music, and drama teacher excelled as Hodge in the group's one act festival production, *Fool's Errand,* for which he received the Best Character Actor award at the provincial festival. Haig also performed in the 1965 one acter, *Dock Brief,* as well as in the major productions, *Our Town, Romanoff and Juliet,* and *The Queen and the Rebels.* Within the teaching community, Haig became noted for the exceptional field experiences which he provided for his students. In order to make the history of western Canada more meaningful, Haig organized numerous expeditions, in which he and his students traced the routes of various explorers.

This interest eventually led to Haig's leaving the teaching profession in order to establish the Lethbridge Historical Research Centre.

Glen Seeman was probably the most versatile actor among the more youthful members of the club. Seeman, a local lad, whose family owned one of the major jewelry stores in the city, joined the cast of *Little Red Riding Hood* (1966), and then he became a very active member of the club until its demise. He also participated in other local theatre societies until family and work (Royal Trust Company) responsibilities became too demanding. To fill other youthful roles, the Pritchards enticed some of their own children onto the stage, the most active of whom was their oldest son, Jay. Other young men such as Jack Horn and Bruce Brandson showed considerable acting potential; however, they were involved with the group for only a short period of time.

Two members who truly seemed to blossom under the careful guidance of Joy and Fred Pritchard were Bud Iverson and Muriel Matheson. Iverson was an automobile mechanic who worked under the supervision of Earl Colpitts at the Beny garage. Colpitts convinced Iverson to audition for *I Remember Mama*; Iverson was cast in the part of Uncle Chris. Later that year (1964), Iverson was awarded Best Supporting Actor for his role of Gus in Our Town Workshop's entry in the Lethbridge and District One Act Festival, *The Dumb Waiter*. Following that, he performed in most of the major productions staged by the company. In 1966 Iverson was recognized as the Best Supporting Actor for his portrayal of Astor in Harold Pinter's *The Caretaker*. Adjudicator Peter Boretski said of Iverson's performance, "This man fully realized his part . . . superb. . . . He gave a beautifully relaxed, stunned, bovine, very, very fine performance."[147] Although Iverson tended to be cast in serious dramatic roles, he thoroughly enjoyed playing the light comic roles of Burl (a pig) and the short sighted, Halterton Hullabaloo, in the children's theatre productions, *Three Little Pigs* and *Little Red Riding Hood,* respectively. Shortly after Iverson's portrayal of Zor in the 1967 Alberta Regional Festival production, *The Wheel*, he moved from Lethbridge and his absence was truly felt among performers and patrons, alike.

Muriel (Mo) Matheson's debut performance with the Our Town Workshop was in the one act festival production of *Fool's Errand* (November, 1963). At the provincial festival, the adjudicator, Tom Kerr, remarked that she "had a very good attack and she sustained her character throughout the play very well."[148] Kerr, then, selected Matheson as the Best Character Actress. In the following two years, Matheson garnered two additional rewards: Best Actress for her portrayal of: Dodo in Our Town's *A Phoenix Too Frequent,* presented at the Lethbridge and District One Act Festival (1965) and Best Character Actress for Elisabetta, the Queen, in *The Queen and the Rebels* (1965 Alberta Regional Festival). It should be remembered that Matheson's husband, Bill, was also honored for his acting in this production. Muriel Matheson also appeared as Aunt Trina in *I Remember Mamma* for Our Town Workshop, and she participated in productions of the Playgoers Club as well as Lethbridge Musical Theatre. In conclusion, Matheson developed into a makeup specialist whose skills were eagerly sought by the various local groups.

Drama Festival Competition

Within a year after VE Day (on May 4, 1946), the revived Alberta Drama League (ADL) sponsored the Alberta Drama Festival at Western Canada High School, Calgary. Although the Alberta Drama League had not functioned in any official way since 1939, continuity was provided for the new executive because of the fact that the long time secretary treasurer, Gwillym Edwards, of Calgary, was named president. During the first couple of years following the reorganization, he was assisted by Mrs. D.W. Hays (Medicine Hat) as vice-president and Charles Sweetlove (Edmonton) as secretary-treasurer.[149] In 1948 there was a complete turnover of the executive with Arthur Graham (Coleman) taking over the reins, assisted by Betty Mitchell (Calgary - vice-president) and Ray Whitehouse (Edmonton - secretary-treasurer). Edwards's contribution was maintained during the 1948-49 season by creating the position of past president. Later, in 1955 Edwards was named honorary president, a position which he retained until 1960. During the period 1949-`. 2, the presidents were succeeded every year or two by their former vice-presidents. In 1949 Betty Mitchell replaced Arthur Graham; in 1951 Elizabeth Sterling Haynes succeeded Mitchell, and the following year, Elodia Christensen took over from the ailing Sterling Haynes.[150] Henceforth, the executive became quite stable; Christensen retained the president's chair for most of the eleven years, 1952-63. Although she stepped down in favor of Dave Cormack (Calgary) for the 1960-61 season, she presided, again, for two more terms after that before handing over the reins to Rod E. Ashburner (Medicine Hat), who retained the position until the Alberta Drama League was disbanded in 1967. Other executive members who made extensive contributions to the League, included: Frank Glenfield (secretary-treasurer); Dean Rolfson, Esther Nelson, Alice Polley, Doris Oliver, and Mrs. Merton E. McAffer (secretaries); C.R. Matthews and Murray Robison (treasurers). Southwestern Alberta zone representatives to the Alberta Drama League included: Elodia Christensen, Maybelle Bryans, Murray Robison, Harry Baalim, Kaye Watson, Sandy McCallum, and Fred Pritchard.[151]

It seems appropriate here to say a little bit more about the drama career of Elodia (Peterson) Christensen. Peterson was born in Utah in February 1901, but shortly thereafter, she moved with her family to Stirling, Alberta, where she lived throughout most of the rest of her life. Stirling is primarily a Mormon village located a few miles southeast of Lethbridge. Shortly after Elodia's marriage to Carl Harold Christensen in December 1920, she took on the task of directing her first play.[152] This was the beginning of a very active drama career for Christensen, who also raised three children, acted as village postmistress for forty-one years, was treasurer of the Stirling School district for thirty-one years, and assisted her scoutmaster husband for nine years. In January 1956 Christensen was honored by her community for thirty-five years of service to local drama. During these years, she had directed numerous plays and had served conscientiously on the Taylor Stake Drama Board.[153] By 1949 her reputation had extended well beyond the confines of southern Alberta, so she was invited to attend meetings of the Alberta Drama League. The following year, she was named zone chairman for the ADL, and then, succeeded to the positions of vice-president and president. An additional honor came her way in 1955-56; she was selected as a recipient of the prestigious Canadian Drama Award (CDA). Although her activities associated with the Alberta Drama League and the DDF were rather demanding, Christensen continued to be active in community and church drama. In 1954 she directed *The Exodus*, a play which was presented to the LDS conference in Salt Lake City, Utah; in 1956, she was appointed Divisional Drama Supervisor for the LDS Church in southern Alberta, a position which she held for a number of years.

Throughout the eighteen years in which Christensen was associated with the ADL, she retained the love and respect of everyone with whom she was associated. Theatre practitioners from every segment of society (local, provincial, and national) appreciated her warmth, on the one hand, and her strength, on the other. To paraphrase Murray Robison, "Elodia exuded an air of dignity; she was always a lady, who at the same time, provided incredible leadership." In addition to stimulating participation in the DDF, Christensen gave particular impetus to the establishment and growth of the Alberta one act festival movement.[154] Through 1949, one act plays were still allowed to compete in the Alberta Regional Drama Festival; however, from that time on, the ARDF was strictly a three act festival. This void was filled in 1953 when the Alberta Drama League introduced the Alberta

One Act Festival, to be preceded by regional festivals in the various zones into which the province was divided. Alberta one act festivals were held in Red Deer for the first decade; the last Red Deer Festival, sponsored by the Alberta Drama League, was May 10, 11, 1963. In November of that same year, the Alberta One Act Festival was moved to Banff, where it continued, annually, until the Alberta Drama League discontinued its activities.

It was during the latter years of Christensen's presidency that the League began to question the competitive nature of the festivals. This concern with competition was also voiced at the Western Canadian Community Theatre Conference held in Banff in November 1963. The conference, which was sponsored by the drama division of the Alberta government's recreational and cultural development branch, attracted 85 delegates from Alberta and British Columbia (including the presidents of the British Columbia Drama Association and the Alberta Drama League, Bill Zuellner and Rod Ashburner, respectively). According to the *Edmonton Journal,* the conference concluded that, "non-competitive drama festivals are the big hope for the drama festival movement. . . ."[155] At the same time, the DDF was struggling with this question as well. In addition, the DDF was concerned about the quality of the DDF and about the role of professional theatre in Canada.[156] Eventually, the Alberta Drama League determined that drama festivals were passé, and therefore, the executive decided to gradually dissolve its operations. After all, the larger cities of Edmonton and Calgary had not been represented for many years. Ironically, Joyce Doolittle brought Calgary back into the three act festival for competition in 1964, 1965, and 1966, capturing the best play award in each of these years. But "the die was cast"; the Alberta Drama League closed its books following the centennial festivals of 1967. Elodia Christensen, who had already retired from her various civic duties in Stirling, could now retire from her external drama responsibilities as well. Fortunately, she could look back with great pride on a job well done and on one which was highly appreciated. Christensen lived to be 81 years of age; she died in Medicine Hat on January 11, 1983. At that time, Joan Waterfield, writing in her weekly column for the *Lethbridge Herald*, penned the following most appropriate tribute:[157]

> The death in Medicine Hat of Elodia Christensen, formerly of Stirling, is a sad blow to those who grew to know her through her interest and work in community drama. Elodia was a woman of grace and conviction, of great personal warmth and of indefatigable strength in her promotion of theatre at the grassroots.

The Alberta Regional Festival

Although the Lethbridge Playgoers did not re-enter festival competition until 1952, other theatre groups in southern Alberta demonstrated an early interest in the festivals. In 1946 subregional festivals, adjudicated by Sydney Risk, Drama instructor, University of Alberta, were held in Lethbridge, Coleman, and Calgary. Formal arrangements for the 1946 Lethbridge subregional festival were handled by Marian Brandley; the festival was conducted under the auspices of the local Mutual Improvement Association of the LDS Church. LDS dramatic societies from Cardston, Raymond, and Lethbridge competed in this subregional festival.[158] In Coleman, the local Lions Club festival was the only community drama festival to be maintained in Alberta throughout the war. When the Lions Club 5th annual drama festival was accorded subregional status in 1946, drama groups from Cardston, Coleman, Bellevue, and Blairmore competed for the right to represent that area at the Calgary Regional Festival.

Emerging from the three subregional festivals were Calgary Workshop 14, Cardston Drama Club, Coleman Players, and Cardston Players. *John Doe*, the Calgary production under the direction of Conrad Bain was declared the winner by adjudicator Elizabeth Sterling Haynes. Alice Dowdle, director and leading lady in the Cardston Players' production, *To Die With a Smile,* was chosen as the best actress of the festival, an honor which she shared with Polly Purvis of the Coleman Players.[159] Lethbridge residents recall proudly that Conrad Bain and his twin brother, Bonner, were born in Lethbridge and spent a number of their younger years in the city where they attended Bowman and Central elementary schools. After enrolling in Western Canada High School, Calgary, Conrad came under the influence of Betty Mitchell, the school's extraordinary drama teacher.[160] In the school's 1942 production of *Our Town,* directed by Betty Mitchell, Bain's performance was so outstanding that he was awarded a scholarship to the Banff School of Fine Arts. Shortly thereafter, Bain enlisted in the Canadian Dental Corps, and while stationed in Calgary, he wrote, directed, and acted in a play for the 33rd Company. During most of his three years of service, Bain was assigned to the POW camps in Lethbridge and Medicine Hat. In Lethbridge, he assisted Dr. Wayne Matkin. Following his release from military service, he helped to found Workshop 14 (Calgary), for whom he directed their first festival entry, *John Doe.* Bain subsequently graduated from the American Academy of Dramatic Arts in New York City in 1948 and later joined the faculty.[161] He also became an extremely successful stage actor and television star. Readers will particularly remember his portrayals of Arthur Harmon and Philip Drummond in the T.V. situation comedies *Maude* and *Different Strokes,* respectively.

Edmonton was selected for the 1947 Regional Festival which followed subregional festivals held in Calgary, Coleman, and Edmonton. Provincial competitors were narrowed down to Edmonton Community Theatre, Calgary Theatre Players, Medicine Hat Little Theatre, and the Cardston Drama Club. Adjudicator, R.G.H. Orchard (professor of Drama, U of A) selected the Edmonton production, directed by Eva O. Howard, to represent the Alberta Region at the reorganized DDF which was held in London, Ontario that year (May 6-9), and which was to be adjudicated by Emrys Jones. Jones, professor of drama at the University of Saskatchewan, was born in Wales, but he came to Canada as a child and received his public schooling in Edmonton and then graduated from the University of Alberta. Subsequently, he studied drama at the universities of Columbia and Cornell.[162]

In 1948, following subregional festivals in Calgary, Banff, Medicine Hat, Coleman, Edmonton, and Peace River, the Edmonton Community Players, directed by E.S. Haynes was selected as the top Alberta entry. After that, the larger communities began to dominate the Alberta Regional Festival with entries coming primarily from Calgary, Edmonton, Lethbridge, Medicine Hat, and Red Deer. In addition, subregional festivals were generally eliminated; however, as illustrated earlier, final competitors were selected for some of the successive festivals by roving adjudicators.[163] As far as major honors are concerned, Betty Mitchell's Workshop 14 captured the best play award in nine of the Alberta Regional Festivals in which it competed. In reality, this group was dominant in the festival until 1956. During the first eleven festivals, the only two times when Workshop 14 didn't capture this award were the two years when the company did not compete (1947, 1953). On those two occasions, the coveted best play award was presented to Edmonton companies [Edmonton Community Theatre Players and Studio Theatre (University of Alberta), respectively]. From 1957 through 1970, the Alberta Regional Festival was dominated by theatre companies from southern Alberta, although, as was noted earlier, Joyce Doolittle's Calgary companies severely challenged this southern domination from 1964-66. Honors bestowed on southern Alberta groups are illustrated in Table 5-12.

As can be seen from Table 5-12, Coaldale Little Theatre was the most successful southern Alberta competitor in the Alberta Regional Festivals. In fact, next to Calgary Workshop 14, Coaldale's productions were selected for the best play award more often than any other group. In addition, Murray Robison's selection as best director on five occasions rank him second in the category after

TABLE 5-12

Alberta Regional Three Act Festival Awards
Southern Alberta Recipients (1946-1970)*

Year	Company	*BEST PLAY*	Year	Company	*BEST PLAY*
1957	MHCT	Stalag 17	1962	PL	The Dark at the Top of the Stairs
1958	CLT	All Summer Long	1963	CLT	The Well of the Saints
1959	MHCT	Diary of Anne Frank	1967	CLT	Teach Me How to Cry
1960	MHCT	Come Back Little Sheba	1969	LMT	Bus Stop
1961	CLT	The Beautiful People	1970	PL	The Hostage

Year	Company	*BEST DIRECTOR*	Year	Company	*BEST DIRECTOR*
1956	CLT	Murray Robison	1962	PL	Denise Black
1957	MHCT	Henry Allergoth	1963	CLT	Murray Robison
1958	CLT	Murray Robison	1966	OTW	Fred Pritchard
1959	MHCT	Henry Allergoth	1967	CLT	Murray Robison
1960	PL	Sam Pitt	1970	PL	Dick Mells
1961	CLT	Murray Robison			

Year	Company	*BEST ACTOR*	Year	Company	*BEST ACTOR*
1957	MHCT	Garry Mitchell	1963	CLT	Sandy McCallum
1958	PL	George Hall	1964	PL	Syd Clarke
1960	PL	Sandy McCallum	1965	OTW	Bill Matheson
1961	CLT	Russell Wiber	1967	CLT	Ed Bayly
1962	PL	Cliff Black	1970	U of L	Charles Schott

Year	Company	*BEST ACTRESS*	Year	Company	*BEST ACTRESS*
1946	CaP	Alice Dowdle	1962	PL	Jean Ede
1946	CoLP	Polly Purvis	1963	CLT	Peggy Mallalieu
1954	PL	Mary Waters	1965	OTW	Joan Waterfield
1955	MHCT	Evanthea Evangelos	1967	PL	Joan Waterfield
1956	CLT	Jennie Emery	1970	PL	Lois Dongworth
1960	MHCT	June Ferguson	1970	PL	Sheila Pisko

Year	Company	*BEST SUPPORTING ACTOR*	Year	Company	*BEST SUPPORTING ACTOR*
1957	MHCT	John Komanchuk	1964	PL	George Mann
1958	CLT	Sandy McCallum	1966	OTW	Bud Iverson
1960	MHCT	Wayne Chesley	1967	PL	George Mann
1961	CLT	Sandy McCallum	1970	PL & U of L	Charles Schott, Jr.
1963	PL	Derek Charnley			

Year	Company	*BEST SUPPORTING ACTRESS*	Year	Company	*BEST SUPPORTING ACTRESS*
1953	PL	Mary Waters (Heinitz)	1963	PL	Joan Perkinson
1956	CLT	Theresa King	1964	PL	Sharon Bolen (Magee)
1957	CLT	Jennie Emery	1966	MHCT	Sandra Brown
1960	PL	Kaye Watson (Robison)	1967	MHCT	Jean Van Wert
1961	CLT	Theresa King	1970	U of L	Nora Needham

Year	Company	*BEST CHARACTER ACTOR*	Year	Company	*BEST CHARACTER ACTOR*
1959	MHCT	Russell Stone	1964	MHCT	Richard Wray
1961	CLT	Fred Pritchard	1966	OTW	Bill Matheson
1963	PL	George Mann	1970	PL	Bill Matheson

Year	Company	*BEST CHARACTER ACTRESS*	Year	Company	*BEST CHARACTER ACTRESS*
1956	CLT	Peggy Mallalieu	1964	PL	Jean Ede
1958	PL	Brenda Cordwell	1965	OTW	Muriel Matheson
1959	MHCT	Jennifer Kerr	1966	MHCT	Margaret Phillips
1960	PL	Joan Waterfield	1967	CLT	Peggy Mallalieu
1961	PL	Denise Black	1970	PL	Hazel Skaronski
1962	PL	Helen (James) Bennett			
1963	MHCT	Lois Dongworth			

Year	Company	*BEST STAGE MANAGER*	Year	Company	*BEST STAGE MANAGER*
1961	CLT	Ivan Meyers	1965	CLT	Ivan Meyers
1962	PL	Norville Getty	1967	CLT	Ivan Meyers
1963	CLT	Ivan Meyers	1970	U of L	Weste Jensen
1964	MHCT	-			

Year	Company	*BEST VISUAL DESIGNER*	Year	Company	*BEST VISUAL DESIGNER*
1957	MHCT	Fred Kirkpatrick	1964	PL	-
1960	PL	Corne Martens	1965	CLT	Ed Bayly
1962	PL	-	1966	OTW	-
1963	CLT	Katherine & Elizabeth Brauer	1967	CLT	M. Robison
			1967	MHCT	Ron McAffer (special award)
			1970	PL	Ed Bayly

*CLT	Coaldale Little Theatre		MHCT	Medicine Hat Civic Theatre
CaP	Cardston Players		OTW	Our Town Workshop
ColP	Coleman Players		PL	Playgoers of Lethbridge
LMT	Lethbridge Musical Theatre			

Betty Mitchell who captured the honor seven times. Medicine Hat Civic Theatre, under the direction of Henry Allergoth and Dorothy Jones, was also rather successful.

Murray Robison and Ernest G. Sterndale Bennett (1963)
Photo: Sterndale Bennett Family

When one reviews the total number of awards presented to the various southern Alberta companies, it becomes apparent that each of the companies achieved considerable success. It is also true, however, that certain productions tended to dominate the awards presented in any one year. For example, Coaldale took a majority of the awards in 1956, 1961, 1963, and 1967; Playgoers of Lethbridge excelled in 1960, 1962, 1964, and 1970; Medicine Hat gained supremacy in 1957 and 1959; and the Our Town Workshop garnered most of the awards in 1966. Individuals who received multiple onstage awards at the Regional Drama Festivals included: Sandy McCallum (who garnered four acting awards), George Mann (three), Bill Matheson (three), Peggy Mallalieu (three), Joan Waterfield (three), Jennie Emery (two), Mary Waters (two), Lois Dongworth (two), Theresa King (two). Ivan Meyers, who was honored four times, was the only multiple winner in the stage management category, whereas Ed Bayly was the only multiple winner to gain awards for acting as well as backstage participation (one best actor award plus two awards for best visual presentation).

Alberta Regional Festival Winners: Jean Ede, Cliff Black, Denise Black
Photo: City of Lethbridge Archives and Records Management

Hosting the Regional Festival

During the years 1946-1952, the Alberta Regional Drama Festival generally alternated its location between Edmonton and Calgary. The exception to this was the year, 1948, when the festival was held in Medicine Hat. Then, in 1953 Lethbridge became the host, and for the period 1953-1967, the festival tended to move between Alberta's four major cities, although Red Deer acted as host in 1962. During the era under discussion, the Alberta Regional Drama Festival was held in Lethbridge in 1953, 1957, 1963, and 1967. (It seems somewhat appropriate that the final regional festival sponsored by the Alberta Drama League should occur in Lethbridge, the home of the founder of the League, E.G. Sterndale Bennett.) Special festival committees were established in the host communities in order to organize the festival activities. The Lethbridge committees for 1953 and 1957 were both chaired by Lethbridge Playgoer, Harry Baalim; whereas, the two committees in the 1960s were presided over by the city's development officer, Dennis S. O'Connell. Most of the committee members in 1953 and 1957 were active members of the Playgoers Club, whereas in the 1960s, the committees included more local business and professional members as well as representatives from the Coaldale Little Theatre. Specific membership in these four committees is shown in Table 5-13.[164]

Ed Bayly and Kaye Robison in Playboy of the Western World, *produced by Coaldale Little Theatre, 1968*
Photo: Coaldale Public Library

The 1967 festival was not the last three act festival to be held in Lethbridge. Although there was no official regional festival held in Alberta in 1968, a number of interested local citizens, in cooperation with the Lethbridge Chamber of Commerce, decided to fill the void by sponsoring a major Western Canada Arts Festival in Lethbridge. In August 1967 a Western Canada Arts Festival Association was formed with Len Ankers as president.[165] Considerable enthusiasm was generated for this idea, and four western theatre companies agreed to participate in the non-competitive festival which was scheduled for the Yates Memorial Centre, April 17-22, 1968. Coaldale Little Theatre, the only local participant, presented *Playboy of the Western World*. The other amateur participants

TABLE 5-13
Alberta Regional Festival Committees
Lethbridge, Alberta

POSITION	1953	1957	1963	1967
Chair	Harry Baalim	H. Baalim	D.S. O'Connell	D.S. O'Connell
Secretary	Lydia Turbis	Doris Balcovske	Vera Ferguson	Kaye (Watson) Robison
Treasurer		C.R. Matthews	Kay MacLeod	Ian Kinnell
Publicity	Hugh Buchanan	Daphne Manson, Sandy McCallum, Bill Bagshaw	K. Macleod	Joan Waterfield
Stage Manager	Tom Ferguson	Bruce Busby	R.E. Shackleford	Ed Bayly
Prod. Assistant	Glen Adamson, Farrel Oler	G. Adamson		
Props	Jessie Baalim	F. Oler	K. Watson and Phyl Ellerbeck	K. Robison
Wardrobe	J. Waterfield	P. Ellerbeck	K. Watson and P. Ellerbeck	K. Robison
Entertainment	Camille Hay	C. Hay	G.S. Neils	Jack Lakie
Advanced Tickets	Eleanor Matkin	Cliff Black	Ted Scheurkogel & Peggy McCann	
Program	C.R. Matthews	Lydia Turbis	Ed Davidson	E. Davidson
Welcoming Committee	L. Connor	L. Connor		
Box Office	H.G. Stretton	Audrey Baines	D.A. Shackleford	P. McCann
House Manager	H.B. Halifax			
Registration, Info. & Accommodation		E. Matkin	Ron Nixon	Jean Ede.
Vice Chairman, Arrangements			D.G.W. Sutherland	
Vice Chairman, Drama			Tom Ferguson	
Trophies			G.K. Thompson	Vaughn Hembroff
House Committee				L. Ankers
Executive Members		Mary Waters & H. Buchanan		
Regional President ADL				Fred Pritchard
City Rec. Director				Dick Mells

were White Rock Players (*Barefoot in the Park*), Regina Little Theatre (*Lo and Behold*), and Edmonton's All Saints Friendship Guild (*The Hollow Crown*). Adjudication for the festival was given by Firman Brown from the Theatre Department, University of Montana. An additional evening of superb theatre was presented at the festival by a professional theatre company from Calgary, Calgary MAC 14. Betty Mitchell informs us that Calgary Workshop 14 had, in December 1965, amalgamated with the Young Musicians and Actors Club (MAC) to form the MAC 14 Society.[166] Then, on July 1, 1967, this society obtained a stock contract with Actor's Equity and became a professional theatre company operating out of the Calgary Allied Arts Centre. In 1968 Calgary MAC 14 became Theatre Calgary.[167]

The Western Canada Festival also sponsored a drama seminar consisting of three panel discussions on various aspects of theatre, plus a luncheon with special guest speaker, Dr. Firman Brown. The panel discussions, which were chaired by Jack McCreath, supervisor of the drama division of the provincial government's cultural affairs branch, focussed on: Community Theatre, Vicarious Aspects of Theatre, and Child Drama. The panelists were: Margaret Faulkes, child drama specialist from the University of Alberta; Professor B.B. Engels, University of Alberta; Kay Grieve, Calgary; and Ron Wigmore, manager, Edmonton Jubilee Auditorium.[168]

Because of the considerable success which this festival achieved, it was decided to try to make it an annual event and to broaden its scope, somewhat. Through the efforts of Dick Mells and Fred Pritchard, an application was made to the DDF to include a provincial segment of the DDF in the 1969 Western Canada Arts Festival.[169] The DDF agreed, and plans were made accordingly. Unfortunately, three of the clubs which originally planned to participate had to withdraw for various reasons. These clubs were the Playgoers of Lethbridge, the Our Town Workshop,and the University of Lethbridge Players. This left the Lethbridge Musical Theatre production of *Bus Stop*, directed by Dick Mells, as the only competitor.[170] Although DDF rules required a minimum of three competitors, it was decided to relax the rules on this occasion. Therefore, the DDF dispatched adjudicator Dennis Sweeting to Lethbridge where he described the production as "a lot of fun" and "well worth seeing."[171] He was, however, somewhat critical of the "lack of shading in characters"; nevertheless, he complimented the actor, Don Runquist, by saying, "Mr. Runquist was as nice a Virgil as I've ever seen." No awards were presented at this festival; neither was *Bus Stop* selected as a finalist in the DDF which was held in Kelowna, British Columbia, that year. Other entertainment provided by the 1969 Western Canada Arts Festival included: an evening with Rich Little; a musical recital by students of the Lethbridge Registered Music Teachers' Branch; a film showing of the controversial CBC film, *Warrendale*; a play, *Dear Liar*, produced by Theatre Saskatchewan; and an evening of dramatic readings by Mrs. Jean McIntyre, presented in conjunction with two short plays, *The Bespoke Overcoat* (Grande Prairie Little Theatre) and *Red Peppers* (Playgoers Club of Lethbridge).[172] Shortly thereafter, Playgoers presented Red Peppers at the Lethbridge Provincial Jail to about 200 inmates.[173]

In 1970 Lethbridge was able to attract enough plays to constitute an official regional festival. Two Lethbridge entries, *The Hostage* and *The Miser*, produced by Playgoers and the University of Lethbridge, respectively, were joined by *Luv,* presented by the Medicine Hat Civic Theatre. The Lethbridge entries shared all of the awards; Dick Mells was awarded best director for *The Hostage*, which was also selected by adjudicator, Roberta Dolby, as the best play of the festival, and which, subsequently, was invited to Winnipeg to compete in the final DDF. Unfortunately, DDF adjudicator, Guy Beaulne, was not quite so enthusiastic about the Lethbridge production. His critical comments, nevertheless, were both positive and negative as the following excerpt from the *Lethbridge Herald* indicates:[174]

. . . Guy Beaulne described The Hostage . . . as a "well directed, enjoyable production" but "losing much in confusion of movement and voices.". . . some of the actors were too young for the parts they played and tended to lose their characters when they were not the focus of attention. He said, however that the production had "got the juice out of the comedy" and was "rich in entertainment."

It is obvious that Beaulne recognized considerable talent among the Playgoers since he selected Sheila Pisko to be the recipient of the Grace Elliott-Trudeau award for the best actor or actress under 26 years of age and listed numerous Lethbridge participants, Hazel Skaronski, Phil Story, Jim Elliott, and Jack Warburton, as contenders for other awards.

Shortly after the Winnipeg festival, another member of *The Hostage* cast, Charles (Chip) Schott, Jr., received some exciting news; he had been accepted into the acting division of the National Theatre School.[175] Schott also appeared in the University of Lethbridge production of *The Miser* with his father, Charles, who played the title role. In fact, during the Alberta Festival, Schott, Jr., was awarded Best Supporting Actor for his work in both of these plays. Following his training at the NTS, Schott joined the mime company, Theatre Beyond Words, resident in Niagara-on-the-Lake, Ontario.[176]

Following the 1970 DDF, Theatre Canada was created to supersede the DDF. Theatre Canada was charged with holding "an annual national showcase of the best of Canadian theatre at the National Arts Centre in Ottawa."[177] Participation in the non-competitive showcase would be by invitation, only. Playgoers of Lethbridge was honored to be among the twenty-two theatre organizations across Canada to be invited to the first national festival sponsored by Theatre Canada, in Ottawa, May 17-22, 1971. Playgoers' director, Dick Mells, chose the musical play, *Fings Ain't Wot They Used T'Be*. Unfortunately, the club eventually had to decline the invitation because of what it termed "insurmountable financial difficulties."[178] President Jack Warburton also commented that the club did not think it appropriate to approach city council and local business firms, again, although they had responded very generously to the Playgoers' needs in 1970. So, the year 1970 brought to an end the extensive major festival activity that had absorbed so much of the time and energy of local community theatre organizations in and around Lethbridge. Before concluding this discussion on festival activities, however, let us review the one act festival movement.

One Act Festivals

The Alberta Drama League organized the Alberta One Act Festival in 1953 with basically the same structure as the DDF, whereby, zone festivals were preliminary to the final Alberta festival. One significant difference existed between the two festivals: during the early years of the one act festival, it provided for both junior and senior competition. This practice lasted until the late 1950s.

Lethbridge and District festivals were held regularly from 1953-1959, but they became rather sporadic during the 1960s because Coaldale Little Theatre became involved in a number of rather extensive and demanding workshops, Playgoers of Lethbridge concentrated its efforts on staging at least two major productions per year, Our Town Workshop was not organized until late 1962, and the ADL disbanded in 1967.

Although a number of local and district groups participated in the Lethbridge zone festivals, the best play award was regularly garnered by one of the three groups referred to above. Coaldale Little Theatre was the most successful competitor, taking the best play award on five different occasions, and even though it withdrew from the 1955 Alberta One Act Festival, the club participated in the provincial festival six times. An analysis of the zone festivals illustrates a very interesting fact: Coaldale Little Theatre achieved best play in every local one act festival in which it competed. This was true even on the one occasion when Murray Robison did not direct the festival play; in 1959 Peggy Mallalieu directed *The Jack and the Joker.*

Coaldale Little Theatre was so successful in local competition that in 1955 it opted out of the provincial finals in favor of Playgoers so that the latter group could benefit from the experience of the additional adjudication.[179] Actually, Playgoers' production, *Lonesome Like*, received a very good reception from the Alberta One Act Drama Festival adjudicator, Elizabeth Sterling Haynes, who sincerely praised the leading players, Anita Susman and Leo Lancaster and who, as mentioned earlier, awarded a small BSFA's scholarship to director, Mary Waters. Playgoers of Lethbridge were obviously encouraged by this experience and proceeded to capture best play honors in the two successive local festivals. During those latter two festivals, Playgoers entered seven one act plays. In addition, two members of the club, Bruce Busby and Mary Waters, handled the directing chores for other local theatre companies. The 1957 festival also witnessed three entries from the Chinook Theatre Guild, which had enrolled a number of Playgoers' members. No local festival was held in 1958; however, Playgoers entered two plays in the 1959 festival. After this, as explained earlier, Playgoers withdrew from one act festival competition until 1973 in order to concentrate on major productions. As can be seen in Tables 5-14 and 5-15, Playgoers took the best play award at the Lethbridge and District Festival on two occasions and participated in three provincial festivals.

The Our Town Workshop took up the slack left by the withdrawal of Playgoers. Immediately after establishing the Our Town Workshop, Pritchard entered her group in the April 1963 zone festival. Their production of *Chinook* was selected to proceed to Red Deer in May. Following this latter festival, the Alberta Drama League decided to change the date of the provincial festival to November and to move the venue to Banff; therefore, there were two sets of zone and provincial festivals that year. Our Town Workshop was the only local entrant for the preliminary Lethbridge zone festival held in the fall 1963. Murray Robison was asked to make comments on the two plays presented by the group: *Fool's Errand* and *Red Peppers*, the latter of which was a non-competitive entry. Following this presentation, both plays were invited to participate in the Banff festival; *Red Peppers* was again entered in the non-competitive category. Because the local musician, Nellie Mann, was not able to accompany the group to Banff, Jack McCreath "volunteered" to take over the piano playing duties for *Red Peppers*. At Banff, *Fool's Errand* was selected as the best play.[180] Encouraged by this success, Our Town Workshop entered three plays in the 1964 zone festival; however, Murray Robison's production of *The Tinker's Wedding* took top honors both at home and at the provincial festival. No more zone festivals were held in Lethbridge under the auspices of the Alberta Drama League, but Our Town Workshop was invited to participate in the 1965 Banff festival with its production of *The Dock Brief*. So, like Playgoers of Lethbridge, the Our Town Workshop represented the Lethbridge zone at three provincial festivals. The 1965 festival was the last provincial one act festival sponsored by the ADL in which individuals from Lethbridge and district participated. For a resume of the various productions presented at the Alberta One Act Festivals by Lethbridge and district groups, see Table 5-15. Table 5-14, on the other hand, summarizes the various honors and awards bestowed on participants in the Lethbridge and District One Act Festivals. It should be noted that the number and type of awards presented at the festivals varied considerably from one year to the next. During the first festival (1953), for example, no individual awards were presented. Nevertheless, adjudicators, Sue Laycock and Esther Nelson, of Edmonton, did recommend six honorable mentions: Cloe Boyden and Jean Jensen (Alberta Stake MIA), Kay Salmon (Taylor Stake MIA), Carol Steed (Lethbridge Stake MIA), Carolle Eaves (Coaldale MIA), and Peggy McCann (Coaldale Little Theatre).[181] In 1954 best actor and best actress awards were added at the zone festival; in 1956 and thereafter, best supporting actors and actresses were recognized when performances warranted such recognition.

TABLE 5-14

Awards: Lethbridge & District One Act Festival (1953-1964)

Year	Group*	*BEST PLAY*	Year	Group*	*BEST PLAY*
1953	CLT	The Case of the Crushed Petunias	1959	CLT	The Jack & the Joker
1954	CLT	Riders to the Sea	Apr/63	OTW	Chinook
1955	CLT	Catherine Parr	Nov/63	OTW	Fool's Errand
1956	PL	Bathsheba of Saaremaa	1964	CLT	The Tinker's Wedding
1957	PL	From Paradise to Butte			

Year	Group	*BEST ACTOR*	Year	Group	*BEST ACTOR*
1954	PL	Jack Gibson	1959	CLT	Sandy McCallum
1955	SYP	Wally Kemp	Apr/63	OTW	Fred Pritchard
1956	PL	Bruce Busby	1964	OTW	Jim Elliott
1957	PL	Bill Matheson			

Year	Group	*BEST ACTRESS*	Year	Group	*BEST ACTRESS*
1954	Coutts	Gwen Brosz	1959	CLT	Jean Mannington
1955	PL	Anita Susman	Apr/63	OTW	Joan Waterfield
1956	PL	Elsie Biddell	1964	CLT	Yvonne Robison
1957	PL	Theresa King		OTW	Muriel Matheson

Year	Group	*BEST SUPPORTING ACTOR*	Year	Group	*BEST SUPPORTING ACTRESS*
1956	PL	Colin Turner	1956	PL	Kaye Watson
1957	CTG	Don Eccleston	1957	CTG	Yvonne Kennedy
1959	PL	Peter Hornsby	1959	CLT	Peggy McCann
Apr/63	Vulcan	Louis Shaw	Apr/63	Vulcan	Margaret Shaw
1964	OTW	Bud Iverson	1964	CLT	Jennie Emery

Year	Group	*BEST VISUAL DESIGNER*			
1964	CLT	Ed Bayly			

*CLT	Coaldale Little Theatre		MHCT	Medicine Hat Civic Theatre	
CTG	Chinook Theatre Guild		OTW	Our Town Workshop	
PL	Playgoers of Lethbridge		SYP	Southminster Young Peoples	

The competitive element was less noticeable at the provincial festivals. In the early days, there was a tendency to award scholarships where it was felt they would do the most good, either for the individual, the theatre company, or the community. Thus, in 1955 three directors were granted scholarships. But as time passed, individual awards became more common. Lethbridge and district recipients of provincial one act festival awards are listed in Table 5-16.

Lethbridge Musical Theatre (LMT)

In the fall of 1963, an extraordinarily important artistic event took place in Lethbridge when the Lethbridge Musical Theatre (LMT) was formed under the chairmanship of Gordon Moir. This group

TABLE 5-15

Alberta One Act Festival
Lethbridge and District Participants (1953-1965)

YEAR	GROUP	PRODUCTION
1953	CLT	The Case of the Crushed Petunias
1954	CLT	Riders to the Sea
1955	PL	Lonesome Like
1956	PL	Bathsheba of Saaremaa
1957	PL	From Paradise to Butte
1959	CLT	The Jack and the Joker
1960	CLT	The Devil Among the Skins
1963	OTW	Chinook
Nov/63	OTW	Fool's Errand & Red Peppers (non-comp.)
1964	CLT	The Tinker's Wedding
1965	OTW	The Dock Brief
1965	CLT	The Golden Goose (non-comp.)

TABLE 5-16

Alberta One Act Festival
Lethbridge and District Award Winners (1953-1965)

YEAR	AWARD	RECIPIENT	THEATRE/ COMPANY
1955	Honorable Mention	Anita Susman	PL
	Honorable Mention	Leo Lancaster	PL
	Directing Scholarship	Mary Waters	PL
	Best Play	An act from *Our Town*	MHCT
1956	Honorable Mention	Elsie Biddell	PL
	Honorable Mention	Sandy McCallum	PL
1957	Best Actor	Bill Matheson	PL
	Honorable Mention	Howard Palmer	PL
1959	Best Supporting Actor	Fred Pritchard	CLT
1960	Best Actress	Joy Pritchard	CLT
	Best Supporting Actor	Ed Davidson	CLT
NOV/63	Best Play	Fool's Errand	OTW
	Best Character Actress	Muriel Matheson	OTW
	Best Character Actor	Bruce Haig	OTW
	Best Actress	Gwen Brosz	MHCT
1964	Best Play	The Tinker's Wedding	CLT
	Best Actor	Ed Bayly	CLT
	Best Character Actress	Jennie Emery	CLT
	Best Director	Murray Robison	CLT

was dedicated to the production of Broadway musicals, an aim which had not been manifest in Lethbridge since 1935 when Playgoers produced *The Gingham Girl*. In the interim, various local organizations had produced a number of operettas but these efforts lasted for only a short time. On the other hand, the Lethbridge Musical Theatre was destined to become an institution in Lethbridge following the success of its initial production, *Finian's Rainbow*, at the Capitol Theatre in April 1964. The outstanding success which Lethbridge Musical Theatre achieved is due primarily to the tireless efforts of a few conscientious executive members and to the artistic dedication of three remarkably talented individuals who set a very high standard for all successors: Muriel Jolliffe (choreographer), Dick Mells (producer-director), and Albert Rodnunsky (musical director).

Jolliffe moved to Lethbridge from England in the spring of 1958 with her husband, Ray. Born in London, England, but raised in Portsmouth, Muriel began dancing at the age of three. Her initial training was in tap dancing, but in her early teens, she became interested in ballet. Her talent was such that by the age of seventeen she was lured to London where she trained under such well known artists as Anne Severskaya and Letty Littlewood, and where she was accepted as a member of the Royal Academy of Dancing. Later, she joined the Ballet Montmartre (an Anglo-Commonwealth - French touring company) in its tour of England and the European continent. Following her marriage to Ray Jolliffe in 1954, Jolliffe devoted herself to her family (two children) and to teaching.[182]

Upon her arrival in Lethbridge, Jolliffe lent immediate assistance to Joy Camden, director of the Lethbridge branch of the Canadian School of Ballet, which was affiliated with the Royal Winnipeg Ballet School.[183] In the fall of 1959, Camden took up a teaching position in Vancouver and turned over the Lethbridge instruction to Muriel Jolliffe. Although the Vancouver move was originally considered to be temporary, Camden announced in 1960 that she would not return to Lethbridge; therefore, Jolliffe officially took over the school (renamed the Jolliffe Academy of Dancing) and quickly established herself as an outstanding teacher, choreographer, adjudicator, examiner, and critic. She continued the tradition of presenting an annual recital, and by 1964 her students were prepared to offer a full ballet, *Cinderella*. In addition to directing her school, Jolliffe's other local activities during this era included choreographer for the Lethbridge Musical Theatre, Lethbridge summer musicals, and numerous other local productions as well as writer, director and choreographer for a series of Christmas pantomimes.

Albert Rodnunsky was hired by the Lethbridge Public School Board in September 1960 to give orchestral instruction to local junior and senior high school students. Rodnunsky was a student of the piano and cello and had also studied to be a conductor under Pierre Monteaux at the Domaine School of Conducting in Hancock, Maine.[184] Following this training, he took up a position as conductor of the Youth Orchestra of the Winnipeg Symphony where he was employed when contacted by the Lethbridge school superintendent. Upon arriving in Lethbridge, Rodnunsky assessed the local musical scene and determined that there was a need for a locally based symphony orchestra, and that there was probably a sufficient number of trained musicians in the district to man a full sized orchestra. He personally telephoned about 150 local and district musicians and invited them to an organizational meeting to be held September 14, 1960; only 17 showed up. Undaunted, Rodnunsky called a second meeting for a week later; 34 musicians responded to this invitation. Within a short while, however, Rodnunsky had attracted a complement of about seventy musicians, and therefore, the first full sized symphony orchestra, in the history of Lethbridge, was established.[185] It too, became a solid musical institution in the city, although it suffered a slight decline in interest on the part of the public and the musicians for a short period of time in the late 1960s.[186] Nevertheless, the symphony recovered from these doldrums and developed into a highly respected musical organization.

Shortly after the orchestra was established, Rodnunsky formed the Lethbridge Symphony Choir which joined with the orchestra for the presentation in May 1961 of Handel's "Creation."[187] The organization of a Junior Symphony followed in September 1962. Rodnunsky soon turned the baton for this latter group over to a local teacher and bass player, Bill Ivison, who was assisted by a teaching colleague and future member of the Our Town Workshop, Bruce Haig.[188] Within those first two years, Rodnunsky, aided by the Lethbridge Symphony Association, greatly transformed the musical life of the city of Lethbridge. Besides presenting a series of orchestral and choir concerts, the Lethbridge Symphony, with the assistance of the Symphony Women's League, organized and sponsored various workshops. In addition, a weekly radio program, designed to broaden the musical appreciation of local teenagers, was instituted with the assistance of interested citizens such as Cam Cathcart and Joe Shannon (radio broadcasters), Joan Waterfield (actress), and Nellie Mann (musician).[189]

In 1962 the Lethbridge Symphony Association added another dimension to its concert series – *Review 62*. This evening of entertainment included "pop" numbers by the chorus and orchestra as well as various selections by other groups and soloists from southern Alberta. For the next few years, this special concert, featuring numerous local and district artists, took on the title *Southern Showcase*. It was this activity which seriously set the stage for organizing the Lethbridge Musical Theatre as an adjunct of the Symphony Association. Albert Rodnunsky was named musical director for this musical theatre organization; LMT's association with the Lethbridge Symphony continued until 1968, at which time Lethbridge Musical Theatre became an autonomous society.[190]

Dick Mells, a teacher and recreation specialist, moved to Lethbridge from Medicine Hat in the summer 1963 to take up a position as the city's Recreation Director.[191] Mells, a native of New Zealand, had moved to Medicine Hat a few years earlier and had stimulated the development of musical theatre there by directing and producing works such as *Oklahoma!*, *Li'l Abner*, and *Pajama Game*. As soon as he arrived in Lethbridge, Mells made contact with Jolliffe and Rodnunsky, and through the cooperation and encouragement of his immediate supervisor, Gordon Moir, he interested a number of people in the idea of organizing a musical theatre society. Mells took on the task of dramatic director or director-producer for the organization's first sixteen shows, *Finian's Rainbow* (April 1964) through *Camelot* (November 1978).

Mells literally "threw himself" into the theatre scene in Lethbridge. Not only did he take on the task of directing and producing shows for LMT, but in 1966 he also introduced the concept of summer musicals primarily aimed at involving high school and college students. In the spring of 1966, Mells directed *You Can't Take it With You*, the first of many productions for the Playgoers Club of Lethbridge. Later that spring, he directed *Teahouse of the August Moon* for the Our Town Workshop. In the next few years, Mells added numerous other directorial and supervisory activities to his portfolio. In early 1967 he was appointed Superintendent of Cultural Activities for the City of Lethbridge, and consequently, he was relieved of his physical recreation duties.[192] In his new position, Mells's voluntary activities for the city's various theatrical groups increased even further. Besides the aforementioned activities, Mells: collaborated with Bill Matheson in order to develop Matheson's one act play, *Chinook*, into a three act play, which then received a centennial award at the 1967 Alberta Three Act Festival; convinced the Lethbridge Musical Theatre to underwrite his production of the three act comedy, *Bus Stop*, the sole entry in the 1969 Three Act Festival; cooperated with the Allied Arts Council, for whom he directed the summer productions, *Of Mice and Men* and *Romeo and Juliet*; and personally organized cabaret productions of *South Pacific* and *Canterbury Tales* and a Yates Theatre presentation of *Bye, Bye Elsie High* (LCI). Later, Mells (under the auspices of the LMT) entered *Two Gentlemen From Soho* in the Lethbridge and District One Act Festival.

Without question, Jolliffe, Rodnunsky, and Mells brought tremendous energy, enthusiasm, and talent to all of the artistic activities with which they were associated. This fact is well demonstrated in the following analysis of LMT's activities through the 1960s. Following the unqualified success of *Finian's Rainbow* in the spring of 1964, LMT decided to produce another popular show as soon as possible in order to maintain the initial enthusiasm. *Oklahoma!* opened at the Capitol Theatre in November of that same year. Henceforth, the late fall became the regular time for the annual productions of Lethbridge Musical Theatre, and after the 1965 production of *Li'l Abner*, the Yates Memorial Centre became the organization's permanent home. *Li'l Abner* was also the last production with which Albert Rodnunsky was associated. Because Rodnunsky was interested in pursuing his graduate program at the University of Southern California, he took a leave of absence from his local teaching responsibilities in the winter of 1966. During that absence, he accepted an offer from the Edmonton Public School system. Within a few years, Rodnunsky left the teaching profession in order to manage an Edmonton based talent agency, Rozark Artists Ltd., which produced the 1969 grandstand show for Lethbridge Whoop Up Days.[193]

Fortunately, LMT was able to call on two experienced local musicians to take over the musical direction for the 1966 production, *South Pacific* – Dr. Wayne Matkin (choral and vocal director) and Dr. Cliff A. Palmer (orchestra director). As mentioned earlier, Palmer had been concert master for the Lethbridge Symphony since its inception. These responsibilities were demanding for busy professional men, so they were pleased when Rodnunsky's successor, Malcolm MacDonald, a string specialist with Lethbridge public schools, volunteered to take over as musical director for *Show Boat* (1967). Besides, Matkin had a sincere desire to produce the Christmas opera, *Amahl and the Night Visitors*, which he presented through the auspices of the LDS church during the Christmas season in 1967 and again, in 1968. Interestingly enough, MacDonald produced the one act opera, *Sister Angelica*, for a Christmas offering in 1969. Lethbridge Musical Theatre contracted David Peterkin, Music Supervisor for the Alberta Government, to be musical director for *Destry Rides Again* (1968) and *Guys and Dolls* (1969). In his professional capacity, Peterkin had instructed a number of music workshops in Lethbridge. Musical direction for *My Fair Lady* (1970) was shared by two local high school band instructors, Willie Mathis and Jerry Pokarney.

Other production personnel who made an important contribution to the early development and success of Lethbridge Musical Theatre included many people who were also associated with local theatre groups like Playgoers, Coaldale Little Theatre, and Our Town Workshop. Nevertheless, Lazlo Funtek, Art Director of CHCT-TV, Calgary, was contracted to design some of the early productions (*South Pacific, Show Boat*). Funtek designed numerous stage productions in western Canada; he also taught stage design and stage craft at the BSFA. In addition, he conducted lectures on theatrical design at various colleges and universities as well as at provincial drama seminars.[194]

Many of the onstage participants of LMT were also involved in the local theatre scene. Exceptions to this fact could be classified into two groups: external professional performers who were contracted by Lethbridge Musical Theatre for a specific role, and local participants whose artistic interests were primarily of a musical nature. The practice of contracting professionals from outside Lethbridge began with the hiring of Allan James Monk (from Calgary) to play Woody Mahoney in *Finian's Rainbow*. Little did Lethbridge audiences realize that they were being given the opportunity to hear one of Canada's future opera greats. They thoroughly enjoyed his performance and that of the exceptionally talented local cast which had been assembled for this show. Subsequent shows featured the following imports: Doug Crosley (*Oklahoma! & Guys and Dolls*); Ron Nelson (*Li'l*

Abner); Jan Rubes (*South Pacific*); Robert McFerrin, Darryl Sherwood, Bobbi Sherron, and The Californians (*Show Boat*). Doug Crosley was one of Canada's most prominent male "pop" singers of the 1960s. He appeared regularly on the *Juliette Show*, frequently on *Wayne and Shuster*, and he did guest performances on numerous other Canadian as well as American T.V. shows.[195] Calgary critic and president of the Calgary Theatre Singers, Mort Van Ostrand, was ecstatic about his performance of Curly in the LMT production of *Oklahoma!*.[196] Crosley's later portrayal of Sky Masterton in *Guys and Dolls* was also enthusiastically received. Ron Nelson, of Edmonton, came to the role of *Li'l Abner* following extensive opera training and experience at the Toronto Conservatory, Montreal Opera Guild, Banff School of Fine Arts, and the Canadian Opera Company.[197] He had also studied in London, England, and had performed at Stratford and on CBC radio and T.V. Jan Rubes, whose beautiful deep voice was appreciated by Lethbridge opera lovers when he appeared with the Canadian Opera Company, was selected to play Emile de Becque in *South Pacific*. Who, at that time, could predict the exciting musical, film, and T.V. career that lay ahead for Rubes, or that twenty years following his South Pacific performance in Lethbridge, he would be recognized, not only as a magnificent bass singer, but also, as one of North America's finest actors. Robert McFerrin had also appeared previously in southern Alberta – in the Celebrity Concert Series. As Joe in *Show Boat*, his rendition of "Ole Man River" was majestic, as one would expect from a man with his musical credits; he was the first black male to hold a regular contract with the Metropolitan Opera Company. He also appeared on Broadway and at the Hollywood Bowl. On the sound track album for the movie, *Porgy and Bess*, his singing is dubbed for the role played by Sidney Poitier. Joining McFerrin in *Show Boat*, was Bobbie Sherron, who played Queenie. Sherron, originally from New York, was now a resident of Canada where she appeared in numerous radio and T.V. programs and on Winnipeg's Rainbow Stage. In addition, she was a very popular club entertainer. Completing the "external" cast of *Show Boat* were The Californians, a male trio (composed of Peter Bryant, Jonathan Collins, and Henry Morton), who were hired to play the various black stevedores called for by this musical. The male lead in *Show Boat*, Gaylord Ravenal, was portrayed by a Lethbridge native, but then, Calgary resident, Darryl Sherwood. Sherwood's musical career had by this time included numerous festival honors, a singing tour of South Africa, various singing engagements in Canada and the United Stated, and major roles in Calgary musicals.

Joining these professional imports were many extremely talented local actors and singers. Some of the local participants also had considerable acting or singing experience in Lethbridge or elsewhere. Gwen Legge (Sharon McLonergan in *Finian's Rainbow* and Nellie Forbush in *South Pacific*) had appeared in the Vancouver production of the opera *Carmen* and in numerous shows produced by the Vancouver Theatre Under the Stars. She was also a very popular soloist with various choirs in Lethbridge. After *South Pacific*, Legge married Peter Dell, who was shortly transferred from Lethbridge; consequently, southern Alberta lost an exceptionally talented soprano.

When Kathleen Stringam was offered the role of Laurie in *Oklahoma!*, she was exuberant; this was her first major theatrical role. She was, nevertheless, a very competent singer who had studied voice with Mrs. Eileen Higgin of Calgary and with the Banff School of Fine Arts, Opera Division. Following *Oklahoma!*, Stringam moved to Salt Lake City to continue her academic and musical education. While there, she became a member of the professional company, Valley Music Theatre, and she also took numerous roles in university opera and musical productions – roles such as Hedy La Rue in *How to Succeed in Business Without Really Trying* and Mabel in *The Pajama Game*. After this experience, she returned to Lethbridge to participate in the summer musical, *The Pajama Game*, and to play the role of Magnolia in LMT's *Show Boat*. Later, she and her husband settled in the Cardston area where she contributed immeasurably to the musical life of that community; in

1978 she agreed to commute to Lethbridge to play the role of Guenevere in the LMT production of *Camelot.*

Marilyn Ellison, a native of Long Beach, California, was a dance instructor who operated Marilyn's School of Dance in Lethbridge. Prior to moving to Lethbridge, she had participated in a number of musical and dramatic productions for the Masque and Sandal Club in Long Beach, and for Brigham Young University in Logan, Utah. Her marriage to Lethbridge businessman, Howard Ellison, brought her to Lethbridge where she and Howard participated actively in both Playgoers and Lethbridge Musical Theatre. For the latter group, she played Gertie Cummins in *Oklahoma!,* and then, starred as Daisy Mae in *Li'l Abner.* During the next few years, she took on various dancing roles.

Norma MacInnes played three minor chorus parts with Lethbridge Musical Theatre before portraying the lead, Sergeant Sarah Brown, in *Guys and Dolls.* Prior to coming to Lethbridge, this Scottish born lass had performed for a number of years in Vancouver for radio shows and professional stage companies such as Theatre Under the Stars. After coming to Lethbridge, she not only performed for Lethbridge Musical Theatre, but was also called upon to participate in Christmas pantomime productions where she took lead roles in both *Aladdin* and *Cinderella.*

Ellyn Ford was a music specialist with the Lethbridge schools. Ford, a native of Madison, Wisconsin, began her musical theatre career as a high school student when she played Sharon in *Finian's Rainbow.* She also participated in many musical productions at the University of Wisconsin where she graduated with a Bachelor of Music degree. Also, she had been a member of the Wisconsin Theatre Guild and the Diamond Circle Theatre, in Colorado. Her various musical talents were quickly realized when she moved to Lethbridge, and before long, she established herself as a very competent singer, an extraordinary pianist (who could sight read any score), and an excellent choral and vocal director. Her first appearance with LMT was in *Guys and Dolls* where she excited the audiences with her portrayal of Adelaide. The following year, she took the leading role of Frenchy in *Destry Rides Again.* Following her marriage to director, Dick Mells, she basically settled into the roles of accompanist and musical director; however, she did appear on stage, occasionally.

Although Jean Warburton displayed remarkable talent in the summer musical, *The Pajama Game,* the team of Jack and Jean Warburton first burst upon the LMT scene when they played the song and dance duo, Ellie and Frank, in *Show Boat.* From the very beginning, it was obvious that this pair, who exuded such obvious talent, were seasoned performers. In fact, they had participated actively with the Falmouth (England) Operatic Society for over fifteen years.[198] After their 1967 Lethbridge debuts, both Jack and Jean Warburton became perennial favorites in LMT as well as active members of the Playgoers and contributors to other theatrical and musical activities in the city.

In addition to these semi-professional performers, many local amateur actors and musicians helped to bring success to the productions of LMT during the 1960s. Readers are referred to Table 5-17 for a summary of the number of roles performed by the most active actors and singers in the eight LMT productions from 1964-1970.

Performers (some of whom appear in Table 5-17) who primarily took dancing roles included Linda Bauman, Jim Green, Jack Horn, Catherine Leon, Donna Gayle Mullin, Horst Mueller, Sandra Niedermier, Allan Skretting, Margaret Trockstad, and Margaret Welsh. Many of these participants were students at the Jolliffe Academy of Dancing.

Of course, all of this onstage and backstage activity would be useless if it were not for adequate musical accompaniment. Because of the close initial relationship between the Lethbridge Symphony and the LMT, it was natural that most of the pit orchestra players should be selected from members of the Lethbridge Symphony. Once LMT became autonomous, this orchestral relationship also began to diminish. Gradually, the pit orchestra began to recruit more of the local and district junior and senior high school band instructors and their students. In the 1970 pit orchestra (My Fair Lady), at least five of the nineteen players were school music teachers and at least six others were high school students. Musicians participating in the LMT productions from 1964-1970 are listed in Table 5-18. The number in parantheses indicates the number of productions for which that individual played.

TABLE 5-17

Onstage Participants: Lethbridge Musical Theatre (1964-1970)

PARTICIPANT	R	C	T*	PARTICIPANT	R	C	T	PARTICIPANT	R	C	T
Cliff Black	5	2	7	Frank Huszar	1	2	3	Ellyn (Ford) Mells	2	-	2
Kaye (Watson) Robison	4	3	7	Bud Iverson	2	1	3	Ron Francis	-	2	2
Shirley Wilson	1	6	7	Phil Kristiansen	2	1	3	Peter Grantham	2	-	2
Marilyn Ellison	3	2	5	Lily Larter	-	3	3	Shirli Gonzy	-	2	2
Al Greenway	2	3	5	Gwen Legge	2	1	3	Deb Gray	-	2	2
Ike Lanier	2	3	5	Marg McKay	-	3	3	Marion Greenway	-	2	2
Norma MacInnes	1	4	5	Tom Melling	1	2	3	Merry Jo Hahn	-	2	2
Ed Bayly	4	-	4	Bill Matheson	3	-	3	Audrey Harper	-	2	2
Howard Ellison	2	2	4	George Mann	3	-	3	Terri Anne Illingsworth	1	1	2
Dunc Gillispie	1	3	4	Claire Marie Pacaud	-	3	3	Kirk Jensen	-	2	2
Lee Mells	2	2	4	Don Runquist	1	2	3	Linda Kotyk	-	2	2
Michael Sutherland	2	2	4	Frank Ward	2	1	3	Dianne Pokarney	-	2	2
Jack Warburton	3	1	4	Jean Warburton	3	-	3	Bill Rasmussen	-	2	2
Laverne Ankers	-	3	3	Linda (Albertson) Bayly	-	2	2	Karren Runquist	-	2	2
Truus Baird	-	3	3	Bery Allan	-	2	2	Chip Schott	1	1	2
Wendy Carson	-	3	3	Laurel Anderson	-	2	2	Kathleen Stringam	2	-	2
Hazel Durans	-	3	3	Bob Befus	-	2	2	Norm Thomas	2	-	2
Jean Ede	-	3	3	Wayne Barry	2	-	2	Florence Ward	-	2	2
Bill Hacker	-	3	3	Larry Dye	-	2	2				
Sheila (Hawn) Pisko	2	1	3	Georgia Fooks	-	2	2				

*T = Total performances R = Leading or Supporting Role; C = chorus.

It must be acknowledged that excellent artistic endeavors do not become significant community institutions without competent board members to oversee the organizing, budgeting, and scheduling aspects of such an enterprise. Fortunately, a number of community minded professional people and business entrepreneurs were prepared to devote many hours of supervision and hard work to the organization in return for very little recognition. On the other hand, they undoubtedly received much personal satisfaction from their superlative accomplishments. Horace Barrett, a local hardware merchant, was an exemplary president of the LMT executive for two terms; however, his contribution was cut short by his unfortunate death in 1967. Nevertheless, during his short tenure, he demonstrated the ideal characteristics required of a volunteer leader: extremely good organizational skills; a deep concern for, and understanding of, other people; and a sincere interest in the needs of the community. In honor of his dedicated work for LMT, the organization established the Horace Barrett Memorial Trophy to be presented annually to the best performance in the Senior Musical Theatre class at the Lethbridge Kiwanis Music and Speech Arts Festival. The community's appreciation for Barrett and his colleagues' fine organizational and supervising talents was shown, annually, when approximately 6 500 local and district patrons flocked to the fall production.

TABLE 5-18
Pit Musicians: Lethbridge Musical Theatre (1964-1970)

TYPE OF INSTRUMENT	MUSICIANS
Violin/Viola	H. (Mrs. Keith) Ferguson (4), Hugh Laycock (4), Clifford Palmer [concert master (4)], Evan Gushul (3), Alex Palmarchuk (3), Ted James (3), Jack Blech (2), B. Hegland, Don Kirkham, M. Moir
Bass Violin	Fred Leister (8), Bill Ivison (4), F. Duff
Cello	Abe Enns (4), Michael Golia (2), G. Watkinson (2)
Flute	Mardine Francis (3), George Swedish (2), Don Flaig
Reeds	Glenda Colley (3), Clarence Ringland (3), Stewart Campbell (2), Milt Iverson (2), Vaughn Anderson, W. Annon, Allen Block, Ernie Block, Joan Christiansen, H. Falcons, Peggy Foster, A. Frank, P. Gould, Cliff Harvey, Lynette Iverson, Nick Kucheran, Tom Last, P. Lyall, David Mann, Judy Milligan, A. Pomahac, Ray Reynolds, Eileen Runge, Frank Russell, Bill Sikking, Donna Speelman, Dean Takahashi
Trumpet	Grant Erickson (4), Dexter Archibald (2), Joe Dowell (2), Barry Goughnour (2), Jerry Pokarney (2), D. Williams (2), Ross Barnaby, Alan Dahl, Pat Davidson, J. Dobson, G. Duits, Jim Dundass, R. Hall, K. Lancaster, J. Mack, Jerry Mezei
Trombones/Other Brass	Boyd Hunter (3), Grant Ford (2), M. Graham (2), Bruce Haig (2), Morry Marshall (2), Brad Watson (2), Kent Fletcher, George Flynn, Andy Isbister, Rex Little, Norman Nettleton, Robert Rathe, Bruce Schaalje
French Horn	B. Stannard (3), Lorraine Bougham, D. Horug, Philip Matkin, R. Perkinson
Percussion	Ernie Block (5), B. Laycock (2), D. Byrne, B. Francis, S. Purkis
Piano/Organ	D. Botterill (6), Henry Waack (4), W. Haig, Ellyn Mells

Locally Produced Summer Musicals

Through the initiative of Dick Mells and Muriel Jolliffe, Lethbridge Allied Arts Council was convinced that sponsoring summer musicals would be a worthwhile addition to the Council's summer arts program. With the assistance of Ray Jolliffe to organize and supervise the backstage crew, Cathy Evins to design sets, props, and costumes, and Henry Waack to direct the musical activities, the first Allied Arts summer musical, *Babes in Arms*, opened at the Yates Memorial Centre on August 19, 1966.[199] Although some mature members of the Lethbridge theatrical community appeared in appropriate roles, most of the cast consisted of high school, college, and university students since one of the major aims of this project was to provide an educational, yet, "upbeat" summer activity for Lethbridge young people. Allied Arts Council also sponsored the two succeeding musicals, *The Pajama Game* (1967) and *The Boy Friend* (1968); during the summers of 1969 and 1970, LMT backed the summer musicals, *Little Mary Sunshine* and *Your Own Thing*.

Locally Produced Christmas Pantomimes

Muriel Jolliffe, with the cooperation of her husband, Ray, and the Allied Arts Council, were primarily responsible for producing English pantomimes during the Christmas season starting in 1966. Like many of her predecessors, Jolliffe was concerned with giving her dance students opportunities to perform beyond the traditional annual recitals. Certainly, the musicals with which Jolliffe was associated provided invaluable experiences for many of the more mature dancers, but the pantomimes extended those opportunities to dancers of all ages. Muriel Jolliffe wrote, choreographed, and directed the pantomimes; Ray Jolliffe supervised the backstage activities. Many other people, including Muriel's mother, Gladys Carson (costume mistress), helped backstage. Onstage participation was led by Frank Featherstone, a Coaldale teacher, who routinely played the "Dame." Unquestionably, this native of Newport, Wales, was about the most excruciatingly funny "Dame" one could possibly imagine. Featherstone's acting career began with church plays during his youth. In the early 1960s, he emigrated to central Alberta and after two years, he took a teaching position in Coaldale. Later, he was named Vice Principal, and subsequently, Principal at Kate Andrews High School in Coaldale where he agreed, among other duties, to teach the drama courses.[200] Featherstone was a strong supporter of the high school drama festival association which resulted in his being named to the executive of that organization. In 1965 he joined the casts of the two children's shows produced by the Coaldale Little Theatre, *The Red Shoes* and *The Golden Goose*. The following year, he portrayed the zany character, Paul Sycamore, in Playgoers' production of *You Can't Take It With You*, and then during the 1966 Christmas season, he started his love affair with Lethbridge audiences through his participation in the Christmas pantomimes.

In addition to the tradition that the "Dame" be played by a male character actor, the juvenile male lead in the English pantomime is customarily portrayed by a young female; however, this latter practice was not commonly followed in the Lethbridge productions even though Norma MacInnes did play Aladdin in the initial Jolliffe pantomime. Generally, however, a young male (Kirk Jensen) was cast in this role. Other stock characters included the "sweet, young damsel," the innocent but somewhat dull fellow, and the villain. In the early pantomimes, the juvenile female lead was portrayed by young actresses such as Gay Gray, Adele Stephens, and Linda Johnson; the innocent dull fellow became the speciality of Frank Huszar; villains were wickedly portrayed by Dick Mells, Bill Matheson, and George Mann. Of course, additional characters were introduced into the various pantomimes depending upon their plot. Peter Grantham, who had displayed an extraordinary talent when portraying Og in the LMT production of *Finian's Rainbow*, proved to be an excellent choice for pantomime characters such as Buttons, Cinderella's best friend, or Wishee Washee (in *Aladdin*).

Local Dance Schools and Their Activities

During the 1950s a number of dance schools and instructors came and went in Lethbridge. Some of these schools gave instruction on various forms of dance; others tended to specialize. Moore's Academy of Dancing, which maintained schools in Vancouver and Calgary, offered a series of classes in the local Civic Centre; however, most of the academies were operated by resident instructors such as Mrs. M. Qually, Marge Dunlop, Jack Taylor, and Eileen Dodds.[201] Some of the local schools were rather short lived, for example, Phyl Trca's Dancing Academy. It will be recalled that Trca choreographed and danced in a number of YMCA sponsored productions during the late 1940s. The three major local schools, however, were the Dickson Dance Studio, Nettie Livingstone's School of Dance and the Canadian School of Ballet under Joy Camden. In July 1951 Dickson's Studio proudly announced the arrival of Shirley Arnold, a registered tap and ballet instructor.[202] Livingstone (nee Walker) specialized in highland dancing, but she also offered instruction in folk, tap, and novelty dancing as well as baton work. Although a native of Glasgow, this grand champion of highland dance had lived most of her adult life in Lethbridge where she had entertained in Rotary minstrel shows and other productions since the 1920s.[203] In 1956 Livingstone contracted Jean Gauld to assist her.[204] At that time, Gauld was president of the Calgary branch of the Canadian Dance Teacher's Association. Gauld advertised instruction in ballet, tap, acrobatic, character, Scottish, and other national folkdances. In addition, she was prepared to offer "general stage training" and to teach professional routines for stage and T.V.

In June 1953 Joy Camden first presented her students in a dance demonstration held at the Civic Centre. Camden was principal of the Lethbridge Branch of the Canadian School of Ballet, an official training school for the Royal Winnipeg Ballet.[205] Camden, a native of London, England, not only instructed in Lethbridge and district but also gave instruction in Edmonton where she was associated, as ballet mistress and choreographer, with Alberta's first amateur ballet company, Arts Ballet Company '54.[206]

Both Camden and Gauld were invited to participate in the official opening of the Southern Alberta Jubilee Auditorium.[207] They presented two student ballets on Thursday, May 2; the first, *Love Will Find a Way*, was choreographed by Joy Camden; the second, *Maciek is Dead*, was produced by Jean Gauld, whereas Camden arranged the traditional music, and danced the role of Maciekova (Maciek's wife). Shortly after this Jubilee presentation, one of Camden's most successful students, Judy Botterill, who had performed in *Love Will Find a Way*, enrolled in the Royal Ballet School in London, England. On October 31, 1958, Botterill appeared in the ballet corps of the Royal Ballet's production of Moussorgsky's opera, *Boris Godunov*, at the Royal Opera House.[208]. One and a half years later, she danced in the Royal Ballet School's first all student show, Delibe's *Coppelia*.[209] Four years later, this young dancer, who incidently, was the daughter of Norman and Dixie Botterill, manager of radio station CJOC, and accompanist "extraordinaire," respectively, was the featured artist at the annual Jolliffe Evening of Dance.[210] By this time, Camden had moved to Vancouver and Jolliffe had assumed ownership of the Canadian Ballet School which became incorporated as the Jolliffe Academy of Dancing, a school which achieved success and longevity unprecedented in Lethbridge. Other prominent schools in the early 1960s were Marilyn Ellison's School of Dancing and Sillito's Tap School.[211]

The excellent success which Jolliffe achieved with her dancers is evident in the results of the Alberta Dance Festivals which were inaugurated in Lethbridge on February 7, 8, 1964. In fact, Muriel Jolliffe was the driving force behind the festival which was held in Lethbridge for many successive years under the auspices of the Lethbridge Ballet Auxiliary and the Lethbridge Gyro Club. A local dance festival committee was organized to attend to all the routine business.[212]

Being a student at the Jolliffe Academy in the 1960s was an exciting experience. Jolliffe was a true task master, but as illustrated earlier, she provided her students with numerous opportunities to display their talents. Consequently, although most of Jolliffe's students did not conceive of professional dance careers, she developed some exceptionally talented dancers who eventually proceeded to very respectable ballet schools and ballet companies. Five of Jolliffe's students from this era went on to professional careers in dance.[213] At the early age of fifteen, Esther Murillo was awarded a summer scholarship, followed by a regular bursary for study at the National Ballet School in Toronto. Upon graduation from the school, she studied with various European companies before being awarded a contract with Canada's National Ballet, for whom she danced for eight years. When she retired in 1981, she was a first soloist with the company. Jane Lee devoted twenty years to her professional dance career. After leaving the Jolliffe Academy, Lee entered the Rambert Ballet School in London. An extremely varied career in dancing followed. She, together with her husband, Phil Devonshire, participated in various companies in Europe including a singing and dance company, Ballet Zoom. Later, the couple danced with Ballet San Marcos in Lima, Peru. Lee's career also included a contract with London's West-End production of *Peter Pan*. In addition, she spent five years in the London cast of *Cats;* Devonshire was in the show for three years. The couple retired to Victoria, B.C., in 1988. Sherry Lanier spent three years with the Alberta Ballet Company (1971-1974) before continuing her studies in England. In 1978 she joined the Toronto Dance Theatre where she became a principle dancer. Lanier also danced with les Feux Follets in Montreal. A scholarship with Martha Graham took her to New York in 1983. While in New York, she paired with Ohad Naharin, with whom she performed at Carnegie Hall (December 1983). A few years later, a severe injury to her Achilles tendon forced Lanier to retire from dancing. Jim Green, who performed in Christmas pantomimes, summer musicals, and LMT productions signed a contract with the Alberta Ballet Company. Later, he became associated with the Saskatchewan Dance Theatre. However, after relatively few years in the profession, Green accepted a position with the *Toronto Globe and Mail.* Jeremy Leslie-Spinks was still quite young when his family moved to Edmonton where he continued his studies with the Alberta Ballet School. Leslie-Spinks spent a number of years with the Swedish Ballet and assumed the position of Artistic Director with the Alberta Ballet for a short interval. One of Jolliffe's most promising students, her daughter, Carol, was forced to abandon her dream of a professional dancing career because of a congenital knee problem which was diagnosed while she (a winner of three Royal Academy gold medals) was studying at the National Ballet School in London. The prognosis, that two years of professional dancing would result in permanent disability, was extremely disheartening to Carol, especially since she already had a dance contract with Lawrence Gradus of Montreal. Nevertheless, after a few months of deliberation, Jolliffe decided to leave London and return to Lethbridge. There, she married a local realtor, Miles Godlonton. She also joined her mother as an instructor at the Jolliffe Academy. When Muriel gave up teaching in order to devote herself to examining, Carol (Godlonton) assumed full responsibility for the Academy's instruction.[214] In the mid-1960s, a former student of Joy Camden's, Mrs. Romola Ully, opened the Lakeview School, and students from Ully's school achieved considerable success at the dance festivals. In fact, the school captured one of the major group awards at the 1967 festival. The Dawn Higgins Dance Studio rounded out the major private schools. Higgins, who had been an award winner at the 1965 Los Angeles National Dance Teacher's Association festival, advertised instruction in "acrobatic, tap, baton, modern jazz, and character ballet."[215]

Professional Theatre

Unquestionably, this era was a period of considerable theatrical activity, especially of a community, amateur nature. It was also a time when Lethbridge audiences were treated to some of the finest Canadian professional acting, dancing, and musical talent. A professional company, which took up residence in Lethbridge during the summers of 1953-1955, presented a wide range of excellent productions; however, the company was not very successful, financially. Possibly, as suggested earlier, the city had not yet achieved the critical mass of population required to support professional ventures.

The Great Plays Company

Professional theatre, per se, returned to Lethbridge on March 30, 31, 1953, after an absence of many years when Dean Goodman, producer-director of the Great Plays Company presented *Hamlet* at the Capitol Theatre.[216] Goodman, who began his professional career in radio drama at station KOMO in Seattle, was quickly drawn to the theatre. After four years of playing juvenile leads with the Seattle Repertory Theatre (1938-1942), he moved to Hollywood where he studied acting with the famous Russian actress, Maria Ouspenskaya. Later, Goodman was contracted to tour in Shakespearean repertory with John Carradine, who, although his movie reputation was furthered by portraying eccentric and villainous characters, was a trained Shakespearean actor. Further acting and directing experiences in Hollywood, New York, and Seattle greatly advanced Goodman's career. In 1952 he was asked to portray the lead role in the Everyman Theatre's (Vancouver, B.C.) production of *Macbeth*. Later that year, he was offered financial backing to present *Hamlet* during a five month tour of Canada with his own company, the Great Plays Company.[217] In the Lethbridge presentation, Goodman portrayed Hamlet, whereas Mary Matthews played Ophelia. Miss Matthews was a gold medal winner from the Royal Academy in London and had also played Broadway in a recent hit, *Women of Twilight*.[218] Other professionals in the cast included Naydyne Hamilton (Gertrude), Derek Ralston (Claudius), Glyn Jones (Polonius and Osric), Don Pethley (Laertes), William Lawson (Horatio), Leonard Lauk, Arthur Keenan, Frank Lindsay, Andrew Snider, Cheryle Brown, Jack McLaren, and James Gartry. A few local young actors were also given the opportunity to work with this professional troupe. Kent Duncan and Donna Glock were given walk-on parts; Bill Fruet, who had recently gained considerable notice at the Alberta Regional Drama Festival, was accorded a small speaking role. Acting members of the company also shared some of the production chores although some of these tasks were contracted to professional production personnel. The various production assignments for *Hamlet* were:

Producers:	Dean Goodman and Ron MacDonald
Set & Costume Designer:	Gary Ness
Business Manager:	Glyn Jones
Stage Manager:	Arthur Keenan
Props:	James Gartry
Costume Mistress:	Cheryle Brown
Publicity:	Frank Lindsay
Production Manager:	James Onley

The production was very well received in Lethbridge, and following its two night run in the city, Goodman announced that he hoped to return in the fall and once or twice every year, thereafter.[219] At the same time, a group of Lethbridge businessmen, headed by Hugh Buchanan, promised some financial assistance if Goodman would locate the company in Lethbridge during the summer of 1953. Goodman agreed, and after checking out the possible facilities, he decided to operate out of the Recreation Hut at the Kenyon Airport – an air-conditioned space which could seat 400 patrons, and which had an "adequate stage."[220] The Company opened with *The Voice of the Turtle* on June 15-17, and then played at the RCAF Station in Claresholm on June 18. Individual tickets sold for $1.25; season tickets were also available. Over the summer, fifteen different plays were produced in Lethbridge. Most of these productions were also toured to Waterton and Claresholm and occasionally to other southern Alberta communities such as Medicine Hat and Pincher Creek. Personnel comprising the company were somewhat different from those who visited Lethbridge in March. In addition, the company's membership changed as the summer progressed. The cast for *The Voice of the Turtle* (directed by Dean Goodman) included: Dean Goodman, Mary Matthews, and Nadyne Hamilton. Jack Medhurst (stage designer) joined the company from Calgary where he was associated with Children's Theatre at Mount Royal College. While in Calgary, Medhurst also designed sets for ice revues and operas. As the summer advanced, the Company was augmented by Robert "Mike" Hemingway (Hollywood), Cheryle Brown (Seattle), Gary Ferguson (Seattle), Cliff Sherwood (England), Anne Christensen, John Rivet, Bevonne Patterson, Bruce Busby, Marie Keenan, James Onley, and Len Ontkean. Although Dean Goodman directed most of the fifteen productions that summer, some directorial responsibilities were assigned to James Onley, Len Ontkean, and Mary Matthews, the latter of whom was called upon to direct Claudia, a play in which she had previously appeared for six months in London, England. James Onley directed *See How They Run* as well as *The Drunkard*; in the production of *See How They Run*, Derek Ralston recreated the role which he had played in the 1948 North American premiere in Ottawa (a Command Performance for the Governor General of Canada). Len Ontkean, a professional actor-director and a former resident of Lethbridge, was contracted to direct *Born Yesterday*, in which he also portrayed the lead male character, Harry Brock. Ontkean's interest in the theatre was passed on to his son, Michael, who spent part of his childhood in Lethbridge, and who in the early 1970s, became a household name through his association with the ABC Television Network series, *The Rookies*.[221] Michael Ontkean also appeared on the stage (for example, Stratford) and in numerous movies. Canadian movie buffs were pleased to witness his very fine performance in the 1989 Canadian film, *Bye Bye Blues*.[222]

Technical responsibilities were shared by various members of the company, but some tasks were formally assigned. Technical Director was Arthur Keenan, Set Designers were Gary Ferguson and Jack Medhurst, Stage Manager was Bruce Busby, and Props were handled by Kent Duncan (of Lethbridge), who also appeared in minor parts. Other locals who participated in the summer's productions (primarily in minor acting roles) included Stan Sawicki, Mary Waters, Jean Block, Yvonne Robison, Theresa King, Marion McKendry, and nine year old, Alan Whapham.

Unfortunately, the Great Plays Company suffered a major setback when a fire at the Recreation Hut destroyed about $3 000 worth of sets, props, costumes, and personal effects.[223] The Hut, itself, was sufficiently damaged that the Company had to seek out another performance facility. The ongoing production, *Goodbye Again*, was moved to the Legion Memorial Hall; *Born Yesterday* and all subsequent productions in Lethbridge were staged at the Civic Sports Centre. Although the company suffered this financial loss, and although the receipts at the door were not always adequate, the company decided to present three plays beyond those originally scheduled; therefore, Goodman and his players remained in Lethbridge for about three weeks after the original closing date of September 7. Following their final performance of *Bell, Book and Candle* on September 26, 1953, the company took a week's holiday which was followed by a tour to a few Alberta and Saskatchewan communities.

In the spring of 1954, Goodman announced that he would make Lethbridge his summer home, again, that year.[224] The twelve week season began on Tuesday, June 15, with *The Moon is Blue* (underwritten by the Lethbridge Playgoers Club), and it ended on September 11, with the comedy, *Miranda*. During the first half of the season, plays were scheduled for the Civic Centre on Tuesday and Friday evenings. On Wednesday, Thursday, and Saturday, the plays were toured to Medicine Hat, Claresholm, and Calgary. After the first three shows, however, the Calgary performing facility was closed. Goodman momentarily considered substituting Waterton for Calgary, but his experience during the summer of 1953 reminded him that Waterton had no truly adequate facility. Unfortunately, attendance at the Lethbridge performances was mediocre. Apparently the Company could count on an average attendance of 200 in both Medicine Hat and Claresholm but could only attract about 100 to each Lethbridge performance. Goodman voiced considerable concern about meeting his weekly payroll of $510.[225] There were usually about ten people on the payroll, although the company members changed, somewhat, over the summer.

The Moon is Blue featured Dean Goodman, Cheryle Brown, and John Farmer. Ralph Robinson of Lethbridge made a brief appearance. John Farmer was also the stage manager – a position which he maintained throughout the summer. Mahlon Vanderlain performed in only one show, *Laura*. Cheryle Brown departed after performing in the first three productions. After this, and following the addition of Bruce MacLeod, Liza Benedict, Robert Hobbs, Edward Stevlingson, Sybil Siegel, Sally Sherman, and John Bouchard, the company remained fairly stable, although Siegel departed near the end of the season and was replaced by Hilda Armstrong. Celia Stanton, of Claresholm, was also incorporated into the company as of late August; she appeared in *Petticoat Fever*, *Suspect*, and *Miranda*. In addition to Ralph Robinson, other local amateur actors who were offered parts of varying challenge, that summer, included Mary Waters; Daphne Manson and her son, Brian; Cliff Black; Joan Perkinson; Jack Maynard; and Sydney Huckvale.

At the end of July, Goodman readjusted his performance schedule so that the Lethbridge productions appeared on Friday and Saturday nights. The Saturday night performances were booked into The Whoop Up Guest Ranch (under the stars) or Alan Watson School. The Friday-Saturday schedule did draw more patrons; however, the reasons for this might also include factors related to weather, facilities, and type of productions. *Philadelphia Story* drew particularly large and enthusiastic crowds.[226] Nevertheless, a rather slow summer took its toll on the company, and it was in no mood to extend the 1954 season, although Dean Goodman, while remaining to clear up his business in Lethbridge, presented a one man show, *A Night With Dean Goodman*, on September 18 at Alan Watson School prior to taking it on a tour of southern Alberta. *A Night With Dean Goodman* consisted of selections from the works of Edgar Allan Poe, Ogden Nash, Elizabeth Browning, and William Shakespeare. A rather small audience attended.[227]

After the 1954 summer season, some members of the Great Plays Company joined the Lancaster Company of British Columbia – a company which presented *Romeo and Juliet* at the LCI on November 29. Also that fall, it was reported that the Great Plays Company had been absorbed by Rocky Mountain Productions Limited – an organization which was to engage in the production and exhibition of many types of entertainment, including radio and film. Dean Goodman was named a director of the new organization whose subsidiary, Great Plays Company, produced and toured plays – the first of which, *I Like It Here*, was booked to play at the LDS auditorium in Lethbridge on January 28, 29, 1955; they received an enthusiastic reception.[228]

Surprisingly, Goodman decided to give Lethbridge a third summer of professional theatre. He and his assistant producer-actor, Robert Jackson, a former Hollywood associate, decided that they could make a success of the venture if they involved local people in some of the decision making processes. So, a local advisory board was set up to advise on the selection of plays and to aid in the sale and distribution of tickets.[229]

Professionals associated with the 1955 season included Dean Goodman, Robert Jackson, Rosemarie Meyerhoff (who appeared with the Lancaster Company in the fall of 1954), Matt Zimmerman, Arthur Silva, Jane Smith, Gary Mitchell, Robert Collins, Abigail Arundel, and

Charlotte McDowell. Local amateur participants included Bruce Busby, who had previously left the Great Plays Company to reside in Lethbridge; Denise Black; Georgina Ozar; Joyce Williams; Jean Northan; Sydney Huckvale; and the future Liberal Senator, Joyce Fairbairn.

Lethbridge performances were booked into the Civic Centre and Susie Bawden School. Six different productions were offered to the local patrons; however, audiences were smaller than ever. After the August 5th performance of *Springtime for Harry,* for which only twenty-one patrons showed up, the company had no other choice but to "pull up stakes." The company cancelled the remainder of the season, repaid ticket holders, and closed the books on the Great Plays Company.[230] So this ill-fated relationship between Lethbridge and the Great Plays Company – a relationship which was basically a one way affair – was ingloriously terminated. It is apparent to this writer that the various members of the company, especially the director, Dean Goodman, gave much more than they received. They provided a good variety of solid entertainment, and according to the *Lethbridge Herald* reviews, their presentations were skillfully produced and well acted. Goodman was consistently praised for his directing as well as for his acting. Unfortunately, the citizens of Lethbridge did not respond accordingly. Regardless of this lack of support, Goodman remained in the city until early September in order to meet a commitment he had made with the local Golden Jubilee Committee to direct the historical pageant, *Saga of a Prairie Town,* written by Harry Baalim. Upon leaving Lethbridge, Goodman settled in San Francisco where he made an impressive contribution to the professional stage through his acting and directing. He also became involved in numerous films and television projects. As well, his theatrical contribution encompassed writing (for example, a history of theatrical productions in San Francisco) and teaching (he was contracted to offer courses at both San Francisco State University and San Francisco Community College).[231] Many years would pass before professional theatre would again attempt to locate in Lethbridge.

Other Professional Theatre

For three years, the Great Plays Company had provided Lethbridge with most of its professional legitimate theatre. The only exception to this was the production of *Romeo and Juliet* by the Lancaster Company (referred to earlier). The fall of 1955 brought two additional productions to Lethbridge – the original *Black Hills Passion Play* starring Josef Meier, and the one man show by Eric Christmas. *The Passion Play* returned to Lethbridge in 1960.

In the winter of 1955-56, a new era of professional touring began in Canada, and Lethbridge was treated to this experience through the trans-Canada tours of the Canadian Players.[232] Lethbridge audiences were thrilled to see "drama at its best" performed by a Canadian company which had received glowing reviews even from New York critics."[233] The company performed *Macbeth* and *St. Joan* at the Capitol Theatre in February 1956. It also toured to Lethbridge during the winter of most of the succeeding years through 1964. The *Lethbridge Herald* reviewer continually praised the performances except for the 1961 production of *The Caucasian Chalk Circle* which it described as "cheap burlesque."[234]

During the following eight years, Lethbridge audiences looked forward with considerable anticipation to the next offering of the Canadian Players, and almost without exception, their high hopes were fulfilled; therefore, they longed for other first class Canadian professional theatre – a yearning, which was partially satisfied when Mavor Moore decided to tour his latest edition of the musical revue, *Spring Thaw,* to western Canada for the first time in 1964.[235] Although Lethbridge audiences were delighted with this production and its successors, little did they realize what a great contribution some of these entertainers such as Alan Lund, Barbara Hamilton, Dave Broadfoot,

Peter Mews, Donald Harron, Catharine McKinnon, and Dinah Christie would make to the Canadian cultural scene for many years to come.

Unfortunately, by the time that the Canadian Confederation and Centennial celebrations were in full swing (1964-67), the era of touring Canadian professional drama was about to come to a close. The Canadian Players completed their tours to Lethbridge with the production, *All About Us*, which played to an audience of 800 in the Capitol Theatre on December 2, 1964. During the following three years, two unique dramatic events toured to the city. In September 1965 the touring pageant, *The Fathers of Confederation*, was presented, and Lethbridge audiences were honored to witness, personally, the work of established Canadian actors such as Robert Christie, Andrew Allen, and Sean Mulcahy. During March of 1966 and 1967, Les Jeunes Comédiens (of Quebec) presented productions in French – rare experiences for Lethbridge – yet obviously much appreciated if judged by the number of patrons in attendance.[236] In the 1967 year, Centennial productions included: *Spring Thaw* or *My Country What's It To You*, the Vancouver Festival Society's *100 Years of Musical Comedy*, and a performance by the Royal Winnipeg Ballet. On February 26, 1968, local audiences enjoyed the final Lethbridge performance of *Spring Thaw*.

By this time, the Alberta Drama League had been disbanded and there was fear that both professional and amateur theatre in the city would wither away. However, spring 1968 witnessed another rare experience (at least during the past 25 years): the presentation of a New York touring cast in the musical, *Stop the World, I Want to Get Off*. Also, as mentioned earlier, the Western Canada Arts Festival committee was created in Lethbridge, and in 1968 and 1969 it booked professional performances by the Alberta Ballet Company, MAC Theatre Company, and Theatre Saskatchewan.

But on the whole, the professional legitimate theatre scene was nearly finished in Lethbridge. Fortunately, for those patrons who enjoyed the various forms of musical theatre, their theatre calendars were somewhat more fulfilling. Throughout the 1950s and 1960s, Lethbridge audiences were treated to professional ballet presented by both the Royal Winnipeg Ballet and the the National Ballet Company of Canada, as well as the occasional other company, under the auspices of organizations such as the Celebrity Concert Canada Limited, The Overture Association, or the local Allied Arts Council. Lethbridge and district was very supportive of these two major dance companies, and the local dance teachers were pleased with the prospects of increased career opportunities for their students. In 1955 formal contact was established with the Royal Winnipeg Ballet when the local Canadian School of Ballet, under the direction of Joy Camden, was recognized as an official branch of the Winnipeg Ballet school. Some Lethbridge and district dancers also became associated with these professional dance companies during this era. In the 1950s, at least three residents or former residents of Lethbridge and district came under contract with the Winnipeg Ballet. Although Marina Katronis had moved to Vancouver from Lethbridge at the age of four, Lethbridge citizens still laid claim to this fine young artist when she became a major dancer with the Winnipeg company.[237] Roger Fisher, who was born and raised in Stirling and who attended the University of Alberta where he became a member of the Golden Bears basketball team, showed a flair for dance, and therefore, he enrolled in dance classes at the Banff School of Fine Arts. He then danced for a number of years with Vancouver's Theatre Under the Stars and later, appeared in Heino Heiden's *Daphne and Chloe* before joining the Royal Winnipeg Ballet.[238] Another district dancer (from Coutts and Pincher Creek), Dalton Davis, attended the BSFA and then performed in Vancouver and with the Quebec City Ballet before joining the Royal Winnipeg Ballet for the 1957-58 season. Later, Davis accepted a ballet scholarship at the Arts Education School in London.[239] Probably the most successful dancer to originate from the Lethbridge district in this era was Grant Strate, who hailed from Cardston. While attending the University of Alberta, Strate won the best actor award in a university drama competition. He also became interested in dance and proceeded to take lessons from Laine Metz Kritz. In 1951 he auditioned for Celia Franca who admired his dramatic abilities, so she signed him to a contract with the fledgling National Ballet to dance dramatic roles such as Hilarion in *Giselle* and Dr. Coppelius in *Coppelia*. Strate achieved immediate critical acclaim and soon became one of the most prominent dancers and choreographers in the company.[240] Some years later, Strate established and helped develop dance programs at two major Canadian universities. In 1971 Strate was named the founding chairman of the Department of Dance at York; in 1980 he became Director, Centre for the Arts, Simon Fraser University.

In the realm of popular dance entertainment, the name of George Patey comes to mind. After graduating from the LCI, Patey was attracted to the west coast where he teamed up with partners such as Jean Robinson and Eli DuMonde to perform in clubs such as the Cave Cabaret in Vancouver, in musical productions such as the United Casting's production of *Cuban Color Box* (Vancouver), and in other specialty entertainments.[241]

The Canadian Opera Company performed *Opera Backstage* on its first Lethbridge appearance in December 1952. Its final appearance in the city, *Orpheus in the Underworld,* closed out the theatre season in 1970. During the interim, the appearances of the Canadian Opera Company were sporadic. The performance of the Wagner Opera Company of New York on November 2, 1957, and the touring productions by the Banff Opera School, which played Lethbridge during the summers of 1958-1969, helped to fill in the gaps. As Leighton informs us, "Banff became a summer production centre for students from the University of Toronto's Opera Training School."[242] The Banff School of Fine Arts also toured the original Bill Soly musical, *Come North, Come North*, to Lethbridge in August 1966.

Professional Entertainment

Professional theatrical entertainments were relatively rare during this era. The days of vaudeville, minstrel shows, and musical revues were long gone. Most of the popular entertainment now took the form of musical variety shows, which, during this era, featured entertainers like Hank Snow and Webb Pierce (from the Grand Ol' Opry) and other western entertainment groups, on the one hand, or Scottish entertainers associated with the White Heather Concert Company or the Breath of Scotland Variety Show, on the other hand. The White Heather Concert Company made its debut in Lethbridge on October 5, 1955; it appeared annually through 1965 and semi-annually through 1970. The show was consistently sold out (at the 800 seat Capital Theatre) weeks before the presentation.

Popular entertainments of a more theatrical nature included the odd musical revue, infrequent ice shows, annual grandstand shows associated with the Lethbridge Exhibition, the ever popular circus, and magic shows. In November 1949 World and Olympic figure skating champion, Canada's own Barbara Ann Scott received an overwhelming reception from 4 200 fans when she performed with *Skating Sensations of 1950* at the Lethbridge Arena.[243] Two other ice shows, *Ice Fantasy of 1953* and *Ice Fantasy of 1955*, both produced by Roy Lisogar, were offered at the Arena, but after this, most of the other major producers felt that the Arena's facilities and seating capacity were inadequate. Professional skating shows returned to Lethbridge when the 5 000 seat Sportsplex (built for the 1975 Canada Winter Games) was completed in late 1974. Besides musical acts, the grandstand shows traditionally included high wire acts, acrobatics, stand up comedians, magicians, and ventriloquists. Throughout most of these years, the acts were booked by the following agencies who held contracts with the various fair circuits: Gus Sun-Irving Grossman, Sam Snyder, Charles Zemater, KBD Enterprises, Bob DePaola, Frank E. Roche, and Tom Drake. Most of these agencies were located in such places as Des Moines (Iowa), and Chicago. As such, the local Exhibition Board had very little say about the shows. In their desire to maintain more control, the Board sought out producers and agents more closely associated with Lethbridge. Therefore, in 1969 they contracted the grandstand show to Rozark Productions of Edmonton which, as was explained earlier, was headed by Albert Rodnunsky. Unfortunately, the 1969 grandstand show was not a success, so the Board contracted Muriel Jolliffe to produce the show in 1970. Severe rainstorms disrupted this latter production.

The Clyde Beatty Circus was the major circus attraction through the early 1950s, but circus tents did not appear through the years, 1955-59. Then, a number of circuses and wild west shows of various sizes and qualities began to vie for patrons, and in June 1964 an annual tradition became instituted – the Shrine Circus which was actually the Hubert Castle Circus sponsored by the Shriners' Club. Other service clubs such as the Gyro Club also sponsored the occasional circus or other popular entertainments.

As has been illustrated throughout this book, magicians, hypnotists, and illusionists always attracted good audiences in Lethbridge, and this continued to be so during the 1950s and 1960s. This fact is attested to by the list of such performers: George Haddad, Dr. Kit, Dr. Morton Green, Mandrake the Magician, Lee Grabel, Tribini, Cole, and Reveen. But it was Reveen who really captured local attention; his full week runs at the Capitol and Yates Theatres throughout the years 1962-70 were extraordinarily successful at the box office.

6

An Era of Musical Theatre (1971 - 1988)

Community Setting

During the 1970s and 1980s, Lethbridge experienced remarkable political stability together with considerable economic prosperity. The civic government, imbued with the value of planned growth, was headed by a local pharmacist, Andrew Charles "Andy" Anderson, who held the post of mayor from March 1968 until October 1986. His successor, David Carpenter, a chartered accountant and local businessman, maintained a similar administration. In provincial politics, Lethbridge became P.C. territory in 1975 and its conversion was awarded by having Lethbridge East MLA, Dick Johnston, named to the cabinet. In the late 1980s, Johnston was joined in the cabinet by his West Lethbridge colleague, John Gogo. In federal politics, the P.C. party maintained its stranglehold on the constituency. Membership in the Canadian Senate was, of course, a different matter; southern Alberta had been represented by Liberal Senator, James Gladstone, from 1958-1970. Later, Joyce Fairbairn, another Liberal, who had distinguished herself in Canadian politics as legislative assistant to Prime Minister Pierre Elliott Trudeau, was named to the Senate in 1984.[1]

The city's economic prosperity was closely associated with the boom conditions which the province experienced during most of the 1970s because of the expanding gas and oil industry. Unfortunately, Alberta's good fortune attracted the attention of the Federal Liberal government which, consequently, introduced the National Energy Policy in order to gain greater control over the country's resource industries. A consequent power struggle between the federal and Alberta governments seriously disrupted the province's oil and gas industry. This economic situation was exacerbated in the early 1980s when the OPEC nations began to flood the world market with low priced oil. The Alberta Government was soon faced with deficit budgets – a phenomenon which Albertans had not experienced for many years. Government spending was cut radically in a number of essential service areas such as education, health, and welfare.

Locally, extensive economic growth and development through the 1970s, sustained Lethbridge during the recession years of the mid-1980s. Institutional, commercial, and residential building, all of which proceeded at a rapid pace during the 1970s, was undoubtedly stimulated by the establishment of the University of Lethbridge. Construction at the new campus in west Lethbridge began in 1970; by the fall of 1971, the $16 million academic and residence building, designed by Vancouver's internationally renowned architect, Arthur Erickson, was partially ready for occupancy. The university's official opening took place September 22-24, 1972.[2] After that, capital projects on the campus succeeded one another quite regularly. Building construction at the LCC campus complemented the university developments. Additional major public construction during this era included the new Lethbridge Public Library, the $4 million Canada Games Sportsplex (1974), the $10.5

million laboratory and administration complex at the Agriculture Canada Research Station (1976), and the $117 million Regional Hospital (the single most expensive project in the history of Lethbridge).[3] These capital expenditures illustrate how important public institutions were to the city of Lethbridge. In 1988 the four largest employers in the city were, in order: The City Administration, The Lethbridge Public School Board, The Regional Hospital, and The University of Lethbridge. These public expenditures also provided Lethbridge with an economic stability which attracted considerable commercial interest. Complementary commercial development, including two large downtown malls, supports the belief that consumerism was popular in the 1970s and '80s. Other social movements which had a direct effect upon the social structure of Lethbridge include: corporatism, nationalism, multiculturalism, and professionalism. Much of the commercial change was related to the growth of major retail corporations; also, the retail shops in the new shopping malls were, primarily, national outlets commonly located in malls throughout the country. But traditional local institutions such as the Lethbridge Brewery and the *Lethbridge Herald* also succumbed to the corporate takeover. Unfortunately, the Molson's acquisition of the local brewery resulted in the eventual closing of this pioneer plant. The Thomson Newspaper chain takeover of the *Lethbridge Herald* was also rather disruptive.

Nationalism and multiculturalism received a tremendous boost from the Canadian Centennial celebrations of 1967. In Lethbridge, these two movements were symbolically linked together in the construction of the Nikka Yuko Centennial Garden, which was officially opened by "Prince and Princess Takamasu, brother and sister-in-law of the Emperor of Japan," on July 16, 1967, and which was dedicated to the contribution which Japanese culture had made to Canada.[4] Throughout 1967 multicultural activities flourished in Canada; this interest was maintained in Lethbridge for successive years through various folk festivals. The University of Lethbridge, through the efforts of Professor Bahir Bilgin, formerly from Turkey, introduced the idea of an International Festival of music, dance, crafts, and food. Multicultural programs and festivals became regular components of Canada Day and, later, Heritage Day. Besides these multicultural festivities, which recognized the cultural contribution of numerous ethnic groups, more specific programs concentrating on individual ethnic cultures also became commonplace. This is especially true with regard to indigenous societies. Both the University of Lethbridge and the Lethbridge Community College recognized the unique cultures of surrounding Indian groups through annual Native Awareness festivals. Interestingly enough, the importance given to multiculturalism did, in fact, add to Canadian nationalism because Canadians could finally identify with a significantly "unique" and, therefore, distinguishing feature of their culture: a belief in cultural pluralism. Unfortunately, enthusiasm for this social ideal seemed to dim considerably in the 1980s.

To a large extent, professionalism developed out of the extension of higher education to a greater and greater proportion of the Canadian population. This movement was certainly evident in Lethbridge as enrollments at both institutions of post-secondary education grew well beyond expectations and well beyond the growth of the young adult population. Coincidental with this growth was a demand for more openings in the various professional schools and faculties, especially those directly related to business or management. The extraordinary growth of the management program at the University of Lethbridge during the 1980s clearly illustrates this trend.

The movements which briefly have been discussed here seriously affected the role of the theatre in Canadian society. Some of these movements had a more direct, obvious, and immediate effect than others; professionalism and nationalism were most keenly felt. The following discussion will review some of the developments related to the theatre in Canada. Later, we will investigate the influence which these developments had upon the theatre in Lethbridge.

Canadian Theatrical Developments

During the 1970s and '80s, the regional theatres consolidated their status in the Canadian arts community; many of these companies built magnificent permanent theatres or rehabilitated existing legitimate or movie theatres. Although Canada Council provided some grant money for capital construction, much of the required funds were obtained from public donations, a fact which underscores the public's growing commitment to the Canadian professional theatre institution. John Howse, writing for *Maclean's* magazine, illustrates how Edmonton's Citadel Theatre exemplified some of these developments:[5]

> It started out in a 274-seat Salvation Army hall with a modest production of Edward Albee's *Who's Afraid of Virginia Woolf.* Now, 25 years later, housed in a handsome glass-and-brick structure that occupies a whole city block, The Citadel Theatre is a commanding presence in the heart of downtown Edmonton ... the Citadel has attracted top talent and the largest subscription base of any nonprofit company in the country.

Theatre London and the Bastion Theatre Co. of Victoria represent companies which located in rehabilitated existing theatres. Kathleen Fraser informs us that a major restoration and reconstruction project, priced at $5.5 million, was begun on the Grand Theatre in London in 1975. Fraser also reports that $3 million was raised before the construction began.[6] The Bastion Theatre Co., which was originally founded as an amateur company in 1963, but which turned professional in 1971, took up residence in the 837 seat McPherson Theatre. According to Robert Lawrence the company also operated "a theatre school and a theatre-in-education program (with the University of Victoria)." Unfortunately, the company accumulated a deficit of $184 000 by mid-1988 and decided to suspend operations as of November "pending a consultant's review of its operations."[7]

Theatre New Brunswick had the good fortune of inheriting the 1 000 seat Playhouse which had been financed by a gift from the Lord Beaverbrook estate. In 1971 a reconstruction plan was begun which, among other changes, added a fly gallery and reduced the seating to 763. Theatre New Brunswick achieved remarkable success as illustrated in the following quotation by Edward Mullaly.[8]

> In the 1985-86 season, Theatre New Brunswick's budget rose to $1.3 million and its audience averaged 11 000 per production. .... While its base remains in Fredericton, Theatre New Brunswick now tours all of its mainstage productions to nine provincial centres, and travels occasionally to other provinces. Its bilingual Young Company performs over 300 times a year in schools throughout the Maritimes.

In 1985 Theatre Calgary moved to the 750 seat Max Bell Theatre in the city's new Centre for the Performing Arts. Theatre Calgary's financial situation fluctuated considerably over the years; however, as Joyce Doolittle informs us:[9]

> Theatre Calgary received more than one third of its three million dollar budget for 1985-6 from the Canada Council, Alberta Culture, The Alberta Foundation for the Performing Arts, and the Calgary Regional Arts Foundation. Private and corporate donations fluctuate widely. .... However, in two decades it has grown from a modest grassroots operation to a multi-million dollar business with high artistic standards and a respectable record of Canadian premieres.

The above quotation suggests that financing of Canada's regional theatres was shared by governmental agencies, Canadian corporations and businesses, and private citizens. During the formative years of the regional movement, Canada Council provided the major financial stimulant.

However, Czarnecki reports that, "In its 1969-70 annual report, the Canada Council notified its clients that a time of austerity was at hand," and subsequently, the purchasing power of the Canada Council grants diminished considerably.[10] Peter Roberts, director of Canada Council between 1985-1988, stated that the biggest challenge which faced the Canada Council during his tenure as director was trying to develop a "system of priorities." He went on to report that, as his term of office drew to a close, the Council was "giving its foremost consideration to support for the creative person – writer, playwright, music composer, choreographer. . . ."[11] Incidently, Roberts was a graduate of the Lethbridge Collegiate Institute, and later, he was selected as a University of Alberta graduate for a Rhodes Scholarship at Oxford. Before taking on his post with the Canada Council, Roberts spent a number of years in the foreign service culminating that career as envoy to the Soviet Union.

Unfortunately, according to Czarnecki, just as Canada Council grants to Canadian professional theatres were being trimmed, business contributions also dropped in value. Reduced public and private subsidies resulted in greater dependence on box office receipts which, in turn, forced the regional theatres to cater more and more to audience tastes in order to remain solvent. At this time, Canadian middle class regional audiences seemed to prefer the tried and proved mainline plays penned by successful American and British playwrights. Therefore, as Czarnecki comments:[12]

> . . . increased reliance on box office only strengthened the intrinsic conservatism of the regionals' boards. In 1971, an inevitable confrontation between boards and artists insured that most regionals never again mounted provocative theatre.

But up and coming young theatre professionals were not pleased with these developments in the regional theatres. Consequently, according to Renate Usmiani, "Alternate companies set themselves up in protest against the 'colonial' attitudes of the directors of regional theatres; . . . " Usmiani continues:[13]

> The Canadian alternative theatre movement shared with its American and European counterparts a strong political orientation; rejection of the traditional author-actor-director triangle; the use of non-traditional space; a new approach to the audience; improvisations and collective creation; "poor theatre" techniques and an emphasis on "process" rather than "product." What distinguishes it from parallel movements in other countries, however, is a passionate and militant nationalism.

During the 1970s, a large number of alternative theatre companies were developed in Canada. Many had very short life spans, for example, Edmonton's Theatre 3; however, numerous others became fairly permanent elements of Canadian culture. Jack Gray informs us that in 1983 there were 120 professional theatre companies in Canada compared to four in 1957 when the Canada Council was formed.[14] About 100 of these companies could be categorized as alternative theatre companies; many of the English Canadian companies patterned their operations after two Toronto models: Toronto Workshop Productions (TWP) and Theatre Passe Muraille. Lethbridge readers will be particularly interested in the fact that TWP was founded by George Luscombe, a former student of Sterndale Bennett's. In 1961 Luscombe was appointed permanent director of TWP which, at that time, was an amateur organization. Their first major success, *Hey, Rube!,* was a collective creation which, according to Usmiani, proved to be a great success.[15] Usmiani also tells us that:

> Since 1963, TWP has been a professional company, working in three genres: collective creation, free adaptation of classic and scripted plays. For the first eight years, the company performed in the basement of an old factory in Toronto's West End, with seating capacity for one hundred on bleachers around an open stage. In 1967, it moved to its present theatre facilities in downtown Toronto where the new house seats three hundred in an open stage arrangement. . . . TWP pioneered the use of

collective creation in English Canada; these productions were usually built around a current social or political problem.

Lethbridge theatregoers were captivated by TWP's most financially successful production, *Ten Lost Years*, when it toured to Lethbridge and played the Yates Centre on November 7, 1974. The Lethbridge reception was not unlike that received throughout the country. The Canadian theatre historian, Alan Filewod informs us that:[16]

> Luscombe's most popular shows have been those in which his theatrical brilliance has been matched by his passion for politics. His ideological affiliation with the traditional left-wing issues of trade unionism and internationalism was expressed in a trilogy of documentaries on working-class history: *Ten Lost Years* (1974), *The Mac-Paps* (1979), and *The Wobbly* (1983).

After 25 years at the helm of TWP, Luscombe resigned his position as artistic director in 1986. He will always be remembered as a significant pioneer in the Canadian alternate theatre movement – a movement which has had considerable impact on theatre in Alberta's two major urban centres. During the 1970s and '80s, Edmonton audiences gave considerable support to companies such as Theatre Network, Phoenix Theatre, Catalyst Theatre, Nexus, Workshop West, and Northern Lights Theatre; whereas, Calgary patrons appreciated the productions of companies such as Alberta Theatre Projects, Lunchbox Theatre, Arété Physical Comedy Company, Sun-Ergos Theatre and Dance, and Loose Moose Theatre. Some Lethbridge theatre practitioners also experimented with the alternate theatre mode. Young thespians, under the supervision of Peter Mueller (an MFA graduate from the University of Alberta), functioned in the mid-1970s for a short period of time as Stage Three. Later, in 1982-83, Richard Epp, drama instructor at the University of Lethbridge, operated Southern Stage. Neither of these experiments resulted in a permanent professional theatre company in Lethbridge.

In a 1985 article, Usmiani claims that "the movement of the 1970s has largely run its course" and that:[17]

> Those alternate theatres of the earlier period which still operate are by now considered "mainstream", although the original concerns are still pursued. The new alternates have shifted their interest from political theatre and the promotion of new Canadian plays to experimentation with style and technique, and often return to the classics as a base.

Coincidental with these developments, were changes taking place in some of the regional theatres. Mark Czarnecki summarizes the changes as follows:[18]

> Placed in the 20 year historical perspective of regional theatre, the changes apparent in 1984 were decidedly beneficial to the growth of Canadian theatre. Out of 13 theatres, at least four – the Centaur, the Globe, MTC and TNB – had become committed to rooting themselves in local soil and growing theatre from the playwright up. At Halifax's Neptune, Tom Kerr, formerly of Kelowna, B.C., was gradually shifting his theatre in that direction, while Gordon McDougall at the Citadel promised to continue innovative programming.

By the late 1980s, many professional theatre companies in Canada were committed to three C programming – contemporary plays, classical plays, and Canadian plays. This latter commitment provided encouragement for aspiring Canadian playwrights. Two such playwrights whose origins were in southern Alberta are Gordon Pengilly and John Krizanc. Pengilly was born and raised on a farm near Stirling, Alberta, the home of Elodia Christensen. He attended the University of Alberta where he received a BA degree in English and an MFA degree in playwriting. By 1986, at the age of 33, Pengilly had authored about twenty-five television, radio, and stage plays as well as screenplays. He had also written three musicals including *Kootenai*, which was commissioned by the Cardston Musical Theatre. Included among his stage plays were *Hard Hats and Stolen Hearts*, which toured Canada in 1977-78 and also played New York; *Swipe*, an allegorical drama, which was produced by the University of Lethbridge, Department of Dramatic Arts in February 1990; and the one act play, *Seeds*, which was undoubtedly his most frequently produced play.[19]

Although Krizanc was born in Lethbridge, he was geographically mobile in his youth, finally settling in Toronto. His playwriting career started at an early age; in fact, the Theatre Department of York University produced his *Crimes of Innocence* when he was twenty years of age. As Richard P. Knowles notes, Krizanc's other plays, awards, and activities include:[20]

> *Uterine Knights*, produced in 1979 by Toronto's Necessary Angel Theatre Company; the award winning *Tamara* (1987), . . . and *Prague*, first produced in 1984 at Tarragon Theatre, Toronto, and awarded the Governor General's 1987 Award for Drama. . . . He is chairman of the publishing committee of the Playwrights Union of Canada.

Many of the summer theatre festival companies emphasized one or other of the above mentioned programming C's. Certainly, the Stratford festival stressed the classics, although it also incorporated operetta, musical theatre, and the occasional Canadian contemporary play into its season. With regard to this latter development, it is significant that John Neville included Lethbridge playwright Richard Epp's *Intimate Admiration* in the 1986 summer season. *Intimate Admiration* is a two person play based upon the love letters of Anton Chekhov and his wife, Olga Knipper (a Moscow actress). Further status was accorded Epp's play when Neville chose, personally, to play the part of Chekhov; Lucy Peacock portrayed Olga.[21] *Intimate Admiration* was also presented by Theatre Calgary's Extension Department at the Max Bell Theatre for two performances on February 16, 1986.[22]

Although the Shaw festival's original mandate was to produce the plays of George Bernard Shaw, other playwrights such as Coward, Chekhov, Wilder, Feydeau, Ben Travers, Brecht, and Alan Bennett were gradually introduced. Nevertheless, contemporary Canadian plays were definitely not featured. The Charlottetown festival retained its aim of producing modern Canadian musical theatre. The Blyth Summer festival in Blyth, Ontario, and the Chilliwack Theatre Festival devoted themselves to original Canadian works often dealing with local history and local issues. Unfortunately, Festival Lennoxville, whose mandate was the staging of high quality productions of English Canadian plays, survived for little more than a decade.[23] Other summer festival companies such as Stephenville (NFL) Festival Co., White Rock Summer Theatre, Red Barn Theatre (Jackson's Point, Ontario), Muskoka Festival (Gravenhurst, Ontario), and Le Théâtre des Prairies (Notre-Dame des Prairies, Comté Joliette, Quebec) presented varied programs.

The 1980s witnessed the rise of more authentic theatre festivals, in which various theatre companies participated. Edmonton's Fringe Festival, which was a prime example, had its debut during the week of August 14-22, 1982, with 220 performances of 45 different productions staged primarily by Edmonton, and to a lesser extent, by Calgary companies and freelance professionals. During the succeeding years, the festival grew tremendously in every dimension. In 1982, 7 500 tickets were sold; in 1987, 170 000 patrons witnessed performances of 150 different productions.[24] By this time, professional companies from other parts of Canada and elsewhere began to participate more actively in "The Fringe," although the provincial contingent still dominated. The festival became so extensive that it required a full time administrator; therefore, the originator of the Fringe, Brian Paisley, artistic director of Edmonton's Chinook Theatre for ten years, resigned this position in the spring 1987 "to concentrate his time and energy on the Fringe Festival. . . . Paisley . . . offered to produce the festival on contract for the next three years."[25]

Similar festivals arose in other Canadian cities: Montreal (Le Festival International de Mime and Le Festival de théâtre des Amériques), Quebec (Quinzaine Interantionale du Théâtre), Toronto (du Maurier World Stage Festival), Winnipeg (Bread and Dreams). The Toronto and Montreal festivals attracted participants from more distant places and generally accommodated both Anglophone and Francophone productions. These recent developments encouraged Mark Czarnecki to comment that, "Canada finally has the beginnings of a genuine festival culture."[26]

The dramatic growth of Canada's professional theatre stimulated the growth of professional training programs throughout the country. Colleges, universities, theatre companies, arts centres, and the National Theatre School introduced or expanded programs devoted to training theatre professionals in all aspects of legitimate and musical theatre as well as in theatre management. The province of Alberta was certainly a major participant in this development. The Banff School of Fine Arts increased its presence as a professional training institution, especially after being granted autonomy by the government of Alberta on April 1, 1978. An independent Board of Governors was given a mandate to expand the programs at the renamed Banff Centre for Continuing Education.[27] Colleges such as Grant McEwan (Edmonton), Mount Royal (Calgary), Keyano (Fort McMurray), and Red Deer prided themselves on their theatre programs. The universities of Alberta and Calgary vied for status in the Canadian theatre training community. Even the fledgling Department of Dramatic Arts at the University of Lethbridge introduced, in 1985, a BFA degree program in drama aimed at preparing professional actors and designers. By this time, the department had made a distinct impact on Lethbridge and district theatre. Its graduates assumed teaching positions at all levels of the educational system as well as positions in various areas of professional theatre.

Local Theatre Facilities

The University of Lethbridge figured most prominently in the provision of theatre performance spaces during the 1970s and 1980s. Because the university did not appoint a full time drama instructor until July 1, 1971, the first academic building constructed on the new campus did not contain any special facilities for dramatic performance. After David Spinks arrived from Birmingham, England, to chair the new Department of Dramatic Arts, he began to inspect the new academic residence complex at the University of Lethbridge for any space which could conceivably be converted into an acting area. But no such space became available until the Physical Education Building was completed in late 1972. At that time, Spinks cornered a fairly good sized storage area in the basement, and this area became known as the University of Lethbridge Drama Studio. A 1977 extension to the Physical Education/Fine Arts building provided a much superior space: the Theatre Laboratory.

The University's Board of Governors had, however, contracted the local architectural firm of Robins, Watson, and Baunton in 1971 to begin plans for a Performing Arts centre on the campus. This early commitment on the part of the university's governing body reflected the fact that the university had, from its inception, placed considerable emphasis on the fine arts because the community of Lethbridge had traditionally been very supportive of the arts. Unfortunately, the Alberta government was not prepared to provide additional capital funds at that time, so construction was delayed for a number of years. Nevertheless, planning continued; the architects met with faculty members, they engaged numerous consultants, and they presented a detailed design proposal in May 1978. The government gave final approval on August 27, 1978, and construction on the $11.6 million dollar Performing Arts Building began in October.[28] The final outcome was a magnificent facility for teaching, rehearsing or practicing, performing, and creating the various forms of art.

Performance areas included a 203-seat dual purpose recital hall and film theatre, a two story flexible experimental theatre which could accommodate approximately 200 patrons, a similarly sized drama education studio, an additional drama studio, and a 450 seat proscenium type theatre. Although the building proved to be both aesthetic and functional in many ways, it suffered from two major drawbacks: accessibility and shortage of gallery space for the visual arts. Convenient parking was at a premium; the long walk to the Performing Arts Building, and the descent to the bowels of the building (where the theatre and recital hall foyers are situated) discouraged many possible patrons from attending performances there. The art gallery suffered from these problems as well; however, it was plagued by other concerns which were not predicted when the building was first envisioned. The university art collection quickly became so extensive that the gallery could display only a very small part of the permanent collection. It soon became apparent to everyone concerned about the university's art collection that a much larger gallery was required.

The experimental theatre is basically a large, square room with no fixed furnishings; it has no formal seating arrangements – rather:[29]

> . . . seating platforms for up to 200 people can be moved around to accommodate the stage configuration required by the play – theatre in the round, for example. . . . The most unique feature . . is the lighting grid system, similar in concept to that found at the Carnegie-Mellon University Theatre in Pittsburgh, Pennsylvania. The system consists of a suspended steel mesh grid about 16 feet above the floor. The grid enables drama students to walk anywhere above the room and hang lights from any position, . . . The mesh grid also provides much quicker and safer access to lights by eliminating the need for ladders. Like the drama workshop, the experimental theatre has a floating floor for acoustical reasons, plus resilience.

This theatre is also equipped with a control booth which contains appropriate lighting and sound boards.

A special section of the *Lethbridge Herald* published on September 5, 1981 to commemorate the official opening of the Performing Arts Centre (September 10-12), described the University Theatre in the following way:[30]

> The theatre's spacious wings, adjoining workshop, 15 foot flyloft, and 30-seat orchestra pit enable the theatre to mount any professional or amateur production, including those of the technically demanding Canadian Opera Company. . . . The sound control section oversees a[n] intercom system wired throughout the entire theatre complex, including the catwalks, flyloft and dressing room. The lighting section houses a computerized light control board . . . Low velocity airconditioning eliminates the swishing sounds and drafts of cooled air common to many air-conditioned buildings. . . . The 42m wide by 36m deep stage is fully trapped in removable sections. . . . a spring floor covers the stage . . . . The 54 square metre orchestra pit is one metre lower than the stage . . . – the pit can be removed and extra seats placed right up to the stage. . . . Forty-three lines are suspended in the loft's soaring reaches, including six lines of lights, the main drape and the orchestra's acoustical shell. . . . Five catwalks cross the stage and theatre, connecting all lighting positions above the stage and audience, as well as the control booth at the back of the theatre. . . . Immediately north of the stage . . . is the two storey drama workshop.

Without question, the theatre was a magnificent addition to the campus, which, together with the experimental theatre and the recital hall, provided the university and the City of Lethbridge with facilities which were the envy of many similar sized communities. To a very large extent, these facilities (particularly the main theatre and the recital hall) have developed into community venues. They are, in fact, administered separately from the university's fine arts departments, and from the beginning, the professional theatre managers, Brian B. McCurdy and his successor Don Acaster, were charged with the task of trying to make these facilities pay for themselves. The manager is responsible for booking all events in the University Theatre and the recital hall and "for the organization and co-organization of facilities and services of these events."[31] Even productions and recitals for the drama and music departments must be formally booked. The facilities were made available for rent by local as well as touring amateur and professional organizations. In addition, the managers organized a number of very popular dance, musical, and theatrical series.

McCurdy was hired as of January 2, 1981, and the University Theatre was first booked on March 18-21, 1981, for the Department of Dramatic Arts' production of *The Cherry Orchard* directed by Richard Epp. About six months later, the official opening of the Performing Arts Centre was held in conjunction with Fall Convocation, at which time the university conferred four honorary Dr. of Laws' degrees; the recipients were Liona Boyd (classical guitarist), Peter Ustinov (actor, director, novelist, and playwright), Frank Lynch-Staunton (respected southern Alberta citizen and Lieutenant-Governor of the province), and Arthur Erickson (architect). Liona Boyd and Peter Ustinov gave a gala performance on the evening of September 12, 1981.

Shortly after this occasion, McCurdy introduced the first two series of touring professionals to perform at the University Theatre (see Table 6-1). By comparison, seven distinct series were scheduled during 1987-88 including: Dance Canada Danse, All That Jazz, The Lively Stage, Music, The Entertainers, Kids' Concerts, and Family Treats (by the Alberta Ballet). Each of the first six series offered three different performers or organizations. In addition, two special musical events, Andre Gagnon (pianist) and His Trio, and Murray McLaughlan (Canadian award winning country vocalist), were offered to the public. A number of these series were financially assisted by the support of local commercial sponsors – CJOC radio, 2 and 7 Lethbridge Television (CFAC-T.V.), the *Lethbridge Herald*, and Canbra Foods. External assistance was provided by Alberta Culture.[32] Unfortunately, throughout this era, touring legitimate theatre companies appeared rarely; most of the series were devoted to musical performances, including some musical theatre (opera) and dance. Dance companies were particularly amenable to touring. It should be kept in mind that, prior to the establishment of these series, the University of Lethbridge, through the director of Continuing Education, and often, in association with the Allied Arts Council, had arranged for various professional artists to perform in Lethbridge.

Although the University of Lethbridge Theatre was equipped with some facilities which the Yates Centre was not, some community theatre groups such as the Playgoers Club and the Lethbridge Musical Theatre preferred to book the Yates, primarily because of accessibility. In addition, with more of the touring groups performing at the University of Lethbridge Theatre, more opportunity was opened up at the Yates for rehearsal time. However, both theatres were booked fairly constantly. Since the University Theatre accommodated approximately 450 patrons, the local call for a larger theatre was still not met. The 5 000 seat Lethbridge Sportsplex, which was constructed for the 1975 Canada Winter Games, was frequently used for larger stage shows – particularly of a musical nature, for example, Harry Belafonte and Nana Mouskouri. Entertainers such as Reveen and the occasional theatrical production such as the musical, *The Best Little Whorehouse in Texas* (starring Stella Parton), were also booked there. Unfortunately, this facility lacked the atmosphere, the acoustics, and the comfort of a true theatre.

Many citizens in Lethbridge continued to decry the lack of appropriate theatre facilities for large scale productions, on the one hand, and for intimate theatre, on the other hand. The city did provide funds in the latter 1980s for a more intimate theatre space. For many years, the manager of the Yates Memorial Centre, Ed Bayly, and many of the users of the Centre, argued for more workshop, storage, and rehearsal space. But, of course, the city fathers had to deal with many requests for improved cultural facilities. Finally, in June 1987 the architectural firm of Watson and Horton was retained to plan renovations for the existing building and to design a major addition which would include a large basement workshop and storage area as well as a rehearsal or intimate theatre space (similar to the University of Lethbridge Experimental Theatre). Construction of the addition began in 1988, and then, on the initiative of George Mann, and with the support of the Playgoers Club of Lethbridge, the Allied Arts Council suggested to City Council that the new facility be named the Sterndale Bennett Theatre in honor of Ernest, Belle, and Hilda Sterndale Bennett. City Council approved the name on January 9, 1989.[33] In addition, plans were formulated to hold an official opening on April 21, 1990, followed by a week of festivities. The Playgoers Club, having been invited to participate in the opening week's celebrations, chose to produce the three act comedy *The Whole Town's Talking* by Anita Loos and John Emerson as well as the readers' theatre presentation, *The Hollow Crown*, devised by John Barton with directors, George Mann and Linda Bayly, respectively. The *Whole Town's Talking* was selected in remembrance of the fact that Ernest Sterndale Bennett not only directed the play for Playgoers in 1925 but also starred in it as Chester; a young entrepreneur. Belle Sterndale Bennett portrayed Lettie Lythe, a motion picture star. Among the other artistic groups which performed during the opening was St. Augustine's Choir under the direction of Alan Young. Included in the selections presented by the choir, was the motet, "God is a Spirit," composed by Sir William Sterndale Bennett, Ernest's grandfather.

TABLE 6-1
Performing Arts Series, University of Lethbridge Theatre (1981-82)

Music Series One		Festival of Dance Series	
Date	**Organization**	**Date**	**Organization**
SEPT 18	The Calgary Philharmonic	NOV 9	Theatre Ballet of Canada
OCT 9	Lois Marshall (soprano)	NOV 16	Dancemakers
OCT 29	Anton Kuerti and the Orford String Quartet	NOV 23	Danny Grossman Dance Theatre
JAN 22	Erik Schultz and the Edmonton Chamber Players Orchestra	APR 15	Alberta Ballet Co.
MAR 12	Tudor Singers of Montreal		

Locally Produced Theatre

One significant fact which will become quite evident from the following analysis of both amateur and professional theatre in Lethbridge during this era is the dominant role which musical theatre played. Musical theatre is defined, here, as all theatrical productions which rely heavily upon a musical component: opera, operetta, musical comedy, musical revue, English pantomime, and dance productions. Interest in musical theatre was also stimulated by the spectacular musicals which opened in Toronto and then toured to many Canadian metropolitan urban centers throughout the latter part of this era (*Cats, Les Misérables,* and *Phantom of the Opera*). Another interesting feature of Lethbridge theatre at this time was its continuing reliance upon amateur productions. Although professional theatre had become dominant in most urban Canadian centres, this was certainly not the trend in Lethbridge; however, there were various aborted attempts at establishing local professional companies. Also, very few professional companies toured to Lethbridge, although the number of dance companies increased considerably. Nevertheless, the influence of professionalism was felt very strongly by a number of youthful thespians who had their interest whetted and reinforced by the many opportunities provided for theatrical training and involvement within the city, and who then proceeded into professional theatre careers. The following discussion will analyze these developments more specifically.

Youth Oriented Theatre

Summer Musicals and Related Productions

With the support of the Allied Arts Council, Dick Mells, Muriel Jolliffe, and Ellyn Mells (musical director) revived the summer musicals in 1973. This activity ended in 1979 when Dick Mells decided to move to Fort McMurray, Alberta. Although these musicals were basically recreational in purpose, they undoubtedly did contribute to the dramatic development of the many young people who were attracted to this theatrical activity and who were provided with excellent opportunities to perform and to work backstage in association with a number of the city's foremost theatrical practitioners such as Joan Waterfield. Waterfield assisted backstage and front of house for most of the productions and also portrayed the role of Nurse in *Romeo and Juliet.* Table 6-2 lists the various summer productions from 1966-1979; Table 6-3 ranks the performers who were most actively engaged in these summer shows.

Veterans such as Al Greenway (who played the leading role, Ben Rumsen, in *Paint Your Wagon*) are discussed thoroughly in the community theatre sections of this book, so the ensuing discussion will focus on the most active young participants – those for whom the summer theatre was primarily created. Albert Azzara was, undoubtedly, one of the most enthusiastic and committed young actors the city ever produced. Throughout his years at Winston Churchill High School (WCHS), Azzara was an outstanding contributor to the school's drama programs. Azzara became involved with the summer musicals in 1973 when he joined the cast of *West Side Story* playing the role of Bernardo. In the 1977 version of the same musical, he portrayed A-rab. In the interim, he took the role of Available Jones (*Li'l Abner*) and Jake Whipance (*Paint Your Wagon*). In the 1977 summer companion piece, *Romeo and Juliet*, he played both a servant and a prince. It was, however, the summer of 1975 that Azzara showed amazing dramatic potential when he thrilled local audiences with his portrayal of the not too bright drifter, Lenny, in *Of Mice and Men.* Azzara also caught the attention of Murray Robison who proceeded to cast him in a number of productions for the Attic Theatre. In addition, Azzara participated in University of Lethbridge productions as well as in numerous productions for Playgoers and Lethbridge Musical Theatre.

When sixteen year old Lorretta Bailey auditioned for *Paint Your Wagon* (1976), she displayed a very pleasant voice as well as a vulnerable stage personality. Because of her age and lack of experience, she was cast in a minor role, Bubbles. She returned as Estella in the 1977 summer production of *West Side Story*; the following summer, she portrayed the oldest daughter, Tzeitel, in *Fiddler on the Roof.* At that time, Bailey had just graduated from WCHS where she had participated in the various productions. In the fall of 1978, she enrolled at the University of Lethbridge where she planned to complete a degree in drama. She also became involved in two of Dick Mells's freelance productions, *South Pacific* and *Bye Bye Elsie High*. Her university career was interrupted by marriage to a fellow performer, Greg Martin, and a move to Fort McMurray where she became active in shows which Dick Mells produced. A later move to Edmonton provided her with the opportunity to complete a Fine Arts program (in 1987) and to pursue a professional career in the theatre.[34] Involvement with various professional companies in Edmonton resulted in roles in *Pirates of Penzance, Annie, Hurleyburly*, and the Christmas pantomime, *Aladdin*, which also featured two other Lethbridge products, Jeff Haslam and David Mann. Bailey made her film debut, as a monster, in *Prom Night II - Hello Marylou* and was contracted to do a number of T.V. commercials. In early 1989 she "landed" a dream role, Eponine, one of the leading characters in the Toronto production of *Les Miserables* to be staged at the Royal Alexandra Theatre. Following the opening night performance of March 16, 1989, Ray Conlogue of the *Toronto Globe and Mail* said of Bailey's performance:[35]

> Lorretta Bailey is a vigorous and hard scrabble Eponine, the daughter of thieves who knows that she can't compete against Cosette for the love of Marius; she does full justice to the exuberant demands of the music. . . .

Throughout the Toronto run of the show, Bailey received ongoing praise for her portrayal.

TABLE 6-2

Summer Productions: Allied Arts Council and Lethbridge Musical Theatre
Lethbridge, Alberta (1966-1979)

DATE/SPONSOR	PRODUCTION	DIRECTOR(S)
Aug 17,20; 26,27/66	*Babes in Arms*	Dick Mells [prod dir], Muriel Jolliffe [chor], Henry Waack [mus dir]
Aug 29-31 - Sept 2/67	*The Pajama Game*	Dick Mells [prod dir], Muriel Jolliffe, Henry Waack
Aug 27-31/68	*The Boy Friend*	Dick Mells, Muriel Jolliffe, Henry Waack, Cathy Evins [designer]
Aug 18-23/69	*Little Mary Sunshine*	Dick Mells, Muriel Jolliffe, Henry Waack & Ellyn Mells [mus dirs]
Aug 21,22; 29,30/70	*Your Own Thing*	Lee Drew [dir], Dick Mells [prod], Darlene Snyder [chor], Lily Larter [mus dir]
Aug 21-25/73	*West Side Story*	Dick Mells, Muriel Jolliffe, Ellyn Mells
Aug 20-24/74	*Damn Yankees*	Dick Mells, Muriel Jolliffe, Ellyn Mells
Aug 12-16/75	*Li'l Abner*	Dick Mells, Muriel Jolliffe, Ellyn Mells
Aug 20-23/75	*Of Mice and Men*	Dick Mells
Aug 24-28/76	*Paint Your Wagon*	Dick Mells, Carol Jolliffe [chor], Ellyn Mells, Cathy Chirka & Shelagh Stefan [mus dirs]
Aug 24,26; Sept 1,3/77	*West Side Story*	Dick Mells (assisted by David Mann & Mike Wright), Muriel Jolliffe, Ellyn Mells
Aug 25,27,31; Sept 2/77	*Romeo & Juliet*	Dick Mells
Aug 30 - Sept 2/78	*Fiddler on the Roof*	Dick Mells, Carol (Jolliffe) Godlonton [chor], Arla Bach [mus dir]
Aug 21-25/79	*Godspell*	Dick Mells, Carol Godlonton, Bruce Mackay [mus dir]

TABLE 6-3

Major Onstage Participants
Summer Productions: Allied Arts Council/LMT
Lethbridge, Alberta (1966-1979)

Participant	# of Roles			Participant	# of Roles		
	1966-70	1973-79	T		1966-70	1973-79	T
Albert Azzara		6	6	Lilian Kolodziej		3	3
Lorretta Bailey		3	3	David Mann		5	5
Cliff Black	3		3	Laurin Mann		4	4
David Cunningham		3	3	Greg Martin		5	5
Michael Day		6	6	Sheri McFadden		4	4
Al Greenway	1	7	8	Randy Rae		4	4
Deb Grey		5	5	Mark Russell		3	3
Marlin Howg		3	3	Chip Seibert		3	3
Michael Hoyt		3	3	Mark Switzer		3	3
Kirk Jensen	1	3	4	Jack Warburton	2	1	3
Karen Kay		3	3				

Greg Martin also had his interest in theatre whetted at WCHS and he made a significant contribution to the summer productions by portraying Lonesome Polecat (*Li'l Abner*), Julio Valveras (*Paint Your Wagon*), Motel Kamzoil (*Fiddler on the Roof*), and Curly (*Of Mice and Men*).In other community theatre projects, Martin was a major participant in *Bye Bye Elsie High*, which featured selections from the musical, *Grease*; he also played the artful Dodger and Squire Dap in LMT's *Oliver and Camelot*, respectively, and Merv in Playgoers' 1978 festival production, *The Rehearsal*. Shortly thereafter, Martin left Lethbridge but he did continue to be active in the theatre.

Marlin Howg also showed considerable potential while a high school student at WCHS, primarily because he was endowed with so much energy and enthusiasm. He was also an active competitor in the musical theatre section of the Lethbridge Music Festival. In his first summer musical, he was cast as one of the ball players (Smokey #8) in *Damn Yankees* (1974). The *Lethbridge Herald* columnist, Joan Waterfield, referred to "some truly exciting star-lights. . . . Like the unbeatable comedy of Mike Day and Marlin Howg bringing down the house with 'The Game.'"[36] In 1975 Howg did a superlative job of playing Marryin' Sam in *Li'l Abner*, and then, he followed up this role with that of Salem Trumbell in *Paint Your Wagon*. During the following two summers, Howg participated in the provincial musical theatre workshops directed by Alan Lund. He then lent strong support to the cast of LMT's *Annie Get Your Gun* in the role of Tommy Keeler.

Mark Russell showed considerable comedic talent while performing in WCHS productions and in *Bye Bye Elsie High*. His good humor was also appreciated in LMT productions such as *Annie Get Your Gun* (Pawnee Bill] and *Camelot* (Sir Lionel).In the summer productions, Russell portrayed Lieutenant Schrank in *West Side Story,* a Friar in *Romeo and Juliet*, and the lead, Tevye, in *Fiddler on the Roof.* His performance in this latter role suggested that Russell was one of the finest actors to come out of the local youth theatre programs. Shortly after this show, Russell left Lethbridge for a number of years, but he returned in the late 1980s to make a substantial contribution to local theatre.

Mark Switzer joined the summer musicals in 1977 when he took the role of Riff in *West Side Story* which he succeeded in the next two summers with roles in *Fiddler on the Roof* and *Godspell*. His talents were later pursued by LMT who cast him in major roles in *The King and I* and *Down Memory Lane*. In the meantime, he married the former Lea Blaquiere, a leading lady in various LMT productions. Unfortunately, their family and business responsibilities kept them from being seriously involved in local theatre for a number of years after 1985.

Deb Grey, Randy Rae, and David Cunningham were also active participants in the musicals at WCHS. Grey was a particularly good vocalist who was also a staunch member of various local choirs. In the summer musicals, Grey played numerous supporting roles plus the leading romantic role of Elizabeth Woodling in *Paint Your Wagon*. Rae's major role was that of Hairless Joe in *Li'l Abner*. Cunningham tended to play secondary roles such as Zeke in *Li'l Abner* and Edgar P. Crocker in *Paint Your Wagon*. In the summer plays, Grey portrayed Juliet in *Romeo and Juliet*, Rae played Carlson, and Cunningham portrayed Whit in *Of Mice and Men*.

Lillian Kolodziej, a graduate of Catholic Central High School, made her summer musical debut playing the role of Marguerita (a Shark girl) in *West Side Story* (1973). She followed this up with Chi Chi in *Li'l Abner* and Sarah Woodling in *Paint Your Wagon*. Kolodziej also participated in Dick Mells's dinner theatre production of *South Pacific* as well as in the English pantomime, Aladdin. She was also attracted to LMT where she joined the chorus of *Oliver*, portrayed Flora from Frisco in *No No Nanette*, and then, was selected to play the title role in *Annie Get Your Gun*. Joan Waterfield's review of this latter production commented on Kolodziej's performance, as follows:[37]

> A honey of a star has been found in Lilian Kolodziej – a winning winsome Annie . . . Her every moment on stage is a revelation of singing-acting talent that seizes the comedic side of the role, yet imbues it with a vulnerability that is immensely appealing.

Kolodziej also played the principal girl in two Christmas pantomimes.

Kirk Jensen was a graduate of Kate Andrews High School in Coaldale where he came under the instruction of Frank Featherstone. While still in high school, he appeared in the LMT production of *Destry Rides Again* and in the summer musical *Your Own Thing*. Then, Jensen enrolled in the University of Lethbridge where he qualified as a teacher. During his university years, Jensen participated in numerous university productions as well as in *My Fair Lady* and *Fiddler on the Roof* for LMT, and in *A Midsummer Night's Dream* and *Black Comedy* for Playgoers. He also portrayed the juvenile male lead in a number of Christmas pantomimes. His extensive list of credits during these few years also included acting in Dick Mells's production of *Canterbury Tales* and directing the WCHS production of *Finian's Rainbow*. With regard to other summer productions, Jensen took the roles of Action in *West Side Story* (1973), Senator Phogbound in *Li'l Abner,* and Crooks in *Of Mice and Men.* He also stage managed the latter two shows. In the fall of 1976, Jensen played Billy Early in LMT's *No, No, Nanette*. The review of this latter production states, "Mr. Jensen, who gave a fine performance helped to bring the Charleston back to life during 'You Can Dance With Any Girl'."[38]

Following graduation from the Lethbridge Collegiate Institute (LCI), Michael Hoyt completed the program at the Canadian Mime School and then attended the University of Lethbridge. While he was still a high school student, Hoyt was cast as Pepe in the 1973 summer show *West Side Story*.

In 1977 he returned to the summer productions and portrayed two leading characters, Bernardo in *West Side Story* and Romeo in *Romeo and Juliet*. Later that fall, he played The Wild Horse (principal Indian dancer) in LMT's *Annie Get Your Gun* immediately after appearing as Nugget (the lead horse) in the University of Lethbridge's production of *Equus*. Hoyt also had the honor of playing a horse in the Citadel Theatre's (Edmonton) production of that same Peter Shaffer play.

David Mann showed considerable talent in drama, music, art, and literature. His first public stage performance occurred in the summer of 1967 when he was cast as Clarence and his Classy Clarinet in the University of Oregon's Carnival Theatre production of *Gypsy*. His father, George, portrayed Rose's companion, Herbie. Probably his most exciting experience arose while attending high school in Boulder, Colorado; he was cast to portray the lead juvenile delinquent in a twenty-four minute training film for volunteer juvenile court officers, *A Second Chance,* produced by Spenfilm, Inc., Boulder, Colorado. On his return to Lethbridge, Mann became very active in musicals both at the LCI and WCHS. Upon graduating from the LCI, he was awarded a D.R. Yates Fine Arts Scholarship. Mann was a staunch founding member of the local Youth Theatre and an active participant in the summer shows, where his debut performance was General Bullmoose in *Li'l Abner*. He followed this up with lead parts, Joe Hardy and Tony, in *Damn Yankees* and *West Side Story*, respectively. He also portrayed Mercutio in *Romeo and Juliet* as well as Lenny's companion, George, in *Of Mice and Men*. With regard to musical theatre, Mann was a recipient of the Horace Barrett award for senior musical theatre competition in the Lethbridge Kiwanis Music Festival. Mann was also an active participant with Playgoers, LMT, Coaldale Little Theatre, Attic Theatre, Christmas panto-mime, and the University of Lethbridge, Department of Dramatic Arts. He, then, headed for Edmonton to begin a career in professional theatre – a career in which he was to achieve considerable success.[39] In addition, he was accepted into the 1983 master acting class at Banff, where he portrayed Sir Toby Belch in *Twelfth Night,* directed by Bernard Hopkins.

Laurin Mann, like her brother, David, displayed a very early interest in acting. This interest was first manifest when she participated in the musicals at the LCI. Laurin Mann shared the 1973 D.R. Yates Fine Arts Scholarship with Dawn McCaugherty. Mann's first summer musical role was Harriet Scragg in *Li'l Abner*. Then, her versatility as an actress was clearly demonstrated in the summer of 1977 when she portrayed Lady Capulet in *Romeo and Juliet* and Rosalia in *West Side Story*. Mann also achieved accolades for her entries in musical theatre competition at the Kiwanis Music Festival; her rendering of "Adelaide's Lament" from *Guys and Dolls* was awarded the highest honor in the senior class. Mann's interest in the theatre was also piqued by the success which she achieved as a member of the Lethbridge Youth Theatre. Later, Mann participated in LMT (*No, No, Nanette*), in Playgoers [*Come Blow your Horn,* the 1975 summer melodrama, and in *Priscilla Pringle's Predicament* (1983)], and in various Christmas pantomimes. Murray Robison perceived an exceptional talent in Laurin and cast her in three of his Attic Theatre productions. Undoubtedly, this experience with Robison encouraged Mann to seek a career in the theatre. A summer in Banff (1976) as a participant in the Senior Acting course where she played Goody Rickby in *The Scarecrow* (by Percy MacKaye), directed by Charles Werner Moore, also stimulated her profes-sional interests. After completing her B.A. in English and Drama at the University of Lethbridge, Mann pursued an MFA degree in acting at the University of Oregon. Upon graduating from this program, she acted in Eugene and Boston. Then, she returned to Lethbridge for a year to teach drama at the University of Lethbridge; she also performed in Playgoers' reenactment of *Priscilla Pringle's Predicament,* and she took the female lead in the Southern Stage production of *Christmas Pudding*. The following year, she accepted a one year appointment at Queen's University, after which she participated in professional theatre in Toronto and other southern Ontario communities.[40]

Michael Day's participation in high school productions and summer musicals was very extensive. Day enjoyed the pleasures of early musical theatre success while still at the LCI where he captured two major roles. His summer musical portrayals included Earthquake McGoon in *Li'l Abner,* Riff and Glad Hand in *West Side Story* (1973 & 1977, respectively). After graduating from university, Day began his teaching career in Lethbridge. He also became involved with Playgoers and LMT, for whom he primarily contributed backstage.

Another graduate of the LCI, David Chipman (Chip) Seibert attended the University of Lethbridge where he participated in *J.B.* (1977). He also performed in a few Playgoers' productions in 1976 and 1977: *The Time of Your Life, Ernie's Incredible Illucinations,* and *Comedy of Errors.* The innocent, young male lead was his forte in the Christmas pantomimes. Seibert's onstage potential was in stage movement and dancing; this aptitude was shown most vividly in his performance of Pappy Yokum in the summer musical, *Li'l Abner.* He also displayed his flair for stage movement in his portrayals of Deisel (a Jet) in *West Side Story* and Jasper in *Paint Your Wagon.* Seibert's talent for movement was quickly recognized by Muriel Jolliffe who nurtured this late bloomer and then sent him off to ballet school where he very quickly proved his latent talent; he, then, danced for professional dance companies in Canada and New Zealand before becoming a professional costume and set designer.[41]

The LCI also nurtured the dramatic interests of Sheri McFadden. In the summer productions in which McFadden was cast, she took four very important but quite contrasting roles: Rosalia in *West Side Story* (1973); the female lead, Lola ("Whatever Lola Wants"), in *Damn Yankees*; Appasionata Von Climax in *Li'l Abner;* and Curley's wife in *Of Mice and Men.* She was also one of the lead performers in Dick Mells's production of *Canterbury Tales,* and she performed in Playgoers' Fiftieth Anniversary shows, *Black Comedy* and *Oh, What a Lovely War.* Shortly after these latter two productions, McFadden received word that she had been accepted into the Canadian Theatre School.[42] She later performed in professional and amateur theatre in various Canadian communities. Then, returning to Lethbridge, she married a local automobile salesman, Rob Thomson, and began to raise a family. Nevertheless, (McFadden) Thomson continued to be active in amateur theatre. She also earned the credentials to become a professional speech teacher.

Karen Kay, a professional lab technologist and supervisor of the Histopathology department at the Lethbridge Regional (earlier, Lethbridge Municipal) Hospital, was a diligent worker and consistent participant in most of the local theatre companies, as will become very obvious to readers as they progress through this chapter. Her contribution to the Allied Arts Council was also greatly appreciated by her colleagues on the executive. With regard to the summer productions, she portrayed Miss Weston in *Damn Yankees,* Lady Montague in *Romeo and Juliet,* and Francesca in *West Side Story* (1977). Besides being an accomplished singer, Kay was an excellent dancer, and therefore, she was an invaluable member of the chorus in numerous local musicals.

Christmas Pantomimes

The Jolliffe family maintained the annual Christmas pantomimes throughout the 1970s, but then, Muriel found that the demands on her time had become too excessive, so this tradition was basically drawn to a close after the 1979 production. Nevertheless, in 1985 she was convinced to cooperate with Centre Stage Productions to produce another version of *The Queen of Hearts,* however, that cooperative venture did not continue.

The usual stock characters (described in Chapter 5) appeared in the Pantomimes of this era as well. Although there was no "Dame" in the 1971 production of *Old King Cole,* Frank Featherstone returned in this familiar and very popular role in *The Old Woman in the Shoe* (1972) and *Sinbad*

(1973), after which he decided to let some of the younger fellows try their hand at it. In 1974 Tony Dimnik, who had been very impressive as one of the fathers in the LCC production of *The Fantasticks*, superbly carried off the role of the wicked stepmother in Cinderella. Then, Dimnik left Lethbridge to pursue other career and educational interests, so Eric Low was enticed into playing the Dame, which he did on four separate occasions (1975, '76, '79 and 1985). Low's domination of the role was interrupted by his temporary relocation in Victoria in order to pursue graduate studies in theatre. During Low's two year absence, Albert Azzara further illustrated the breadth of his young acting talent by portraying Mother Goose (1977) and Sinbad's mother (1978). On numerous other occasions, Azzara portrayed the "villain of the piece" or other characters. Others who commonly fit into the villain category were Mike Day, Karen Kay, David Mann, and Laurin Mann. As mentioned earlier, the lead juvenile girl was regularly played by Linda Johnson in the early 1970s, but then, others such as Lillian Kolodziej, Dawn McCaugherty, Flora Erdos, and Narda McCarroll took on this role. The juvenile male lead was usually taken by Kirk Jensen or Chip Seibert; whereas, Frank Huszar maintained his hold on the naive and somewhat dull associate. The balletic fairy or princess was regularly portrayed by Carol (Jolliffe) Godlonton. Other dancers from the Jolliffe Academy such as Gerry Tomiyama and Mark Litchfield contributed their talents to the dancing and movement elements. Muriel Jolliffe's sister, Wendy Carson, who cooperated with Mark Litchfield to give remarkably human characteristics to Henry the Horse in *Babes in the Woods* (1970), also personified the Goose in *Mother Goose* (1977). Others who were multiple participants in the Pantomimes from 1971-1985 included Bryan Francis and Pat Hammond.

TABLE 6-4

Locally Produced Christmas Pantomimes
Yates Memorial Centre
Lethbridge, Alberta (1966-1985)

DATE	SPONSOR	PRODUCTION	DATE	SPONSOR	PRODUCTION
Dec 28-30/66 Jan 5-7/67	AAC	*Aladdin*	Dec 26-28/74	AAC	*Cinderella*
Dec 28-30/67 Jan 5,6/68	AAC	*Cinderella*	Dec 26,27,29,30/75	AAC	*Aladdin*
Dec 26-28/68	CLT	*Mother Goose*	Dec 26-29/76	AAC	*The Queen of Hearts*
Dec 26-27/69	AAC	*The Queen of Hearts*	Dec 26-29/77	AAC	*Mother Goose*
Dec 26; 28,29/70	AAC	*Babes in the Woods*	Dec 26-29/78	AAC	*Sinbad*
Dec 26-28/71	AAC	*Old King Cole*	Dec 26-29/79	AAC	*Dick Whittington & His Cat*
Dec 26-29/72	AAC	*Old Woman in the Shoe*	Dec 26-28/85	Centre Stage	*The Queen of Hearts*

Musical accompaniment was regularly provided by piano and drums. Henry Waack (piano) and Ernie Block (drums), who referred to themselves as "Block and Waack 'em," played for the early shows. Susan (Young) Garrie played the piano during the early 1970s (as she did with the Lethbridge Musical Theatre). In the later years, pianists such as Ellyn Mells, Debra Mann, Margaret Dean, and Susan Sametz volunteered their talents; Bruce Robin, Willie Mathis, and Ernie Block maintained the beat, although Robin was the most consistent performer on the drums.

Local Dance Schools

As is obvious from the preceding discussion, the Jolliffe Academy of Dancing continued to be a very vital organization throughout the 1970s and '80s. In addition, Jolliffe received further recognition for her various efforts on behalf of dance. She received numerous invitations to adjudicate, to guest teach, and to conduct workshops. For example, in the spring and summer of 1975, alone, she: adjudicated dance events at the Sault Ste. Marie, Ontario, Festival of Music, Speech and Dance; hosted a workshop on "character" at the Canadian Conference on Dance held at the University of Alberta; and taught ballet character and mime at the summer session for the Alberta Ballet Co.[43]

The year prior to this, Jolliffe was invited to Lima, Peru, to choreograph three ballets for the resident professional company there, Universidad Nacional Mayor De San Marcos.[44] She had previously choreographed a pas de deux for her former pupil, Jane Lee, and Jane's husband, Phil Devonshire, who were now associated with this Lima company. In 1977 Jolliffe was awarded a life membership in the Alberta Professional Dance Teachers Association in recognition of the many years of superlative contribution which she had made to the development of dance in Alberta. Later that year, Jolliffe could smile at the fact that twenty-two year old Chip Seibert won a place in the National Ballet school after less than one year of formal training under her tutelage.[45] Jolliffe's accomplishments also resulted in her being honored with an Alberta Achievement award for outstanding contribution to community arts.

It is true, however, that a number of other dancing schools and instructors also contributed to the continued development of dance and its appreciation during this era. The Lakeview School of Dance, under the direction of Romola Ully, always attracted a large number of students. In 1979 Ully turned the school over to her daughter, Kim, who renamed the school, Studio One.[46] Kim's early dance training had been provided by her mother who, later, turned her over to Muriel Jolliffe. During her tutorial years, Kim participated in numerous recitals and festivals. In 1975 she was the featured dancer at the opening ceremonies of the Canada Winter Games. Later, she performed for a number of theatrical organizations such as the Alberta Musical Theatre, Edmonton, and the National Tap Dance Company of Canada.[47] Once in charge of Studio One, Kim contracted a number of other teachers to assist her with the various forms of dance, for example, the Hollywood dance instructor, Al Gilbert, who was also professor of tap dance at California State University at Fullerton.[48] Later, ballet teachers such as Elizabeth Wells and Jacqui Stuart joined Ully as ballet mistresses.[49] A former Jolliffe student, Wendy Spoulos, also joined the staff.

Dawn's Dancing Studio, operated by Dawn (Higgins) May, continued to function during the 1970s. Later, May's move from Lethbridge left a void in contemporary dance instruction that was eventually filled by Joy Ackerman, a specialist in tap, jazz, and acrobatic dancing. Ackerman moved to Lethbridge in the spring of 1984 to establish Joy's Dance Factory. Ackerman received her early training in Edmonton, which she supplemented with advanced studies in Los Angeles and Chicago. She then settled in Medicine Hat to offer instruction there and in neighboring communities such as Foremost where she became associated with their longstanding musical theatre company.[50] Soon, Ackerman was attracted to Lethbridge where she continued with her emphasis on tap, jazz, and acrobatic dancing, but where she also placed a priority on the performing arts. Ballet was also taught by instructors such as Deborah Le Maistre.[51] Dance Factory students such as Tara Fenton, Lisa DeBow, and Jessica and Tiffany Knight were featured in numerous recitals and ethnic programs each year; they also participated regularly in festival competition where they achieved considerable success.

Also, in 1984 Mark Litchfield and Candy Williams combined forces to found Danceworks Dance Studio, a school which emphasized both jazz dance and ballet. Because both Litchfield and Williams participated in local theatre quite considerably, their contributions to local theatre are discussed elsewhere in this volume.

Other dance schools and teachers who offered dance instruction for various periods of time during the 1970s and 1980s include St. Patrick's School of Irish Dancing; the Linda Kohn School; the Reid School of Highland Dancing; Patricia Livingston (Nicholas Sheran Community School); and Esther Murillo (following her retirement from the National Ballet). Other teachers came and went. Some dance instruction was also offered by the university and the college.

Dancers from these various academies who sought out careers in dance, either as teachers or performers, include the following: Vanessa Plettell, Wendy Spoulos, Gerry Tomiyama, Tara Fenton, Mark Litchfield, Tiffany and Jessica Knight, and Kendra Moore.[52] Meg Beckel retained her interest in dance by becoming a corporate fund raiser for the National Ballet. Although most of the local dance students proceeded into nondance related careers (Sandra Niedermier – school principal, Linda Bauman – university librarian, Margaret Welsh – public relations, Dean Collett – medical doctor, Candice Elzinga – actor), the physical and mental discipline which they acquired through their dance training would prove beneficial throughout their lives.

With the exception of the dance schools, and to some extent, the public school drama programs, no local institutions had been established with the explicit mandate of nurturing and training young theatre aspirants. However, the decade of the 1970s witnessed the emergence of a number of organizations and institutions whose aims specifically included the development of latent dramatic talent; their purpose was educational in that they placed more emphasis on theatrical instruction than on performance. The following discussion will review the activities of four of these institutions: Lethbridge Youth Theatre, University of Lethbridge (Department of Dramatic Arts), Lethbridge Community College (Dramatics Arts program), and the Lethbridge Summer School for the Performing Arts.

Lethbridge Youth Theatre

The Lethbridge Youth Theatre was established under the auspices of the local Allied Arts Council in April 1970 by the business manager of the Council and long time member of Playgoers, Joan Waterfield. At that time, Waterfield was also a daily program hostess for the CFCN-T.V. show, *In Conversation*, and regular weekly arts commentator for the *Lethbridge Herald*. Waterfield invited interested youths (ages 13-30) to study all facets of the theatre with the ultimate aim of creating more discriminating patrons. About thirty young people accepted the initial invitation; however, by September 1971 Waterfield estimated the membership at eighty. Many of these members took their dramatic education very seriously and complemented their Youth Theatre experiences with drama courses in the local high schools, the college, and the university. Initially, the group concentrated on Children's Theatre and performed their offerings at the Bowman Arts Centre. In the summers of 1972 and 1973, the Lethbridge Youth Theatre's Shoestring Players combined forces with a local federally sponsored Opportunities for Youth drama group, the Sunshine Players, to present children's theatre. Some of the members of this latter group were alumni of the Lethbridge Youth Theatre.

In May 1971 Waterfield's Youth Theatre entered two plays in the Lethbridge Festival of Community Theatre: *Ah-Tish Mit*, directed by a *Lethbridge Herald* staff writer and drama critic, Christine Puhl, and *The In Group*, directed by Joan Waterfield. When the provincial one act festival was resurrected in 1973, the Lethbridge Youth Theatre again participated with two entries, one of which, *Babel Rap* (presented by the Bowman Players), took the honors at the Lethbridge and District Festival. The Lethbridge Youth Theatre duplicated this feat in 1974 when *Elizabeth and the Lexicon* (directed by Joan Waterfield) captured the Lethbridge and District Festival.[53]

Former Youth Theatre members speak very highly of their experience in the Lethbridge Youth Theatre, and those who were selected for special honors to be bestowed upon them for their contribution to the group, cherished these honors with great pride. The "Chris" was such an honor. For three years, Doris Balcovske donated a trophy and a scholarship (tenable at the University of Lethbridge) in memory of her father, Chris Gibson, to the member(s) of the Youth Theatre showing the greatest dramatic promise. The first award was presented to David Mann in 1972. The following year, Laurin Mann shared the award with Dawn McCaugherty. That year, Waterfield also selected Eilonwy Morgan to be honored with the Director's Award given to the "most willing and wanting" youngster.[54] Morgan also showed considerable talent for playwriting, and some of her plays were produced by the Lethbridge Youth Theatre as well as by the Lethbridge Playgoers. The final Chris award was shared by Jim Robinson and Liz Waterfield. Shortly thereafter, Waterfield disbanded the Youth Theatre; she felt it had served its purpose of providing the youth of Lethbridge with the opportunity to experience a broader perspective of theatre – a purpose which was now being fulfilled by local post secondary institutions which had recently introduced a variety of drama programs.

Lethbridge Junior College

Actually, the first dramatic society established in Lethbridge at a post-secondary educational institution was the Lethbridge Junior College Drama Club which was organized in the fall of 1965 by the sociology instructor, George Mann. Mann entered the club in the Alberta College One Act Festival with the Noel Coward play, *Ways and Means*. The festival was held in Red Deer in mid-February 1966, and the leading man in the Lethbridge production, Michael Clemis, was honored with the best actor award.[55] Then, Mann's leave of absence from the college prevented him from maintaining the club beyond the 1965-1966 term. By the time he returned to Lethbridge, the college had divided into the two institutions described earlier. His contract was transferred to the University of Lethbridge where a recently appointed member of the English Department, Dr. Brian Tyson, had established the University of Lethbridge Dramatic Society.

University of Lethbridge Productions

The University of Lethbridge Dramatic Society, under Tyson's direction, produced three plays, one each in the spring of 1969, 1970, and 1971 (*School For Scandal, The Miser*, and *A Man For All Seasons*, respectively). The production of *The Miser* was entered in the Alberta Regional Festival of the DDF. Both Charles Schott Sr. and Jr. received regional awards for their acting, as did Nora Needham; Weste Jensen was selected best stage manager.[56] By the time that *A Man For All Seasons* was presented, the Department of Dramatic Arts had been established at the University of Lethbridge and a chairman had been appointed; Tyson was happy to turn over the directing and producing responsibilities to the new department. During the next few years, Tyson authored a number of award winning plays.[57]

Although the University of Lethbridge was founded on July 1, 1967, a dramatic arts department was not approved by the Board of Governors until the summer of 1969.[58] David Spinks was appointed as the initial Chairman, effective July 1, 1971. Prior to joining the University of Lethbridge, Spinks was associated with West Midlands College, University of Birmingham, England. Spinks was primarily interested in children's theatre and improvisation, and he proved to be an extraordinarily talented instructor in these areas. When the U of L introduced an award for teaching excellence, Spinks was honored as one of the first recipients. Spinks's popularity as an instructor, production supervisor, and general advisor attracted so many students to the drama offerings that it became apparent that additional faculty were required immediately; nevertheless, the university was faced with a period of fiscal restraint, so funds for adequate faculty appointments were not forthcoming. During the next few years, the workload on Spinks was horrendous. Since a season of faculty directed productions was inconceivable, numerous student directed productions were mounted (under the supervision of Spinks) through the auspices of courses in directing and production. Actually, the students involved in these programs gained invaluable experience because they had to rely a great deal on their own initiative. This might explain why so many of these students were attracted to the alternate theatre movement.

When Spinks took a leave of absence in 1974, Dr. Terry Theodore was hired to assume the position as acting chairman, and Richard Epp, who had recently graduated (with an MFA) from the University of Victoria, was hired as an academic assistant; Epp's position also included technical director. A student, Bryan Francis, was called upon to perform the responsibilities of technician. (Francis later studied technical theatre at the University of Victoria, and then became associated with professional companies in British Columbia, particularly, in Kamloops). Theodore was very interested in the production process, and he perceived that his outlet for this interest lay in the city's community theatre. He, therefore, took on the task of directing a major production, *The Crucible*, for Playgoers in April 1975. He also entered *A Swan Song* (sponsored by the University of Lethbridge) in the 1975 one act festival. Subsequently, he directed *The Dirty Old Man* as Playgoers' entry in the 1976 festival.

As is apparent from the foregoing discussion, Theodore remained at the university for an additional year following Spinks's return from his leave of absence; therefore, the Department of Dramatic Arts then had the "luxury" of three full time faculty members since Epp was also appointed as a regular member of the faculty. Epp expanded the students' repertoire of dramatic experiences by introducing them to the genre of readers' theatre. In addition, he too, entered the 1975 one act festival with a troupe referred to as the Westside Players, who performed *The First Plateau,* written by Epp, himself. Epp quickly distinguished himself as a playwright; he authored one act plays, plays for radio and television, and a number of full length plays such as *Treasures*, which was awarded first prize ($800) in the adult full length category of the 1978 Alberta Culture playwriting competition.[59] Epp's other major works include: *Notes on The New Man, Christmas Pudding, Kristallnacht,* and *Intimate Admiration.* As was mentioned earlier, he had the honor of having this latter play performed at the Stratford, Ontario Festival. Epp was also an excellent actor who was sought out by his colleagues and by professional companies such as Theatre Calgary to perform in their productions. As a director, he introduced recent Canadian works as well as a number of the classics to his students and to many Lethbridge theatre goers. In March 1977 his production of Archibald Macleish's play, *J.B.*, was the initial offering at the University of Lethbridge Drama Lab. Four years later, his production of Chekhov's *The Cherry Orchard*, which opened the University Theatre in March 1981, gave evidence that Epp was a promising scholar of Chekhov.

Following Theodore's departure from the University of Lethbridge in 1976, Spinks and Epp were joined by Chesley Skinner who became a permanent member of the faculty. Henceforth, the university took its commitment to the Department of Dramatic Arts more seriously, but it still required about ten more years before the department could boast of a faculty large enough to cover the basic areas of theatre instruction. Table 6-5 lists the faculty members who were associated with the Department of Dramatic Arts from 1971 through 1988.

Ches Skinner had a wealth of training and experience in educational and community drama before joining the University of Lethbridge department. He had studied drama at Memorial University,

Illinois State University, the University of Birmingham, and the Banff School of Fine Arts. He also taught in Newfoundland high schools and authored a 20 part series on drama in school for the Newfoundland Department of Education.[60] After teaching in Lethbridge for a number of years, he completed his Ph.D. degree in the History of Theatre (specializing in 19th century theatre) from Michigan State University. At the University of Lethbridge, he established a reputation as a very sensitive director and a very conscientious teacher; his direction of *The Shadow Box* was particularly memorable. Skinner was an executive member of the Association for Canadian Theatre History throughout the latter half of the 1980s.

TABLE 6-5

Faculty & Associates - Department of Dramatic Arts
University of Lethbridge (1971-1988)

MEMBER	TIME OF APPOINTMENT	AREA OF DRAMATIC EXPERTISE
David Spinks	1971-1990	Developmental, Children's, Improvisational
Richard Epp	1974-	Acting, Directing, Playwriting
Terry Theodore	1974-76	Acting, Directing, History
Ches Skinner	1976-	Directing, History
Brian Parkinson	1977-	Acting, Directing
Aristides Gazetas	1980-82	Technical
John A. Johnston	1980-	Master Carpenter, Design, Scenic artistry
Sara Stanley	1981-	Developmental, Children's
Vivien Frow	1982-84	Costuming
Terry Bennett	1983-	Technical Theatre, Design
Leslie Robison-Greene	1984-	Costuming

Brian Parkinson was born in England, but his family was geographically mobile; therefore, he received a varied cross cultural education. He completed his B.A. degree in Theatre and English at the University of British Columbia and his M.A. in Drama and Theatre Arts at Leeds University (England). While at Leeds, Parkinson also became the resident assistant director of the Leeds Playhouse Theatre Company which was an A class professional company. He then qualified for a professional teaching certificate at UBC and took a high school teaching position at the Steveston Senior High School in Richmond, B.C. before being attracted to the University of Lethbridge.[61] In the production process, Parkinson was particularly instrumental in introducing his students to French playwrights such as Moliere and Feydeau. Additional contributions for which Parkinson will be remembered are the creation of two summer theatre projects, one at the University (TheatreXtra) and one in the town of Fort Macleod (Great West Summer Theatre Co.). Both of these developments will be discussed more thoroughly later.

John A. Johnston (commonly known as Jay) joined the department in 1980 as master carpenter. Johnston, a talented artist, completed an Honors BFA in sculpture at the University of Windsor. He also studied contemporary abstract painting at the University of Reading, England and restoration carpentry at Eastfield Village in Albany, New York, where he devoted six summers to this activity.Then, he literally "fell into theatre" when the position of master carpenter for Susan Rubes's Young People's Theatre Centre in Toronto was offered to him. He was later attracted to the University of Lethbridge in order to express all of his various talents. In addition to contributing to various productions, Johnston also taught stagecraft and supervised independent study and portfolio projects. Beyond his university responsibilities, Johnston contributed his artistic talents to sets for various movies and T.V. productions.[62] In addition, community theatre societies in Lethbridge, particularly Playgoers and LMT, benefitted greatly from his valuable advice and assistance; also, Johnston, a member of the Associated Designers of Canada (ADC), devoted many hours to designing and painting sets for these groups.

Sara Stanley, an MFA graduate from the University of Alberta, headed up the drama program at the Medicine Hat College for a number of years before joining the University of Lethbridge where she helped to relieve some of the student demand for instruction in improvisation and children's theatre.[63] In addition to teaching and directing regular departmental productions, she worked diligently to maintain the summer project, TheatreXtra.

Although Aristides Gazetas was hired in 1980 to teach design and to supervise the technical aspects of the department's productions, his main theatrical interests centred more on cinema. Accordingly, he was appointed to study the possibility of developing a department of film at the University.[64] Within the Department of Dramatic Arts, Gazetas's responsibilities were taken over by J. Johnston during the 1982-83 season, after which the faculty design position was filled by Terry Bennett whose MFA in design was awarded by the University of Texas, and whose formal training was complemented by a wealth of experience in professional and educational theatre.[65]

Leslie Robison-Greene, an MFA graduate from the University of Illinois, was hired to replace the professional costumer, Vivien Frow, who had been persuaded by David Spinks to come from England to fill the position of costumer until such time as the department could find an appropriate academic candidate. Eventually, Robison-Greene applied and was signed to a contract, effective July 1, 1984.[66] In addition to being a very effective member of the department, Robison-Greene extended considerable advice and assistance to summer projects and to local theatre groups such as Centre Stage Productions Society and Lethbridge Musical Theatre.

The academic program of the Department of Dramatic Arts developed rather slowly as a result of budget restraints placed on hiring. Because of limited course offerings during the first few years, the department cooperated with other departments, especially English, to round out its program. Fortunately, the Department of English had two faculty members, Brian Tyson and Edward Mikhail, whose expertise in dramatic literature was highly recognized. Early graduates such as Neil Boyden were, however, forced to petition the General Faculties Council for permission to graduate with a Bachelor of Arts and Science degree majoring in English and Drama.[67] By the mid-1970s, a multidisciplinary major in Drama and English was regularized by the Faculty of Arts and Science. In 1977 the university introduced a major in dramatic arts which meant that students could, henceforth, graduate with a Bachelor of Arts and Science degree in this major. Shortly thereafter, the Faculty of Education introduced a major in Drama Education.[68] When the department's faculty was eventually rounded out, a BFA proposal was approved by the various academic councils; the Board of Governors passed the proposal in June 1985 – specialization was restricted to performance or design.

These developments provided increasing opportunities for local and district students to have their various dramatic interests and talents nurtured. Consequently, a growing number of these students considered the dramatic arts to be a basis for their future careers and then proceeded into teaching or the professional theatre.Many of these students also brought considerable academic distinction to the Department. Two notable graduates were Karen Bernstein and Sally Scott. In the fall of 1981, Bernstein was honored as the first student to be awarded the Agnes Turcotte Memorial Scholarship which was established by Judge L.S. Turcotte, Chancellor Emeritus, to recognize academic proficiency and outstanding artistic talent.The award was open to senior students majoring in drama, music, or art.[69] Then, in 1986 Scott was selected as the gold medal recipient for the Faculty of Arts and Science.

Oedipus Rex *produced by the Department of Dramatic Arts, University*
of Lethbridge in the Experimental Theatre, February, 1985
Photo: Phil Boras, University of Lethbridge

Throughout these years, the members of the drama department were under considerable pressure to meet enrolment demands. Teacher-student ratios were exceptionally high – chairpersons regularly forfeited the course reduction which was normally accorded to departmental administrators. Nevertheless, the department not only offered a full range of courses during the regular semesters but also attempted to provide a variety of courses in the summer. In 1983 a significant new dimension was introduced into the department's offerings when Brian Parkinson became aware of the availability of funds for supporting a summer work project for students. He applied for a federal student employment grant to support a small summer repertory company at the university (to be known as TheatreXtra). Approval was granted and the first such project was launched that summer; assistance was provided by Sara Stanley and John A. Johnston, who maintained their association with TheatreXtra throughout the decade. The project continued through the successive summers, although funding became problematic in the later 1980s.[70] After the summer of 1984, Parkinson basically withdrew from TheatreXtra because of his responsibilities with the Great West Summer

Theatre Company. Other members of the department such as Ches Skinner and Leslie Robison-Greene took over some of the directorial chores as did Eric Low, an occasional sessional lecturer for the department.

Lethbridge Community College

Although the University of Lethbridge gradually expanded its drama offerings, the same could not be said for the Lethbridge Community College which introduced some drama courses in 1972 and maintained a marginal interest in such courses for about five years but then suspended this program. Betty Sorenson, B.A., M.A., was hired to offer drama instruction at the college for this short period of time. The College's dramatic society, the Harlequin Players, directed by Betty Sorenson, provided the community with some very entertaining theatre of various forms (see Table 6-6). Susan Young provided musical accompaniment, when needed. The most active students are listed in Table 6-7.

The Lethbridge Allied Arts Council (AAC)

After reading the previous pages of this book, one is abundantly aware of the tremendous scope of the activities developed or sponsored by the Allied Arts Council: summer musicals, Christmas pantomimes, Youth Theatre, summer educational programs, and touring professional and semiprofessional performers and companies. With regard to drama related educational programs in the early 1970s, Joan Waterfield provided the basic instruction; in the mid-1970s, Sandi Balcovske was contracted to develop courses in children's theatre, improvisational drama, and puppets and masks.[71] Then, in 1982 the AAC, in cooperation with Alberta Culture, the City of Lethbridge, Lethbridge Musical Theatre, and Playgoers of Lethbridge, sponsored the Lethbridge Performing Arts Summer School which offered a comprehensive one week drama seminar for students aged 12-16 years.[72] Instruction was provided in acting, makeup, speech, movement, and stage craft; instructors included Debbie Waterfield, Joan Waterfield, Fran Rude, Cherie Baunton, and Ed Bayly.

The idea of a summer performing arts school was originally conceived by Joan Waterfield who discussed the need for it with Fred Keating (Alberta Culture). Nevertheless, Wes Stefan and Kim Ully initiated such a school in the summer of 1980 through the sponsorship of LMT and Alberta Culture.[73] The facilities of Studio One Dance Academy were used for the classes. Although plans were laid for an annual summer school, Alberta Culture withdrew its funding after the first year, so the proposed 1981 session was cancelled. Then, Joan Waterfield and Cherie Baunton combined forces to persuade the Allied Arts Council to help fund an annual summer school. With additional financial assistance from Alberta Culture, the dream of a regular Lethbridge Summer School for the Performing Arts became a reality in 1982. Students paid a modest registration fee and were required to arrange their own board and room. In 1983 an advanced section was added, and in 1984 the instruction was extended to seventeen year olds; three separate classes were offered: to 12 year olds, to 13-14 year olds, and to 15-17 year olds, respectively. The latter program was also stretched into a two week course.[74] As the 1980s progressed, other local theatre practitioners such as Mardi Renyk(makeup), Dawn McCaugherty (acting), and Candy Williams (movement) were called upon to share their expertise.

The Great West Summer Theatre Company (GWSTC)

In concluding this review of youth oriented and educational or developmental drama, it seems appropriate to discuss the productions and personnel of the Great West Summer Theatre Company which was founded by Brian Parkinson in Fort Macleod in the summer of 1983. The appropriateness of this suggestion arises because Brian Parkinson was a faculty member at the University of

TABLE 6-6

Lethbridge Community College Productions: (1972-77)

DATE	TYPE	PRODUCTIONS
NOV, DEC/72	Evening of One Act Plays	1. *Act Without Words* by Samuel Beckett 2. *The Ten Worst Things About a Man* by Jean Kerr 3. *The Black Box* by Clive Haubold
Fall/72	Radio Drama	
MAR 1-3/73	Musical	*You're a Good Man, Charlie Brown* by Clark Gesner
NOV 1-3/73	Play	*Thurber Carnival* by James Thurber
MAR 7-9/74	Musical	*The Fantasticks* by Tom Jones & Harvey Schmidt
OCT, NOV/74	Rock Musical Play	*Aesop's Falables*
MAR/75	Play	*Dial M for Murder*
NOV/75	Melodrama	*Only an Orphan Girl*
DEC/76	Melodrama	*The Plight of the Widow's Daughter* or *The West Was Never Like This*
MAR/77	Musical	*The Diary of Adam & Eve* (from *The Apple Tree* - based on stories by Mark Twain, Frank R. Stockton & A. Jules Feiffer)

TABLE 6-7

Student Participants
L.C.C. Harlequin Players (1972-1977)

Most Active	Mark Cambell Tony Dimnik	Sherry Kennedy	Kim Hall
Moderately Active	Paul Cohen	Kelly Fiddick	Allan La Fayette
Active	Kristine Ackerman Mike Bennett Alexis Carr Patsy Crawford Candice Croft Jim Gledhill Lucretia Feaviour	Ron Forsythe Jim Gray Annette Hammond Dixie Hobbs Dale Johnson Kathy Langston Bill Mallalieu	Bob Mothersell Lorne Petty Bruce Stremel Penny Takahashi Debbie Thiessen Dalyce Van Cleave Kathy Zelinsky

Lethbridge, many of the company were from Lethbridge, and the shows became so popular that the company became identified with all of southern Alberta rather than with Fort Macleod, alone.

Parkinson established the GWSTC at the invitation of Jim Mountain who was associated with the Heritage Canada's Main Street Project.It was suggested that the company operate out of the town's Empress Theatre during the summer months.[75] The Empress, constructed in the centre of main street in 1912, had served the community well as a venue for concerts, live theatre, and movies.[76] The local Fort Players presented their productions there as of the early 1980s. But the theatre, last renovated in 1937, was in dire need of rehabilitation; however, the slim movie crowds and the odd live production did not warrant such expense. With the promise of a resident summer company, the owners were convinced to upgrade the facility, especially, with some financial assistance from the various levels of government. The summer project was approved; Parkinson quickly formalized the operation, received some funding from Alberta Culture, and cast the melodramas: *Egad What a Cad* and *Dastardly Deed at the Grill.* Jim Mountain preferred that the company be made up exclusively of local Macleod residents but Parkinson found that this requirement was too restrictive.[77] Although the admission price was extraordinarily reasonable ($1.00 - adult; $0.50 - children under 12), the houses were quite disappointing; they averaged about fifteen per performance. An unusually good Friday night audience numbered about forty. Undaunted, Parkinson persevered during the next two summers when the productions included: That *Sally Gal*; *Dracula, the Musical*; an extended version of *Curse You Jack Dalton;* and *Puttin' on the Glitz.* During this formative period, a number of changes in the shows' format were evident. Although the Main Street officials envisioned productions with a distinct historical mandate, historical authenticity was sacrificed. Also, the shows gradually took on the form of a musical revue. Audiences responded accordingly, and houses of 150-160 became commonplace for *Puttin' on the Glitz.* In 1986 *Shake, Rattle and Roll* drew almost 10 000 patrons. The demand was so overwhelming that additional shows had to be added. The reputation of the company was now solidly established; residents of southern Alberta awaited the new summer season with great anticipation; locals paid numerous repeat visits to the shows; visitors to the area were entertained with an evening out to the Fort Macleod productions. Succeeding productions were: *The Great West Picture Show* (1987); *That Was Now, This Is Then* (1988); and *The Last Resort* (1989).[78] Throughout these seven summers, the company remained under the careful supervision of Parkinson who provided his expertise free of charge. Parkinson always considered this work to be an extension of his research and performance responsibilities as a university faculty member. In addition, he found the creative process associated with developing the shows to be very exhilarating.

As the years passed, the company's resources improved considerably because of increased government grants as well as increased box office receipts.The latter was accomplished because of larger houses but also because of higher admission prices as illustrated below:

	1983	1984	1985	1986	1987	1988	1989
Adult	$1.00	$2.00-$3.00	$3.50	$3.50	$4.00	$5.00	$6.00
Student			$2.00	$2.00	$2.50	$3.00	$4.00
Child	$0.50	$0.50-$1.00	$1.00	$1.00	$1.00	$2.00	$3.00

Parkinson involved his company, which ranged from 9-13 members, in the whole creative process; nevertheless, the extent of that involvement depended upon the varying abilities and the past experiences of the troupe members. He always prepared for the new summer show by developing a fairly well defined idea and plotline. Then, he encouraged brainstorming and researching by the company. The collected material, including historical data and music, would be developed

TABLE 6-8

Company Members:* Great West Summer Theatre Co.
Fort Macleod, Alberta (1983-1989)
(Director: Brian Parkinson)

MEMBER	83	84	85	86	87	88	89	MEMBER	83	84	85	86	87	88	89
Jeff Carlson				X	X		X	Karl Meintzer		X	X				
Candice Elzinga				X	X			Norton Moranz					X		X
Ryan Hart					X		X	Rhonda Nugent						X	X
Richard Hamilton	X	X						Roman Phob					X	X	X
Greg Jarvie			X	X				Kelly Roberts			X	X	X	X	X
Marselle Jobs			X	X				Jaybo Russell				X	X	X	
David Loney				X	X	X		Mark Russell					X	X	X
Robert Macleod		X	X					Roger Schultz					X		X
Narda McCarroll				X	X	X	X	Ron Tracey		X	X				

* Member for 2 or more summers

into a production by the company as a whole; however, Parkinson remained the final arbiter and thus he determined the final product. Students who were involved in this process were primarily University of Lethbridge students, and they were usually residents of Lethbridge or Fort Macleod although a few came from other communities. It is also true that, beginning in 1986, the company membership became fairly stable, and, as can be seen from Table 6-8, a number of these students participated for three or four summers.

Locally Produced Community Theatre

The Playgoers Club of Lethbridge

Although the Lethbridge Playgoers were forced to decline the invitation to participate in Theatre Canada in 1971, the club did produce the musical *Fings Ain't Wot They Used T'Be* for presentation at the Yates Memorial Centre. Nevertheless, Playgoers had been in a bit of the doldrums since 1966 and were thus able to mount only one production a year during the years 1966-1972, inclusive.The recurring problem which returned to haunt the Playgoers during this period, was the lack of alternative directors. However, the 50th anniversary year for Playgoers (1973) and its celebration tended to give the club a needed shot in the arm. In addition, the reintroduction of the one act festival movement in 1973 gave the club added incentive. In 1974 two novice directors, Ed Bayly and Joan Waterfield, "tried their stuff" and discovered the joys of directing.They became the club's most productive directors in the period, 1974-1977. As can be seen from Table 6-9, Playgoers experienced a period of considerable activity from 1974-78. After this, Bayly and Waterfield were happy to encourage others to try their hand at directing.The most prolific director to emerge during the succeeding period was Fran Rude. After Rude left the Lethbridge Playgoers to found the Centre

Stage Productions Society, the mantle of leading director fell into the hands of Neil Boyden (see Table 6-10).

Although Dick Mells's interests substantially dominated the activities of the Playgoers Club from 1966-1973 inclusive, his association with the organization withered, thereafter, as he became more involved in other theatrical ventures. Following the success of *The Hostage* in 1970, Mells directed four of the succeeding five Playgoers' productions: *Fings Ain't Wot They Used T'Be* (1971), *A Midsummer Night's Dream* (1972), and two pieces for Playgoers' 50th anniversary celebration (1973), *Black Comedy* and *Oh, What a Lovely War*. Mells's interest in musical theatre is evident, here, since two of these productions were basically musicals. After the 1973 celebration, Mells turned his attention to reviving the summer musicals and to directing some freelance presentations.

TABLE 6-9

Playgoers of Lethbridge: Productions (1971-1988)

TYPE OF PRODUCTION	71	72	73	74	75	76	77	78	79	80	81	82	83	84	85	86	87	88	TOTAL
MAJOR PLAY		1		2	2	2	2	1	1			1	1	1	1	1	1	1	18
MAJOR MUSICAL	1		1						1										3
ONE ACT PLAY			2	2		3	3	2	1	1	1		2	1	5	3			26
MELODRAMA				1	2	2	1	1							1	2			10
READERS' THEATRE								2		1				2		4		1	10
MISC.*				1										2		2			5
TOTALS	1	1	3	5	5	7	6	6	2	3	1	1	5	4	9	10	1	2	72

* Convention entertainment and promotional productions

Table 6-10 confirms the fact that Ed Bayly and Joan Waterfield were, by far, the most active directors for the Playgoers Club during this era. Bayly tended to concentrate on one act plays (including festival productions), melodramas, and readers' theatre; whereas, Waterfield focussed almost exclusively on directing one and three act plays. Because of Bayly's responsibilities at the Yates Memorial Centre, and because of his extensive contribution to design, backstage, and executive activities for both Playgoers and Lethbridge Musical Theatre, he found it difficult to devote the time required for directing major productions. However, he was the driving force behind getting Playgoers involved in performing melodramas at the annual Lethbridge Exhibition (Whoop Up Days). In fact, Bayly wrote the melodrama, *Priscilla Pringle's Predicament* or *All's Swell That Ends Swell*, in the spring of 1974 and then directed three casts so that the production could run frequently, each day, throughout the 1974 Fair. *Priscilla Pringle's Predicament* proved so popular that the Playgoers and Bayly produced it many times after for convention programs and non-competitive entertainment at local festivals. Bayly directed a number of other melodramas for the local fair including *Polly Pardon Gets Her Own Back* or *Kitty Litter Strikes Again* (1977) which he also penned. Unfortunately, the association with the Exhibition ended after the summer of 1978, primarily because the Exhibition Board could not provide a truly adequate venue for these presentations. The most popular readers' theatre presentation, directed by Bayly, was a Richard Epp adaptation of *The Christmas Carol*. Admission proceeds and royalty payments to Richard Epp were donated to the Unitarian Service Committee. In 1987 and 1988 Bayly took on the responsibility of directing the annual Lethbridge Musical Theatre productions, *The Sound of Music* and *South Pacific,* respectively. Bayly's achievements were recognized in the early 1980s, by being awarded an Alberta Achievement Award in the Community Service category for his contribution to the arts (Drama) in Lethbridge.

TABLE 6-10

Playgoers of Lethbridge: Directors (1971-1988)*

DIRECTOR	MAJOR PLAY	1 ACT	MELODRAMA	MUSICAL	READERS' THEATRE	TOTAL
Ed Bayly	-	3	7	-	4	14
Joan Waterfield	5	7	-	-	1	13
Neil Boyden	3	2	2	-	-	7
Dick Mells	1	1	-	2	-	4
Fran Rude	3	1	-	-	-	4
Cherie Baunton	-	1	-	-	2	3
George Mann	2	-	1	-	-	3
Eric Low	1	1	-	-	-	2
Marty Oordt	-	-	-	-	2	2
Wes Stefan	1	-	-	1**	-	2
Terry Theodore	1	1	-	-	-	2
Keith Harris	-	-	-	1**	-	1
David Poole	1	-	-	-	-	1
TOTAL	18	17	10	4	9	58

* 1 Major production or more than 1 Little Theatre Production
** Co-director

Waterfield, too, was honored with a similar Achievement Award. She had maintained her involvement with the local media throughout the period under discussion; however, her regular weekly column in the *Lethbridge Herald* and her commentaries on CFCN-T.V. gradually focussed almost exclusively on movie reviews. With regard to live theatre, Waterfield's interests turned more and more to directing. Her directing activities with Playgoers stretched from the spring of 1974 until the spring of 1986, although this activity tended to be concentrated in the years 1974-77 and 1983-86. In 1986 she took on the task of directing the LMT production of *Hello Dolly*. Unfortunately, during a rehearsal of this latter musical, Waterfield backed off of the Yates stage, fell into the orchestra pit, and suffered a compound fracture of the leg; Ed Bayly was called upon to fill in for Waterfield until she could return to the show. Although she completed the directing task, the accident curtailed her theatrical activities for a period of time, thereafter. She returned to the stage in the Playgoers' 1989 production of *Steel Magnolias*.

Fran Rude was a woman of many talents. She was an accomplished singer, she became an expert in theatrical makeup, she enjoyed acting, and she developed into one of the city's most ardent directors. Rude (nee Young) moved to Lethbridge from Montreal in the spring of 1964 to take up a position with the YMCA. She later became employed by Alberta Social Services. In the early 1970s, she sought out dramatic instruction from Murray Robison and faculty members at the University of Lethbridge. She made her local stage debut (with Playgoers) in the musical *Oh, What a Lovely War* (1973) and then, she became an active contributor to all facets of the club's activities. Rude's directing debut with Playgoers, the one act festival production, *Canadian Gothic*, was very auspicious in that the play was selected to represent the Lethbridge and District Zone at the Alberta One Act Festival. At the latter festival, Rude was awarded a special drama achievement award for her "sensitive direction."[79] Encouraged by this success, Rude proceeded to take directing very seriously, and in the next few years, she directed three major productions for Playgoers: *Walsh* (1979), *Da* (1983), and *The Miracle Worker* (1985). During this time, she also freelanced when she directed *How the Other Half Loves* (1981) in collaboration with Neil Boyden, who agreed to produce the play in Coaldale.Playgoers sponsored a run of this play in Lethbridge following its presentation in Coaldale. It was also in 1981 that Rude took on directing responsibilities for Lethbridge Musical Theatre, for whom she directed three regular fall productions plus the special 20th anniversary production, *Down Memory Lane*, in the spring 1984. Then, in 1985 she spearheaded the organization of Centre Stage Productions Society, whose initial production, *Chorus Line,* was presented at the Yates Memorial Centre in the fall of 1985.

Neil Boyden was a young drama teacher at R.I. Baker School in Coaldale. Raised on a farm near Lethbridge, he attended the University of Lethbridge and specialized in English and drama education. After Murray Robison resigned his position at the R.I. Baker School, Boyden succeeded him. As Neil stated, "The exit of Murray Robison . . . left a void that no one could fill.The only alternative was to begin again in a different direction."[80] Rather than following the tradition of legitimate theatre which Robison had maintained, Boyden concentrated on the production of musicals; at first, with students only, but later, with the participation of some adults from the community.Of course, he always relied upon production assistance from his colleagues and associates: vocal instruction (Henny Hildebrand); choreography (Laurin Mann, Gerry Tomiyama); stage management (Wilma Wiebe); props (Murray Robison). Examples of Boyden's musicals are: *Anne of Green Gables, The Land of Oz, You're a Good Man Charlie Brown, Tom Sawyer, West Side Story,* and *Annie.*

Boyden's dramatic activities at the R.I. Baker School were seriously disrupted on June 8, 1977, when the school's gymnasium and stage were burned to the ground. The County School Committee was quick to plan a replacement for the gym, and Boyden was able to convince them and other responsible parties that the performing arts required more adequate facilities than a stage associated with a sport's gym. Boyden conceived of a flexible 3 000 square foot performing arts room and suggested that it be dedicated to Murray Robison. The governing bodies agreed; the new facility was officially opened on November 9, 1979, with a program of selected works from Boyden's previous musicals. The next night, Boyden began his run of *Oliver,* the first Baker show in which Boyden cast adult members of the community. Notably, Frank Featherstone took the part of Fagin – a role which he had so masterfully portrayed for LMT in 1974. In 1981 Boyden collaborated with Fran Rude to produce *How the Other Half Loves,* which included Frank Featherstone in the cast. As it turned out, this was Featherstone's farewell performance in southern Alberta; he retired from his teaching and school administrative post at Kate Andrews School and moved to Vancouver Island. With the new performing arts facility in place, Coaldale quickly became the annual venue for the

Lethbridge and District High School Drama festival, and Boyden became recognized as a most efficient organizer and cordial host of the festival. Boyden's organizing talents were also recognized by his colleagues who perennially returned him to the position of president of the area's High School Drama Association.

It was extremely fortunate for Playgoers that Neil Boyden became associated with the club in the mid-1980s. Because of the name which he had established for himself in southern Alberta drama circles, Boyden quickly vaulted into prominence with the club. In 1985 he was elected president – the first executive position he held in the club. In addition, his willingness to direct was greatly appreciated, especially since Fran Rude was about to leave the club and Joan Waterfield and Ed Bayly were becoming more deeply involved with directing for Lethbridge Musical Theatre. Neil Boyden's debut directing task with Playgoers was the one act play, *Funeral Tea*, which he presented at the public library theatre gallery on June 15, 1985. During the next four years, Boyden became the primary director for the Playgoers Club. He directed the four succeeding major productions: *On Golden Pond* (1986), *The Odd Couple* (female version [1987]), *The Teahouse of the August Moon* (1988), and *Steel Magnolias* (1989), the latter of which actually falls beyond the time frame of Table 6-11 and this book. He also directed a number of other short but special works for Playgoers such as a computer promotion sketch and a melodrama, *Run to the Roundhouse Nellie* (which was performed on numerous occasions in the spring and summer of 1986).

Playgoers of Lethbridge: Acting Personnel

The acting core of Playgoers during the years 1971 - 1988 is illustrated in Table 6-11. Some of these members participated in the club's activities throughout this period; others were involved for various lengths of time. The tenure of active membership has been indicated in most instances.

Generally, it can be said that the members who were involved with the club for fewer than ten years can be placed into one of four categories: (1) young members who participated in their late teens or early twenties and then left Lethbridge to pursue advanced education or careers; (2) members who participated in Playgoers for a period of time and then withdrew because of other interests or demands; (3) geographically mobile members who resided in Lethbridge for varying but somewhat limited periods of time; (4) people who became involved off and on but did not have the time or inclination to become highly involved. Of course, these categories are not necessarily mutually exclusive; some participants might fit into more than one category. Let us begin our analysis of onstage involvement by reviewing the participation of the long term members first.

Ed Bayly was, without question, the most sought after actor in the club. His acting credits for Playgoers in the period 1971-1988 exceeded those of all other members of the club throughout its entire history. One of the reasons for this is the fact that Bayly was extraordinarily capable of portraying characters of various ages. Being relatively young when he joined Playgoers, he was generally called upon to portray youthful parts, and he continued to portray the "juvenile lead" for many years, thereafter. But Bayly was also noted for his marvellous character portrayals, some of which were elderly men. In 1966 Bayly, in his late 20s, played the role of grandpa in *You Can't Take It With You* and received considerable praise from adjudicator, Peter Boretski. In 1983 he succeeded in convincing us, again, of his supreme ability when he portrayed the elderly title role in Hugh Leonard's play, *Da.* A year later, he played the youthful murderer, Sam Blaine, in *Suddenly at Home.* Bayly's repertoire of characters stretched from beggars to high class gentlemen and from old country folk heroes to elderly prospectors. His facility with dialects also opened up numberable acting opportunities. He portrayed Irish, Welsh, numerous English, American, and Canadian characters of various social classes with equal ease. In addition to his superb acting, Bayly had many other talents that made him indispensible to the Lethbridge theatrical community. Throughout all the years that he was associated with the Yates Centre, he was always willing and able to assist in

TABLE 6-11

Onstage Participants (3 or More Roles)
Lethbridge Playgoers (1971-1988)

PARTICIPANT	N	TENURE*	PARTICIPANT	N	TENURE
Ed Bayly	30	T	Janice (Tilley) Brown	4	76-78; 85-88
Bob Baunton	13	73-86	Lois Dongworth	4	T
Linda Bayly	12	T	Pat Hammond	4	74-81
Cathy Evins	10	T	Kate Johnstone	4	84-85
Frank Huszar	10	T	Karen Kay	4	73-88
Garry Johnson	10	T	Lawrence Kotkas	4	82-86
George Mann	10	T	Jane McCoy	4	72-80
Hazel Skaronski**	10	T	Ray Mercer	4	71-73
Bill Matheson	9	71-75	Sheila Pisko	4	71-73; 85-88
Cherie Baunton	9	73-86	Lee Prindle	4	86-88
Albert Azzara	8	74-79	Fran Rude	4	73-85
Barbara Day	8	74-86	Wes Stefan	4	71-76
Frank Featherstone	8	72-80	Jean Warburton	4	71-79
Phil Story	8	T	Candy Williams	4	79-85
Mike Day	7	74-88	Mark Campbell	3	76-78
Linda Johnson	7	T	Gail Holland	3	76-88
Mardi Renyk	7	T	Winstan Jones	3	72-85
Nora Rose	6	74-77	Laurin Mann	3	75-76; 82-83
Deb Waterfield	6	77-85	Doug Petherbridge	3	78-84
Al Greenway	5	71-73	Chip Seibert	3	76-77
Eric Low	5	75-88	Ken Sinclair	3	79-88
Kaye Robison**	5	T	Joan Waterfield**	3	T
Jack Warburton	5	71-73			
*period of involvement; T = throughout the era **Honorary Life Membership awarded Feb. 1, 1986					

the most helpful and courteous way, the various groups using the facility. His talents and abilities were endless. In the twenty-five year period from 1963-1988, his theatrical talents were manifest in acting, singing, designing (sets and lights), directing, playwriting, stage managing, set construct-ing, scenic painting, and technical directing. In many ways, Bayly's life and career represent the very best of amateur theatre in Lethbridge. His British origins are reminiscent of the many British immigrants who contributed so much to the local theatre. On the other hand, because he was only 15 years of age when his family moved to Lethbridge, and because he gained most of his theatrical experience in Lethbridge, he also represented the many young dramatic enthusiasts whose talents were nurtured by sincere local teachers or directors. Bayly's devotion to all aspects of the theatrical enterprise also reminds us of the founder of Playgoers, E.G. Sterndale Bennett. Bayly is a worthy representative of the traditions and goals set down in the club's original constitution and, therefore, it is significant that the name of Bayly became so synonymous with that of Playgoers. Bayly's acting talents, together with his many other abilities, achieved for him by the mid-1980s the reputation of being the most competent and respected all round male thespian in Lethbridge.

Bayly's wife, Linda, was noted for being a very responsible person, an exceptionally hard worker, and a member who could be counted upon to provide competent assistance wherever it was needed. Linda was an effective executive member, production manager, program organizer, and deeply committed, loyal supporter of Playgoers. In addition, she made extensive contributions to the Lethbridge and District Music Festival, to the Lethbridge Musical Theatre, and to the LDS Church. After joining the crew for *The Madwoman of Chaillot* (1968), Linda Albertson (Bayly) worked diligently backstage for a number of years before being enticed onstage by Ed to play a part in various presentations of *Priscilla Pringle's Predicament.* She then proceeded to perform in most of the succeeding summer melodramas where she displayed considerable comic ability. Unfortunately, her great dependability backstage probably kept her from being cast in many acting roles. Onstage, she is probably best remembered for her portrayals of Mickey (in the female version of The Odd *Couple*), and Clairee (in *Steel Magnolias*).

Bob and Cherie Baunton were New Zealanders who emigrated to Canada in the early 1970s. Bob was an engineer who became associated with a local architectural firm. His professional training fitted him very well for stage construction work. Baunton was very athletic and ruggedly handsome which gave visual credence to roguish and villainous type characters. Although Baunton was generally cast in supporting roles, he proved himself equal to more demanding roles in *How the Other Half Loves* (1981) and *Suddenly at Home* (1984). These roles also required considerable acting scope as they ranged from a broad comic character to a treacherous murderer. Petite and attractive, Cherie Baunton, a certified speech teacher, was a devoted worker in all aspects of the Playgoers' activities. She performed effectively on the executive, she contributed immeasurably to the costume department, she tried her hand at directing, and she added to the acting component. With reference to Baunton's debut performance in *Black Comedy* (1973), the *Herald* reviewer, Lynn Van Luven, stated, "Cherie Baunton as Miss Furneval is priceless as the strait-laced spinster who 'discovers' the enjoyable sin of imbibing spirits."[81] From that time on, Cherie Baunton provided excellent support in numerous Playgoers' productions. Her outstanding major role was, however, Teresa Phillips, in Rude's production of *How the Other Half Loves*. In addition to her contribution to Playgoers, Baunton participated in LMT, taught numerous speech workshops, and raised four children. When the Bauntons decided to return to New Zealand in 1986, the Playgoers club established an award in Cherie's name to be presented annually at the Lethbridge and District Kiwanis Music and Speech Arts Festival.

After establishing her artistic career in Lethbridge, Cathy Evins proceeded to display her acting talent with her outrageous Playgoers' debut in *Arsenic and Old Lace.* As Lynne Van Luven of the Herald said: "Consistently strong, believable and spunky, Cathy Evins as Abby Brewster was the undisputed star in the opening performance."[82] During the next six years or so, Evins literally threw herself into meeting the various needs of Playgoers. From 1974 to 1982 she performed in four major productions, numerous melodramas, and a readers' theatre presentation. She portrayed a maid, a servant, a sweet young thing, a good gentlewoman, and a domineering, crippled mother; she also designed at least seven major production sets, she acted as prop mistress for numerous productions, she directed a one act festival play, *The Rehearsal* (1978), she took on the responsibility of General Director (1978-80), and she presided over the club in 1980. After 1982 her participation with Playgoers was curtailed somewhat as she became more deeply involved with Lethbridge Musical Theatre. However, she could still be relied upon to help backstage, particularly with props. She also appeared in the one act plays, *Spreading the News* and *Funeral Tea,* both of which were produced in 1985.[83]

Frank Huszar is probably best remembered for his performances in the Christmas pantomimes. He was also a very solid member of the chorus in numerous LMT productions. Actually, his local acting career began in 1967 with CLT; then, in the early 1970s he became a fairly regular supporting actor in Playgoers, appearing in numerous one act plays, melodramas, and in the major productions, *The Crucible* and *A Midsummer Night's Dream.* Undoubtedly, his greatest impact on the audience while performing for Playgoers came in 1987 when he portrayed Jesus Costazuela in the female version of *The Odd Couple.* His comic work was so incredible in that role that he was later selected to play the leading role of Chester in the club's revival of *The Whole Town's Talking* (1990).

Garry Johnson, a social welfare worker for Alberta Social Services, made his acting debut with the club in the 1974 summer melodrama, *Priscilla Pringle's Predicament,* where he was outstanding as the mountie, Sergeant Presson. In fact, Johnson fit the part so well that members identified him with the role; therefore, he was called upon to reprise the part every time Playgoers did *Priscilla.* . . . But Johnson is also remembered for his hilarious portrayals of Dad and Charlie in the one act festival play, *Ernie's Incredible Illucinations,* and the three acter, *On Golden Pond,* respectively. Throughout his association with Playgoers, Johnson also gave invaluable service backstage where he showed exceptional organizing and supervising talent as production manager.

Johnson's wife, Linda, debuted with Playgoers in the production of *A Midsummer Night's Dream* (1972). She also became a perennial performer in the melodrama where she not only portrayed the title role in *Priscilla's* . . , but also excelled as Sergeant Presson's trusty dog, Rex. Primarily, Linda helped backstage, and she, like Garry, showed great skill in organizing the production personnel. Then, in 1987 Johnson was given the opportunity to play a major role, Renee, in *The Odd Couple.* This experience gave her the added confidence to try directing but that adventure had to wait until 1990, and thereafter.

George Mann's involvement with Playgoers was interrupted during the early 1970s while he completed his Ph.D. degree at the University of Colorado. Then, in 1974 he joined the set construction crew for the spring production, *Breath of Spring,* and portrayed the role of Teddy Brewster in the fall presentation, *Arsenic and Old Lace.* Throughout this era, Mann appeared in two additional major productions, three short plays, numerous melodramas, and most of the readers' theatre presentations which Playgoers produced. He is probably best remembered for the villainous characters he played in the various melodramas and for his 1986 portrayal of Norman Thayer in *On Golden Pond.* Certainly, he believed that Norman was the high point in his acting career for Playgoers. In addition, Mann directed two major productions, *Come Blow Your Horn* (1975) and

Never Too Late (1982), as well as the melodrama, *She Was Only a Farmer's Daughter* (summer, 1975). He was also responsible for organizing the 1986 "Bash" which recognized the lengthy contributions of Kaye Robison, Hazel Skaronski, and Joan Waterfield by honoring them with lifetime memberships in the club.Finally, in 1988 Mann spearheaded the movement to name the new acting facility at the Yates Memorial Centre, the Sterndale Bennett Theatre.

Mardi Renyk graduated from Catholic Central High School in Lethbridge, completed her teacher education at the University of Alberta, and served in Africa as a CUSO volunteer before returning to Lethbridge to devote herself to homemaking and to raising her family. She functioned, occasionally, as a beauty parlor receptionist, and therefore, gained an appreciation for the skills involved in proper hairdressing and makeup. She made valuable contacts with operators who contributed to the hairstyling and makeup components of local productions. Renyk, herself, developed into one of the city's most competent stage makeup artists. She headed this department for many LMT and Playgoers' productions. Renyk, a slim, beautiful woman, ideally suited ingenue roles such as Elaine Harper in *Arsenic and Old Lace* (1974). However, her role as the servant, Helga, in *Life With Father,* and later, some vaudeville work which she did for club meetings, uncovered a flair for comedy. Unfortunately, family, work, and advanced educational demands kept her from participating as actively onstage during the 1980s as she had during the earlier decade.

Phil Story continued to provide excellent support both onstage and backstage for the various community theatre organizations in Lethbridge. Onstage, he carved out a career for himself either as a policeman or as an indigent. He also played "folksy" characters extremely well as is evidenced by the fact that he received another honorable mention for his acting in the 1985 festival production of *Spreading the News*. On that occasion, both adjudicators, Dick Mells and Rick McNair, praised him for his acting.

A number of University of Lethbridge students became involved with Playgoers in the mid-1970s. Albert Azzara made his debut with Playgoers in 1974 when he played a young man in the one act festival entry, *Hello Out There,* directed by another young student member, Jim Veenstra. This was the first production in which Azzara was cast opposite Laurin Mann; however that combination was repeated numerous times, especially for the Attic Theatre. Later that summer, Azzara portrayed Sergeant Presson in the club's initial offering of *Priscilla Pringle's Predicament.* He returned to the melodrama format in the summer of 1978 when he performed in his own offering, *Truckers Are a Girl's Best Friend.* [Deb (Anderson) Waterfield was also in the cast.] Azzara appeared in three major productions for Playgoers, three one act plays, and two melodramas. His major challenge was probably portraying Louis, the Metis scout in *Walsh* (1979). However, his greatest triumphs locally were undoubtedly in Dick Mells's production, *Of Mice and Men,* and in various plays under the direction of Murray Robison. After leaving Lethbridge to take up a teaching career in Red Deer, Azzara became a significant contributor to amateur community theatre in that community.

Eric Low, the youngest son of the former leader of the Social Credit party, Solon E. Low, was raised in Raymond and attended the Universities of Alberta, Lethbridge, and Victoria. After completing some graduate theatre courses at the University of Victoria, Low returned to Lethbridge where he did some sessional teaching for the Department of Dramatic Arts, Universityof Lethbridge, and worked part time in local schools. Low was endowed with an extremely rich, deep voice, and he was capable of playing a variety of roles. In addition, he had a keen interest in directing. Accordingly, he directed personal productions, university offerings, plays for Playgoers, and presentations for Centre Stage Productions. For Playgoers, Low directed *Comedy of Errors* (1977) and the one act festival play, *The New Play* (1976). He appeared in three major productions as well as in two shorter plays produced for festival competition. Low's wife, Jody (nee Snow), was a specialist in technical theatre who provided this expertise to various groups in Lethbridge including Playgoers, but she became most closely associated with Centre Stage Productions.

Debbie Waterfield (nee Anderson) excited Lethbridge audiences with her portrayal of Nurse Kelly in the *Miracle Worker* (1985), but all of the theatre people who had observed her various performances over the years had long realized the exceptional talent of this young lady. Deb Waterfield was a "graduate" of the Lethbridge Youth Theatre and later showed considerable potential in *The Shadow Box* (1978) and *Twelfth Night* (1970) at the University of Lethbridge. It was at that time, that she became quite active in Playgoers; first, by portraying some minor roles, Luce in *A Comedy of Errors* (1977) and Maggie in *Life With Father* (1977). In 1978 she participated in readers' theatre, the summer melodrama, and in the one act festival winner, *Canadian Gothic,* in which she portrayed Jean. She then left Lethbridge for a period of time, but returned in the mid-1980s to resume her university studies and to participate in the university productions, *Waiting for the Parade* (1982) and *The Importance of Being Earnest* (1986). Just prior to this last production, she married another University of Lethbridge drama major, Brian Solberg.

Janice Tilley graduated from the University of Lethbridge with a B.Ed. degree. Her university studies, career, marriage, and motherhood interrupted her participation in local theatre. Nevertheless, she managed to act in the odd production; the year 1985 saw her participate in two one act productions, *Funeral Tea* and *Yes Dear* for Playgoers, the latter of which was a festival contender. Tilley also appeared as the daughter in *'Night Mother* for Centre Stage Productions. This was undoubtedly her most demanding role in community theatre.

Pat Hammond alternated the role of Sergeant Presson in the first Playgoers' summer melodrama. In addition, he appeared in *Comedy of Errors* and in *Walsh.* With regard to the latter production, the *Lethbridge Herald* critic, Arthur McDougall, said of Hammond's portrayal of Clarence, a NWMP recruit:[84]

> Pat Hammond as the new recruit, eager to go into battle but finally immersed in the human tragedy he sees around him, could have been a "stock" character but this actor's technique and intelligence rescues the part from triviality.

Hammond concluded his association with Playgoers by directing a short play, *Optimism,* presented at the Public Library Theatre Gallery in December 1981 under the auspices of Joan Waterfield's Shoestring Theatre. At the University of Lethbridge, he participated in a number of productions including: *Twelfth Night, The Cherry Orchard,* and *Tartuffe*; in the latter production, he delightfully played the title role. Hammond was also very convincing in the Attic Theatre production of *The Rainmaker,* in which, he played the naive younger son.

A number of veteran Playgoers left the club after participating with it for varying periods of time because they felt their dramatic interest could be best served elsewhere. This was particularly true in the early 1970s when members like Al Greenway, Ellyn Mells, Ray Mercer, and Jack and Jean Warburton began to concentrate on musical theatre. These members had been particularly attracted to Playgoers because of Dick Mells's association with it and because he occasionally added some kind of musical theatre to Playgoers' seasons. Actually, Jean Warburton maintained her membership for many succeeding years and continued to work backstage, off and on, for Playgoers and also took a cameo role in the 1979 production of *Walsh.*

The creation of Centre Stage Productions Society in 1985 not only meant the loss of Fran Rude to Playgoers, but Candy Williams and Hazel Skaronski also felt they could make a more useful contribution to the new group. Skaronski was accorded a lifetime membership in Playgoers in 1986 for more than twenty-five years of valuable contribution to the club. Her work in the costuming area had been invaluable; in addition, her acting, as described in Chapter Five, was remarkable.Her contributions continued unabated until around 1986 when she basically retired from the club and from the executive position of treasurer which she had held continuously since 1981 and on occasions, previously. In the period 1974-1985, Skaronski appeared in four major productions, five one act plays, and one summer melodrama for Playgoers. In the 1974 melodrama, she was one of the original Priscillas. Later that year, she convulsed local audiences with her portrayal of the Fairy Godmother in Jolliffe's Christmas pantomime, *Cinderella*. Skaronski's performances were always priceless and evoked critical comment such as:[85]

> ... Ms. Skaronski created an inspired "Hattie," (*Breath of Spring*, 1974)

> ... characterization was excellent [extracted & changed (*Night Must Fall*, 1976)]

> ... she is a very believable character (*Da*, 1983)

To cap off her acting career with Playgoers, Skaronski received honorable mention for her performance as Mrs. Tully in Playgoers' 1985 Alberta One Act Festival production, *Spreading the News*.

The following discussion will analyze the onstage participation of four very active Playgoers whose association with the club was curtailed because of their move from the city: Bill Matheson, Frank Featherstone, Nora Rose, and Kaye Robison. These extremely talented actors were also major contributors to LMT; in addition, Nora Rose was a trained professional soprano who was highly sought after for concert performances. The first three of these members also had in common the fact that their participation in the club's activities was, primarily, onstage although Matheson sat on the executive for a few years and was president during the 50th anniversary year, 1973. From 1971 through 1974, Matheson appeared in the two Playgoers' musicals, three major productions, two one act plays, and *Priscilla Pringle's Predicament* (as one of the original villains). Whether playing a leading role or a supporting role, and whether playing a Shakespearean nobleman or a slimy Jonathan Brewster (*Arsenic and Old Lace*), Matheson could always be counted upon to do a masterful job.

Frank Featherstone was also an extremely reliable performer, who, although his real forte was farce, also brought strength to the many straight supporting roles which he played: Witherspoon, the director of the mental institution in *Arsenic and Old Lace;* the blustery Brigadier in *Breath of Spring*; or the Inspector of Police in *Night Must Fall*. He was also convincing and very amusing as the leading character, Clarence Day, Sr., in *Life With Father*. Also, Lethbridge audiences will never forget his riotously funny presentation of Frank Foster in Fran Rude's production of *How the Other Half Loves*.

Featherstone's wife in *Life With Father* was Nora Rose who had also starred in *Arsenic and Old Lace* as the spinster, Martha Brewster. Rose, who was, as mentioned earlier, a trained concert singer, was truly challenged by the parts in which she was cast for Playgoers. But she illustrated what a good sport she was by performing in the two melodramas, Priscilla ... and *She Was Only a Farmer's Daughter;* she too, played one of the original Priscillas. In addition, Rose appeared in The *Time of Your Life* and in the one act festival play, *Steinway Grand*. She also tried her hand at directing a festival play, *Birdbath*, by Leonard Melfi which was awarded first place standing at the Lethbridge and District One Act Festival in 1976.[86] Besides appearing in Playgoers' productions, Rose participated in the three major productions which Brian Tyson directed for the University of Lethbridge Dramatic Society. She also took the title role of Mame in the LMT production. Shortly thereafter, Rose and her husband, Bob, a dedicated backstage assistant, moved to Calgary.

Kaye Robison's presence was felt both on and offstage throughout this period until she and Murray moved to Medicine Hat in 1986. Prior to the move, her activities were spread to Coaldale Little Theatre, Attic Theatre, LMT, and Playgoers. Her marriage to Murray Robison brought her into the fold of CLT, as was explained earlier. She also became Murray's "right hand person" in the Attic Theatre, which operated from 1974 to early 1979. Nevertheless, Kaye maintained her membership in Playgoers throughout this period, and Murray, later, joined the organization. They both contributed backstage to most of the productions of Playgoers during the era of the Attic Theatre.In addition, Kaye took major roles in *Breath of Spring* (1974) and *Come Blow Your Horn* (1975). When the Robisons closed their Attic Theatre, they simply increased their efforts on behalf of Playgoers and LMT. Murray directed Kaye, Hazel Skaronski, and George Mann in the sketch, *Catherine Parr or Alexander's Horse,* which was presented at the public library to commemorate Playgoers' gift to the library of a lighting system for the theatre gallery. Murray also took over the reins of General Director for the year, 1986. Prior to this, Kaye had taken on the supporting role of Grace Kimbrough in *Never Too Late* (1982). Then, after thrilling audiences for many years through her association with various community theatre groups, she gave a magnificent farewell performance as Ethel Thayer in Playgoers' 1986 production of *On Golden Pond.* As the *Lethbridge Herald* critic commented:[87]

> Kaye Robison . . . , sparkles on stage. Her sense of timing keeps the play moving as she bustles and bristles, coaxing old Norman from his self-pitying moods.

This triumph occurred just a few days after Robison had been presented with a lifetime membership in Playgoers for over thirty years of devoted effort.

Playgoers of Lethbridge: Production Personnel

Table 6-12 clearly shows that the production tasks were shared by a relatively small number of very dedicated members, many of whom also appeared fairly regularly onstage. A majority of the supervisors listed in Table 6-12 also assisted in numerous other capacities backstage. This fact will become apparent in the following analysis of the contributions made by the most involved backstage participants.

In the area of set design, Playgoers relied heavily on the artistic talents of Cathy Evins and Ed Bayly during most of this era; however, in the latter part of the 1980s, John A. Johnston and Roger Schultz added their creative talents to the club's productions. All of these designers also aided in the construction and painting of the sets. The role of production manager usually involved organizing the entire production process and supervising the various technical department heads. Frequently, the production manager also acted as stage manager and supervisor of the set construction. Most of the members involved with these responsibilities were acknowledged in earlier discussions; however, it seems appropriate, here, to note the contributions of Bob Rose, Fred McKay, and Herb Matis. Rose, a local businessman and the son of founding Playgoers, Fred and Bessie Rose, became involved in backstage work in order to support the dramatic activities of his wife, Nora. As so often happens, he proved to be an invaluable asset to the club. McKay, manager of the Lethbridge Gulf Service bulk plant, encouraged his wife Marg to audition for Lethbridge Musical Theatre. She, then, became a very active participant, and Fred lent his support to Marg and to his young daughter, Dawn, by volunteering to help with set construction. Before long, his very helpful assistance was called upon by Playgoers, as well. Matis graduated from Kate Andrews High School in Coaldale, and after exploring a number of career possibilities, specialized in carpentry which he quickly mastered and which gained for him a reputation as a very fine finishing carpenter and cabinet maker. Matis began his backstage work when he was called upon by Ray Jolliffe to assist with the sets for the Christmas pantomimes. His interest in working backstage was further piqued by the fact this his young niece, Carla Serkin, developed a strong interest in acting and singing, which was stimulated by participation in the local music festival. In 1982 Serkin was cast as the young girl, Amaryllis, in the LMT production *The Music Man* directed by Fran Rude. Then, in 1985 she captivated local audiences with her portrayal of the blind girl, Helen Keller, in Playgoers' *The Miracle Worker,* also under the direction of Rude. When Rude founded Centre Stage Productions Society, Matis lent his expertise to that group.Regardless of the time and effort which he devoted to Centre Stage's productions, Matis continued to provide leadership, instruction, creativity, and hours of personal craftsmanship to the construction needs of Playgoers and LMT. His contribution to the work of community theatre in Lethbridge was outstanding; in fact, it was beyond measure.

TABLE 6-12

Production Supervisors
Playgoers of Lethbridge (1971-1989)

Set Designer & Decorator	Cathy Evins (9), Ed Bayly (5), J.A. Johnston (4), Roger Schultz (2), Elizabeth Blair
Production Manager	Linda Bayly (7), Linda Johnson (2), Garry Johnson (2), Bob Baunton, Mike Day, Karen Kay, Garry Kohn, Dawn McCaugherty, Fran Rude, Jody Snow, Hazel Skaronski
Stage Manager	Bob Baunton (2), Ern Bayly (2), Linda Bayly (2), Fred McKay (2), Ed Bayly, Mike Day, Frank Huszar, Garry Johnson, Kate Johnstone, John Malcolm, Anne Reid, Bob Rose, Jody Snow, Candy Williams, Jonathan White
Master Carpenter	Ed Bayly (5), Fred McKay (4), Herb Matis (3), Bob Rose (3), Bob Baunton, Garry Johnson, Bill Mains, George Mann, Don Ryane, Ken Sinclair
Costume Designer and/or Costume Mistress	Gail Holland (6), Anne Reid (4), Barb Day (2), Donna Kampen (2), Fran Bayly, Elisa Chalmers, Cathy Evins, Ruth Liska, Ellyn Mells, Sheila Pisko, Mardi Renyk, Kaye Robison, Hazel Skaronski
Sound	Brian Tedder (5), Eric Low (3), Sandi Balcovske, Larry Etling, Muriel Jolliffe, Jody Snow
Lighting Designer and/or Operator	Ed Bayly (9), Brian Tedder (3), Bob Reed (2), Jody Snow (2), Mike Day, Barry Hegland, Frank Huszar, David Mann, Murray Robison, Bruce Sekella, Kathy Sharp, Bert Timmermans
Makeup Artist	Fran Rude (9), Muriel Matheson (4), Mardi Renyk (3), Jean Warburton, (2), Lois Dongworth, Eileen Cashmore, Bryan Francis, Ginny Hoffarth, Marg McKay, Kaye Robison, Betty Sorenson, Linda Thomsen, Candy Williams, (Sue Koshman - hair stylings)
Publicity	Ed Bayly, Lea Blaquiere, Simon Cashmore, Lois Dongworth, Bill Matheson, Brian Sakamoto, Phil Story, Keith Weston
House Manager	Karen Kay (4), Khym Goslin (3), Doris Balcosvske (2), Eileen Cashmore, Peter Durrans, Marion Greenway, Linda Johnson, George Mann, Laurin Mann, Jackie Mark, Shirley A. Walkey, Bryce Walton
Props Coordinator	Cathy Evins (5), Heather Joyce (2), Anne Reid (2), Linda Bayly, Cherie Baunton, Eileen Cashmore, Denise Dobek, Yvonne Fredrick, Linda Johnson, Kate Johnstone, Vicki McKay, Nora Rose, Gerry Tomiyama, Lee Van Andel

The design and construction of costumes gradually shifted to members such as Anne Reid, Gail Holland, Barbara Day, and Donna Kampen. Reid, a library clerk at the Lethbridge Public Library, lent her artistic creativity in numerous backstage activities such as costuming, set decorating, painting, as well as manufacturing and supervising properties. She appeared onstage in only one Playgoers production (*Canadian Gothic*). Since she did not particularly enjoy that experience, she devoted herself to backstage activities for Playgoers and LMT. She also held a number of executive positions for Playgoers including president. Holland, a graduate of the Lethbridge Collegiate Institute and a specialist in the teaching of the gifted, became associated with Playgoers in 1976 when she participated both on and backstage with *The Time of Your Life*. Although she also was involved in some Christmas readers' theatre, her only other appearance onstage for Playgoers was as Vera in *The Odd Couple* (1987). Mostly, Holland loved designing and building costumes, which she did on numerous occasions for both Playgoers and LMT. She also enjoyed researching the background of various productions and playwrights. Barbara Day was another local school teacher who devoted a great deal of time to backstage work. Nevertheless, she also performed a number of supporting roles for Playgoers. Donna Kampen owned and operated a local bookstore for a number of years, and then completed her teacher education at the University of Lethbridge.Her business and professional association with Mardi Renyk introduced her to local theatre organizations where she became involved in makeup duties and costume construction. It soon became apparent that Kampen was highly skillful in the costuming department, so both Playgoers and LMT quickly took advantage of her expertise.

Lighting design was generally handled by Ed Bayly, although other specialists like Jody (Snow) Low and Bob Reed also aided this process. In the 1980s Bayly began to nurture an interest in this area expressed by Brian Tedder. Tedder, a media specialist with the local public school system, was naturally attracted to the area of sound as well. With additional experience in the theatre, he became involved in stage management. He performed all three roles for both Playgoers and LMT. He even ventured onto the stage for the occasional supporting role, the most notable of which was the court clerk in *Hello Dolly* (LMT [1986]).

In concluding this discussion about production assistance, mention should be made of the help provided by Eileen Cashmore, Karen Kay, Sue Koshman, and Khym Goslin. Cashmore, wife of a local orthopedic surgeon, was one of those "unsung workers" who volunteers to help out wherever assistance is needed. Consequently, she spent many hours working on costumes, props, and makeup for Playgoers, LMT, and Centre Stage. Her efforts were formally recognized by LMT in 1989 when she was awarded a backstage Lemmy. Karen Kay was also noted for her willing assistance both on and backstage for Playgoers, LMT, Christmas pantomime, and Centre Stage Productions. Because of her natural leadership qualities and because of her training in dance, Kay was frequently given the responsibility of dance captain in musical shows. Her organizing abilities were also called upon frequently to plan and supervise the front of house personnel.Her advice and assistance was invaluable when planning social occasions such as receptions. Koshman, owner and operator of two of the city's foremost beauty salons, was frequently called upon by the various local theatrical companies to provide expert advice and assistance related to hair stylings. Her expertise was verified by the more than thirty trophies which she garnered for excellence in her field.[88] Koshman also tread the boards in some local musical theatre productions. Khym Goslin was a graduate in Physical Education from the University of Lethbridge where he also spent a term as student union president. He later worked for the YMCA and engaged in a small sportswear business, but his desire to stimulate a greater general interest in physical recreation, led him into the teaching profession. As a member of Playgoers, Goslin proved to be an excellent host and therefore became conscripted as house manager. He also did excellent work in designing and organizing posters and programs, he was a tireless worker backstage, and he proved to have considerable acting talent in his one major role, Captain Fisby, in *Teahouse of the August Moon* (1988).

Other Locally Produced Theatre

Although the Playgoers Club was the most stable and consistent legitimate theatre organization in the city, it was by no means the only one. A number of other groups came into being for various periods of time – mostly rather short periods. Many of these other groups could not be called true amateur or community theatre organizations. Some of them, in fact, had professional aspirations and were composed of a selected company. Others came into being simply to participate in specific events such as festivals or historical pageants. Then, there was the Attic Theatre which performed for invited audiences, only. In addition, there was a certain amount of church sponsored theatre. Other local theatrical events included the annual skating carnivals sponsored by the Lethbridge Figure Skating Club and some synchronized swimming activities. During this era, local skating professionals such as Sonja Davis concentrated on the exhibition of local skaters.[89] Nevertheless, a number of champion Canadian skaters were also incorporated into the annual revues. In the latter half of the 1970s, the Lethbridge Synchronized Swim Club, organized and instructed by Linda Stephens, Jackie Hall, Val Patterson, Penny O'Brien, Ursula Kasting, and Melanie Ellis added another dimension to the genre of athletic theatre.

Church sponsored theatrical groups from the LDS congregations were quite active in the first half of the 1970s. Georgia (Green) Fooks gave direction to the musical comedy, *Blue Ribbon Affair* (1970), the operetta, *Pirates of Penzance* (1973), and the LDS musical drama, *The Promised Valley* (1974); whereas, Betty Sorenson directed *HMS Pinafore* (1975). In the latter half of the 1980s, Rita Peterson took on the task of directing two shows:the Agatha Christie mystery, *The Mousetrap*, and a production based on the Book of Mormon, *Saturday's Warrior*. Peterson also participated in a number of musical theatre productions for LMT and Centre Stage Productions.

In the interim, that is, in the early 1980s, it was the New Hope Christian Centre which became the major producer of church sponsored theatre. Like the presentations of Agnes Davidson's Southminster Players many years earlier, the productions of the New Hope Christian Centre were sectarian in nature and were seen as contributing to the spiritual development of the actors and patrons, alike.

Local students organized federally sponsored Opportunities for Youth theatre groups for the summers of 1971 through 1973. The first of these groups dedicated themselves, primarily, to offering 2-4 week classes in various aspects of the theatre to interested youths, aged 12-21. The coordinator of this group, a University of Lethbridge student, Genevieve Pratt, gathered together a staff of five other students: Gordon Filbert (to teach acting [U of A student]); Cindy Zak (design [U of A]); Wendy (Robison) Nishimura (movement [UofL]); BillPratt (stage craft [U of L]), and Betty Selkirk (secretary).[90] Nishimura, by the way, was Murray and Yvonne Robison's daughter; her experience in the theatre, combined with her years of ballet instruction under Muriel Jolliffe, made her an ideal candidate for the movement position.One unfortunate problem, which created some concern for this group and for the future of such projects, was the fact that they attracted only about one-half of the enrolments which they had anticipated.[91] Nevertheless, the federal government did fund another group of students (calling themselves the Sunshine Players) during the following two summers.[92]

The Sunshine Players took a somewhat different approach to their mandate. Not only did they organize a summer workshop program (in creative drama), they also performed in Lethbridge and toured some of their productions to neighboring communities. During the first summer, this group emphasized children's theatre, but during the second summer, they decided to produce more sophisticated drama. Membership in the Sunshine Players changed considerably from 1972 to 1973;

however, the two U of L students who spearheaded the proposal, Sandi Balcovske and Bob Bainborough, returned for the second year. Other members of the 1972 troupe included Lois Dongworth, Kirk Jensen, Patricia Parks, and Doug Smith, the latter of whom had created quite a sensation with his portrayal of Fagin in the LCI production of *Oliver*. The 1973 troupe included David Diamond, Scott Dobbie, Jain Kurany, David Mann, James Rae, and Jane Wilson. Later, the Lethbridge trio of Balcovske, Bainborough, and Mann became core members of the Edmonton Catalyst Theatre and the Edmonton Second City. As a member of the 25th Street Theatre in Saskatoon, Bainborough was involved in the creation of the original production of *Paper Wheat;* he was also in the cast. Later, he and Balcovske spent a number of years with the Toronto Second City Company. Mann preferred to do more scripted work and therefore became associated with various companies such as Theatre Network, Workshop West, Phoenix Theatre (Edmonton); Alberta Theatre Projects (Calgary); and Kam Theatre (Thunder Bay).

Two societies which planned to become resident professional companies were Stage Three and Southern Stage. Stage Three was organized in 1978 with Peter Mueller, a recent U of A MFA graduate, as artistic director.The original company was comprised mostly of University of Lethbridge students and former graduates of Catholic Central High School. Stage Three made its debut at the 1978 Lethbridge and District One Act festival. Its entry, *Zoo Story,* which was directed by Pat Slemko and featured Jason Slemko and Les Smolnicky, was selected as runner up; nevertheless, it was invited to participate in the Alberta One Act Festival. Following this, the troupe operated out of the Catholic Central Drama Centre during the summers 1978 through 1980, after which the company disbanded. Mueller also took on the responsibility of directing the historical pageant, *Who We Were*, which was commissioned to help celebrate Alberta's 75th anniversary as a province.The pageant was designed to be presented in an outdoor setting at Indian Battle Park. Unfortunately, the weather did not cooperate very well that summer. In addition, the script was somewhat panned by the local critic, Arthur McDougall. Mueller, then, decided to concentrate his efforts on teaching and on operating a local business venture. The Historama Society planned to present the pageant, again, in the summer of 1981; however, these plans were eventually cancelled because of insufficient funds.[93] It should be mentioned, that one of Mueller's protegees, Larry Erdos, wrote, directed, and "starred" in *How to Beat a Computer While Stoned on Acid* at the U of L Experimental Theatre (April 1982), under the auspices of what Erdos called the Psyche Theatre. (Erdos was still a very active drama student at the U of L.) His mentor, Peter Mueller, reviewed the play for the *Lethbridge Herald* and displayed admirable objectivity when he reported that this "innovative play becomes tedious."[94]

Southern Stage, founded in 1982 by artistic director, Richard Epp, took a somewhat more aggressive approach to its professional mandate. The company's initial advisory committee was composed of local theatre personalities, Richard Epp, Ed Bayly, and Joan Waterfield as well as some local business professionals, Danny Huszar, Isabelle Hamilton, Cam and Sharon Peat. For the initial offering, Epp invited professional director, Sharon Bakker, of Calgary, to direct Epp's play, *Christmas Pudding*, which was inspired by Dickins's *The Christmas Carol*. *Christmas Pudding* was set in a prairie community and centred around the Scrooge-like chairman of the school board who was portrayed by Laurin Mann. All other adult members of the cast, Karen Bernstein, Larry Erdos, Richard Epp, and Brian Tyson, as well as the production personnel, were local amateurs and university students or staff. The production was very amusing and an ideal Christmas presentation; however, the anticipation of filling the 500 seat Yates Centre theatre for ten performances was somewhat too optimistic. Undaunted, the society produced *Mass Appeal* by Bill C. Davis and directed by Richard Epp (September 20-25, 1983). Professional actors, Warren Graves and Francis

Damberger, were engaged to play the two priests. The company again depended upon a voluntary but highly competent production team including specialists from the university such as David Hignell and J. Johnston. Although the production was presented under the auspices of the Allied Arts Council, and although the *Lethbridge Herald* review by Joan Waterfield was quite enthusiastic, audiences, again, were not sufficient to sustain the company, so it closed its books after this second offering.

Undoubtedly, the most unique theatrical experiment in Lethbridge during this era was the Attic Theatre which, in fact, operated out of the third story attic of the large home which Murray and Kaye Robison purchased in Lethbridge after moving from Coaldale in 1974. Robison converted the attic space into an intimate theatre which could accommodate about thirty patrons. With the partial assistance of the $500 donation presented to him by Coaldale Little Theatre, Robison furnished his new theatre with a lighting and sound system as well as with curtains. Robison then proceeded to offer youth and adult classes in various aspects of the theatre and to produce one and three act plays, for which the production duties were shared between Kaye and Murray. Generally, Murray directed the production, constructed and painted the set, and designed the lights and sound effects. Kaye took on the responsibilities of business manager, costumer, and set dresser. She also portrayed a number of roles in the various major productions. During the five years in which the Robisons owned the Attic property, they produced seven plays – three major plays, two one act festival productions, one Attic Youth Theatre production (*Rise and Shine*), and a one act festival production under the auspices of Coaldale Little Theatre (*The Case of the Crushed Petunias*). The latter presentation featured Linda Bayly, Bill Matheson, Phil Story, and Fran Rude. Rude, who also functioned as assistant director for *The Rainmaker*, credited Robison with seriously stimulating her interest in directing – another example of Robison's influence in the local theatre scene.

George Mann's approach to acting and directing were also greatly influenced by his experience with Attic Theatre. Mann had the good fortune to be cast in all three of the major productions presented at the Attic; he portrayed the father, H. C. Curry, in *The Rainmaker,* Joseph in *My Three Angels*, and Papa in *Papa is All.* In the latter production, he was cast opposite his wife, Nellie, who played Mama and his daughter, Laurin, who played their daughter, Emma. Laurin also played George Mann's daughter, Lizzie, in *The Rainmaker,* where she acted opposite Albert Azzara (the rainmaker).

Robison also cast these two young people in the one act festival production, *Where Have All the Lightning Bugs Gone.* Unquestionably, these three roles which Laurin Mann portrayed at the Attic Theatre were extremely challenging, and the response which she received from the patrons who had the pleasure of witnessing these performances, together with the inner pleasure which she derived from creating these roles, greatly encouraged her to seek a professional career in the theatre. Azzara, who was equally inspired by Murray Robison and the Attic Theatre to maintain his deep interest in the theatre, also portrayed a third role for Attic Theatre – one of the trio of thieves in *My Three Angels*. Others who played multiple roles in Attic Theatre productions were Kaye Robison, Phil Story, Bob Baunton, and Neil Boyden. Besides Kaye Robison and Phil Story, two other former participants in Coaldale Little Theatre performed in Attic Theatre productions: Peggy Mallalieu's role in *My Three Angels* was her theatrical swan song and it culminated almost 25 years of local theatre activity, primarily, under the direction of Murray Robison; David Mann had the pleasure of performing in *Mooney's Kid Don't Cry.* Two years previously, Mann had acted under the direction of Robison in CLT's production of *Butterflies are Free.*

Like Coaldale Little Theatre, the Attic Theatre became a fairly consistent participant in festival competition, which, at the time of Attic's existence, was confined to the one act festival. The following discussion will review the fortunes of the Attic Theatre and other participating societies in the Lethbridge and District One Act festivals during this era.

The One Act Festival

The drama festival movement was partially reactivated when the Allied Arts Council responded to the suggestion by its Executive Director, Joan Waterfield, that it sponsor a festival of community theatre at the Yates Memorial Centre on May 25 and 27, 1971. Most of the participants were school and youth groups; Murray Robison was responsible for directing three of the productions, whereas the Lethbridge Youth Theatre and the Shoestring Players under the direction of Chris Puhl and Joan Waterfield, respectively, contributed two productions. Three members of the Youth Theatre, Sheri McFadden, Laurin Mann, and Rachel Luca, also presented a short play, *The Spoken Word*. Two additional plays were staged by Wilson Jr. High School under the direction of David Lynagh, and Kate Andrews High School supervised by Frank Featherstone. A mime presented by the Jolliffe Academy of Dancing concluded the festival.

The Allied Arts Council, under president Keith L. Lowings, envisioned the festival becoming an annual event alongside the Alberta Dance Festival and the Kiwanis Music Festival.[95] However, it was not until February 1973 that a regular one act festival was instituted in the province under the auspices of the Alberta Drama Festival Association whose local representative was Joan Waterfield. Preliminary festivals, sponsored by local groups such as the Lethbridge Allied Arts Council, were also organized. Local festival winners were then invited to participate in the provincial festival.The Bowman Players (a division of the Lethbridge Youth Theatre), under the direction of Jim Veenstra, took the 1973 local honors with *Babel Rap*. The production, which featured Albert Azzara and David Moline, was described by adjudicator, Brian Tyson, as " . . . a fascinating play . . . I was delighted with what I saw."[96] The following year, the Lethbridge Youth Theatre repeated its winning ways by capturing the local honors, again. On this occasion, Joan Waterfield directed Dawn McCaugherty and Debbie and Laurie Anderson in *Eliza and the Lexicon*. By 1975 the local festival began to attract many more entrants.Attic Theatre's entry, *Mooney's Kid Don't Cry* (featuring David Mann and Patricia Matheson – the daughter of Muriel and Bill Matheson), was chosen as the best production; it was joined by the U of L production, *The Swan Song*, at the provincial festival. Both plays were very well received by the provincial festival adjudicator, John Murrell.[97] By the mid-1970s, the festival was well established, and it continued to be an important component of the amateur theatre movement in Alberta throughout the remainder of this era. Unfortunately, the Lethbridge zone festival was cancelled on five occasions in the 1980s because of a shortage of entries.

The Playgoers presented a noncompetitive entry, *Pyramus and Thisbe,* in the 1973 festival; then the club returned to festival competition in 1974. Henceforth, Playgoers was the most consistent participant in the local festivals. In 1976, 1977, and 1986, productions by the Playgoers Club were the only entries. In other years, Playgoers was joined by numerous other societies from the city and district. Occasionally, troupes such as Kintown Players and the Quarter Theatre Troupe were organized with the sole purpose of participating in the festival. The Kintown Players was founded by Doug Hinds in order to showcase his play, *Thursday's Child Has Far To Go*. Hinds co-directed the play and also portrayed the leading role of Joe, a "55 year old unemployed incipient alcoholic. . . ."[98] Adjudicator, Dick Mells, described the production as "outstanding" and sent it to the provincial one act festival. In October 1980, Hinds, who was then living in Calgary, toured a Calgary group to Lethbridge to present two of his plays, *Death Certificate* and *Thursday's Child. . . .*[99] The Quarter Theatre Troupe was created by Eric Low in 1975. Some years later, he and Rebecca Dwyer, in their two person production, *The Golden Fleece* by A.R. Gurney, Jr., took the honors at the 1983 Lethbridge Regional one act festival.[100]

The provincial festival gradually introduced some competition. In the late 1970s, some monetary drama achievement awards were issued at the discretion of the adjudicator. In 1978 Fran Rude was recognized for her sensitive direction of Playgoers' production, *Canadian Gothic*.[101] By the mid-1980s, awards were presented for best play, best actor, and best actress.[102]

Locally Produced Musical Theatre

Although the activity of drama societies fluctuated considerably during this era, there was one form of theatre which did not waver – musical theatre. In the early 1970s, Gilbert Paterson Community School produced a few student operettas; then, in 1977 it presented a combined student and adult (community) musical, *The Music Man*, which featured Jack Hunter and Lea Blaquiere (Switzer). The most sustained interest in musical theatre was, however, shown by the Lethbridge Musical Theatre. Then, in 1985 Centre Stage Productions Society was founded and emphasized musicals in its production season. Musical theatre was also a very popular genre in some of the neighboring communities. As illustrated earlier, Neil Boyden introduced school and community musicals at R.I. Baker School in Coaldale. Gradually, the communities of Cardston and Raymond joined the musical theatre bandwagon. When the music specialist, Dr. Ralph Kennard, settled in Cardston, he encouraged the Cardston Community Theatre to produce various kinds of musical theatre – musical comedy, operetta, and even opera [*Hansel and Gretel* (May 2-7, 1981)]. In the spring of 1980, Cardston toured *The Sound of Music* (under the direction of Terry Petrie) to the Yates Memorial Centre in Lethbridge where it was very well received.[103] Although this practice of touring was not continued, the Cardston annual musical productions attracted many Lethbridge patrons to the southern community throughout the 1980s. In the late 1980s, the Raymond Opera Society offered musicals such as *Fiddler on the Roof, Oliver, Paint Your Wagon,* and *My Fair Lady.*

Lethbridge Musical Theatre (LMT)

LMT, under the very capable guidance of executive members such as Vaughn Hembroff, Bob Fenton, Ross Whitmore, Ernie Lawson, Lenore Beyer, and Ken Mills maintained its love affair with Lethbridge audiences throughout the 1970s and 80s [with the possible exception of the presentation *Once Upon a Mattress* (1980) which lost $5 584].[104] Dick Mells continued to direct the musicals through 1978; Muriel Jolliffe provided choreography for most of the shows from 1971 through the spring of 1984. Musical direction (by the orchestra leader and the vocal coach) came under the supervision of a number of people – not unlike the situation during the earlier era.

Once Dick Mells decided to leave Lethbridge in 1979, the LMT executive drafted a resolution that directors should be contracted for two successive productions, only; therefore, Wes Stefan was selected to direct the 1979 and 1980 productions. Stefan was born and raised in Lethbridge, he attended the Lethbridge Junior College, and then transferred to the University of Alberta where he graduated with a B.Ed. degree. His oratorical skills were evidenced early when, as a high school student, he won a trip to the United Nations in New York as a result of his entry in the United Nations Youth Speaking contest sponsored by the Order of the Odd Fellows.[105] While living in Edmonton, Stefan became involved as an actor and as a director with University of Alberta dramatic productions. In addition, he participated in shows produced by the Citadel and the Walterdale Theatres. His professional experience also included acting in numerous radio and television broadcasts for CBC.[106] In 1971 Stefan returned to Lethbridge and took up a teaching position with the Lethbridge public school board; he also joined the cast of Playgoers' *Fings Ain't Wot They Used T'Be.* In 1976 Stefan agreed to direct *The Time of Your Life* for Playgoers, and in 1980 he was cast as the troubadour in Playgoers' *The Fantasticks.* During the rehearsal period of this show, he was called upon to assist director, Keith Harris. Although Stefan participated in at least one other production for Playgoers [*The Exhibition* - a one act festival production (1989)], he devoted most of his artistic talents to Lethbridge Musical Theatre.

Following Stefan's two year contract to direct for LMT, Fran Rude was appointed director. She was faced with the task of selecting a show which would help LMT recover from its deficit. She chose *The King and I;* it was a smash hit as was its successor, *The Music Man.* Following upon these successes, the executive decided to extend Rude's contract for a third regular fall production, *Kiss Me Kate,* and for the special spring commemorative presentation, *Down Memory Lane.* The subsequent two shows, *Brigadoon* and *Cabaret,* were directed by the visiting professional director, Jack McCreath, who had recently retired from his position with the Alberta Department of Culture. Because McCreath was establishing himself in Victoria, B.C., at this time, and because he had to fulfill some other professional commitments, he required a competent assistant director to conduct rehearsals during his absences. This task fell upon the shoulders of Wes Stefan. In 1986 *Hello Dolly* was directed by Joan Waterfield. It was during the rehearsals of this musical that Waterfield had the terrible accident when she backed into the orchestra pit. Although she quickly returned to complete the directing assignment (with the assistance of Ed Bayly and the choreographers, Theresa Dee and Joy Ackerman), Waterfield thought it best not to take up her contract for the following year. Ed Bayly agreed to direct *The Sound of Music,* followed by a revival of *South Pacific.* Mark Russell was contracted to direct the shows for 1989 and 1990, *Oklahoma!* and *Anything Goes,* respectively. Waterfield portrayed Mrs. Harcourt in the latter show.

Exceptions to Jolliffe's participation as choreographer were the two shows directed by Wes Stefan: *The Pajama Game* (1979) and *Once Upon a Mattress* (1980). After LMT's 20th anniversary year presentation, *Down Memory Lane* (spring 1984), Jolliffe began to devote herself more to examining and adjudicating. She was invited to become an examiner for the Royal Academy of Dance (RAD), for which she was a Life Member. In order to meet the demands of examining throughout Canada and Europe, she was forced to withdraw considerably from many of her local activities. In recognition of her outstanding contribution to LMT, Jolliffe was named a Life Member. Fortunately, the city, then, had a number of new young dance teachers willing to attempt choreography for LMT.

When Wes Stefan was contracted to direct *The Pajama Game,* he asked Kim Ully to take over the choreography. Because Stefan had cooperated with the Ullys in some of their dance, modelling, and performing activities, he was aware of Kim's creative potential. So well did Ully live up to Stefan's anticipations, that he requested her to choreograph the succeeding show, *Once Upon a Mattress.* The director of Joy's Dance Factory, Joy Ackerman, was called upon to choreograph the following four productions. Because of family and career pressures, Ackerman sought some assistance for *Hello Dolly* and *The Sound of Music.* Theresa Dee, an acquaintance of Ackerman's from Medicine Hat, took on the major responsibility for the former production, whereas a former Jolliffe student, and an instructor at Studio One, Wendy Spoulos, assisted with the choreography for the latter one. Then Spoulos and Patricia Livingstone cooperated to choreograph *South Pacific.*

Orchestra leaders tended to be selected from local junior and senior high band directors; this task rotated quite regularly in the early 1970s, but then, the selection focused on Bob Brunelle who conducted ten of the nineteen shows produced by LMT between 1971- 1988. Tanya Arnold conducted the orchestra for the last two shows of this era. The musicians associated with these shows are listed in Table 6-13; the numbers in parentheses refer to the number of shows in which the musician participated.

TABLE 6-13

Pit Musicians: Lethbridge Musical Theatre Productions
Lethbridge, Alberta (1971-1988)

TYPE OF INSTRUMENT	MUSICIANS
Baton (Conductor)	Bob Brunelle (10), Jerry Pokarney (3), Tanya Arnold (2), Stewart Grant, Willie Mathis, Ellyn Mells, Larry Yelland
Violin/Viola	Norbert Boehm (3), Alex Palmarchuk (3), Susan Schaefer (3), Irene Tamajka (3), Edith Francis (2)Phil Minty (2), Michael Pauls (2), Jack Blech, Megan Falk, Barbara Haney, Jeanne Newman, Jodie Ross
Cello	Blair Amundsen, David Conroy, Perry Foster
Bass Violin	Fred Leister (6), Randy Paskuski (4), Keith Landry (2), Rick Blair, Rudy Habijanac, Bill Ivison
Flute	Paddy O'Connell (6), Christy Pokarney (6), Sara Francis (2), Rosalind Harvey (2), Wanda Eddy, Susan Foster, Melanie-Jane Hughes, Sara Laying, Betty Leister, Heather Packard, Cheryl Porkka, Pat Robb, Susan Staples
Oboe	Colleen Heynen (2), Judy Cummins, Walter Falk, Chuck Hendrickson
Bassoon	Tanya Arnold (5), Lorraine Daw, Dee Dee Fulwiler, Susan Harker, Gordon Hunt, Loren Mitchell
Other Woodwinds	Joan Robin (10), Max Wilson (4), Jamie Day (3), Brian Pritchard (3), Doug Scales (3), Rebecca Blair (2), Ernie Block (2), Margaret "Peggy" (Foster) Mezei (2), Brian Thorlacius (2), Shireen Calman, Marlene Carter, Nancy Dewit, Bib Findlay, Don Globa, Nick Kucheran, Donna Peard, Marcie Pitman, Bruce Redstone, Sheila Rogers, Lori Leister Schacher, Joyce Schmidt, Greg Skafte, David Smith, Scott Sommerfeldt, Nancy Walker, Hal Weaver, Karen Wilms, Debbie Wudrick
Trumpet & French Horn	Grant Erickson (14), Jerry Pokarney (11), Jeff Anderson (3), Mark Ward (3), Tom Doyle (2), Glen Hewitt (2), Derek Graham, Brad Hembroff, Tracey Lowe, Gil MacKay, Vondis Miller, Don Peard, Don Robb, Lyle Skretting, Ed Staples
Trombone	Gerald Rogers (11), Boyd Hunter (6), Bob Brunelle (3), Terry Nishida (3), Sandra Brunelle (2), Grant Erickson (2), Dave Robin (2), Ken Rogers (2), John Dewitt, Ron Garnett, Tom Little, Deanne May, Michael McClary
French Horn	Kirk Ramsay (2), Christopher Rose (2), Tom Staples (2), William Blair, Jack Calder, Tania Ellis, Blaine McClary, Susan Racz, Karen Stelter
Other Brass	Drew Bryant, Grant Freeman, Bob Greig, Cathy McDowell, Don Peard, Peter Sametz
Guitar/Banjo/Mandolin	Dale Ketcheson (5), Ron Beyers, Rick Blair, Scott Kanashiro, Alex Palmarchuk
Electric Bass	Richard Erickson (3), Greg Paskuski (3), Ernie Block
Accordian	Violet Nagy, Annabelle Pruegger
Piper	Alistair Gilchrist
Harp	Marie Woodrow
Electric Keyboard	Sandra Brunelle (3), Rob Morrison (3), Richard Burke (2), Steven Erickson
Percussion	Neil Sheets (7), Bruce Robin (5), Kurt Ellison (2), Remo Baceda, Donald Bell, Ernie Block, Cathy Chirka, Brad Clarke, Dave Keister, Mark Mazur, Paul Walker
Piano	Bonnie Jean (Brown) Pokarney (8), Elinor Lawson (4), Susan (Young) Garrie (4), Ellen Mells (3), Shelagh Stefan (2), Marilyn Sinclair, Larry Yelland

Vocal direction for *Fiddler on the Roof* (1971) was provided by Willie Mathis, music instructor at Winston Churchill High School. Ellyn Mells was vocal director for all of the successive musicals directed by her husband, Dick. Ellyn Mells also conducted the orchestra for *Oliver*. Stefan engaged his wife, Shelagh, a local teacher, as vocal director for *Pajama Game*, whereas Arla Burbank, another local teacher, took over the vocal instruction for *Once Upon a Mattress* and all of the shows directed by Fran Rude except *Down Memory Lane*, for which the overall musical direction was turned over to a newcomer to the city, Larry Yelland. It was during the rehearsals of this latter show that a former Lethbridge resident and music graduate of the University of Lethbridge, Mark Ward, was encouraged to commute from Medicine Hat to perform some of the selections which Yelland had planned to sing but relinquished because the logistics of being musical director and performer were insurmountable. Ward, who was generally recognized as a very competent trumpet player, proved himself to be an excellent singer, as well; consequently, he was asked to take over the vocal direction for *Brigadoon*. Throughout many of these productions, rehearsal pianist, Bonnie Jean Brown, also assisted with vocal direction. Brown, incidently, was the daughter of George Jr., and Lorna Brown and had, therefore, been surrounded by music throughout her life. Now, as accompanist and vocal coach, she was about to follow in the revered footsteps of her grandmother, Katherine Brown. Bonnie became another third generation artist to contribute her talent to the Lethbridge musical and theatrical scene. She took over the reins as vocal director for *Camelot* and the three successive productions.

Having reviewed the personnel who directed the various performance activities associated with musical theatre, let us now turn to a more specific analysis of those performers. About 400 different individuals appeared in the LMT productions between 1971 and 1988, inclusive, and of these, about three quarters appeared in one show, only. About one half of the remaining participants performed in two of the nineteen shows. Therefore, about fifty performers appeared in three or more of these productions. The varying levels of involvement by the participants who performed in at least four productions during this era are illustrated in Table 6-14.

Jack Warburton and Maura K. Wedge in LMT's 1972 production of Man of La Mancha
Photo: Jean Warburton, *Lethbridge Herald*

Before discussing the onstage activities engaged in by the performers listed in Table 6-14, it should be mentioned that very few professional performers were contracted by LMT to participate in these productions. In fact, only two external professionals were hired during this era, Maura K. Wedge and Christopher Lyle, who played Aldonza in *Man of La Mancha* and Emile De Becque in *South Pacific*, respectively. Wedge, who lived in Greenwich Village, New York, was a Broadway

TABLE 6-14

Onstage Participants: Lethbridge Musical Theatre
Lethbridge, Alberta (1971 - 1988)

PARTICIPANT	S	C	T*	PARTICIPANT	S	C	T
Marg McKay	1	12	13	Sherie Rae	1	4	5
Al Greenway	6	5	11	Fran Rude	2	3	5
Jean Warburton	7	4	11	Wendy Spoulos	1	4	5
Jack Warburton	10	0	10	Linda Bayly	1	3	4
Karen Kay	0	10	10	Lyndon Bray	4	0	4
Ray Mercer	6	3	9	Mike Day	0	4	4
Wes Stefan	9	0	9	Karen Dobek	1	3	4
Dawn Flexhaug	2	5	7	Lois Dongworth	4	0	4
George Mann	6	1	7	George Gallant	4	0	4
Roger Schultz	6	1	7	Frank Huszar	1	3	4
Candy Williams	3	4	7	Narda McCarroll	1	3	4
Mark Campbell	5	1	6	Neana Meeks	3	1	4
Sandra McFarlane	5	1	6	Laurie Meyers	0	4	4
Albert Azzara	3	2	5	Ken Sinclair	3	1	4
Jeff Carlson	1	4	5	Lea Switzer	3	1	4
Cathy Hawn	0	5	5	Jack Tyreman	2	2	4
Phil Kristiansen	2	3	5	Joan Waterfield	3	1	4

S = major or supporting speaking role; C = chorus; T = Total

star who played Aldonza in both the Broadway and national touring companies. She repeated this Broadway and touring feat as Nancy in *Oliver*. Wedge also performed in numerous other Broadway and New York productions as well as on major T.V. shows such as *The Merv Griffin Show* and *The Ed Sullivan Show*.[107] A few years after her appearance in Lethbridge, her associates were saddened to hear of her death as a result of cancer. Lyle, a young operatic baritone from Calgary, had performed in New York at the After Dinner Opera Company, an Off-Broadway facility. In addition, he appeared in various operas at Banff, Des Moines (Iowa), and Calgary as well as in musicals in Calgary and Kalamazoo. Lyle also completed a successful concert tour in Europe.[108]

Local professionals and other participants who had had considerable professional experience, included: Nora Rose, Lea (Blaquiere) Switzer, Sheri (McFadden) Thomson, Wes Stefan, and

Kathleen (Stringam) Thompson, the latter of whom was discussed thoroughly in Chapter Five. A soloist with a number of major choirs in Winnipeg and Calgary, Rose also appeared as Mercedes in the Southern Alberta Opera Association's presentation of *Carmen*. She was a winner of the Metropolitan Opera District Auditions held in Winnipeg in 1964. Later, while residing in Lethbridge, Rose was recognized as Best Supporting Actress in the Alberta Regional Drama Festival for her portrayal of Frosine in *The Miser*. She also performed in the summer musical, *The Boyfriend,* and took the title role of Mame in LMT's production.[109] Lea (Blaquiere) Switzer (nee Pohjokas) portrayed Sylvia Potter-Porter in *Annie Get Your Gun* as well as the lead roles, Anna Leonowens *(The King and I)* and Lilli Vanessi/Katherine *(Kiss Me Kate)*, for LMT. She was also involved in a few other Lethbridge productions. Prior to moving to Lethbridge, she had spent five years in Iran where she was a member of the Tehran International Theatre and performed in their productions: *The Miser, Butterflies Are Free, A Midsummer Night's Dream,* and *Guys and Dolls.*[110] After studying at the National Theatre School in Montreal, Sheri Thomson developed an extensive professional career in Calgary where she appeared in numerous productions at the Pleides Theatre and the Glenmore Dinner Theatre. She also performed in some musicals under the direction of Harold Baldridge. In addition, Thomson gained television and film credits before returning to Lethbridge to participate, once again, in LMT where she had made her debut in *My Fair Lady* when she was still in high school. After resettling in Lethbridge, Thomson took the role of Pegeen in *Mame* and later, the lead roles, Babe in *Pajama Game* and Sally Bowles in *Cabaret.*[111] In addition, she portrayed the mother, M'Lynn in Playgoers *Steel Magnolias*. Stefan's theatrical career prior to his returning to Lethbridge has been referred to elsewhere in this volume; therefore, the following discussion will review only his performance activities with LMT. Stefan's debut with LMT was a memorable one; he portrayed the young adventurer, Nikos, in *Zorba* and it was immediately apparent that LMT had attracted a great talent; later performances quickly verified that early assessment. All of the roles which Stefan performed for LMT were leading or major roles and he proved himself capable of portraying characters of all social levels from the nobility (King Arthur in *Camelot*) to shady, "low-life" individuals such as Bill Sykes in *Oliver*. A review of his other portrayals, all of which were well developed and superbly performed, will quickly illustrate his versatility: Frank Butler [sharp shooter *(Annie Get Your Gun)*]; King Sextimus the Silent [villain *(Once Upon a Mattress)*]; The King [*(The King and I)*]; Petruchio/Fred Graham *(Kiss Me Kate)*; Herr Schultz [elderly Jewish gentleman *(Cabaret)*]; Captain Georg von Trapp [the children's father *(The Sound of Music)*].

In this introduction to LMT performers, it should also be noted that some major participants whose contribution somewhat stretched over the time periods covered in chapters 5 and 6, are not listed in either Table 5-17 or 6-14 because their participation in each era did not meet the criteria for inclusion. Had the two periods been combined, Frank Featherstone and Chet Wayne would have (and should have) been included. Featherstone joined LMT for *My Fair Lady,* in which he played Alfie Doolittle. The following year, he scored another hit with his portrayal of Lazar Woolfe in *Fiddler on the Roof.* His most memorable role with LMT was, undoubtedly, Fagin in *Oliver*. He then completed his association with LMT by portraying King Pellinore in *Camelot. My Fair Lady* also introduced Chet Wayne to Lethbridge audiences; he took on the role of Colonel Pickering. The program for this show relates the following most interesting background:

> [Wayne] was associate-director of NBC's "Today" show (when it was hosted by Dave Garroway), after which he devoted his time to educational radio, a period which procured him a Peabody award and four National Grants from the Ford Foundation for his radio series. . . . In 1960, he was an assistant-director on location for the filming of "Exodus."

Wayne came to Lethbridge to teach communication arts at the Lethbridge Community College, and during the period under discussion, he took on the following supporting roles for LMT: Baptista in *Kiss Me Kate,* Henry in *South Pacific*, and Herr Zeller in *Sound of Music*.

Karen Kay and Marg McKay were the most staunch members of the LMT chorus. Kay, of course, also made her presence felt in the various dance numbers, most notably as Uncle Thomas in the "Uncle Tom's Cabin" ballet for *The King and I*. Although McKay appeared in more LMT productions than any other person, she stepped out of the chorus only once in order to portray the gentlewoman, Hattie, in *Kiss Me Kate*. Both Kay and McKay also contributed much time and effort to the deliberations of the LMT executive, and both participated in Playgoers and Centre Stage productions. McKay's daughter, Dawn Flexhaug, another major participant in the chorus, also contributed immeasurably to the executive functions of LMT. The dance chorus benefitted particularly from the efforts of Candy Chiselle Williams and Wendy Spoulos.

The following analysis will discuss the various theatrical activities of participants listed in Table 6-14 who portrayed five or more leading roles.

Jack Warburton continued to captivate Lethbridge audiences with his exceptional talents until a brain tumor abruptly ended his participation in the mid-1980s. Prior to that, Jack had absolutely thrilled local audiences with his portrayal of Tevye in *Fiddler on the Roof*. His performance helped to solidify the contention that Lethbridge performers were equal to, and in many cases superior to, professional imports. (This attitude was freely expressed after 1970 when Bill Matheson and Sheila Pisko had so marvelously carried the lead roles in *My Fair Lady*). Warburton, who later portrayed the title role in *Zorba,* was also the ideal "sidekick," for example, Sancho Panza (*Man of La Mancha*) and Marcellus Washburn (*The Music Man*). Two years after this latter production, Warburton made his last appearance with LMT when he performed in the medley of selections from twenty years of LMT shows, *Down Memory Lane*. At each performance of this show, the audience broke into spontaneous applause when Jack stepped forth to sing "If I Were a Rich Man" from *Fiddler on the Roof*. About four years later, the executive of LMT awarded Jack an honorary lifetime membership in the organization.[112]

During the early years of Jack's disability, Jean Warburton withdrew from active participation in local theatre; however, she maintained close informal ties with LMT, Centre Stage, and Playgoers, whose members provided her with considerable social support. When she was able to arrange for more assistance in caring for Jack's needs, she plunged back into musical theatre by taking on three major roles in 1988 and 1989: Bloody Mary in *South Pacific*, Aunt Eller in *Oklahoma,* and a major singing role in Centre Stage's concert version of *Follies*. Petite, extremely attractive, and possessed of a glorious deep voice with an extraordinary range, Jean Warburton was a truly professional and versatile performer. She was equally at home in major roles such as Nancy in *Oliver,* supporting roles such as the "wacky" friend, Vera Charles, in *Mame,* or in the chorus. She will be remembered particularly for her exceptional renderings of "As Long as He Needs Me" (*Oliver*), "I'm Still Here" [*Follies*-(Centre Stage Productions Society)], "Bali Ha'i" (*South Pacific*), and numerous selections in *Down Memory Lane*.

Al Greenway proved himself to be a versatile performer, and therefore, he was seen in numerous character roles for LMT, summer musicals, Playgoers, and Centre Stage. In addition, he frequently appeared in local T.V. commercials. In Lethbridge musical theatre circles, Greenway's performances of Big Julie (*Guys and Dolls*) were considered to be outstanding. Reference is made here to performances because Greenway portrayed the same role for both LMT and Centre Stage, even though almost twenty years lapsed between the two productions.

Although Ray Mercer did not appear in a LMT production following his portrayal of the anvil salesman, Charlie Cowell, in *The Music Man* (1982), he performed in almost every show prior to that once he was introduced to the organization through backstage participation for *My Fair Lady* (1970). Mercer primarily played supporting roles; however, he did take the leading male role, Jimmy Smith, in *No, No, Nanette.* In addition, Mercer appeared with Playgoers and Centre Stage Productions.

Generally, George Mann was noted for his portrayal of supporting character roles such as the Rabbi in *Fiddler on the Roof,* Gremio in *Kiss Me Kate*, and Rudolph in *Hello Dolly*; however, he also performed in *Down Memory Lane.* Two of his most memorable character roles were the Innkeeper/Governor in *Man of La Mancha* and Mayor Shinn in *The Music Man.* In both of these shows, he played opposite one of his favorite stage wives, Joan Waterfield, who also portrayed Mrs. Higgins and Golde in *My Fair Lady* and *Fiddler on the Roof*, respectively.

Once Mark Campbell completed his radio and T.V. course at the L.C.C. and settled into his announcing position with a local radio station, he began to get more and more involved in local theatre societies. His first major role with LMT was Chief Sitting Bull in *Annie Get Your Gun* (1977). Two years later, he played the leading male character, Sid Sorokin, in *Pajama Game.* In addition, he played the minstrel in *Once Upon a Mattress,* the secondary lead, Jeff Douglass, in *Brigadoon* and a chorus member in *The King and I.* Undoubtedly, Campbell's most amusing role was that of Fast Eddie in *Kiss Me Kate.* Campbell also participated in summer musicals, in Playgoers, and in Centre Stage Productions Society.

In the early 1980s, a number of young high school students and recent high school graduates became associated with LMT and very quickly developed a reputation for dependability, on the one hand, and considerable talent, on the other. Included among the quite active youthful members of the organization were Jeff Haslam, Roger Schultz, Sandra MacFarlane, Jeff Carlson, Narda McCarroll, and Candice Elzinga. Schultz and MacFarlane were graduates of Winston Churchill High School and both were awarded D.R. Yates Fine Arts scholarships upon their graduation. It was in *Once Upon a Mattress* that Schultz first displayed some of his many talents to LMT audiences. As the LMT program for this show states, "His natural sense of movement makes him ideal for the role of Sir Harluce, one of the court dancers." In the succeeding show, *The King and I,* Schultz again intrigued local patrons with his unique portrayal of Simon Legree in the "Uncle Tom's Cabin" ballet. Because Schultz was also an excellent singer as well as a tall, slim, and handsome young man, he was a director's dream. Since he was also an extremely hard worker, he was an ideal colleague on and offstage. He was cast in six shows, successively, for LMT. His last appearance for LMT was in 1985 when he so remarkably portrayed the extremely complex character of the Master of Ceremonies (Emcee) in *Cabaret.* Following that show, Schultz became more involved in his drama studies at the U of L (in design) and in a number of Centre Stage musicals. Schultz was also one of the outstanding performers in the summer revues staged by the Great West Summer Theatre Co. in Fort Macleod. In the fall of 1989, Schultz moved to Edmonton to establish a professional career in the theatre.

MacFarlane was a very successful competitor in the Kiwanis Music Festivals. She had established her reputation as an exceptional singer before she joined LMT as a member of the chorus in *Camelot* (1978). Then, in 1981 she was cast as the young princess, Tuptin, in *The King and I,* and her beautiful voice joined together with that of the fine tenor, Lyndon Bray, in the strains of "We Kiss in a Shadow." *Down Memory Lane* also benefitted from MacFarlane's participation as did *Cabaret* and *Hello Dolly.* But it was the role of Fiona MacLaren in *Brigadoon* which really gave her the opportunity to show off her exceptional vocal talent. MacFarlane was able to identify quite considerably with the part since she had been raised in a very strong Scottish household where she had been encouraged to participate in many Scottish concerts and Robbie Burns nights. But MacFarlane was not only a highly accomplished singer, she was also quite a versatile young actress, as is evidenced by the fact that she so convincingly carried the part of the "slob," Olive Madison, in Playgoers' production of *The Odd Couple* (female version).

Jeff Haslam was one of the most talented prospective actors to graduate from the LCI, where he had been an extremely active participant in the school's drama offerings. While still in high school, he was cast as Sir Hastle in LMT's *Once Upon a Mattress*. Later, when attending the University of Lethbridge, Haslam became quite committed to community theatre. In the fall of 1982, he captivated local audiences and fellow actors with his portrayal of Tommy Djilas in *The Music Man* (LMT). In February 1983 Haslam appeared in Playgoers' one act festival production, *A Bench at the Edge*. Later that spring, Haslam directed the LCI production of *Patio,* which was entered in the Lethbridge Regional High School Drama Festival. Out of 15 entrants, *Patio* and *Where Have All the Lightning Bugs Gone* (Willow Creek Composite High School, Claresholm) were selected to proceed to the provincial high school festival.[113] Haslam capped off his local theatrical endeavors with a superb performance as young Charlie in Playgoers production of *Da*. Haslam's subsequent transfer to the U of A in order to complete a BFA program deprived Lethbridge of witnessing further this fine actor's development. Following graduation Haslam achieved considerable success in his chosen professional field of acting.[114]

Carlson, McCarroll, and Elzinga were still LCI students when they joined the chorus of *The Music Man*. Following three years of apprenticeship in the chorus, this youthful trio were ready to go solo, and each made an impressive individual debut in the Centre Stage production of *A Chorus Line* – a rather appropriate debut, considering their prior experiences. Following this, Elzinga enrolled in the BFA acting program at the University of Alberta, whereas the others continued their studies at the U of L. McCarroll emerged as a supporting player in the immediately succeeding LMT production, *Cabaret*. The summer of 1986 introduced these three aspiring thespians to the patrons of the Great West Summer Theatre Co. Much to the enjoyment of these patrons, the trio returned for succeeding years although Elzinga discontinued her relationship with the company after the summer of 1987. Carlson attracted considerable attention when he portrayed the youthful clerk, Barnaby, in the 1986 LMT production of *Hello Dolly*. Both he and McCarroll contributed effectively to Centre Stage, to U of L productions, and to the 1985 Christmas pantomime. Carlson also pleased LMT audiences with his interpretation of Curly in the 1989 production of *Oklahoma!*.

Three other young participants, not raised in Lethbridge, George Gallant, Lyndon Bray, and Neana Meeks, made valuable contributions to both LMT and Centre Stage Productions Society during the 1980s. Meeks, who also portrayed Florence Ungar in Playgoers' *The Odd Couple,* was raised in the Raymond area. She was tall, slim, attractive, and endowed with a beautiful soprano voice which brought her many accolades at festival competition. She studied voice seriously while attending Brigham Young University. Shortly after settling back in southern Alberta, Meeks was cast in the lead role of Marian (the librarian) in *The Music Man* (1987), for which she did a superb job. Her other major roles for LMT were a singer in *Down Memory Lane* and Minnie Fay in *Hello Dolly*. In the former production, her rendition of "Why Do I Love You" from *Show Boat* was thrilling. Because of Meek's very true and beautiful voice, she was asked to participate as a soloist in numerous university and church choral concerts as well as in other musical theatre companies such as Centre Stage Productions. Her return to university studies made it difficult for her to meet the many requests for her participation. Wherever and whenever she appeared, her talents were always greatly appreciated.

When George Gallant moved to Lethbridge in the mid-1980s, he already had considerable musical theatre experience which began, for him, in high school and then continued through his association with the Beth Israel Players, productions at S.A.I.T. (where he enrolled in the Television, Stage and Radio Arts program), and some freelance productions in Calgary. Prior to moving to Lethbridge, he worked in T.V. in Swift Current, Saskatchewan, for three years. An appointment with CFAC-T.V. in Lethbridge opened up many opportunities to engage in live theatre and numerous T.V. productions. His debut performance for LMT was in the 1984 production of *Brigadoon,* where he played the role of the young Scottish lad, Charles Dalrymple. The following year, he was cast as the romantic lead, Clifford Bradshaw, in *Cabaret,* which he performed about two months after playing Richie in Centre Stage Productions' *A Chorus Line.* This youthful appearing, congenial tenor quickly captivated the hearts of Lethbridge performers and patrons, alike. Before long, he was being sought out to play one major role after another. For LMT, he demonstrated pure innocence in his portrayal of Cornelius Hackl in *Hello Dolly* and sincere tenderness in his role of Lt. Cable in *South Pacific.* Gallant also appeared in at least seven musical productions for Centre Stage Productions including two lead roles, Jesus in *Jesus Christ Superstar* and Guy Masterson in *Guys and Dolls.*

TABLE 6-15

Lemmy Award Winners*
Lethbridge Musical Theatre (1964 -1988)

YEAR	ONSTAGE	BACKSTAGE	YEAR	ONSTAGE	BACKSTAGE
1965	Kaye Robison		1977	Ray Mercer	Shirley Ann Walkey
1966		Ray Jolliffe	1978	Frank Featherstone	Mardi Renyk
1967	Shirley Wilson		1979	Dawn Flexhaug	Barb Stefan
1968		Ern & Fran Bayly	1980	Karen Kay	Rod Flexhaug
1969	Norma MacInnes	Ed Bayly	1981	Linda Bayly	Gail Holland
1970	Al Greenway	Freda Walton	1982	George Mann	Cherie Baunton
1971	Marg McKay	Marg Kokott	1983	Candy Williams	Hazel Skaronski
1972	Joan Waterfield	Cathy Schwass	1984	Mark Campbell	Marj Dalke
1973	Jack & Jean Warburton	Cathy Evins	1985	Wes Stefan	Eleanor Fenton
1974	Albert Azzara	Fred McKay	1986	Sandra MacFarlane	Brian Tedder
1975	Phil Kristiansen	Nora Hawn	1987	Roger Schultz	Donna Kampen
1976	Fran Rude	Anne Reid	1988	George Gallant	Eileen Cashmore

*No formal distinction of onstage or backstage made until 1969

An associate of Gallant's at CFAC-T.V., Lyndon Bray, was a well trained singer who also took musical theatre very seriously. Unfortunately, Bray was a resident of Lethbridge for only a very few years, but during that time, he made quite an impression upon the musical theatre scene. He had come to Lethbridge from Moose Jaw, Saskatchewan, where he had performed a number of lead roles in community theatre. Upon arriving in Lethbridge, he immediately was cast to play the young prince in *The King and I.* The following year, he took the leading role of Professor Harold Hill in *The Music Man* and later, portrayed Bill Calhoun/Lucentio in *Kiss Me Kate* and the male lead, Tommy Albright, in *Brigadoon.* Bray also performed for Centre Stage, but then, television career opportunities attracted him elsewhere.

The work of the backstage personnel for LMT basically revolved around two outstandingly dedicated people, Ed Bayly and Cathy Evins. Because they were both very artistic individuals, they engaged in the process of design; Bayly concentrated on set, lighting, and sound design; whereas, Evins created many of the costume designs and properties. Evins also added her artistic talents to set painting and set dressing. In addition, both she and Bayly took on the position of production manager, which involved the overall organization and supervision of the production process. Evins performed this role on four or five occasions and Bayly on one official occasion. Bayly, nevertheless, carried on many of these functions in an informal fashion while supervising the light, sound, and construction crews. Speaking of production responsibilities, it should be mentioned that Dick Mells acted as producer for most of the musicals which he directed. Another very consistent department head was Mardi Renyk who inherited the makeup supervision from Fran Rude in 1977, and then retained the position throughout the era under discussion. Others who made a major contribution to the backstage activities of LMT from 1971-1988 can be gleaned from the appendices.

As a conclusion to this discussion about the LMT, it seems appropriate to list the various Lemmy recipients. Lemmy award winners were chosen annually by a vote of the executive, the director, the production manager, and previous Lemmy recipients associated with the ongoing production. The role of the electors was to select the most deserving onstage and backstage participant who had also made an outstanding contribution to a number of previous shows. The list in Table 6-15, substantiates the contribution which many of the people previously discussed made to the success of LMT.

Centre Stage Productions Society (CSPS)

Centre Stage Productions Society was formed in the spring of 1985 as a successor to the then defunct Stage Three Theatre Company.[115] The society immediately announced its first production, *A Chorus Line,* to be staged at the Yates Memorial Centre in September 1985. Within the following year, Centre Stage Productions also staged the "musical reminiscence," *We'll Meet Again*, in conjunction with the Royal Canada Legion. During the next three years, the society produced two to four shows per year, and of the nine shows offered between September 1985 and September 1988, seven were musicals. Eight of these nine shows were directed by Fran Rude (artistic director), and the musicals were all choreographed by Candy Chiselle Williams. The other consistent participant behind the scenes was Jody Low who designed the lighting and took on the task of production manager, and who in 1988 was named to the executive as technical director. Musical direction and orchestral leadership was usually handled by John S. Reid, but Don Robb and Edward Johnson also performed this task, occasionally. Vocal direction was primarily turned over to Kenneth Rogers; however, Arla Burbank acted in this capacity as well. With regard to technical assistance, the organization was able to call upon the expertise of university personnel since the society decided to produce most of their shows at the university – experts such as David Hignell, technical director of the university theatre; Leslie Robison, costumer, University of Lethbridge, Department of Dramatic Arts; and John A. Johnstone, master carpenter and designer. However, community minded participants from Playgoers and LMT such as Herb Matis, Hazel Skaronski, Fred McKay, Sue Koshman, Brian Tedder, Roger Schultz, and Cliff Stoakley provided much of the backstage work.

With regard to onstage participation, it would seem appropriate to distinguish between the legitimate theatre productions and the musical theatre ones. From 1985-1989, Centre Stage Productions produced two plays: a drama, *'Night Mother,* directed by Eric Low and a comedy, *Noises Off,* directed by Fran Rude. The first play had a cast of two – the mother, played by Lois Dongworth and the daughter, portrayed by Janice Tilley. *Noises Off* had a considerably larger cast. Winstan Jones and Candy Chiselle Williams proved themselves to be excellent stage comedians. With a few exceptions, most of the actors in these plays did not appear in the musicals. The musicals were generally selected to showcase the talents of George Gallant and Rhonda Ruston, with Gallant playing such lead roles as Jesus in *Jesus Christ Superstar* and Sky Masterson in *Guys and Dolls,* while Ruston took the title role in *Evita,* the leading female role in *Guys and Dolls,* Sarah Brown, and the leading character in *I'm Getting My Act Together and Taking It On the Road.* Gallant's contributions to local theatre have been well documented in the discussion on LMT. Most of Ruston's consistent theatrical activities centered around Centre Stage Productions, for which she was a founding member, and one who was highly dedicated to its development as an important component of the local drama scene. Ruston's roots in local drama reached back to WCHS where she appeared as Gertie Cummins in *Oklahoma!.* She also participated in the summer musicals, *Damn Yankees* and *Li'l Abner,* taking the roles of Meg Boyd and Moonbeam McSwine, respectively. As a University of Lethbridge student she appeared in such productions as *Equus.* Her law studies forced her to leave Lethbridge for a few years; when she returned to practice law, she also became very active in politics; Ruston ran in the provincial election as a Liberal candidate. Ruston's return to the Lethbridge stage occurred in the spring of 1984 when she performed in *Down Memory Lane* for LMT directed by Fran Rude. Rude was obviously very impressed with Ruston's talent and also perceived that Ruston's legal knowledge and her general capabilities would make her an ideal person to help launch Centre Stage Productions Society. Unquestionably, this was a very wise decision; Ruston proved to be just as valuable behind the scenes as she was on the stage.

Al Greenway, Mark Litchfield, and Roger Schultz were also important ingredients in a number of musicals for CSPS. As was his forte, Greenway portrayed numerous supporting characters including his reprise of Big Julie in *Guys and Dolls.* Speaking of *Guys and Dolls,* Rude also enticed Tom Melling to repeat his portrayal of Arvide Abernathy so that Lethbridge audiences could, once again, enjoy his beautiful rendition of "More I Cannot Wish You." Litchfield and Schultz contributed immeasurably to the dance and movement elements of the Centre Stage musicals. Schultz also designed the sets for *Guys and Dolls.* He would have been a natural for one of the dancers in *A Chorus Line;* however, he was rehearsing probably the most challenging role of his youthful career, the M.C. in LMT's *Cabaret.* Litchfield, who earned a B.A. in dance from Brigham Young University, was dance captain for a number of Centre Stage musicals. He made his Centre Stage debut as the choreographer, Zack, in *A Chorus Line,* after which he also sang and danced in *We'll Meet Again* and in *Evita.* Then, he played a major role, Nathan Detroit in Centre Stage's production of *Guys and Dolls.* In order to perform in this latter production, Litchfield had to commute about 150 miles from the town of Hanna (north of Medicine Hat), where he had just taken a teaching position. While in Hanna, he directed and produced the musical, *Little Shop of Horrors.* Litchfield too, was a home grown product whose talent for stage movement was apparent in high school and pantomime productions. WCHS invited him to play King Simon, the villain in the ballet sequence "Uncle Tom's Cabin" in the musical, *The King and I.* At the L.C.I., his dancing talents were put to the test when portraying Birdie (the rock & roll star) in *Bye Bye Birdie.* The following year, he played a carnival boy in *Carousel* at the L.C.I. As a student at the Jolliffe Academy of Dance, Litchfield was also involved in a number of Christmas pantomimes where his introduction to this genre in 1970 was as the back end of Henry the Horse in *Babes in the Woods.* The next year, he was one of the fiddlers in *Old King Cole* and the following year, he danced a "Pas de Deux" with Carol Jolliffe in *The Old Woman in the Shoe.* During the succeeding dozen or so years, Litchfield: attended BYU; participated in various dance and theatre organizations in Utah such as the International Folk Company, Orchesis Modern Dance Company, BYU Ballet Company, and the Black Forest Dinner Theatre; and worked at a number of odd jobs. In 1976 he returned home for a period of time and became involved in the pantomime, *The Queen of Hearts.* In the mid-1980s, he settled back in Lethbridge in order to complete his teacher education at the University of Lethbridge. Almost immediately, he joined the LMT cast of *Brigadoon* where he was called upon to dance a Scottish sword dance with Roger Schultz. He then joined forces with Candy Chiselle Williams to form Danceworks Studio in Lethbridge. Because of his association with Williams, it was natural that he should become deeply committed to the activities of Centre Stage Productions until his teaching career temporarily took him away from Lethbridge. In 1989 he announced that he would be returning to Lethbridge to join Williams as a full time staff member at Danceworks.

TABLE 6-16

Executive Members
Centre Stage Productions Society
Lethbridge, Alberta (1985 - 1988)

POSITION	1985	1986	1987	1988
President	Rick Braund	Gloria Serkin	Winstan Jones	Rhonda Ruston
Vice President	Gloria Serkin	Winstan Jones	Rhonda Ruston	Rosemarie Guttiker
Secretary	Hazel Skaronski	Hazel Skaronski	Gloria Dummitt	John Duell
Treasurer	Hazel Skaronski	Hazel Skaronski	Gloria Dummit	Diane Bennett
Artistic Director	Fran Rude	Fran Rude	Fran Rude	Fran Rude
Publicist				Cliff Stoakley
Technical Director				Jody Low
Directors	Rhonda Ruston Winstan Jones Candy Williams	Herb Matis John Duell Carla Newbould Rhonda Ruston Candy Williams	Wilma Wiebe John Duell Doris Balcovske Rosemarie Gattiker Reno Lizzi Candy Williams Jean Warburton	Wilma Wiebe Jean Warburton Candy Williams Doris Balcovske Doug Alger Barbara Bartlett

Many of the actors and singers who participated in Centre Stage Productions were active in LMT and other local theatre groups, but a few of them were primarily associated with Centre Stage. The following discussion will focus on the activities of these latter individuals. Chris Davidson made his Centre Stage debut as the Apostle, Thaddeus, in *Jesus Christ Superstar!* Then, he portrayed Benny Southstreet in *Guys and Dolls.* Davidson was also very helpful backstage, primarily, with set construction. Stephen Graham, a native of Lethbridge, was a computing science student at the University of Lethbridge; he was also a member of the U of L Jazz Band. His community stage experience began in the 1985 pantomime, *Queen of Hearts.* He then became more directly involved with Centre Stage by taking roles in *Evita, Jesus Christ, Superstar!,* and *Guys and Dolls.* Rhonda Nugent and Sheena Lawson gave excellent musical support to *Guys and Dolls, Follies,* and *I'm Getting My Act Together and Taking It On the Road.* Martin Madge appeared in U of L productions such as *Oh, What a Lovely War,* and he began his association with Centre Stage by taking the role of Caiaphas in *Jesus Christ, Superstar!* He followed this up with the role of Harry the Horse in *Guys and Dolls* and then, his rich voice was added to the cast of *I'm Getting My Act Together and Taking It On the Road. Jesus Christ,Superstar!* introduced a very talented singer to Lethbridge audiences – David Mikuliak, a music major at the University of Lethbridge. Mikuliak's strong baritone voice was also utilized in the concert version of *Follies* and in later Centre Stage productions. Mikuliak's vocal talent was such that he would make an impressive contribution to music and musical theatre wherever he were to reside.[116]

Throughout the short three and one-half year history discussed here, Centre Stage Productions Society was an extremely active organization, especially when one considers the demands inherent in producing musical comedy. The organization was very fortunate in having an artistic director, Fran Rude, who was prepared to devote the extraordinary amount of time required in directing so many successive productions. In her turn, she was blessed with highly dedicated and ambitious assistants such as Candy Williams, John Reid, and Jody Low. And, as mentioned on numerous occasions in this text, artistic ambition needs the support of rational board members who can give the appropriate organizational and fiscal leadership. Considering the tremendous monetary demands placed on the organization in producing so many successive musical productions, the executives were surprisingly effective. The organization was a master at publicity; it attracted numerous corporate and private patrons; and it developed a very strong following among the local theatre audience. The various members of the executive are shown in Table 6-16. Certainly, the success of Centre Stage helped to solidify musical theatre as the dominant form of local theatre during the era under discussion.

Touring Theatre

Although many of the theatre and dance companies which toured to Lethbridge in this era were professional companies in that the members were associated with the Canadian Actors Equity Association or its American equivalent, some of the companies were semiprofessional or associated with educational institutions. Companies which stressed children's theatre and those that aroused the social conscience tended to belong to the latter category. As can be seen from Table 6-17, quite a number of touring companies catered to children and families. In addition, one of the most frequent visitors to the city, not referred to in Table 6-17, was the children's theatre troupe from the University of Montana at Missoula, which often performed in various city and district schools.

Contemporary social problems were the focus for the touring Catalyst Theatre Co. from Edmonton. This troupe, under the careful supervision of U of A professor, David Barnett, generally toured the province through the sponsorship of the Alberta Alcohol and Drug Abuse Commission (AADAC). The young members of the company were regularly set the task of researching a social problem, after which they improvised a production designed to illustrate various concerns associated with that problem. Original music and lyrics were frequently developed to emphasize some of the ideas. Following each public performance, time would be devoted to a public discussion of the problem. The first such production to play Lethbridge was *Drinks Before Dinner*, which was presented at the Bowman Arts Centre in August 1977. The company was then referred to as the Intimate Theatre of Alcohol Awareness and one member of the company was Lethbridgite, Sandi Balcovske. Gerry Potter, who later founded Workshop West Playwright's Theatre in Edmonton, was also in the company. The following year, Catalyst Theatre toured *The Black Creek Project*. The company added the following members to its Lethbridge contingent: Carol Virtue, Malcolm Baines, and Michael Hoyt. In 1979 a former U of L student, Philip Kuntz, joined the cast of *On and Off the*

TABLE 6-17

Professional Touring Companies
Lethbridge, Alberta (1971-1988)

TYPES OF PRODUCTION CO.	1971-76	1977-82	1983-88	TOTAL
Legitimate Theatre	-	-	-	-
English Co.	4	8	5	17
French	1	7	2	10
Other Ethnic	-	1	1	2
Social Drama	-	7	1	8
One Person Play	-	3	4	7
Dinner Theatre	-	1	8	9
TOTAL	5	27	21	53
Musical Theatre	-	-	-	-
Musical Comedy & Revue	4	4	9	17
Musical Plays	1	3	3	7
Opera	2	2	-	4
Operetta	-	1	2	3
TOTAL	7	10	14	31
Family & Variety Th.	-	-	-	-
Children's Theatre	3	6	4	13
Puppet Theatre	-	6	4	10
Mime, Mask Th.	2	6	6	14
TOTAL	5	18	14	37
Dance	-	-	-	-
Ballet	4	11	24	39
Contemporary Dance	2	8	9	19
Ethnic	2	1	4	7
TOTAL	8	20	37	65
CUMULATIVE TOTAL	25	75	86	186

Street. It was also in that year that Bob Bainborough and David Mann became participants in Catalyst Theatre. Mann directed the final Catalyst production to tour to Lethbridge, *Family Portrait*, which played the Lethbridge Labor Club on February 23, 1984.

It should be noted that many of the historical or biographical productions that were brought to Lethbridge also showed a concern for social and psychological issues – issues such as unemployment, ethnic relationships, and the effects of war. Illustrative of these productions were *Ten Lost Years* (Toronto Workshop Productions); *Years of Sorrow, Years of Shame* (Theatre Calgary Stage Coach Players); *Billy Bishop Goes to War* (Workshop West, Edmonton, and the Vancouver East Cultural Centre); and *Hess* (Michael Burrell). The first two shows referred to here were based on works written by Barry Broadfoot.

Table 6-17 reveals a number of other interesting facts. The touring of French Canadian companies was common in the period 1977-82, but rather uncommon in the period just prior to this and the period following. One person plays became quite popular in the late 1970s, and that popularity continued throughout the 1980s. In addition, dinner theatre productions (from Calgary) were attracted to Lethbridge in the later years until Lethbridge established its own resident dinner theatre company.[117] Touring to Lethbridge was rather limited in the period, 1971-76, but it multiplied almost four fold in the next six year period and then remained high in the later period. The touring of plays increased dramatically between 1977-82 but then decreased, somewhat. Much of this decrease was brought about because of the diminution of Catalyst productions. Musical theatre increased quite consistently over the entire era, with musical comedy and musical revue retaining their general popularity. Opera and operetta was toured very rarely. Opera productions which did appear here were presented by opera associations from Edmonton and Calgary. Family oriented theatre also increased dramatically in the late 1970s, and then remained quite consistent throughout the period under discussion. Two of the favorite types of theatre with a broad age appeal were puppet theatre and mime theatre. With regard to the former theatre, Lethbridge audiences were entranced by the Puppetmongers Powell of Toronto and the Merrytime Clown Puppet Co. of Halifax, each of which appeared on one occasion, only. The Mermaid Puppet Theatre of Halifax toured to the city twice as did the Théâtre sans fil of Montreal – once with *The Hobbit* and later with *The Lord of the Rings*. But the most frequent visitor and certainly one of the most popular companies to play Lethbridge was Diane Depuy's Famous People Players, from Toronto – a group that was particularly remarkable because of its involvement of mentally handicapped persons. Most of the companies mentioned in this discussion were well recognized Canadian puppet companies.[118]

Like puppet theatre, mime theatre has universal appeal; in addition, a mime production can communicate to people from various cultural and language backgrounds. It is not surprising, then, to note that some of the mime companies which toured to Canadian cities were international groups such as the Theatre of the Balustrade of Prague and the troupe, Cvoci (both from Czechoslovakia), or Francophone groups such as Théâtre Nouveau from New Brunswick. But much of Canada's mime theatre developed out of the Canadian Mime Theatre, founded at Niagara-on-the-Lake by Adrian Pecknold.[119] "In 1974, the company established the Canadian Mime School – under the direction of Myra Benson. . . ." (In turn, The Arété Physical Comedy Co. of Calgary was established by graduates of this school). In 1977 other associates of the Canadian Mime Theatre formed the Theatre Beyond Words in Niagara-on-the-Lake. This company made its first trip to Lethbridge in the spring of 1979 when it brought its famous *Potato People*. The company appeared, again, in 1983 with *Uncle Clarence's Visit*. This company had a special affinity to Lethbridge because a former resident, Charles Schott, was a regular member of the troupe. Ron East, a student of Lecoq mime tradition, brought his Mime Theatre Unlimited to Lethbridge in 1976; his show at the public library was described as "stunning and hilarious."[120]

In was dance companies which truly sustained the touring tradition. Thanks to the Alberta Ballet Co. (Edmonton), the ballet tradition was maintained through the doldrums of the early 1970s. In the late 1970s and throughout the 1980s, dance developed into the predominant form of touring theatre. In Lethbridge, this development was spurred by the subscription series which were introduced by the theatre managers at the University of Lethbridge. The Alberta Ballet continued to be an important component of the dance series; however, numerous other companies such as the Royal Winnipeg Ballet, Les Grands Ballets Canadiens, and Ballet British Columbia were frequent visitors. Contemporary dance companies such as the Danny Grossman Dance Co., Anna Wyman Dance Theatre of Vancouver, Toronto Dance Theatre, and Les Ballets Jazz de Montréal graced the stage of the University of Lethbridge theatre on numerous occasions.

Other features which characterized this era of touring professional theatre but which are not shown in Table 6-17, are analyzed in the following discussion. To begin with, most of the companies were Canadian. A few exceptions to this feature were noted earlier when discussing mime theatre. American productions were rare, although two musicals are noteworthy: *The Best Little Whore*house *in Texas*, starring Stella Parton and Blake Emmons, played the Sportsplex in September 1983, and Gazebo Theatre One from Santa Barbara, California, performed *Godspell* in September 1974. The latter production featured a former Lethbridge young man, Brad Murdock. Another outstanding feature of this era was the fact that, although the regional theatres such as Theatre Calgary, Citadel, and Neptune toured some productions, most of the legitimate shows were brought to Lethbridge by alternate theatre companies, particularly the Arts Club Theatre (Vancouver) and Theatre Network (Edmonton). In conclusion, it seems fairly apparent that most of the toured productions fit pretty well into "mainstream," traditional theatre.

As far as professional theatrical entertainment is concerned, the spectacular ice shows such as the *Ice Capades* and the odd special show, for example, *The Toller Cranston Ice Show,* captured a very wide audience. Undoubtedly, the many television ice specials, and the televising of numerous competitions such as *Skate Canada* as well as the World and the Olympic championships helped to heighten the interest in professional ice shows. Also, the completion of the Lethbridge Sportsplex for the 1975 Canada Winter Games provided an extremely pleasant venue for these shows.

Of course, the circus retained its popularity, but this era brought more regularity and stability into the business as two major service groups, the Shriners' Club and the Gyro Club, became annual sponsors. The Shrine Circus staked claim to a late spring date, whereas the Gyro Club's circus settled into the city in the late summer. As this era progressed, the Sportsplex became the popular venue for housing these shows, as well.

Another annual entertainment feature, the Lethbridge Exhibition (Whoop Up Days), continued unabated, although it was disrupted, somewhat, in the mid-1970s by the construction of a new grandstand facility which was officially opened on June 21, 1978, with a production featuring 70 local performers under the direction of Dick Mells, assisted by choreographer, Muriel Jolliffe. Musical arrangements for the production were by Allan Rae, a former Raymond, Alberta, resident who had "scored works for the CBC, films, and major orchestras."[121] The stage settings were designed by Ed Bayly. In general, professional entertainers who were contracted to perform for the Exhibition Grandstand shows were musical entertainers, for example, impersonators of Elvis Presley. But magicians, illusionists, and hypnotists continued to be favorite entertainers in Lethbridge. Quite a variety of these entertainers visited Lethbridge in the 1970s, but Reveen maintained his prominence in this field; consequently, he generally appeared in Lethbridge at least once per year and, frequently, more often. Also, his visits in the city were rather extended.

The Electronic Media

The electronic media played a very important role in not only maintaining but actually stimulating an interest in many of the forms of entertainment discussed in this chapter. When we talk about electronic media, we usually refer to radio, film, television, and ancillary industries such as audio and video recording. Radio became increasingly dependent upon recordings, especially musical recordings. In many Canadian cities (and Lethbridge was no exception to this), local radio stations specialized in advertising, in airing popular music, and in presenting local "news, weather, and sports." As such, Lethbridge radio became an important means by which local theatrical events were advertised to the public. Little effort, however, was devoted to commentary or review. A much more important role was that of popularizing contemporary musical artists and their music, which, in turn, contributed to the growing demand for live presentations by these various artists. Recognizing this demand, organizations such as the Lethbridge and District Exhibition Board eventually replaced the traditional vaudeville type of grandstand entertainers with popular musical artists.

The CBC AM, FM, and stereo radio outlets maintained a somewhat broader mandate – CBC AM and FM placed much more emphasis on news commentary; whereas, CBC stereo emphasized classical music and some drama. Drama production on CBC was somewhat more prevalent in the early 1970s than in the later years when CBC budgets were drastically reduced. In the early years, some Lethbridge actors were contracted to perform in various CBC productions. Wes Stefan's work with CBC has been discussed previously. In addition, Jack Warburton was signed in 1970 to a CBC contract to perform in his first radio part – the lead in a radio adaptation of *A Matter of Grave Importance* by the Dublin writer, Michael Judge. The production was aired on CBC radio on December 21, 1970.[122]

Throughout this book, reference has been made to movies which were filmed, at least partially, in the Lethbridge area and to movie actors who had some association with the area. Southern Alberta became a very popular area for film production during the 1970s and early 1980s. Numerous international films such as *Superman I* and *The Silver Streak* hired many local extras for the crowd scenes which were shot in district communities like Barons, which was renamed Smallville for the Superman movie.[123] A number of Canadian movies were also shot in and around Lethbridge – the first of these, and appropriately so, was *Slip Stream,* the screenplay of which was written by Bill Fruet. Another movie, filmed in the Spring Coulee area and in Lethbridge, with numerous local extras including Muriel Jolliffe and some of her students, *Days of Heaven,* was released in the fall of 1978. A dressing room in the Jolliffe dance studio was used as a setting for a Chicago tenement room. The movie, directed by Terence Malick, starred Richard Gere, Brooke Adams, Sam Shepherd, and Linda Manz.[124] In 1980 a number of Lethbridge residents, including me, were contracted to portray roles in *Pure Escape.*[125] The movie was financed by Canadian backers, and it was produced by a Canadian company; nevertheless, it starred James Garner and Billie Dee Williams under the direction of Stuart Margolin. Canadian stars included Dixie Seatle and Chris Wiggins. Unfortunately, the financial backers withdrew their support before the film was completed, so the filming was abandoned. In the meantime, a movie made for television, *Amber Waves,* starring Dennis Weaver and Kurt Russell, was also filmed, partially, in this area.[126] Lethbridge Playgoer, Kaye Robison, was cast in a small speaking part. The Magrath-Cardston Marching Band was recruited to lead the parade which was filmed for the movie. In the mid-1980s, CBC-T.V. filmed part of a musical fantasy, *Floating,* in the southern Alberta foothills. The production, which starred Canadian singers, Murray McLaughlan and Buffy Sainte Marie, and which featured members of the Blood Indian tribe, was part of the 1985 *Canada Day Spectacular* broadcast by CBC.[127] During the year 1987, two international films were shot in and around Lethbridge. In the early part of the year, Bo Ho Films of Hong Kong filmed some scenes of *Eastern Condor* at the Lethbridge Correctional Centre. The film starred the Hong Kong actor, Samo Hung; the scenes filmed in Lethbridge featured a local man, Ken Hamilton, as a guard at the centre.[128] Later that year, Sundown Productions Ltd., filmed some scenes for *Summer Lightning,* a movie which starred Debra Winger and Tom Berenger. A number of local extras were also used.[129]

The year 1987 also brought the film festival movement to southwestern Alberta. In March the Department of Continuing Education, University of Lethbridge, in cooperation with the World Citizens' Centre, and with the financial assistance of CUSO, presented an International Film Festival which emphasized "life in various nations of the world."[130] In October the community of Pincher Creek became the site for the first "World Festival of Aboriginal Film." During the four day festival, about 140 films were screened.[131] Henceforth, this festival became an annual event.

The expansion of television broadcasating and production had considerable effect upon the local theatre scene. Although city residents received three direct T.V. signals, only two of these T.V. stations broadcast much locally produced material. CBC-T.V. (Calgary) broadcast via a local transmitter, only. CFCN-T.V., the CTV affiliate which was closely associated with CFCN-T.V., Calgary, produced some local shows in addition to news segments which were incorporated into the Calgary news broadcasts. The non network station, CFAC-T.V. (Lethbridge), presented a number of locally produced shows other than the usual news, weather, and sports programs. Two unique presentations, written, directed, and produced by the local staff – *A Gladstone Mountain* Christmas and *Christmas in Lethbridge* – were programs of story and music about the Christmas tradition performed by local actors and musicians. This latter activity had two major effects on the local theatrical scene. The first effect was that some people hired to work in this field made exceptional personal contributions to local theatre, for example, Lyndon Bray and George Gallant. In addition, production activity involved a number of local musicians and actors and, therefore, broadened their performance experiences. As this era came to a close, there was some promise that local T.V. production would increase considerably in the future.

Epilogue

This analysis of the history of theatrical production in Lethbridge illustrates that a number of external and internal factors combine to determine the type, quality, and extent of theatre presented in a community – factors which may be classified as conditional, dynamic, or structural. Conditional factors are defined here as circumstances over which the community has very little direct control; yet, circumstances which tend to set conditions or limits upon the development of the community and its social institutions. Conditional variables which have proved to be influential in the development of theatre in Lethbridge include geographical location, population size, technological development, and historical time. Dynamic factors include social, political, and economic forces, all of which tend to stimulate change in society. Structural factors refer to the manner in which a social phenomenon is organized and the way in which it relates with other organizations in society and in the local community. These latter variables tend to be fairly stable and somewhat change resistant.

The most obvious conditional factor isolated in this study is the geographical location of the community in association with its accessibility by various means of transportation and communication and its proximity to major centres of population – urban areas. Location has always played an important role in the development of Lethbridge. Since its founding in 1885, Lethbridge has been a somewhat isolated community – tucked away in the southwest corner of Alberta. Calgary, located a distance of approximately 140 miles (224 km) northwest of Lethbridge, is the closest major urban area. Other metropolitan centres such as Edmonton, Regina, Spokane, and Vancouver range in distance from 350 to 750 miles (560 to 1 200 km).

From the perspective of theatrical touring companies, Lethbridge has generally been considered an out of the way place. Trans-continental transportation routes consistently bypassed Lethbridge; therefore theatrical troupes traditionally were forced to make side trips to the city. It is true that during the era of passenger rail service in Lethbridge (after 1893, and until the mid-1950s), companies could travel from Calgary to Lethbridge and then to Medicine Hat or vice versa. However, connecting schedules were not always convenient. The subsequent Lethbridge-Calgary dayliner, which operated until 1971, was certainly not adequate to meet the needs of touring companies. In addition, rather poor air service existed between the two cities until the late 1970s. In view of this isolated situation, it is not surprising that Lethbridge relied a great deal upon indigenous theatre. Considering the size of the community, it is also not surprising that this indigenous theatre was almost exclusively amateur.

Sociologists concerned with community studies have determined that community size relates specifically to the range and variety of services and facilities available within a particular community. It has been determined that North American cities must reach a certain critical size before they can support various cultural activities or facilities. Canadian experience seems to suggest that for year round professional theatre to flourish, the critical community size is somewhat in excess of 100,000 residents. For considerable competition and extensive variety to exist (regional theatres, alternate theatres, resident opera and ballet companies), a minimum population of 500 000 is required. However, these resident requirements do not necessarily apply to summer or festival theatre since many other variables (often related to the tourist industry) intervene: such theatre attracts audiences from an extensive geographical area.

Lethbridge has had neither the critical mass of population nor the tourist appeal to support full time or even seasonal professional theatre. Although Lethbridge has consistently maintained its status as the third largest city in Alberta, its relative size compared to Edmonton and Calgary has decreased regularly. In 1905 the population of Lethbridge was about one-third that of each of the larger cities; in the late 1980s its population of about 60 000 was around one-twelfth that of either of these two metropolitan centres. Much of this changing differential has resulted from the increasing importance of the oil and gas industry compared to the agricultural and coal industries. In fact, Red Deer, located mid-way between Calgary and Edmonton has recently grown much more quickly than Lethbridge, and by 1988 it was seriously challenging Lethbridge's third place status.

Recent attempts in Lethbridge to establish professional theatre indicate that a population of 60 000 is not sufficient, in and of itself, to support such theatre. Professional theatre in Lethbridge must attract large numbers of patrons from its service area or from its tourist visitors. But unpredictable winter weather would probably discourage most neighboring residents from subscribing to a season of professional theatre in Lethbridge. In addition, southern Albertans have rarely proved to be amenable to summer theatre. Tourists, on the other hand, are often more eager to attend summer productions. Unfortunately, Lethbridge is not seen as a destination point for most tourists, and although there are a number of excellent vacation areas in the vicinity (for example, Waterton-Glacier International Peace Park), Lethbridge is too far away (80 or more miles or 128 km) to entice these visitors to travel "just to see a show" unless that show, itself were to become a major attraction or unless tourists became more aware of the many outstanding but generally unknown attractions of Lethbridge and district, for example, Nikka Yuko Japanese Garden (Lethbridge), Head-Smashed-In Buffalo Jump (Fort Macleod), Remington Alberta Carriage Centre (Cardston).

A successful contemporary venture in southern Alberta – Bryan Parkinson's Great West Summer Theatre Company (now, New West Theatre Company) demonstrates that quasi professional theatre can succeed in Lethbridge if the following conditions exist: 1) the production has a broad appeal (for example, a comical musical revue), 2) the patrons are attracted from the entire service area population, 3) the organization is sufficiently funded so that it can survive until its "product" has been generally accepted and the company has been established as an important local institution, and 4) the company adheres to high production standards. To some extent, the New West productions have become an important tourist attraction.

Touring companies are influenced by the size of the market since size is a fairly good predictor of ticket sales and of prices which can be charged for those tickets. (The larger the population – the larger the segment of upper income patrons.) Higher priced companies are obviously attracted to larger centres, unless the companies are subsidized to the point where they can absorb a loss at the box office. When touring of American productions was paramount, most of the companies which played Montreal, Toronto, and Vancouver did not venture into the hinterland. Of course, the two eastern cities had the advantage of being located near New York, the major American theatre centre at that time. Vancouver, on the other hand, was simply considered another stop on the West Coast touring route. Major national and international companies that did tour to prairie cities such as Winnipeg, Calgary, or Edmonton frequently did not play smaller communities such as Moose Jaw, Medicine Hat, Lethbridge, or Red Deer. To a very large extent, this is still true today.

Besides problems relating to accessibility and size of community, another concern of touring companies (as well as local companies) is the availability of an appropriate performing facility. Although theatrical societies and organizations have various needs, most troupes are interested in the size (seating capacity) of the potential auditorium, the dimensions and fittings of the stage, the lighting and sound equipment, the acoustics, the backstage facilities (dressing rooms, scene dock, storage area), the rental agreements, and the management of the theatre. Throughout this text, it has been shown that no one facility can meet the needs of the various genres of theatre. Generally speaking, the smaller the community, the more limited are the types and accoutrements of performing facilities. But this is not necessarily true. Other factors such as historical time and the relative importance placed upon various kinds of activity may be more influential than size. For example, even though the city's population has increased about fivefold since the second decade of the twentieth century, the seating capacity of the two presently existing major legitimate theatres in Lethbridge is considerably less than that of the two early theatres: the Majestic and the Morris. It must be kept in mind that live theatre was, during the heyday of the Majestic and the Morris theatres, the dominant form of community entertainment. With regard to the concerns of modern contemporary Lethbridge, it is evident that present theatrical facilities are not adequate, especially for large scale productions. A larger auditorium would certainly attract more touring companies and entertainers. However, one must be cognizant of the fact that in a Canadian community, patron admission would be responsible for covering most of the cost of operating such a facility.

Technological advancements have had both positive and negative effects on live theatre. Many cause and effect relationships are quite obvious; others are more problematic. This study has demonstrated that there is a relationship between the growing importance of the movie industry and the declining role of live theatre in the 1930s. On face value, it would appear that the movie industry literally destroyed live theatre during the Depression. However, we must keep these developments in perspective and realize that a number of forces were operating together at that time. Certainly, the economic situation was a significant intervening variable. Actually, developments in radio, film, phonograph, and television have often complemented live theatre by stimulating an interest in performers and productions.

Socio-dynamic factors frequently originate beyond the boundaries of the local community. This study has clearly shown that major national and international developments can have serious consequences for theatrical activities of even the most isolated communities. Economic and political effects resulting from the Depression of the 1930s and from the two World Wars of the twentieth century are thoroughly documented in this study and elsewhere. Sociologists refer to some of these consequences as manifest since they are readily apparent to most people. But unanticipated or latent consequences such as the following can be equally significant: the emergence of popular military concert parties; the downsizing of theatrical productions; the exposure of large numbers of service men and women to other cultures and their return to Canadian communities with greater expectations; the introduction of numerous theatrically experienced immigrants into Canadian society, some of whom become major contributors to national and local theatrical organizations; and the realization that Canadian society can compete with similar industrialized societies, even in the realm of the arts.

Social movements arise when large numbers of people become organized or alerted to support and encourage change. Four movements which were discussed quite specifically in this book are the Little Theatre movement, the festival movement, nationalism, and professionalism. The effects of another movement, egalitarianism, on Canadian theatre are less evident, probably because the movement has grown rather slowly and unevenly over an extended period of time. Nevertheless, egalitarianism is reflected in changes which have occurred in the structure of theatrical organizations during the past one hundred years. This movement is most clearly demonstrated in Lethbridge when reviewing the decision making process of local theatre societies. A survey of early theatrical societies in Lethbridge clearly shows that the major participants in these activities tended to be members of the leading families – the community elite. Prominent business and professional men filled the executive positions in the various theatrical societies; also, the NWMP participants were primarily officers.

Elitism was still evident during the early twentieth century; nevertheless, the artistic direction of most of the theatrical organizations became the prerogative of more middle class individuals – theatre managers, salesmen, music teachers, auctioneers. During the first two decades of the Playgoers' existence, the club appealed to the general public to become involved as official members. As we have seen from this study, membership did not imply participation in the productions or in the executive; rather, active involvement was confined to a fairly small core of members. In addition, the major executive positions continued to be dominated by lawyers and local entrepreneurs.

World War II contributed greatly to the growth of the middle class and this growth is reflected in the composition of Playgoers' executives following the reestablishment of the club in 1951. Since then, executives have been primarily comprised of homemakers and of individuals from middle class occupations such as the following: teaching, social work, retail sales, secretaryship, and librarianship. It is also interesting to note that executive members from more recently founded societies such as LMT and Centre Stage Productions Society are representative of the middle classes.

Although the wives of prominent men performed in early local productions, they rarely filled decision making positions until the mid-1920s and thereafter. In addition, artistic direction was primarily carried out by males – Deane, Dunne, Hincks, Harper, Waddington, Sterndale Bennett. It is true that women occasionally took on the task of directing operettas. At that time, directors of operetta emphasized musical direction – very little thought or attention was given to acting; therefore, the director's main qualification was competency in musical performance, and many of the women in the community were well trained musicians.

When choreography became an essential part of musical theatre, its direction was the domain of local dance instructors who were almost exclusively female. Mark Litchfield was the first male to gain equality in this field; however, his contribution did not begin until 1985.

With the coming of the Little Theatre movement in the 1920s, women began to take on somewhat more responsible roles in local theatre societies. In Lethbridge, Belle Sterndale Bennett and Maybelle Bryans became artistic directors; in Edmonton, Calgary, and Medicine Hat, the names of Elizabeth Sterling Haynes, Betty Mitchell, and Joan Hays became synonymous with Little Theatre. But it took until World War II before Playgoers elected a woman president. Since 1955, when the majority of the club's executive were female, women have played an increasingly important role in the decision making process.

Although no woman has held the position of president or vice president of LMT, women have functioned in all of the other executive positions. Other positions which have tended to be sex-linked are secretaries (female) and production managers (male). With regard to Centre Stage Productions Society, Fran Rude was the driving force behind its creation, and numerous women were represented on the Board.

Another force affecting theatrical production in Canada is the social structure of Canadian theatre, that is, the manner in which Canadian theatre is organized and operated. Throughout the history of Lethbridge, theatre production has been influenced by theatrical developments beyond its borders – and in some ways, Lethbridge theatre practitioners have helped to influence these outside developments. This mutual influence occurs because numerous individuals and organizations within the theatre community became associated with (linked to) each other in various ways. Frequently, these linkages are interpersonal (theatrical agents, individual theatre managers, Chautauqua organizers); others are more organizational in their interconnections [control agencies (Chautauqua organizations, the Theatre Syndicate), booking agencies (United Booking Office, British-Canadian Theatre Association Society), funding agencies (Carnegie Foundation, Canada Council), governmental departments (Alberta Department of Culture and Multiculturalism), educational institutions (Banff School of Fine Arts, University departments of extension), regulating bodies (censor boards), and sponsoring agents (Allied Arts Council, Celebrity Concerts)].

Many of the social structures which link the local theatrical scene to the broader cultural matrix have encouraged the development of local theatre, whereas others have hindered or thwarted that development. Regardless of this latter possibility, local theatre must seek external linkages in order to be truly viable. Unfortunately, theatre in Lethbridge seems to exist in more of a vacuum today than probably any other time in its history. The demise of the DDF and the coincidental growth of professional theatre in Canada have had deleterious effects upon theatre in small and medium sized communities. The national festival provided opportunities for local groups to become more aware of what other community theatre groups were accomplishing. The scheduling of Regional Festivals in communities like Lethbridge heightened the theatrical awareness of local theatrical practitioners and patrons, alike. The nationally or internationally renowned adjudicator helped to communicate contemporary conventions, expectations, and trends. The competitive spirit made local groups more cognizant of higher standards of production. Since the DDF was discontinued in 1970, little effort has been made to include the amateur in the Canadian theatrical community.

Some social structures which have developed in Alberta to fill this void are the Alberta Drama Festival Association (ADFA) and the Alberta Conference for Theatre (ACT). The former group has reestablished the provincial one act festival, whereas the latter group aims to "ensure the growth of theatre in Alberta through the cooperative efforts of the various community, educational, and professional" theatre constituencies in the province. Both associations so far have had very limited success in creating the necessary linkages.

The professional theatre movement has pretty well ignored the needs of patrons in communities such as Lethbridge. When regional theatres were first developed, neighboring communities anticipated that these theatres would serve the region in various direct ways. This has certainly not been the case in Lethbridge. The existence of Theatre Calgary has had very little effect on the citizens of Lethbridge or its theatrical community. Its outreach program has been rather minimal, although it has been very cooperative in providing or recommending professional instructors for short term workshop programs.

In fact, very few productions from either the regional theatre or alternate theatres have been toured to Lethbridge in the last thirty years. When most of the professional theatre companies tour, they do so through reciprocal arrangements with other professional companies; therefore, touring productions play to audiences which already have a fair access to professional theatre. Of course, this kind of exchange makes financial sense. Professional theatre is, after all, a business and, as such, it must balance its books in order to survive. Because touring is expensive, Canadian theatre companies need greater subsidization in order to more completely meet the needs of many Canadian citizens who do not live in the metropolitan areas. Possibly, a special Canadian Arts Council should be funded to establish regional theatre societies whose mandate would be to tour professional productions to neighboring smaller communities.

The Department of Dramatic Arts, University of Lethbridge, performs an important role in the linkage process. By their very nature, universities are cosmopolitan in their orientation, that is, they identify more with the larger social world than with the local community. Nevertheless, the community benefits immeasurably from these external connections. Lethbridge is especially fortunate for a city of its size to be the site of a provincially funded university. Certainly, the Department of Dramatic Arts has added an important dimension to the city's artistic culture while also meeting the career needs of a growing number of students.

As a teaching and learning institution, the University of Lethbridge has provided needed opportunities for interested people to train for careers in the theatre or in ancillary fields. In order to do this effectively, the department members must keep abreast of developments within the Canadian professional theatre. Linkage also occurs through programming. In a sense, the Department provides the community with its only alternate theatre. As far as productions are concerned the department is the city's centre of 3 C programming (classical, Canadian, and contemporary). It is primarily through the university that local patrons are introduced to some contemporary Canadian playwrights. And, although the department's offerings have rarely included Shakespeare, they have presented playwrights such as Chekhov, Moliere, and Ibsen. Generally speaking, local community groups are not in a position to produce classical theatre, and they are certainly not in touch with contemporary Canadian drama. Contemporary plays and musicals which are performed by local groups still tend to be Broadway hits like *Steel Magnolias* or *Sweeney Todd*. Unfortunately, a linkage between the department and the amateur theatre community has not been forged very well. Certain faculty and staff, particularly in the technical areas, have been truly instructional and helpful to local groups. On the other hand, the academic faculty has had little interaction with local amateur theatre, although they have been very willing to adjudicate numerous local festivals. Their reluctance to become involved with community theatre groups is undoubtedly due to factors such as their need to meet the heavy teaching and research demands placed upon them by the university, their commitment to the academic discipline, their cosmopolitan orientation, and their role in nurturing a professional outlook among their students. Nevertheless, it would be ideal if these highly trained faculty could share more of their expertise with the local groups. Both the amateurs and their patrons would benefit greatly. In fact, it is quite likely that university productions could also profit from the infusion of some local theatre practitioners. Like Sterndale Bennett, let us aim for excellence in the theatre whether amateur, professional, [or educational].

Social structures persist because of norms: accepted guidelines of appropriate behavior. The normative structure of Canadian theatre creates linkages in that certain theatrical customs or conventions are considered right or proper regardless of where the theatre functions. But, regardless of how institutionalized these conventions become, changes in them do occur. Small and isolated communities such as Lethbridge are more likely to adhere to production practices or forms of theatre long after they have been generally abandoned in major theatre centres, for example, minstrel shows. In addition, theatrical avant-garde would be an unlikely experience in Lethbridge, except, within the university's offerings. Rather, one would expect community theatre groups to present a full menu of mainline theatre.

Because norms create predictability, the various social components that constitute a social structure develop status based upon how well those elements meet the needs or expectations of the participants in that structure. Expectations are based upon direct contact with these various elements or upon expectations communicated by various informants. When expectations are consistently met, a relationship becomes institutionalized. With regard to theatre in Lethbridge, certain touring companies established a reputation for consistent excellence and therefore always drew capacity crowds. This was true of certain stock companies such as the Allen Players, of the military concert vaudeville groups such as the Dumbells, and of the theatrical troupe, The Canadian Players. In a community the size of Lethbridge, word of mouth is an important form of advertising and therefore a sustained relationship between audience and performing companies or individuals is one of the best guarantees for financial success. Of course, there are exceptions to this. Certain performers and productions have well established reputations which are communicated successfully through the mass media. This too, has been true throughout the history of Lethbridge.

Lethbridge experience has shown that the satisfaction of expectations can also result in strong audience commitment to local theatre societies. Certainly, love affairs have existed between Lethbridge patrons and the Playgoers of Lethbridge (especially during the Sterndale Bennett era), the Lethbridge Musical Theatre, the Christmas pantomime, and the New West Theatre Company. Coaldale Little Theatre also enjoyed this type of relationship with its community. Unfortunately, history also illustrates that this relationship can be quite tenuous. Playgoers' status in the community slipped considerably after the Sterndale Bennetts departed. Of course, the Depression greatly aided this process. LMT also experienced a lack of audience commitment whenever it tried to produce something out of the ordinary. Because of their limited theatrical experiences, Lethbridge audiences do not adapt readily to the unusual. In musical theatre, they demand popular Broadway successes. Lesser known shows such as *Once Upon a Mattress* and *The Mystery of Edwin Drood* are doomed to financial failure. Lethbridge audiences must learn to give their local companies greater creative leeway.

Local theatre is also determined by a number of other internal local community factors such as political orientation, population composition, economic structure, educational level, tradition of artistic endeavor, and social structure of the organization involved in presenting theatre. In Lethbridge, many of these factors combine to create a rather conservative community (which probably contributes to its tendency to prefer main line theatre). In addition, the city as a whole reflects a middle class culture: home and family are paramount, religion is significant, law and order are revered, and public education (both Protestant and Catholic) is respected. The educational level of the community is undoubtedly above average for a city of its size. To begin with, the Alberta population generally ranks fairly high in school retention. The high school dropout rate is relatively low. In addition, this wealthy, clean, attractive city has considerable appeal for people in professional occupations. The Agricultural Research Station has traditionally employed numerous research scientists and para professionals, and since the mid-1960s, the college has employed numerous highly educated people of a rather practical orientation. On the other hand, the establishment of the university has contributed to a somewhat more liberal outlook. Nevertheless, the long tradition of artistic endeavor in this city has complemented the conservative perspective, and any effort to change that perspective will undoubtedly meet considerable opposition. Most Lethbridge patrons of the theatre attend productions to be entertained; they do not want to be lectured or educated. Not that they are necessarily opposed to these functions; they simply consider that such a task should be reserved for the schools and churches, not the theatre.

With regard to the social structure of Lethbridge's community and theatre organizations, two generalizations come to mind. Local theatre societies have been structured in two quite diverse ways: democratically and autocratically. Playgoers and LMT tend to represent the more democratic forms, whereas Coaldale Little Theatre, Our Town Workshop, and Centre Stage Productions Society tend to fall more under the autocratic mode. This study of theatre in Lethbridge illustrates that each of these types has its strengths and weaknesses. The democratically run groups have experienced longevity, whereas the autocratically oriented ones tend to disintegrate when the leader (artistic director) leaves. On the other hand, autocratic leadership seems to result in more creativity and more experimentation. Obviously, the ideal compromise would combine a democratically elected board of competent individuals to oversee fiscal matters, and a dedicated, theatrically informed artistic director who can envision a well balanced season of challenging and entertaining productions. This could then be combined with a subscription ticket sales program.

However, another system suggests itself, and this may be preferable for a city the size of Lethbridge where a number of theatrical societies vie for audiences. This system requires an acceptable division of labor and a coordinated calendar of productions. Rarely, if ever, is a single theatre organization capable of effectively producing all genres of theatre. Therefore it is suggested here that the various community groups specialize – some could become dedicated to children's theatre, some to contemporary Canadian drama, others to mainline theatre. Even musical theatre groups could develop specific mandates. But for this to work effectively, it would also seem necessary to agree on a coordinated season of events, for example one musical theatre group could produce in the fall, the other in the spring. This would be advantageous to both participants and patrons. Patrons like to budget their entertainment dollars. In addition, they prefer to spread out their entertainment experiences. Participants, too, like to be involved in various forms of theatre and to participate with various groups, but if they are asked to do too much at any one time of the year they quickly become burned out. It must always be kept in mind that amateurs are basically volunteers who engage in backstage and onstage activities in their leisure hours. Amateur theatre can be extremely demanding, but it can also be very personally rewarding. A major psychological reward arises from the personal satisfaction which one attains from artistic achievement such as developing a character or designing a set, a lighting scheme, or a wardrobe which the individual feels makes an important contribution to the production. But, first and foremost, theatre is a social endeavor, and in this regard the audience's response is most important. Beyond this, most amateurs hope that their amateur colleagues and the community as a whole appreciate their efforts. Occasional recognition from professional peers would also be very rewarding. It should be recognized by all members of the Canadian theatrical community that amateur theatre societies still perform the very important function of maintaining a theatrical tradition in towns and cities which are not in a position to support professional theatre. In turn, amateur societies must take on the responsibility of presenting quality productions.

Chapter One: Notes

[1] Johnston and den Otter, 38, report that Nicholas Sheran began his mining operation in the riverbottom in 1874.

[2] Johnston and den Otter, 40

[3] *Ibid*, 37

[4] *Lethbridge News (L.N.)* 2 August 1899, 2

[5] *L.N.* 29 June 1897, 1

[6] *L.N.* 20 September 1899, 8

[7] *L.N.* 3 May 1900, 3

[8] Johnston and den Otter, 50

[9] *L.N.* 28 May 1886, 3

[10] *Macleod Gazette* 9 April 1891, 3

[11] Johnston & den Otter, 44

[12] Edwards, 19

[13] *L.N.* 24 December 1885, 3

[14] *L.N.* 1 December 1886, 3. Bourgoin's Saloon was located on the southwest corner of Baroness Street (1st Ave. South) and Smith Street (4th St. South).

[15] *L.N.* 18 December 1885, 3

[16] Stuart (b), 47

[17] *L.N.* 22 December 1887, 2; 10 September 1888, 2

[18] *L.N.* 19 December 1888, 3

[19] *L.N.* 20 October 1886, 3

[20] *L.N.* 25 February 1887, 5

[21] *L.N.* 14 December 1887, 3; 22 December 1887, 3

[22] *L.N.* 26 January 1888, 3

[23] Deane, 1916a, 37

[24] Deane, 1916b

[25] *L.N.* 28 September 1887, 1; provisional directors were J.H. Cavanah, H. Bentley, and John Craig. The original company was comprised of C.A. Magrath, T. McNabb, H. Martin, E.T. Galt, C.F.P. Conybeare, and T.D. Kevin.

[26] *L.N.* 2 June 1891, 3; 7 October 1891, 3; 25 November 1891, 3; 10 February 1892, 3

[27] *L.N.* 15 October 1890, 3

[28] *L.N.* 12 July 1889, 8

[29] *L.N.* 17 May 1899, 8. The Oliver Block was located on the west side of Round Street (5th St. S.) between Redpath (3rd Ave.) and Dufferin (4th Ave.).

[30] *L.N.* 23 November 1899, 7

[31] Although the Bijou Theatre opened in 1907, it was not equipped for live theatre.

[32] *L.N.* 18 August 1886, 4

[33] *L.N.* 22 December 1887, 3

[34] *L.H.* 14 December 1887, 3. The scene was the morning conversation between Sir Peter and Lady Teazle—performed by Miss Duff and M. Tabor.

[35] *L.N.* 19 July 1888, 3; *Regina Leader*, 17 January 1888, 4; 31 January 1888, 4; 21 February 1888, 4; 28 February 1888, 4

[36] February 1888 Program, Sir Galt Alexander Museum, Lethbridge, William Baker, Historian, University of Lethbridge, reports the following presentations: *Ici on parle français* (1884 & 1887); *Dearest Mama* (1896); *Steeple Chase* and W.S. Gilbert's *Engaged* (January 1888); *Turkish Bath* and Gilbert's *Sweethearts* (February 1888)

[37] Deane, 1916b

[38] *L.N.* 22 August 1888, 3

[39] *Saskatchewan Herald*, 10 May 1886, 1; *Regina Leader*, 28 February, 1888, 4

[40] *L.N.* 23 February 1898, 8

[41] *L.N.* 21 November 1888, 3

[42] *L.N.* 4 December 1889, 3

[43] *Macleod Gazette*, 14 February 1889, 1

[44] Deane, 1916b

[45] *Lethbridge Herald (L.H.)*, 11 July 1935, 112

[46] *L.N.* 19 March 1890, 3

[47] *L.N.* 30 December 1891, 4

[48] *L.N.* 24 February 1892, 3; 2 March 1892, 3

[49] Higginbotham, 168

[50] *L.N.* 11 May 1892, 3

[51] *Macleod Gazette*, 1 July 1890, 3; *L.N.* 2 July 1890, 3. The *Macleod Gazette* reports that the wedding took place in Winnipeg. Bernadette Carpenter confirms the *L.N.* report that the wedding occurred in St. Paul.

[52] *L.N.* 18 May 1897, 1

[53] *L.N.* 16 November 1899, 8

[54] *L.N.* 11 April 1901, 1

[55] *L.H.* 3 January 1907, 4 reports that the pallbearers were J.D. Higginbotham, C.F.P. Conybeare, G.W. Robinson, G. H. Johnston, M. Barford, and Dr. F.N. Mewburn.

[56] *L.N.* 24 June 1941, 7

[57] Johnston and den Otter, 68

[58] Skinner, 14

[59] *Regina Leader*, 31 January 1888; 28 February 1888, 4; 24 April 1888, 1

[60] *Macleod Gazette* 14 March 1890, 3; *L.N.* 29 January 1890, 3

[61] *L.N.* 6 April 1892, 3

[62] Johnston, 3,4, notes that the Library Hall, which was located in the western end of what in the 1970s became known as Centre Site, had been converted from the "Galt Company's No. 1 Boarding House."

[63] *L.N.* 2 January 1891, 3; other performers were T. Glenwright, W. Waghorn, and Mrs. T. McNabb, whose husband was mayor of Lethbridge in 1894 (see Johnston & den Otter, 232)

[64] *L.N.* 10 February 1892, 3

[65] *L.N.* 27 July 1892, 3

[66] *L.N.* 16 October 1895, 1; 15 April 1896, 1

[67] *L.N.* 15 September 1898, 8

[68] *L.N.* 9 January 1891, 3; 16 January 1891, 3

[69] *L.N.* 15 September 1891, 3

[70] *L.N.* 6 February 1902, 3; 20 March 1902, 1

[71] *L.N.* 8 May 1902, 8

[72] *L.N.* 13 September 1898, 8

[73] *L.N.* 15 December 1898, 2

[74] *L.N.* 13 September 1899, 1; 27 September 1899, 1; for a related article about the Castle Square Opera Company, see 18 January 1900, 5. Whether or not MacKenzie actually joined the Chicago-based opera company is impossible to determine; however, the *Lethbridge News* later reported the intriguing coincidence that the *Pirates of Penzance* was performed by Pincher Creek amateurs under the direction of W. McKenzie. Although the surnames are spelled differently, it seems conceivable that William MacKenzie and W. McKenzie could be the same.

[75] *L.N.* 30 August 1899, 1

[76] *L.N.* 13 September 1900, 1

[77] *L.N.* 31 January 1901, 1

[78] *L.N.* 23 February 1889, 3

[79] *L.N.* 20 February 1889, 3

[80] *L.N.* 9 August 1900, 8. Later, Cunningham became a partner in one of the city's major lumber retail outlets.

[81] *L.N.* 25 April 1901, 2

[82] *L.N.* 19 September 1901, 1

[83] *L.N.* 29 May 1902, 2

[84] *L.N.* 21 April 1904, 4

[85] *L.N.* 5 April 1900, 8

[86] *L.N.* 9 February 1905, 4

[87] Johnston & den Otter, 29

[88] Orrell, 16

[89] *Macleod Gazette*, 30 June 1893, 3

[90]Edwards, 53

[91]*Macleod Gazette*, 12 August 1898, 4; 19 August 1898, 4

[92]*L.N.* 17 August 1898, 8

[93]Edwards, 34

[94]Stuart (b), 60

[95]Arrell, 91,92

[96]Edwards, 138

[97]Edwards, 187-196

[98]Smith, Bill, 7

[99]*L.N.* 5 November 1902, 8

[100]*L.N.* 22 October 1903, 4

[101]*L.N.* 1 February 1900, 8

[102]Blum, 20

[103]Gerould, 14

[104]*L.N.* 10 May 1899, 1; *Macleod Gazette*, 5 May 1899, 4.

[105]This lack of review for major productions was not uncommon at that time. However, the *Calgary Herald* (8 May 1899, 1; 11 May 1899, 1; 16 May 1899, 4; 17 May 1899, 4) verifies that the company was in Cranbrook, B.C. around May 7 and played the Alexander Hall in Calgary on May 16 and 17.

[106]Evans, 184

[107]Higginbotham, 218

[108]*L.N.* 2 November 1899, 2

[109]*L.N.* 24 August 1898, 8

[110]*Macleod Gazette*, 26 August 1898, 1

[111]Evans, 277

[112]*L.N.* 23 August 1899, 8

[113]*L.N.* 8 February 1894, 3

[114]*L.N.* 27 June 1894, 3

[115]By permission from *Webster's Ninth New Collegiate Dictionary*, 1991 by Merriam-Webster Inc., publisher of the Merriam-Webster (R) dictionaries, 662; see also Rhode, 3; Brownlow and Kobal, 26, 28, 54

[116]Ackery, 54; Griffith, Mayer and Bowser, *The Movies*, 1970, 2. Copyright © 1957, 1970 by Arthur Mayer and Ann Griffith. © Renewed 1981 by Arthur Mayer, Ann Griffith and Eileen Bowser. Reprinted by permission of Simon and Schuster, Inc.

[117]*L.N.* 28 September 1900, 8

[118]*L.N.* 22 July 1902, 4

[119]*L.N.* 6 October 1905, 1

Chapter Two: Notes

[1]Dr. L.G. DeVeber, who sat in the North-West Territorial Assembly from 1898-1905, was re-elected in the first Alberta election. When elevated to the Senate, his seat was filled by William C. Simmons (Liberal). Donald McNabb (Labor) held the seat for part of 1909; he was succeeded by William A. Buchanan (Liberal). Both DeVeber and Buchanan held Cabinet positions (see Johnston and den Otter, 233).

[2]Johnston & den Otter, 230

[3]Johnston & den Otter, 81

[4]For photographs of the bridge, see Fooks, 48, 92

[5]*Lethbridge Herald (L.H.).* 2 April 1910, 10, 20

[6]For a thorough analysis of the various socio-economic consequences brought about by the boom years, the subsequent World War I years, and the postwar years, readers are referred to Johnston and den Otter, *Lethbridge: A Centennial History.*

[7]Johnston & den Otter, 106

[8]*L.N.* 27 March 1902, 2

[9]*L.N.* 25 August 1904, 4

[10]*L.H.* 11 April 1907, 14

[11]*L.H.* 14 March 1907, 9; 7 April 1908, 1

[12]*L.H.* 15 August 1907, 10; 19 September 1907, 7

[13]*L.H.* 18 May 1908, 1

[14]*L.H.* 6 October 1908, 4; 9 October 1908, 6; 7 November 1908, 6

[15]*L.H.* 27 November 1908, 6

[16]*L.H.* 27 February 1909, 2nd section, 6; 7th section, 4; An S.S. Kresge store replaced the Hill Block in 1950; *L.H.* 3 July 1950, 7

[17]*L.H.* 20 November 1911, 5

[18]*L.H.* 7 October 1912, 10

[19]*L.H.* 19 May 1917, 9; In the 1980s this site became the location of the Lethbridge Centre Cinemas.

[20]*L.H.* 1 December 1908, 3

[21]*L.H.* 19 January 1909, 3

[22]*L.H.* 12 July 1909, 1; 17 August 1909, 4; 11 November 1909, 5; 15 November 1909, 3,8,9

[23]*L.H.* 1 February 1939, 7. The Arcade, located at 325 - 5th Street South, was sold to Mr. Patterson in 1911 and, subsequently, to R.W. Wallace who retained ownership until 1939.

[24]*L.H.* 10 July 1909, 1,4; 12 July 1909, 6

[25]*L.H.* 18 June 1910, 7,11; 20 June 1910, 10

[26]*L.H.* 28 January 1911, 11

[27]*L.H.* 21 June 1920, 5

[28]*L.H.* 24 January 1921, 8; 4 January 1944, 7; 25 April 1970, 16; King, Dora, 6,7; A.W. Shackleford was born to Mr. & Mrs. A.E. Shackleford in the fall of 1899 in Romford, England. The family moved to Calgary in 1909. Aspiring to be an engineering draughtsman, A.W. attended the Provincial Institute of Technology and Art; however, employment opportunities in theatre management derailed his early aspirations. Mr. & Mrs. A.W. Shackleford moved to Lethbridge in January 1921.

[29]Rogers and Company was engaged in a number of business enterprises: they operated the Roger's Purebred Stock Farm and the Cadillac (later, the Studebaker) Garage on 9th Street South. They also invested in oil and gas exploration—with some considerable success.

[30]*L.H.* 9 October 1908, 6

[31]*L.H* 9 October 1908, 6; 14 April 1910, 9

[32]*L.N.* 9 December 1908, 3; 13 August 1909, 8; 17 August 1909, 4

[33]*L.H.* 8 July 1909, 3

[34]*L.H.* 13 April 1910, 12; 29 April 1910, 8

[35]*L.H.* 13 November 1911, 6

[36]*L.H.* 13 November 1911, 6

[37]*L.H.* 13 December 1911, 12

[38]Goffin, 195

[39]*L.H.* 2 September 1913, 3

[40]*L.H.* 9 February 1915, 3; 10 February 1915, 3; 29 September 1915, 2

[41]*L.H.* 10 October 1918, 5

[42]*L.H.* 16 May 1921, 11

[43]*L.H.* 18 December 1911, 12

[44]*L.H.* 30 December 1940, 2

[45]*L.H.* 17 August 1915, 2

[46]*L.H.* 6 January 1913, 5

[47]*L.H.* 6 October 1909, 1

[48]*L.H.* 8 February 1910, 5; 9 February 1910, 4; 10 February 1910, 8; 12 February 1910, 6

[49]*L.H.* 7 February 1910, 5

[50]*L.H.* 22 January 1910, 5

[51]*L.H.* 19 October 1910, 7

[52]*L.H.* 30 December 1910, 10

[53]*L.H.* 7 December 1911, 5; 20 January 1912, 5; 16 November 1916, 14

[54]*L.H.* 19 February 1912, 7

[55]*L.H.* 16 November 1912, 14

[56]*L.H.* 21 December 1912, 11

[57]*L.H.* 19 May 1913, 9

[58]*L.H.* 6 May 1921, 11; 12 July 1921, 9

[59]*L.H.* 15 December 1921, 7

[60]*L.H.* 29 May 1945, 7

[61]*L.H.* 17 January 1922, 7; 7 February 1922, 7

[62]*L.H.* 17 August 1909, 5; 8 April 1911, 2

[63]Johnston and den Otter, 106

[64]St. Denis (1880-1968), dancer, choreographer, and teacher, became world famous for her modern dance interpretations of Oriental, Native American, and religious themes. St. Denis married dancer, choreographer, teacher, director, and writer, Ted Shawn (1891-1972), in 1914. For more information about St. Denis and Shawn, see Anderson, Shelton, or Terry.

[65]The original Denishawn studio was established in 1915. Its original alumni included Martha Graham, Charles Weidman, and Doris Humphrey. Lillian and Dorothy Gish and other movie stars such as Mabel Norman and Carol Dempster also attended sessions at the school. Soon, Denishawn franchised studios were opened throughout the United States. Denishawn remained in operation until 1931.

[66]*Medicine Hat Daily News (M.H.D.N.)* 30 August 1917, 17; *L.H.* 1 September 1917, 2; *Calgary Herald* 1 September 1917, 3; 17 September 1917, 8; *M.H.D.N.* 8 June 1918, 4; 19 September 1918, 4; 29 November 1918, 4; 1 April 1918, 4 (see also *C.H.* 3 September 1919, 3; 1 September 1920, 3; 1 September 1921, 3)

[67]Programs provided by Lawrence Adams, Dance Collection Danse

[68]*L.H.* 19 January 1909, 5

[69]*Moose Jaw Daily Times* 14 April 1910, 1

[70]*L.H.* 28 June 1906, 8; 11 July 1935, 7; the building has had many tenants since then, but the street level premises has generally been referred to as the Spudnut Shop.

[71]*L.H.* 18 June 1910, 12

[72]*L.H.* 28 February 1910, 4

[73]*L.H.* 2 February 1911, 9. For many years, thereafter, Bessie Hazell (Mrs. Fred Rose) and her sisters, Minnie (Mrs. Ralph Thrall) and Nellie (Mrs. Hazelton Moore), made immeasurable contributions to the musical and theatrical culture of Lethbridge and district.

[74]*L.H.* 26 October 1912, 20

[75]*L.H.* 25 January 1913, 7; 28 January 1913, 10; 1 February 1913, 5

[76]*L.H.* 24 June 1913, 3

[77]*L.H.* 13 December 1913, 11; 12 December 1913, 7

[78]*L.H.* 22 November 1921, 8; 30 November 1921, 7

[79]Blum, 35,42

[80]*L.H.* 14 December 1910, 9

[81]*L.H.* 5 December 1914, 9

[82]Mrs. Ritchie's name was Louie, however, she was frequently referred to as Louise.

[83]*L.H.* 28 December 1918, 7

[84]*L.H.* 9 March 1922, 10

[85]*L.H.* 13 December 1921, 10

[86]*L.H.* 30 April 1915, 9; 11 May 1915, 3; 14 May 1915, 9; 4 June 1915, 7

[87]Kallman, Potvin and Winters, 982

[88]*L.H.* 4 February 1921, 8

[89]*L.H.* 9 June 1921, 9; 2 September 1921, 11

[90]*L.H.* 12 February 1913, 16

[91]Blum, 21

[92]*L.H.* 8 December 1927, 10

[93]*L.H.* 12 December 1922, 10

[94]Malabar Ltd. (Malabar's) "The Costume Shop", which has its office in Toronto, rents costumes and accessories and sells makeup to customers throughout Canada. The major outlets were in Toronto and Winnipeg. According to the *MHDN* of 24 December 1920, page 15, the Winnipeg outlet was operating at that time.

[95]*M.H.D.N.* 3 January 1921, 7; 20 January 1921, 1; 21 January 1921, 1; 22 January 1921, 1

[96]Stuart, (b) 50

[97]Stuart, (b) 67-69

[98]*L.H.* 1 April 1909, 5; 2 April 1909, 3; 5 April 1909, 3; 13 April 1909, 5

[99]Johnston & den Otter, 114

[100]Edwards, 42-46

[101]*L.H.* 19 November 1910, 10

[102]*L.H.* 6 August 1946, 7

[103]Twomey and McClure, 269

[104]Shulman & Youman, 133

[105]*L.H.* 6 August 1946, 7

[106]Jackson, 89-91

[107]Jackson, 95

[108]Orrell, 117

[109]Twomey & McClure, 104; Vallance, 72

[110]Parish, et al., 442

[111]Blum, 168, 170

[112]Guthrie, 2

[113]Guthrie, 4

[114]Guiles, 75, 94-95

[115]Blum, 132

[116]Blum, 79

[117]Atkinson, 6

[118]Mordden, 26-27

[119]Spitzer, 28

[120]Blum, 59

[121]Blum, 59, 66, 67, 105, 153

[122]Blum, 122

[123]Blum, 146

[124]Blum, 152

[125]Blum, 104

[126]Blum, 213

[127]Blum, 159

[128]Blum, 93; McCabe, 270

[129]Blum, 131; McCabe, 272

[130]Atkinson, 212, 213

[131]Stuart,(b) 51

[132]Stuart, (b) 79

[133]Johnston & den Otter, 106; Jameson, 3-5; 29

[134]*L.H.* 25 August 1917, 11

[135]Smith, Bill, 13

[136]Laurie, 359-365

[137]Gilbert, 54. Reprinted by permission of Curtis Brown, Ltd.

[138]Smith, Bill, 13

[139]Csida & Csida, 225, 226

[140]Ackery, 57

[141]Orrell, 131

[142]*L.H.* 21 January 1909, 5; 1 February 1909, 4; 4 February 1909, 4; 20 February 1909, 3; 7 June-10 July 1909 (passim)

[143]Slide, 99; Adamson, 35-47

[144]*L.H.* 27 August 1913, 3; 26 August 1913, 3

[145]*L.H.* 13 January 1912, 9

[146]Curran and Porter, 44, 57, note that the Gaumont Company was an early example of foreign film companies operating in England, but that Leon Gaumont discontinued his business in England in the early 1920s.

[147]*L.H.* 13 January 1914, 3; 17 January 1914, 3

[148]*L.H.* 11 April 1922, 8

[149]*L.H.* 27 May 1916, 1

[150]*L.H.* 26 July 1920, 8; 28 July 1920, 8

[151]*L.H.* 15 April 1922, 8; *Calgary Herald* 24 March 1922, 10

Chapter Three: Notes

[1]*L.H.* 21 January 1922, 7

[2]*L.H.* 8 February 1924, 7

[3]MacGregor, 255; *L.H.* 1 October 1924, 7; 27 May 1927, 1

[4]*L.H.* 11 May 1922, 7

[5]*L.H.* 18 July 1922, 7

[6]*L.H.* 17 April 1928, 7

[7]*L.H.* 14 January 1928, 7

[8]*L.H.* 13 February 1928, 7

[9]*L.H.* 31 December 1930, 9

[10]MacGregor, 259

[11]MacGregor, 249

[12]*L.H.* 26 March 1929, 7

[13]*L.H.* 15 July 1929, 1

[14]*L.H.* 23 September 1929, 1

[15]*L.H.* 11 September 1930, 7; 29 October 1931, 7

[16]*L.H.* 15 September 1930, 7; 16 January 1931, 7

[17]*L.H.* 29 September 1930, 7; 1 December 1930, 7

[18]MacGregor, 263

[19]*L.H.* 17 June 1931, 7

[20]*L.H.* 2 December 1930, 7; 20 January 1931, 7; 3 February 1931, 7; 11 February 1931, 1. Palmer, 247 states that by 1932, 20 percent of Lethbridge's population was receiving relief.

[21]From Oscar G. Brockett, *History of the Theatre*, Fifth Edition. © 1987 by Allyn and Bacon, 626. Reprinted with permission.

[22]From the *Oxford Companion to Canadian Theatre* edited by Eugene Benson and L.W. Conolly, © Oxford University Press Canada 1989, 304. Used by permission of the publisher.

[23]Brockett, 627

[24]Gardner in Benson and Conolly (b), 304

[25]Interview: George Mann with A.W. Shackleford

[26]Shackleford was associated with Famous Players Corporation for approximately 60 years. Later in his career, he established Lethbridge Cablenet and served as its president through its formative years. In the realm of community service, he was involved with civic politics through the years 1939-1961 and served as mayor of Lethbridge for ten of these years. Other civic responsibilities included: Chairman, Lethbridge Exhibition Board; President, Lethbridge Junior Band; Chairman, Cancer Society; Chairman, Lethbridge Community Chest. In addition, he participated actively in the Lethbridge Gyro Club, the city's Board of Trade, St. Augustine's Anglican Parish and the Alberta Theatre Operators Association. A.W. Shackleford died on May 30, 1992 at the age of 92.

[27]*L.H.* 30 September 1924, 1; 6 December 1924, 8, 13. For additional references relating to the death of Rogers, see *L.H.* 1 October 1924, 17; 4 October 1924, 7; 6 October 1924, 7; 11 October 1924, 7

[28]*L.H.* 25 April 1970, 16

[29]*L.H.* 27 October 1928, 7; 30 October 1928, 7

[30]*L.H.* 25 May 1929, 11; 21 June 1929, 9

[31]*L.H.* 5 October 1929, 8; 7 October 1929, 8; 9 October 1929, 8-10

[32]*L.H.* 20 October 1924, 7

[33]*L.H.* 1 November 1924, 9

[34]*L.H.* 21 May 1926, 7

[35]*L.H.* 27 April 1929, 11

[36]*L.H.* 9 May 1929, 7; 10 May 1929, 10

[37]*L.H.* 18 April 1931, 5; 30 March 1931, 6

[38]*L.H.* 20 June 1932, 7

[39]*L.H.* 29 October 1932, 7; 11 March 1933, 7

[40]*L.H.* 22 February 1933, 6; 11 March 1933, 7; 2 October 1934, 2

[41]*L.H.* 27 March 1933, 7; 26 May 1933, 7

[42]*L.H.* 22 October 1928, 7; 2 November 1928, 11; 17 November 1928, 7; 22 December 1928, 7

[43]*L.H.* 9 November 1928, 9

[44]*L.H.* 20 April 1929, 2

[45]*L.H.* 13 July 1932, 7; 18 July 1932, 2

[46]Letters of Muriel Ritchie; Sheridan, 57-64; 91-94; informs us that Tom's daughter, Joan Sterndale Bennett, took formal dramatic training at the Royal Academy of Dramatic Art, and then joined the Players' Theatre at Covent Garden. Her first appearance for the Players' Theatre was in *The Shoemaker's Last* by Geoffrey Thomas which began its run on 1 February 1939. For the Christmas season of 1939, Joan Sterndale Bennett appeared in the Player's pantomime production of *Wittington Jnr. and His Cat*, in which Peter Ustinov also participated. Almost a year later, the Players' Theatre moved to Albermarle Street where they remained throughout W.W. II. In January 1946 the company took up residence in the former Forum Cinema on Villiers Street near Charing Cross Underground Station where it remained for many years, thereafter. Joan Sterndale Bennett was a core member of the company throughout this period. Then, she was cast in the role of Madame Dubonnet in the club's production of the musical, *The Boy Friend*. She played the role for three and a half years in London's west end.

[47]E.G. Sterndale Bennett: personal papers

[48]E.G. Sterndale Bennett: personal papers

[49]Letter: To Whom It May Concern: J. Chalmers, M.E.I.C., John Quinlan and Company, General Contractors, Westmount, P.Q.

[50]*M.H.D.N.* 21 February 1921, 4; 21 January 1921, 1; 24 January 1921, 6; 27 January 1921, 5; 2 February 1921, 1

[51]*L.H.* 13 January 1923, 8; E.G. Sterndale Bennett: personal papers

[52]*L.H.* 22 January 1923, 7

[53]*L.H.* 16 February 1923, 14. It is also noted that in the original constitution the apostrophe in the club's title was dropped. Since then, the club has officially been referred to as the *Playgoers Club of Lethbridge*. Unofficially, it is usually called *Playgoers of Lethbridge, Lethbridge Playgoers* or simply *Playgoers*.

[54]*L.H.* 10 April 1923, 10

[55]*L.H.* 10 April 1923, 10

[56]*L.H.* 6 June 1923, 14

[57]*L.H.* 4 December 1932, 8; 30 September 1926, 14; 26 March 1927, 11; 23 April 1927, 12; 20 May 1930, 7

[58]*Edmonton Journal*, 23 February 1931, 14; *Calgary Herald*, 14 February 1930, 14; 23 February 1931, 13; *Edmonton Bulletin*, 22 February 1932, 6

[59]*L.H.* 7 February 1924, 7

[60]*L.H.* 9 October 1928, 14

[61]*Toronto Globe*, 12 April 1930, 19; Alberta Drama League Festival Programs, 1930, 1931, 1932

[62]*L.H.* 31 October 1932, 6

[63]*L.H.* 28 April 1924, 7

[64]*L.H.* 31 January 1928, 7

[65]Letter of 22 August 1933 addressed to E.G. Sterndale Bennett by J. Rosewarn, Secretary, Playgoers Club.

[66]Sterndale Bennett archives: programs, newspaper clippings; The *Mail and Empire*, 13 October 1933; *The Globe*, 13 October 1933; 8 November 1933; *The Evening Telegram*, 8 December 1933; *Daily Star*, 13

October 1933; 4 December 1933; Interviews: Robert Christie, Olive (Williams) Cranston, Georgie (Baird) Lewis

[67]Sterndale Bennett: personal papers; letter: M.W. Onyon, Commander, R.W., Inspecting torpedo officer, British Admiralty Delegation, N.Y.: 27 March 1945

[68]Hoffman, 218

[69]L.H. 18 February 1958, 9

[70]Sterndale Bennett: personal writings

[71]Playgoers scrapbooks

[72]L.H. 28 March 1912, 11; 2 January 1914, 3

[73]L.H. 10 April 1923, 10; 4 December 1923, 4; 28 November 1924, 11

[74]Calgary Herald, 17 February 1930, 15; Edmonton Bulletin, 22 February 1932, 6

[75]L.H. 27 October 1932, 9 summarizes the membership as follows: 1923 - 327; 1924 - 361; 1925 - 331; 1926 - 576; 1927 - 659; 1928 - 575; 1929 - 682; 1930 - 520; 1931 - 629; 1932 - 800.

[76]L.H. 27 October 1932, 9

[77]L.H. 28 November 1932, 6; 3 December 1932, 7

[78]L.H. 18 March 1927, 18

[79]L.H. 12 June 1931, 7

[80]L.H. 19 September 1931, 7. A Lethbridge Herald article of 23 February 1931, 6 describes Brockington further as a "brilliant after-dinner speaker and keen reviewer of things theatrical." In 1936, Brockington was named the first Chairman of the Canadian Broadcasting Corporation, a position which he held until 1939 when he became a special assistant to Prime Minister Mackenzie King. He was also appointed as a member of the first Canada Council (see The Canadian Encyclopedia, 285)

[81]L.H. 18 February 1932, 7; Calgary Albertan, 19 February 1932, 3

[82]Playgoers' archives

[83]Regular minstrel performers were R. Barrowman, Bill Craig, Bill Armstrong, Bob Lawrence and the Chapman Brothers; regular soloists were Minnie Thrall, Fred Rose, Tom Smith, William Stott, Ben B. Martin, Hazelton Moore.

[84]L.H. 21 September 1928, 20

[85]L.H. 26 October 1931, 7

[86]L.H. 18 March 1927, 12; 8 October 1927, 14

[87]Atkinson, 168

[88]Parish, et al., p. 128; Charles Coburn appeared in about seventy movies before his death in 1961.

[89]Lerner, 99

[90]Atkinson, 358

[91]Atkinson, 129, 252, 358

[92]L.H. 18 March 1924, 8

[93]L.H. 2 November 1926, 12; 19 February 1927, 14

[94]Goffin, 198

[95]L.H. 28 July 1926, 8

[96]L.H. 5 March 1918, 9; 26 December 1918, 5; M.H.D.N. 6 March 1918, 4

[97]L.H. 5 October 1921, 5

[98]O'Neill, 195-198

[99]L.H. 4 March 1940, 6

[100]L.H. 25 February 1920, 5

[101]L.H. 4 October 1920, 8; 6 October 1920, 8; 9 October 1920, 10

[102]L.H. 12 October 1920, 13

[103]L.H. 12 December 1921, 8

[104]L.H. 25 February 1920, 5

[105]O'Neill, 198, states that the Dumbells was initially comprised of eight performers including: Captain Plunkett, Ivor E. (Jack) Ayre, Elmer A. Belding, Ted Charter and Allan Murray.

[106]L.H. 23 February 1920, 5, 8

[107]O'Neill, 204

[108]Sources: Lethbridge Herald; Stuart (b), 52; O'Neil, 198-204; Medicine Hat Daily News 8 May 1920, 11. A news release in the latter reference described Marie's (Al. G. Murray's) first outfit in the following way: "...Marie was garbed with gauze, secured from the dressing station and gunny sacking under it to give stiffness and shape. A pair of lady's stockings were found in a billet and a pair of military socks were cut to give the effect of shoes. A curtain was swiped from the Estaminet to make a blouse, a shrapnel helmet covered with gauze and decorated with a spray of carrot tops was Marie's hat, while a frayed piece of rope made the wig. Needless to say Marie as the first woman entertainer on the military front made a tremendous hit."

[109]L.H. 26 November 1923, 8

[110]L.H. 28 December 1926, 18

[111]L.H. 5 January 1926, 8

[112]L.H. 17 October 1927, 7

[113]L.H. 30 January 1924, 8

[114]L.H. 8 February 1927, 8; 8 March 1927, 12

[115]L.H. 11 February 1928, 12

[116]L.H. 23 February 1929, 14; 15 June 1935, 7

[117]L.H. 24 November 1930, 5

[118]L.H. 21 November 1930, 5

[119]L.H. 26 November 1930, 5

[120]L.H. 13 November 1931, 9

[121]L.H. 17 November 1931, 6

[122]L.H. 2 March 1940, 7; 4 March 1940 6, 7; 5 March 1940, 7

[123]L.H. 22 January 1945, 7

[124]L.H. 29 June 1977, 7

[125]Pember (1983), 254. Reprinted with the permission of Macmillan Publishing Company, publisher of the Fifth Edition of Mass Media in America by Don R. Pember. Copyright © 1987 by Macmillan Publishing Company.

[126]From: Mass Media III: An Introduction to Modern Communication by Ray Eldon Hiebert, Donald F. Ungurait, Thomas Bohn. © 1982 by Longman Publishing Group, 305. Reprinted with permission from Longman Publishing Group.

[127]L.H. 15 October 1928, 12; Medicine Hat Daily News, 1 December 1920, 14. Occasionally, more than one of Semon's films would show in Lethbridge at the same time, for example, on February 5, 1925, Dull Care played the Empress Theatre while Her Boy Friend was exhibited at the Palace. Fay Wray, 34, who referred to Semon as "comedian and director," informs us that he played Scarecrow in the first Wizard of Oz which he also directed. Prior to his starring in movies, this native from West Point, Mississippi, played juvenile roles in his father's theatre company, became a magician and a newspaper cartoonist, and toured as a tumbler in vaudeville. He was married to the film actress, Dorothy Dawn.

[128]Hiebert, et al., 287

[129]L.H. 25 September 1929, 7; 7 October 1929, 8

[130]Black & Whitney, 288

[131]L.H. 24 December 1930, 5, 10; 5 January 1931, 5; 7 March 1931, 7. In 1931 the Empress Theatre accepted one bushel of wheat as the equivalent of fifty-five cents, one bushel of barley as thirty-five cents, and oats as twenty-five cents.

[132]L.H. 8 October 1927, 14

[133]L.H. Jubilee Edition, 14 June 1935, 11

[134]L.H. 4 May 1928, 16; 5 May 1928, 10

[135]Haver, 43

[136]Haver, 40

[137]L.H. 28 September 1931, 7

[138]Harris, 48. In Nikki, Leach played a character named Cary Lockwood. Apparently, the surname, Grant, was selected randomly from a telephone directory.

[139]Haver, 63

[140]Wray, 257-262 (Filmography)

[141]Wray, 254, 1-10

[142]L.H. 29 September 1931, 7; 2 October 1931, 7

[143]Pember, 128

Chapter Four: Notes

[1]*L.H.* 21 April 1933, 1; 26 April 1933, 1

[2]MacGregor, 262-270, 283, 284

[3]*L.H.* 22 August 1935, 1

[4]MacGregor, 270

[5]MacGregor, 284; *L.H.* 31 May 1943, 1

[6]Johnston & den Otter, 233; *L.H.* 9 August 1944, 1

[7]Johnston & den Otter, 230

[8]*L.H.* 31 December 1937, 13; 31 December 1938, 15; 30 December 1939, section 2, 1

[9]*L.H.* 1 August 1939, 7

[10]*L.H.* 11 September 1939, 1. Street paving projects continued, a new $100,000 LDS church and auditorium on 5th Avenue between 11th and 12th Street was undertaken, new quarters were completed for the British Canadian Trust Company as well as the Greyhound Bus Company; the Broder Canning Company completed an extensive vegetable canning factory which opened in August 1941. A few months before this opening, Western Airlines inaugurated flights between Lethbridge and Great Falls, Montana (see *L.H.* 28 May 1941, 6).

[11]*L.H.* 25 October 1939, 7

[12]*L.H.* 20 July 1940, 7; 23 July 1940, 7

[13]Johnston & den Otter, 139

[14]*L.H.* 7 November 1941, (special edition); 1 December 1944, 1. Kenyon Airport (south of Lethbridge) was opened on 13 June 1939.

[15]*L.H.* 14 January 1942, 1; 21 March 1942, 6; 17 April 1942, 7; 16 May 1942, 7; 30 May 1942, 7; 9 June 1942, 6

[16]*L.H.* 22 September 1988, 1; 21 July 1942, 7; see also 24 August 1942, 7; 12 December 1942, 7

[17]*L.H.* 28 April 1941, 1

[18]*L.H.* 30 September 1942, 1

[19]*L.H.* 31 December 1942, 1; The North African campaign was gathering momentum; on the Russian front, the Nazi siege of Stalingrad was almost broken as the year came to a close.

[20]*L.H.* 9 April 1942, 7

[21]Thomson, 738-751. Russian troops were on the march to Latvia and the Ukraine (recapturing Kiev); Allied troops captured Tunisia and Sicily and invaded Italy, which successively: surrendered, deposed Mussolini, and declared war on its former ally, Germany.

[22]*L.H.* 22 May 1943, 7; 7 August 1943, 7; 18 November 1943, 7; 30 November 1943, 6; 1 December 1943, 9; 2 December 1943, 6; 3 December 1943, 9

[23]*L.H.* 13 January 1943, 6

[24]The Allies began their northern offensive on D Day, June 6, 1944, when their troops invaded the beaches of Normandy. Elsewhere, in the Pacific, the Allies achieved victory in Burma, and the American forces

were fighting their way through the Marshal Islands, the Marianas, Dutch New Guinea, and the Philippines (see Thomson, 738-752).

[25]*L.H.* 16 September 1944, 1

[26]*L.H.* 28 October 1944, 7; 1 December 1944, 1

[27]Thomson, 761

[28]*L.H.* 10 September 1945, 1; 31 January 1946, 1

[29]*L.H.* 31 December 1948, 15

[30]*L.H.* 16 November 1939, 39. Festival competition continued in Saskatchewan and British Columbia.

[31]*L.H.* 28 July 1936, 7

[32]*L.H.* 31 May 1938, 7

[33]*L.H.* 7 October 1950, 25, 29

[34]*L.H.* 13 November 1942, 7. The Purity Dairy vacated the Majestic Theatre building in 1970, at which time it was sold to another dairy company. A few years later, the building was badly damaged by fire, and subsequently, was replaced in the mid 1980s by a one-story professional office complex.

[35]*L.H.* 22 November 1937, 7; 4 January 1938, 7; 22 June 1971, 11

[36]*L.H.* 16 October 1940, 7; 16 November 1940, 7; 30 December 1940, 2. The new Lealta Theatre was located on the southwest corner of 3rd Avenue and 13th Street North.

[37]*L.H.* 18 April 1941, 7

[38]Day & Potts, 15-16; see also Leighton, 18; *L.H.* 13 March 1933, 7

[39]Leighton, 23

[40]Leighton, 18-23

[41]*L.H.* 19 March 1936, 13; see also Leighton, 43

[42]*L.H.* 24 July 1937, 10

[43]Day & Potts, 25

[44]Day & Potts, 23

[45]*L.H.* 1 August 1939, 12

[46]*L.H.* 11 April 1938, 8. Brockett, 627 states that Koch founded the "influential Carolina Playmakers in 1918."

[47]Rutland, ix

[48]*L.H.* 17 April 1939, 8

[49]Plant, 23

[50]*L.H.* 9 June 1939, 8

[51]*L.H.* 13 March 1940, 10

[52]*L.H.* 1 April 1941, 8

[53]*L.H.* 30 June 1941, 7

[54]University of Lethbridge Honorary Degree Citation

[55]University of Lethbridge Honorary Degree Citation. For a more complete chronology of Ringwood's life and career, see Anthony, 13-17; Rutland, VIII - X

[56]Gardner in Benson and Connolly (b), 308. Gardner, 302, 303, also informs us that Governor General Earl Grey primarily sponsored Anglophone musical and dramatic competitions during the years 1907-1911; also, in 1908, "eighteen Cercles on Montreal Island entered the first all-French amateur festival, the Concours de l'île.

[57]*Calgary Herald*, 23 February 1931, 13; *Edmonton Journal*, 23 February 1931, 10

[58]*L.H.* 1 November 1932, 6; 4 November 1932, 8

[59]Day & Potts, 14

[60]Telephone interview: George Mann with Robert M. Hume.

[61]*Calgary Herald*, 19 March 1937, 24

[62]*L.H.* 17 April 1939, 6

[63]*L.H.* 13 April 1942, 8

[64]*L.H.* 13 March 1933, 7

[65]*L.H.* 26 February 1934, 7

[66]*L.H.* 8 February 1936, 11

[67]*L.H.* 22 March 1937, 4

[68]*L.H.* 4 March 1934, 8. Donald Buchanan was a son of W.A. Buchanan, publisher of the *Lethbridge Herald.*

[69]*L.H.* 5 June 1936, 7; 17 October 1936, 6; 9 March 1937, 8; 22 March 1937, 9

[70]DDF Program, 1937; L.H. 30 April 1937, 12

[71]*L.H.* 23 February 1931, 6

[72]*L.H.* 26 February 1934, 8; 27 February 1934, 7

[73]*L.H.* 19 August 1940, 7

[74]*L.H.* 4 January 1941, 7 states that Johnson did not return to Lethbridge because of an offer from the Disney Studio. In fact, no contract was completed.

[75]*L.H.* 30 January 1933, 7; 8 June 1933, 6; 18 September 1944, 7

[76]*L.H.* 9 March 1933, 7

[77]*L.H.* 27 March 1935, 9; 26 October 1935, 11

[78]*L.H.* 5 September 1936, 7; 8 September 1936, 6; 9 September 1936, 7

[79]*L.H.* 8 June 1933, 6; 3 July 1933, 7

[80]*L.H.* 4 March 1933, 7

[81]*L.H.* 14 June 1933, 11; 18 September 1934, 7; 23 September 1935, 7; 12 October 1935, 7; 6 April 1937, 7; 9 October 1937, 10; 13 November 1937, 7

[82]*L.H.* 10 May 1939, 8

[83] *L.H.* 16 January 1937, 8

[84] *L.H.* 16 November 1937, 7

[85] *L.H.* 6 April 1937, 7

[86] *L.H.* 15 March 1938, 8

[87] L.H. 18 March 1937, 7

[88] *L.H.* 6 April 1937, 7

[89] *L.H.* 4 April 1939, 6; 10 May 1939, 8

[90] *L.H.* 29 March 1939, 7

[91] *L.H.* 10 May 1939, 8

[92] *L.H.* 21 November 1953, 14; 26 March 1955, 5; interview notes supplied by Lawrence Adams, Dance Collection Danse; personal interviews

[93] *L.H.* 8 November 1935, 6. Other featured dancers were Bernadette's brother, Crawford Fisher, and Allan Lewis who performed a tap dance routine. Stafford Peat and Vivian Buffett danced a ballroom dance number.

[94] *L.H.* 6 November 1935, 8

[95] *L.H.* 25 June 1957, 9

[96] *L.H.* 28 April 1934, 7; 17 November 1936, 6

[97] *L.H.* 10 May 1965, 10; 14 May 1965, 16

[98] *L.H.* 18 February 1932, 7

[99] *L.H.* 12 June 1925, 14

[100] *L.H.* 21 May 1938, 8, 9

[101] During World War II, Robin Ritchie served in both the army and the airforce. Following his release from the armed services, Ritchie became a career personnel officer and eventually joined the federal civil service in Halifax. Finding that the bureaucratic life was not personally satisfying, Ritchie entered the Anglican ministry after graduating from King's College in Halifax (1964). His calling led him to South Africa but the stay there was short-lived; he was formally asked to leave the country because of his anti apartheid sentiments. The Robin Ritchie family then moved to England.

[102] *L.H.* 11 December 1934, 7

[103] *L.H.* 14 December 1937, 7

[104] *L.H.* 21 October 1937, 8

[105] *L.H.* 12 February 1940, 1

[106] *L.H.* 13 December 1928, 7; 25 February 1939, 10

[107] Haig, 103; *L.H.* 1 June 1943, 7; 10 December 1954, 10; 3 February 1955, 11

[108] In 1990 Brown was named to the Canadian Association of Broadcasters' Hall of Fame

[109] *L.H.* 2 January 1952, 8

[110] *L.H.* 8 September 1959, 14

[111] *L.H.* 22 April 1937, 23; 10 March 1938, 11

[112] *L.H.* 25 July 1944, 6

[113] *L.H.* 5 September 1956, 16

[114] *L.H.* 12 April 1940, 8

[115] *L.H.* 18 November 1941, 7

[116] *L.H.* 21 December 1940, 11

[117] *L.H.* 18 November 1941, 7

[118] *L.H.* 6 April 1942, 8; 17 April 1942, 6

[119] *L.H.* 11 April 1942, 8

[120] *L.H.* 2 March 1944, 6; 26 July 1944, 8; Patrick O'Neill in Benson & Connolly (b), 31 states, "A new sixth group put together 'About Faces of 1944'—starring Margaret Cross..."

[121] *L.H.* 26 July 1944, 7

[122] *L.H.* 5 May 1947, 6

[123] *L.H.* 9 February 1952, 8

[124] *L.H.* 2 June 1952, 7

[125] *L.H.* 17 April 1942, 6

[126] *L.H.* 18 April 1945, 7; 20 April 1945, 6; see also Haig, 642

[127] *L.H.* 27 March 1928, 14

[128] *L.H.* 3 September 1957, 3

[129] *L.H.* 29 November 1947, 8; Blum, 336; *L.H.* 19 August 1946, 7; 17 September 1946, 6; 22 September 1946, 8

[130] *L.H.* 23 March 1942, 7

[131] L.H. 12 October 1943, 6, 7

[132] *L.H.* 23 October 1928, 11

[133] Kallman, Potvin and Winters, 982

[134] McNeil & Wolfe, 208, 215

[135] Kallman, Potvin and Winters, 982

[136] Kallman, Potvin and Winters, 983

[137] *L.H.* 24 December 1943, 8; 20 September 1944, 8; 20 March 1945, 8

[138] *L.H.* 19 August 1936, 9; 18 February 1939, 8; interview notes supplied by Lawrence Adams, Dance Collection Danse; interview: Eildon Kondaks

[139] *L.H.* 2 June 1943, 2; 4 June 1943, 7

[140] *L.H.* 19 June 1943, 11

[141] *L.H.* 29 December 1941, 6; 28 November 1944, 6

[142] *L.H.* 12 February 1945, 7

[143] *L.H.* 19 March 1943, 2; 27 March 1943, 2

[144] *L.H.* 26 October 1943, 8

[145] *L.H.* 6 January 1934, 7

[146] *L.H.* 10 February 1934, 6; 27 March 1935, 7

[147] L.H. 19 July 1940, 7

[148] *L.H.* 24 February 1940, 14

[149] *L.H.* 6 February 1943, 7; 9 February 1943, 7

[150] *L.H.* 7 April 1938, 7

[151] *L.H.* 24 July 1940, 8; 15 August 1940, 8

[152] *L.H.* 19 October 1940, 13; 21 October 1940, 8; 22 October, 8; 23 October 1940, 8; 24 October 1940, 9

[153] *L.H.* 7 May 1945, 7

[154] *L.H.* 20 June 1941, 9

[155] *L.H.* 1 August 1941, 2; 2 August 1941, 10; 4 August 1941, 8; 25 August 1941, 8

[156] *L.H.* 21 February 1944, 6

[1]MacGregor, 298

[2]*L.H.* 5 July 1946, 1; 2 January 1947, 7; 17 September 1949, 2nd section, 46-47; 31 December 1948, 17

[3]*L.H.* 31 December 1954, 22; "Main Street" was basically transported from 5th Street South to 4th Avenue South

[4]*L.H.* 31 December 1956, 23

[5]*L.H.* 31 December 1960, 9

[6]*L.H.* 21 September 1957, 10

[7]*L.H.* 19 January 1957, 9; 31 December 1957, 18-23

[8]*L.H.* 16 October 1965, 14

[9]*L.H.* 29 July 1966, 1

[10]*L.H.* 18 January 1968, 9. In 1991-92, the University's budget was about $43 million.

[11]*L.H.* 8 October 1970, 15; 4 June 1970, 10; 28 January 1969, 13; the malls were College Mall and Centre Village Mall

[12]From *English-Canadian Theatre* by Eugene Benson and L.W. Conolly, © Oxford University Press Canada 1987, 86. Used by permission of the publisher; Usmiani in A. Wagner (a), 148

[13]Benson & Conolly (a), 70; Patterson & Gould, 170-178

[14]Patterson and Gould, 212-216

[15]*L.H.* 25 May 1955, 16; Patterson and Gould, 215-216

[16]Patterson & Gould, 218

[17]Horenblas in A. Wagner (a), 148

[18]Benson and Conolly (a), 68; Leighton, 48; *L.H.* 17 September 1946, 6

[19]*L.H.* 18 July 1955, 11; Leighton, 71-73

[20]Czarnecki in A. Wagner (a), 35

[21]Walsh, passim

[22]Peake in A. Wagner (a), 102

[23]Patterson and Gould, 196-198

[24]Dyba, 139

[25]*L.H.* 25 March 1958, 18; 10 April 1958, 14; 1 October 1970, 9

[26]*L.H.* 3 April 1964, 18; 26 February 1960, 12; 28 July 1970, 9

[27]*L.H.* 8 October 1969, 17; 10 August 1968, 13. Following their discharge from the armed services after World War II, Doug and Bob Shackleford became associated with their father's theatre business.

[28]*L.H.* 12 January 1954, 9

[29]Johnston and den Otter, p. 173

[30]*L.H.* 15 December 1964, 9

[31]*L.H.* 12 January 1965, 9

[32]*L.H.* 11 January 1965, 11; 10 July 1966, 12

[33]*L.H.* 2 May 1966, 1, 9-10; Official Yates Spring Program

[34]Personal interview: Dr. Wayne Matkin

[35]*L.H.* 1 May 1946, 7; 3 May 1946, 6; 6 May 1946, 7

[36]*L.H.* 21 October 1961, 14; 14 October 1961, 10

[37]*L.H.* 23 September 1959, 16; 3 September 1968, 10

[38]*L.H.* 22 February 1950, 6

[39]*L.H.* 18 November 1950, 6; 11 December 1950, 7; 12 December 1950, 7

[40]*L.H.* 10 January 1951, 6

[41]*L.H.* 18 January 1951, 8; 27 January 1951, 6; 14 November 1951, 7

[42]*L.H.* 8 January 1951, 18

[43]*L.H.* 9 April 1957, 4; 12 April 1957, 4; 16 April 1957, 4; for rebuttals and further discussion see *L.H.* 10 April 1957, 4; 11 April 1957, 4; 17 April 1957, 4

[44]*L.H.* 18 June 1955, 13; see also 27 November 1951, 7

[45]*L.H.* 9 May 1953, 9

[46]*L.H.* 23 January 1952, 1, 2

[47]Personal interview: Yvonne Hohm

[48]According to the fifth Director of the National Gallery, Jean Sutherland Boggs (56), Donald Buchanan had also been active in founding the National Industrial Design Council (in 1948), the Canadian Film Institute, and the magazine *Canadian Art* which he edited from 1944-1959. In this latter year, Buchanan was named Acting Director of the National Gallery. After a few months in this role, Buchanan resigned from the Gallery. In 1963 he was appointed to the Gallery's Board of Trustees. From the *National Gallery of Canada* by Jean Sutherland Boggs, © Oxford University Press Canada 1971. Used by permission of the publisher.

[49]*L.H.* 22 June 1954, 10; the Burton W. James scholarship was established to honor James who had been Chairman of the Drama Division at the BSFA from 1947 until his death in 1951 (see *L.H.* 12 June 1953, 9)

[50]*L.H.* 25 April 1955, 10

[51]*L.H.* 30 September 1953, 18

[52]*L.H.* 4 November 1961, 3

[53]*L.H.* 7 November 1970, 9

[54]*L.H.* 27 January 1973, 7; 22 June 1973, 13; *Calgary Herald* 30 January 1973, 14. The screenplay was based on Fruet's play of the same name.

[55]*L.H.* 25 May 1973, 14

[56]Programs: Little Theatre Group of Toronto [*They Went Thataway* (12 August 1954)], Mountain Playhouse [*George Washington Slept Here* (1954 season)], The Crest Theatre [*A Jig for the Gypsy* (14 September, 1954)]; Letter of Contract to Bill Lazaruk from Brian Maller, Administrator; Murray and Donald Davis Ltd., The Crest Theatre (31 August, 1954)

[57]Playgoers' Newsletter, 19 October 1955 (Playgoers Scrapbooks)

[58]*L.H.* 29 November 1955, 10

[59]*L.H.* 4 May 1959, 9

[60]Interview: Kaye Robison

[61]*L.H.* 3 July 1942, 8; 11 July 1947, 8

[62]*L.H.* 4 June 1968, 10; 21 September 1968, 18; 26 October 1968, 3; 13 August 1971, 12

[63]*L.H.* 5 August 1970, 14; Coaldale Historical Society, 680-681 (see also *L.H.* 1 October 1987, A3)

[64]*L.H.* 13 April 1971, 10

[65]*L.H.* 11 January 1965, 11

[66]*L.H.* 26 November 1968, 12

[67]*L.H.* 27 March 1968, 18; 25 November 1989, B11

[68]Sandi Balcovske was nominated for Dora Mavor Moore awards (Toronto's annual theatre awards) in directing for the Second City productions, *When Bush Comes to Shove* (1990) and *New Democrats on the Block* (1991).

[69]*L.H.* 23 March 1964, 1, 2

[70]*L.H.* 28 March 1960, 1, 2

[71]*L.H.* 29 May 1969, 14; James taught at every level in the Lethbridge public schools; she retired from her position at the LCI in June 1969

[72]*L.H.* 5 March 1955, 9; 9 March 1955, 14

[73]*L.H.* 11 February 1957, 1, 2; 7 February 1957, 1, 2

[74]*L.H.* 25 March 1958, 18; 12 March 1988, 3

[75]*L.H.* 28 March 1960, 1, 2

[76]*L.H.* 12 April 1965, 1; 13 March 1967, 1, 15; 18 November 1963, 1, 2

[77]*L.H.* 4 December 1962, 10

[78]*L.H.* 1 February 1986, C1

[79]*L.H.* 1 April 1963, 1, 2

[80]*L.H.* 22 May 1962, 3; 30 October 1962, 10

[81]*L.H.* 12 March 1970, 1

[82]*L.H.* 25 May 1970, 10

[83]*L.H.* 8 April 1954, 10

[84]*L.H.* 7 January 1966, 1, 2; 5 January 1966, 17

[85]*L.H.* 8 November 1963, 9

[86]*L.H.* 18 April 1963, 10; 1 May 1963, 17; 9 May 1963, 12; 10 May 1963, 12

[87]*L.H.* 13 March 1967, 15

[88]L.H. 4 April 1957, 9; 29 April 1957, 1; 1 May 1957, 4

[89]Jubilee Program

[90]L.H. 21 May 1963, 2

[91]L.H. 16 May 1963, 1, 2

[92]L.H. 14 August 1957, 13; 5 July 1963, 10

[93]L.H. 5 July 1963, 10

[94]L.H. 7 February 1964, 10 (see also, L.H. 10 June 1971, 14)

[95]The recording is a Caedmon production.

[96]L.H. 14 February 1966, 2

[97]L.H. 1 April 1963, 2; 23 March 1964, 1, 2; 13 March 1967, 1, 15

[98]L.H. 1 April 1963, 1, 2

[99]L.H. 25 May 1970, 10

[100]L.H. 6 August 1966, 12

[101]L.H. 18 June 1955, 13

[102]L.H. 9 May 1957, 10

[103]L.H. 1 December 1955, 14

[104]L.H. 25 March 1958, 9; 10 January 1959, 13; 1 October 1959, 9; 7 January 1961, 12; 4 October 1961, 8; 21 October 1961, 3; 11 January 1963, 10; 11 January 1964, 23; 12 February 1965, 3; 8 October 1965, 12

[105]L.H. 26 November 1963, 10

[106]L.H. 8 November 1963, 9

[107]L.H. 13 March 1967, 10; Interview: Murray & Kaye Robison. The Lethbridge Herald incorrectly reported that the dwarf sketch was a portrait donated by Playgoers.

[108]Personal interviews: Murray Robison

[109]L.H. 18 March 1952, 7; Interview: Murray Robison

[110]L.H. 12 June 1953, 9

[111]Personal interviews: Murray Robison, Jennie Emery

[112]L.H. 12 April 1965, 1

[113]Interview & review notes: Murray Robison. The Lethbridge Herald report of 25 April 1967, 3, incorrectly referred to the Vernon play as Gilliam.

[114]Since 1966, a local dance teacher, Muriel Jolliffe, had been organizing and directing Christmas pantomimes under the auspices of the Allied Arts Council. In 1968 Coaldale Little Theatre agreed to produce the annual presentation and to provide backstage assistance and onstage participants, where necessary.

[115]L.H. 11 March 1955, 9; 25 April 1955, 10

[116]L.H. 22 November 1960, 3

[117]6 November 1965, 6

[118]L.H. 18 January 1956, 15; 20 January 1956, 1

[119]L.H. 6 November 1959, 12; 7 November 1959, 13; 23 November 1959, 1

[120]L.H. 20 January 1956, 1; 1 April 1963, 1, 2; 13 March 1967, 1, 15

[121]L.H. 13 March 1958, 1

[122]L.H. 20 January 1956, 1; 20 March 1961, 1

[123]L.H. 1 April 1957, 1,2

[124]L.H. 30 October 1964, 11

[125]L.H. 4 April 1953, 13; 7 November 1959, 13

[126]L.H. 20 January 1956, 1

[127]L.H. 17 March 1958, 1

[128]L.H. 20 March 1961, 1

[129]L.H. 30 October 1964, 11; 13 March 1967, 1, 15

[130]L.H. 17 March 1958, 1; 20 March 1961, 1

[131]Personal interview: Audrey Davidson

[132]L.H. 2 February 1989, A2

[133]L.H. 20 March 1961, 1; 1 April 1963, 1, 2; 12 April 1965, 1; 13 March 1967, 1, 15

[134]L.H. 5 August 1970, 14

[135]L.H. 1 April 1963, 1, 2; 12 April 1965, 1; 18 November 1964, 20

[136]L.H. 4 August 1973, 5

[137]Coaldale Historical Society, 351

[138]L.H. 27 March 1965, 18

[139]Personal interview: Joy Pritchard

[140]Alberta Drama League, Lethbridge District One Act Drama Festival programs, 1955, 1956 (Playgoers' scrapbooks)

[141]L.H. 22 November 1960, 3; 20 March 1961, 1

[142]L.H. 26 March 1962, 9

[143]L.H. 2 March 1963, 14; 11 March 1963, 3, 10; 13 March 1963, 16

[144]L.H. clipping, 1968, Our Town Workshop Scrapbook

[145]personal interview: Joy Pritchard

[146]Scrapbook: Our Town Workshop

[147]L.H. 31 March 1966, 2; see also M.H.D.N. 4 April 1966, 3

[148]L.H. 18 November 1963, 1

[149]L.H. 4 March 1966, 7; C.H. 8 March 1946, 15; M.H.D.N. 25 March 1948, 3; L.H. 9 March 1948, 8; L.H. 31 January 1950, 8

[150]L.H. 11 April 1951, 5; 31 January 1950, 8

[151]Alberta Regional Festival programs

[152]L.H. 16 December 1955, 14; 16 January 1956, 8; 13 January 1983, B8

[153]The Church of Jesus Christ of Latter Day Saints divides the territory which it serves into large administrative districts, each of which contains smaller units called Stakes. The Taylor Stake covered a section of southern Alberta centred on the town of Raymond.

[154]L.H. 6 February 1957, 13

[155]Edmonton Journal, 30 November 1963, 23

[156]Lee, 304-315

[157]L.H. 15 January 1983, 131

[158]L.H. 23 March 1946, 6

[159]John Doe advanced to the Western Drama Festival held in Winnipeg on May 25. The other competitors were Regina Little Theatre (Mooncalf Mugford) and Vancouver Little Theatre (The Terrible Meek). Mooncalf Mugford was the victor; its director, Hilda Buckley, was also singled out as the best actress (see C.H. 27 May 1946, 14).

[160]Calgary Herald, 27 March 1946, 8; Dyba, 57

[161]L.H. 3 February 1954, 22; 8 April 1958, 10; 14 February 1975, 17; 17 February 1975, 2, 20; see also: King, Ag, 10-16; Dyba, 124

[162]DDF Program, 1947; David Gardner in Benson & Conolly (b), 306

[163]L.H. 11 April 1951, 5

[164]Alberta Regional Festival programs

[165]L.H. 30 August 1967, 5

[166]Dyba, 139

[167]L.H. 17 March 1967, 3; Dyba 139

[168]L.H. 6 April 1968, 14

[169]L.H. 9 September 1968, 9

[170]L.H. 18 December 1968, 13

[171]L.H. 14 March 1969, 14

[172]Program: Western Canada Arts Festival; see also L.H. 10 January 1969, 10; 6 February 1969, 10; 14 February 1969, 14; 19 February 1969, 3; 24 February 1969, 9; 4 March 1969, 10; 7 March 1969, 7; 10 March 1969, 10; 11 March 1969, 9; 12 March 1969, 18; 14 March 1969, 14; 15 March 1969, 17; 17 March 1969, 12

[173]L.H. 27 March 1969, 14

[174]L.H. 19 May 1970, 1

[175]L.H. 26 June 1970, 11

[176]Informant: Charles Schott

[177]L.H. 23 May 1970, 2

[178]L.H. 17 April 1971, 13

[179]L.H. 11 March 1955, 9

[180]L.H. 18 November 1963, 1, 2

[181]L.H. 4 April 1953, 13

[182]L.H. 23 September 1959, 12; 4 February 1968, 10

183 *L.H.* 16 January 1954, 11

184 *L.H.* 1 November 1960, 10. The Lethbridge Symphony Association, spearheaded by Dr. and Mrs. W.A. Nelson, was incorporated in February 1961 with Dr. B. Wayne Matkin as its first president.

185 *L.H.* 1 November 1960, 10

186 *L.H.* 15 August 1969, 7

187 *L.H.* 16 May 1961, 13

188 *L.H.* 6 September 1962, 12

189 *L.H.* 18 September 1961, 3

190 *L.H.* 15 August 1969, 7

191 *L.H.* 23 July 1963, 10

192 *L.H.* 4 January 1967, 18

193 *L.H.* 29 June 1966, 17; 17 July 1969, 11

194 LMT 1967 program, *South Pacific*

195 Much of the personal background data relating to professional and semi-professional performers was obtained from notes in the various Lethbridge Musical Theatre programs.

196 *L.H.* 21 November 1964, 13

197 *L.H.* 9 August 1963, 10; see also Leighton, 71

198 *L.H.* 18 November 1977 Leisure & T.V. Week, 2

199 *L.H.* 20 August 1966, 14

200 Coaldale Historical Society, 349

201 *L.H.* 26 April 1951, 3; 27 September 1951, 7

202 *L.H.* 19 July 1951, 3

203 *L.H.* 15 September 1951, 8

204 *L.H.* 1 September 1956, 14; personal interview: Mrs. Nettie Livingstone

205 *L.H.* 1 June 1953, 10; 16 January 1954, 10

206 *L.H.* 18 January 1955, 10. The first performance of this group, under director-producer, Edythe Heavener, occurred in Edmonton's Victoria Composite High School in February 1955.

207 Official Opening program: Southern Alberta Jubilee Auditorium

208 *L.H.* 25 October 1958, 16

209 *L.H.* 1 April 1959, 22

210 *L.H.* 29 May 1961

211 *L.H.* 4 September 1962, 3

212 *L.H.* 8 February 1964, 13. The 1967 dance festival committee included: President, Dr. Keith Lowings; Secretary, Jean Dogterom; Treasurer, Jack Kimber; Honorary President, Joe Balla; Technical Advisor, Muriel Jolliffe and Executive Members, Terry Bland, Jintie Welsh, Betty Ridley, and Ray Jolliffe.

213 *L.H.* 18 January 1975, 17; 3 September 1988, B12; *L.H. Campus* Vol. 1, #14, 4 February 1982, 7.

214 *L.H.* 31 October 1987, C1, Interview: George Mann with Muriel Jolliffe.

215 *L.H.* 2 September 1965, 3

216 *L.H.* 21 March 1953, 3, 9

217 *L.H.* 21 March 1953, 9

218 *L.H.* 28 May 1953, 9

219 *L.H.* 1 April 1953, 13

220 *L.H.* 20 May 1953, 9

221 *L.H.* 2 November 1974, 7

222 *L.H.* 30 August 1989, B7. Later, Ontkean became identified with the role, Sheriff Harry S. Truman, which he played in the T.V. series, *Twin Peaks.*

223 *L.H.* 21 July 1953, 10

224 *L.H.* 27 April 1954, 10

225 *L.H.* 10 July 1954, 14

226 *L.H.* 21 August 1954, 9

227 *L.H.* 18 September 1954, 10; 20 September 1954, 10

228 *L.H.* 27 January 1954, 3; 29 January 1954, 9

229 *L.H.* 3 June 1955, 3. The Board was comprised of Harry and Jessie Baalim, Denise Black, Stan Sawicki, Agnes Stafford, Reno Lizzi, Lena Connor, Mrs. W.O. Hay, and Mrs. W.E. Huckvale.

230 *L.H.* 6 August 1955, 10

231 Telephone interview and correspondence: Dean Goodman with George Mann. Since 1955, Goodman has directed and acted for numerous professional stage companies in San Francisco. In 1978 he received the Bay Area Theatre Critics award for his role in *The Little Foxes.* His acting career was still going strong in 1992 when he appeared in a one-man show, *Windows and Mirrors,* at the Phoenix Theatre, San Francisco. Throughout his professional theatrical career, Goodman has produced, directed, or acted in approximately 400 plays. In addition, his film and T.V. credits include: Mr. Bennington, the Chairman of the Board, in the 1987 Lucus/Coppola movie, *Tucker,* and a major part in the made-for-cable film, *Fear;* guest appearances in television drama (including a recurring role in *Santa Barbara);* industrial films; and T.V. commercials. In 1986 he published *San Francisco Stages: A Concise History (1849-1986).* He was also a weekly contributor to *Drama-Logue,* a Hollywood trade paper.

232 *L.H.* 3 February 1956, 9; see also Patterson and Gould, 215-218

233 *L.H.* 25 May 1955, 16

234 *L.H.* 3 March 1961, 14

235 *L.H.* 4 December 1964, 11; 25 January 1965, 18; 1 February 1965, 9; see also Pettigrew and Portman (a), 19

236 *L.H.* 17 March 1967, 9

237 *L.H.* 24 January 1952, 7; 11 May 1954, 10; 30 September 1957, 18

238 *L.H.* 24 January 1952, 7

239 *L.H.* 3 December, 1958, 14

240 *L.H.* 24 March 1954, 13; 7 January 1958, 11; 18 February 1958, 9; 30 October 1958, 18

241 *L.H.* 2 February 1951, 2; 3 February 1955, 11

242 Leighton, 73

243 *L.H.* 15 November 1949, 6

Chapter Six: Notes

1 *L.H.* 7 September 1971, 1, 4. Senator Gladstone died on 4 September 1971.

2 *L.H.* 27 September 1971, 9; 21 September 1972, 1; 23 September 1972, 1, 17-19; 25 September 1972, 1, 13, 14

3 *L.H.* 8 March 1991, 1

4 Johnston & den Otter, 191

5 *Maclean's* 9 October 1989, 62

6 Fraser in Benson & Conolly (b), 242-243

7 Lawrence in Benson & Conolly (b), 46

8 Mullaly in Benson & Conolly (b), 542

9 Doolittle in Benson & Conolly (b), 527

10 Czarnecki in A. Wagner (a), 41

11 University of Alberta Alumni Association, Autumn 1988, 20

12 Czarnecki in A. Wagner (a), 41-44

13 Usmiani in A. Wagner (a), 49

14 Gray in A. Wagner (a), 24

15 Usmiani in A. Wager (a), 50

16 Filewod in Benson & Conolly (b), 315

17 Usmiani in A. Wagner (a), 57

18 Czarnecki in A.Wagner (a), 46

19 *L.H.* 21 March 1986, A5; 8 February 1990, C4

20 Knowles in Benson & Conolly (b), 286-287. The Department of Dramatic Arts, University of Lethbridge produced *Prague* in the winter of 1992.

21 Personal interview: Richard Epp; see also *L.H.* 27 June 1987, A11

22 *L.H.* 25 January 1986, A10; Theatre Calgary program

[23]Young & Young in *Canadian Theatre Review*, 29 (Winter, 81), 112-120

[24]Day in *CTR*, 45 (Winter, 1985), 43; Wallace in *CTR*, 49 (Winter, 1986), 117; Nothof in *CTR*, 54 (Spring, 1988), 89

[25]Nothof in *CTR*, 50 (Spring, 1987), 72

[26]Czarnecki in *CTR*, 45 (Winter, 1985), 11

[27]*L.H.* 27 January 1978, 7; Leighton, 7, 154

[28]*L.H.* 5 September 1981, E2

[29]*L.H.* 5 September 1981, B7

[30]*L.H.* 5 September 1981, E2

[31]*L.H.* 5 September 1981, E9

[32]Brochure: Performing Arts Series: School of Fine Arts, U of L 1987-88

[33]*L.H.* 10 January 1989, A5; see also *L.H.* 24 June 1987, A3

[34]*L.H.* 29 April 1989, B11

[35]*Toronto Globe and Mail*, 17 March 1989, A13

[36]*L.H.* 23 August 1974, 7

[37]*L.H.* 12 November 1979, 14

[38]*L.H.* 16 November 1976, 11

[39]In 1990 David Mann received the Sterling Award (named for Elizabeth Sterling Haynes) as Best Supporting Actor for his portrayal of Huey Maximillian Bonfigliano in the Phoenix Theatre (Edmonton) production of *Italian American Reconciliation*.

[40]In 1990 Laurin Mann began a Ph.D. program in Theatre History at the University of Toronto.

[41]Siebert's first costume designs were for the Alberta Ballet Company's presentation, *Passages*. He studied at the Helen Lefeaux School of Fashion Design where he was recognized as an outstanding student. He has since designed for dance companies throughout Canada and the United States.

[42]*L.H.* 7 June 1974, 13

[43]*L.H.* 8 April 1975, 16; 2 June 1975, 17; 12 July 1975, 3, 4

[44]*L.H.* 24 May 1974, 7

[45]*L.H.* 4 August 1977, 16

[46]A sister, Lori Ully, specialized in modelling and operated the very successful Silhouette Academy of Modelling in the city. Another younger sister, Teri Jo, was a featured singer and dancer in the 1985 Centre Stage production of *A Chorus Line*.

[47]*L.H.* 13 August 1985, A12

[48]*L.H.* 10 March 1970, 16

[49]*L.H.* 22 August 1981, B1, 2; 31 October 1987, C1

[50]*L.H.* 21 June 1984, A11

[51]*L.H.* 9 June 1989, C4

[52]In the early 1990s, Tiffany Knight was with the National Ballet, while Kendra Moore danced with the Austin Texas Ballet.

[53]*L.H.* 9 February 1974, 8

[54]*L.H.* 5 January 1974, B4

[55]*L.H.* 14 February 1966, 2. Other actors in the production were: Gloria Kunkel, Roy Kariatsumari, Frank Cummins, Sandra Tiberg, Beverly Hamilton, Don Gray, Judy Fairfield, and Heintz Fredrick. [About twenty years later, Beverly (Hamilton) Merkley formed the very successful Star Singers, an organization devoted to the development of musical theatre performance among Lethbridge children and youth]. Backstage assistance was provided by: Maureen Byrne, Marjorie Lane, Peggy Matthews, Jim Connor, Bill McIntyre, Marilyn Enes, Cheryl Hall and Richard Ringdahl.

[56]Shortly thereafter, Jensen was killed in an automobile accident.

[57]Tyson's plays took awards in the following Alberta playwriting competitions: 1972 Three Act, *Love Play*, 3rd prize; 1972 One Act, *Lines of Enquiry*, 2nd; 1973 One Act, *Companion Piece*, 2nd; 1975 One Act, *Political Asylum* 1st. *Companion Piece* was also published in *Canadian Drama*, Fall 1980. *Lines of Enquiry* was broadcast over radio station CKUA in April 1973; *Graft* was heard on CBC radio in February 1976.

[58]*L.H.* 17 August 1969, 9

[59]*L.H.* 29 March 1978, 14; program: *Kristallnacht*

[60]*L.H.* 5 September 1981, E9

[61]Personal interview: Brian Parkinson

[62]Personal interview: John A. Johnston

[63]U of L Calendar

[64]Seminar Program: The Education of a Film Maker, March 19-21, 1982

[65]U of L Calendar

[66]U of L Calendar

[67]Personal interview: Neil Boyden

[68]U of L Calendar

[69]*L.H.* 5 September 1981, E9; 9 April 1987, B6; U of L Convocation program, 11 September 1981.

[70]By the end of the decade, provincial funding was withdrawn and TheatreXtra was discontinued.

[71]*L.H.* 25 May 1974, 8

[72]*L.H.* 10 April 1982, D14; 31 July 1982, B2

[73]*L.H.* 31 December 1980, B3

[74]*L.H.* 16 April 1983, A10; 22 July 1983, A3; 7 April 1984, A11; registration applications; personal interview: Joan Waterfield

[75]Personal interview: Brian Parkinson

[76]Parkinson in Benson & Conolly; (b) 197-198

[77]Personal interview: Brian Parkinson. All additional information about the Great West Summer Theatre Co. was obtained from Brian Parkinson, director. The original

company was comprised of the following nine members: Sherry Bachue, Robert Chomiak, Sophia David, Richard Hamilton, Lori Isberg, Judy Ann McCarthy, Buffy McGale, Melwyn Morning Bull and Vivian Walper.

[78]In the summer of 1990, the company moved to the Yates Memorial Centre in Lethbridge; as well it changed its name to the New West Summer Theatre Company.

[79]*L.H.* 6 March 1978, 18

[80]Coaldale Historical Society, 351

[81]*L.H.* 22 May 1973, 14

[82]*L.H.* 18 October 1974, 16

[83]In 1991 Evins was awarded a joint Special Achievement scroll by Playgoers and LMT; she was also recognized as a Life Time Member by Playgoers. Evins died in July, 1992.

[84]*L.H.* 17 October 1979, 35

[85]*L.H.* 26 April 1974, 8; 22 October 1976, 16; 6 May 1983, A12

[86]*L.H.* 23 July 1974, 4; 23 February 1976, 15; 22 April 1976, 14; 25 February 1977, 7; 21 October 1977, 6

[87]*L.H.* 6 February 1986, A11

[88]Haig, 468

[89]Noted local skaters were Mark and Janet Hominuke, Bill and Cory Jo Petrunik, Donna Rude, Grant Sorenson, Anne Lanier, Maura Knowles, Holy McGuire, Mickey Brown, Jennifer Chue, and Natalie Reimer.

[90]*L.H.* 16 June 1971, 14

[91]*L.H.* 14 July 1971, 20

[92]*L.H.* 27 May 1972, 15; 14 January 1973, 22

[93]*L.H.* 31 December, 1980, B3; 1 August 1981, B2

[94]*L.H.* 17 April 1982, C11

[95]*L.H.* 20 May 1971, 7; 22, 6 May 1971, 17; 25 May 1971, 16; 31 May 1971, 10; festival program

[96]*L.H.* 26 February 1973, 12

[97]*L.H.*, 20 February 1975, 18; unidentified clipping, Playgoers' scrapbook

[98]*L.H.* 26 February 1979, 5

[99]*L.H.* 31 December 1980, B3

[100]*L.H.* 28 February 1983, A2

[101]*L.H.* 6 March 1978, 18

[102]In 1989 Mark Russell was named Best Actor for his portrayal of Woodruff Gately in *PVT Wars*; in 1990, Sheila Pisko captured Best Actress for Marion in *On Tidy Endings*.

[103]*L.H.* 26 April 1980, B10

[104]*L.H.* 16 July 1981, B4

[105]*L.H.* 6 April 1959, 9

[106]*L.H.* 29 December 1970, 11; LMT program, *The King and I*

[107]LMT program: *Man of La Mancha*

[108]LMT program: *South Pacific*, 1988

[109]LMT program: *Mame*

[110]LMT programs: *The King and I*; *Kiss Me Kate*

[111]LMT programs: *Pajama Game*; *Cabaret*

[112]Jack Warburton died in early 1991.

[113]*L.H.* 27 April 1983, A3

[114]In 1989 Haslam was awarded a Sterling Award for outstanding performance by an actor in a supporting role for his portrayal in *Burn This* (Citadel Theatre).

[115]The original executive of CSPS consisted of Rick Braund (president), Gloria Serkin (vice president), Hazel Skaronski (treasurer), Fran Rude (artistic director), Rhonda Ruston, Winstan Jones, and Candy Williams (business directors).

[116]In the early 1990s, Mikuliak graduated from the University of Lethbridge with Bachelor of Music and Bachelor of Education degrees. He offered vocal instruction in the Conservatory program, University of Lethbridge, he sat on the Board of Marquee Theatre Workshop, he performed in productions for LMT, and he took on the task as vocal director for a number of LMT productions.

[117]In 1989 Mark Russell spearheaded the establishment of a resident dinner theatre company in Lethbridge, The Round Street Dinner Theatre. He interested some young local entrepreneurs in financing the theatre, and he became artistic director. Russell remained as artistic director when new owners took over the theatre and renamed it Stages. Lack of patronage support led to its closure in the spring of 1991.

[118]Rewa in Benson and Conolly (b), 439-441

[119]Rewa in Benson and Conolly (b), 340

[120]Rewa in Benson and Conolly (b), 340; *L.H.* 19 May 1976. 13

[121]*L.H.* 7 June 1978, 14

[122]*L.H.* 4 December 1970, 18

[123]*L.H.* 3 August 1977, 14; 13 August 1977, 11

[124]*L.H.* 7 October 1978, 16

[125]*L.H.* 31 December 1980, B3

[126]*L.H.* 23 August 1979, 13; 18 September 1979, 12

[127]*L.H.* 4 September 1984, A5

[128]*L.H.* 14 January 1987, B4

[129]*L.H.* 19 June 1987, C6

[130]*L.H.* 10 March 1987, B7

[131]*L.H.* 9 October 1987, A5

APPENDICES

Key to the Appendices

The following abbreviations are used throughout the Appendices presented in this text:

1. Organization and Performance Facilities

AAC	Allied Arts Council
ADL	Alberta Drama League
ADFA	Alberta Drama Festival Association
A1AF	Alberta One Act Festival
ARF	Alberta Regional Festival (DDF)
BAC	Bowman Arts Centre
BCH	Building Company's Hall
BMH	NWMP Barracks Mess Hall
Cap	Capitol Theatre
CCH	Catholic Central High School
CT	Colonial Theatre
DDF	Dominion Drama Festival
Emp	Empress Theatre
LCC	Lethbridge Community College
LCI	Lethbridge Collegiate Institute
LDS	Church of Latter Day Saints
LL	Lethbridge Lodge
LT	Lyceum Theatre
LTT	Lyceum Tent Theatre
LUH	Labor Union Hall
MT	Majestic Theatre
MoT	Morris Theatre
NHCC	New Hope Christian Centre
OH	Oliver's Hall
OT	Orpheum Theatre
Par	Paramount Theatre
PLib	Public Library
R1AF	Regional (District) One Act Festival
SACH	St. Augustine's Church Hall
Sm. Ch.	Southminister Church
ST	Sherman Theatre
Sppx	Sportsplex
UL	University of Lethbridge
VT	Variety Theatre
WCHS	Winston Churchill High School

2. Newspapers References:

M.G.	*Macleod Gazette*
C.H.	*Calgary Herald*
MHDN	*Medicine Hat Daily News*
S.H.	*Saskatchewan Herald*

• References are read as follows:

(*M.G.* December 15/35/7; 21/6,9) - *Macleod Gazette*, December 15, 1935, page 7 and December 21, 1935, pp. 6 and 9.

• References to local newspapers are cited as follows:

(Nov 17/43/8) - *Lethbridge News* or *Lethbridge Herald*, November 17, 1943, p.8

• References prior to December 1905 refer to the *Lethbridge News*.

• References after November 1905 refer to the *Lethbridge Herald*.

Professional Theatre Productions[*]
(Plays, Musical Theatre, Opera)
Lethbridge, Alberta (1885–1988)

DATE/PLACE	COMPANY AND/OR PERFORMER(S)	PERFORMANCE(S)/REFERENCE/CRITIQUE
MAY 30-JUN 1; 6,7/89 - *Barracks Mess Hall (BMH)*	Keene Theatre Co. with Miss Carolyn Gage	Fanchon the Cricket; East Lynne; The Pearl of Savoy; Kathleen Mavourneen; Damon & Pythias (Jun 5/3; 12/3) - *Miss Gage is a young actress of promise*
AUG 23; SEPT 4-6/90 - *BMH*	Caroline Gage Co. with Kent Thomas & Lydia Knott	Mr. Barnes of New York; The Octoroon (Aug 27/3; Sept 3/3; 10/3) - *played to slim houses*
DEC 31/90 - JAN 2/91 - *BMH*	Star Theatre Co. Managers: Quinn and Hughes	The Silver King; Kathleen Mavourneen; The Tragedy of Seven Deals (Jan 6/3) - *couldn't do justice to large cast play like "The Silver King"*
MAY 16 - 19, 21/92 - *Bldg. Co's Hall (BCH)*	Caroline Gage Co.	Pygmalion & Galatea; The Honeymoon; Oliver Twist; Camille; Damon & Pythias (May 18/3; 25/3) - *a strong troupe. Miss Gage's acting is ahead of anything ever given in Lethbridge*
AUG 4, 5/93 - *BCH*	Oliver Comedy Co. with Miss Cricket Oliver	Peck's Bad Boy and variety (Aug 10/1) - *highly enjoyable*
JAN 20 - 25/95 - *BCH*	Fraser Co. with Mollie Jeffries, Ivy Summers, Will Stedman	Rose Garland; The Little Duchess; Face to Face; Esmeralda; East Lynne; Our Boys; Jane (Jan 15/1; 22/1; 29/1)
FEB 27 - MAR 1/96 - *BCH*	Fraser Co.	Woman Against Woman; Charlie's Aunt; The Private Secretary; Fanchon the Cricket (Feb 19/1; 26/1; Mar 4/1) - *well satisfied audience*
APR 20-25/96 - *BCH*	Wilbur Stock Co., Miss Alice Roseland	The Golden Giant Mine; Shadow of Wealth; The Octoroon; The Streets of New York; The Two Orphans; Muldoon's Picnic (Apr 22/1; 29/1) - *All good except last one; a weak & trashy affair*
NOV 16-21/96 - *BCH*	Katie Putnam Co.	Love Finds a Way; Erma the Elf; The Old Lime Kiln; Lena the Madcap; Old Curiosity Shop; Meg's Diversion; Little Rebel (Nov 4/1; 11/1; 18/1) - *"Old Lime Kiln" was best*
APR 19-24/97 - *BCH*	Harry Lindley Comedy Co. with Clara Mathes	The Shadows of a Great City; Queena; The Weavers; Flower of the Forest; Little Lord Fauntleroy; Myrtle Finds; Arabian Nights (Apr 21/2) - *one of the best troupes to ever visit here*
AUG 14, 16-21/97 - *BCH*	Harry Lindley Co.	The Mail Girl; The Castaways; Lynwood; The Gold King; The Galley Slave; Tenderfoot Divine; Little Lord Fauntleroy; The Inside Track (Aug 18/1; 25/1) - *Mr. Lindley is a star comedian; an improved co.*
APR 29,30; MAY 26-28/98 - *BCH*	Orris-Ober Co.	The Circus Girl; Trilby; Jerry the Tramp; Mr. Wright of Wall Street; Mother and Son (May 4/8; 26/8; Jun 1/8) - *not as well attended as should be*
DEC 29,30/98 - *BCH*	French Comedy Co.	Hands Across the Sea; The Fair Rebel (Dec 15/8; 29/8) - *best show in town for some time*
APR 10-13/99 - *BCH*	Lyceum Co. (amalgamation of Imperial & Nelson Stock Cos.) under management of E. Shipman	All the Comforts of a Home; Under Two Flags; Alabama; Othello, The Moor (Apr 13/8) - *Company appeared for 80 nights in Winnipeg. Othello presented for first time to a territorial audience*
APR 28,29; MAY 1/99 - *BCH*	Andrew McPhee's Company; cast of 26 including: F.G. King, Mlle La Tina (world's only lady drum major)	Fanchon the Cricket; Uncle Tom's Cabin; Temptation and Money; The Wife's Peril (Apr 20/8; 27/8; May 3/8) - *largest company to visit Lethbridge - Audiences were well pleased & loud in their praises*
MAY 10,11/99 - *BCH*	Bittner Theatre Co.	Dramatic & vaudeville company - At Gay Long Branch; Michael Strogoff (May 10/8) - *drama & vaudeville of the highest quality*
MAY 12/99 - *BCH*	Metropolitan Opera Co.	The Mikado (May 10/8) - *largest advanced sale of tickets for any show*
JUN 30, JUL 1/99 - *BCH*	The Boston Comedy Co.	Ten Nights in a Barroom; The Old Homestead (Jun 28/2; Jul 5/8) - *very fair presentation*
AUG 29-31/99 - *Oliver's Hall (OH)*	Harry Lindley Co.; Harry Lindley and Adelaide Flint	Our Boys; Everybody's Friend (Aug 30/2,8; Sept 6/8) - *complimentary benefit tendered the Fire Co.*
NOV 2,3/99 - *OH*	French Theatre Co., Mr. R.E. French	Melodrama: The Black Flag (Nov 2/2; 9/8) - *their efforts here to entertain were well appreciated*

*Touring companies primarily; resident companies are identified

DATE/PLACE	COMPANY AND/OR PERFORMER(S)	PERFORMANCE(S)/REFERENCE/CRITIQUE
APR 12,13/00 - *OH*	Columbia Comedy Co. including "celebrated" Somers Family, 16 artists and orchestra	Speciality acts; <u>A Stranger in New York</u>; <u>Escape From The Law</u> (Apr 12/8; 19/8)
JUN 12-16/00 - *OH*	Clara Mathes & Co.	<u>Brown's in Town</u>; <u>Lady Audley's Secret</u>; <u>Cupid</u>; <u>A Wife Wanted</u>; <u>Ingomar</u>; <u>Jack Shephard</u> (Jun 14/1) - *Miss Mathes is an actress of great power and ability*
OCT 9-12/00 - *OH*	R.E. French Theatre Co.	<u>A Cheerful Liar</u>; <u>Just Before Dawn</u>; <u>The Silver King</u>; <u>Quo Vadis</u> (Oct 11/8; 19/8) - *delighted audiences - drama of power and pathos so well received*
AUG 5-7/01 - *OH*	Stultz Theatre Co.	<u>Was She To Blame?</u>; <u>Jack's Lost Paradise</u> (Aug 8/1) - *nothing but favorable comments*
DEC 9-14/01 - *OH*	Clara Mathes assisted by Miss A. Hardie of Lethbridge	<u>Romeo & Juliet</u>; <u>Under Two Flags</u>; <u>La Belle Marie</u>; <u>The Young Wife</u>; <u>Nell Gwynne</u>; <u>The Legion of Honor</u> (Dec 12/7; 19/2) - *very capable co.; Miss Mathes is a high class finished actress*
FEB 25/02 - *OH*	Russell Comedy Co.	<u>The Two Partners</u> (Jan 27/8) - *fair crowd*
MAR 26/02 - *OH*	Otto Frechtl's Co.	<u>Peck's Bad Boy</u> and variety (Mar 27/1) - *not of highest order but above average for similar travelling shows*
JUN 20/02 - *OH*	The "Too Rich to Marry" Co.	<u>Too Rich to Marry</u> (Jun 25/8) - *The performance is highly spoken of. Played to a fair house*
AUG 4-9/02 - *OH*	Harry Lindley Co.	<u>The Golden Cliff</u>; <u>Are You a Mason?</u>; <u>David Harum</u>; <u>A Pretty Sinner</u>; <u>The Hand of Fate</u>; <u>The Weavers</u>; <u>Little Lord Fauntleroy</u>; <u>British Born</u> (Aug 6/1) - *the plays are well presented; the specialties are first rate and very interesting*
AUG 11-16/02 - *OH*	Clara Hanmer Co.	<u>Master and Man</u>; <u>Brother Against Brother</u>; <u>La Belle Marie</u>; <u>Woman Against Woman</u> & others (Aug 13/8) - *very favorable, good specialty acts*
SEPT 15/02 - *OH*	"A Wise Member" Comedy Co. Dir: C.B. Marvin	Musical farce comedy; <u>A Wise Member</u> (Sept 10/8; 18/8) (*$0.75 - $1.00*) - *played to a poor house but actors took their parts well*
JAN 9,10/03 - *OH*	Wilson's "Mammoth Uncle Tom's Cabin" & "Ten Nights in a Bar Room Co."; 25 people & pack of "genuine southern Blood Hounds"	"Three hours of high class amusement" (Jan 7/8) (*$0.25, $0.50, $0.75*)
MAR 20,21/03 - *OH*	A. McPhee Co.	<u>Only A Farmer's Daughter</u>; <u>Little Lord Fauntleroy</u>; <u>The Two Orphans</u> (Mar 26/1) - *principal parts were well taken*
APR 9-13/03 - *OH*	Harold Nelson & Co.	<u>Ingomar</u>; <u>Richelieu</u>; <u>Don Caesar de Bazan</u>; <u>Mistress Nell</u>; <u>Hamlet</u>; <u>Merchant of Venice</u> (Apr 9/4; 16/3) - *actor of exceptional power - well balanced company*
JUN 2/03 - *OH*	Mr. Harold Nelson & Co.	<u>Othello</u> (Jun 4/4) (*$0.50 - $0.75*) - *it is regretted that the company could give only one performance*
JUL 13-16/03 - *OH*	Clara Mathes & Co.	<u>A Royal Spy</u>; <u>A Fatal Error</u>; <u>In the Reign of the Emperor</u>; <u>A Race for Congress</u> (Jul 9/4; 16/4) - *the company has a good reputation throughout the country*
OCT 31, NOV 2/03 - *OH*	Mr. Harold Nelson "Distinguished Canadian actor" & Co. with Clifford Bruce & Florence McLeay	<u>Quo Vadis</u>; <u>The Merchant of Venice</u> (Oct 29/4; Nov 5/4) - *presented in a highly artistic manner*
DEC 16-18/03 - *OH*	Harold Nelson & Co.	<u>Richelieu</u>; <u>The Taming of the Shrew</u>; <u>A Set of Turquoise</u>; <u>Hamlet</u> (Dec 10/7; 17/8) - *excellent presentation*
JAN 1,2/04 - *OH*	Cornyn's National Stock Co. with Horace Noble	<u>The Prisoner of Zenda</u>; <u>Work and Wages</u>; <u>Resurrection</u> (Jan 7/4) - *favored with good audiences & created a very favorable impression*
FEB 3; MAR 7/04 - *OH*	C.P. Walker, Manager, Winnipeg Theatre presents	Comedies by George Broadhurst <u>What Happened to Jones?</u>; <u>Why Smith Left Home</u> (Jan 28/4; Feb 4/4) - *the company is strong & well-balanced and Mr. Millard Reid is an actor of exceptional ability*
FEB 16, 17/04 - *OH*	Aaron Johnson Co.	<u>Jack O'Diamonds</u>; <u>Hazel Kirke</u> (Feb 11/4; 18/4) - *an excellent presentation*
MAY 9,10; 13,14/04 - *OH*	Clara Mathes & Co.	<u>Tennessee's Partner</u>; <u>A Daughter of Erin</u>; <u>Soldier Boy</u>; <u>The Silver Dagger</u> (May 5/4; 12/1; 19/4) - *audiences were not as large as the merits of the company warranted*
JUN 24/04 - *OH*	C.P. Walker presents Beggar Prince Opera Co. with F.W. Walters, G. Bronti, Frank Wade & Stanley Felch	<u>La Mascotte</u> (Jun 23/3; 30/4) - *audience was kept laughing throughout*
SEPT 5-10/04 - *OH*	Buchanan Stock Co. with Robert Buchanan & Adelaide Harlane	<u>Fanchon the Merry Cricket</u>; <u>King's Evidence</u>; <u>The Deputy Sheriff 'Maud Muller'</u>; <u>Fate</u>; <u>Hustling For a Wife</u>; <u>An Eye on Hubby</u> (Aug 25/4; Sept 1/4; 8/4) - *a company of refinement & rare professional ability - poor house*

DATE/PLACE	COMPANY AND/OR PERFORMER(S)	PERFORMANCE(S)/REFERENCE/CRITIQUE
SEPT 19,20/04 - *OH*	Shirley Co. with Jessie Shirley and Harry W. Smith	The Princess of Patches; Camille (Sept 15/1; 22/4) *($0.75 - $1.00) - two excellent presentations*
OCT 7/04 - *OH*	C.P. Walker's Comedians	My Friend From India (Oct 6/2) *($0.75 - $1.00)*
OCT 10/04 - *OH*	Stuart's Comic Players, James F. Post and Mary Ashley	Farce comedy, U and I (Oct 6/4; Oct 13/4) - *a full feast of merriment*
OCT 31; NOV 1/04 - *OH*	Harold Nelson & Co. presented by C.P. Walker	Heart & Sword; Faust (Sept 22/4; Oct 20/1,4; Nov 4/4) *($0.75 - $1.00) - only terms of highest praise can be applied to the work of Mr. Nelson*
NOV 11/04 - *OH*	C. P. Walker's Comedians with George Berry and William Yule	Brown's in Town (Nov 10/4; 16/4) - *unstinted amusement*
NOV 28,29/04 - *OH*	Beggar Prince Opera Co. with Irene Palmer, Messrs. Walters, Bronti, Wade	Fra Diavolo by Auber; Giroflé-Girofla by Lecocq (Nov 10/1,2,4; 16/1,2) *($0.75 - $1.00) - unqualified satisfaction*
DEC 19-23/04 - *OH*	Clara Mathes & Co.	A Nutmeg Match; The Grand Duchess; A Russian Spy; Du Barry (Nov 24/4; Dec 8/8; 15/8; 22/2) *($0.35 - $0.50) - very favorable comment*
JAN 23-28/05 - *OH*	Summers Stock Co. with George Summers & Belle Stevenson	The Gambler's Wife & others *($0.25 - $0.75) - Mr. Summers...a newcomer here...company is one of the best*
FEB 28; APR 13/05 - *OH*	C.P. Walker presents Mr. Harold Nelson & Co. with Helene Scott	Paul Kauver by Steele McKay, Richelieu (Feb 16/2; 23/4; Mar 23/4; Apr 20/5) *($0.75 - $1.00) - personnel of the company is of exceptional merit throughout*
JUN 19-24/05 - *OH*	The Sherman & Platt Stock Co.	The Christian; Lost Paradise; Sherlock Holmes; The Highwayman (Jun 20/3,4) *($0.25, $0.35, $0.50) - most creditable performance*
JUL 17,21/05 - *OH*	Edward R. Salter presents William Morris & Co.	Fabio Romani (Jul 7/1; 18/1,4; 25/2) - *a very pleasing presentation - poor crowds*
JUL 27/05 - *OH*	Mr. William Yule & Co.	One act plays: His Lordship the Burglar; A Happy Pair; The Baron's Wager (Jul 21/1,4; 28/4) - *played to a full house...put on a good show*
SEPT 13/05 - *OH*	Mr. Edward R. Salter presents Margaret Neville (former member of Sir Henry Irving's Co.)	The Lady of Lyons by Lytton (Sept 1/2,3; 8/1; 15/4) - *one of the very few really good companies to visit Lethbridge this year*
OCT 18,19/05 - *OH*	Arthur J. Aylesworth Production	Hooligan's Troubles (Oct 13/1,3,4; 17/4; 20/4) - *a very funny show*
NOV 9-11/05 - *OH*	Sherman & Platt Stock Co. with Hayden Stevenson	The Henrietta; Because She Loved Him So; Lend Me Your Wife; The Village Gossip; Gerry From Kerry (Nov 7/4; 10/3,4; 14/4) *($0.35 - $0.50) - direct from a 22 week run at Calgary - vaudeville performances between acts - gave great pleasure to large audience*
NOV 17,18/05 - *OH*	Mr.C.P. Walker presents "The Eminent Actor", Mr. Harold Nelson with Clifford Lane Bruce, Helen Scott & Co.	Prince Otto by Otis Skinner, Francisca de Rimini (Nov 14/3; 21/2) *($0.75 - $1.00) - the most important dramatic event in the early season*
DEC 4/05 - *OH*	Roscian Comic Opera Co. of 30 participants with Claude Amsden, Frank Walters	John Phillip Sousa's comic opera: El Capitan (Nov 24/5,6) *(admission: $1.00) - unquestionably the best comic opera co. that ever toured Western Canada*
FEB 27,28/06 - *OH*	Andrew McPhee & Co.	Woman Against Woman; The Hand of Man (Feb 21/3; Mar 1/4) - *company of 25 with band and orchestra drew crowded houses*
MAR 1,2/06 - *OH*	Juvenile Bostonians Opera Co.	The Gypsy Girl; Tips (Feb 23/3; Mar 2/4) - *unanimous applause*
JUN 2/06 - *OH*	Juvenile Bostonians, Babe Mason	Oriental opera, The Land of Boo-Loo (May 31/9) - *return engagement*
JUN 13/06 - *OH*	Roscian Opera Co. with Winifred Crowley	The Mikado - (Jun 7/2)
JUN 25-30/06 - *Tent (T)*	Sharpley Theatre Co. with Passie Mae Lester and Add Sharpley	Various unidentified plays - (Jun 14/8; 21/8) *($0.25 - $0.50) - under water proof pavilion*
SEPT 5/06 - *OH*	Roscian Opera, F.W. Walters, Misses Crowley and Nola	Martha by Flotow (Aug 30/5,10; Sept 6/7) - *delightful*
NOV 15,16/06 - *OH*	Amsden's Musical Co. with Claude Amsden & Hazel Davenport	The Mascot; The Governor's Wife (Nov 15/9)
NOV 23/06 - *OH*	Ed. F. Adams N.Y. Co.	Melodrama Out in Idaho by H. Webb Chamberlain (Nov 27/7,9)
DEC 21,22/06 - *OH*	Harold Nelson & Clifford Lane Bruce	Prisoner of Zenda; A Soldier of Fortune (Dec 13/2,3) *($0.75 - $1.00) - most talented group of the year*
JAN 7,8/07 - *OH*	Juvenile Bostonians	Dorothy; The Gypsy Girl (Jan 3/4; 24/7) *($0.75 - $1.00)*
JAN 18/07 - *OH*	Roscian Opera Co.	Said Pasha (Jan 17/7)
MAR 29,30/07 - *OH*	Amsden Musical Co.	Comic opera, Olivette; The Governor's Wife (Mar 28/11)

DATE/PLACE	COMPANY AND/OR PERFORMER(S)	PERFORMANCE(S)/REFERENCE/CRITIQUE
JUL 25/07 - *Hill's Hall*	Pride of N.Y. Co. directed by Charles A. Young	Musical comedy, The Girl From Frisco (Jul 29/9) (*$0.50 - $1.00*)
AUG 30,31; SEPT 2/07 - *Tent-Public Square*	Dick P. Sutton presents "The Gillettes" with Irene North & Co.	Shall We Forgive Her; The Honor of a Cowboy; Old Pals (Aug 29/2)
SEPT 2-7/07 - *Tent-Public Square*	Claman Comedy Co.	A Pair of Country Kids; Wedded But No Wife; A Woman's Secret; Down on the Farm (Aug 29/2) (*$0.50 - $0.75*)
OCT 26/07 - *Labor Union Hall (LUH)*	Harold Nelson, Clifford Lane Bruce, Helene Scott & Joseph De Stefani	The Egyptian of Pompeii (Oct 24/8)
NOV 14/07 - *LUH*	Stetson's Original Big Double Uncle Tom's Cabin Co.	Uncle Tom's Cabin & other entertainment (Nov 14/3) (*$0.75 - $1.00*)
NOV 23/07 - *LUH*	R.B. Price presents	The Two Orphans (Nov 21/2,6,9) (*$0.50 - $1.00*) - *a famous classic*
FEB 29-MAR 4/08 - *OH*	Arington Comedians with Miss Mayme Arington; Polmatier Sisters Orchestra	An American Girl; A Texas Ranger; Jim the Westerner (Feb 25/3; Mar 2/4) (*$0.75 - $1.00*) - *average troupe*
MAR 6,7/08 - *OH*	Dominion Comedy Co. with Francis Murray and Blanche Smaill	A Run Away Match; Winning a Woman; and vaudeville (Mar 2/2,4; 4/3,4; 6/2)
MAR 11/08 - *OH*	Beggar Prince Opera Co. with Ethel Balch & Jay C. Taylor	The Mikado (Mar 2/4; 3/3; 4/4; 6/2; 7/3)
APR 6-11/08 - *OH*	Arington Comedians; Polmatier Sisters	The Golden Giant Mine; The Black Flag; and others (Apr 1/3; 7/3; 8/4) (*$0.50 - $1.00*)
APR 14/08 - *OH*	Jeanette Carew	No Mother to Guide Her (Apr 9/2; 11/4; 14/4)
OCT 12/08 - *OH*	Harold Nelson & Co.	The Holy City (Oct 1/6; 13/3) - *vivid and realistic - inadequate stage*
OCT 26-31/08 - *OH*	Tom Marks & Co.	The Detective; Jerry the Tramp; The Hippocrite; That Irish Boarder; In North Carolina; Because She Loved Him So; Buster Brown (Oct 23/6; 24/5; 26/3; 27/4; 28/4; 30/4) (*$0.35 - $0.50*) - *brighter than the usual company*
NOV 30/08 - *Lyceum Th. (LT)*	National Opera Co.	Comic Opera, His Highness the Bey by Joe Howard (Nov 27/3; Dec 1/3) - *a very creditable reproduction; best thing in its line to come to the city this year*
JAN 5-9/09 - *LT*	Tom Marks Stock Co.	The Rose of Kerry; Dublin Dan; Lorna Stanley; The Red Cross Nurse; The Night Before New Year's; The Prodigal Son; Buster Brown; The Irish Immigrant (Jan 2/6; 5/6; 7/5; 8/3; 9/5) (*$0.25 - $0.35 - $0.50*)
JAN 20-21/09 - *LT*	Mr. W.L. Stewart presents The Stoddard Stock Co.	The Christian; The Devil (Jan 19/4; 20/2)
FEB 8-13; 15-20/09 - *LT*	George H. Summers Stock Co. with Miss Belle Stevenson	David Harem; Sweet Clover; The Lion & the Mouse; Paid in Full; Caught in the Rain; A Texas Steer (Feb 4/3; 6/3; 8/3; 9/4; 11/3; 15/3; 16/4)
MAR 1/09 - *LT*	Frederic Clark & Co.	Count of Monte Cristo (Feb 27/3) (*$0.25 - $1.00*)
MAR 8-13/09 - *LT*	Tom Marks & Co.	Soldier's Sweetheart; That Irish Boarder; A False Step; Irish Detective; Jerry the Tramp; Hippocrite; Dublin Dan (Mar 12/5; 13/9) (*$0.25 or $0.20 & a potato for the matinee - $0.50 - $0.75 evenings*)
MAR 15-20; 22-27/09 - *LT*	Theodore Lorch & Metropolitan Players	The Lieutenant & the Cowboy; Dr. Jekyll & Mr. Hyde; Struggle for Gold; Strong Heart; Piney Ridge; Trilby; A Gilded Fool (Mar 13/3; 15/6; 17/3; 18/6; 20/6; 22/4) (*$0.25 - $0.50 - $0.75*) - *an actor of the highest order...supported by competent artists*
MAR 29 - APR 1; 19-21/09 - *LT*	Jeanne Russell Co. with Ray Brandon, Mrs. William Yule, and Jane Dorsey	In Missouri; The Squaw Man; Woman Against Woman (Mar 29/4; Apr 1/5; 21/6) (*$0.25 - $0.75*)
APR 2-10; 12-17/09 - *LT*	Ray F. Brandon's Players with E. Loring Kelly, Betty Barrows & Florence Matthews	The Heart of Kentucky; Charlie's Aunt; Jessie James; The Parish Priest; The Power of the Cross (Apr 2/3; 5/3; 10/6; 12/14; 17/3) (*$0.25 - $0.35 - $0.50*) - *proved to be very good and the audience was well pleased*
APR 22-24; 26-28/09 - *LT*	The Stultz Stock Co.	Was She to Blame; One of the Family; Ole Olson; East Lynne; Rip Van Winkle; Bells of Shannon (Apr 21/5; 24/3; 26/3; 27/4; 28/5) (*$0.25 - $0.35 - $0.50*) - *made an excellent impression*
MAY 17-24/09 - *LT*	Theodore Lorch & Metropolitan Players	Old Heidelburg; Dr. Jekyll & Mr. Hyde; Carmen; Trist; The Lieutenant & the Cowboy; The Bells (May 17/5; 21/3; Jun 2/4) (*$0.25 - $0.50 - $0.75*)
JUN 2,3/09 - *LT*	San Francisco Opera Co. with Teddy Webb	Florodora by Leslie Stuart; King Dodo by Gustav Luders (May 27/2,5; Jun 1/4; 2/4,5) - *captivated the big audience*
JUN 21,22/09 - *LT*	Boston Grand Opera Co.	Lucia di Lammermoor; Faust (Jun 17/5; 22/5) (*$1.00 - $2.00*) - *unrestrained enthusiasm*

DATE/PLACE	COMPANY AND/OR PERFORMER(S)	PERFORMANCE(S)/REFERENCE/CRITIQUE
JUL 22/09 - *Lyceum Tent Th. (LTT)*	Pollard's Opera Co.	Musical farce, <u>Widow O'Brien</u> (Jul 20/4,5,8; 21/4; 22/4) - *corner Redpath & Glyn Streets*
JUL 26-31; AUG 5-7; 9-11/09 - *LTT*	Jeanne Russell	Secret Service; The Little Minister; The Squaw Man; Moths; Jesse James; <u>The Devil</u>; The Flag of Truce; The American Girl; The Heart of Kentucky; <u>An Englishman's Home</u> (Aug 4/7; 9/7) *($0.25 - $0.75)*
AUG 19/09 - *LTT*	unidentified co.	Musical comedy, <u>The Show Girl</u> (Aug 17/4) *($0.50 - $1.00)*
SEPT 22;28/09 - *(T) Cutbill St. near Barracks*	McPhee's Tent Theatre Co.	Comedy drama, For Her Brother's Sake; <u>The Girl I Love</u> (Sept 27/4) *($0.25 - $0.50)*
NOV 15-20; 22/09 - *(LT) reopening*	Deloy Comedians with Myrtle Deloy & Joe Kelsey	The Merry Widow, Junior; The Mayor of Tokyo; Dr. Dippie; <u>Hogan's Alley</u> (Nov 15/3,9; 16/3; 18/5; 20/12; 27/7) - *ranks first with any seen in this city*
NOV 23-24/09 - *LT*	Juvenile Bostonians	<u>Berta's Billion</u> (Nov 20/7)
NOV 29 - DEC 4; 6-11/09 - *LT*	Allen Players with Verna Felton	Zaza; The Truth; In the Bishop's Carriage; Tennessee's Partner; Zira; All Due to Diana; Jim the Westerner; Under Two Flags; The Second Mrs. Tanqueray; Sherlock Holmes; Camille; <u>Our New Girl</u> (Nov 29/7; Dec 11/7) *($0.25 - $0.75)*
DEC 13-18; 19-25/09 - *LT*	Stoddard Players with Miss Leah Stoddard and Mr. W.L. Stewart	The Man on the Box; Charlie's Aunt; Tom Moore; The Devil; The Wolf; The Music Master; The Girl of the Golden West; The Idler; <u>The Gold Mine</u> (Dec 11/7; 13/7; 17/3,11; 18/9; 20/4; 23/11; 24/7) *($0.25 - $0.50 - $0.75)* - *decided hit; finished & well trained stage artists*
DEC 27/09-JAN 1/10 - *LT*	San Francisco Opera Co. with Mabel Day, Teddy Webb, James Stevens	The Geisha; The Runaway Girl; The Gay Parisienne; Oh, What I Know About You; The Time, The Place & The Girl; <u>The Toymaker</u> (Dec 24/3,8; 28/4; 29/3; 30/4; 31/5) *($0.50 - $0.75 - $1.00 - $1.50)*
JAN 3-8/10 - *LT*	Jeanne Russell & Co.	Polly Primrose; Mrs. Temple's Telegram; Sunday; Cousin Kate; When We Were Twenty-One; <u>The Thief</u> (Dec 31/5; Jan 4/1; 6/1; 7/3) *($0.25 - $0.75)*
JAN 10-15; 17-22/10 - *LT*	Marks Brothers	Kidnapped by the Gypsies; Brother Against Brother; The Moonshiner's Revenge; Two Nights in Rome; Down Where the Orange Blossoms Grow; For His Sister's Sake; His Mother's Vindication; The Jail Bird; Irish Molly O; <u>Betty of the Bowery</u>; No Mother to Guide Her (Jan 8/4; 11/1; 14/4) *($0.25 - $0.75)*
JAN 21/10 - *Griffith (Majestic) Theatre Opening*	John P. Slocum Co. with Miss Texas Guinan	Comic opera, <u>The Gay Musician</u> by Julian Edwards (Jan 19/3; 20/4; 21/9; 22/5) *($1.00 - $2.00) - positively the original production...75 in company*
JAN 24-27; 29; 31-FEB 5/10 - *LT*	Stoddard Players	The Divorcons; Paid in Full; The Gold Mine; Ten Nights in a Barroom; Charlie's Aunt; The Brixton Burglary; <u>Damon & Pythias</u> (Jan 24/8; 26/8; Feb 2/8) *($0.25 - $1.00)*
JAN 28/10 - *LT*	The Bonnie Briar Bush Co.	Ian Maclaren's Scottish idyll, <u>The Bonnie Briar Bush</u> (Jan 24/5) *($0.25 - $1.00)*
FEB 7-13/10 - *Griffith (Majestic) Theatre Formal Opening*	Jeanne Russell Co.	The Little Minister; Friends; Mrs. Temple's Telegram; The Squaw Man; <u>The Heart of Kentucky</u> (Jan 31/3; Feb 5/5; 8/5; 11/12) *($0.35 - $0.50 - $0.75)*
FEB 7-13/10 - *LT*	Summers Stock Co. with Belle Stevenson & W.F. Blake	The Great Divide; The Lion & the Mouse; The Witching Hour; May Blossom; <u>Mrs. Diana's Defence</u>; Brown's in Town (Feb 2/7; 5/7; 7/7,8; 8/8; 10/8; 11/12)
FEB 14-25/10 - *Majestic Theatre "The Real Final Completion, Christening and Opening"*	The Summers Stock Co.	The Witching Hour; The Professor's Love Story; Leah Kleschna; The Middleman; The Fighting Hope; The Christian; Niebe; <u>The Bachelor's Honeymoon</u> (Feb 14/8; 16/5; 17/4; 18/4,10; 19/6,7; 21/8)
FEB 28-MAR 1/10 - *Majestic (MT)* MAR 2-5/10 - *LT*	Burt Imsen Dramatic Co.	The Parisian Princess; The Black Sheep; The Black Hand; East Lynne; <u>Down East</u>; The Farmer's Daughter (Feb 26/8; Mar 3/8)
MAR 14-19; 21-26/10 - *MT*	Jeanne Russell Co.	Polly Primrose; The American Girl; Cousin Kate; Jesse James; The Two Orphans; The Man From Home; <u>Faust</u>; Old Cronies (Mar 15/10; 17/10; 21/4; 25/12) - *Faust was the biggest spectacular production ever seen in Lethbridge*
MAR 28-APR 2/10 - *MT*	Summers Stock Co. with Belle Stevenson & W.F. Blake	A Prisoner of War; The Christian; A Bachelor's Honeymoon; Leah Kleschna; <u>May Blossoms</u> (Mar 26/6,12; 28/6; 30/10)
APR 20/10 - *MT*	Juvenile Bostonians	<u>The Ransom</u> (Apr 13/12; 14/5; 16/6)
APR 28/10 - *MT*	Grace Cameron & Co.	<u>Nancy</u> (Apr 22/12; 27/12) - *dainty singing comedienne in 4 act comedy success*
APR 29-30/10 - *MT*	Royal Chef Co. with Florence Sinnet & Princess Teto	<u>Royal Chef</u>; A Knight For a Day (Apr 26/12; 28/12) *($0.50 - $2.00)*

DATE/PLACE	COMPANY AND/OR PERFORMER(S)	PERFORMANCE(S)/REFERENCE/CRITIQUE
MAY 5-7; 9-14; 16,17; 19; 21/10 - *MT* MAY 18/10 - *LT*	The Partello Stock Co. with Alice Kennedy & Jack Westerman	The College Girl; Lena Rivers; A Royal Prisoner; The Man From the West; How Baxter Butted In; Tempest & Sunshine; The Bachelor's Romance (May 2/6; 7/4; 9/12; 10/12; 16/8) - *Canada's best stock company - Toronto*
MAY 23,24/10 - *MT*	Claman Co.	Are You Crazy (May 19/8; 23/7,12) (*$0.50 - $1.00*)
MAY 27/10 - *MT*	Mme. Harriet R. Labadie	Dramatic reading of 5 act play, A Servant in the House (May 25/8)
JUN 7,8/10 - *MT*	unidentified co. with Miss Ernestine Morris	Augusta J. Evins novel dramatized by Grace Hayward, St. Elmo (Jun 1/4,11,12; 2/9; 4/10; 8/9) - *one of the best things here in some time*
JUN 29-JUL 2/10 - *MT*	unidentified co. of 16 participants	Farce comedy and mystery, What Happened to Jones; Sherlock Holmes (Jun 29/5,8)
AUG 16,17/10 - *MT*	William P. Cullen Co. with Gus Weinburg and the original Kangaroo Girls	The Burgomaster (Aug 13/8; 16/3; 17/8) (*$0.50 - $2.00*) - *enthusiasm reigned throughout*
SEPT 14,21; OCT 24/10 - *MT*	Harold Nelson & Associated Players	Pierre of the Plains; The Wolf (Sept 13/3; 19/5; Oct 22/12) (*$0.50 - $1.00*)
OCT 3,4/10 - *MT*	Partello Co.	The House of a Thousand Candles; Mabel Talliferio's Polly of the Circus (Oct 1/7; 4/7) (*$0.25 - $1.00*) - *an unusual play*
OCT 7,8/10 - *MT*	Juvenile Bostonians with Rose (Patsie) Henry & cast of 20 girls	The Ransom; The Rose of Blandeen (Oct 5/8,11) (*$0.50 - $1.50*)
OCT 22/10 - *MT*	unidentified co. "direct from Winnipeg"	Mrs. Wiggs of the Cabbage Patch (Oct 20/6) (*$0.75 - $1.50*)
OCT 25,26/10 - *MT*	C.P. Walker presents	12th Night; As You Like It (Oct 22/12)
OCT 29/10 - *MT*	unidentified co.	Among the Kennebee (Oct 29/8) - *beautiful down East play*
NOV 7-12; 14-17,19/10 - *MT*	Allen Players with H. Irving Kennedy & Verna Felton	The Defiance of Doris; Zaga; The Man From Mexico; Dad's Girl; Mrs. Hobbs; The Second Mrs. Tanqueray; Three of Us; When We Were 21; Second in Command; The Prodigal Son; The Heir to the Hoorah (Nov 5/3; 12/7; 19/10) (*$0.25 - $0.75*) - *one of the most successful dramatic stock company engagements*
NOV 22,23/10 - *MT*	Gilson & Bradfield present: J.B. Wilson, Rose Ainsworth & Co.	A Bachelor's Honeymoon (Nov 19/2,10; 22/6) (*$0.25 - $1.75*)
DEC 26,27/10 - *MT*	W.L. Stewart presents: Miss Leah Stoddard & Co.	Musical mix-up, My Wife's Family (Dec 20/11) - *fun, rolicking, rippling, riotous*
DEC 31/10 - *MT*	Mason Brothers Co. of 20	Uncle Tom's Cabin (Dec 30/5) - *first and only performance in Canada*
JAN 2-7/11 - *MT*	Sanford Dodge supported by Adele Nickerson & Co.	The Three Musketeers; The Gladiator; The Merchant of Venice; Othello; Faust; Romeo & Juliet (Dec 30/5; 31/5; Jan 3/7) (*$0.25 - $1.00*)
JAN 9/11 - *MT*	Wm. P. Cullen presents Gus Weinburg & Co.	Musical comedy by Pixley & Luders, The Burgomaster (Jan 9/7) (*$0.50 - $2.00*)
JAN 10-14/11 - *MT*	Partello Co.	The Travelling Salesman; Carmen; Father and the Boys (Jan 9/7; 12/8) (*$0.25 - $0.75*)
JAN 30/11 - *MT*	C.P. Walker presents	Musical comedy, Managing Mildred (Jan 27/5)
FEB 3,4/11 - *MT*	Miss Hazel Kirke & Co.	Girl show, A Stubborn Cinderella (Jan 25/11; 31/5) (*$0.50 - $2.00*) - *497 times in Chicago*
FEB 6-11; 13-18/11 - *MT*	Summers Stock Co.	The Wrong Mr. Wright; The Girl & the Baron; The Private Secretary; David Harum; Melting Pot; June; Rip Van Winkle; Seven Days; The Black Flag; The Man From Ottawa; The Bells; Facing the Music (Feb 7/7; 8/5; 9/5; 10/5; 11/9; 13/5; 14/8; 15/7; 16/7; 17/10; 18/5) (*$0.25 - $0.75*)
FEB 20-25/11 - *MT*	Partello Co.	The Lost Paradise; The Virginian; Camille; The Spoilers; The Blue Mouse; The Small Town Girl; Salomy Jane (Feb 16/7; 20/8) (*$0.25 - $0.75*)
MAR 2-4; 14-16/11 - *MT*	George B. Howard & Co. with Robert K. McKim	The Easterner; The Witching Hour; Hello Bill; Christopher, Jr.; Other People's Money; The Marriage of Kitty (Feb 28/7; Mar 2/6; 10/10; 14/10) (*$0.25 - $0.75*)
MAR 17,18/11 - *MT*	John P. Slocum Opera Co.	The Kissing Girl (Mar 13/5)
MAR 20-23; 27-APR 3/11 - *MT*	Maude Henderson & Co.	Dora Thorne; Piney Ridge; The Dope Fiend; Slaves of the Orient; The American Girl; The King's Rival; Paid in Full; The Gambler; 45 Minutes From Broadway (Mar 16/7; 24/8; Apr 1/10)
MAR 24,25/11 - *MT*	unidentified co.	D. Hope Leonard's operetta, Alice in Wonderland (Mar 21/10)
APR 17-23/11 - *MT*	Oliver J. Eckhardt & Co. with Ethel Tucker, Whit Brandon, Ethelyn Noble, Georgia Nichols, Sheridan Davidson	Mrs. Temple's Telegram; A Wicked Woman; RUA Mason; The Marriage of Kitty; The Charity Child; Brown's in Town (Apr 17/5) - *company is worthy of a large audience*

DATE/PLACE	COMPANY AND/OR PERFORMER(S)	PERFORMANCE(S)/REFERENCE/CRITIQUE
APR 24,25/11 - *MT*	Samuel E. Rork's Musical Production	The Queen of the Moulin Rouge (Apr 20/5; 21/8,11) - *immense company & augmented orchestra - original company*
MAY 5,6/11 - *MT*	Max Dill Opera Co. with Max Dill, the great German comedian	Musical comedy, A Lonesome Town (May 3/5,9) (*$0.50 - $2.00*)
MAY 17/11 - *MT*	United Play Co.	Comedy The Climax by Edward Locke (May 13/10; 16/3) (*$0.50 - $2.00*)
MAY 20-24/11 - *MT*	Mr. John Griffith supported by Edith Trotter & Co.	Faust; Othello; The Bells (May 18/5)
MAY 26,27/11 - *MT*	F.A. Wade presents	Musical, Isle of Spice (May 16/3; 19/5; 22/8) (*$0.50 - $1.00*)
MAY 30-JUN 1/11 - *MT*	Simpson Hogg & Lilliputian Opera Co.	San Toy; HMS Pinafore; Gondoliers (May 27/5)
JUN 2/11 - *MT*	Luber & Co. with Olga Nethersole	The Redemption of Evelyn Vaudray (May 27/5) (*$0.75 - $3.00*) - *England's most emotional actress*
JUN 3/11 - *MT*	Frederick Shipman presents Albert Chevalier & musicians	"England's greatest character actor in scenes" (May 30/7) (*$0.75 - $2.00*)
JUN 5/11 - *MT*	New York Co. direct from Amsterdam Theatre	The Barrier (May 26/7; 30/1) (*$0.50 - $1.50*)
JUN 6-10/11 - *MT*	Miss May Roberts, Victor Gellard & Co.	The Thief; The Judge & the Girl (Jun 2/5; 3/5; 8/5)
JUN 16-17/11 - *MT*	Boyle Woolfolk presents Max Bloom	Musical comedy, A Winning Miss (Jun 12/8)
JUN 26,27/11 - *MT*	Harry H. Watson & Co. of 40	Musical, The Cat and the Fiddle (Jun 23/5,12)
JUL 20-22/11 - *MT*	Sherman & Cleveland present	Musical comedies, The Rajah; The Honeymoon Trail; Cupid's Handicap (Jul 22/9)
JUL 24,25/11 - *MT*	Clarence Bennett's Co.	The Squaw Man by Edwin Milton Royle (Jul 22/5; 24/7) (*$0.50 - $1.00*)
AUG 7,8/11 - *MT*	H.E. Pierce & Co. with Frank Patton, Horace Noble, Frank Fanning	In Wyoming (Aug 2/5,7)
AUG 14/11 - *MT*	Jess Harris, Betty Caldwell & a cast of 40	Musical comedy, The Flower of the Ranch (Aug 10/5)
AUG 19/11 - *MT*	Boyle Woolfolk presents Max Bloom	Musical, The Sunny Side of Broadway (Aug 19/10)
SEPT 6,7,9/11 - *MT*	Royal Lilliputian Opera Co.	The Gondoliers; San Toy by Sidney Jones; Human Hearts (Sept 2/10) (*$0.50 - $1.00*) - *30 clever children*
SEPT 15,16/11 - *MT*	Shubert Production with Paul Gilmore	The Humming Bird; The Bachelor (Sept 12/5; 13/7) (*$0.50 - $1.50*) - *original New York production*
SEPT 25/11 - *MT*	Walters Stock Co.	Corianton by Orestes U. Bean (Sept 25/5) (*$0.25 - $0.75*)
SEPT 30/11 - *MT*	Max Bloom presented by Boyle Woolfolk	Musical farce, The Telephone (Sept 26/6)
OCT 2,3/11 - *MT*	David Brattstrom & Co.	Yon Yonson (Sept 30/8)
OCT 19-21/11 - *MT*	Sherman Stock Co.	Brown of Harvard; The Gay Mr. Thompkins (Oct 14/10; 16/6; 21/7) - *highly creditable production*
OCT 23,24; NOV 11/11 - *MT*	W.B. Sherman & F.W. Healey present	Musical comedy, Madam & Sherry (Oct 14/10; 21/7; Nov 4/8) (*$1.00 - $2.50*) - *from New Amsterdam Theatre, New York*
OCT 25/11 - *MT*	Wm. Yule & Co. with the famous Blue Ribbon Chorus	45 Minutes From Broadway by George M. Cohan (Oct 14/10; 21/7)
OCT 26/11 - *MT*	Wm. K. Spark's N.Y. Production	When Knighthood Was in Flower (Oct 16/6; 21/7)
OCT 30-NOV 1/11 - *MT*	Juvenile Bostonians, with Patsie Henry	The Ransom; The Dream Girl; The Rose of Blandeen (Oct 31/8) - *audience was quite enthusiastic*
NOV 6-8; 16,17/11 - *MT*	H.D. Mars presents Majestic Stock Co.	Brewster's Millions; The Third Degree; My Friend From India; Girls (Nov 2/6; 4/8; 6/7; 17/11; 18/15) (*$0.25 - $0.75*)
NOV 27-DEC 1,4,5; 7-9/11 - *MT*	Allen Players with Verna Felton	The Resurrection; The Spoilers; The Lion and the Mouse; The Bishop's Carriage; Sapho; A Stranger in a Strange Land; The Christian; The Undertow; Second in Command; The Road to Yesterday; Our New Girl (Nov 23/11; 25/5; 27/7; 30/5; Dec 2/10; 4/5; 7/5; 9/8) (*$0.25 - $0.75*) - *can candidly commend the work of the Allen Players*
DEC 6/11 - *MT*	William Yule & Co.	The Rivals (Dec 2/10; 5/5; 6/15; 7/5; 11/7) (*$0.75 - $1.50*) - *much improved company since "45 Minutes From Broadway"*

DATE/PLACE	COMPANY AND/OR PERFORMER(S)	PERFORMANCE(S)/REFERENCE/CRITIQUE
DEC 25-30/11 - *MT*	Oliver J. Eckhardt & Co.	RUA Moose; Shepherd of the Hills; The Boston Friend of Bowser; Way Down East; The Bishop's Carriage; The Charity Child; Mrs. Temple's Telegram; Brown's in Town (Dec 20/5; 23/7; 26/5; 27/5; 29/6) - *performance of a highly creditable character; meritorious work*
JAN 8,9/12 - *MT*	W.D. Reed presents C. James Bancroft	Farce comedy, The Private Secretary (Jan 2/5; 9/6) - *eminent English comedian*
JAN 12,13/12 - *MT*	Lewis A. Till presents Canadian favorite Clifford Lane Bruce & Co.	The Thief (Jan 9/6; 13/9) *($0.25 - $1.50) - great play, well presented*
FEB 5,6/12 - *MT*	Willam Hawtry, "Distinguished English comedian"	Dear Old Billy (Jan 31/6) *($0.50 - $2.00) - excellent standard*
FEB 9-10/12 - *MT*	All Star English Co. (original co.)	Henry Seton Merriman's With Edged Tools (Feb 8/5; 10/13) *($0.50 - $1.00) - one of most satisfying all round acting units*
FEB 12-17/12 - *MT*	George H. Summers & Co.	The Wrong Mr. Wright; Baby Mine; David Harum; The Music Master; Ishmael; An American Abroad (Feb 12/6; 17/7) - *the company taken as a unit is the best of its kind*
FEB 19-23; 29-MAR 2/12 - *MT*	Jeanne Russell Co.	The Devil; Emanuella; The American Girl; The Man From Home; The Half Breed; Moths of Society; Cousin Kate; Charley's Aunt; The Little Minister (Feb 19/8 - Mar 1 - *passim) - capacity audiences*
FEB 24; 26-27/12 - *MT*	James Bancroft & Co. (direct from New Amsterdam Theatre, N.Y.)	The Barrier; The New Boy (Feb 21/7; 22/7) - *attracts & thrills large audience*
MAR 4-10/12 - *MT*	Tom Marks & Co.	5 big vaudeville acts per night & Irish comedies, His Irish Honor; The Peacemaker; Wanted, A Wife; The Irish Detective; In North Carolina; Jerry the Tramp (Mar 2/8; 5/6) *($0.25 - $0.75) - laughter reigned supreme*
MAR 11-13; 18-20/12 - *MT*	George Summers & Co.	Alias Jimmy Valentine; Jim the Penman; There and Back; The Man From Mexico; Baby Mine; The Gentleman From Mississippi (Mar 7/5) *($0.25 - $0.75) - Mr. Summers knows his business*
MAR 29,30/12 - *MT*	A New York Touring Co.	The Girl From Rectors (Mar 28/11) - *direct from Weber's Music Hall, New York - above average co. is wasting its time with this production*
APR 4-6; 8-13,15/12 - *MT*	Ardoth & Bock Musical Theatre Co.	Musical comedies, Hiram; Tim Toolin's Tear; Finnegan's Flats; The Matchmaker; Zig Zag Alley (Apr 1/7; 6/9; 11/8; 13/5)
APR 17/12 - *MT*	Jeanne Towler & Co.	The White Sister by Viola Allen (Apr 13/5; 17/10) - *not an attractive play*
APR 22-24; MAY 3/12 - *MT*	Sanford Dodge supported by Adele Nickerson & Co.	Nero, the Gladiator; Faust; Julius Caesar; Damon and Pythias (Apr 22/7; 23/11; 24/11; May 3/9) - *company worthy of respect, played to slim audience; May 3 - Benefit for Titanic Relief*
APR 26,27/12 - *MT*	unidentified co.	Three Weeks by Elinor Glyn (Apr 26/8) - *sensation of two continents - does not however resemble the book*
APR 29,30/12 - *MT*	Mort H. Singers presents Olive Vale	Musical review Miss Nobody From Starland (Apr 29/7; 30/10) - *large delighted audience*
MAY 10,11/12 - *MT*	H.E. Pierce & Co.	In Wyoming by Willard Mack (May 10/13; 11/9) - *small crowds...satisfactory production*
MAY 13,14/12 - *MT*	Clara Greenwood & Co. directed by John F. Sullivan	The White Squaw by Della Clark (May 14/7) - *uncommonly well staged*
MAY 24,25/12 - *MT*	Fred Byers & Co.	The Girl & the Tramp (May 25/15)
MAY 28,29/12 - *MT*	Clarence Bennett & Co.	The Squaw Man; The Stampede by C.B. Demille (May 29/7) - *solid entertainment*
JUN 3-5/12 - *MT*	Sherman-Cleveland Opera Co.	Follies of 1911; The Time, the Place & the Girl; A Stubborn Cinderella; A Lonesome Town (Jun 3/7; 4/7) - *large audience...creditable performance*
JUN 7/12 - *MT*	Constance Crawley & London Co.	The Broken Law (Jun 7/11; 8/9) - *social drama...fine acting*
JUN 15/12 - *MT*	Ollie Mack & Pearl Golding & Co.	Comedy, Casey Jones (Jun 13/6)
JUL 1/12 - *MT*	Bob Fitzsimmons and all star cast	A Fight for Love by Hal Reid (Jul 1/5)
JUL 2,5,6/12 - *MT*	Harry Bulger & Co. comedian & opera star	The Flirting Princess (Jul 2/7; 6/8) - *original Chicago cast of 52 people - best musical comedy seen here this season*
JUL 10/12 - *MT*	A.G. Delaneter & William Morris present	Beverley of Graustark (Jul 10/7; 13/8) *($0.50 - $1.50) - original broadway production - 25 actors - utterly worthless...weak acting co.*
JUL 11-13/12 - *MT*	unidentified co.	Cowboy melodramas, The Texas Ranger; Under Southern Skies; Jesse James (Jul 11/7)

DATE/PLACE	COMPANY AND/OR PERFORMER(S)	PERFORMANCE(S)/REFERENCE/CRITIQUE
JUL 15-19; AUG 19-24/12 - *MT*	Constance Crawley and Co. with Mr. Arthur Maude	The Second Mrs. Tanqueray; The Broken Law; The Passport; Magna; The Marriage of Kitty; The Divorcons; Romeo & Juliet (Jul 13/8; 15/5; Aug 17/14) ($0.50 - $1.00)
JUL 20/12 - *MT*	Margaret Illington	The Kindling by Charles Kenyon (Jul 20/7; 22/5) - *gifted emotional actress*
SEPT 2/12 - *MT*	W.E. Lorraine presents Charles J. Conklin	Rip Van Winkle (Aug 29/5; Sept 3/7) - *natural and creditable performance*
SEPT 5,6/12 - *MT*	Billy "Single" Clifford & Co.	The Girl, the Man & the Game (Sept 3/7; 4/7; 6/7) ($0.25 - $2.00) - *it appealed in every way to audience*
SEPT 26/12 - *MT*	Norton and Rith present Frank F. Farrel	Comedy The Missouri Girl by Fred Raymond (Sept 24/7; 26/7) ($0.25 - $1.00) - *full house found it very amusing*
OCT 7-9/12 - *MT*	Pollard's Juvenile Opera Co.	Sergeant Blue; The Toymaker; The Mikado (Oct 5/13; 8/7) ($0.25 - $1.50) - *large enthusiastic audience*
OCT 10,11/12 - *MT*	Sheehen English Opera Co.	Il Trovatore (Verdi); The Chimes of Normandy by Robert Planquette (Oct 5/13; 11/14) ($0.50 - $2.50) - *gave general satisfaction*
OCT 24-26/12 - *Morris Th. (MoT)*	Charles Picquet & the English Opera Singers	Musical play, Managing Mildred (Oct 14/12) - *a delightful burlesque of musical comedy*
OCT 26/12 - *MT*	Paul Gilmore & Co.	The Havoc (Oct 24/12; 29/10) ($0.50 - $1.50) - *unusually smooth performance which delighted the large audience*
NOV 4/12 - *YMCA*	Cyril Hayes	Dramatic recital (Nov 4/7) ($0.50)
NOV 6-12/12 - *MoT*	Allen Players with Verna Felton	The Girl From Texas; The Third Degree; A Contented Woman; Nell Gwynne; The Great Divide; Whose Baby Are You; The Deep Purple; Alias Jimmy Valentine (Nov 6/7; 7/7; 9/11; 12/10) - *another triumph for the Allen players*
NOV 6/12 - *MT*	Alice Nielsen & Co. of Opera Stars	Operatic selections & shortened version of The Barber of Seville (Nov 1/11; 2/9; 6/7) - *artistic success; financial failure*
NOV 16/12 - *MT*	John C. Fisher presents Zoe Barnett & cast of 62	Musical comedy, The Red Rose (Nov 9/11) - *greatest musical comedy success - delights capacity audience*
DEC 23-28,30/12 - *MoT*	Allen Players with Verna Felton	Ready Money; The Fighting Hope; Merely Mary Ann; The House of One Thousand Candles; The College Widow; A Contented Woman; Alias Jimmy Valentine (Dec 21/22; 26/6)
DEC 31/12; JAN 1/13 - *MT*	Miss Annie Adams & Co.	The Butler's Secret (Dec 27/7; 30/5) ($0.25 - $1.00) - *mother of Maude Adams*
JAN 2-4/13 - *MoT*	Allen Players with Verna Felton	The Deep Purple; The Regenerator; The Widow From Tokyo (Jan 2/7; 3/7; 4/10)
JAN 17/13 - *MT*	Ed Rowland & E. Clifford presentation	The Rosary by Edward E. Rose (Jan 17/9; 18/7) - *well worth seeing*
FEB 6/13 - *MT*	Lewis Waller with Madge Titherage	A Marriage of Convenience (Jan 28/7; Feb 4/3) ($0.50 - $2.00) - *win Laurels; his art pulses with innate expression*
FEB 28-MAR 1/13 - *MT*	Frank A. Miller presents	The Girl From Tokyo (Feb 28/3; Mar 1/3)
MAR 7,9/13 - *MoT*	Allen Players with Verna Felton	Madame X; The Easiest Way (Mar 8/3)
MAR 12-15/13 - *MoT*	Oliver J. Eckhardt's Ideal Stock Co.	The Man on the Box; Way Down East; The Deep Purple; Baby Mine; Bought and Paid For (Mar 10/3; 13/3; 14/3) - *greatly enjoyed by crowded house*
MAR 18-20; 31; APR 1/13 - *MoT*	Juvenile Bostonians	The Dream Girl; The Princess Chic; Olivette; The Rose of Blandeen; The Daughter of the Regiment (Mar 17/3; 18/3)
MAR 21,22/13 - *MT*	Harry Buckler & Baby Wilson	The Bachelor's Baby by Francis Wilson (Mar 18/3) - *not a single dull moment*
MAR 28,29/13 - *MT*	Gus Hill presents Co. of 50 people	Mutt and Jeff (Mar 24/3; 25/3; 29/3) - *an excellent company*
APR 24/13 - *MoT*	The Beggar Prince Comic Opera Co.	The Beggar Prince (Apr 24/3) ($0.50 - $1.00)
MAY 12-24/13 - *MoT*	Frank Rich Co. (Eastern)	The Girl From Panama; Variety Isle; The Merry Widow(ers); My Friend From Australia; The Rolicking Girl and The Tramps; A Scotch High Ball; Madame Excuse Me; Papa's Boy (May 12/3; 15/3; 16/3; 20/3; 23/3) ($0.25 - $0.30 - $.50) - *the best musical comedy company that we have seen*
MAY 17/13 - *MT*	M.H. Wilkes Producer with Hal Johnson	The Arrival of Kitty (May 15/3) (female impressionist)
MAY 26,27/13 - *MT*	George W. McGregor & English Co.	Comedy, Passer's By (May 23/3) ($0.50 - $2.00)
MAY 30,31/13 - *MT*	Allardt-Mooser Woolfolk Circuit presents Max Bloom	Musical, Sunny Side of Broadway (May 29/3; 30/3; 31/3) - *very high standard*

DATE/PLACE	COMPANY AND/OR PERFORMER(S)	PERFORMANCE(S)/REFERENCE/CRITIQUE
JUN 2/13 - *MT*	Le Comte & Flesher presents Tim Arnold and cast of 50	Musical, <u>The Prince of Tonight</u> (May 30/3) - *crowded house - musicals popular with Lethbridge audience*
JUN 6,7/13 - *MT*	Allardt Woolfolk Inc. presents Jessie Huston & Thomas Whiffen	Musical, <u>The Time, the Place & the Girl</u> by Joe Howard (Jun 5/3; 7/3) - *all that could be expected*
JUN 13,14/13 - *MT*	J.W. Everett & Co.	<u>The Bell Hop</u> (Jun 11/3; 14/3) - *slim audience*
JUN 20,21/13 - *MT*	William Morris and Thurston & Co. present	Musical, <u>Whose Little Gal Are You</u> (Jun 19/3; 21/3) ($0.25 - $0.75) - *very entertaining performance*
JUN 27-28/13 - *MT*	Raymond Paine & Co.	Musical, <u>The Girl Question</u> (Jun 24/3; 27/7; 28/3) - *the best of the weekend operas at Majestic*
JUL 5/13 - *MT*	Direct from Astor Theatre, New York; English cast including Amelia Summers	Drama, <u>Fine Feathers</u> (Jul 2/3; 7/3) - *exposition of the perfect art of acting*
JUL 7/13 - *MT*	Stetson's Uncle Tom's Cabin Co.	<u>Uncle Tom's Cabin</u> (Jul 5/3; 8/3) - *a meritorious company drew a fairly good audience*
AUG 9/13 - *MT*	Billy "Single" Clifford	Musical, <u>Believe Me</u> (Aug 7/3; 9/3) ($0.25 - $1.50)
AUG 25-27/13 - *MT*	Miss Minnie Palmer presents the Marx Brothers	Musical, <u>Mr. Green's Reception</u> (Aug 26/3; 27/3) - *exhilaratingly funny*
SEPT 6/13 - *MT*	Direct from Gaiety Theatre, N.Y.; Cohan & Harris present	Comedy, <u>Officer 666</u> - (Sept 6/3) ($0.50 - $2.00)
OCT 4/13 - *Sherman Th. (ST)*	Henry B. Harris Estate Production	Comedy, <u>The Country Boy</u> by Edgar Selwyn (Oct 4/9) ($0.50 - $1.00)
OCT 9/13 - *ST*	Hoyt Theatre Comedy presented by F. Mayo Bradfield	<u>A Bachelor's Honeymoon</u> (Oct 4/9; 9/3; 10/3) ($0.50 - $1.00) - *large audience enjoyed it*
OCT 11/13 - *MT*	Sheenan & Beck present Miss Olive Vail and cast of 40	<u>The Girl From Mumms</u> (Oct 4/9; 6/3) ($0.25 - $2.00) - *decidedly good show; full house*
OCT 16; 20,21/13 - *ST*	F. Stuart Whyte presents The Versatiles	<u>The Canada Express</u>; <u>Up the River</u> (Oct 13/3; 17/3) - *every member an artiste*
OCT 18/13 - *ST*	unidentified co.	Musical drama, <u>Freckles</u> (Oct 13/3) ($0.50 - $1.00)
OCT 30,31/13 - *MT*	Klaw & Erlanger present Frank Ireson	<u>The Barrier</u> by Rex Beach (Oct 22/3)
OCT 31-NOV 1/13 - *ST*	Boston Opera Co. of 20 artists	Comic opera, <u>The Beggar Prince</u>; <u>Said Pasha</u>; <u>Giroflé-Girofla</u> (Oct 27/3; 31/3)
NOV 8/13 - *MT*	Lee Morrison Producing Co.	<u>What Happened to Mary</u> (Nov 6/3) - *from Fulton Theatre, New York*
NOV 10,11/13 - *MT*	Juvenile Bostonians	<u>Princess Chic</u>; <u>My Tango Maid</u> (Nov 8/8)
NOV 12,13/13 - *MT*	Pollard Australian Juvenile Opera Co.	<u>The Last Waltz</u>; <u>The Mikado</u> (Nov 8/8)
NOV 14,15/13 - *MT*	Lawrence Brough & all English Co. with Olga Esme	Farcical comedy, <u>The Lady of Ostend</u> (Nov 14/3)
NOV 21,22/13 - *MT*	William A. Brady Ltd. with Robert Ober	<u>Ready Money</u> (Nov 21/3) - *left nothing to be desired*
NOV 29/13 - *MT*	Fisher & Stevens International Musical Comedy Co.	<u>The Pink Lady</u> by Ivan Caryll (Nov 20/3; 29/3; Dec 1/3) ($0.50 - $2.50) - *a brilliant and well deserved success*
DEC 20/13 - *MT*	Frank Farrell, Mildred Ford and Co. as stage characters Zeke & Daisy	Domestic comedy, <u>The Missouri Girl</u> (Dec 19/3) - *delightful rich humor*
DEC 25,26/13 - *MT*	Julius Cahn presents George B. Howard	<u>David Harum</u> (Dec 23/3) - *metropolitan cast*
JAN 12/14 - *MT*	Liebler & Co. Big N.Y. Success	<u>The Deep Purple</u> by Paul Armstrong (Jan 10/3; 12/3) ($0.25 - $1.50)
JAN 19/14 - *MT*	William Cranston's Scottish Players with Dawsey McNaughton	<u>Bunty Pulls the Strings</u> (Jan 19/3; 20/3) - *Lethbridge playgoers were regaled*
JAN 19-21/14 - *ST*	Eugene West & Cathrine Henry present one act plays; Miss Dorothy Young of Lethbridge joins the cast	<u>Taming a Husband</u>; <u>From Scotland Yard</u>; <u>Weather Bound</u>; <u>Blanche</u>; <u>A Sure Thing</u>; <u>Live & Let Live</u> (Jan 17/3; 21/3) - *the most talented & versatile performers*
FEB 6,7/14 - *MT*	Lewis Meyer's All British Co.	Comedy, <u>The Glad Eye</u> (Jan 31/3; Feb 7/8) - *best of its kind ever presented at the Majestic*
FEB 9/14 - *MT*	United Play Co. Inc.	<u>Graustark</u> (Feb 9/3; 10/3) - *rather second-rate & not worth $1.50*
FEB 13,14/14 - *MT*	Edward W. Rowland & Edwin Clifford	<u>The Rosary</u> (Feb 9/3; 14/3) - *splendid show - poor house*
MAR 2-7/14 - *ST*	Tom Marks & Co.	<u>The Golden Rule</u>; <u>The Hidden Secret</u>; <u>The Trust Attorney</u>; <u>His Irish Honor</u>; <u>Bought & Paid For</u>; <u>The Peacemaker</u> (Mar 2/3; 3/3) ($0.25 - $0.50) - *exceptionally fine performers*

DATE/PLACE	COMPANY AND/OR PERFORMER(S)	PERFORMANCE(S)/REFERENCE/CRITIQUE
MAR 17,18/14 - *MT*	British Canadian Theatre Organization Society presents John Martin-Harvey	The Only Way; The Breed of the Tresham (Mar 17/3) - *strongest acting ever seen in this city - monster audience*
MAR 27,28/14 - *MT*	Gus Hill presents	Musical, Mutt & Jeff in Panama (Mar 28/3)
MAR 30-APR 3/14 - *ST*	Oliver Eckhardt Stock Co.	Bought and Paid For; A Woman's Way (Mar 31/3; Apr 2/3) - *established themselves as firm favorites*
APR 11/14 - *ST*	Sherman & Aylesworth Production with Frank Ireson	The Holy City (Apr 11/3)
APR 30-MAY 2/14 - *ST*	Frank Morton Co.	Musical, 50 Miles From Broadway; Irish comedy, Duke of Ireland; Ship Ahoy (Apr 29/3; May 1/3; 2/3) - *reviewer is not too enthusiastic about the musical - Irish comedy is pleasing*
MAY 15/14 - *MT*	American Play Co. with Margaret Illington	Within the Law (May 15/3; 16/3) - *made fine impression*
JUN 23,24/14 - *ST*	Gertrude Ritchie	The Shepherd of the Hills (Jun 20/3) - *creditable interpretation of an interesting play*
AUG 17/14 - *MT*	William Elliott presents	Kitty MacKay by Catherine Chisholm Cushing (Aug 11/2) ($0.50 - $1.00) - *original N.Y. production - (full page ad)*
OCT 12,13/14 - *MT*	F. Stuart Whyte presents The Versatiles	Scottie in Japan; The Canadian Express (Oct 13/2) - *general chorus of approval*
DEC 7-8/14 - *MT*	Theo Johnston presents the Von Glaser Stock Co.	The Bonnie Briar Bush; What Happened to Jones (Dec 7/3; 8/3)- *a distinctly pleasing performance*
FEB 1; APR 2,3/15 - *MT*	Whitney Opera Co.	The Chocolate Soldier by Oscar Straus (Feb 1/3; 2/3; Mar 29/3) - *meritorious production for standing room only crowds*
FEB 12,13/15 - *MT*	E. Dorosh/Russian Ukrainian Players	Classic Russian dramas (Feb 10/3)
FEB 19,20/15 - *MT*	Gus Hill presents	Mutt & Jeff in Mexico (Feb 18/3; 20/3) - *2 hours of laughter and entertainment*
MAR 6; 29,30/15 - *MT*	Theo Johnston presents Guy Harrington & Bessie MacAllister	The Brixton Burglary; Peg O' My Heart (Mar 1/3; 29/2,3) ($0.25 - $1.00)
MAR 8,9/15 - *MT*	John P. Slocum presents Charles Clear	Musical comedy, The Quaker Girl (Mar 8/3; 9/3) - *splendidly presented*
APR 21-24/15 - *MT*	Juvenile Bostonians Opera Co.	The Isle of Spice; My Tango Maid; King Dodo; Fantana (Apr 19/3)
MAY 24/15 - *MT*	John Cort presents Marie Tempest & Co. with W. Grahame Browne	The Marriage of Kitty; Nearly Married (May 17/3) - *Lethbridge people see all too little of talented dramatists such as these*
JUN 8,9/15 - *MT*	B.C. Hilliam & Co. presents 1915 Follies	The Follies in France (Jun 7/2) ($0.25 - $0.75) - *a real treat*
AUG 14,16/15 - *MT*	La Salle Musical Comedy Co. of Chicago with Billy Gross	The Matinee Girl; Fascinating Flora (Aug 9/2; 16/2) ($0.25 - $0.50) - *a big hit*
OCT 1,2; DEC 28,29/15 - *MT*	F. Stuart Whyte presents The Versatiles	Musical comedy, The Girl From Nowhere (Oct 2/2; Dec 22/2) - *first class*
OCT 20/15 - *MT*	Oliver Morosco presents Prima Donna Mdme. G. Johnstone-Bishop and cast	Peg 'O My Heart (Oct 19/2) - *a hit*
NOV 4-6/15 - *MT*	Juvenile Bostonians Opera Co.	Tipperary Mary; The Dream Girl (Nov 3/5)
NOV 11/15 - *MT*	Klaw & Erlanger/All Star New York Co. in Eugene Walter's dramatization	The Trail of the Lonesome Pine by John Fox, Jr. (Nov 11/2; 12/2) ($0.50 - $1.50) - *a hit*
DEC 13-18/15 - *MT*	George H. Summers Stock Co.	The Lion and the Mouse; The Rejuvenation of Aunt Mary; The Boss; The House Next Door; Green Stockings; David Harum (Dec 7/2; 13/2; 14/2) ($0.25 - $0.75) - *most creditable performance*
JAN 11-15; 17-19/16 - Orpheum Th. (*OT*)	Odell Stock Co.	The Coming Man; Two Married Men in an Uptown Flat; Over the Garden Wall (Jan 18/2)
JAN 17-19; 24-25/16 - *MT*	William A. Brady Ltd. with Albert Brown and Co.	The White Feather by Eugene Walter; Too Many Cooks (Jan 12/2; 18/2)
FEB 15-16/16 - *MT*	United Producing Co. with Margaret Illington	Within the Law by Bayard Veiller (Feb 15/2; 16/2) - *a great drama*
MAR 14,15; APR 12/16 - *MT*	United Producing Co. (William Brady Inc.)	The White Feather by Eugene Walter (Mar 14/2)
MAR 21,22/16 - *MT*	F. Stuart Whyte presents Zara Clinton & Billy Oswald	Musical comedy, Florodora (Mar 14/2; 17/6; 22/5) - *all Canadian production*
APR 17,18/16 - *MT*	Gus Hill presents	Mutt & Jeff in College (Apr 11/2) ($0.25 - $1.00)

DATE/PLACE	COMPANY AND/OR PERFORMER(S)	PERFORMANCE(S)/REFERENCE/CRITIQUE
MAY 8,9/16 - MT	Gus Hill presents	Muscial comedy, Bringing Up Father (May 9/2) - infinite enjoyment
MAY 8/16 - OT	J.K. Park assisted by Kitty Allen & Co.	Sketches, The Patriot & the Spy; Princess of Siam; Dissolution of Partnership; Between the Devil & the Kaiser (May 8/2) ($0.25) - eminent Scottish character actor - wonderful effect
JUN 3/16 - MT	Slocum & Co. Metropolitan Cast with Charles McNaughton	Musical comedy, Nobody Home (Jun 3/7)
JUN 6/16 - MT	B.E. Lang presents Juvenile Bostonians: Babe Mason, Patsie Henry	The Girl in the Cabaret (Jun 5/3)
JUN 9/16 - MT	A.H. Woods presents	Kick In by Willard Mack (Jun 6/2)
JUL 22/16 - MT	Barnum & Aylesworth present	Uncle Tom's Cabin (Jul 22/2) - ($0.25 - $1.00)
AUG 21/16 - MT	unidentified co.	Melodramatic farce, Officer 666 by Austin McHugh (Aug 21/2) ($0.25 - $1.00)
SEPT 4/16 - MT	United Producing Co.	Charlie's Aunt (Sept 2/2)
SEPT 22/16 - MT	Garrette & Benson present British Cast	Military drama, Somewhere in France (Sept 22/2) ($0.25 - $1.00) - well worth seeing
SEPT 29,30/16 - MT	United Producing Co. presents Betty Harrison and Co.	French musical farce, Alma, Where Do You Live (Sept 29/5) - good fun - classy performers
OCT 2/16 - MT	W.B. Sherman presents	Kick In (Sept 29/5)
OCT 16,17/16 - MT	F. Stuart Whyte presents Zara Clifton, Billy Oswald & Co.	English pantomime, Aladdin & His Wonderful Lamp (Oct 17/7) - makes a great hit here - first pantomime brought to Canada
OCT 9/16 - OT	O'Neill & Walmsley with Hazel Kirke	The Two Pikers (Oct 6/11)
OCT 18/16 - MT	L.C. Yeoman presents Virginia Hardy and cast	Winning of Barbara Worth (Oct 16/3) ($0.25 - $1.00) - the original company
OCT 21/16 - MT	Juvenile Bostonians	The Rose of Honolulu (Oct 20/5) ($0.25 - $1.00)
NOV 6-8/16 - MT	Oliver Eckhardt Players	Sweet Clover; Lena Rivers; The Girl in the Taxi (Nov 3/3; 7/6) - Benefit Performance, Nov 9 for Tobacco fund for boys in the trenches - not a weak member
NOV 10/16 - MT	unidentified road show co.	Ten Nights in a Barroom by T.S. Arthur - gave a good portrayal
NOV 20/16 - MT	Henry Savage presents	Comedy, Every Woman (Nov 20/5) ($0.50 - $2.00) - superior acting
NOV 29/16 - MT	A.S. Stern & Co.	Twin Beds (Nov 29/5) - a real comedy
DEC 1,2/16 - MT	unidentified road co.	Modern morality play, The Girl He Couldn't Buy by Sumner Nichol (Nov 29/5) - enjoyed by appreciative audience
DEC 9/16 - MT	United Producing Co.	Peg 'O My Heart (Dec 4/5)
DEC 30/16 - MT	W.E. Sherman presents	East Lynne (Dec 29/5)
JAN 12,13/17 - MT	George H. Summers	Comedy drama In Walked Jimmy (Jan 12/5; 13/5) ($0.25 - $1.00) - one of finest ever seen in Lethbridge
JAN 20/17 - MT	Frank Ireson	The Rosary (Jan 20/5) ($0.25 - $1.00)
JAN 29,30/17 - MT	Albert Brown	The Black Feather by W.H. Tremayne (Jan 29/5)
JAN 31-FEB 3/17 - MT	The Oliver Eckhardt Players	Tess of the Storm Country; Broadway Jones; Merely Mary Ann; The Only Son (Jan 29/5)
MAR 9,10/17 - MT	W.B. Sherman presents	Musical comedy, The Man in the Moon (Mar 3/5; 10/5) - scored one of the biggest hits of the season
MAR 12,13/17 - MT	Albert Brown	A Little Bit of Fluff by Walter Ellis (Mar 13/5) - each part perfectly cast
MAR 17/17 - MT	May Robson & Co.	The Making Over of Mrs. Matt by James Forbes (Mar 10/5) ($0.50 - $1.50)
MAR 19,20/17 - MT	Selwyn & Co.	Farce comedy, Fair and Warmer by Avery Hopwood (Mar 20/5) ($0.50 - $1.50)
MAR 24/17 - MT	W.B. Sherman presents	Little Peggy O'Moore (Mar 22/5)
MAR 29/17 - MT	Frank Ireson	The Barrier (Mar 29/5)
APR 16/17 - MT	Gus Hill presents	Mutt & Jeff's Wedding (Apr 16/5) ($0.25 - $1.00) - house packed to the roof
APR 16/17 - OT	Ralston & Wolf/The California Bells	The Elopers (Apr 16/5) ($0.25 - $0.35)
MAY 7-12; 14-19; 21-26; 27-31/17 - OT	Harris & Proy's Musical Comedy Co.	Grape Nut Isle; A Day in Paris; Isles of Smiles; The Rose of Panama; Murphy's Night Out; Muldoon's Picnic; The College Widow; College Chumps (May 7/5; 11/5; 18/5; 24/5) ($0.35 - $0.50) - a great show

DATE/PLACE	COMPANY AND/OR PERFORMER(S)	PERFORMANCE(S)/REFERENCE/CRITIQUE
MAY 23,24/17 - *MT*	All Star N.Y. Road Show with Charles Gramlich & Blanche Wilcox	Musical comedy, <u>Little Miss Innocence</u> (May 18/5) *($0.25 - $1.00)*
MAY 28/17 - *MT*	Ed C. Armstrong presents Baby Dolls	Musical extravaganza, <u>The Follies of Pleasure</u> (May 25/5)
JUN 5-7/17 - *MT*	Juvenile Bostonians with Patsie Henry	<u>Bonnie Jean</u>; <u>The Isle of Dreams</u>; <u>Hello Hawaii</u> (Jun 6/5) - *as good as ever*
JUN 8,9/17 - *MT*	United Producing Co. presents Hazel Wood	Musical drama, <u>Freckles</u> (Jun 6/5) - *a splendid dramatization*
JUL 21/17 - *MT*	John Cort presents original N.Y. Co.	New York musical comedy success, <u>Flora Bella</u> (Jul 21/5) *($0.50 - $2.00)*
AUG 6-11/17 - *OT*	Harris & Proy Musical Comedy Co.	<u>The Slaves of the Orient</u>; <u>In Panama</u>; <u>Off to the Races</u>; <u>Nearly a Hero</u> (Aug 6/5)
AUG 15-17/17 - *MT*	United Producing Co.	Musical comedy, <u>Step Lively</u> (Aug 11/5; 16/5) *($0.50 - $1.00)* - *smiles galore and keen enjoyment*
AUG 27-29/17 - *MT*	Nina Gleason & Co.	<u>Her Unborn Child</u> (Aug 21/5; 28/7) - *very powerful morality play by superb company*
OCT 6/17 - *MT*	Norton & Bunnel Inc. presents	Musical, <u>The Million Dollar Doll</u> (Oct 1/5)
OCT 22/17 - *MT*	F. Stuart Whyte Production	English pantomime, <u>Robinson Crusoe</u> (Oct 22/5; 23/5) *($0.50 - $1.50)* - *best balanced, most clever company of real artists*
OCT 26,27/17 - *MT*	Rowland-Clifford Gatts Inc.	<u>In Old Kentucky</u> (Oct 22/5)
NOV 5,6/17 - *MT*	United Producing Co. with Billy Oswald	<u>Henpecked Henry</u> (Nov 5/5)
NOV 12/17 - *MT*	Albert Brown	<u>The Love of a King</u> (Nov 12/5) *($0.50 - $1.50)*
DEC 24-26/17 - *MT*	John E. Kellerd	Shakespeare's plays, <u>Hamlet</u>; <u>The Merchant of Venice</u>; <u>Macbeth</u>; <u>Othello</u> (Dec 19/5; 24/5)
DEC 27,28/17 - *MT*	Eastern Producers Ltd. present James Blaine	Farce comedy, <u>Oh, Bill</u> (Dec 24/5) - *Canada's most popular comedian*
JAN 7/18 - *MT*	Frank Ireson	<u>My Mother's Rosary</u> (Jan 2/5; 8/5) - *capably presented*
JAN 14/18 - *MT*	San Carlo Grand Opera Co. with Edvidge Vaccari	<u>Lucia di Lammermoor</u> by Donizetti (Jan 8/5)
JAN 18,19; FEB 20/18 - *MT*	New York cast supporting Rae Martin	<u>The Brat</u> by Maude Fulton (Jan 18/5; Feb 14/3,5) - *one of finest impersonations of any character*
JAN 21-25/18 - *MT*	Maude Henderson Co.	<u>The Lure of Wealth</u>; <u>The Wages of Sin</u>; <u>Master & Man</u>; <u>The Tie That Binds</u> (Jan 21/5) *($0.25 - $0.75)* - *well balanced company*
JAN 28,29/18 - *MT*	Albert Brown & Co.	<u>The White Feather</u>; <u>The Love of a King</u> (Jan 22/5; 29/5) - *scored a most decided hit*
FEB 1,2; 8,9/18 - *MT*	United Producing Co. with Julius Velie & May B. Hurst	<u>The Isle of Dreams</u>; <u>Mrs. Wiggs of the Cabbage Patch</u> (Feb 1/5; 2/5; 8/5) - *capable company*
FEB 12/18 - *MT*	N. Y. Touring Co.	<u>Watch Your Step</u> by Irving Berlin (Feb 12/5) *($0.75 - $2.50)*
MAR 2,11/18 - *MT*	Klaw & Erlanger and George C. Tyler present Elsa Ryan & N.Y. Touring Co.	<u>Out There</u> by J. Hartley Manners (Mar 2/5) *($0.50 - $1.50)*
MAR 4,5; APR 8/18 - *MT*	Calgary Great War Veteran's Association presents Sgt. Gittus & Co. of 50 Veterans	4 act play, <u>The Volunteer</u> by Sgt. G.D. Gittus (Mar 4/5; 5/9; Apr 8/5) *($0.50 - $1.00)* - *real army life*
MAR 6/18 - *MT*	United Producing Co./Belva Morrell	<u>The Wolf</u> by Eugene Walter (Mar 6/5) *($0.50 - $1.00)*
MAR 16/18 - *MT*	English actress Phyllis Neilson-Terry	<u>Maggy</u> (Mar 16/5) *($0.50 - $2.00)* - *Ellen Terry's niece*
MAR 22/18 - *MT*	Walter C. Jordan & Robert Campbell present English Touring Co.	Military comedy, <u>Seven Days Leave</u> (Mar 16/5)
APR 9,10/18 - *MT*	B.E. Lang presents Juvenile Bostonians with Doris Canfield	Musical play, <u>The Girl From Over There</u> (Apr 9/5; 10/5)
APR 22-23/18 - *MT*	Ed Rowland presents Wanda Ludlow, Oscar O'Shea & Co.	<u>The Marriage Question</u> (Apr 16/5; 23/5) *($0.25 - $1.00)* - *excellent performance*
MAY 6/18 - *MT*	Max Figman and Lolita Robertson & N.Y. Co.	<u>Nothing But the Truth</u> by James Montgomery (May 6/5) *($0.50 - $1.50)*
MAY 8/18 - *MT*	May Robson & N.Y. Cast	Farce, <u>A Little Bit Old Fashioned</u> by Anna Nichols (May 8/5)
MAY 23/18 - *MT*	United Producing Co.	<u>A Daughter of the Sun</u> by Lorin J. Howard & Ralph T. Kettering (May 23/5) *($0.50 - $1.50)*
JUN 10-28/18 - *OT*	The Londonian Belles	Musical comedies, <u>College Days</u>; <u>Too Much Mustard</u>; <u>A Trip to Paris</u>; <u>Waiter & Chef</u>; <u>Variety Isle</u> (Jun 10/5; 14/5) - *large and appreciative audience*

DATE/PLACE	COMPANY AND/OR PERFORMER(S)	PERFORMANCE(S)/REFERENCE/CRITIQUE
JUN 14,15/18 - *MT*	United Producing Co. with Billy Oswald	Musical farce, <u>You're Next</u> (Jun 14/5; 15/5) - *a real hearty laugh*
JUN 25,26/18 - *MT*	Lambert Producing Co. presents Dorothy La Vern	<u>The Other Man's Wife</u> by Victor E. Lambert (Jun 25/5) (*$0.50 - $1.00*) - *all star aggregation*
JUL 18-20/18 - *OT*	The Russell Musical Comedy Co.	<u>The Doctor Shop</u>; <u>Gay Coney Island</u>; <u>Hogarty and Fogarty</u> (Jul 19/5)
JUL 23,24/18 - *MT*	United Producing Co. presents Belva Morrell	<u>Peg O' My Heart</u> by J. Hartley Manners (Jul 19/5; 24/5) (*$0.50 - $1.00*) - *a most pleasing offering*
JUL 25-27/18 - *MT*	Juvenile Bostonians	<u>Daydreams</u>; <u>The Hill From Over There</u>; & vaudeville (Jul 27/5; Aug 1/5)
SEPT 23/18 - *MT*	Le Comte & Flesher present	Musical, <u>My Soldier Girl</u> (Sept 20/5) (*$0.50 - $1.50*)
OCT 11,12/18 - *MT*	A N.Y. Co. with Daisy Carleton	<u>My Irish Cinderella</u> (Oct 11/5)
OCT 13-NOV 29/18	- LETHBRIDGE THEATRES CLOSED	BECAUSE OF PROVINCIAL INFLUENZA EPIDEMIC
DEC 9,10/18 - *MT*	unidentified co.	<u>The Unmarried Mother</u> by Florence Edna May (Dec 9/5) (*$0.50 - $1.00*)
DEC 20/18 - *MT*	Henry Miller presents a N.Y. Cast with Alice Haynes	<u>Daddy Long Legs</u> by Jean Webster (Dec 21/5) (*$0.50 - $1.50*) - *a delightful play*
DEC 25,26/18 - *MT*	Sergeant George D. Gittus (late 12th C.M.R.) Cast of War Veterans	Five act military comedy drama, <u>Private Murphy C.B.</u> by Sgt. George D. Gittus (Dec 23/5; 24/5)
JAN 17,18/19 - *MT*	San Carlo Grand Opera Co.	<u>Cavalleria Rusticana</u> & <u>Pagliacci</u> (Jan 17/5) (*$1.00 - $3.00*)
FEB 1/19 - *MT*	Richard Carle & Co.	Musical comedy, <u>Fur & Frills</u> (Feb 1/5)
FEB 3; MAR 4/19 - *MT*	F. Stuart Whyte presents	3rd Annual English pantomime, <u>Cinderella</u> (Feb 3/5; Mar 1/5)
FEB 15; APR 16/19 - *MT*	A New York Co.	<u>Turn to the Right</u> (Feb 15/5; Apr 14/5) (*$0.50 - $1.50*)
MAR 5,6/19 - *MT*	Gus Hill presents	<u>Mutt & Jeff in the Woolly West</u> (Mar 6/5) - *best Mutt and Jeff show seen here*
MAR 10,11/19 - *MT*	Oliver Morosco presents Charlotte Greenwood & Co.	Musical comedy, <u>So Long Letty</u> (Mar 8/5) (*$0.50 - $2.00*) - *big Broadway hit*
MAR 24,25/19 - *MT*	A N.Y. Cast with Paul Gilmore, Harry Radford and Horace Sinclair	<u>The Better 'Ole</u> (Mar 25/5) - *made a splendid impression*
MAR 31/19 - *MT*	Louise Price and Charlotte Walker	<u>The Trail of the Lonesome Pine</u> by Eugene Walker (Mar 31/5)
APR 2/19 - *MT*	George H. Bubb presents	Farce, <u>Ikey & Abey in Society</u> (Apr 3/5) (*$0.50 - $1.00*) - *unadulterated fun*
APR 11/19 - *MT*	National Productions Co. Inc. with George Summers	<u>The Girl He Left Behind</u> (Apr 12/5) (*$0.50 - $1.00*) - *one of most all round pleasing shows*
MAY 5/19 - *MT*	Oliver Morosco presents	Hawaiian romantic play, <u>The Bird of Paradise</u> (May 5/5)
MAY 17/19 - *MT*	Klaw and Erlanger present Claire Mersereau	<u>Pollyanna</u> by Catherine Chisholm Cushing (May 17/2) (*$0.50 - $2.00*)
JUN 20/19 - *MT*	Selwyn & Co. with Elsa Ryan	<u>Tea for Three</u> (Jun 21/5) (*$0.50 - $1.50*) - *shows wonderful finesse*
OCT 3,4/19 - *MT*	Theatre Guild Inc.	Melodrama, <u>John Ferguson</u> by Sgt. John G. Ervine (Oct 3/5) (*$0.50 - $2.00*)
OCT 8/19 - *MT*	B.E. Lang presents Billy Oswald	<u>I Love a Lassie</u> (Oct 8/5) - *added still further to his local popularity*
OCT 10,11/19 - *MT*	A.S. Stern & Selwyn Co.	<u>Twin Beds</u> by Salisbury Field & Margaret Mayo (Oct 10/5)
OCT 13,14/19 - *MT*	Colonial Comedy Co. of Vancouver	<u>The End of a Perfect Day</u> (Oct 15/4) (*$0.50 - $1.00*) - *witty, wholesome & well put on*
OCT 17,18/19 - *MT*	unidentifed touring co.	<u>In Old Kentucky</u> (Oct 17/5) (*$0.50 - $1.00*) - *staged elaborately and well*
OCT 24,25/19 - *MT*	John Cort presents	Musical review, <u>Flo Flo & Her Perfect '36'</u> (Oct 25/5) (*$0.50 - $2.00*) - *done to everyone's satisfaction*
OCT 29,30/19 - *MT*	Milton Schuster presents	Musical comedy, <u>Make Yourself at Home</u> (Oct 30/5) (*$0.50 - $1.50*) - *good show*
NOV 7,8/19 - *MT*	N.Y. Touring Co./Kathryn Givney	Comedy-Drama, <u>The Revelations of a Wife</u> (Nov 8/5) - *well liked*
NOV 21,22/19 - *MT*	Clifford Devereux & Co./Zinita Graf	<u>School for Scandal</u>; <u>Arms & the Man</u> (Nov 21/5) - *finely expressed...large audience*
NOV 28,29/19 - *MT*	Stewart Walker presents N.Y. Co.	Booth Tarkington's <u>Seventeen</u> (Nov 29/5) (*$0.50 - $2.00*) - *wonderful show*
DEC 17,18/19 - *MT*	Comstock Elliott Co.	Musical comedy, <u>Oh Boy</u> (Dec 18/5) (*$0.50 - $2.00*) - *scores big success*
JAN 7/20 - *MT*	Charles Dillingham's Production with co. of 65	Musical comedy, <u>Chin-Chin</u> (Dec 31/5; Jan 7/5) (*$1.00 - $2.50*) - *two years at Globe Theatre, N.Y.*

DATE/PLACE	COMPANY AND/OR PERFORMER(S)	PERFORMANCE(S)/REFERENCE/CRITIQUE
JAN 20/20 - *MT*	George Broadhurst presents Miss Norton & Paul Nicholson	She Walked in Her Sleep (Jan 20/5) (*$0.50 - $2.00*)
JAN 28; MAR 1/20 - *MT*	Percy Hutchison with Miss Muriel Martin-Harvey presented by F. Ray Comstock & Morris Gest	The Luck of the Navy by Clifford Mills (Jan 28/5; Mar 1/5) - *first eminent English actor to visit since 1914. Exactly as presented for performance - Queen Mary*
FEB 6/20 - *MT*	Augustus Pitou Inc. presents May Robson	Comedy, Tish by Mary Roberts Rhinehart (Feb 6/5) (*$0.75 - $2.00*) - *original Chicago cast*
FEB 9,10/20 - *MT*	F. Stuart Whyte presents Zara Clinton	English pantomime, Red Riding Hood (Feb 9/5) (*$1.00 - $2.00*)
FEB 21/20 - *MT*	Billy Oswald, "Scottish comedian"	The Goose Girl (Feb 21/5) (*0.50 - $1.00*)
MAR 6/20 - *MT*	John M. Sheesley Inc. presents Gertrude Hutcheson and Metro cast	Musical, Let's Go (May 6/5) (*$0.50 - $2.00*)
MAR 10,11/20 - *Colonial Th. (CT)*	Kulolia's Native Hawaiians	Musical play, The Paradise of the Pacific (Mar 6/5) - *gave a good measure of entertainment*
APR 9,10/20 - *MT*	Percy Hutchison & his Queen's Theatre Co.	General Post (Apr 8/5; 9/5) - *exactly as presented at London's Haymarket Theatre*
APR 16,17/20 - *MT*	Tyrone Power	The Servant in the House; The Little Brother (Apr 8/5; 16/5; 17/5) (*$0.75 - $2.00*) - *eminent British actor; a masterpiece*
APR 30; MAY 1/20 - *MT*	Gus Hill presents	Mutt & Jeff's Dream (Apr 30/5)
MAY 4/20 - *N. Leth. United Ch.*	Theresa M. Siegit	Dramatic reader & entertainer (May 3/5) - *reads whole plays*
MAY 26/20 - *MT*	Guy Bates Post	The Masquerader (May 26/5) (*$1.00 - $2.50*) - *season's most notable dramatic event*
JUN 17,18/20 - *MT*	Una Carpenter	A Night in Honolulu (Jun 18/5) - *throughly enjoyed by a good audience*
JUN 28/20 - *MT*	unidentified touring co.	Peck's Bad Boy (Jun 28/5) (*$0.50 - $1.00*)
JUL 17/20 - *MT*	William P. Springer presents	Pal 'O Mine (Jul 17/5)
AUG 11-17/20 - *T*	Keighley New York Players	Chautauqua, It Pays to Advertise (Aug 10/8)
AUG 28/20 - *MT*	Ralph Dunbar presents	Robin Hood (Aug 28/8) (*$1.00 - $2.00*)
SEPT 4; 14/20 - *MT*	Max Bloom	Novelties of 1920 (Sept 4/8)
SEPT 20/20 - *MT*	Royal English Opera Co./Jefferson De Angelis and Hana Schimozumi, Edith Benmin, J. Humbird Duffy	The Mikado (Sept 20/8)
SEPT 22,23/20 - *CT*	Blakes Original Native Hawaiian Dancers & Singers	Musical comedy, Hello Hawaii (Sept 20/8)
SEPT 25/20 - *MT*	Harvey Orr's New York Co.	Musical comedy, Come Along Mary (Sept 20/8)
OCT 16/20 - *MT*	Lewers & Compton present Edward Lewers and British Cast	Comedy, Grumpy (Oct 16/12)
NOV 23,24/20 - *MT*	Ray Comstock & Morris Gest Production	Experience (Nov 24/8) (*$1.00 - $2.00*) - *gripping drama*
NOV 27; 29,30; DEC 3,4/20 - *MT*	F. Stuart Whyte presents Dororthy McKay; Zara Clinton	English pantomime, Babes in the Woods; and operettas San Toy; The Geisha (Nov 27/12; 29/8; 30/10; Dec 3/8) (*$1.00 - $2.00*)
DEC 11,12/20 - *MT*	F. Ray Comstock & Morris Gest present	The Wanderer (Dec 11/12) (*$1.00 - $2.50*)
DEC 29-JAN 3/21 - *MT*	Arlie Marks & Co. (daughter of Tom Marks)	Repertoire of late dramatic successes including Why Women Divorce Men (Dec 29/8) (*$0.50 - $1.00*) - *biggest and best stock company in Canada*
JAN 7,8/21 - *MT*	Trans-Canada Theatre Society & Percy Hutchison present H.V. Esmond, Eva Moore and English Co.	H.V. Edmond's, The Law Divine (Jan 7/8; 8/8) - *a dramatic treat - played to a very slim house - exactly as staged over 400 times in London*
FEB 11,12/21 - *MT*	Maude Henderson & Co.	Our New Minister; Snug Harbour (Feb 11/8) (*$0.50 - $1.00*) - *excellent company*
FEB 14/21 - *MT*	Ukrainian Dramatic Society	Freedom (Feb 14/8) (*$0.50 - $1.50*)
MAR 8/21 - *MT*	Boston English Opera Co. (65 members)	Ruddigore by Gilbert & Sullivan (Mar 8/8) (*$1.00 - $2.00*)
APR 1/21 - *MT*	Augustus Pitou Inc./May Robson	Comedy Nobody's Fool by Alan Dale (Apr 1/9) (*$0.75 - $2.00*)
APR 5,6/21 - *MT*	Oliver J. Eckhardt & Co.	Farce, The Naughty Bride (Apr 5/9) (*$0.50 - $1.50*) - *rewarding experience*

DATE/PLACE	COMPANY AND/OR PERFORMER(S)	PERFORMANCE(S)/REFERENCE/CRITIQUE
MAY 24/21 - MT (matinee/evening)	John E. Kellard in Shakespeare's	The Merchant of Venice; Julius Caesar (May 23/12) ($0.50 - $2.00)
OCT 21/21 - CT	Trans-Canada Theatre Society; Anglo Canadian Comedies Ltd. present the English Comedian Lawrence D'Orsay with Kitty Coleman & Co.	Tootlums (Oct 21/9; 22/9) ($1.00 - $1.50) - very enjoyable play
NOV 25,26/21 - CT	Marc Klaw Inc. & Trans-Canada Theatre Society, London cast including Walter Edwin	Comedy, French Leave by Reginald Berkeley directed by Charles D. Coburn (Nov 26/10) ($0.75 - $2.00) - sparkling comedy by fine cast
DEC 31/21 - MT	E.H. Robins presents Graham Velsey	Comedy romance, Just Suppose by A.E. Thomas (Dec 3/8) ($0.50 - $2.00)
MAY 26,27/22 - Chautauqua	Reed Metro Players	English comedy, Mrs. Temple's Telegram (Jun 17/7)
NOV 24,25/22 - MT	Tom McKnight & Co. with Miss Dorothy (Babe) McKay "Canada's Sweetheart"	Musical revue, Every Girl (Nov 24/8) ($0.75 - $1.50) - first big road show of the season
DEC 11-14; 18,19/22 - CT	Maude Henderson Co. with Anna Hughes & George P. Gray	Smiling Through; Turn to the Right; The Shepherd of the Hills (Dec 7/8; 12/8; 16/8) ($0.50 - $0.75) - created a splendid impression
JAN 20/23 - MT	Wagenhals & Kemper present a Toronto Co. with Kate Blancke	The Bat by Mary Roberts Rhinehart & Avery Hopwood (Jan 17/8; 22/8) ($0.75 - $2.00) - acting of a very fine order
JAN 22,23/23 - MT	The Hildebrand Dramatic Co. from Regina	Farce comedies, 3 Live Ghosts; Some Baby (Jan 23/8) - provides laughs
MAY 24,25/23 - MT	Joe Bennett & Co.	The Telephone Tangle (May 19/9)
SEPT 6,7/23 - MT	Margaret Marriott, Bryon Aldenn and Grand Players of Calgary	Comedy, Adam & Eve (Sept 1/8; 7/8) - very creative show - 40 weeks in Calgary
OCT 25,26/23 - MT	Lawrence Deas presents Chappelle & Stinnette and Co. direct from Empire Palace, London, England	"Colored" musical comedy success, Plantation Day (Oct 26/10) ($1.00 - $1.50) - very clever & very entertaining
NOV 8,9; 22,23; DEC 27,28/23 - MT	Margaret Marriott & the Grand Players	Cappy Ricks; Buddies; Polly With a Past (Nov 9/8; 23/8; Dec 28/8) - highly pleasing to crowded house
DEC 10,11/23 - MT	Kilbourn-Gordon Inc. presents N.Y. Touring Co.	The Cat & the Canary by John Willard (Dec 11/8) ($0.50 - $2.00) - superb cast
DEC 31; JAN 1/24 - MT	George M. Cohan presents Mr. & Mrs. C. Coburn	Comedy, So This is London (Dec 24/8) ($1.00 - $2.50)
FEB 9/24 - MT	Margaret Marriott & the Grand Players	The Acquittal by George M. Cohan (Feb 2/8)
MAR 10,11/24 - MT	Stanley J. Vermilyea presents	Musical comedy, The Maid of the Mts. (Mar 1/8; 10/8; 11/8) ($0.75 - $2.00) - not too balanced cast
MAR 28,29/24 - MT	Sir John Martin-Harvey supported by Miss N. de Silva (Lady Martin-Harvey)	A Cigarette Maker's Romance; The Burgomaster of Stilemonde; The Breed of the Treshams (Mar 18/8; 21/8; 28/8; 29/8) - theatre packed...a memorable evening - the curtain calls were incessant
MAY 2,3/24 - MT	unidentified road co.	The Unwanted Child by Florence Edna May (May 2/8) ($0.50 - $1.00)
MAY 9,10/24 - MT	John Golden presents Thomas Jefferson & Bessie Bacon	Comedy, Lightnin (May 3/10; 10/8) ($0.75 - $2.50) - 3 years in New York; 2 years in Chicago - fun at its best - deserved far better patronage
NOV 13,14/24 - MT	Theatrical Enterprises Ltd. with Lucille Sears and Mary Marble	Comedy, The First Year by John Golden (Nov 13/8; 14/8) ($0.50 - $2.00) - excellent show...poor attendance
JAN 26,27; FEB 23/24 - MT	Percy Hutchison & his Queen's Theatre Co.	Farce, Nightie Night; Brewster's Millions (Jan 27/7; Feb 24/9) ($0.50 - $2.00) - tickled big audience
FEB 2/25 - MT	Lee & J.J. Shubert present the original Century Theatre New York cast	Blossom Time by Franz Schubert (Feb 3/8) - greatly enjoyed by overflowing crowd
MAR 16,17/25 - MT	E.J. Carpenter presents cartoon, musical comedy	Bringing Up Father in Ireland by George McManus (Mar 17/8) - crowded theatre
MAR 20,21/25 - MT	Stetson's Production	Uncle Tom's Cabin (Mar 20/8) - 54th annual tour
APR 6,7/25 - MT	Brandon Light Opera Co. (50 singers)	Robin Hood by R. DeKoven; The Bohemian Girl by M.W. Balfe (Mar 28/9; Apr 7/12; 8/8) ($0.75 - $2.00) - rare treat...hugely enjoyed
SEPT 29/25 - MT	Brandon Light Opera Co.	The Mikado (Sept 29/8)
NOV 2,3; DEC 8/25 - MT	Cameron Matthews & English Comedy Co.	The Dover Road by A.A. Milne; Too Many Husbands (Nov 3/8; Dec 9/16) - presented with the highest capability - 1st trans-continental tour

DATE/PLACE	COMPANY AND/OR PERFORMER(S)	PERFORMANCE(S)/REFERENCE/CRITIQUE
NOV 30, DEC 1/25 - *Palace Th. (PT)*	W. Leonard Howe, Doreen Thompson	Narration & vocals related to movie, <u>The Man They Could Not Hang</u> (Nov 30/8)
JAN 4/26 - *MT*	Captain Plunkett presents English Comedian G.P. Huntley	Musical comedy, <u>Three Little Maids</u> (Jan 5/8; Oct 11/27/7) - *SRO - completely good performance - G.P.H. died, Oct. 1927*
JAN 18,19/26 - *MT*	Rochester American Opera Co. with Vladimir Rosing	<u>Faust</u>; <u>I Pagliacci</u>; <u>Cavalleria Rusticana</u> (Jan 19/7; 20/14) - *intimate opera*
JAN 22,23/26 - *MT*	Julia Arthur presented by Bertram C. Whitney	<u>St. Joan</u> by G.B. Shaw (Jan 23/9) *($0.75 - $2.00) - splendid performance*
FEB 1,2/26 - *MT*	Robert B. Mantell & Genevieve Hamper and Co.	<u>Merchant of Venice</u>; <u>Macbeth</u> (Feb 2/7,10; 3/8) - *"a gifted Shylock", good, all round performance*
FEB 26,27/26 - *MT*	Sir John Martin-Harvey, Miss N. De Silva	<u>Garrick</u>; <u>The Only Way</u> (Feb 27/7) - *curtain call after curtain call*
APR 5-11/26 - *MT*	Arlie Marks & Co. of 15 performers	Plays & vaudeville, <u>My Irish Cinderella</u>; <u>When Dreams Come True</u>; <u>Where is Your Wife</u>; <u>Mother's Irish Rose</u>; <u>The Lure</u>; <u>45 Minutes From Broadway</u> (Mar 30/8; Apr 8/8) - *commendable show*
OCT 18,19/26 - *MT*	John H. Schuberg presents a Charles E. Royal Production	<u>So This is Canada</u> by W.S. Atkinson (Oct 19/12) *($0.50 - $1.50)*
NOV 1,2/26 - *MT*	P.R. Allen presents Verna Felton	<u>So This is London</u> by George M. Cohan (Nov 2/12) - *admirable piece of acting*
JAN 31, FEB 1/27 - *MT*	Lee & J.J. Shubert present N.Y. Century Theatre Production	<u>Blossom Time</u> (Jan 31/7,6; Feb 1/10) - *packed to the doors - cast includes Alberta baritone, Knight MacGregor*
FEB 18,19/27 - *MT*	P.R. Allen presents Verna Felton & Co.	<u>The Whole Town's Talking</u> (Feb 19/14) *($0.75 - $1.50) - favorite actress pleases audience*
FEB 23/27 - *MT*	Chinese National League of Canada presents Chinese romantic epic	<u>The Lady General</u>; Proceeds to Chinese War Memorial Fund (Feb 24/10) - *packed theatre; acclaim exotic drama. English version printed on program.*
APR 4,5/27 - *MT*	Miss Nichol's Chicago & Detroit Co.	<u>Abie's Irish Rose</u> by Anne Nichol (Apr 5/10) *($0.75 - $2.00 + tax) - delights audience*
APR 20,21/27 - *MT*	Cameron Matthews & Co.	Mystery play, <u>The Gorilla</u> (Apr 11/12; 21/12) - *theatrical novelty of much merit*
OCT 21,22/27 - *MT*	Lang, O'Neill & Lang present London Co. of 50 performers with David Lee & Lillian Barnes	English pantomime, <u>Aladdin</u> (Oct 18/12) *($0.50 - $2.50)*
OCT 24,25/27 - *MT*	Clyde H. Gordinier presents Calgary Stock Co. in Earl Carroll's comedy success	<u>Laff That Off</u> (Oct 22/10; 25/14) *($0.50 - $1.00) - light but pleasing comedy*
NOV 14/27 - *YMCA*	Walt McRaye	<u>Wake Up Canada</u> (Nov 14/7)
NOV 25,26/27 - *MT*	Basil Horsfall's Opera film with stage appearances by members of National Opera Co.	<u>The Bohemian Girl</u> (Nov 12/15,16; 26/16) - *makes fine impression*
FEB 24,25/28 - *MT*	F. Stuart Whyte presents	English pantomime, <u>Dick Whittington & His Cat</u> (Feb 25/12) *($0.50 - $2.00) - the girl show of the season; well received*
MAR 15-17/28 - *MT*	Seymour Hicks, Ellaline Terriss and London Co.	<u>Mr. What's His Name</u>; <u>Sleeping Partners</u>; <u>Scrooge</u>; <u>The Man in Dress Clothes</u> (Mar 6/10; 16/9; 17/16; 19/8) *($0.75 - $2.50) - Hicks & talented London Co. received ovation*
APR 6,7/28 - *MT*	L.A. Lambert presents Opera-film with live cast of National Opera Co.	<u>William Tell</u> (Apr 5/18; 7/14) - *exquisite voice blending*
APR 12,13/28 - *MT*	Horsfall's Opera film with National Opera	<u>Il Trovatore</u> (Apr 10/14; 12/12)
OCT 26,27/28 - *MT*	Arthur Hammerstein presents	<u>Rose Marie</u> by Friml and Stothart (Oct 27/10) *($1.50 - $3.50) - one of the greatest musical shows yet seen in Lethbridge*
NOV 2,3; DEC 7/8/28 - *MT*	Gordon McLeod & his English Co. with Lilian Christine	<u>Miss Elizabeth's Prisoner</u>; <u>A Bill of Divorcement</u> (Nov 3/18; Dec 8/12) *($0.50 - $2.00) - charming portrayal - highly finished performance*
NOV 9,10/28 - *MT*	F. Ray Comstock & Morris Gest present Stratford-Upon-Avon Festival Co.	<u>Taming of the Shrew</u>; <u>Merchant of Venice</u>; <u>Merry Wives of Windsor</u> (Nov 10/13) *($0.50 - $3.00) - brilliant presentation*
DEC 11-15/28 - *MT*	Maurice Colburne Theatrical Co. of England presents Boliol Holloway in Shaw's	<u>You Never Can Tell</u>; <u>Candida</u>; <u>The Dark Lady of the Sonnets</u>; <u>Fanny's First Play</u> (Dec 10/12; 12/12; 14/22) *($0.75 - $2.00) - delights audience - superb* entertainment
MAR 1,2/29 - *MT*	Brandsby William & London Co. with Kathleen Saintsburg	<u>Oliver Twist</u> (Mar 2/12) *($0.75 - $2.00) - impressive...highly meritorious* performance

DATE/PLACE	COMPANY AND/OR PERFORMER(S)	PERFORMANCE(S)/REFERENCE/CRITIQUE
AUG 2-8/29 - *(T) 9th St. between 3rd & 4th Ave.*	Toronto Operatic Co., Chautauqua Players & others	Chautauqua, novelty musical numbers and 3 act comedies: Peg 'O My Heart; The Patsy (Aug 3/7,8; 8/7) - *good performances - adult season ticket $2.25. Return of Chautauqua after many years*
OCT 25,26/29 - *MT*	Philip Rodway presents English comedian Wee Georgie Wood, Fred Conquest	English pantomime, Humpty Dumpty (Oct 22/8; 23/8; 26/8) - *co. of 60 delights large audience*
NOV 1,2/29 - *MT*	Gilbert Miller by arrangement with Maurice Brown presents Basil Gil, Hugh Williams, Walter Hudd, Forester Harvey and all male cast	Journey's End by R.C. Sheriff (Nov 1/8; 2/8) ($1.10 - $2.75) - *gripping drama*
DEC 6,7/29 - *MT*	Gordon McLeod and English Co. with Lilian Christine	Mystery thriller, The Ringer by Edgar Wallace (Dec 7/5) ($0.75 - $2.00) - *real thriller proves delightful*
AUG 1-7/30 - *T*	Martin Erwin Players, Chautauqua	Broken Dishes; Pollyanna; Jack and the Beanstalk (Aug 2/7; 4/7; 7/7)
JAN 5,6/31 - *MT*	Simon Ord presents London Road Show Co. with Jean Clyde	Scottish comedy, Marigold by Allen Harker & F.R. Pryor (Dec 29/5; 31/5; Jan 6/5) - *delights large audience - from Kingsway Theatre, London*
JAN 8-14/31 - *T*	Chautauqua with Mulvaney Light Opera Co., Festival Co., Meredith Players and others	Selections & scenes from light opera, plays: Skidding; Bought & Paid For (Dec 29/5; 31/5; Jan 6/5) - *acting & singing well balanced...play was enthusiastically received*
JAN 23; 25-30; FEB 1-5/32 - *MT*	Majestic Players with George A. Secord present tabloid versions of "latest N.Y. & London stage successes (as added attraction with movies)	This Woman Business; Some Baby; A Lucky Break; Don't Lie to Your Wife (Jan 20/2; 25/2; 27/2; 30/2; Feb 3/2) ($0.25 - $0.35) - *resident company*
FEB 27/32 - *MT*	Sir John & Lady Martin-Harvey & London Co. with Cyril Dane	The King's Message (Feb 29/7) - *enraptured & enthralled large audiences*
JUN 9-11, 13/32 - *T*	Martin Erwin Players, Chautauqua	New Brooms; Merely Mary Ann (Jun 10/9; 11/7) - *enjoyed by large crowd*
APR 14,15/33 - *MT*	Passion Play Co. of Calgary directed by John J. Hennessey	Passion Play (Apr 6/6; 7/9; 15/7) - *well cast...given sympathetic treatment*
JUN 27-30/33 - *T*	Peerless Canadian Players, Chautauqua	Sun Up; A Pair of Sixes (Jun 24/7; 26/7; 28/9)
DEC 18/33 - *MT*	Scottish Musical Comedy Co.	The Cotter's Saturday Night by Robert Burns (Dec 15/6; 19/6) ($0.50 - $1.00 & tax)
FEB 24/34 - *MT*	Scottish Musical Players (Musical Comedy Co.)	The Bonnie Briar Bush; Tam O' Shanter (Feb 22/4; 27/6) - *capacity crowd is delighted*
DEC 3/34 - *MT*	Scottish Musical Players	Bonnie Prince Charles; The Cotter's Saturday Night (Nov 24/2; 28/6; Dec 4/7) ($0.25 - $1.00) - *well received by large audiences*
FEB 14,15/36 - *MT*	Edward Harvey presents his English Co. (auspices of Lions Club)	Comedy The Bachelor Husband (Feb 1/2; 15/7) ($0.35 - $1.00) - *plenty of laughs*
MAR 23/41 - *Capitol Th. (Cap)*	Jan Chamberlain (Toronto actress)	One woman show (Mar 24/8) - *clever show...responsive audience*
APR 3/43 - *Southminster Ch.*	Jan Chamberlain	Character sketches (Mar 20/8)
AUG 27/45 - *LDS Auditorium*	Professor Joseph F. Smith, director, Drama Division Banff School of Fine Arts	Reading, The Flying Yorkshireman by Eric Knight (Aug 28/7)
JAN 23/48 - *Cap*	Theatre Under the Stars on tour with Shirley Neher, Winnifred Hatt, Derek McDermot & Karl Norman	Musical revue A Night in Vienna (Jan 10/2; 20/7; 24/8) ($0.25 - $1.00) - *delights large audience...an artistic treat*
MAR 8-10/50 - *Cap*	Murray & Donald present John Pratt, Murray Matheson & all Canadian cast	Musical Comedy Revue, There Goes Yesterday (Feb 24/7; Mar 1/6; 6/8,11) ($1.00 - $2.00)
DEC 10/52 - *Cap*	Canadian Opera Co./Herman Geiger-Torel with Jan Rubes, Mary Morrison, Ernest Adams, Joan Ivey, Andrew MacMillan, Patricia Snell	Opera Backstage (Dec 2/10; 3/18; 4/10; 8/10; 11/11,12) - *enthusiastic applause*
MAR 30,31/53 - *Cap*	The Canadian Professional Theatre Guild presents Great Plays Inc. (Vancouver)/Dean Goodman with Mary Matthews	Hamlet (Mar 21/9; 30/10; 31/9; Apr 1/13) - *Professional Theatre returns to Lethbridge - fine performance*

DATE/PLACE	COMPANY AND/OR PERFORMER(S)	PERFORMANCE(S)/REFERENCE/CRITIQUE
JUN 15-SEPT 24/53 - *Rec. Hall (Kenyon Air-field), Civic Centre, Legion Memorial Hall, Waterton, Claresholm, Medicine Hat & Taber*	Great Plays Co./Dean Goodman (Resident Summer Stock Co.) with Mary Matthews, Jack Medhurst, Arthur Keenan, Robert "Mike" Hemingway, Cheryle Brown, Gary Ferguson, Cliff Sherwood, Anne Christensen, John Rivet, Bevonne Paterson, Bruce Busby, Marie Kennan, Derek Ralson, James Onley, Len Ontkean	The Voice of the Turtle; For Love or Money; Goodbye Again; Accent on Youth; Yes, My Darling Daughter; The Drunkard; The Skylark; Bell, Book & Candle; John Loves Mary; Claudia; Born Yesterday; Blithe Spirit; See How They Run; Love From a Stranger; There's Always Juliet (May 20/9; Sept 24/10 - *passim*)
JUN 15-SEPT 20/54 - *Civic Centre, Allan Watson School, Ft. Whoop-Up Guest Ranch, Also Medicine Hat, Claresholm, Calgary, Waterton, Barons*	Great Plays Co./Dean Goodman (Resident Summer Stock Co.) with Cheryle Brown, John Farmer, Bruce MacLeod, Liza Benedict, Robert Hobbs, Ed ward Stevlingson, Sybil Siegel, Sally Sherman, John Bouchard, Hilda Armstrong, Celia Stanton, Mahlon Vanderlaan	The Moon is Blue; Light Up the Sky; French Without Tears; I Like It Here; Rebecca; Petticoat Fever; Miranda; Laura; Outward Bound; Personal Appearance; Apron Strings; Philadelphia Story; Suspect; A Night With Dean Goodman (Jun 15 - Sept 13 - *passim*)
NOV 29/54 - *L.C.I. Auditorium*	Lancaster Co. of B.C./Ian Thorne/James Testemale [producer] (auspices of L.C.I.)	Romeo & Juliet with Derek Ralston, Rosemarie Meyerhoff, Ed Stevlingson, Don Pethley, Monica Dudley, Jack Ammon, Vivienne Chadwick, Ian Thorne, Jack Dray, Dale MacDonald (Nov 30/10) - *a hit - audience of 400*
JAN 28,29/55 - *LDS Auditorium*	Great Plays Co./Dean Goodman (in aid of LDS building fund)	I Like It Here (Jan 27/3; 29/9) - *enthusiastic welcome*
JUN 22-AUG 6/55 - *Civic Centre, Susie Bawden School*	Great Plays Co./Dean Goodman (Resident Summer Stock, Lethbridge), with Rosemarie Meyerhoff, Robert Jackson, Mat Zimmerman, Arthur Silva, Jane Smith, Gary Mitchell, Robert Collins, Abagail Arundel, Charlotte McDowell	Two Dozen Roses; Walk the Tight Wire; Goodbye Again; Ten Nights in a Barroom; The Importance of Being Ernest; Springtime for Harry (Jun 23 - Aug 6 - *passim*) - *Company to close books!!*
NOV 18-23/55 - *L.C.I.*	United Church AOTS presents Black Hills Co. with Josef Meier & a cast of 100 including Southminster Choir/A.K. Pulland	Original Black Hills Passion Play (Nov 15/10; 19/9; 21/9; 26/10) - *sell out audience enjoys rich experience*
NOV 28/55 - *L.C.I.*	Eric Christmas (auspices of Playgoers)	One Man Show Christmas Party (Nov 9/3; 14/10; 19/10; 22/3; 29/10) - *variety of characters*
FEB 5/56 - *Cap (auspices of Kiwanis & Rotary Clubs)*	Canadian Players/Douglas Campbell with Frances Hyland, Max Helpman, Bruno Gerussi, Roland Hewgill, John Gardiner, Jack Hutt, Douglas Campbell, George McCowan, John Horton, Bob Gibson, Norma Renault, Margot Blavey	Macbeth; Saint Joan (Jan 18/4; 28/12; 30/10; Feb 1/4, 18; 3/9) [see also May 25/55/16; Jul 26/9; Aug 29/10; Oct 31/55/15] - *Drama at its best - 1st western Canadian tour*
MAR 27,28/57 - *Cap*	Canadian Players/Douglas Campbell with Ann Casson, Tony Van Bridge, Max Helpman, Ted Follows, John Gardiner, Edwin Stephenson, Ann Marginson, Susanne Scott, Irena Mayeska, James Peddie, James Balfour, Alan Zelonska, Jack Hutt	Othello; Man & Superman (Nov 21/56/13; Mar 9/3; 23/10; 26/9; 28/10; 29/10) ($1.50 - $2.50) - *priceless and polished performance*
NOV 2/57 - *Civic Centre*	Wagner Opera Co. (N.Y.)	Carmen by Bizet (Oct 15/16; 26/13; Nov 4/9) - *near capacity crowd shows appreciation*
MAR 16,17/59 - *Cap (auspices of Rotary & Kiwanis Clubs)*	Canadian Players/Tony Van Bridge with Paddy Croft, Bill Glover, Mervyn Blake, Alan Nunn, John Horton, Marigold Charlesworth, Deborah Cass, Peter Needham, Desmond Scott, Jeremy Wilkin, Roberta Maxwell, Christine Bennett, Sydney Sturges, Jane Cleve	Romeo and Juliet; Pygmalion (Feb 28/11; Mar 7/14; 16/9; 17/10) - *played to an appreciative audience*
MAR 7,8/60 - *Cap (auspices of Kiwanis & Rotary Clubs)*	Canadian Players/Tony Van Bridge with William Needles, Eric Christmas, Peter Needham, Bernard Behrens, Deborah Cass, Nancy Kerr, Peter Mannering, Judith Sinclair, David Bedard, Charles Lewsen, Julia Lee, Donna Neufeld, Dan MacDonald, Martin Lager, Gordon Ruttan, Jack Hutt	Comedy of Errors; The Devil's Disciple (Sept 28/59/10; Feb 13/3; Mar 8/9; 9/12) - *a finished and potent performance*
SEPT 19-23/60 - *L.C.I.*	Original Black Hills Co. with Josef Meier (auspices of U.C. AOTS)	Passion Play (Sept 7/17; 15/14; 17/12; 20/9) ($1.00 - $3.00) - *provides a vivid emotional experience*

DATE/PLACE	COMPANY AND/OR PERFORMER(S)	PERFORMANCE(S)/REFERENCE/CRITIQUE 309
DEC 14/60 - *Cap*	Canadian Opera Co. with Jan Rubes, Dodi Protero, Elsie Sawchuk, Donald Young, Sheila Percey, Phil Stark, Alexander Gray, John Arab, Cornelius Opthof	Merry Wives of Windsor by Otto Nicolai (Dec 10/14; 13/18; 15/17) - *a cheerful delight to hear and see* [auspices Overture Concert Association]
MAR 1,2/61 - *Cap*	Canadian Players/George McCowan with Yafa Lerner, Hugh Webster, D. Cass, Judith Coates, Al Kozlik, B. Behrens, Jay Shannon, David White	The Tempest; Caucasian Chalk Circle (Feb 20/16; 27/9; Mar 2/10; 3/14) - *professional finesse but CCC was a cheap burlesque*
DEC 14/61 - *Cap*	Canadian Opera Co./George Brough with Jan Rubes, Dodi Protero, Phil Stark, Peter Mews, Alan Crofoot, Arlene Meadows, Joyce Hill, Joanne Ivey	Orpheus in the Underworld by Jacques Offenbach (Dec 8/12; 15/14) - *a tremendous triumph*
MAR 13,14/62 - *Cap*	Canadian Players/Tony Van Bridge with Henry Ramer, Claude Bede, Nelson Phillips, Gary Krawford, Joseph Rutten, Ken James, James Peddie, Nancy Kerr, Jack Medley, Christopher Newton, Anna Reiser	Julius Caesar; St. Joan (Mar 14/18; 15/12) - *1st - too rapid speech - 2nd - captured the audience* [costumes and settings by Barbara Mattingly]
NOV 20/62 - *Cap*	Canadian Opera Co./Herman Geiger-Torel/W. James Craig (mus dir) with Jan Rubes, John Arab, Sheila Piercey, Frank Pannell, Victor Braun, Tito Dean	La Boheme by Puccini (Sept 22/11; Nov 2/14; 14/8; 19/9; 21/6) - *exciting*
NOV 1/63 - *Cap*	Canadian Opera Co./George Brough with Phil Stark, Elsie Sawchuk, Dodi Protero, Alexander Gray, Heather Thomson, Constance Fisher, Celia Ward, Cornelius Opthof, Peter Van Ginkel	Così fan Tutte by Mozart (Nov 2/14) - *scores triumph*
FEB 3/64 - *Cap*	Mavor Moore presents the Canadian Touring Co./Alan Lund with Barbara Hamilton, Dave Broadfoot, Peter Mews, Bill Cole, Jack Duffy, Dean Regan, Roma Hern, Diane Nyland, Marylyn Stuart, Liane Marshall	Musical review, Spring Thaw (Jan 31/12; Feb 3/11; 4/10) - *1st Western Canadian Tour - delightful*
DEC 2/64 - *Cap* (auspices of Rotary & Kiwanis Clubs)	Canadian Players/Jim Clouser with Hugh Webster, Barb Franklin, Eric House, Bruno Gerussi, Ken James, Jacques Zouvi	All About Us (Nov 24/9; 26/9; Dec 3/14) - *very versatile troupe pleases audience of 800*
JAN 30/65 - *Cap*	Mavor Moore Production/Alan Lund/John Fenwick (mus dir) with Dave Broadfoot, Bill Cole, Peter Mews, Jack Duffy, Marylyn Stuart, Liane Marshall, Gayle Lepine	Spring Thaw (Dec 4/11; Jan 25/15; Feb 1/9) - *top calibre professionals*
SEPT 10,11/65 - *Civic Centre*	Provincial Centennial Committee & City of Lethbridge present: Robert Christie, Andrew Allan and others	Pageant, The Fathers of Confederation by Tommy Tweed (Sept 7/10; 10/14)
JAN 14/66 - *Civic Centre*	Allied Arts Council & Drama Division, Provincial Recreational and Cultural Development Branch	Hogarth Puppets (Jan 11/3; 13/10; 15/14) - *one of the largest troupes in the world; delightful show*
MAR 10/66 - *Cap*	Les Jeunes Comédiens (from Quebec)	Excerpts from Moliere (Mar 3/15)
FEB 27/67 - *Cap*	Robert Johnston Productions/Alan Lund/Fen Watkin (mus dir) with B. Hamilton, P. Mews, D. Regan, Dinah Christie, Douglas Chamberlain, Donald Harron, Catherine McKinnon, Diane Nyland, Ron Tanguay	Spring Thaw or My Country, What's It To You? (20th year) (Jan 16/9; Feb 28/10) - *two packed houses; lots of laughs*
MAR 13/67 - *Yates*	Les Jeunes Comédiens (from Quebec)	French plays, (Mar 14/9) - *500 see the two performances*
SEPT 14,15/67 - *Yates*	Vancouver Festival Society/Aida Broadbent (Festival Canada on Tour) with Karl Norman, Pearl Kerr, Harry Mossfield, Betty Phillips, Shirley Milliner, Ross Laidley	100 Years of Musical Comedy (Sept 12/3,14; 15/4) - *disappointing audience of 250*
FEB 26/68 - *Cap*	Robert Johnson Production/Alan Lund with Pat Armstrong, Douglas Chamberlain, Rita Howell, Dean Regan, Jack Creley, Ed Evanko, Roma Hearn, Robert Jeffrey, Diane Nyland	Musical Revue, Spring Thaw/Alan Lund (dir & chor) (Feb 24/3; 27/14) - *often very funny*

DATE/PLACE	COMPANY AND/OR PERFORMER(S)	PERFORMANCE(S)/REFERENCE/CRITIQUE
MAR 23/68 - *Yates*	Concert Series Management Associates/Jackie Warner, Katie Anders & N.Y. cast	Musical, <u>Stop the World, I Want to Get Off</u> (Mar 22/3; 23/16; 25/10) - *slick production*
APR 16/68 - *Yates*	Calgary MAC 14/Kenneth Dyba with Robert Haley, Joyce Uren	The Owl & The Pussycat (Apr 17/14) - *whacking good production [Western Canada Arts Festival]*
DEC 9/68 - *Yates*	Canadian Opera Co.	The Barber of Selville (Dec 6/14; 10/12) - *sparkling presentation*
MAR 7/69 - *Cap*	The National Shakespeare Co. of N.Y. with Victor Raider-Wexler, Katherine McGrath, Michael Cantine, Don Phenley, Ian Thomson	<u>The Taming of the Shrew</u> (Mar 1/3; 7/13; 8/17) - *lustiness and vigor evident*
MAR 14/69 - *Yates*	Theatre Saskatchewan/Eric Salmon with Sandy Webster, Janet Crowder	<u>Billy Liar</u> (Mar 15/17) - *a treat! [auspices of AAC]*
NOV 13/70 - *Yates*	Canadian Opera Co./John Fenwick (mus dir) with Phil Stark, Dodi Protero, Cornelius Opthof, Elsie Sawchuk, Alan Crofoot, Richard Braun, Linda Boothby, Loro Farell, Anne Linden, Don McManus, Gerard Boyd	<u>Orpheus in the Underworld</u> (Nov 12/14; 14/18) - *Broadway freshness and verve*
JAN 21/71 - *Yates*	Sherman Pituck presents Theatre of the Balustrade of Prague with Ladislav Fialka (sponsored by AAC)	Czechoslovakian mime group (Jan 21/12; 22/11) - *dazzling...refreshing...ebullient good humor*
APR 2/71 - *St. Augustine's*	The Agape Players of Miame, Florida	Musical Drama (Mar 27/9)
NOV 9,10/72 - *U of L*	Théâtre I (Montreal)	**1.** Dr. Faustus by Christopher Marlowe; **2.** <u>Little Theatre of the Green Goose</u> by Galczinski (Sept 28/13; Nov 4/6) - *full house expected*
NOV 29/72 - *U of L Dr. Lab*	Les Jeunes Comédiens du Théâtre du Nouveau Monde (auspices of National Arts Center, Ottawa)	(<u>Quichotte</u> (Nov 18/16) ($0.50 - $1.00) - *10th Cross Canada Tour*
FEB 5-9/73 - *Local Schools*	Theatre Calgary Touring Troupe with Dana Still, Jane Bass & Ken Anderson	(Feb 8/18) - *each presentation is followed by a drama workshop*
FEB 12-16/73 - *Local Schools*	Touring Children's Theatre Group	Evil Ork and her puppets (Feb 19/13)
DEC /73 - *Local Schools*	Theatre Calgary Caravan with Leslie Saunders, Brian Brown, Jean-Pierre Fournier	Two plays by Jonathan Levy (Oct 6/30)
SEPT 5-7/74 - *Yates*	Gazebo Theatre One (Santa Barbara, California) with Lethbridge native son Brad Murdock & Mike Driscoll, Jeanette Collins, Bob Emmens, Paula Byron, Michael Goss, Sandy Sorah, Norman Neil, Cathy McInnis	Musical, <u>Godspell</u> (Aug 7/18; 29/7; Sept 6/16) - *excellent theatre fare*
SEPT 28/74 - *Yates*	Allied Arts Council presents Charlottetown Festival Co. with Mallorie Ann Spiller, Roma Hern, Calvin McRae, Marv Trainor, Sheila McCarthey and others	<u>Anne of Green Gables</u> (Sept 21/8; 30/11) - *enchanting—Anne, a winner*
OCT 24 & 26/74 - *Yates*	AAC presents Citadel Theatre (Edm)/John Neville/Owen Foran, Tom Miller, Margaret Barton, Colin Miller, David Schurmann, Richard Cuffling, Brigid Johnston, Susan Wright, Bob Birch, Richard Partington, Margaret Bard	<u>The Rivals</u> by R. Sheridan (Sept 21/8; Oct 24/7; 25/16) - *near flawless production*
NOV 5/74 - *Yates*	Overture Concert Series Presents Canadian Opera Co. with John Arab, Barbara Collier	<u>La Boheme</u> (Nov 6/14) - *played to a crowd of 425*
NOV 7/74 - *Yates*	AAC presents Toronto Workshop Production	<u>Ten Lost Years</u> from the book by Barry Broadfoot (Sept 21/8; Nov 8/18; 15/11) - *pure gold*
MAY 18/75 - *Yates*	AAC presents Pallisade Arts (Calgary and Jasper)	Musical Comedy Revue <u>Oh Coward!</u> by Roderick Cook (May 9 - Leisure & T.V. Week/11)
JUN 13/75 - *Yates*	Redlight Theatre (Toronto) [sponsored locally by The Women's Place]	<u>Oh, What a Glorious Time We Had</u> by Diane Grant (May 30/9, Jun 14/10) - *group was formed in 1974 to give women experience in the theatre and a forum for their work - sparkling, educational fun; audience of 150*

DATE/PLACE	COMPANY AND/OR PERFORMER(S)	PERFORMANCE(S)/REFERENCE/CRITIQUE
JUN 21,22/75 - *Yates*	Association of United Ukrainian Canadians Theatre 80 (Edm)/Peter Boretski/Gloria Andrichuk (dance dir)/Hazel Skulsky (mus dir) with cast of 55 including Barbara Reese and John Rivet	Musical, <u>Adam's Son</u> by Hannah Polowy & Mitch Sago based on novel <u>Zemlya</u> (Land) by Olga Kobylyanska (May 1/27; Jun 23/14) *($3.50) - prepared for Calgary's centennial celebrations*
JAN 15/76 - *Yates*	Western Opera Association/U of A Singers: George Cotton, Betty Kolodziej, Alan Ord & Merla Aikman	An Evening of Opera including duets, trios & scenes (Jan 16/16) - *pleasant evening [auspices of AAC and Alberta Cultural Development Branch]*
MAY 18/76 - *Pub. Lib.*	Ron East (artistic dir), the Mime Unltd., Toronto Theatre	Mask, mime & clown (May 15/18; 19/13) - *stunning & hilarious [auspices AAC]*
AUG /77 - *Bowman Arts Centre*	The Intimate Theatre of Alcohol Awareness/Sandi Balcovske with Randy Ritz, Susan Gagnon, Paul Johnson, Heather Devine, Jane Olynyk, Gerry Potter	<u>Drinks Before Dinner</u> (Aug 17, Leisure & TV/8; 25/10) [auspices AADAC]
SEPT 12-17/77 - *Yates*	unidentified co.	Musical, <u>My Turn on Earth</u> by Carol Lynn Pearson & Lex de Azevedo (Sept 10/7)
FEB 10/78 - *Yates*	Raymond Clarke (auspices of U of L Department of Drama)	One Man Show, <u>Oscar</u> [a portrait of Oscar Wilde] (Jan 28/17; Feb 11/6) *($2.50) - light weight (Brian Tyson)*
SEPT 8/78 - *U of L*	John Stuart Anderson [British professional actor]	One Man Show <u>Akanaton: King of Egypt</u> (Sept 1/16; 8/7) *($2.00)*
SEPT 23/78 - *U of L*	Irish Canadian Co.	<u>The Year of the Hiker</u> by John B. Deane (Sept 21/8) *($2.50)*
NOV 13-17/78 - *CCH Auditorium & other city schools*	Theatre Calgary Touring Co. Stagecoach Players	<u>Napi</u> [a series of Indian legends] or <u>Pioneers</u> by Dr. Bernardo (Nov 11/10)
DEC 6,7/78 - *Wilson Jr. H.S.; Gilbert Patterson Jr. H.S.*	Catalyst Theatre (Edm)/Lorraine Behman with Carol Virtue, Malcolm Baines and Michael Hoyt (Leth.); Amanda Holoway, Sheila Bennett, Paul Whitney	<u>The Black Creek Project</u> (Dec 7/14)
DEC 9/78 - *Yates*	Le Théâtre Français d'Edmonton	<u>Le Temps d'une Vie</u> by Roland Lepage (Nov 23/6; Dec 2/19) *($3.00 - $4.00) - 1st French language play to be performed at the Yates*
FEB 5/79 - *Yates*	Maxim Mazumdar [auspices of AAC in cooperation with Alberta Culture]	<u>Oscar Remembered</u> dir. by William Hutt (Dec 2/17; Feb 6/7) - *astonishing portrayal (Arthur McDougall)*
FEB 1/79 - *Yates (auspices of U of L Continuing Education & Dept. of Drama)*	The National Arts Centre Theatre Co. dir by John Wood/John Orenstein, Rita Howell, Judy Marshak, Karen Wood, Mary Trainor	<u>Waiting for the Parade</u> by John Murrell (Jan 27/6) - *Murrell really did his homework on this one (Joan Waterfield)*
FEB 14/79 - *Yates*	Sneezy Waters with Keith Glass, George Essery, Joel Zifkim, Jas Butler (musicians)	Musical Play, <u>Hank Williams: The Show He Never Gave</u> by Maynard Collins (Jan 27/6; Feb 12/17; 15/6) - directed by Peter Froehlich - *Waters imitation of Williams was uncanny*
MAR 31/79 - *Pub. Lib.*	Le Théâtre Français d'Edmonton	<u>Le Canard a l'Orange</u> (French translation by M. G. Sauvagion of <u>The Secretary Bird</u> by William Douglas Home (Mar 24/23; 30/6))$2.00 - $3.00)
APR 1/79 - *Yates - AAC Great Performance Series*	<u>Theatre Beyond Words</u> from Niagara-on-the-Lake/Harro Maskow (art dir) with Larry Lefebvre, Paulette Hallich, Robin Paterson	Mime Theatre, <u>Potato People</u> (Mar 24/25; 30/8; Apr 2/23) - *troupe has mastered craft (Arthur McDougall)*
APR 4/79 - *Pub. Lib.*	Théâtre Nouveau (New Brunswick)	A mime about a girl and a clown (Apr 2/24) - *free admission*
MAY 4/79 - *S.A. Art Gallery*	Crossroads Theatre Co. of Cranbrook,B.C.	Music, Pantomime & Poetry, <u>The Child Sketch; The Train Sketch</u> (May 1/9; 3/8; 5/6) - *theatre for children - $2.00 (free for children under 12); delightful & interesting*
MAY 22/79 - *Various Lethbridge locations (auspices of AAC & Canada Council)*	The Greatest Little Travelling Supershow for Young People presents: (1) Kaleido-scope Theatre Production, (2) Theatre Beyond Words, (3) The Mummers Troupe [puppeteers of Newfoundland]	1. <u>Sumidagawa</u> (based on Japanese legend); 2. <u>The Potato People</u>; 3. <u>The Original, Real & Very Illustrious Punch and Judy Puppet Theatre</u> (May 4/16) - *for school children*
SEPT or OCT/79 - *U of L*	Catalyst Theatre/Jan Selman/Brent Thomas (designer)/CAST: Sandi Balcovske, Lorraine Behman, Philip Kuntz, David Mann, Wendell Smith, Paul Whitney, Russ Antonio	<u>On and Off the Street</u> - An original play about juvenile delinquency written by the Company with James R. Sallows. Catalyst Theatre Society is a company whose objectives are to promote and practice the use of theatre for public education and as catalyst for social action.
NOV 17/79 - *Library Theatre Gallery*	Le Théâtre Français d'Edmonton	<u>George Dandin</u> [Le Mari Confondu] by Moliere (Nov 17/11)

DATE/PLACE	COMPANY AND/OR PERFORMER(S)	PERFORMANCE(S)/REFERENCE/CRITIQUE
NOV 17/79 - *Galt School of Nursing Auditorium*	Catalyst Theatre (Edmonton)/with David Mann, Lorraine Behman, Sandi Balcovske, Bruce McFee, Bob Bainborough	Call It a Day - *provokes social review; sponsored by Alberta Alcoholism & Drug Abuse Commission*
FEB 2/80 - *Yates*	25th St. House Theatre (Saskatoon)/(auspices of U of L & Alberta Culture) with Maureen McKeon, James Rankin, Bob Collins	The Queen's Cowboy by Layne Coleman & Bill Hominuke (Jan 30/D6; Feb 4/B7) ($4.00) - *interesting, but flawed play (Arthur McDougall)*
FEB 10/80 - *Pub. Lib.*	Les Tréteaux Des Rocheuses (organized by the Alliance francaise de Calgary)	Two One Act Plays in French: 1. Le Vernissage by Vaclav Havel; 2. Ardele, Ou La Marguerite by Jean Anouilh
FEB 21/80 - *R.I. Baker S., Coaldale*	Stage Coach Players	Docudrama Frank Slide (Feb 22/B2) - *remarkable (Arthur McDougall)*
FEB 22/80 - *Yates*	Allied Arts Great Performance Series/Paul Gaulin Mime Co.	10 Mime Sketches (Feb 5/A7; 20/D9; 23/A6) ($5.00 - $7.00) - *Gaulin knows what he wants and usually gets it from troupe (A. McDougall)*
MAR 1/80 - *Yates*	Southern Alberta Opera Association	Hansel & Gretel by Humperdinck (abridged) (Mar 1/B7)
MAR 13/80 - *Yates*	The Vancouver East Cultural Centre Production on Tour/with Cedric Smith & Ross Douglass (auspices: U of L & C.P. Rail)	Musical play, Billy Bishop Goes to War by John Gray and Eric Peterson (Mar 1/B8; 14/A7) - *blew a full house out of the skies (Arthur McDougall)*
JUN 13-15/80 - *W. C. H.S. Auditorium*	Catalyst Theatre/Sandi Balcovske, Hans Boggild, Sparky Johnson, David Mann, Dena Simon, Paul Whitney	Social Revue City Slickers/(sponsored by AADAC) (Jun 11/C8; 14/B3) - *the show is very well put together*
JUN 13-15/80 - *Yates*	Theatre Calgary (sponsored by Playgoers, Alberta Culture & Alberta Festival of Arts)	The Black Bonspiel of Wullie MacCrimmon by W. O. Mitchell (Jun 7/C8; 16/B3) - *funny but dies lingering death in its last 30 minutes (Arthur McDougall)*
JUL 15/80 - *Yates*	Province of Alberta Anniversary Commission presentation (as part of the Alberta Festival of the Arts)	Premier performance of the Musical Revue, Alberta written & directed by Jack McCreath (Jul 16/C6) - *It is almost a total disaster (Arthur McDougall)*
AUG 14/80 - *Yates*	Caravan Stage Co. on Tour	Caucasian Chalk Circle by Berthold Brecht
AUG 17/80 - *Yates*	The Black Light Theatre of Famous People Players (Toronto)	Black Light Puppet Show (Aug 16/A9; 18/A7) - *deserve raves, ovations (A. McDougall)*
AUG 28/80 - *Yates*	Alberta Anniversary Commission in conjunction with Lethbridge AAC presents Banff Centre Musical Theatre Division production/Michael Bawtree/Howard Cable (mus dir)/Valerie Moore (chor) & Larry McKinnon with CAST of 21: Leslie Yeo, Peter Reardon, Greg Bond, Kathryn Elton, Mary-Lynn Scott, Tammy Rittich, Tracy Dahl & others	Musical, Drummer by David Warrack & Michael Bawtree (Aug 29/A5) - *features fabulous music (Arthur McDougall)*
OCT 11/80 - *Pub. Lib.*	The Puppetmongers Powell (Toronto)	(Oct 10/A5) - *internationally acclaimed puppet co.*
OCT 25/80 - *Yates*	U of L Dept. of Dramatic Arts & Division of Continuing Education/Lampoon Puppet Theatre with Alison & Johan Vandergun	(Oct 4/A8; 7/B3) - *Toronto based troupe; a children's show called Clowning Around will be performed at 2:00 p.m. in the library*
FEB 7/81 - *R.I. Baker Auditorium (Coaldale)*	Theatre Calgary Stage Coach Players/Martin Fishman with Douglas Brown, Heather Lea McCallum, Gayle Murphy, Bruce Parkhouse, Jan Stirling	Years of Sorrow, Years of Shame based on the book by Barry Broadfoot, adapted by Rick McNair (Feb 9/B2) - *Cast given little chance to develop in play but stirs up old emotions*
MAR 21/81 - *C.C. H.S. Dr. Centre*	Le Théâtre de l'Alliance Française de Calgary	Volpone (Mar 21/B11)
APR 15/81 - *Yates*	Southern Alberta Opera Assoc. with Amy Olthuis, John Ghitan, Ross Thompson, Larry Benson, Janet Nicol, Alec Tebbut	The Mikado (Mar 21/B11; Apr 16/A6) - *marvelously funny; but music treated with respect and devotion...a cherished night at the theatre (Arthur McDougall)*
APR 23/81 - *Civic Ctre.*	Merrytime Clown & Puppet Co. (Halifax) with Ron Wagner	(Apr 22/B2; 23/B2) - *one man show especially for children*
MAY 8/81 - *Yates*	Theatre Network (Edmonton)	Eternally Yours
MAY 19 /81 - *U of L Theatre*	Cvoci (from Czechoslovakia)	International Mime Group (May 11/D1) ($1.00 - $2.00)
SEPT 19,20/81 - *Yates*	Famous People Players (Toronto)/Diane Depuy	Scheherazade (Jun 5/A8; Sept 21/B3) - *puppet representation of famous people...magical*

DATE/PLACE	COMPANY AND/OR PERFORMER(S)	PERFORMANCE(S)/REFERENCE/CRITIQUE
OCT 1/81 - *Yates*	James Arrington Productions with James Arrington & Allison Hickman (auspices: Cardston Community Theatre)	The Farley Family Reunion by James Arrington (Sept 22/B3; Oct 2/A10) - *humorous sketches; actors have much to give (A. McDougall)*
OCT 14/81 - *U of L Th.*	U of L Student's Union presents Interlude Mime Theatre	(Oct 2/A10)
NOV /81 - *various schools*	Catalyst Theatre (Edm) with Larry Reese, Robert Clinton & others (auspices of AADAC)	Strut on Demand '81 (Nov 10/B2) - *blasts out message on drug use*
NOV 25/81 - *U of L*	National Arts Centre Co., L'Hexagone	French Play, Je t'aime... Je t'aime (Nov 18/B3)
FEB 22,23/82 - *Lethbridge Lodge Hotel*	David Francis, Tracy Moore, Maurine Thomas	Dinner Theatre production, I Ought to be in Pictures by Neil Simon (Feb 6/A12)
MAR 4/82 - *Yates*	Southern Alberta Touring Council/Judith Le Bane, Stan Kane	La Scala to Broadway (Mar 5/A11)
MAR 11/82 - *Yates (AAC)*	Southern Alberta Opera Co. dir by George Colton with Katharine Megli, Ross Thompson, Larry Benson, Janet Nichol, John Ghitan, Julie Jacques (accomp)	La Boheme [abridged] (Mar 12/B14) - *acting is superb (Pat Robinson)*
MAR 15/82 - *U of L*	U of L Performing Arts Series: Mummenschanz	Modern Mime & Mask production (Feb 3/C6; Feb 6/A12)
MAR 26,27/82 - *Yates (AAC)*	Any Space Theatre Co. dir by Shirley Tooke with Michelle Fansett & James Downing	Jesse and the Bandit Queen by David Freeman (Mar 20/B12)
APR 3/82 - *U of L*	U of L Performing Arts Series: Tamahnous Theatre	We Won't Pay, We Won't Pay by Darjo Fo (Mar 26/B6; Apr 5/A11) - *crass theatrical obscenity (Peter Mueller)*
OCT 15/82 - *Yates (AAC)*	Alberta Theatre Projects (Calgary) dir by Geoff Ferries with Deidre Van Winkle, Grant Cowan, Jack Northmore, Vince Metcalfe	Tom Foolery [based on words and music of Tom Leary] (Sept 4/D11; Oct 12/B14; 16/B9) - *delights 300 patrons (Peter Mueller)*
OCT 16/82 - *L.C.I.*	Le Cercle Molière (Winnipeg)	French plays (Oct 5/B3)
NOV 7,8/82 - *Yates*	Famous People Players	Puppet Theatre by the mentally handicapped (Oct 28/B2)
DEC 20-24; 26-30/82 - *Yates*	Local Semi Professional Co., Southern Stage/R. Epp (art dir)/CAST: Laurin Mann, R. Epp, Brian Tyson, Karen Bernstein, Larry Erdos & children	Christmas Pudding by R. Epp, directed by Sharon Bakker (Calgary) (Nov 23/B5; Dec 21/A3, A12) - *evoked plenty of belly laughs and memories*
JAN 14/83 - *Yates (AAC & U of L Students Union*	Trickster (professional theatre co. from Calgary)/David Chantler	Mime, Clowning, Improv and Dance (Jan 12/A11)
FEB 4/83 - *Yates (AAC)*	Theatre Network (Edmonton)/Stephen Heatly/ musical direction by John Roby/Eddy Arthur, Wally McDonald, Wendell Smith, Robert Clinton, Michelle Fleiger (musicians)	Musical, Country Chorale by Raymond Storey with music by John Roby/CAST: Wendell Smith, Michelle Fleiger, Joyce Seeley, Robert Clinton, K.C. Pavlich, Nola Auguston, Murray McClure (Jan 22/B14) - *always popular*
MAR 24-26/83 - *Labor Club*	Greg Rogers (dir.) with Paul Whitney, Angela Gain, Catharine Brown, Patricia Connor	Dinner Theatre, The Last of the Red Hot Lovers (Mar 18/B6; 25/A14) ($21.95) - *offers real pleasure (Joan Waterfield)*
MAR 25/83 - *U of L Th.*	Brent Fidler	One Man Show, Edgar Allen Poe (Mar 25 TV Week/10)
APR 6/83 - *Yates*	Theatre Beyond Words (Niagara on-the-Lake)	Uncle Clarence's Visit (Mar 16/B15; Apr 6/D3)
APR 15/83 - *Yates*	Citadel Theatre (Edmonton)/Lawrie Seligman/John Dinning/David Gauthier/Dianne Goodman - CAST: Margaret Bard, Paul Soles	Talley's Folly by Lanford Wilson (Apr 9/B10; 13/D5) - *Allied Arts Council 25th anniversary celebration*
SEPT 24/83 - *Sportsplex*	Stella Parton & Blake Emmons	Musical, The Best Little Whorehouse in Texas (Sept 28/C12) - *good show, poor venue*
SEPT 20-25/83 - *Yates (AAC)*	Southern Stage (Lethbridge)/Richard Epp/CAST: Warren Graves, Francis Damberger	Mass Appeal by Bill C. Davis, directed by Richard Epp (Sept 19/D1; 21/A13; 23/C7) - *emotional peaks (J. Waterfield)*

DATE/PLACE	COMPANY AND/OR PERFORMER(S)	PERFORMANCE(S)/REFERENCE/CRITIQUE
SEPT 24/83 - *U of L Th.*	Second City Touring Co. of Toronto with Karen Poce, Bruce Nelson, Michael Myers, Linda Kash, Bruce Hunter and Lethbridge native Bob Bainborough	Comedy, Cabaret, The Entertainers (Sept 22/C5; 26/A3) - *drew a nearly full house*
NOV 5/83 - *U of L Th.*	Workshop West Theatre (Edm) and the Association of Touring Professional Theatres of Alberta/Gerry Potter/CAST: David Le Reaney with Jan Randall (piano)	Musical play, Billy Bishop Goes to War by John Gray & Eric Peterson (Nov 4/C6) *($6.00 - $10.00)*
DEC 10/83 - *Yates (AAC & U of L Students Assoc.)*	Kaleidoscope Theatre of Victoria/Jim Leard	Especially for Children (Dec 2/83; TV Week 10)
FEB 23/84 - *Lethbridge Labor Club*	Catalyst Theatre (Edmonton)/David Mann/Philip Kuntz (mus dir)/CAST: Susan O'Connor, Jack Ackroyd,Bill Johnston, Gayle Murphy, Philip Kuntz (guitar)	Play with music, Family Portrait created by members of Catalyst for its initial production in 1982. Directed by David Mann (Feb 22/B6) - *presented by South Western Alberta Teachers' Convention Association*
MAR 3/84 - *U of L*	Lethbridge Lifelong Hearing Association; U of L Students Union; U of L Continuing Education with assistance of the Touring Office, Canada Council presents Headlines Theatre	Revue, Under the Gun (Feb 18/A12) - *a disarming review*
MAY 5,6/84 - *U of L Th.*	Edmonton Opera Association & Lethbridge Symphony	The Pirates of Penzance by Gilbert & Sullivan (Apr 21/A8; May 4/TV Week/10)
JUL 13,14/84 - *Ft. Whoop-Up*	Studio North (Edmonton)/Mark Schoenberg with Cory Michael Juse & Lynne Fredine	Historical musical, Making Tracks (Jul 14/A10) *($2.00 - $3.50) - troupe's 5th summer production*
AUG 13/84 - *Pub. Lib.*	Loose Moose Theatre Co. (Calgary)	Theatre for Children (Aug 14/A3) - *various sketches*
OCT 10-13/84 - *Lethbridge Lodge*	On-Stage Theatre Productions (Calgary)/Tomas Guzman (dir)/Rivka Schechter (prod)/with Zelda Dean and Terry King	Dinner Theatre, The Marriage Bed or Who's on Top (Oct 2/B9; 11/A12) - *has played to rave reviews in Victoria, Edmonton, Calgary, Red Deer...given an enthusiastic reception here*
OCT 14/84 - *U of L*	Kaze-no-ko (Children of the Wind)	Japanese Troupe for Children's Theatre (Oct 9/B11; 15/B11) - *combines artistry, agility*
OCT 27/84 - *U of L Family Series*	Théâtre sans fil (The No Strings Puppet Theatre)	The Hobbit based on the book by J.R.R. Tolkien (Oct 9/B11; 29/B5) - *delights audience of all ages*
JAN 25/85 - *French Cultural Centre*	The French Theatre (auspices: Alberta Culture)	Four plays by Courteline (Jan 25/A9)
FEB 16/85 - *Yates*	Italian Theatre Group, Teatro Libero (Edm)	Two Italian comedies (Feb 14/A13) [auspices of Canadian Italian Club]
FEB 21-23/85 - *Lethbridge Lodge*	On Stage Theatre Production with Greg Rogers, Grant Lowe, Zelda Dean	Dinner Theatre Comedy, Nina by Andre Roussin (Feb 22/B5) - *not perfect, but still good*
MAR 9/85 - *U of L*	U of L Performing Arts Series/U-Zulu	Musical, Igugu Lethu (Feb 1/A11; Mar 8/B9) - *co. of S. African actors, musicians, singers, dancers*
APR 2/85 - *U of L*	U of L Performing Arts Series/Compagnie Philippe Genty (Theatre of Animation)	Puppetry, theatre and illusion (Mar 30/C10; Apr 2/B5) - *enthusiastically received by critics the world over*
APR 4/85 - *Pub. Lib.*	Loose Moose Theatre Co.	Children's theatre, Zing Bu Bu (pirate tale) (Apr 4/TVWK/12; 16/B5)
APR 26/85 - *Pub. Lib.*	La Société de Théâtre de Calgary	On Ne Danse Plus (Apr 25/A11)
OCT 26/85 - *U of L*	U of L Family Series presents Theatre Beyond Words (Canadian Mime Troupe)	Potato People (Sept 13/C7; Oct 12/B8; 23/B5) *($11.00 - $14.00)*
NOV 19/85 - *U of L*	Arts Club Theatre (Vancouver)/Larry Lillo with Jay Brazeau, Sue Astley, David Marr and others	Twelfth Night (Nov 16/B6; 20/A12) - *a most delightful evening (Joan Waterfield)*
NOV 24/85 - *U of L*	Peter Samelson (U of L Family Series)	Theatre of Illusion (Sept 13/C7; Nov 21/B5)
NOV 28/85 - *U of L*	National Touring Co. (auspices of U of L Student's Union with Russell Leander	Musical, Cotton Patch Gospel by Tom Key, Russell Treyz and Harry Chapin (Nov 26/B6; 29/B7) *($11.00 - $14.00) - entertaining*
FEB 20/86 - *U of L*	Theatre Network (Edm) dir by Stephen Heatley with Susan Sneath, Bonnie Green, Robert Winslow & Brandley Rudy	Something in the Wind by Raymond Storey (Feb 8/C8; 21/A14) *($10.00 - $14.00) - engrossing*
MAR 4,5/86 - *Yates*	The Halifax Neptune Theatre dir by Tom Kerr/John Gray (mus dir)	Original musical comedy, Don Messer's Jubilee by John Gray (Mar 1/A7)

DATE/PLACE	COMPANY AND/OR PERFORMER(S)	PERFORMANCE(S)/REFERENCE/CRITIQUE
MAR 7,8/86 - *Lethbridge Lodge*		Dinner Theatre, <u>California Suite</u> by Neil Simon (Mar 1/A7)
APR 8/86 - *U of L*	(auspices of U of L Student's Union)	<u>The Best of Gilbert & Sullivan</u> (Apr 5/B9)
SEPT 19,20/86 - *LL*		Dinner Theatre, <u>Goodbye, Cruel World</u> (Aug 29/A8)
SEPT 26/86 - *U of L*	Michael Burrell/dir. by Philip Grant	One Man Show, <u>Hess</u> by Burrell (Sept 25/A12; 29B5) - *first performed in 1978 in London—a great actor*
OCT 19/86 - *U of L*	Mermaid Puppet Theatre/Graham Whitehead (dir)	<u>Flights of Fancy</u> (Oct 18/B9)
NOV 25/86 - *U of L*	Arts Club Theatre (Van.)/Bill Millerd	<u>Arms and the Man</u> by G.B. Shaw (Nov 26/B6) - *Shaw would have loved it (Laycock)*
NOV 29/86 - *U of L*	Théâtre Fantastique (Paris-based, American directed theatre co.)	Fantasy production with costumes and masks (Nov 27/B7) - *debut tour of North America*
JAN 23/87 - *U of L*	Arts Club Theatre/Lovie Eli, Lovena Fox, Marcus Mosely, Denis Simpson, Sibel Thrasher	Musical Revue, <u>Ain't Misbehavin'</u> (Jan 21/A7; 26/B5) - *sold out - Quite a show!*
FEB 10/87 - *U of L*	Tapestry Music Theatre/Ken Walsh/Tricia Adams, Jayne Lewis, Allison Grant, Bruce Clayton	Musical play, <u>Gershwin & Gershwin</u> by Larry Fineberg (Feb 9/B7; 11/B7) - *Gershwin magic missed*
MAR 20-21/87 - *LL*	On-Stage Theatre/Mark Turnbull, Patrick Brown, Elizabeth Stepkowski	Dinner Theatre, <u>Not the Count of Monte Cristo</u> (Mar 23/B6) - *lighthearted spoof [from the Glenmore Theatre Co., Calgary]*
MAR 21/87 - *U of L*	Jest in Time Theatre/Sherry-Lee Hunter, Christian Murray & Mary Ellen Maclean	Mime, voice, acting, movement, "takes its inspiration from mime, vaudeville and silent movies" (Mar 23/B6) - *silence can be exciting*
MAY 6/87 - *Galbraith Sch.*	Kaleidoscope Story Theatre Co. (Victoria)	<u>The Three Sillies</u> and other sketches (May 7/B9) - *much to the delight of the young audience*
MAY 6/87 - *Senator Buchanan Sch.*	Quest Productions (Calgary)	Children's Theatre, <u>Dinosaur</u> (May 7/A3)
SEPT 11,12/87 - *LL*		Dinner Theatre, <u>Snacks</u> (Sept 4/A12)
OCT 22/87 - *U of L*	A Theatre Public production/Kenneth Brown/Wm. Vickers	One Man Show, <u>Life After Hockey</u> by Kenneth Brown (Oct 17/B10; 23/C6) *($11.00 - $13.00) - scores big with crowd*
NOV 6,7/87 - *LL*		Dinner Theatre, <u>Sinners</u> (Oct 16/B6) *($25.00)*
DEC 9/87 - *U of L*	Stage II of Troupe America (Minneapolis-St. Paul)/Curt Wollan	<u>The Spirit of Christmas</u> by David Simmons ["a Dicksenian potpourri"] (Dec 5/B6; 10/B8) - *jolly good fun*
APR 9/88 - *U of L*	Christopher Britton	One Man Show, *Einstein* by Gabriel Emmanuel (Apr 11/A10) - *brilliantly portrayed*
NOV 30/88 - *U of L*	Théâtre sans fil (puppet theatre)	<u>The Lord of the Rings</u>

Professional Theatrical Entertainment:
Lethbridge, Alberta (1885–1988)

DATE/PLACE	COMPANY AND/OR PERFORMER(S)	PERFORMANCE(S)/REFERENCE/CRITIQUE
DEC 22/1885 - *Lethbridge Hall (LH)*	Professor T.H. Dunne	Magician [2 hrs magic & mystery] (Dec 18/3; 24/3) - *exceptionally well* performed
APR 27/86 - *LH*	Dolan Comedy Co.; E. Dolan	Vaudeville, "farces, songs and dances" (Apr 30/3) - *well executed*
APR 20, 27/87 - *LH & NWMP Barracks*	King Kennedy	Ventriloquist & magician (Apr 20/4; 27/3)
JUL 10-12/88 - *LH*	Martin's Magical Theatre, Professor Martin & two "young male entertainers"	Legerdemain (Jul 12/3) - *the best entertainment before a Lethbridge audience*
AUG 26,27/89 - *Tent (T)*	Campbell & Seaches Pavilion Show	Vaudeville (Aug 2/3)
OCT 17,19/89 - *Barracks (B)*	J.W. Bengough	Topical Crayon Sketches (Oct 23/3) - *roars of laughter*
JUN 9,10/90 - *B*	Professor Connery & Charles Kelly Co.	Elocutionist/humorist, soloist and guitarist (Jun 11/3) - *one of the best in Lethbridge*
JUN 16/90 - *B*	The Comedy and Specialty Co. with Messrs. Lynch & Costello	3 Farces & variety entertainment (Jun 11/3; 18/3) - *fair house*
OCT 3; NOV 8/90 - *B*	Agnes Knox	Canadian elocutionist (Oct 1/3; 8/3; 22/3) - *unusual talent*
MAR 25/91 - *B*	Professor Tyndall	Mind reader and hypnotist (Mar 24/3)
OCT 14-16/91 - *Bldg. Co.'s Hall (BCH)*	Signor Bosco	Magician (Oct 14/3) - *renowned*
MAR 18,20/93 - *BCH*	Silver Specialty Co.	Vaudeville, gymnastics, slight of hand, comic singing (Mar 23/3)
NOV 23/93 - *BCH*	Professor Rae	Scottish elocutionist & lime light entertainment (Nov 16/3; 30/3) - *not well attended*
AUG 13/94 - *BCH*	Effie Elaine Hext and local artists	Elocutionist (Aug 15/3) - *renowned*
SEPT 17/94 - *BCH*	Pauline Johnson and Owen A. Smily	Poet & humorist (Aug 29/1)
JUL 24/95 - *BCH*	Webbling Sisters	Song and dance (Jul 10/1)
DEC 16,17/95 - *BCH*	Pringle Presentation Co., Dean & Rowland	Ventriloquist & "Black Art Sensation" (Dec 18/1) - *the entertainment was rather amusing*
MAY 11/96 - *BCH*	Neil Burton	Character impersonator & humorist (May 13/1) - *scarcely fulfilled expectations; fair audience*
DEC 12/96 - *BCH*	McKanlass	Banjo King, violinist & soloist (Dec 9/1)
AUG 31-SEPT 2,13/97 - *BCH*	Royal Animatograph & Specialty Co., Messrs. McLeod & Flynn; Mrs. Flynn; Miss Doyle (pianist)	Vaudeville, moving pictures (Aug 25/1) - *1st class vaudeville artists; animatograph is latest Edison invention & is worth price of admission alone*
SEPT 29/97 - *BCH*	Pauline Johnson and Owen A. Smily	Poet, humorist (Sept 29/1; Oct 7/1) - *Prince of entertainers*
OCT 5,6/97 - *BCH*	Cosgrove family	Musical entertainers & kinetoscope showings (Oct 7/1) - *one of best troupes here in some time*
FEB 7,8/98 - *BCH*	R.A. Hardie's "Ideals"	Variety entertainment (Feb 9/1) - *first class items*
FEB 15,16/98 - *BCH*	Cosgrove Co. with Ida Cosgrove, Miss Mackie, Harry Fay	Variety & moving pictures with 1898 model of Edison's kinetoscope (Feb 2/8; 16/1) - *most excellent & deserved better patronage*
OCT 28/99 - *Oliver's Hall (OH)*	J.W. Bengough	Topical & crayon sketches (Sept 27/8; Oct 11/8) - *Canada's most popular* entertainer
NOV 22/99 - *OH*	Owen A. Smily Concert Co.	Humorist (Nov/16/8; 23/7) - *appreciative audience*
JAN 31/1900 - *OH*	Willis Coontown 400 Co. with Charlie Arnold	Ragtime & operatic burlesque: speciality acts, all Black artists (Jan 18/1; Feb 1/8) - *packed house - thoroughly appreciated - largest advance sale since leaving Chicago*
AUG 17/00 - *OH*	Miner East Comedy Co.	Grand Cake Walk and specialty acts (Aug 16/8; 23/8) - *those not present did not miss much of a treat*

DATE/PLACE	COMPANY AND/OR PERFORMER(S)	PERFORMANCE(S)/REFERENCE/CRITIQUE
SEPT 26,27/00 - OH	Emerald Duett Temperance Evangelists	Songs, speech, moving pictures about Boer War (Sept 21/8; 28/8) - *full house*
APR 12/01 - *OH*	Cinematograph	The Queen's Funeral & others (Apr 18/8)
APR 19/01 - *OH*	Professor Payne	Hypnotist & Phrenologist (Apr 25/8) - *amused the small audience*
JUL 1; SEPT 20/01 - OH	Kelly Merry Makers	Entertainers (Jul 4/1; Sept 26/8) - *well received volatile entertainers*
JUL 29,30/01 - OH	Richard's and Pringle's Georgia Minstrels	Black minstrels (Aug 1/1) - *up to average minstrel show but not beyond*
NOV 6,7/01 - OH	"The Black Knight"	Humorous orator (Nov 7/1) - *irresistibly amusing*
JAN 13, MAR 6/02 - OH	Cosgrove Co.	Vaudeville (Jan 16/8) - *unlimited amusement*
MAR 20/02 - *OH*	Scottish Concert & Kinematagraph Co.	Variety Entertainment (Mar 27/8) - *first class*
JUN 19/02 - *OH*	The Clipper Novelty Co.	Vaudeville (June 25/8) ($0.25 - $0.75) - *good show, poor house*
JUL 17/02 - *OH*	Professor Parke's Exhibition Co.	Moving pictures, $10,000 electrical displays; Dawson Mining Scenes and 1800 miles down the mighty Yukon (Jul 16/1; 23/4) - *well patronized*
NOV 3/02 - *OH*	Boston Comedy Co.	Entertainers (Nov 5/4) - *...gave a very amusing entertainment...large audience...kept in a continuous state of hilarity*
DEC 2,5/02 - *OH*	The California Trio and additional entertainers	Humorous musical entertainers, Legerdemain (Dec 3/8; 10/1) - *rounds of applause*
DEC 15-17/02 - *OH*	Professor Zamlock	Magician - trickster, illusionist (Dec 17/6) - *delighted crowded audiences*
DEC 30/02 - *OH*	Scottish Concert Co.: Gavin Spence & Flora MacDonald	Entertainers (Dec 24/6; 31/1) - *heartily enjoyed by large audience*
FEB 16-21/03 - *OH*	The Strollers	Comedy & vaudeville (Jan 28/8; Feb 19/8) - *performance was very good - small audience*
APR 30/03 - *Knox Church*	Florence McLeay	Elocution (May 7/1) - *small but highly delightful audience*
AUG 28/03 - *OH*	Maridor-Goulding Co. (auspices of Lacrosse Club)	Elocution, coronet soloist and entertainers, Rosamond (Sept 3/4) - *favored with a large audience - general satisfaction*
OCT 14,16/03 - *OH*	Fax Concert Co. with James Fax, Ethel Scholfield & Bella Fax (auspices of Guild of St. Monica's)	Song artists, entertainers (Oct 15/1; 22/4) - *large audience...was convulsed with laughter*
OCT 30/03 - *OH*	Firth-Eaton Concert Co.	Entertainment, impersonations (Oct 22/2,4; 29/1; Nov 5/4) - *the company was a decidedly good one*
NOV 13/03 - *OH*	The Cosgrove Family Concert Co.	Entertainment & dance under auspices of Fire Brigade (Nov 12/4; 19/4) - *gave a good entertainment*
JAN 9,11/04 - *OH*	Jolly Entertainers	Variety (Jan 14/4) - *mixed reaction*
FEB 26/04 - *OH*	Miss Pauline Johnson and Mr. Walter McRaye	Poet & humorist (Feb 4/4)
MAR 21/04 - *OH*	Shipman Comedians with Bert Harvey	Entertainment (Mar 17/4; 24/4) - *excellent program*
JUN 6/04 - *OH*	Pauline Johnson & Walt McRaye with assistance by local soloist A.E. Cunningham	Recitations, musical solos, humorous imitation of the "habitants of Quebec" (May 26/4; Jun 2/4; 9/4)
JUL 5/04 - *OH*	Richard & Pringle present Clarence Powell	Georgia Minstrels (Jun 16/4; 30/2,4; Jul 7/4) - *highest salaried colored performer in the world - 28th annual tour - not up to expected*
OCT 24,25/04 - *OH*	The Great Hewett Carnival Co.	Magic & illusion (Oct 20/2)
FEB 9/05 - *Methodist Ch.*	Annie Snyder	Entertainer (Feb 9/4) - *Toronto's most clever entertainer*
JUN 2,3/05 - *OH*	Steel & Freeland Concert Co.	Moving pictures & illustrated songs (May 25/2)
JUN 5; SEPT 25/05 - OH	"The Hottest Coon in Dixie" presented by Mr. Willis - 40 singers, dancers & comedians	Minstrel entertainment (Jun 6/4; Sept 19/4; 22/1) ($0.75 - $1.00) - *company was strengthened for return engagement*
JUN 29/05 - *OH*	The Peerless Entertainers	(Jun 30/4) - *without peers in the realm of bum shows...the audience was disgusted*
AUG 7/05 - *OH*	Professor Buell (auspices of Catholic Church	Entertainer & photographic discussion (Aug 4/4; 8/4) - *well attended & much appreciated*

DATE/PLACE	COMPANY AND/OR PERFORMER(S)	PERFORMANCE(S)/REFERENCE/CRITIQUE
AUG 14/05 - *T*	Cozad's Famous California Shows	Dog & pony show (Aug 8/4; 14/4; 18/1) - *all equipment had dirty antiquainted appearance*
AUG 29,30/05 - *Tent*	Arnold Shows	Entertainment (Aug 25/4; Sept 1/4) - *not too bad*
OCT 6/05 - *OH*	Richard & Pringle's Georgia Minstrels	Minstrel Show (Sept 29/1; Oct 3/4; 10/1) - *entertained very well generally although some can't sing & are a painful imposition*
OCT 11,12/05 - *OH*	"The Richest Coon in Georgia" Co.	Entertainment (Oct 10/4; 13/1) - *good company but played to almost empty house*
NOV 20/05 - *OH*	Patten & Perry Co. of 20 performers	Comedy & specialty acts, musical farce and comedy, Jerry From Kerry (Nov 14/3; 21/5) ($0.50 - $0.75 - $1.00) - *much enjoyed by a crowded house*
APR 27/06 - *OH*	Jimmy Fax & Co.	Comedy, musical acts & variety (Apr 26/5)
JUN 19/06 - *OH*	Mahara's Mammoth Minstrel Carnival - 30 Black performers	Minstrelsy, opera and vaudeville (Jun 14/5) ($0.50 - $0.75 - $1.00)
JUL 4/06 - *OH*	Friscoscope Co.	Vaudeville & moving pictures (Jun 28/6) - *pictures of San Francisco Earthquake*
AUG 29,30/06 - *OH*	Dick P. Sutton Co.	Vaudeville (Aug 23/9) ($0.50 - $0.75 - $1.00)
NOV 1,2/06 - *OH*	Douglas Vaudeville Co.	Variety (Nov 8/9) - *appeared before large house*
NOV 5,6/06 - *OH*	Zinn's Merry Musical Travesty Co.	Walter & Fields musical mixture, Teezy Weezy & The Jolly Musketeers (Nov 1/9,10; 2/4)
NOV 13/06 - *OH*	Patten & Fletcher Production	Jerry From Kerry (Nov 15/9) - *big crowd - high class vaudeville and comedy*
NOV 21,22/06 - *OH*	C.P. Walker presents The Great McEwen	Magic, hypnotism and vaudeville (Nov 15/10)
DEC 6/06 - *OH*	Corkville Coon Minstrels	Grand Minstrel Show (Nov 29/9)
DEC 11/06 - *OH*	Polmatier Sisters Concert Co.	Musical acts (Dec 6/11; 13/11)
DEC 24,25/06 - *OH*	Morris & Douglas Circuit Co.	Vaudeville (Dec 20/11)
FEB 15/07 - *Wesley Ch. (WC)*	unidentified co.	Hiawatha, dramatic recital with still and moving pictures (Feb 14/8) - *Lyceum course*
MAR 16/07 - *WC*	Herbert Leon Cope	Humorous lecturer (Mar 14/9) - *Lyceum course*
APR 30-MAY 4/07 - *OH*	Venetian Glass Blower	Spinning, weaving & blowing glass (Apr 25/2) ($0.15 - $0.25) - *entertaining & instructive*
JUL 8-15/07	Nat Reiss Street Carnival Co.	Grand street carnival (Jun 27/10)
OCT 24-29/07 - *Bijou Theatre*	Blair & McNutty (black-faced comedians)	Vaudeville & moving pictures (Oct 24/10)
NOV 12/07 - *Knights of Pythias Hall (opening)*	Kenny-Harvey Co.	Entertainers (Oct 13/4; Nov 14/5) - *includes four high class artists - thoroughly enjoyed by large crowd*
NOV 15,16/07 - *Labor Union Hall*	Moore Concert Co.	High class vaudeville acts (Nov 14/10)
FEB 12,13; 20/08 - *OH*	Woolf & Lang and Juvenile Bostonians present The Minstrel Maids	Musical novelty (Feb 10/2,4; 11/3) ($0.75 - $1.00) - *a bevy of pretty girls*
APR 25/08 - *OH*	All Star Vaudeville Co. with Thomas R. Curtis & Ella Wilson	Vaudeville, & The Western Girl (Apr 21/3; 25/2)
AUG 21/08 - *OH*	Richard & Pringle's Famous Minstrels with Clarence Powell & Pete Woods	The Meeting of the Alumni; When the Troupe Struck Town (Aug 21/4)
SEPT 3/08 - *OH*	Madam Cellinis & Co.	Vaudeville, mind reading, telepathy, magic (Sept 3/4)
SEPT 26/08 - *OH*	Claman Players	Vaudeville (Sept 23/4)
OCT 12-DEC 31/08 - *Lyceum Th. (LT)*	Various entertainers: The Ingrams, The Fairchilds, Emerson & Van Horn, The Atkins, Weber Sisters, Casey Bros., A.F. Zamlock	Vaudeville & pictures (Oct 6/3,5; 12/3) ($0.15 - $0.25) - *entire change of vaudeville every Monday & Thursday*
OCT 12-DEC 31/08 - *Eureka Th. (ET)*	Various entertainers: Monte La Crosse	Vaudeville, moving pictures & illustrated songs (Oct 12/3) ($0.15 - $0.25)
DEC 15,16/08 - *LT*	Polmatier Sisters Orchestra & Concert Co.	Variety entertainment (Dec 14/3)
DEC 28-JAN 1/08 - *LT*	Brown's Gilt Edge Comedy Co.	Vaudeville (Dec 26/4)
JAN - DEC/09 - *ET*	Various distributors & performers	Moving pictures and vaudeville

DATE/PLACE	COMPANY AND/OR PERFORMER(S)	PERFORMANCE(S)/REFERENCE/CRITIQUE
JAN 20,21/09 - *OH*FEB 22-27/09 - *LT*	Empire Vaudeville Co. with Hickman Miller Co.	Vaudeville & farce, <u>Fevers</u> (Jan 20/4; Feb 20/3) *($0.50 - $0.75)*
MAY 3-8/09 - *LT*	Lyceum All Star Comedy & Vaudeville Co. with Deloy's Comedians and the Spaulding Brothers	Special acts & musical, <u>Hogan's Alley</u> (May 1/6; 4/5) - *direct from Lyceum Theatre, Calgary, after 220 performances - enormous success*
MAY 26-29; 31 - JUN 1/09 - *LT*	Dorothy Lamb & Co. and others	Vaudeville (May 26/8)
JUN 7-12; 14-19; 23-26; 28-JUL 3; JUL 5-10/09 - *LT*	Empire Agency Vaudeville including Professor Willey (hypnotist)	Variety (Jun 8/3; Jul 5/3)
JUL 12-17/09 - *Public Square*	Brown Amusement Co. (local emprissario, Fred Brown) with C.W. Parker Shows	Lethbridge free carnival, "six sensational free acts", 18 shows on the street including Broadway Belles vaudeville (Jul 14/5)
DEC 23/09 - *High School*	Bengough	Canadian cartoonist, reciter & burlesque artist (Dec 24/8) - *one of most delightful evenings*
JAN - DEC/10 - *ET*	Various distributors & performers	Moving pictures and vaudeville
FEB 14-APR 30/10 - *LT*	Pantages Circuit, Various companies & acts including The Scottish Highlanders and The Tyrell Children	Regularly scheduled vaudeville acts - changed bi-weekly (Feb 14/7 - Apr 30/8 - *passim*) - *continuous performance*
MAY 3/10 - *Majestic Th. (MT)*	Jessie McLachlan & Co. with Craighill Sherry	Scottish musical entertainment (May 3/6)
MAY 18/10 - *MT*	Jimmy Fax-Fun Co.	Variety (May 16/8; 18/8,11) *($0.25 - $1.00)*
OCT 27/10 - *MT*	The Five Musical Eckhardts	Novelty musical entertainment (Oct 26/9)
NOV 3-9/10 - *ET*	Christel Brothers	Minstrel show (Nov 3/16) - *direct from Chicago*
NOV 24,25/10 - *MT*	C.P. Walker presents The Merry Musicians	Novelty entertainment (Nov 23/5)
DEC 10/10 - *MT*	James Fax Concert Co.	<u>Fax for Fun</u> variety (Dec 6/7; 27/5) - *under auspices of Garbutt Business College*
JAN - NOV/11 - *ET*	Various distributors & performers	Moving pictures and vaudeville
JAN 19,20/11 - *MT*	Pantages Circuit	Vaudeville (Jan 18/5; 19/7,8) - *direct from Empire Theatre, Calgary*
MAR 13/11 - *MT*	Herbert Booth with Bioscope	Lecture <u>The Early Christians</u> (Mar 8/8)
APR 12/11 - *MT*	Alick Lauder	English musical comedian (Apr 10/5) - *Harry Lauder's brother*
MAY 15,16; 18,19/11 - *MT*	"Mental" Psychic & Mystic Co.	Hypnotism, magic, ventriloquism (May 13/10; 16/5) *($0.25 - $0.75)*
JUL 1/11 - *MT*	Alabama Minstrels	(Jun 29/5) - *not imitators...real Negro singers, dancers, musicians*
SEPT 11-14/11 - *MT*	Mysterious Willard & the Man of Mystery	Magic (Sept 8/5)
NOV 20,25/11 - *MT*	William West's Minstrels	(Nov 14/7; 16/10)
NOV 20/11 - *MoT*	unidentified entertainers	Vaudeville (Nov 20/10) *($0.25 - $0.35)* - *opening of New Morris Theatre*
DEC 1-31/11 - *MoT*	various entertainers	Vaudeville and moving pictures
JAN 1/12 - *MoT*	Musical Eckhardts	Musical entertainment (Dec 27/5)
JAN 18/12 - *MT*	Castle Square Entertainers (Quartette)	Musical variety (Jan 15/6; 19/5) - *best all round entertaining attraction here for many a long day*
JAN 22-27/12 - *MoT*	Miss Rose Fox & her Pickaninnies	Dancing & vocal entertainers (Jan 22/6)
APR 19/12 - *YMCA*	Bengough	"Canada's favorite entertainer" draws, acts, sings, recites; Crayon artist (Apr 18/5) *($0.50 - $0.75)*
APR 22-30/12 - *MoT*	Kenny-Harvey Co.	Musicians, singers, dancers (Apr 20/11; 22/7) - *program extraordinary*
MAY 1/12 - *YMCA*	Polmatier Sisters	Musical entertainers (Apr 30/10) *($0.25 - $1.00)*
MAY 15-18/12 - *MT*	The Great McEwen & Co.	Magician (May 15/7)
JUN 28/12 - *Ball Park*	Miller Brothers & Edward Arlington's 101 Ranch Real Wild West Co.	Wild west show & exhibition (Jun 22/8)
JUL 30-AUG 4/12 - *MT*	Albini Avolo & Co.	Vaudeville (Jul 30/7)
OCT 17-25/12 - *Henderson Lake*	Dry Farming Board of Control Congress	<u>The Terpsifete</u> with allegorical dances, folk dances, pantomime (Oct 14/7; 18/13) - *a great success*

DATE/PLACE	COMPANY AND/OR PERFORMER(S)	PERFORMANCE(S)/REFERENCE/CRITIQUE
NOV 1,2/12 - *MoT*	Otto Weis's Royal Hawaiian Musical Co.	Musical novelties (Nov 1/11)
NOV 4-9; 11-13/12 - *MT*	F. Stuart Whyte's Old Country Pierrots, The Versatiles	In the Campfire's Glow & other musical entertainments (Nov 1/11; 7/7; 13/7) - *excellent performances but not well attended...Manager of Pierrots not pleased with Lethbridge audiences*
JAN 6-8/13 - *MT*	Corbin, the Human Dynamo	Mystery, mirth (Jan 3/7; 6/5; 8/7)
JAN 6-8/13 - *MoT*	Rex Vaudeville Co.	Variety (Jan 6/5)
FEB 20-22; MAR 3-4/13 - *MoT*	Pantages Vaudeville	(Feb 20/3; 21/3; Mar 1/3; 4/3) - *made a decided impression*
FEB 27/13 - *MoT*	Caledonian Entertainers with Baldry Strang	Scottish variety entertainers (Feb 27/3)
MAR 21/13 - *B.O.E. Hall*	Harold Square Entertainers	Variety entertainers (Mar 18/3) (*$0.50 - $1.00*)
APR 13,14/13 - *MoT*	Pantages Circuit	Vaudeville (Apr 13/3)
JUL 8-11/13 - *MoT*	Direct from Calgary Exhibition	Vaudeville (Jul 8/3; 10/3) - *excellent show*
JUL 16/13 - *MoT*	Pantages Circuit	Vaudeville (Jul 16/3)
JUL 28-AUG 8/13 - *MoT*	Webster Circuit acts	Vaudeville (Jul 28/3; 29/3; Aug 8/3) (*$0.10 - $0.35*) - *like old Eureka vaudeville*
SEPT 1,2/13 - *Sherman Th. (ST)*	Utell's Dog Circus	Trained dogs, cats & birds (Sept 2/3) - *interesting and pleasing entertainment*
SEPT 10,11/13 - *ST*	Frank Rich & Company (Western)	Variety entertainment The Wedding Bells (Sept 10/3) (*$025 - $0.50*) - *good fun*
OCT 31/13 - *Empress Th. (Emp)*	Hallowell Concert Co.	Musical entertainment (Oct 27/3)
DEC 1,2/13 - *Bijou*	Musical Eckhardts	Musical entertainment (Nov 29/3)
NOV-DEC/13 - *ST*	Orpheum Circuit	Vaudeville (Nov 15/3)
JAN-MAR/14 - *ST*	Various groups and acts	Vaudeville (*$0.15 - $0.35*)
JAN 2-10/14 - *Emp*	Orpheum Circuit	Vaudeville & pictures (Jan 2/3) (*$0.10 - $0.15*)
MAR 9-11; 16-18,23/14 - *ST*	Pantages Circuit	Vaudeville (Mar 9/3; 17/3)
MAY 21,22/14 - *ST*	Various acts & films	Vaudeville (May 21/3)
JUL 20/14 - *ST*	Grace Russell's Merry Minstrel Maids	Musical variety (Jul 20/3) - *class act*
AUG 3-5/14 - *ST*	Pantages Circuit	Vaudeville (Aug 1/3; 14/3)
OCT 24/14 - *ST*	Richard & Pringle's Georgia Minstrels with Clarence Powell	Black minstrel show (Oct 24/3) - *the real thing*
FEB 10-JUN; AUG/15 - Orpheum Th. (OT)	Various performers	Vaudeville & pictures (Feb 9/3; 10/2) [the former Sherman Theatre] (*$0.10 - $0.15*) - *personally selected by manager Light*
MAR 2-28/15 - *Starland*	Willis and Dell	Vaudeville (Mar 2/3; 8/3) - *Harry C. Willis - new manager of Starland Theatre*
MAY 12/15 - *Variety Th. (VT)*	Various entertainers	Vaudeville & pictures (May 10/3) [formerly, the Bijou Theatre]
JUN 25/15 - *OT*	Culligan's Nashville Students' colored Minstrels	Minstrel show (Jun 25/2) (*$0.10 - $0.25*)
SEPT 1-6/15 - *VT*	Various performers	Vaudeville & films (Sept 1/2)
OCT 1,2/15 - *OT*	The Musical Eckhardts and pictures	Musical entertainers (Sept 30/2; Oct 2/2) - *huge success*
NOV 22-25; NOV 30-DEC 1/15 - *OT*	The Girls in Khaki with Bob Lavelle, George Shady, Mel Butler, Carroll Van	Musical variety Fun in a Cabaret & other shows (Nov 21/2) (*$0.25 - $0.35*) - *capacity crowds*
DEC 1-31/15 - *OT*	Various performers	Vaudeville
JAN 1/16 - *MT*	James Fax & the Fax-Wilson Fun Co.	Variety (Dec 30/2) (*$0.25 - $1.00*)
JAN 3-8; 10-12/16 - *OT*	Pantages Circuit with Odell & Hart and others	Vaudeville & The Two Dandies (Jan 3/2; 12/2)
JAN 20-22/16 - *OT*	The Wheeler Amusement Co.	Vaudeville (Jan 20/2)
JAN 24-DEC 31/16 - *OT*- (selected days)	Pantages Circuit	Vaudeville (Dec 4/5; Jan 18/2) - *same bill as in Calgary*

DATE/PLACE	COMPANY AND/OR PERFORMER(S)	PERFORMANCE(S)/REFERENCE/CRITIQUE
JAN 21-APR/16 - *MT* (*Fri. & Sat. nights*)	Orpheum Circuit	Vaudeville
MAY 15,16/16 - *MT*	Reese Brothers	Africander Minstrels (May 15/2) - *well filled house well pleased*
AUG 16/16 - *OT*	Elite Musical Stock Co.	Musical show & 5 reeler (Aug 11/2) - *taken well with local theatre goers*
AUG 30-SEPT 7,13,16/16 - *OT*	Empire Girls & moving pictures	The King of Bo-Lo-Boo Island; Mike & Ike at Coney Island; The Million Dollar Beauty (Aug 30/2)
OCT 10-14/16 - *OT*	Dr. Herbert Travelutte	"King of Hypnotists" (Oct 10/2) - *greeted elsewhere with packed houses*
FEB 12-15/17 - *OT*	McDonald & Curtis	Vaudeville, burlesque & comedy farces, The Blockhead; Rail Road Bell (Feb 10/5)
FEB 19/17 - *OT*	Musical Eckhardts	Vaudeville (Feb 19/7)
MAR 8-10/17 - *OT*	Burnard Eckhardt presents F.E. Powell	Australian magician (Mar 8/5) (*$0.35*)
MAR 15/17 - *MT*	Fax Wilson Fun Co.	Musical acts (Mar 12/5)
MAY 18,19/17 - *MT*	Kelley-Lane Road Show	Hippodrome vaudeville & sketches, His Night Out; Their First Quarrel (May 18/5; 19/5)
JUN 21; OCT 1/17 - *MT*	Cunning	"The Man of Mystery" (Jun 21/5; Oct 1/5)
AUG 7-13/17 - *Eckstorm Rink*	Chautauqua	22 attractions, lectures, impersonations [S. Platt Jones] (Aug 4/11) - *for the farmers*
OCT 9/17 - *OT*	Powell	The Magician and Mystic (Oct 9/5)
OCT 15-17/17 - *OT*	Culligan Blake's Native Hawaiian Dancers	Novelty dance acts (Oct 12/5)
NOV 15; 19/17 - *OT*	Canadian Concert & Variety Vaudeville Co.	Variety (Nov 15/5; 19/5)
NOV 22/17 - *OT*	"Original" Tennessee Jubilee Singers	Minstrels (Nov 22/5)
DEC 29/17 - *MT*	McDonald Royal Entertainers	Variety (Dec 24/5)
JAN 26/18 - *MT*	unidentified company	Musical & novelty show "Katzenjammer Kids" (Jan 25/5) - *a great big girl show*
FEB 4-7/18 - *OT*	Various acts & films	Vaudeville (Feb 4/5)
FEB 8-19/18 - *OT*	Dr. Herbert I. Travelutte Show	Vaudeville, myrth, mystery "Ali Ben Deb Knows All" (Feb 8/5; 12/5; 14/5) (*$0.10 - $0.50*)
FEB 25/18 - *Wesley Church*	Harry Lauder	Musical entertainment (Feb 14/8)
MAR 25-27/18 - *MT*	The Great Nelson Co.	Vaudeville (Mar 23/5)
JUL 30; AUG 1/18 - *MT*	Juvenile Bostonians	Vaudeville (Jul 30/5) (*$0.25 - $0.50*)
AUG 12-17/18 - (*6 Ave. "A" & 13 St. So.*)	Lethbridge Chautauqua	Variety, lectures, concerts (Aug 8/5; 10/10; 12/17) - *seating for 1400*
SEPT 24-30/18 - *MT*	Dr. Zell Hunt with Nellie Burke	Clairvoyant, Hypnotist (Sept 23/5)
OCT 13-NOV 29/18	**Lethbridge Theatres - CLOSED**	**BECAUSE OF PROVINCIAL INFLUENZA EPIDEMIC**
NOV 29-DEC 29/18 - *Colonial Th. (CT)* (*former Orpheum*)	Resident Colonial Players with Cecille Elliott, Bud Schaffer, Jessie Gay, Al Borde	Vaudeville & sketches: Let's Get a Divorce; The Notorious Helene; A Lady For an Hour; Getting Unmarried (Nov 29/5; Dec 3/5; 6/5; 10/5; 20/5; 23/5; 24/5; 27/5) - *ten piece orchestra*
DEC 3/18 - *MT*	Pantages Circuit	Vaudeville (Dec 3/5)
FEB 5/19 - *MT*	Carter	Magician (Feb 3/5)
MAR 17/19 - *MT*	Buchner's Dixie Jubilee Singers	Spring Chautauqua (Mar 15/5)
FEB 19-22/19 - *MT*	Barnum	Hypnotist (Feb 15/5)
APR 7/19 - *MT*	The Castle Square Entertainers	Spring Chautauqua: Musical variety (Apr 7/5)
MAY 6-8/19 - *CT*	Royal Hawaiian Co. presented by Culligan & Hockwald	Native Hawaiian musical entertainment (May 6/5)
MAY 29/19 - *MT*	Barnum	Magician (May 29/5)
AUG 1,2/19 - *MT*	R.M. Harvey presents	Harvey's Greater Minstrels (Aug 1/5) (*$0.50 - $1.00*) - *great genuine* entertainment
AUG 8-14/19	Chautauqua	Various acts including The White Hussars (Jul 26/13) - *season ticket $2.50*

DATE/PLACE	COMPANY AND/OR PERFORMER(S)	PERFORMANCE(S)/REFERENCE/CRITIQUE
OCT 13-DEC/19 - *CT*	Hippodrome Circuit	Vaudeville: Monday & Tuesday (Oct 8/5; Dec 20/5)
OCT 31, NOV 1/19 - *MT*	The Original Winnipeg Kiddies	Musical revue (Oct 31/5; Nov 1/5) (*$.25 - $1.00*) - *wonderful*
DEC 9/19 - *MT*	Blackstone	Magician (Dec 9/5)
DEC 16/19 - *MT*	Sir Harry Lauder	Musical entertainment (Dec 16/5)
JAN - JUN; SEPT - DEC/20 - *CT*	Hippodrome Circuit	Vaudeville on Monday & Tuesday nights (Jan 7/5; Dec 24/12)
FEB 25; APR 6/20 - *MT*	3rd Canadian Army Division Theatrical Unit (augmented)	The Dumbells in Biff Bing Bang (Feb 21/5; 26/7) - *finest vaudeville to ever visit this city*
MAY 3-5/20 - *MT*	Khaym	Mystery Man of India (May 3/5)
JUN 7,8/20 - *MT*	Gus Hill presents George Wilson and Jimmy Wall & Co.	Gus Hill's minstrels (Jun 7/5)
JUL 3-5/20 - *CT*	Paul Robinson & The California Movie Girls	1920 Bathing Girl Review (Jul 3/5) (*$0.25 - $0.75*)
JUL 9,10/20 - *CT*	Flo Hartley Vaudeville Co.	Cinderella - Up To Date (Jul 8/5)
AUG 11-17/20	Chautauqua	Variety acts (Aug 10/8) - *season ticket $2.50*
AUG 23/20 - *MT*	Harvey's Greatest Minstrels	Minstrel show (Aug 23/8)
SEPT 21/20 - *MT*	Winnipeg Kiddies	1920 Revue (Sept 20/8)
OCT 11,12; NOV 15/20 - *MT*	Cpt. M.W. Plunkett 4th Division Maple Leafs	Original overseas revue Camouflage (Oct 4/8; 11/8; Nov 12/13)
OCT 13,14/20 - *CT*	Musical Eckhardts	1920 vaudeville revue (Oct 11/8)
NOV 17,18/20 - *CT*	Pull Brothers & Co.	Hypnotist, mind reader, illusionist (Nov 15/8)
JAN - MAY/21 - *CT*	Hippodrome circuit (Mon. & Tues.)	Vaudeville (Jan 7/8; May 23/12 - *passim*)
JAN 14,15; FEB 19/21 - *MT*	Cpt. M.W. Plunkett presents the Dumbells in an "all new"	Biff Bing Bang (Jan 14/8; 15/11; Feb 19/8)
APR 9/21 - *MT*	Winnipeg Kiddies	1921 Revue; Vaudeville (Apr 9/9) (*$0.50 - $1.00*)
JUN 16-22/21	Chautauqua	Concerts, lectures, etc. (Jun 7/9)
JUN 17,18/21 - *MT*	Herbert's Greater Minstrels	(Jun 17/9; 18/10) - *delighted large crowd*
AUG 1,2/21 - *CT*	Zantola & Osborne's Road Show	1921 Vaudeville Revue (Aug 1/5; 2/5) (*$0.25 - $0.75*) - *pleasing show*
SEPT 26-29/21 - *CT*	Allendale & Alburtus Co.	Hypnotists & spiritualists (Sept 23/10)
OCT 7,8/21 - *CT*	Captain Fred M. Fisher & Canadian Army Players	Mademoiselle of Armenticres or "The P.B.I." (Oct 7/5) (*$1.00 - $1.50*)
OCT 31;NOV 1/21	The Royal Pierrots (Trans-Canada Theatre Ltd.)	English Music Hall Vaudeville Review (Oct 31/5) (*$0.50 - $1.50*)
NOV 16/21 - *MT*	Lalonde-Proctor Co.	Hawaiian Steel Guitars (Nov 16/9)
NOV 17-19/21 - *MT*	The Musical Eckhardts	Vaudeville (Nov 17/9)
DEC 16,17/21 - *MT*	Cpt. M.W. Plunkett 4th Canadian Army Division The Maple Leafs	1921 edition of Camouflage (Dec 5/8; 16/12; 17/9) - *given thunderous applause*
DEC 30/21 - *MT*	The Calgary Kiddies	1921 Revue (Dec 30/8) (*$0.50 - $1.00*)
JAN 20,21/22 - *MT*	The Great Jackson and Co.	Vaudeville (Jan 19/8)
FEB 3,4/22 - *MT*	Dumbells with "Red" Newman and Ross Hamilton	Biff, Bing, Bang (Feb 4/8) (*$0.50 - $2.00*) - *successfully played New York - scored success here*
FEB 20-25/22 - *MT*	Mem-O-Rea	"The Mental Marvel & added vaudeville (Feb 20/8) (*$0.25 - $0.75*)
MAY 26,27/22 - *MT*	Swift and Daley, William Morrow	Pantages Vaudeville One For Nothing (May 23/8) (*$0.50*)
JUN 22-28/22 - *7 St. & 5 Ave.*	Chautauqua	Concerts, lectures (Jun 10/10; 14/10; 16/13; 17/7)
JUL 19,20/22 - *CT*	Gallarine Sisters	Pantages Vaudeville (Jul 19/8)
JUL 25-27/22 - *MT*	Pantages Circuit with Al Jennings Co.	Vaudeville, The Last of the Law (Jul 24/8)

DATE/PLACE	COMPANY AND/OR PERFORMER(S)	PERFORMANCE(S)/REFERENCE/CRITIQUE
AUG 8 - DEC 5; 14,15/22 - MT	Pantages Circuit	Vaudeville, Thursday & Friday nights: various acts: Blackstone, the Magician; Fashion Plate Minstrels (Aug 8/8 - Dec 11/8 - *passim*)
SEPT 18-20/22 - MT FEB 19-21/23 - CT	Harry Thompson & his Imperial Orchestra; Quintette with Baritone Dewey Washington	Jazz & instrumental novelties (Sept 19/8) - *generous and well deserved applause*
JAN - JUN/23 - MT (selected days); OCT 18,19/23	Pantages Circuit Ruth Budd, Vardon & Perry, Bert Walton, Eva La Rue Margo Raffaro & Jim Gilda George & Mary Usher Six Sheiks of Araby Joe Bennett and Co. Aliko & Co., Eddie Borden & others	Vaudeville Little Cinderella - The Sheik's Favorite; Twenty Minutes in China Town Marriage & Divorce An Arabian Fantasy The Telephone Tangle Grecian mystic (Jan 11/8; Oct 14/8 - *passim*)
MAY 31/23 - MT	The Old Dumbells	Full of Pep (Jun 1/8) - *SRO - pleasing as ever*
JUN 14/23 - MT	Georgia Minstrels	(Jun 9/8; 15/8) ($0.50 - $1.00) - *colored entertainers pleased huge audience*
NOV 26,27/23 - MT	"Originals" (formerly "Old Dumbells")	Rapid Fire (Nov 19/8; 27/8) - *never a dull moment*
JAN 3/24 - MT	Irving's Imperial Midgets	Vaudeville (Jan 2/8) - *direct from London and Paris*
JAN 17/24 - MT	Rusco and Hockwald present	Georgia Minstrels (Jan 14/8) ($0.50 - $1.00)
JAN 29,30/24 - MT	Captain Plunkett's Dumbells	Cheerio 5th Annual Revue (Jan 26/8; 29/8; 30/8) ($1.00 - $2.00) - *breezy & fresh...crowded house*
APR 23/24 - MT	Calgary Kiddies & the McDonald Kilties	1924 Revue (Apr 21/8)
JUN 19,20; JUL 4; AUG 14,15/24 - MT	Pantages Circuit Popular dancers Guy & Pearl Magby, Robert McKim & Elsie Williams; Maude Daniel; Moore & Fields; Marion & Jason	Vaudeville The Bachelor's Bride; Youth; Spilling the Beans; For Goodness Sakes (Jun 20/8; Jul 5/8; 18/8; Aug 15/8)
SEPT 4-6/24 - MT	Richards	Magician (Sept 5/8)
OCT 7/24 - CT	Beck & Walker's Co. with Bubber Carson	"Colored" Minstrels (Oct 6/8)
NOV 24-26/24 - CT	Eddie McLean, Bobby Bryson, Rose Leigh	Vaudeville (Nov 25/8)
DEC 10/24 - MT	The Originals (Old Dumbells)	Stepping Out (Dec 11/7) - *delight packed audience*
DEC 23,24; 26,27/24 - Palace Th. (PT)	Joey and Christine Johnston & movies	Vaudeville, Odds and Ends (Dec 23/8; 26/8) [the former Colonial Theatre]
JAN 12-14/25 - PT	Mr. Dennis O'Brien, et. al.	Vaudeville as added attraction (Jan 13/8) - *former juvenile lead of "The Maid of the Mts." & a singer of the first order*
JAN 19/25 - MT	The Originals (return engagement)	Stepping Out (Jan 20/8) - *exhilarating vim*
JAN 27-29/25 - PT	Victor Durigo & his accordian	Vaudeville (Jan 27/10)
FEB 4; MAR 9,10/25 - MT	The Dumbells in Captain Plunkett's	Ace High; Oh, Yes (Feb 5/8; Mar 9/8; 10/8) - *SRO - pleasing as ever*
FEB 14; 16,17/25 - PT	Bill Marr	Vaudeville as added attraction (Feb 14/8)
MAR 23/25 - PT	The Winnipeg Kiddies	Vaudeville, 1925 Revue (Mar 24/8) - *show of undoubted merit*
APR 9; 27-29/25 - PT	Various acts and movies	Vaudeville (Apr 9/12; 29/8)
AUG 8;10; 17-22/25 - Emp	Elsie & Phillis McGowan; Joey Johnston & the Scottish Laugh Co.	Vaudeville (Aug 8/8; 18/8)
OCT 19,20/25 - MT	The Originals	Thumbs Up (Oct 20/8) - *one of best soldier shows ever seen here*
NOV 2,3/25 - Emp	Fred Karno & Co. and movie	Vaudeville comedy skit Sons of the Sea & 3 other acts (Oct 31/6)
NOV 13,14/25 - PT	Fay the Magician & Mystery Man	Vaudeville (Nov 14/8)
DEC 1-5; 7-9/25 - Emp	Miss Tommy Clancy Vaudeville Co. with Madame Valda and Wilfred Hill	Comedy, The Mollusc (Dec 5/14; 8/8) - *late of the Gaiety Theatre, London*
DEC 7-12/25 - PT	Green the Magician	"Show of Wonders" (Dec 8/8) - *50 minutes of magic & mystery entertainment*
DEC 16,17/25 - PT	Empire Entertainers	Vaudeville [7 big acts] (Dec 16/8)
DEC 14-19/25 - Emp	Maraja	Illusionist & mind reader (Dec 16/8)
DEC 22-25/25; JAN 9,10/26 - PT	Walter Bates and his Lyric Quartette	Musical entertainment (Dec 23/8)

DATE/PLACE	COMPANY AND/OR PERFORMER(S)	PERFORMANCE(S)/REFERENCE/CRITIQUE
JAN 20/26 - *MT*	Pantages with Guy Voyer & Co. etc.	Vaudeville (Jan 18/8)
FEB 8,9/26 - *MT*	Dumbells	Lucky 7 (Feb 9/8) ($0.75 - $2.00) - *excels past efforts*
FEB 10;20/26 - *Emp*	Acadian Players with Sandy McNabb	Vaudeville (Feb 10/8; 20/8)
FEB 22-25/26 - *Emp*	Wing Chong, etc.	Vaudeville (Feb 22/8) ($0.25 - $0.60)
MAR 8,9/26 - *MT*	Plunkett's Dumbells	Three Bags Full (Mar 9/8) - *great show*
MAR 22/26 - *Emp*	Bill Marr	Fire eater (Mar 20/8)
MAR 29,30/26 - *MT*	Dr. Paris & various vaudeville acts	Hypnotist (Mar 29/8; 30/8) - *good deal of merriment*
MAY 10-13/26 - *Emp*	Moore's Plantation Revue	Vaudeville (May 11/10) - *one of peppiest & snappiest programs*
MAY 31-JUN 5/26 - *PT*	Tom Copeland	Scottish novelty vaudeville (May 31/12)
JUL 19,20; 21-23; SEPT 4/26 - *Emp*	Various acts: Winnipeg Ukrainian Girls (Mandolin players), Professor Utell & trained animal circus, Mr. Frost (English co-median)	Vaudeville (Jul 19/6; 23/12; Sept 4/12)
OCT 7-9/26 - *PT*	Joey Johnstone and Ashra	Vaudeville (Oct 7/12)
OCT 29,30/26 - *MT*	Richards	"World's Greatest Magician" (Oct 29/14)
DEC 20,21/26 - *PT*	Jack Strong's Wonder Novelty Show with The Great Omar	Vaudeville, magic (Dec 21/14)
DEC 27,28/26 - *MT*	Cpt. Plunkett's sister show to the Dumbells	Revue of 1926 (Dec 28/7) - *pleasing but not outstanding*
JAN 6-8/27 - *PT*	Joe Marks presents Bert Johnston & Co.	Vaudeville, illusionist, ventriloquist, magic (Jan 5/16; 6/10; 8/12)
JAN 7,8/27 - *Emp*	La Clare S-H-O-W-S	Vaudeville & bear wrestling (Jan 7/12)
JAN 21/27 - *MT*	Cpt. Plunkett (return engagement)	Revue of 1926 (Jan 14/14) ($0.75 - $1.50)
FEB 7,8/27 - *MT*	Cpt. Plunkett and Dumbells	8th Annual Revue Joy Bombs (Feb 8/7) - *sold out; smart & snappy as ever*
FEB 14,15/27 - *Emp*	Bert Taylor (comedian)	A Hegg, Some 'Am & a Honion (Feb 14/10)
MAR 7,8/27 - *MT*	Dumbells	Musical Revue, That's That (Mar 8/12) - *snappy spring revue enjoyed by capacity house*
MAR 14-19; 21-26/27 - *PT*	Hill & Durham, Harry C. Willis	Vaudeville (Mar 18/12; 14/12) - *former manager, local Starland Theatre (Willis)*
MAY 30-JUN 4; 6-11/27 - *Emp*	Ralph Maddison (Canadian tenor) - "the singing miner"	Vaudeville (Jun 1/10) - *critics call him the underground Caruso*
JUN 27-30/27 - *PT*	Joe Marks presents Bert Johnston & Co.	Vaudeville, magic & fun show (Jun 25/16)
OCT 3,4/27 - *PT*	Teddy Sullivan	Vaudeville, concertina wizard (Oct 1/12)
OCT 10,15/27 - *Emp*	Harry C. Willis	Vaudeville comedian (Oct 8/14) - *see Mar 14-19*
OCT 20-22/27 - *PT*	Britain's Mystery Film Girl	Movies & song about world tour (Oct 20/14)
OCT 27-29; NOV 7; 11,12/27 - *Emp*	B.H. Sarsfield; Butler & Darby	Vaudeville, English musical hall entertainer (Oct 27/16; Nov 5/16; 11/16)
DEC 2,3/27 - *MT*	Australian Concert Co.	Vaudeville (Dec 3/14) - *snappy show with many excellent features*
JAN 23/28 - *Emp*	Tom Copeland (Scottish entertainer)	Variety (Jan 24/10)
FEB 1-4/28 - *Emp*	Australian Concert Co. plus Canadian juvenile entertainers Hec Totten and Helen Rullens	Vaudeville (Feb 3/12)
FEB 6-9/28 - *PT*	The Four Playmates	Vaudeville - Capital Theatre (Calgary) Circuit (Feb 8/10; 9/12) - *Pacific coast's most famous quartette*
FEB 10,11/28 - *MT*	The Dumbell's 9th Annual Revue	Oo! La, La! (Feb 11/12) - *highly pleasing to packed house*
FEB 20-25; 27-29; MAR 2-7/28 - *Emp*	Capital Theatre Circuit: Doreen Sisters; The Raney Players; Signor Pette	Vaudeville, dancers, accordianist (Feb 18/12; 25/12; 29/14; Mar 7/12)
MAR 5,6/28 - *PT*	Canadian Juvenile Performers Helen Rullen, Gene and Hec Totten	Vaudeville (Mar 3/16)
MAR 26-31/28 - *PT*	Jean Gauld and Eve Beete	Vaudeville (Mar 27/14) - *the versatile Scot, Canada's champion dancer; dancer petite of London*

DATE/PLACE	COMPANY AND/OR PERFORMER(S)	PERFORMANCE(S)/REFERENCE/CRITIQUE
APRIL 2-5; 28-MAY 5/28 - *PT*	Wing Chong	Vaudeville [1 string violin] (Apr 5/18; 30/12; May 4/16)
APR 19-21; 23-28/28 - *Emp*	The Totten Kids, Harvey & His Red Tux Boys	Vaudeville [Canadian Stage Band] (Apr 20/14; 27/18)
MAY 4-NOV 10/28 - *Emp*	Various acts, Ted Sullivan, David Morgan, Ken Koe, Totten Kids, Darby and Butler, Edmonton Ukrainian Mandolin Orchestra, Gallegher & Co., The Merry Makers, Andy Gump, Les Crane & His Canadians	Vaudeville, concertina wizard, Welsh tenor, Hula dancer, song & dance, magic & comedy, specialty music, trained animals, variety cartoonist, impersonator (May 4/16 - Nov 9/18)
JUL 31/28 - *MT*	The Calgary Kiddies	Musical revue (Jul 28/14; Aug 1/7)
SEPT 20-22/28 - *MT*	Pantages Circuit, Niblo & Spencer, Hillier and Forte	Vaudeville (Sept 21/20) ($0.50 - $1.00)
OCT 1,2/28 - *MT*	Winnipeg Kiddies	Vaudeville (Sept 29/16; Oct 1/10; 2/12)
OCT 15-18/28 - *PT*	Georgian Singers & Players, etc.	Vaudeville, musical entertainment (Oct 17/12)
DEC 6; 12-15; 17-19; 20-22; 24-27/28 - *PT*	Wing Chong, Delroy & Delaney, Oriole McLaughlin, Charles Courtier & other vaudeville acts	One string violin, song & dance, pattern dance, impersonations, vocals (Dec 6/18; 12/22; 17/12; 20/14) - *Little Miss Oriole McLaughlin - late of Our Gang Comedies*
JAN 14,15; 17-19/29 - *PT*	Jimmie Fisher & Baldy Strang's Sunset Artists	Canadian boy comedian; musical entertainment (Jan 15/10; 17/12)
JAN 24-26; MAR 10; JUN 3-6; JUL 25,26; SEPT 23; DEC 9/29 - *Emp*	Totten Family, Thomas & Holmes, Winnipeg Kiddies, Dandy Dixie, Butler and Darby & other vaudeville artists	Juvenile vaudeville stars; Hawaiian music; juvenile revue, minstrels, vaudeville (Jan 24/14; Mar 20/14; Jun 4/8; Jul 26/8; Sept 21/8; Dec 9/5) - *Dandy Dixie Minstrels feature 7 year old boy, Edwin Hall*
JAN 18,19/29 - *MT*	Cpt. Plunkett's Dumbells	10th annual Revue Why Worry (Jan 19/12) ($0.75 - $2.00) - SRO
FEB 22,23/29 - *MT*	Cpt. Plunkett's Dumbells	Here 'Tis (Feb 23/14) ($0.50 - $2.00) - *as bright & breezy as ever*
MAY 9; JUN 1; 6-8; 15-21/29 - *Capital Th. (Cap)*	Ernest Hammond, Joey & Christine Johnston, Omar & other vaudeville artists	Toronto baritone; Comedy & magic; "The Great Psychic" (May 9/8; 31/14; Jun 5/8; 15/8)
NOV 8,9/29 - *MT*	Sandy McNabb and others	Vaudeville (Nov 8/8)
JAN 13,14/30 - *Emp*	Al Nathan & Co.	Vaudeville (Jan 14/5)
APR 14-17/30 - *MT*	Dr. Raymond & Co.	Hypnotist, magician (Apr 14/5; 17/5) ($0.25 - $0.50)
AUG 1-7/30 - *(T)*	Chautauqua [at St. Patrick's School Grounds]	(Aug 2/7; 4/7; 5/7; 7/7) - *opened on last day of Lethbridge Fair*
NOV 25,26/30 - *MT*	The Dumbells	11th Annual Revue, Come Eleven (Nov 19/5; 25/5; 26/5) (0.50 - $1.50) - *pleases capacity house...all that could be desired in such a show*
JAN 8-14/31 - *(T)*	Chautauqua	Variety (Jul 9/7; 11/7; 15/7)
NOV 16,17/31 - *MT*	Cpt M.W. Plunkett's Dumbells	As You Were (Nov 17/6) - *packed house...as popular as ever*
MAR 23,24/32 - *Emp*	Sun Si Guy Co.	Oriental magician (Mar 23/2)
JUN 9-11,13/32	Chautauqua: Lucille Elmore, The Night Hawks, etc.	(Jun 8/7; 10/9; 11/7) ($1.00 - $1.50 for season)
AUG 4/32 - *Cap*	Professor Franklin	Palmist, phrenologist (Aug 4/2)
NOV 26/32 - *MT*	Ted Wilson directs The Carolina Minstrels with 40 entertainers	Minstrelsy (Nov 24/2,6; 25/6) ($0.50 - $0.75)
FEB 14/33 - *MT*	Cpt. M.W. Plunkett presents The Dumbells	14th annual revue Here We Are Again (Feb 15/5) ($0.50 - $1.00) - *bright entertainment pleases crowded house*
APR 3-5/33 - *Cap*	Koram	Crystal Gazer (Apr 1/7)
JUN 27-30/33 - *(T)*	Deep River Plantation Singers, The Lombards	Chatauqua (Jun 24/7; 26/7; 28/9) $1.50 (adult season tickets); $1.00 (children) [St. Patrick's School Grounds]
AUG 14,15/33 - *Cap*	Omar	Psychologist & seer [mentalist] (Aug 12/2,6)
OCT 23/33 - *MT*	Frederic Shipman presents Michio Ito and Co.	"Internationally famed Japanese dancer" (Sept 30/7; Oct 21/7; 24/7) - *masterful...captivated Lethbridge audience*
MAR 28,29/34 - *Cap*	Winnipeg Kiddies with Jimmy Fisher	Varieties of 1934 (Mar 24/7; 27/7)

DATE/PLACE	COMPANY AND/OR PERFORMER(S)	PERFORMANCE(S)/REFERENCE/CRITIQUE
APR 2,3/34 - *Cap*	Calgary Kiddies, Gene & Joyce Totten	Vaudeville (Apr 2/2,3)
FEB 19,20/35 - *Roxy*	Les Nichols	Whistling ventriloquist (Feb 19/2)
JUL 11-13/35 - *Cap*	Purple Sage Riders, The Pioneer Trio	"Frontier" entertainers (Jul 11/2)
OCT 9,10/35 - *Cap*	Jack Rothschild presents Irvin C. Miller's Brown Skin Models	Harlem rhythm & dance routines, novelty musical numbers (Oct 10/6) *(0.15 - $0.50) - packed house*
OCT 28-DEC 16; OCT 28,29; NOV 4,5; 11,12; 18,19; 26, 27; DEC 2; 9; 16/35 - *Cap*	Wilbur Cushman Units Harry Clark Co. Jack Randall & Co. Glen Dale & His Masqueraders Louis Western with Phillip Casino's Band Clifford Wayne Indians with Brown & LaVelle (stars of the Alka Seltzer Hour) Jed Dooley & Co. Art Gleason presents the Musical Town Criers George Lovett & the Masked Mystery Band	Vaudeville stage shows Rancho Grande Revue From Broadway to Bagdad Mardi Gras Night A Night in Avalon Comedy Stars of Hollywood with Jack Tracy & his Hollywood Boulevardiers - March of Rhythms Town Scandals - The Stratosphere Revue [(Oct 28/6 - Dec 13/8 - *(passim)*]
JUN 4,5/36 - *Cap*	Major Bowes presents	Amateurs on Tour (Jun 4/2; 5/2)
NOV 17/36 - *Cap*	El-Wyn (magician, spiritualist)	Midnight Spook Party (Nov 16/7; 19/6) - *thrills audience*
NOV 30-DEC 2/36 - *Cap*	Wing Wing Troupe	Chinese acrobats & jugglers (Nov 28/6; 30/6)
FEB 22,23/37 - *Cap*	Frederic Shipman presents The Tipica Mexican Orchestra	Musical & dance novelty with dancers: Joseph Von Hahn & Marta De Negre (Feb 17/6; 23/6) - *pleases audience*
JUN 21-23/37 - *Cap*	Crockett Family: (stars of KNX Hollywood Barn Dance)	Stage show (Jun 19/2,7) - *plenty of variety*
SEPT 14,15/37 - *Cap*	Major Bowes	Jamboree of 1937 [10 big acts] (Sept 15/2)
SEPT 20/37 - *Cap*	Irvin C. Miller presents	Brown Skin Models (Sept 20/2,7)
OCT 1,2/37 - *Cap*	Angus & Searle, Foley & Leture and others	Vaudeville direct from Grand Theatre, Calgary (Sept 29/2,7; Oct 2/7) - *well received*
JAN 16/38 - *Cap*	Direct from Madame Tussard's Famous Chamber of Horrors	London Ghost Show (Jan 15/2)
AUG 8/38 - *Cap*	Robert Bell Honolulu City Trio & other at-tractions	Hawaiian Follies (Aug 4/7; 9/7) - *pleases large crowds*
MAY 29-31; JUN 1-3/39 - *Roxy*	Professor Gladstone ("Man of Mystery", mental wizard)	Mem-O-Rea (May 26/2; Jun 1/12) - *held over*
MAR 4; APR 19,20/40 - *Cap*	Red Newman, Pat Rafferty, Ross Hamilton, Jack Ayre and The Lowells	"The Stars of the Dumbells" & acrobats, [The Lowells] (Mar 1/6; 4/6,7; 5/7) - *last chance to see Canada's famous entertainers...entertained packed houses*
MAR 12/40 - *Cap*	"Famous youngsters of screen & radio"	Paramount Starlets Revue (Mar 12/2)
MAY 29/40 - *Cap*	The Musical Taits with Winnie Martin Tait & her six children	Musical entertainment (May 29/2; 30/8) - *interesting feature; W.M. Tait was first captain of Edmonton Grads basketball team*
JUN 24,25/40 - *Cap*	Henry Viney & Entertainers	The Big Radio Jamboree (Jun 20/2; 24/2)
MAY 16,17/41 - *Cap*	M. De La Ferre	Impersonator & magician (May 15/7,2)
FEB 13/42 - *Arena*	Hollywood action, Ian Hunter & local acts	Victory Loan Rally (Feb 14/7,9)
MAY 26/43 - *#8 B. & G. School*	Massey Harris presents Pat McIntosh, Betty Robertson & Co.	Combines of 1943 variety show (May 17/8; 25/6; 27/12) - *entertaining the troops in training across the country...an entertaining treat*
JUN 3,4/43 - *#8 B. & G. School*	Calgary Air Training Station; Cast of 32 dir. by F.O. Wishart Campbell	Blackout of 1943 (Jun 2/7; 4/7) - *fine, streamlined entertainment*
MAR 24,25; 27,28/44 - *Rainbow Hall, Hun-garian Hall*	Green the Magician	Show of Wonders (Mar 23/6,7; 24/6) *($0.35) - returns after 9 years*
SEPT 19/44 - *Arena*	Dr. Kotowicz - magician	"International mystery & comedy show" (Sept 18/2; 20/6) *($0.60 - $1.50) - versatile, impressive*
JUN 28/47 - *Arena*	Canadian Productions present	The Happy Gang Show (Jun 20/2; 30/19) - *pleases large crowd of 2000*
SEPT 8/47 - *Arena*	Roy Ward Dickson	Fun parade [stunts and practical jokes by members of audience] (Sept 8/2)
MAY 18/48 - *Arena*	Roy Ward Dickson	The Fun Parade (May 13/10)

DATE/PLACE	COMPANY AND/OR PERFORMER(S)	PERFORMANCE(S)/REFERENCE/CRITIQUE
MAY 20/49 - *Arena*	Roy Ward Dickson	Fun Parade of '49 plus Adam's Take A Chance (May 5/2; 20/2)
MAR 6/50 - *Cap*	Irving Grossman presents (auspices of Lethbridge Gyro Club)	Vaudeville with Bill Warfield, Wally Sands, Tom & Gene Gary, Rosemary Wade (Mar 4/8) *($0.55 - $1.00)*
MAY 27/50 - *Arena*	A. Keith T. Crowe Productions (in aid of Manitoba Relief Fund)	Varieties of 1950 (May 25/3; 27/3; 29/6) - *17 performers, 2 hours of enter-tainment. Thrills spectators*
JUN 15,16/51 - *Civic Centre*	The Great Tex Morton Show (from Australia)	Sharpshooter, Western Singer, Mesmerist, Hypnotist (Jun 14/3) *($1.00 - $1.25 - huge audience held spellbound*
JUN 13/52 - *Trianon Ballroom*	Pat Gerow & His "Western Gang" (stars of CBC - Burns' Chuckwagon Show)	Stage show and dance (Jun 10/10) [RCA recording artist]
SEPT 4/54 - *Civic Centre*	M.J. Randle of Ottawa presents the Variety Touring Co. with Betty Meek, Nancy McCaig, Alan Scott, Mildred Morey, Ernie Bruce	Parade of Stars (Sept 3/10; 7/9) - *sparkling revue* [auspices of ANAF Vets]
SEPT 15,16/54 - *Civic Centre*	George Haddad & Co.	Magician & Hypnotist (Sept 16/10) - *top flight show*
JUN 2,3/55 - *L.C.I.*	George Haddad & Co.	(May 30/3; Jun 1/3) *($0.50 - $1.00)* [in aid of Callow Coach fund]
SEPT 3,4,8/56 - *Cap*	Billy Papons' All Star Revue	Vaudeville (Sept 4/10) - *outstanding show*
SEPT 17,18/56 - *Arena*	The Great Dr. Kit, Hypnotist	(Sept 17/3; 18/10) *($0.75 - $1.50)* - *amazes crowd*
OCT 12/56 - *Ft. Whoop-Up Guest Ranch*	Lee Grabel & Co.	Illusionist (Oct 9/3; 13/14) - *stumped his audience*
MAR 11/57 - *Jewish Synagogue*	Molly Picon (famous Yiddish actress) auspices of Lillian Freeman Chapter of Hadassah	Songs, stories, monologues (Mar 9/16) - *recently appeared in Broadway show, Morning Star*
JUN 22/57 - *Henderson Lake Pav.*	Miss Lillian Randolph & Co.'s Night Club Revue	Variety Entertainment (Jun 14/3) - *portrays Madame Queen on the Amos n' Andy radio/T.V. show*
AUG 21/57 - *Cap*	"Dracula" (direct from Hollywood)	Stage Show: House of the Living Dead (Aug 14/3)
NOV 9/57 - *Civic Centre*	Dr. Morton Green	Hypnotist (Nov 8/3) [auspices of Lethbridge Cosmopolitan Club]
JUN 14/58 - *L.C.I.*	Alexander's Magic Circus with Mandrake the Magician	(May 17/10; Jun 3/6) [auspices of Lethbridge Lion's Club]
FEB 5-10; APR 23-28; Nov 5-10/62 - *Cap*	Reveen presented by Famous Players Theatre [Following 1962, Reveen appeared almost annually at the Capitol, Civic Centre, Sportsplex and/or Yates]	Australian Magician, Hypnotist, Illusionist Trip to Honolulu, (Feb 7/3; 9/3; 10/3) The Hypnotic Circus (Apr 21/3; 27/3; Oct 27/3; 31/3; Jan 18/64/3; Oct 2/65/3; Oct 2/67/3; Feb 5/69/10; Jan 22/70/7; Apr 3/71/7; Aug 28/76/10; Jan 3/78/7; Feb 19/79/15; Apr 26/80/B10; Jan 2/82/D1; Jan 30/84/B11; Mar 1/86/B6)
AUG 19,20/63 - *Cap*	The Buffalo Bill Show	Sharpshooting, ventriloquism, magic, mirth, mystery (Aug 14/3; 19/3) - *company of 20*
MAR 31/66 - *LDS Auditorium*	Patti Royal, Roy Baumgart, Verland Whip-ple, Ken Christensen, Terri Sisters, Ray Lee Combo	Revue, Tonight on Broadway (Mar 30/18)
APR 27/66 - *Cap*	An Oriental Doll Revue	(Apr 15/17; 28/14) - *fail to impress* [auspices of Norbridge Lion's Club]
MAY 9,10/67 - *Arena*	Canadian Armed Forces Tatoo (cast of 25)	Military music, pageantry, comedy, variety battle scenes, etc. (May 9/11)
APR 17,18/67 - *El Rancho*	Cole	Hypnotist (Apr 14/3) [auspice of Lethbridge Minor Baseball Association]
JUN 18/68 - *Civic Centre*	Tommy Scott's "Big Country Caravan" together with Col. Tim McCoy's Wild West Show	(Jun 12/3)
MAR 10/69 - *El Rancho*	Rich Little (Western Canada Arts Festival)	Impersonations (Mar 3/10; 11/9) - *audience called for encores; also entertained at senior citizen's lodges*
DEC 8-10/69 - *Cap*	Trikini	Hypnotist (Nov 27/6) [auspices of downtown Lion's Club]
JUN 3/71 - *Ex. Pavilion*	Colonel Tim McCoy & Co. (sponsored by Green Acres Kiwanis Club)	Wild West Show (May 28/16; 29/6; Jun 3/16) - *80 year old film star performs showman whip tricks*
NOV 6/71 - *Yates*	Lethbridge Overture Concert Series presents Brolin	Moravian Folk Ensemble from Czechoslovakia (Nov 8/13) - *young singers & dancers were the stars of the show*

DATE/PLACE	COMPANY AND/OR PERFORMER(S)	PERFORMANCE(S)/REFERENCE/CRITIQUE 328
JUN 29,30/72 - *Ex. Pavilion*	The Original Ottoman J. Herrman Royal Lippizzan Stallions of Austria	(Jun 21/7; 22/17)
JUN 16/73 - *Fort Whoop-Up*	Wayne and Shuster	Tourist Promotional Skit (Jun 9/13; 18/10) - *also here to promote the official opening of a Gulf service station*
JUL 11/75 - *Sportsplex*	Myron Flore Show with dancers Bobby Burgess & Cissy King	Variety and dance show (Jun 13/7)
AUG 26,27/75 - *Sportsplex*	Ron Sakamoto presents Wonderful World of Horses (Charleston, West Virginia production)	Royal Lippizzan Stallions (Jul 30/15; 22 L&T.V. Week/20; 27/14) (*$3.00 - $5.00*) - *outshines rodeo*
AUG 7/75 - *Japanese Gardens*	Japanese Cultural Goodwill Mission (32 member troupe from Japan)	Japanese dances, music, poetry (Aug 2/10; 8/18) - *witnessed by about 250*
SEPT 27/75 - *Ex. Pavilion (two shows)*	Don Arthur & His Magical Maids	Magic show, Hocus Pocus (Sept 25/10; 29/14) - *show was no gamble for sparse crowd*
APR 24/76 - *Yates*	Association of United Ukrainian Canadians	Heritage '76 - program of music, song, dance (Apr 10/12; 19/12; 26/9) - *cast of 130*
JUL 16/76 - *Yates*	Tamayasu Gojo	Classical Japanese dance, Odori (Jul 15/12; 17/12) - *performed before about 200 persons*
AUG 25/76 - *Sportsplex*	Royal Lippizzan Stallion Show (presented by 1090 CHEC & the Panthouse)	The Wonderful World of Horses (Aug 7/15;20 L&TVWK/5; 26/10) (*$3.00 - $5.00*) - *horse, rider discipline pays off*
OCT 29/77 - *Yates*	The Association of United Ukrainian Canadians of Edmonton	Heritage '77 - an evening of music, song and dance (Oct 24/7)
NOV 30/77 - *U of L*	U of L Student's Union presents	Mandrake the Magician (Nov 24/8)
SEPT 10/78 - *Sportsplex*	The Royal Lippizzan Stallions	(Sept 2/7) (*$5.50 - $6.50*)
OCT 7/78 - *Yates*	Hungarian Cultural Society of Southern Alberta present folk dancers & Martha Gyorgy (featured singer)	A Night in Hungary Folk dance and music [Edmonton, Calgary & Lethbridge Dance groups] (Oct 7/19;10/11) (*3.50*)
JUN 24/79 - *Ex. Grandstand*	R.C.M.P.	Musical Ride (Jun 22/16)
OCT 27/79 - *Paramount*	Association of United Ukrainian Canadians of Edmonton	Ukrainian-Canadian songs, music and dances (Oct 24/23; 25/9)
JUN 29/80 - *Yates*	Ballada (Edm) (auspices of Southern Alberta Ethnic Association)	Romanian music and folk dancing (Jun 21/C6; 28/C5) - *formed in 1975; toured Romania in 1978*
SEPT 4/80 - *Sportsplex*	1090 CHEC & Anglo Stereo present	The Royal Lippizzan Stallions (Aug 21/A5)
OCT 4/80 - *Yates*	Ukrainian Touring Co. including St. John's Cathedral Choir, Zirka Dances, Vodohrai Ensemble, Mandalin Orchestra	Ukrainian Cavalcade - Ukrainian music and folk dances (Jun 26/B3; October 6/B2)
DEC 5/80 - *Sportsplex*	1090 CHEC & Anglo Stereo present The Chinese Acrobats	Taiwan Magic Circus (Nov 20/A9; Dec 6/B1) (*$5.00 - $8.00*) - *colorful show witnessed by 1700*
MAR 7/81 - *Yates*	Tryzub Ukrainian Dance Ensemble (Calgary)	(Mar 9/B1) - *in honor of the 167th anniversary of the Ukraine's greatest poet, Taras Shevchenko*
MAR 25/82 - *Sportsplex*	Lethbridge Herald & CFCN TV present	The Up With People Show: song and dance variety (Mar 5/A10)
APR 17/82 - *Yates*	Trembita Ensemble of the Association of United Ukrainian Canadians of Edmonton & Calgary Hopak Dancers	Heritage '82, music, song & dance (Apr 12/A5; 19/B3) - *evening of nostalgia*
OCT 10/82 - *Paramount*	The Hungarian Cultural Society of Southern Alberta	4th Annual Western Canadian Hungarian Folk Dance Festival (Oct 2/A8) (*$2.00*)
MAY 19/83 - *Sportsplex*	Peking National Acrobats: China Railway Acrobatic Troupe	(May 14/A9) - *formed in 1956* [presented by 1090 CHEC and Gold & Gold Productions]
SEPT 7/84 - *U of L*	Cheremosh Ukrainian Dance Co. (formed in 1969 by Chester Kuc)	Ethnic Dance (Sept 4/B11) (*$15.00*)
NOV 10/84 - *U of L*	Performing Arts Family Series: The Chinese Magic Revue of Taiwan	Magic, Acrobatics (Nov 3/A8; 7/C16; 12/B7) - *entertaining (Joan Waterfield)*
FEB 10/85 - *U of L (The Entertainment Series)*	Kodo - Demon Drummers & Dancers of Sado	Festival Drum Routines & dances (Jan 12/C3)

DATE/PLACE	COMPANY AND/OR PERFORMER(S)	PERFORMANCE(S)/REFERENCE/CRITIQUE
SEPT 13/85 - *Ex. Grandstand*	RCMP/Vern Baugh (officer in charge)/Corporal Darrell Karnes and Jerry McCarty (instructors)	Musical Ride (Sept 13/A3; 14/A1) - *3500 watch the famous ride - a Lethbridge Centennial presentation*
JAN 9/86 - *Yates*	1090 CHEC & Gold Key Auto present	The Stars of the Orient - acrobats, magicians, martial arts, dance & circus (Jan 8/B5; 10/A4) - *thrills city audiences (John Farrington)*
FEB 1/86 - *U of L*	Bob Berky & Michael Moschen	Vaudeville, The Alchemedians (Jan 25/B6)
MAR 18/86 - *U of L*	Polka Dot Door (from children's T.V. show)	From TV to Stage with Polkaroo, Marigold, Humpty Dumpty and Bear (Mar 14/B9; 19/B13) - *especially for children - a hit*
FEB 22/87 - *University Drive Alliance Church*	Maralee Dawn	"Canada's Foremost Ventriloquist" (Feb 21/A5)
MAR 1/87 - *PLib*	Derek Scott (former Lethbridge resident)	Clown\magic\comedi\juggler vaudeville routines (Mar 2/A3) - *delights audience*
MAR 23/87 - *LCC*	Chicago-based Second City National Touring Co.	(Mar 21/B6)
APR 5/87 - *Yates*	Mr. Dressup (Ernie Coombs of Toronto) with Jim Parker (vocalist)	Family entertainment (Apr 6/A9) - *provides excitement, enjoyment*
JUN 2/87 - *Sppx*	The Royal Lippizzan Stallions	(May 23/B6; 28/A12) - *an American production based in Miami*
OCT 3/87 - *U of L*	Robert Morgan	Morgan's Journey (Sept 19/B11) - *Magical play for children and family audiences* (Oct 5/B11) - *every inch a delight (C. Laycock)*
JAN 30/88 - *Fiddler's Chalet (Restaurant)*	Sir Unicorn Entertainment Inc. (Edm.)/David Thiel, Robert Woodburg & others	Participant murder mystery performance Skulduggery (Feb 1/B9) - *enjoyed by full house*
FEB 20/88 - *U of L*	The Acrobats of the Pagoda of the Plentiful Lands from Harbin	Chinese acrobats assembled by the Chinese Ministry of Culture (Feb 22/B9) - *weave a spell...audiences marvelled*
FEB 29/88 - *Fiddler's Chalet*	Sir Unicorn Entertainment Inc.	Murder mystery performance, Sgt. Pepper's Homicide Club Band (Feb 1/B9)
APR 5/88 - *Yates*	Brian Foley presents the Scott Walker Production Inc.	Children's theatre & ballet, Snow White and the Seven Dwarfs (Mar 18/B9; Apr 2/B10; 6/B9) - *enthusiastic response*
MAY 7/88	Trickster and Pepper the Clown	Clown techniques, gymnastics, physical comedy (Apr 21/B8)

Ice Shows: Professional and Semi Professional
Lethbridge, Alberta (1927–1988)

DATE PLACE	COMPANY AND/OR PERFORMER	PERFORMANCE/REFERENCE/CRITIQUE
FEB 3/27 - *Arena*	Gordon Thompson	(February 2/9) - *world's greatest skater*
DEC 3/37 - *Arena*	Glencoe Club (Calgary)/Muffie McHugh & Ian Mackie	Lion's Club Ice Carnival (Dec 1/11; 4/6) - *2000 spectators*
MAR 11/12/38 - *Arena*	Glencoe Club, Calgary/Rhona & Cliff Thaell (British champions)	Ice Ballet & skating carnival (Mar 8/8)
DEC 16,17/38 - *Arena*	Glencoe Club/Shirley Martin, Helen Cantwell, Muffie McHugh, Harry Reddy, Mary Lou Moore	(Feb 17/7)
FEB 28/40 - *Arena*	Hope Braine (Australia); Margaret Manahan (England) & cast of 50	The Cracked Ice Follies of 1940 (Feb 24/14; 27/8,10; 29/8) - *thrilling - enthusiastically received*
FEB 8,9/43 - *Arena*	Megan Taylor & Co.	Stars of the Winterland Ice Revue (Feb 6/7; 9/7)
MAR 31-APR 1/44 - *Arena*	Ian Mackie production/Muffie (McHugh) McKenzie & local skaters	(Ice Cabaret (Apr 1/7; 3/2,7) - *a fine show*
MAR 9,10/45 - *Arena*	Glencoe Club of Calgary/Marjorie Jean Miller, Betty Atkinson, Charles Hain	Ice Carnival (Mar 5/2; 8/6; 12/7)
MAR 8,9/46 - *Arena*	Glencoe Club/B. Atkinson, C. Hain, I. Mackie, Edward & Gladys Rushka, Ralph & Betty Fogal	Ice Carnival (Feb 27/6; Mar 9/7)
MAR 28,29/47 - *Arena*	Glencoe Club directed by Betty Cornwall/Don & Ethel Higgins (Lethbridge)	Ice Carnival (Mar 19/6; 22/7; 26/12; 29/6) - *smartly staged* [auspices of the Kinsmen Club]
NOV 14,15/49 - *Arena*	Barbara Ann Scott & cast of 50	Skating Sensations of 1950 (Nov 10/8; 15/6) - *audience of 4200 thrilled*
JAN 19,20/53 - *Arena*	Roy Lisogar production/Gloria Dawn (auspices of Lethbridge Elk's Club)	Ice Fantasy of 1953 (Jan 19/9; 20/9; 21/10) - *talent galore in Canadian ice show*
NOV 26,27/54 - *Arena*	Roy Lisogar/Lorie Perkins, Christine Peebles, Joyce McFarlane, Chas. Murphy, Ken Hoeffert (auspices - Kinsmen Club)	Ice Fantasy of 1955 (Nov 25/3,9; 27/9; 29/12) (24 acts) - *colorful, sparkling*
OCT 10-13/74 - *Canada Games Sportsplex*	Karen Magnussen, Adelle Boucher, Montaigne & Blake, Ken Shook, Ann-Margaret Frei, Vic Zoble, Glenn Parriott, Sherri Thrapp, Rick Earhart & former Lethbridge resident, Chris Shedlowski	Ice Capades [33rd edition] (Sept 16/6; Oct 1/7; 7/7; 11/16; 15/18) - *crowd loved it* [world champion - K. Magnussen]
OCT 15-19/75 - *Sportsplex*	K. Magnussen, Sashi Kuchiki, Donna Arquilla, A-M. Frei, Titch Stock, Dan Henry, Lisa Illsley, K. Shook, Adelle Boucher, Lee Meadows	Ice Capades (Oct 15/14; 16/10) - *nothing short of spectacular*
OCT 8-10/76 - *Sportsplex*	Don Knight (Canadian & North American champion), Julie Johnson, Jean-Pierre	Ice Capades (September 18/6; Oct 9/2) ($2.00 - $5.00) - *capacity crowd for opening performance*
NOV 11/76 - *Sportsplex*	Hurok Productions/Toller Cranston (Canadian Senior Men's Champion) and other noted skaters	The Ice Show (Oct 12/8; 25/7; Nov 12/10) - *They are all outstanding including Brian Foley (choreographer & director) and Ellen Burka (choreographer)* [A Dennis Bass production of the Ice Show scheduled for November 20/77 was cancelled]
OCT 12,13/77 - *Sportsplex*	Lynn Nightingale, Ron Shaver	Ice Capades (Sept 17/20) - ($3.00 - $5.50)
MAR 22/78 - *Sportsplex*	1978 World Champions including Linda Fratianne	World Figure Skating Tour (Mar 7/25) ($5.50 - $6.50)
OCT 14/83 - *Sportsplex*	A Famous Artists Event/John Curry (Olympic, World & European champion), Jo Jo Starbuck, David Sontee	Symphony on Ice (Sept 24/B8) - ($9.00 - $11.00)
SEPT 27/86 - *Sportsplex*	Jayne Torvill & Christopher Dean (World & Olympic Champion ice dancers)	Ice Show (Aug 29/A8; Sept 25/A13; 29/B5) - *thrill audience*

DATE *PLACE*	COMPANY AND/OR PERFORMER	PERFORMANCE/REFERENCE/CRITIQUE
NOV 7/86 - *Sportsplex*	Skarratt Productions (Hamilton) present Soviet Stars on Ice (Kiev)	<u>Ice Revue</u> (Nov 7/C8; 8/A3)
FEB 4-7/87 - *Sportsplex*	Tom Scallen presents Paul Martini & Barbara Underhill (Canadian and World Pairs Champions)	<u>Ice Capades</u> *($10.00 - $12.00)* [special rates for seniors, youth and groups] (Feb 5/A11) - *thrilled Lethbridge crowd*

Ice Shows: Lethbridge Figure Skating Club
Lethbridge, Alberta (1948–1988)

DATE/PLACE	PROFESSIONALS & GUEST ARTISTS	PRODUCTION/PARTICIPANTS/REFERENCE(S)
APR 2,3/48 - *Arena*	Assisted by Glencoe Club (Calgary)/Dominion champions: Wally Diestelmeyer, Suzanne Morrow, Pierette Paquin, Donald Tobin	Ice Fantasy directed by Ralph & Betty Fogal (local pros) - *50 local junior skaters; 30 from Glencoe Club*
MAR 4,5/49 - *Arena*	Beth Fogal & Helen Little/Ethel and Don Higgins, Muffy McHugh MacKenzie and Peggy O'Grady (Glencoe Club, Calgary)	Ice Revue, Figure Fancies/ACT Boys Band/Fr. Hosek/George Brown (m.c.) (Mar 5/7) - *warmly applauded*
MAR 24,25/50 - *Arena*	Shirley Ingham, David Pencosky, Robert Clossen (Spokane)	World Cruise George Brown (m.c.) (Mar 22/6; 25/7) - *Dazzling - black light effects by Bob Reed and Winter Royer*
MAR 2,3/51 - *Arena*	Lethbridge Figure Skating Club with guest skaters: Gayle Wakely & David Spalding [gold medalists from Connaught F.S.C. Vancouver], Dave Pencosky [Spokane]	Ice Carnival, Dreamer's Holiday (Jan 29/7; Feb 26/7; Mar 5/7) - *nearly 8000 attended*
FEB 29-MAR 1/52 - *Arena*	Lethbridge Figure Skating Club	Ice Show, Happy Holidays: Sally Price, Iris Kirk, Mary Lyn Fairbairn, Everal Borgal (Feb 22/3; 23/6,7; 26/8; 28/7; 29/7; Mar 1/7; 3/7) - *Theme: 10 holidays; brilliant*
FEB 20,21/53	Lethbridge Figure Skating Club/Mrs. Fay Morris assisted by Helen Little	Ice Capers of '53 music by Katherine Brown (Feb 21/10; 23/10) - *well received; draws 6000*
FEB 12,13/54	Fay Morris	Ice Capers of '54, Cinderella Linda Beeling, Beverley Johnson, Madeline Burr, Donna Farstad, Barbara Smyth, Sandra Fogal, Frank Beerling, Carolyn Arnold & others (Feb 12/9,11; 12/9,11; 13/10) - *enchanting and beautiful*
MAR 15,16/63 - *Arena*	Sonja Currie Jacobson & Peggy Currie	Ice Carnival (Jan 17/9; Mar 1/77; 9/12) - *1st local ice show in many years*
MAR 13,14/64	Sonja Currie Jacobson	Ice Show, Calendar Carnival (Mar 14/13) - *filled with laughter, enchantment & grace*
APR 23/65 - *Arena*	Sonja Jacobson and Peggy Currie	Calendar Carnival '65: Sandra & Carol Fogal (Mar 30/9)
MAR 18,19/66 - *Arena*	Sonja Currie Jacobson	Calendar Carnival '66: Paul Thomas [Calgary] and 100 skaters from Lethbridge and District (Mar 12/3,17; 19/13) - *thrilled by a stunning display of skating*
MAR 17/67 - *Arena*	Sonja Jacobson with Muriel Jolliffe [choreographer]	Ice Centennial: James Allen, Laureen Hunt (Calgary) & local skaters (Mar 15/18; 18/18) - *Hippo on skates is highlight*
FEB 2,3/68 - *Arena*	Wendy & Peggy Currie with choreography by Muriel Jolliffe	Annual Ice Carnival, Around the World in 90 Minutes: Corby Coffin [B.C.'s senior men's champion] (Jan 26/10; Feb 1/10; 3/14) - *sharp, appealing show*
MAR 28,29/69 - *Arena*	Sonja Davis assisted by Joan Catonio (joined by Taber Skating Club choreographed by Beth Fogal)	Disneyland on Ice: Suzie Zonda & Frank Nowasad [Calgary] (Mar 29/16) - *enjoyable*
MAR 6-7/70 - *Arena*	Sonja Davis & Joan Catonio (in association with Taber Skating Club)	Ice Revue, Up the Down Escalator: Urs Stenbrecker (Mar 7/13)
MAR 5,6/71 - *Arena*	Sonja Davis assisted by Debbie Stimson with guest artist Don Jackson world figure skating champion	Carnival, The Nutcracker: Donna Rude, Mark & Janet Hominuke, Anne Lanier, Bill Petrunik, Maura Knowles, Holly McGuire, Mickey Brown, Grant Sorenson, Jennifer Chue & others (Feb 27/17; Mar 4/8; 5/11; 6/14) - *150 enthralled the capacity crowd of 1800 on first night*
MAR 17,18/72 - *Henderson Lake Ice Centre*	Sonja Davis with guest star, Don Jackson	Ice Show, Land of Oz: Mark and Jennifer Hominuke, Donna Rude, Bill Petrunik, Grant Sorenson (Mar 4/11; 18/17) - *showed hard work*
APR 13,14/73 - *Henderson Ice Centre*	Sonja Davis	Local Ice Show, Winnie the Pooh: Wally Macguire, Dan Dorohoy, Sonja Davis and the LFSC (Apr 14/16) - *enjoyed by a full house*
MAR 29,30/74 - *Henderson Ice Centre*	with guest, Don Jackson	Ice Revue, Treasure Island (Mar 20/23; 30/13)
FEB 6,7/75 - *Centre Village Mall*	Amateur Figure Skaters from Southern Alberta	Mini Ice Capades (Feb 5/31)
APR 18,19/75 - *Sportsplex*	LFSC/presents Donald Jackson & Camille Rebus and local club members	Ice Carnival, Arabian Nights (Apr 9/24; 17/13; 19/9) - *($1.25 - $2.50) - a real treat*

DATE/PLACE	PROFESSIONALS & GUEST ARTISTS	PRODUCTION/PARTICIPANTS/REFERENCE(S)
APR 2,3/76 - *Sportsplex*	Donald Fraser & Candace Jones (1976 Canadian Pairs champions) with Camille Rebus (Canadian Jr. Women's Champion)	That's Our Entertainment (Mar 24/28; 30/33) - *cast of 300*
MAR 18/77 - *Sportsplex*	LFSC with guest artists Brian Pockar; Lorna Wighton and John Dowding	Figure Skating Carnival, Alice in Wonderland (Mar 18/5) - *($1.00 - $3.00)*
MAR 18/78 - *Sportsplex*	featuring Donald Jackson (World Champion)	The Best of the Seventies: Bill & Cori-Jo Petrunik (Mar 11/8) - *($1.00 - $3.00)* - *cast of 300*
MAR 24/79 - *Sportsplex*	guest artists Peggy McLean (Calgary) and Natalie Reimer (Lethbridge)	Ice Galaxy 1979 (Mar 20/23; 26/16)
MAR 24/84 - *Sportsplex*	guest artists Linda & John Ivanich (Vancouver), Dennis Coi (Kitimat)	Annual Ice Show (Mar 26/A3) - *more than 150 club participants*
MAR 30/85 - *Sportsplex*		Annual Ice Show, Jungle Book (Apr 1/A3)
MAR 22/86 - *Henderson Ice Centre*	Sasha Boyd with Mitch Miller [prod-dir]	Annual Ice Carnival, Mary Poppins (Mar 24/A3) - *enthusiastic crowd*
APR 4/87 - *Sportsplex*	with featured artists, Michelle Menzies & Kevin Wheeler (Canadian Junior Pairs Champions)	Annual Ice Show Showboat (Mar 26/A5; Apr 4/B7; 6/A5) - *did themselves proud*
MAR 26/88 - *Nicholas Sheran Ice Centre*		Annual Ice Carnival, Fantasy on Ice (Mar 28/A3)

Professional Dance Performances
Lethbridge, Alberta (1952–1988)

DATE/PLACE	COMPANY AND/OR PERFORMER(S)	PERFORMANCE(S)/REFERENCE
JAN 23,24/52 - *Cap*	Royal Winnipeg Ballet/Gweneth Lloyd with Arnold Spohr, Eva Von Gencsy	(Jan 24/7) - *scores hit with two different programs*
NOV 13,14/52 - *Cap*	National Ballet Co. of Canada/Celia Franca with David Adams, Lois Smith, Earl Kraul	(Nov 12/13; 13/9; 14/13; 15/10) ($2.00 - $3.25) - *outstanding, memorable*
JAN 21,22/53 - *Cap*	Royal Winnipeg Ballet/G. Lloyd with A. Spohr & Jean Stoneham	(Jan 3/10; 7/13; 13/10; 16/9; 20/10; 22/9,10) ($1.75 - $3.25) - *superb*
OCT 16/53 - *Cap*	Ballet Russe de Monte Carlo/Serge Denham	(Oct 14/14; 17/14) - *auspicious season opener*
JAN 28/54 - *L.C.I.*	Kay Armstrong's Professional Dance Theatre	Ballet & dance mime (Jan 23/14; 26/10; 29/14) - *an interesting evening*
MAR 25,26/54 - *Cap*	National Ballet Co. of Canada/C. Franca	(Mar 26/3,10; 27/10) - *small audience - company hampered by small stage*
MAY 14/54 - *Cap*	Royal Winnipeg Ballet/G.L. with A.S., Carlie Carter, Marina Katronis	(May 15/18) - *is a hit again*
FEB 14/57 - *Cap*	Royal Winnipeg Ballet with Ruthanna Boris & Frank Hobi	(Feb 13/22; 15/13) ($1.50 - $2.50) - *six curtain calls*
MAY 3/58 - *Cap*	National Ballet Co. of Canada/C.F. (first sponsored program by the Lethbridge Allied Arts Council [AAC])	(Apr 29/10; May 2/9; 5/10) - *thrills audience despite pitifully inadequate stage*
FEB 3/59 - *Cap*	Royal Winnipeg Ballet/Arnold Spohr (sponsored by local Beta Sigma Phi Sorority) with Marilyn Young, Rachel Browne, Naomi Kimura & others	(Feb 3/11; 4/11) - *capacity crowd enjoys pleasing offer*
OCT 9/59 - *Cap*	Royal Winnipeg Ballet/A.S.	(Sept 30/18; Oct 7/8; 10/6) - *an evening of real enjoyment*
MAR 1/65 - *Cap*	Royal Winnipeg Ballet/Arnold Spohr with Sonia Taverner, Fredric Strobel, Richard Rutherford, Jim Clouser, Lynette Fry	(Feb 17/18; 27/3; Mar 2/10) ($2.00 - $3.00) - *danced way into hearts of capacity audience*
NOV 13/67 - *Yates*	Royal Winnipeg Ballet/Arnold Spohr/Brian MacDonald (chor) with Christine Hennessy, Richard Rutherford, Sheila Mackinnon, David Moroni	(Nov 13/16; 14/10) - *enthusiastically endorsed by audience of 400*
APR 15/68 - *Yates*	Alberta Ballet Co. (1966) Western Canada Arts Festival	(Apr 16/10) - *youthful liveliness shown*
SEPT 29/69 - *Cap*	Royal Winnipeg Ballet/Arnold Spohr & Bill MacDonald with Richard Rutherford, Sheila MacKinnon, David Maroni	(Sept 18/14; 29/14; 30/12) - *confident & versatile - Linda Lee Thomas (of Cardston) is accompanist*
APR 9/72 - *Yates*	Alberta Ballet Co./Ruth Carse [auspices of AAC] with Lethbridge participant: Sherry Lanier	Carnival of the Animals; Pas de Deux (The Nutcracker); Coppelia (Mar 22/20; Apr 5/7; 10/13)
MAR 14/74 - *Yates*	Anna Wyman Dance Theatre of Vancouver (sponsored by AAC)	Recital of contemporary dances and creative improvisations (Mar 7/7; 9/25; 14/18) - *first dance group to receive a Canada Council grant*
MAY 6/75 - *Yates*	Alberta Ballet Co. with Merrilee Hodgins, Shelly Cromie, Margo Gurst, Anne Stevenson	Ballet and All That Jazz (May 7/13) - *300 in attendance [sponsored locally by the Canadian Mental Health Association]*
SEPT 2/75 - *Yates*	AAC & Alberta Dept. of Culture present National Folk Ballet of Korea (a troupe of children organized in 1962)	The Little Angels (Jun 6 - Leisure & T.V. Week/15; Jul 23/38; Aug 23/13; 30/13; Sept 3/13) - *captivated 500 theatre goers*
OCT 17/75 - *U of L Gym*	U of L & The Tibetan Community of Southern Alberta present The Tibetan Dance & Drama Society of DHARNSALA	LHAMO (a combination of song, dance, drama & mime) (Oct 11/14; 14/31) ($0.50 - $1.50) - *troupe of Tibetan refugees currently touring North America*
JAN 31/76 - *Yates*	Entre-Six (a company of six dancers from Quebec) dir by Lawrence Gradus	Ballet: Six short works (Feb 2/14) - *350 attend*
FEB 26/76 - *Yates*	Alberta Ballet Co. directed by Jeremy Leslie-Spinks (auspices of Canada Mental Health Assoc., Lethbridge Branch)	Five dance selections choreographed by Frank Ohman, Wayne McKnight & J.L.S. (Feb 27/16) - *Company founded by Ruth Carse shows poise & grace*
OCT 5/76 - *Yates*	AAC presents The Ballet Ys of Canada (Toronto)	(Oct 1/17; 6/12) ($3.50) - *about 200 persons attended*
MAY 20/77 - *Yates*	AAC presents Alberta Ballet Co./Brydon Paige with Anne Stevenson and Wayne McKnight	Danses Concertantes & others (May 13, TVWK/7,8) ($4.00) - *founded in 1966 by Ruth Carse*

DATE/PLACE	COMPANY AND/OR PERFORMER(S)	PERFORMANCE(S)/REFERENCE
JUL 31/77 - *Ex. Pavilion*	Japanese Canadian Centennial 77 Society/Nikka Festival Dancers (Toronto & Vancouver)/Harry Aoki (mus dir)	Ethnic Dances (Jul 28/24)
JAN 17/78 - *Yates & U of L*	AAC presents The Toronto Dance Theatre	Evening of Dance (Jan 12/25; 17/10) *($5.00)*
JAN 27/79 - *Yates*	Royal Winnipeg Ballet with Margaret Slota & Bill Lark [auspices of AAC in cooperation with Alberta Culture]	Grand Pas Espagnol; Adagietto; Sebastian; Les Patineurs (Dec 2/17; Jan 29/14) - *capacity crowd*
JAN 31/79 - *Yates*	Lethbridge Overture Concert Society presents a Russian troupe: Roussianka with members of Moscow Folk Ballet	Music, song and dance (Jan 27/8; Feb 1/17) - *about 400 attended*
MAR 20/79 - *Yates*	AAC Great Performances Series/Jose Greco, Nan Lorca, Alexandra Greco & Antonio Villa (piano), Aurro Champion (flamenco guitar)	An Evening with Jose Greco & Friends (Mar 21/11) - *Greco is incredible, magnificent but needs support (Arthur McDougall)*
OCT 23/79 - *Yates*	Overture Concert Association presents the Mini Bolshoi from Russia	Ballet (Oct 24/23) - *disappointing (Arthur McDougall)*
NOV 8/79 - *Yates (AAC)*	Entresix Dance Co. of Montreal directed by Lawrence Gradus	Chamber Dance Performance (Nov 3/8) - *company was launched at Dance Canada '74*
DEC 14,15/79 - *Yates (AAC)*	Alberta Ballet/Brydon Paige, Lambros Lambrou (chor) with Lillian Baldyga, Svea Eklof, Michel Rahn, Mariane Beausejour, Leanne Simpson, Kim Derenne	Alice in Wonderland; Julianna Variations; Sundances (Dec 8/6; 15/6) - *recovers after trifle stodgy start (Arthur McDougall)*
AUG 1/80 - *Yates*	AAC & Alberta Culture present the David Y.H. Lui production starring Frank Augustyn, Ann Marie De Angelo, Ulysses Dove, Evelyn Hart, Valentina Kozlova, Leonid Kozlov, David Peregrine, Danilo Radojevic, Marianna Tcherkassky, Donna Wood	Dance, Dance, Dance! (Jul 12/B9; Aug 2/C10) *($2.50 - $5.00)* - *a triumph; a very special event enjoyed by overflow audience (Arthur McDougall)*
NOV 3/80 - *Yates*	The Toronto Dance Theatre (auspices of U of L)	Stepping Out (Oct 17/B3; 18/A10) *($5.00)*
APR 2/81 - *Yates*	The Royal Winnipeg Ballet with Evelyn Hart, David Peregrine & Patti Caplette	Two classical and two contemporary works (Mar 21/B11; Apr 3/B1) - *lives up to its reputation (Arthur McDougall)*
NOV 9/81 - *U of L*	Theatre Ballet of Canada/Larry Gradus (art dir)/(auspices of AAC and U of L)	Tribute; Rain Garden; Symetric Inquietante (Jun 24/A8; Nov 10/A5) - *visual excellence (A. McDougall)*
NOV 16/81 - *U of L*	Dancemakers [founded in 1974] [U of L Festival of Dance Series] (auspices of AAC and U of L)	Contemporary Dance (Jun 24/A8; Nov 17/B6) - *shows freshness, amazing versatility (A. McDougall)*
NOV 23/81 - *U of L*	Danny Grossman Dance Co. (auspices of AAC & U of L)	5 Contemporary Dances (Jun 24/A8; Nov 24/B3) - *reveals choreographer's genius*
APR 15/82 - *U of L*	Alberta Ballet Co. dir by Brydon Paige with Svea Eklof, Michel Rahn, Mariane Beausejour	Firebird; The Venetian Twins; Sundance choreographed by Lambros Lambrou (Apr 16/A9) - *good dancing & choreography; weak lights and sets (Muriel Jolliffe)*
JUL 27/82 - *Yates*	Baha'i Community of Lethbridge presents Ottawa's Ballet SHAYDA	Drama in dance, The Martyrs (Jul 23/B3; 31/A6)
SEPT 17/82 - *U of L*	U of L Dance Series/Les Grands Ballet Canadiens	(Sept 20/B3) - *mixed review (Muriel Jolliffe)*
OCT 1/82 - *Yates*	Calgary City Ballet/Laszlo Tamasik with Mary Sullivan	(Sept 29/B2; Oct 2/A7) - *Sullivan projected an engaging charisma (Muriel Jolliffe)*
NOV 2/82 - *U of L*	U of Dance Series/Bella Lewitzky Dance Co.	(Nov 3/C13) - *lacks human element (Muriel Jolliffe)*
NOV 26,27/82 - *Yates*	Alberta Ballet Co. dir & chor by Brydon Paige/Mariane Beausejour, Scott Harris, Sandra Currie	The Nutcracker (Sept 24/B3; Oct 1/B3) - *40 young local dancers are selected by M. Jolliffe*
MAR 19,20/83 - *U of L*	Royal Winnipeg Ballet with Susan Bennett, David Peregrine, Patti Caplette, Daniel Nelson, John Kaminski, Julie Whittaker	U of A Gala performance (Mar 21/B6) - *lacked spark, excitement (Muriel Jolliffe)*
SEPT 28/83 - *U of L*	National Ballet of Canada/Constantine Palsalas (chor) with Veronica Tennant, Kevin Pugh, Amalia Schelhorn, David Dixon, Sabina Allemann, Nadia Potts, Raymond Smith, Yoko Ichino (selected members)	Ballet excerpts from Napoli, Conciones, Kettentanz (Sept 29/A1, A8) - *sold out crowd; Pugh steals show*
OCT 22/83 - *U of L Th.*	U of L Family Series presents Kasatka Cossacks (founded by Mikhail Berkut in London)	(Oct 21/A11; 24/D1) - *dancers are sons & daughters of Soviet expatriates; 2 sold out performances*
DEC 23/83 - *U of L*	U of L Dance Series/Alberta Ballet Co.	The Nutcracker (Nov 12/D1; Dec 2/TV Week/10)
JAN 21/84 - *U of L*	U of L Dance Series/Les Ballets Jazz De Montreal	(Jan 13/TV Week 10)
MAR 6/84 - *U of L*	U of L Dance Series/Jennifer Muller & The Works	(Mar 2/TV Week/10)

DATE/PLACE	COMPANY AND/OR PERFORMER(S)	PERFORMANCE(S)/REFERENCE
APR 6-8/84 - *U of L*	U of L Dance Series/Alberta Ballet Co./Brydon Paige/Mariane Beausejour	Cinderella (Mar 10/C1)
SEPT 16,17/84 - *U of L*	U of L Dance Series/Les Grands Ballets Canadiens	(Sept 8/C2; 14/C7) (*$10.00 - $13.00*) - *organized in 1958*
NOV 7,9/84 - *U of L* (*Dance Series*)	American Ballet Comedy of N.Y./Bob Boyer (chor) with Sandra Chinn, Judy Fielman, Amy Flood, Laurie Goodman, Zane Rankin, Veronica Yurasits	16 different dance numbers (Nov 8/A10) - *blends wit, satire with good dancing (Muriel Jolliffe)*
NOV 29-DEC 2/84 - *U of L*	Alberta Ballet Co./Brydon Paige	The Nutcracker (Nov 23/B6) (*$10.00 - $13.00*)
DEC 15/84 - *U of L*	U of L Family Series/The National Tap Dance Co. of Canada	The Tin Soldier (Dec 17/B7) - *delightful show represented to full house (Romola Ully)*
JAN 31, FEB 1/85 - *U of L* (*Dance Series*)	The Royal Winnipeg Ballet/Vicente Nebrada (chor)/with Sarah Slipper, Andre Lewis, Colin Horsburgh, Alain Charron and others	(Feb 1/A4) - *good performance but with some disappointments (Muriel Jolliffe)*
FEB 14/85 - *U of L*	U of L Dance Series/Alberta Ballet/Brydon Paige	Coppelia (Feb 15/A10) - *a treat (M. Jolliffe)*
MAY 10/85 - *U of L*	Calgary City Ballet	An Evening of Dance (May 3/C4) (*$5.00 - $7.00*)
JUN 15/85 - *U of L*	Houston Ballet/Ben Stevenson (art dir) with Kenneth McCombie, Janie Parker	Swan Lake (May 29/A7; 30/A9)
OCT 6/85 - *U of L*	The National Ballet of Canada with Sabrina Alleman & Gregory Osborne	An Evening of Short Ballets (Sept 28/A12; Oct 1/B9)
OCT 27,28/85 - *U of L*	Les Ballets Jazz de Montreal	(Oct 12/B8)
NOV 21/85 - *U of L*	Anna Wyman Dance Theatre	5 varied dances (Nov 22/A4) - *all dancers in their own right (Muriel Jolliffe)*
FEB 22/86 - *U of L* Th.	U of L Performing Arts Series: Yugoslavian Dance Co. Frulica/Dragoslav Dzadzevic (chor)	National dances (Feb 8/C8; 25/B7) (*$10.00 - $14.00*) - *exciting*
MAR 21,22/86 - *U of L*	Theatre Ballet of Canada/Margery Lambert (Ballet Mistress)/Lawrence Gradus (art dir)	Ballets, Moralities; Tribute; Valse Fantaise; Full Moon and others (Mar 19/B12; 21/A10; 24/B7) - *Moralities, Tribute rescue ho-hum ballet (Muriel Jolliffe)*
APR 11-13/86 - *U of L*	Alberta Ballet Co./Brydon Paige/Mariane Beausejour, Lillian Bertolino, Claude Caron and others	Cinderella (Apr 3/A7; 14/A7) *enjoyed the overall improvement in the calibre of dancing (Muriel Jolliffe)*
MAY 23/86 - *Yates*	Saskatchewan Theatre Ballet/Robyn Allen (chor)/with Marie Nychka, Martin Vallee, Martha Leonard [formed in 1982] (auspices locally of World Citizen's Centre & SalvAide in aid of health care in El Salvador)	New Canadian Ballets: 1. They Planted Many Seeds; 2. Breaking the Silence (May 20/B7; 24/A3; 26/A7)
SEPT 16,17/86 - *U of L*	Alberta Ballet/Brydon Paige/M. Beausejour, Claude Caron, John Davie, Lillian Bertolino, Lorna McConnell, Seung-Hae Joo, Cheryl Graden	20th Anniversary Gala 1. Pineapple Poll based on Gilbert's ballad the "Bumboat Woman's Story" and musical selections from Sullivan's operettas 2. In Passing by Reid Anderson (world premiere) (Sept 17/B4) - *wonderful night*
OCT 5/86 - *U of L*	Cloud Gate - Taipei Contemporary Dance Theatre/Lin Hwai-Min	Acrobatic - physical dance (Oct 1/D1; 6/A4) - *worth standing ovation (M. Jolliffe)*
NOV 2,3/86 - *U of L*	Les Grands Ballets Canadiens/chor by James Kudelka/Kevin Irving, Josee Ledaux, Jean-Hughes Rochette	Carmina Burana by Fernand Nault (M. Jolliffe) (Nov 3/B5) - *final ballet beautifully danced*
DEC 4-7/86 - *U of L*	Alberta Ballet Co./Brydon Paige/Desiree Champion, Mario Marcil	The Nutcracker (Dec 5/C6) - *delightful entertainment*
FEB 26/87 - *U of L*	Ballet Sovietski (ten couples from Kirov, Bolshoi and other major Soviet companies)	A program of pas de deux's ensembles and classical folk dances (Feb 27/B8) - *somewhat uneven*
APR 2,3/87 - *U of L*	Royal Winnipeg Ballet/David Peregrine, Svea Eklov	(Apr 3/B6) - *continues to delight and captivate*
APR 7/87 - *Public Library (PLib)*	Hyon Ok Kim (Korean dancer)	Modern dance presentation (Apr 7/A11; 8/B8) - *trained in Chinese martial arts of Shaolin & T'ai-Chi-Chuan*
OCT 24/87 - *U of L*	National Tap Dance Co. of Canada/William Orlowski (artistic dir)	Fascinating Rhythms featuring Oliver Button is a Sissy and other routines (Oct 23/A13; 26/B9) - *company founded by Orlowski and Steve Dymond - a hit*
NOV 10/87 - *U of L*	Les Ballets Jazz de Montreal	A Celebration of Dance (Nov 11/C9) - *excites crowd*

DATE/PLACE	COMPANY AND/OR PERFORMER(S)	PERFORMANCE(S)/REFERENCE
DEC 11,12/87 - *U of L*	Alberta Ballet Co./Brydon Page/M. Beausejour, Claude Caron	The Nutcracker (Nov 25/B7; Dec 11/D7; 14/B9) - *sheer beauty, magic*
JAN 28/88 - *U of L*	Ballet British Columbia/Annette av Paul [art consultant] & Reid Anderson [art dir]	(Jan 29/B6) - *The highlight...Return to the Strange Land choreographed by Jiri Kylian*
MAR 17-20/88 - *U of L*	Alberta Ballet Co./Brydon Paige/M. Beausejour, Claude Caron, Luke Vanier	The Snow Maiden (Mar 16/C7; 21/B9) - *farewell performance of Mariane Beausejour*
APR 16/88 - *U of L*	Judith Marcuse Repertory Dance Co. of Canada	(Apr 15/C4)

Local Dance Recitals, Programs and Festivals
Lethbridge, Alberta (1917–1988)

DATE/PLACE	ACADEMY AND/OR DIRECTOR/ DANCERS	PRESENTATION/REFERENCE
JAN 19/1917 - *Majestic*	Gladys Attree School of Dance (auspices of IODE - returned soldiers' funds)	Evening of Dance, <u>A Midwinter Night's Frolic</u> (Jan 20/5) - *($0.25 - $0.50) - one of best entertainments ever in the city*
JAN 11,12/18 - *Majestic*	Gladys Attree assisted by Kathleen Southard, Calgary (auspices of IODE - Halifax Orphan's fund)	Evening of Song and Dance (Jan 12/11) - *fine entertainment*
APR 10; MAY 15/19 - *Colonial*	Gladys Attree with Hilda Church, Doris Smith, Helena, Lorna & Adair Simpson, Myrl O'Hagan, Ursula Elton, Emma, Gladys & Orisa Green, Thelma Noble, Ethel Jones, Gwen Bowman, Jean Brymner, Myrtle Leech and Mona Waddell	Classical Dances (Apr 10/5; May 14/5,11; 15/5) - *a score of artistically beautiful dances*
FEB 25-27/26 - *Palace*	Hilda Church (added attraction with movie)	Spanish Prologue & Clown Routine (Feb 25/8) - *special lighting effects & new scenery*
NOV 11,12/27 - *Palace*	Gladys Attree (juvenile dancers) with Evelyn Rashbrook	Acrobatic Dancing; Black Bottom Dance (Nov 11/16)
NOV 14-16/27; JAN 2,3/28 - *Palace*	Hilda Church	<u>Dance Revue</u> (Nov 12/16; Dec 31/12)
AUG 6-11/28 - *Palace*	Gladys Attree with Evelyn Rashbrook and Lola Strand	Acrobatic & Soft Shoe Novelty Dances (Jul 30/10)
JUN 7/30 - *Majestic*	Alice Murdock assisted by song and dance artist from Calgary	<u>Revue of 1930</u> (May 10/11; Jun 6/5; 7/5; 9/5) - *Lethbridge girls in the school's first Lethbridge review*
JUN /31	Alice Murdock	2nd Annual Dance Revue
JUN 3/32 - *Capitol*	Bernadette Fisher with B.F., Eildon Brander, Dorothy Craddock, Alma Bourgett	<u>Dance Revue</u> (Jun 2/2; 3/2; 4/6) - *theatregoers were pleased with Miss Fisher's first revue*
JUN 4/32 - *YMCA*	Alice Murdock with guest artists from Calgary & Medicine Hat	<u>Dance Revue</u> (Jun 6/6) - *toe ballet work was outstanding*
JUN 2,3/33 - *Capitol*	Bernadette Fisher with B.F. & Eildon Brander	<u>Dance Recital</u> (Jun 1/9)
FEB 10/34 - *Majestic*	Mrs. Fred Humby School with Bill Sykes [m.c.], musical accompaniment by Mrs. P. Cull, Mrs. Charles Daniel, Mrs. W.J. Nelson [piano], J.P. Alexander [violin], J. Moore [pipes]	Musical & Dance Revue, <u>Tour of the World</u> - Guest Artists: Tom Pizzey, Audrey Leonard, Charles Daniel, Mrs. C. Geiger, Janet McIlvena, Mrs. C.F. Steele, Mrs. Blanche Roy, Mrs. C. Jackson, G. Evans, Jack Coffay, Tom Smith & others (Feb 12/6) - *a colorful revue*
APR 2,3/34 - *Capitol*	Bernadette Fisher	Dance Routine in conjunction with stage appearance of the Calgary Kiddies (Apr 2/2)
MAR 2/35 - *Majestic*	Mrs. Fred Humby	<u>Spring Dance Revue</u> assisted by George Brown [violin], Hugh McIlvena [clarinet], S.L. Chappell [drums], J. Moore [bag pipes] (Mar 4/9) - *a delightful treat*
JUN 7/35 - *Majestic*	Bernadette Fisher's School of Dance directed by Eildon Brander with Eildon Brander, Elaine Heninger, Ila Hicks, Dorothy Swancesky, Nuwana Stoddard, Stafford Peat	<u>Dance Revue</u> assisted by George Brown & orchestra, Lyn Jordan [lighting] (Jun 8/11) - *an event of infinite variety, originality & artistic arrangement*
JUN 14/35 - *Capitol*	Alice Murdock/Lola Strand [dirs] with Denise Sydal, Birdie Metcalfe, Mary Ponech, Audrey Chiswick	<u>Dance Revue</u> (Jun 13/9; 15/8) - *a lively revue*
APR 30/36 - *Majestic*	Mrs. Fred Humby	Russian ballet & pantomime: <u>The Quest of the Fire Bird</u> (May 1/6) - *successfully presented*
MAY 22/36 - *Majestic*	Bernadette Fisher with 80 dancers including E. Brander, E. Heninger, D. Craddock, D. Swancesky, Kathleen Brewerton, Lorraine Fletcher, Aileen Mackwood	A fairy ballet; <u>The Enchanted Princess</u> with assistance from: Mrs. F.E. Fisher [costumes], Mrs. A.I. Ethel Brander [mus dir], L. Jordan [scenic design & painting], T. Ferguson [set construction] (May 23/8) - *clever dancers delighted big crowd*

DATE/PLACE	ACADEMY AND/OR DIRECTOR/ DANCERS	PRESENTATION/REFERENCE
JUN 10,11/36 - *Capitol*	Alice Murdock/Lola Strand [dirs]	Black and white dance revue (Jun 6/7) - *tap dancing & acrobatic work were outstanding*
DEC 19/36 - *Capitol*	Bernadette Fisher/Eildon Brander [dirs]	Children's matinee production: Santa's Doll Shop (Dec 18/2)
MAR 8/37 - *Majestic*	Fisher/Brander School	Dance Frolic in association with Playgoers Little Theatre Evening (Mar 9/8)
MAY 28/37 - *Capitol*	Eildon Brander with Evelyn Fooks, Collette Green, Dalton Elton, Beverly Knowlton, Patsy Garrison	Revue, Pictures From Alice in Wonderland with assistance from musical trio: Rubelle G. Murray [violin], Ethel Brander [piano], Gordon Henderson [cello] (May 27/2; 28/7) - *ingenuity & charm*
JUN 9,10/37 - *Capitol*	Alice Murdock/Lola Strand	Revue, Anchors Away (Jun 9/2; 10/8) - *adagio dancing is notable*
DEC 13/37 - *Majestic*	Lola Strand Dancers	Dance Revue (Dec 14/7) - *in association with Playgoers Evening of Little Theatre*
DEC 20,21/37 - *Capitol*	Eildon Brander assisted by Ambassador's Orchestra	Revue; Christmas Parade (Dec 20/2; 21/7) - *entertaining & colorful*
FEB 1/38 - *Majestic*	Eildon Brander School	Dance Interlude (Feb 2/8) - *in association with Playgoers Evening of Little Theatre*
JUNE 6/38 - *Capitol*	Eildon Brander with E.B., Kathleen Brewerton	Revue with assistance from Aileen Jones, Ethel Brander, Walter Hays [pianists] (Jun 7/8) - *delightful*
JUN 15/38 - *Arena*	Lola Strand's Dancers with Jerry Bastyan's Orchestra & singers: Verna Russell, Elaine Hansen, Marguerite Herman, Irene Tanner	Dance Revue, Swingtime and Jitney Dance (Jun 16/8) - *over 80 dances*
FEB 27/39 - *Majestic*	Eildon Brander School	Dance Revue, Toy Shop (Feb 28/6) - *in association with Playgoers Evening of Little Theatre*
MAR/APR/44 - *various halls*	Jean Gauld School	(Mar 21/7; Apr 5/7) - *participants in the Victory Revue*
APR 19,31/45	Jean Gauld School	(Apr 19/7, 20/6) - *participants in Springtime Revue*
JUN 13-15/46 - *Capitol*	Jean Gauld School	Dance Revue (Jun 13/2)
MAY 8,10/47 - *YMCA*	Joyce Hall School of Dance	(May 8/7,9; 6/10,7) - *participants in YMCA So-Ed Club's minstrel show*
JUN 17/55 - *LCI (auspice of Lethbridge Ballet Auxiliary)*	Lethbridge Branch, Canadian School of Ballet/Joy Camden with Pamela Dray [studio assist], Judy Botterill, Ginny Cernolavek, Kirstie Gentleman	Dance Recital assisted by Mrs. George Willoughby [costumes], Mrs. Leigh [scenery], Tom Ferguson [stage mgr], Carol Wood and Dixie Botterill [accomp]
FEB 13/56 - *Capitol*	Canadian School of Ballet/Joy Camden with Harry Baalim [stage dir] and Dixie Botterill [accomp], Judy Botterill, Mary Leigh, Kathryn Stringam, Lynn Jones	Evening of the Dance (Jan 21/16; 28/16; Feb 7/11; 11/3,16; 14/11) - *a big hit* Guest Artist: Linda Gay Flitton, Calgary
MAY /56 - *Canadian Legion Memorial Hall*	Mrs. N. Livingstone	Springtime Dance Revue (May 19/14) - *program held recently was entertaining*
JUN 11/56 - *Wilson Jr. High School*	Jack Taylor School of Dance	Revue [dancing, singing, comedy] (Jun 9/3,10)
JUN 15/56 - *LCI (auspices of Leth. Ballet Auxiliary)*	Canadian School of Ballet/Joy Camden	Demonstrations: Ballet technique, Highland Folk Dancing (Jun 13/3)
JUN 17/57 - *Capitol (auspices of Leth. Ballet Auxiliary)*	Canadian School of Ballet/Joy Camden with Judy Botterill, Eleanor Noble, Kirstie Gentleman and others	Evening of Dance (Jun 15/3; 18/11) Harry Baalim [stage mgr], Roberta Bremner [accomp] - *wholehearted applause*
FEB 17/58 - *Capitol (Leth. Ballet Auxiliary)*	Canadian School of Ballet/Joy Camden assisted by Eleanor Watson	Evening of Dance (Feb 14/11; 15/14; 18/9) - *superb program; sets by Ted Godwin & members of the '55 Club*
JUN 23/58 - *Capitol*	Eileen Dodds School of Dancing	Musical extravaganza, Dancing Stars of Tomorrow & children's ballet; Red Riding Hood (Jun 15/3; 18/11; 21/3)
JUN 27/58 - *Civic Center*	Canadian School of Ballet/Joy Camden	Ballet and Folk Dance Demonstration (Jun 27/3)
JUN 15/59 - *Capitol (Leth. Ballet Auxiliary)*	Canadian School of Ballet/Joy Camden assisted by Muriel Jolliffe	An Evening of Dance (Jun 16/9) - *the ballerinas were outstanding*
MAR 28/60 - *Capitol (Leth. Ballet Auxiliary)*	Canadian School of Ballet/Muriel Jolliffe with Gay Hahn [accomp]	Evening of Dance (Mar 16/17; 29/10) - *the dancing was excellent*

DATE/PLACE	ACADEMY AND/OR DIRECTOR/ DANCERS	PRESENTATION/REFERENCE
MAY 29/61 - *Capitol*	Jolliffe Academy of Dancing with featured artist, Judy Botterill	Evening of Dance (May 27/3,16) Dixie Botterill [accomp]
JUN 4/62 - *Capitol*	Muriel Jolliffe Academy (auspices of Lethbridge Ballet Auxiliary)	Evening of Dance (May 26/3; Jun 2/18; 5/15) - *near capacity audience enjoys successful performance*
JUN 10/63 - *Capitol*	Jolliffe Academy/Muriel Jolliffe	Evening of Dance (Jun 8/13; 11/10) - *well received by audience of 600*
FEB 7,8/64	Alberta Professional Dance Teacher's Association Local Sponsors: Lethbridge Gyro Club & Lethbridge Ballet Auxiliary	1st Annual Dance Festival; Adjudicator: Gweneth Lloyd (Feb 8/13; 10/13) - *300 entries*
JUN 8/64 - *Capitol*	Jolliffe Academy with dancers: Sandra Niedermier, Linda Bauman, Catherine Leon, Wendy Robison	Evening of Dance Guests: Peter Grantham, Dean Collet (Jun 4/3; 9/12) - *ballet as it can be*
MAR 5-7/65 - *Civic Center*	Lethbridge Gyro Club & Lethbridge Ballet Auxiliary	Annual Dance Festival; Adjudicators: Gweneth Lloyd, Grace Macdonald (Feb 6/10; 8/13)
JUN 7/65 - *Capitol*	Jolliffe Academy with S. Niedermier, C. Leon, W. Robison, Horst Mueller, Donna G. Mullin, Janice Rice, Darlene Snyder, Sherry Lanier, Terri Anne Illingsworth, Janice Gurney, Janis Cottrell, Kathryn Low, Carol Jolliffe	Evening of Dance including ballet, Cinderella (Jun 7/9; 8/10) - *a triumph*
FEB 3-5/66 - *Civic Centre*	Lethbridge Gyro Club & Lethbridge Ballet Auxiliary	Annual Dance Festival, Adjudicators: Gweneth Lloyd, Duncan Cameron (Dec 2/65/14; Jan 17/10; Feb 1/10; 7/10)
JUN 3,4/66 - *Yates Memorial Centre*	Jolliffe Academy with guest performances by Peter Grantham & Bob Befus	Children's ballet, Pepper, by junior dancers The Dancing Princess by senior dancers (Jun 3/14; 4/16) - *Muriel Jolliffe really knows her stuff*
MAR 2-4/67 - *Civic Centre & Yates*	Jolliffe Academy, Lethbridge Gyro Club & Lethbridge Ballet Auxiliary - Ray & Muriel Jolliffe as technical advisors	Annual Dance Festival, Adjudicators: Adeline Duncan, Reginald Hawe (Mar 6/11)
JUN 2,3/67 - *Yates*	Jolliffe Academy with guests: Frank Featherstone and Peter Grantham	Short Ballets, Divertissement & Pinocchio (May 27/3; Jun 3/3) - *some 55 dancers*
JUN 10/67 - *Hamilton Jr. High School*	Dawn's Dancing Studio/Dawn Higgins	Danskapades of 1967 (Jun 8/3)
MAR 5-9/68	Lethbridge Gyro Club & Lethbridge Ballet Auxiliary	5th Annual Alberta Dance Festival Adjudicators: David Latoff (Montreal), Heather Jolley (B.C.) (Mar 8/10)
MAY 28/68 - *Yates*	Lakeview School of Dance/Mrs. Romola Ully	Dance Revue (May 23/3)
JUN 1/68 - *Yates*	Jolliffe Academy	An original ballet, Who Done It? (May 24/3; Jun 1/13)
MAR 5-8/69 - *Yates*	Lethbridge Gyro Club & Lethbridge Ballet Auxiliary	6th Annual Alberta Dance Festival Adjudicators: Adeline Duncan, Carole Chadwick, Dot Blakely (Feb 25/10; Mar 4/10; 6/11; 8/17; 10/10)
MAY 23,24; JUN 2/69 - *Yates*	Jolliffe Academy with Esther Murillo, Jim Green, Margaret Welsh, Elizabeth Zalys & others	Ballet, Sleeping Beauty (May 20/13; 22/14; 24/16; Jun 2/7) - Assisted by Carol Watkinson [set design], Gladys Carson [costumes], Ray Jolliffe [set construction] - *standing ovation*
MAY 28/69	Lakeview School of Dance/Romola Ully	Dance Recital (May 23/7)
MAY 30,31/69 - *Yates*	Dawn's Dancing Studio	Danskapade of '69 (May 30/7)
MAR 12-14/70 - *Yates*	Gyro Club & Lethbridge Ballet Auxiliary	7th Annual Dance Festival & Festival of Stars; Adjudicators: Don Gillies, Heather Jolley, Dorothy Carter (Mar 11/18, 16/10)
JUN 10/70 - *Yates*	Jolliffe Academy (auspices of Lethbridge Ballet Auxiliary)	An Evening of Dance (Jun 8/10)
MAR 9-13/71 - *Yates*	Lethbridge Ballet Auxiliary & Lethbridge Gyro Club	8th Alberta Dance Festival (Mar 2/10; 10/18) Adjs: Gweneth Lloyd, Sandra Bold Jones, Brian Foley
MAY 21,22/73 - *Yates*	Jolliffe Academy/M. Jolliffe/Carol Jolliffe, Mark Litchfield, David Mann, Lori Ully, Christine Lowings, Karen Kay and academy students	Comedy Ballet Pineapple Poll (May 22/14) Included in Playgoers Golden Jubilee Festival
MAY 27/71 - *Yates*	Jolliffe Academy [AAC Festival of Community Theatre]	Mime (May 27/14)

DATE/PLACE	ACADEMY AND/OR DIRECTOR/ DANCERS	PRESENTATION/REFERENCE
MAR 13-20/72 - *Yates*	Lethbridge Ballet Auxiliary & Lethbridge Gyro Club	9th Alberta Dance Festival - Adjs: Lois Smith (ballet), Dorothy Kerr (Highland dance), Roland (tap and stage dancing) (Mar 18/18; 20/11)
JUN 5/72 - *Yates*	Jolliffe Academy with guests: Mark Litchfield & Kirk Jensen	An Evening of Dance 1. Coppelia with Carol Jolliffe; 2. From the Classroom (Jun 3/7; 3/18)
MAY 21,22/83 - *Yates*	Jolliffe Academy/M. Jolliffe/Carol Jolliffe, Mark Litchfield, David Mann, Lori Ully, Christine Lowings, Karen Kay and academy students	Comedy Ballet Pineapple Poll (May 22/14) - *included in Playgoers Golden Jubilee Festival*
JUN 4,5/73 - *Yates*	Jolliffe Academy of Dance	Evening of Dance (Jun 1/13)
FEB 28/74 - *U of L*	Jolliffe Academy (sponsored by U of L Folk Arts Council)	Free ballet, Coppelia
MAR /74 - *Yates*	St. Patrick's School of Irish Dancing	1st St. Patrick's Day Dance Concert
JUN 3-5/74 - *Yates*	Jolliffe Academy with guest narrator, Ed Bayly	Evening of Dance; 1. Les Sylphides; 2. Alice in Wonderland; 3. Jazz Ballet (May 24/6,7)
JUN 8/74 - *Yates*	Dawn's Dancing Studio	Dance Recital
FEB/75 - *Sportsplex*	Jolliffe Academy/M. Jolliffe	Comedy Ballet Pineapple Poll Opening Ceremonies: Canada Winter Games
MAR 16/75 - *Yates*	St. Patrick's School of Irish Dancing	2nd Annual St. Patrick's Day Concert (Mar 17/16)
JUN 2,3/75 - *Yates*	Jolliffe Academy of Dance	Evening of Dance (May 16, Leisure & TV Week/10; Jun 3/10) - *enjoyed by 450*
AUG 4/75 - *Yates*	Lethbridge Heritage Day Program	Cultural displays & ethnic dancing (Aug 5/16) - *witnessed by 600*
SEPT 30/75 - *CJOC T.V.*	Jolliffe Academy of Dance/Muriel Jolliffe	Ballet, Genesis (Sept 26, L&TV Week/20) - *T.V. production filmed at the Yates*
JUN 7,8/76 - *Yates*	Jolliffe Academy	Evening of Dance including masquerade & the short modern work, Metamorphosis (Jun 8/11) - *graceful*
JAN 27/77 - *Yates*	The Alberta Highland Dancing Association (Lethbridge Branch)	"Dance & Sing with Scotland" (Jan 24/9; 28/14)
MAY 29/77 - *Civic Centre*	Japanese Canadian Centennial Dancers Odori	Variety dance concert (May 14/14; 28/14) - *to mark centennial of Japanese immigration to Canada*
JUN 4,5/77 - *Yates*	Ukrainian Canadian Youth Association	Ethnic Cultural Spring Concert of music and dance (Jun 1/28) - *($2.00 - $3.50)*
JUN 5/77 - *Yates*	Hungarian Cultural Society of S.A. presents Calgary Hungarian Wildrose Dancers	Ethnic Concert (Jun 4/6) - *($3.50)*
JUN 14,15/77 - *Yates*	Jolliffe Academy	Evening of Dance (Jun 9/6)
FEB 22/78 - *Yates*	Alberta Highland Dancing Association featuring Jack Whyte (nationally known star of TV & stage and Miss Jill Young [champion dancer])	Dance & Sing with Scotland (Feb 16/5; 18/16)
JUN 12,13/78 - *Yates*	Jolliffe Academy	Evening of Dance (Jun 7/38)
JUN 21/78 - *Grandstand*	Jolliffe Academy/M. Jolliffe	Comedy Ballet Pineapple Poll Opening Ceremonies: Lethbridge Exhibition's new grandstand (Jun 7/78/14)
FEB 21/79 - *Sportsplex*	Alberta Highland Dancing Association	Dance & Sing With Scotland (Feb 17/21)
MAR 18/79 - *Yates*	St. Patrick's School of Irish Dancing dir. by Bernie Forrester (auspices of Irish Canadian Society of Lethbridge)	Annual St. Patrick's Day Concert (Mar 10/19; 14/30)
MAY 6/79 - *Yates*	Momiji Dances/Mrs. Chiyoko Hirano	A Glimpse of Japan (Apr 21/20; May 5/8)
MAY 12/79 - *Civic Centre*	Alberta Highland Dancing Association (auspices of Lethbridge Branch)	1st Highland Dance Competition (May 9/15; 14/17) - *210 contestants; 300 spectators*
JUN 18,19/79 - *Yates*	Jolliffe Academy	Evening of Dance (Jun 15/6)
FEB 28/80 - *Yates*	Alberta Highland Dancing Association	Dance & Sing With Scotland (Feb 23/A6)
APR 26/80 - *Yates*	Momiji Dancers with guest artists from Calgary and Vancouver	Matsuri (Apr 9/D5) - *classical & folk dancing*
MAY /80 - *Civic Centre*	Alberta Highland Dancing Association	2nd annual competition

DATE/PLACE	ACADEMY AND/OR DIRECTOR/ DANCERS	PRESENTATION/REFERENCE
JUN 10/80 - *Yates*	Jolliffe Academy	Evening of Dance including an original ballet The Selfish Giant based on the Oscar Wilde Story (Jun 7/C6)
JUN 29/80 - *Henderson Lake*	Japanese dancers/Chito Kimura	Traditional Japanese dancing (Jun 30/B2) - *60 participants aged 4-84*
AUG 23/80 - *Indian Battle Park*	Lethbridge Folk Club in cooperation with the Alberta 75th Commission present various professional & local singers, musicians and dancers	Art and Musical Festival including folk dances (Jul 3/B1)
FEB 5/81 - *Yates*	Lethbridge Highland Dance Association with guest artist Kerry O'Brien (Edmonton)	Dance & Sing with Scotland (Feb 7/A10) (Kohn School of Dancing)
MAY 9/81 - *Civic Centre*	Lethbride Highland Dance Association	3rd annual open competition (May 6/C11) LETHBRIDGE TROPHY WINNERS: Charlotte Haig, Twila Bechley, Suzanne Miasey....*250 dancers participated*
MAY 23/81 - *Yates*	Studio One Dance Academy	Revue '81 (May 22/A6)
JUN 8,9/81 - *Yates*	Jolliffe Academy/Muriel Jolliffe with Esther Smith-McGowan, Chip Seibert	Evening of Dances featuring an original children's ballet, A Bird of Magic (Jun 8/B3)
JUN 28/81 - *Nikka Yuko*	Canada Japan Friendship Society	Japanese Summer Dance Festival (June 25/B3; 29/B3)
AUG 7/81 - *Nikka Yuko*	Momiji Dancers	Japanese Dancing (Aug 1/B2) - *in conjunction with Alberta Summer Games*
FEB 17/82 - *Yates*	Alberta Highland Dancing Association	Dance & Sing With Scotland (Feb 6/A12)
MAR 20/82 - *Yates*	Momiji Dancers	Furusato [folk dancing] (Mar 15/B9) - *($4.00 - $4.50)*
APR 24,25/82 - *Yates*	Alberta Highland Dance Association	17th Annual Alberta Festival (Apr 26/B1) - *Lethbridge trophy winner - Karen Oler*
JUN 15/82 - *Yates*	Jolliffe Academy	An Evening of Dance - **1.** A Child's Dream; **2.** Divertissement (Jun 11/A8; 14/B2) - *more than 90 performers*
MAY 26-28/83 - *Yates*	Studio One Dance Academy/Kim Ully	Evening of Dance Review '83: Ballet, tap, jazz (May 26/B6) - *Ully has studied in New York, Los Angeles and Toronto; sold out for all performances*
JUN 13,14/83 - *Yates*	Jolliffe Academy	Evening of Dance featuring an original children's ballet, The Nightingale (Jun 11/A10)
FEB 21/84 - *Yates*	Lethbridge Highland Dancing Association	Annual concert (Feb 21/B6)
MAY 31-JUN 2/84 - *Yates*	Studio One Dance Academy/Romola Ully with instructors Kim Docherty, Joanne Flanagan, Wendy Spoulos	Kids World; Thriller; Pinocchio; Jazz routine (May 31/C1)
JUN 12/84 - *Yates*	Jolliffe Academy/Muriel Jolliffe, Carol Godlonton	Ballet, The Snow Queen (Jun 6/A3) - *($3.50)*
JUN 21-23/84 - *Yates*	Joy's Dance Factory/Joy Ackerman	Evening of tap, jazz and ballet (Jun 21/A11)
APR 6/85 - *Yates*	Momiji Dancers/Chiyoko Hirano	Lethbridge Centennial Show (Mar 11/A2) with guest artists from Calgary & Vancouver
APR 28/85 - *Yates*	Joy's Dance Factory/Joy Ackerman	Centennial Festival Dance Preview: evening of show dances including jazz, tap, ballet & musical theatre (Apr 16/B5; 29/B5) - *a strong line up of dancers*
MAY 4/85 - *Yates*	Lethbridge Ethnic Association	Spring Fling, Ethnic music & dance (May 3/C4)
MAY 10/85 - *Exhibition Pavilion*	Native Student Association	5th Annual Pow-Wow (May 8/B8)
MAY 30-JUN 1/85 - *Yates*	Studio One Dance Academy/Romola & Kim Ully	Dance Review (May 31/A4) - *it was magnificent*
JUN 10,11/85 - *Yates*	The Jolliffe Academy/Carol Godlonton/Meriel Kingston, Kathryn Preuss, Julie Amundsen and others	25th Annual Evening of Dance featuring an original children's ballet, The Hollow Tree (Jun 7/A11,A16; 12/A10) - *($4.50)*
AUG 1/85 - *Sportsplex*	Southern Alberta Ethnic Association	Heritage Day Program - Ethnic crafts, music, dances (Aug 6/A3)
DEC 20/85 - *Exhibition Pavilion*	Lethbridge & District Exhibition Board with organizers Art Calling Last (Standoff) & Lee Buckskin	1st Christmas Pow-Wow (Dec 21/A1)

DATE/PLACE	ACADEMY AND/OR DIRECTOR/ DANCERS	PRESENTATION/REFERENCE
APR 20/86 - *Yates*	Joy's Dance Factory presents jazz, tap, classical & character ballet, musical theatre	4th Annual Evening of Dance, A Festival of Stars (Apr 16/A10; 21/A7)
MAY 31/86 - *Yates*	Studio One Dance Academy/Kim Ully	Evening of Dance & Award Presentations (Jun 2/A3) - *Romola Ully recognized for 25 years association with Studio One*
JUN 9,10/86	Jolliffe Academy/Carol Godlonton	26th Annual Evening of Dance - ballet, modern, national dances, Pepper & the Magic Buckles (Jun 5/A11; 10/B7)
JUN 13/86 - *Yates*	Danceworks/Candy Williams & Mark Litchfield	Dance Recital (Jun 11/B5)
JUL 13/86 - *Nikka Yuko*	Honpa Japanese Buddhist Church	Japanese dances (Jul 14/A4)
OCT 19/86 - *Yates*	Lethbridge Delibab Dancers	Hungarian Dances (Oct 20/A3) - *celebrate 100 years in southern Alberta*
NOV 2/86 - *Yates*	Tryzub Dance Ensemble	Ukrainian Dances (Nov 3/A3) - *Ukrainian independence concert*
MAR 4/87	Dance Gala Danse Canada/Muriel Jolliffe (National coordinator)	1st annual regional festival (Mar 5/A5) - *110 entries in the zone competition of the nationwide Canada dance gala*
APR 25,26/87 - *U of L; CCHS*	Alberta Highland Dancing Association	Alberta Championship Highland Dance Competition (Apr 27/A3)
MAY /87 - *Wilson Jr. High*	Lethbridge Highland Dancing Association]	Local dance competition
MAY 8,9/87 - *Yates*	Dance Gala Danse Canada (coordinated by M. Jolliffe) with adjudicators Christine Richardson and Ruth Carse	Provincial competition (May 11/B4)
JUN 8,9/87 - *Yates*	Jolliffe Academy of Dancing/Carol Godlonton/Meriel Kingston, Corinne Smith, Marlene Nagy	An Evening of Dance (Jun 8/B9; 9/A9) - *a brand of unspoiled magic - a thrill*
JUN 17-20/87 - *Yates*	Joy's Dance Factory	7th Recital - 2 performances by beginning students, 3 by senior students (Jun 18/B5; 20/A3)
JUN 27/87 - *Yates*	Danceworks	Recital, 9 To 5 at 4/4 Time (Jun 24/B5; 26/A10; 29/B9)
MAR 4-5/88 - *Yates (auspices AAC)*	Dance Gala Danse Canada with adjs. Shelley Cromie and Eva Christiansen	(Mar 8/A9) - *southern Alberta dancers strut their stuff*
APR 9/88 - *Yates*	Momiji Dancers (Lethbridge) and guests Kaedi Dancers (Calgary)	10th annual Japanese Dance festival (Mar 28/B11; Apr 11/A11) - *Yasumi Uechi steals this show*
JUN 2-4/88 - *Yates*	Studio One Dance Academy/K. Ully, J. Stuart, E. Murillo (chor)	Revue '88 Phantom of the Opera (May 24/B9; 25/B9; 26/B7; Jun 3/C6) - *three hour show*
JUN 6/88 - *Yates*	Jolliffe Academy of Dancing/Carol Godlonton	An Evening of Dance (Jun 7/B6)
JUN 18/88 - *Yates*	Danceworks Dance Studio/Candy Chiselle-Williams	Annual recital, Storefront Theatre (Jun 16/C4; 20/A9)
JUN 22-25/88 - *Yates*	Joy's Dance Factory/Deborah LeMaistre, Patricia Livingstone	Annual dance revue (May 25/B9; Jun 25/B8)

Community Theatre Productions
Lethbridge, Alberta (1887 - 1988)

DATE/PLACE	GROUP/DIRECTOR(S)	PRODUCTION/CAST/REFERENCES
DEC 20/1887 - *NWMP Barracks*	Lethbridge Amateurs (in aid of St. Augustine's Church)	Variety entertainment including short farce <u>Martyr to Science</u>: cast unknown (Dec 14/3; 22/3) - *great laughter; provoked hilarious mirth*
AUG 16/88 - *Barracks*	Lethbridge Amateurs/Capt. R.B. Deane (in aid of St. Augustine's Church)	Variety entertainment including short sketch <u>Cut Off With a Shilling</u>: R.B. Deane, Mr. & Mrs. White-Fraser (Aug 22/3) - *best of its kind*
NOV 20,21/88 - *Barracks*	Lethbridge Amateurs/Capt. Deane (in aid of the Recreation Room, NWMP Barracks)	<u>The Chimney Corner</u>; Ici on parle français: R.B. Deane, Mrs. White-Fraser & others (Nov 21/3) - *acting throughout was very good*
FEB 18,19/89 - *unknown hall* FEB 28/89 - *Macleod*	Lethbridge Sunflower Minstrels/John Gamble	Minstrel Show, Messrs. Gamble, Dougherty, Hutchinson, Welch, Jardine, Gordon, Calvert (Feb 20/3) - *exceeded most sanguine expectations*
DEC 3/89 - *Barracks*	Lethbridge Amateurs/Capt. Deane (in aid of St. Augustine's Church)	Music & Drama including <u>Dearest Mama</u>: Messrs. R.B. Deane, C.C. McCaul, N.T. Macleod, H.F. Greenwood; Mrs. Neale; Misses Duff, Jardine (Dec 4/3) - *acting could scarcely have been improved upon*
MAR 17,18/90 - *Barracks* MAR 20/90 - *Macleod Town Hall*	Lethbridge Amateurs/Capt. Deane	<u>The Wonderful Woman</u>: Messrs. Deane, Greenwood, McCaul, Dunn; Mesdames Neale, H. Bentley, R.B. Deane - *first dress play in the Territories* <u>Betsy Baker</u>*: H. Martin, N.T. Macleod; Misses Duff, Jardine (Mar 19/3)
JAN 13/91 - *Barracks*	Lethbridge Amateurs/Mrs. F.R. Godwin/Mrs. Neale [accomp] (in aid of fencing fund: Protestant cemetery)	Operetta, <u>The Pedlar</u>: Mesdames C.F.P. Conybeare, Godwin; Miss Jardine; N.T. Macleod; Sgt. W.G. Cleveland (Jan 15/3) - *complete success in every way*
MAR 31/91 - *Barracks*	Calgary IOOF Lodge #1	<u>The Initiation of a Candidate</u> (Mar 31/3) - *variety entertainment including drama*
SEPT 10/91 - *Barracks*	Lethbridge Amateurs/Capt. Deane/Mrs. Godwin/Miss Sherlock [accomp] (auspices of Lethbridge Building Co.)	Ici on parle français: Messrs. Deane, Dunne, Martin; Mesdames Neale, Bentley, Godwin <u>The Pedlar</u>: Miss Enid Martin; Mesdames Godwin, Deacon; N.T. Macleod, Sgt. W.G. Cleveland (Sept 15/3) - *all parts exceedingly well performed*
NOV 30; DEC 1/91 - *A.R.&C. Co.'s Library*	A.R. & C. Co. Employees Literary Society/T.H. Dunne (in aid of A.R.&C. Co.'s Library)	Farce, <u>Turn Him Out</u>: Messrs. T. Dunne, T. Glenwright, W. Waghorn; Mesdames T. McNabb, T.H. Dunne - Burlesque, <u>Bombastes Furioso</u> (Dec 2/3) - *in every particular, all that could be desired*
DEC 23/91 - *Bldg. Co.'s Hall (opening)*	Lethbridge Amateurs/Capt. Deane	<u>The Porter's Knot</u>: Messrs. R.B. Deane, Clarke, Champness, G.W. Robinson, Martin; Mesdames H. Bentley, Neale 4 Act, <u>Illustrious Stranger</u>: Messrs. Oliver, Dunne, Macleod, Martin; Mesdames Godwin, Deacon (Dec 30/4) - *new scenery is the best in the northwest*
FEB 8,9/92 - *A.R.&C. Co.*	A.R. & C. Co. Employees/T.H. Dunne	<u>Luke the Laborer</u>: Messrs. Dunne, W. Waghorn, E. Davis, W.W. Walmsley, T. Glenwright, J. Barclay, H. Gregory, J. Wallwork, D. Creighton, Jr.; Mrs. T.H. Dunne; Misses E. Wallwork, E. McKay; <u>Slasher & Crasher</u>: H. Gregory (Feb 10/3) - *some forgetting of lines deterred the effectiveness*
MAY 4/92 - *Bldg. Co.*	Lethbridge Amateurs/Capt. Deane	3 act comedy by W. J. Byron, <u>Not Such a Fool as He Looks</u>: Messrs. Deane, Dunne, Martin; Mesdames Neale, Conybeare; Miss Jardine; Corporal Matthews (May 11/3) - *one of the best*
DEC 3/94 - *Bldg. Co.*	Lethbridge Amateurs/Capt. Deane/Mrs. Godwin (in aid of First United Church)	2 act farce, <u>Who Killed Cock Robin</u>: Messrs. Deane, N.T. Macleod; Mrs. H. Bentley, Miss Simpson (Dec 5/1) - *very good program*
JAN 3/95 - *Bldg. Co.*	Lethbridge Amateurs/NWMP/Mrs. Neale (in aid of St. Aloysius Convent)	<u>To Paris & Back for Five Pounds</u>: cast unknown (Jan 15/1) - *carried out without a hitch but not well attended*
APR 10,11/96 - *Bldg. Co.*	Columbia Minstrels from Medicine Hat (in aid of Galt Hospital	Minstrel show, (Apr 15/1) - *deserved larger audiences*
JUN 21/97 - *Bldg. Co.*	Cardston Mutual Improvement Assoc. Dramatic Co. (assisted by Cardston Orchestral Band)	<u>Time & The Hour</u>: W.H. Steed, Lola Stoddard, Dora Hinman & others (Jun 23/1)
DEC 12-15/98 - *Bldg. Co.*	Lethbridge Operatic Society/William MacKenzie/Jessie Glover/Mrs. Neale [accomp]/Messrs. Case and Withers [lighting]	Operetta, <u>Pirates of Penzance</u> by Gilbert & Sullivan; double cast: Jessie Glover; Mesdames A. Southard, C.F.P. Conybeare (Miss Stafford), W. Laurie (Mrs. Alexander); Misses McIntyre (Mrs. J.D. Higgin), Finnis (Miss Robb); Messrs. James (G.H. Johnston), R. Sage, (J.D. Higinbotham), Reg Claris (CFP Conybeare) (Dec 8/8; 15/2) - *truly wonderful - two casts did justice to their parts*

*Replaced in the Macleod offering by *Cut Off With A Shilling* with R.B. Deane, Mr. & Mrs. White-Fraser

DATE/PLACE	GROUP/DIRECTOR(S)	PRODUCTION/CAST/REFERENCES
MAR 20,21/99 - *Bldg. Co.*	Georgia Minstrels from Medicine Hat (benefit for widow of M.H. bridge accident victim)	Minstrel show (Mar 23/8)
OCT 23/99 - *S.A. Citadel*	Salvation Army	Ten Virgins (Oct 26/8) - *attracted a large audience*
NOV 10-11/99 - *Oliver's Hall*	Medicine Hat Drama Club (in aid of M.H. Hospital)	For a Brother's Sin; Queen's Evidence (Nov 9/8; 6/2)
MAR 12/1900 - *Oliver's*	Magrath Amateur Comedy Co. (in aid of Magrath LDS Church organ fund)	Dutch Jake; The Yankee Pedlar; The Toodles; The Spectre Bridegroom (Mar 15/8)
JAN 24,25/01 - *Oliver's*	Lethbridge Operatic Society/Miss Haas/Mrs. Neale [piano]/J.C. Kelly [violin]/A. Pirie, E.M. Kevin [stage mgrs]/H. Case [lighting]	Operetta, Gypsy Queen: Mesdames F.W. Downer, J. Kirkpatrick; Miss Haas; Messrs. G.H. Johnston, E. M. Kevin and chorus (Jan 31/1) - *scored a surprising success*
APR 9/01 - *Oliver's*	Lethbridge Amateurs/Capt. Deane (in aid of St. Augustine's rectory fund)	Variety entertainment including Dearest Mama: Messrs. Deane, W.C. Ives, W.H. MacDonald, J. Greenwood; Mesdames Conybeare, Bentley; Miss Lily Deane (Apr 11/1) - *decided success*
APR 23-25/01 - *Oliver's*	Lethbridge Amateur Minstrels/E.A. Cunningham [mus dir]	Minstrel show, The White Eyed Coterie: A.E. Humphries, E. Kevin, J. Howard, E. Jarvis, T. Clayton, T. Burnett, A. Scott, C.B. Bowman, F.D. Anderson, G.W. Robinson, G.H. Johnston, T. Lewis, G. Kerr, C.D. Simpson, H. Case, D. Kain, W. Burnett, T.C. Douglas, G. Burnett, E. Sharman, G. Sutton, J. Henderson, C. Leonard, C.J. Atkinson, Major Burnett (Apr 25/2) - *most conspicuously successful local event in history of our town*
OCT /01 - *Citadel*	Salvation Army	Passion play (Oct 10/8)
MAY 27-29/02 - *Oliver's*	Lethbridge Amateur Minstrel Club/A.E. Cunningham [mus dir]/Professor Conradie [orch leader]/Messrs. Conradie, Albiston, J. McCaig, M. Boskaski, C. Leonard, J.A. Barclay [orch]	Minstrel Show - W.E. Humphries, H. Case, A. Niven, G. Sutton, R. McIntosh, W. & T. Burnett, Jim Salisbury, G.W. Robinson, W. McKay, G.H. Johnston, J. Murray, J. Scott, C. Fraser, F.D. Anderson, Sgt. Balderson & others (May 29/2) - *not as good as its predecessor*
APR 12,13/04	Lethbridge IOOF (in aid of Galt Hospital)/H.T. Cherry [stage mgr]/H. Case [electrician]/Mr. Kennedy [stage carpenter]	Farcical Entertainment, High Illustrious Grand Hiankidink (HIGH): Head of the Order of Hercules: Messrs. Goddard, Nedham, Appleby, Read, Bennett & others (Apr 14/4; 21/1) - *scarcely a break in the laughter provoking situations*
APR 28/04 - *Oliver's*	Ladies of St. Monica's Guild/Reverend Mr. Chivers, A.E. Cunningham [mus dirs]/Mrs. Neale [accompanist]/A. Nedham, J. McCaig, Little, Gaskell, Rusbaski [orch]	Ladies minstrel show, cast unknown (Apr 21/4) - *a grand success*
FEB 6,7/05 - *Oliver's*	Brigham Young Drama Society of Raymond (assisted by Miss Sloan & Mr. D.H. Elton of Cardston)	4 act comedy, The Merry Cobbler: B.S. Young, D.H. Elton, Miss Sloan & others (Feb 9/4) - *gave much pleasure to slim audiences*
DEC 6/06 - *Oliver's*	Lethbridge Amateurs/George Harper	Grand Minstrel Show: Sid Jackson (Colonel), S. Niven, Mr. Miller [end men]; Messrs. Armstrong, Dobbin, F. Harrop, J.R. Shearer, W.M. McKay, H. Kilmer, E. Sloan, J. Eakin, F. German (Dec 13/4) - *reflected credit on de Boss Harper*
JAN 19-21/09 - *St. Augustine's Hall*	Lethbridge Opera & Dramatic Club/Allan E. Allen/Rev. Mr. J.S. Chivers [mus dir]/C.F.P. Conybeare [book]	Operetta, The Darling of the Geishas: Messrs. A.E. Allen, D. May, G.E. Fleming, H.R. Cooper, G.W. Robinson; Mesdames G. Rogers, S. Jackson, C.F.P. Conybeare, A. Southard; Misses Bawden, Elaine Conybeare & chorus (Jan 20/1; 21/3; 22/4) - *persistent round of applause*
JAN 25,26/09 - *Eureka*	Lethbridge Amateurs/Richard Hincks (in aid of the young Men's Club of Lethbridge)	3 act comedy, Sweet Lavender by A.W. Pineo: Messrs. G.E. Fleming, J. Eakin, L.L. Asquith, R. Hincks, R.H. Williams, T.E. Patteson, A. Whitton; Misses Beryl Nimmons, Mary Hings, Agnes Patteson, E. Williams (Jan 26/3) - *projection was weak but Mr. Hincks has play in hand; makes every part count*
APR 29-MAY 1/09 - *Lyceum*	Richard Hincks & Co. of Lethbridge Amateurs	**1.** Apr 29,30; Three Act Farce, Dandy Dick: Richard Hincks, Mary Hings, & others **2.** May 1 (matinee & evening); Sweet Lavender: (see Jan 24 cast list) (Apr 30/1; May 1/2) - *staging is letter perfect*
AUG 2,3/09 - *Lyceum Tent* AUG 7 - *Raymond*	Richard Hincks & Co.	Dandy Dick: R. Hincks; Mrs. Rankin; Misses Hings, Anderson, Neale (Aug 3/09/3)

DATE/PLACE	GROUP/DIRECTOR(S)	PRODUCTION/CAST/REFERENCES
DEC 13/10 - *Majestic* (MT)	Richard Hincks & Co. of Lethbridge Amateurs	Series of farce comedies: **1.** April Fools: R. Hincks, Frank Waddington, L.L. Asquith **2.** Little Toddlekins: R. Hincks, F. Waddington, L.L. Asquith, Grace McLeod, Mary Hings, Mrs. A. L. Hings **3.** Packing Up: R. Hincks, L.L. Asquith, Grace McLeod **4.** The Fair Equestrienne: R. Hincks, L.L. Asquith, Mary Hings (Dec 8/7; 14/9) ($0.25 - $1.00) - *Mr. Hincks's drole humor was at all times entertaining. Audience was tickled by the good comedy.*
DEC 31/10 - *MT*	Knights of Pythias	Minstrel show, cast unknown (Dec 8/9; 20/11)
JAN 30/11 - *MT*	Musical Drama Club of the Conservatory of Music/G. Harper/Mrs. Jenkins [accomp]	Nautical Comedy Opera, Billee Taylor: 75 performers including Bessie Hazel, Ada Wright, Irene McLachlan, Elaine Conybeare, Frank Waddington, Harold (Al) Cooper, George Spencer, Richard Hincks, James Dawson & chorus (Feb 2/9) - *a finished company of performers*
APR 27/11 - *Eureka & toured to Magrath*	Drama Club/(Conservatory of Music)/George Harper	Comedy-Drama, Nevada or The Lost Mine: H. Cooper, Fred Rose, E. Chandler, H. Nicholson, Bernard McKay, Harry Pilling, L.V. Butler, Chris Gibson, Gladys Downer, Mary Simpson (Apr 25/11; 28/9) - *well staged - cast acquitted themselves in a most able manner*
MAY 10-13/11 - *MT*	Lethbridge Amateurs trained by professional mgr. & dir. of Queen Zephra Co., Harry J. Booth. Magnificent scenic display in addition to 35 musical numbers	Operetta, Queen Zephra: 150 local participants - H.C. Booth (professional), Ada Wright, Marjorie Glayzer, Annie Davidson, Edith Jones, Douglas McNair, Mrs. Douglas, Jean Crawford, Lucy Warren, Percy Morris, Lyle Fairhurst, Robert Niven, Doloras Warren, Robert Ross, Eva Bissett, Ursula Elton, Val Pearson, Vernon Pearson, Fred T. Robins, Charles Woods, Albert Woods & chorus (May 11/9) - *holds a prominent place among amateur productions*
FEB 16-17/12 - *Morris* (MoT)	Al Morris & Co. of Lethbridge Amateurs	Al Morris Minstrels: Al Morris [Interlocutor], Thomas, James and Harry Chapman, G.E. Fleming, E.L. Jarvis, R. Barrowman [cartoonist] (Feb 17/3) - *superior to many touring companies*
OCT 21-24/12 - *MT*	Conservatory Musical Drama Club/George Harper, Mrs. F. Waddington [accomp]	Revival, Billee Taylor: F. Waddington, Harold (Al) Cooper, J.P. Petts, H. Nicholson, G. Spencer, Ruth Freeman, Ada Wright, Edith Jones, Elaine Conybeare [solo dance] & chorus (Oct 22/7) ($0.50 - $1.50) - *acquitted themselves with credit*
MAY 12-14/13 - *MT*	Lethbridge Musical & Dramatic Society/G. Harper/George Mitford [mus dir] Mrs. F. Waddington [accomp]	Operetta The Country Girl: Misses Dorothy Young, Ruth Freeman, Mary Simpson, Nellie Duncan, Beck; Mesdames Bourke, C.R. Peters, E.J. Sehl; Messrs. F. Rose, J. Petts, B.S. Young, G. Robinson, F. Waddington, H. Nicholson, E.L. Jarvis, Mrs. F.E. Fisher (Elaine Conybeare) [solo dance] and chorus (May 13/1; 14/3) - *presented with a dash of professionalism*
JUN 25,26/13 - *MT*	Lethbridge Musical & Dramatic Society/B.S. Young replaced G. Harper	Revival The Country Girl: cast replacements: G.E. Fleming, Mr. & Mrs. V. Brown, Charles Sydal, Mr. Rhodes (Jun 26/3) - *best performance yet*
OCT 17,18/13 - *MT*	St. Patrick's Minstrels from Medicine Hat	Minstrel Show (Oct 18/3) - *pleases Lethbridge audience*
DEC 11-13/13; JAN 1/14 - *MT*	Lethbridge Musical & Dramatic Society/B.S. Young (assisted by Messrs. Adams & Edwards)/T. Roberts [orch conductor]/Mrs. F. Waddington [accomp]	Operetta San Toy: B.S. Young, G.E. Fleming, Frank Waddington, F. Rose, H.A. Nicholson, Richard Hincks, E.C. Guilbault, G.W. Robinson, Mr. Salt, Fred Downer, Jr.; Dorothy Young; Mesdames W.S. Harvey, E.J. Sehl, Agnes Dowselty, Snell & chorus (Dec 9/3; 12/7; Jan 2/3) - *there was a lack of "ginger" in the production*
APR 24-25/14 - *Sherman* (ST)	Al Morris & Co.	Merry Minstrels: Al Morris, Tom, Harry & James Chapman, Jack Wilson, Bob Barrowman (Apr 25/3) - *furious roars of laughter were almost continuous*
DEC 4/14 - *MT*	Richard Hincks & Co. (auspices of IODE)	Patriotic concert including comic sketch, A Sister to Assist 'Er: L.L. Asquith, F. Waddington (Dec 5/9) - *vernacular which convulsed the audience with laughter*
DEC 25,26/14 - *ST*	(Lethbridge) Columbia Minstrels/Len S. Brown	Minstrel Show: R. Barrowman [Interlocutor] Chapman Bros., Len Brown, H. Cooper, Joseph Simpson, Harry Parsons (Dec 26/3) - *did themselves proud*
FEB 15,16/15 - *MT*	Lethbridge Amateurs/Len S. Brown (auspices of IODE)	Farce, Are You a Mason?: Mesdames J.N. Ritchie, R.T. Brymner, L.S. Brown, F.E. Fisher (i.e. Elaine Conybeare); Misses Ethel Conybeare, Mary Simpson, Bessie Hazell; Messrs. F.O. Hyde, S.J. Shepherd, G.E. Fleming, L.S. Brown, R.T. Brymner, G.W. Robinson (Feb 16/3; 17/3)
APR 30/15 - *St. Augustine's Hall* MAY 11/15 - *Burgman's Hall*	Ladies of St. Augustine's W.A. (in aid of St. Mary's Anglican Church)	Short play, Sunbonnets: Misses Susie Bawden, Angela Bawden, Ashton, Hanrahan, Nimmons, Bentley, Eleanor Walsh, Mary Simpson; Mesdames Brymner, Stephens; Messrs. Cooper, Brymner (Apr 30/9; May 11/3)
MAY 13,14/15 - *St. Basil's Auditorium* JUN 3/15 - *MT*	Joint auspices: St. Patrick's Drama Society and IODE	Roman drama, Fabiola: E. Kennedy, G. Tennant, J. Vaselenak, L. Close, H. Mayer, W. Supina, S. Kosko, C. Walsh; Misses M. Delay, B. Dorjoume, M. Vaselenak, M. Moore, K. McCormack (May 14/9; Jun 4/7) - *a good dramatization of a heavy play*

DATE/PLACE	GROUP/DIRECTOR(S)	PRODUCTION/CAST/REFERENCES
AUG 16/15 - *Orpheum* (*OT*)	Richard Hincks & Co. (in aid of the IODE & the Nursing Mission)	Comic sketches: **1.** A Sister to Assist 'Er: L.L. Asquith, F. Waddington **2.** Packing Up: Mr. & Mrs. L. Asquith, R. Hincks **3.** The Brute Simmons: R. Hincks, L.L. Asquith, F. Waddington (Aug 17/5) - *a very delightful treat*
SEPT 27,28/15 - *MT*	(Lethbridge) Columbia Minstrels/Len S. Brown (in aid of the Patriotic Fund	Minstrel Show: unidentified cast (Sept 27/2,3)
APR 27/16 - *MT*	IODE/Richard Hincks	Concert including unidentified sketch with F. Waddington, R. Hincks, E.C. Guilbault (Apr 28/5)
NOV 9/16 - *MT*	Auspices of Lethbridge Sports and Amusement Club (Tobacco fund benefit)	Boxing & wrestling matches; included "black and white" sketch, untitled, Len S. Brown & associate (Nov 10/3)- *better than many professional vaudeville performers seen here*
JAN 1/17 - *MT*	Medicine Hat Opera Society/George Stewart [mus dir]	Operetta, Tom Jones by Edward German: (Jan 3/5) - *best amateur production ever witnessed in Lethbridge*
APR 9,10/17 - *MT*	Richard Hincks & Co. (in aid of Red Cross)	3 act farce, Dandy Dick, R. Hincks, F. Waddington, G.E. Fleming, C.R. Matthews, R. Hincks, Jr., George Kemm, Mr. Manson; Mesdames Louise Ritchie, G.E. Fleming; Misses S. Bawden, W. Stitt (Apr 10/6)
JAN 1/18 - *MT*	Medicine Hat Opera Society/George Stewart	Operetta, Erminie by Jacobowski (Jan 2/10) (*$0.50 - $1.50*) - *one of the best amateur productions in the West*
APR 1,2/18 - *MT*	Richard Hincks & Co.	3 act comedy, His Excellency the Governor: R. Hincks, F. Waddington, Mrs. J.N. Ritchie, Mrs. Snow, Miss F. Donald, R. Hincks, Jr., A.C. Raworth, C. R. Matthews, F.O. Hyde, George Kemm (Apr 2/7) - *successfully presented to a crowded house; R. Hincks surpassed himself*
JUN 10/18	Lethbridge Amateurs/Mrs. Pawson (Coaldale) auspices of the Great War Veteran's Association	Vaudeville including sketches: **1.** The Parlor Snake: Winnifred Lingard, Leo Coombs, Jessie Ross, Mary Clark, M.V. Coombs, L.S. Brown, W.B. Ferguson **2.** The Rehearsal: G.A. McIntosh, L.S. Brown, W.B. Ferguson, M.V. Coombs (Jun 11/9)
DEC 27,28/18 - *MT*	Richard Hincks & Co. (in support of tobacco fund for soldiers overseas & in aid of the Nursing Mission)	**Short Plays:** **1.** The Changeling by W.W. Jacobs: A.C. Raworth, Alfred Henshaw, C.R. Matthews, Alfred Stokes, R. Hincks, Mrs. Henshaw **2.** The Collaborators by Daisy McGeoch: R. Hincks, Mrs. J.N. Ritchie **3.** Cinders by Lily Tinsley: Mrs. A.E. Snow, Frank Waddington **4.** The Playgoers by A.W. Pineo: Richard & Mrs. Hincks, R. Hincks, Jr., F. Waddington, Mrs. Donald, Mrs. Buchanan, Mrs. A.E. Snow (Dec 28/7) - *one of the best evenings of amateur entertainment*
JAN 1/19 - *MT*	Raymond Drama Society	Comedy drama, The Stubborn Motor Car by Anthony E. Willis: Ruth Stevens & others (Dec 28/7)
MAR 1/19 - *MT*	Calgary Rotary Club	Minstrel show (Mar 3/8) - *pleasing production*
JAN 1/20 - *MT*	Medicine Hat Opera Society	Operetta, San Toy: (Jan 2/5) - *very favorable impression*
JAN 15/20 - *MT*	Raymond Drama Society (auspices of Lethbridge Boy Scouts)	The Squire's Daughter by Walter M. Wills (Jan 15/5)
JAN 21/21 - *MT*	Lethbridge Amateurs (auspices of IODE)	Variety concert including comedy, Dearest Mama, Roy Keivill, Eric Ings, G.E. Fleming, Frank Cope, Minnie Hazell, Mrs. Dorothy Edwards, Mrs. C.F.P. Conybeare (Jan 22/7) - *shows signs of hasty production but still went down well*
FEB 3,4; 21/21 - *St. Augustine's Hall* JUN 8, SEPT 2/21 - *MT*	Waddington Family & Co./Frank Waddington/Mrs. Waddington, Mrs. Frank Colpman, Eileen Waddington [accomp]	Musical and variety entertainment, Black & White Pierrots: F. Waddington, Geoffrey Waddington, Eileen Waddington, Miss Paterson, Frank Colpman, James Cranney, Betty Wise (Feb 4/8; Jun 9/9; Sept 2/11) - *truly fine entertainment*
NOV 28,29/21 - *MT*	Local Amateurs/Messrs. Jordan & MacDonald (claimed to be N.Y. promoters & directors) Benefit for Canadian Army and Navy Veterans	Scandals of 21: unidentified cast (Nov 22/8; 30/7) - *the biggest scandal was that the promoters skipped town with the proceeds of $300*
DEC 12,13/21 - *MT*	Lethbridge Rotary Club/Robert Barrowman/C.J. Ferguson [mus dir]/Bob Winters [props]/Guy Roy [electrician]/girls' dances staged by Hilda Church	**1.** Rotary Minstrels: Rose Pomeroy, Bill Craig [Interlocutor], Bill Armstrong, G. Fleming, Hugh Crawford, A.C. Ades, Harry & Tom Chapman, Roy Keivill, Edward G. Hazell, George Davies, C.J. Ferguson, Pat Moore, Pat Paterson, Tom Fetterly, Garrett W. Green, Aileen Long, Mrs. Milhouse, Mrs. N. Bletcher **2.** One Act Farce, The Village Fire Brigade: Ernest Gaskell Sterndale Bennett, Elizabeth Belle Sterndale Bennett, George Dixon Short Rural Comedy, School Days: Allan Watson, Roy Davidson (Dec 13/10) - *real big hit; 1st annual Rotary production*

DATE/PLACE	GROUP/DIRECTOR(S)	PRODUCTION/CAST/REFERENCES	348
MAY 8,9/22 - *MT*	Richard Hincks & Co.	1. His Excellency the Governor: R. Hincks, Mrs. J.N. [Louie] Ritchie, Mr. & Mrs. E.G. Sterndale Bennett, Rose Pomeroy, R. Hincks, Jr.; Messrs. Rowley, Evans, Hicks, Butler 2. The Bathroom Door: Miss Bawden, Miss Louise Smith, Mrs. Sick, A.W. Raworth, R. Keivill, Jim Jackson (May 9/10) - *well played & well received but some first night nervousness*	
DEC 4/22 - *St. Basil's School*	Amateur Theatrical Society of St. Patrick's Parish	Operetta, The Wild Rose: Kathleen McCormick, Anne Bakos, Henry Viney & others (Dec 5/8) - *sincere and unaffected; the only male (Henry Viney) did himself proud*	
DEC 11-13/22 - *MT*	Rotary Club of Lethbridge/C.J. Ferguson [mus dir], George Brown [orch dir], Robert Barrowman [dir], Rose Pomeroy [chor dir], Dougal McNabb [stage mgr], Webster Burton [props], C. Watson [lights], Mr. & Mrs. George Brown, Messrs, D. Hay, D. Scott, T. Routledge, H. McIlvena, R. Van Heck, N. Meyers, A. McIlvena, A.W. Maxwell [orch]	Musical comedy, The Czar of Zanzibar written locally by Robert Barrowman: E.G. Sterndale Bennett, E.G. Hazell, F. Rose, W.J. Armstrong, Robert W. Long, D. McKillop, George R. Dixon, Thomas Chapman, Harry Chapman, Rev. Mr. R. Cripps, Garrett W. Green, Roy Keivill, J.H. Rivers, A.C. Saunders, George Cope, B.B. Hoyt & chorus (Dec 12/10) - *scored another success*	
MAR 12,13/23 - *MT*	C.P.R. Social & Athletic Club/E.F. Layton [orch leader]	Can Pac Minstrels: Phil Sangster, R. Barrowman, D.H. Elton, J. Harvey, Mr. Wesley & others (Mar 13/12) - *a little ragged; chorus was good*	
NOV 19,20/23 - *MT*	Rotary Club/C.J. Ferguson [mus dir]/George Brown [orch leader]	1. Minstrel & Variety Show: Dave Elton, Ed Hazell, Bill Armstrong, Tom Chapman, William Stott, Phil Sangster, Roy Keivill, Roy Davidson, Robert Barrowman, Avril Little 2. Short Play: The Sleeping Car dir. by Belle Sterndale Bennett with Camille Connor, Ernie Wilson, Tom Ridpath, George Davies, Bill Armstrong 3. A Musical Sketch, Indian Days dir. by Rose Pomeroy with M. Hazell, Bill Beattie & chorus (Nov 16/8; 20/7) - *Rotary once more wins laurels; capacity crowd enjoys performance*	
MAR 4/24 - *First United Ch.*	Coaldale United Church Ladies Aid	Comedy, The Farmerette (Mar 3/8)	
MAR 5,6/24 - *YMCA*	YMCA Bazaar Committee	Bazaar program including sketch, Suppressed Desires: E.G. & E.B. Sterndale Bennett, Louie Ritchie (Feb 23/7; Mar 6/7) - *roles all practically perfectly interpreted*	
NOV 17,18/24 - *MT*	Rotary Club/George E. Bower [mus dir]	1. Minstrel and Variety Show: Bill Craig [Interlocutor], Hugh Crawford, Phil Sangster, Bill Armstrong, Roy Keivill, Bob Winter, Norman Peat, Bill Beattie, Tom Ness, Haze Moore, Bob Lawrence 2. Farce, Isn't It Exciting, dir. by Belle Sterndale Bennett with E.G. Sterndale Bennett, E.N. Sturrock, George Holman, Fred Rose, Nan Thomas (Nov 15/9; 18/7; 25/7) - *all the usual pep; audience is delighted; net proceeds of $1250*	
FEB 19-21/25 - *MT*	Lethbridge Elks Club/C.H. Lewis of Chicago	Musical Comedy, The Beauty Shop: 80 in cast including: Charles Hiscocks, Roy Keivill, A.S. Bennie, A.C. Raworth, Art McIlvena, R.S. Rannard, Phil Sangster, Barbara Miles, Minnie Thrall, Anita Rooney, Gwyn Thomas, Hilda Church, Helen F. King, Millie Wakelen, George Parsons, Eleanor Lindsay, Marjorie McElroy, Kathleen Sick, Doran Miles, A.J. Gleam, Tommy Owens (Feb 12/8; 18/8; 20/7) - *with only a fortnight's training, the first act was weak; some judicious paring needed, but audience was generally well entertained*	
MAR 13,14/25 - *YMCA*	YMCA/G.E. Bower [mus dir]	Minstrel Show: Phil Sangster, Roy Keivill, Hod Seamans, Carl Sandquist, Lyn Fairbairn, C.J. Broderick, H.D. Ellis, A. McAlpine, B. Long, F.M. Rose [Interlocutor] & 80 boys including Charlie Dawson, Malcolm Matheson, Alfred Morris, G. Keel, Clinton Constantinescu (Mar 5/8; 14/7)	
OCT 15-17/25 - *MT*	Gyro Club/Miss E.M. Jones of Chicago who toured with sets & costumes	Oh! Oh! Kachoo: 80 local participants including: Mrs. E.L. Connor, Fred Teague, Mrs. Emil Sick, Minnie Thrall, Haze Moore, Hilda Church, Kathleen MacKenzie, Walter Cross (Oct 16/7) (*$0.75 - $1.50*) - *went swimmingly*	
FEB 18-20/26 - *MT*	Elks Club	Comedy with music, The Tailor Made Man cast of 70 including: Robert Hume, C.R. Matthews, F. Teague, P. Sangster, C.E. Hiscocks, George Frost, Natalie Bletcher, Ruth Holman, Molly Walton, Kathleen Gordon, John Vaselenak, G. Parsons, R.S. Rannard, Eleanor Lindsay (Feb 19/7) - *relished by audience*	

DATE/PLACE	GROUP/DIRECTOR(S)	PRODUCTION/CAST/REFERENCES
OCT 21-23/26 - *MT*	Gyro Club/George Brown's Palace Theatre Orchestra	Gyro Cheerio Revue: cast of 100 including: F. Teague, Eleanor Fleming, Katherine MacKenzie, Camille Connor, Minnie Thrall, Georgina Reardon, Anna & Lucille Barber, Ruth Matson, Margaret Flinn, A.W. Raworth, Haze Moore, Lyn Fairbairn, Helen Wright, Dixie Daniel, Hilda and Betty Church, Marguerite Hill, [A.W. Shackleford & P. Sangster (female impersonators)] Sketch, The Woman Intervenes: E.B. & E.G. Sterndale Bennett, Bill Russell, Fred Rose (Oct 16/10; 22/7) - *presented remarkably well to a meagre crowd on opening night*
JAN 24-26/27 - *MT*	Elks Club/C.H. Lewis of Chicago	Comic Opera, Foxy Quiller by Reginald De Koven: E. Lindsay, G. Parsons, B.B. Martin, Isobel Teague, Hugh McIlvena, R.S. Rannard, Molly Watson, A. Raworth, Al Walton, Cleve Ross, G. Frost, R.M. Hume; Chas. A. Thomas, Marguerite Matthews, Margaret Mulvahil & chorus (Jan 22/10; 25/10) - *first night's hesitation but entertaining performance*
MAY 17/27 - *Moose Hall*	St. Mary's Vestry/S. Harrison	Drama-Comedy, A Poor Married Man: Ida Leigh, Luck Moore, Nellie Ward, Mrs. W.G. Ward, W.A. Taylor, S. Harrison [replaced Fred Ingram], A. Darlington, Rev. W.T.H. Cripps (May 14/12; 18/12) - *thoroughly enjoyed by audience; stage settings loaned by Playgoers' Club*
FEB 20/28 - *St. Basil's Ch.*	Coalhurst Drama Society	Deacon Dubs (Feb 18/12)
NOV 25,26/29 - *MT*	Rotary Club	**1.** Minstrel Show, Vaudeville & Concert: Norris Stoltze, "Pat" Patterson, Bob Lawrence, Chapman Brothers, Tom Smith, [Alice Murdock & Lola Strand (dance routine)] **2.** Playlet with E.B. & E.G. Sterndale Bennett, D. A. Struther (Nov 13/8; 21/11; 26/7) - *Rotary show returns after lapse of some years; captivates capacity audience; chorus was particularly good*
DEC 15,16/30 - *St. Augustine's Hall*	St. Augustine's Men's Society/E.G. Sterndale Bennett [mus dir]	Minstrel Show; Percy Gaynor, Bob Lawrence, A. Rudd, E.A. Sharman [Interlocutor], "Martha" Robin & Chorus (Dec 15/7; 16/10) - *evening of hilarious good fellowship*
FEB 27/31 - *Wesley Hall*	Wesley Black Raven Tuxis Square/Harvey Greenway [dir]/Mrs. Layton [mus dir]/Fred Nuttal [props]/Clancy Davidson [stage mgr]/F.W. Wilkins [bus mgr]/A. McAlpine [sets]	Minstrel Show, Gentlemen Be Seated: Bill Davidson [Interlocutor], Ted Bryans, Joe Saunder, Allan Moore, Dick Shillington and chorus Skit, Hello There: Eugene Forster, Wilfred Melvin Skit, Long Distance: Cleve Hill, Bill Delf, Stewart Fulton, David Menzie, Jean Reagh, Margaret Dunham (Feb 28/6)
MAR 2,3/31 - *St. Basil's*	Knights of St. Michael & St. Theresa	3 Act Farce, Go Slow Mary (Mar 2/7)
APR 9/31 - *St. Augustine's*	United Church Hustlers (auspices of St. Augustine's Tuxis Square)	Minstrel Show, A Night in Darky Town (Apr 9/7) - *well received on previous performances*
APR 24/31 - *St. Andrew's Ch.*	St. Andrew's Church Choir	Operetta, Miss Polly's Patchwork Quilt: Mesdames T. McGregor, C. Hogg, F. Morris, Webster, Park; Misses: Mary Webster, Harriette Lindsay, Jean Forbes, Florence Hill, Mary Garrett, Lillian Reid, Elizabeth Crowe, Helen Blackbourne; Messrs. W. Cowan, J. Bannerman, E. Sinclair, J. Carpenter, G. & W. Milne, F. Shippobotham, T. Lawrence, W. Park (Apr 21/7; 25/9) - *very pleasant & entertaining program*
MAR 10-12/32 - *First United Ch.*	First United Church Hustlers	Minstrel Show (Mar 7/7)
DEC 4,5/33 - *MT*	Lethbridge Rotary Club/Robert Barrowman/Francis "Morse" Stevenson conducting Henderson's Orchestra; Assisting Artists: Hungarian Dancers, A. Murray [violin], Miss J. Scott [monologue], Mrs. J. Smith [vaudeville sketch]	**1.** Minstrel Show, E.E. Eisenhauer [Interlocutor], Bill Armstrong, Bob Lawrence, George Lomas, R. St. Armour, Karl Rasmussen, Charles Daniel, Lynn Gibb, Byron Tanner, Ben Martin, Tom Smith **2.** Skit, Wagon Lits - Mrs. E.L. Connor, A.W. Shackleford, P.M. De Jourdan, George Bohner, Louis Gaetz, G.E.A. Rice (Dec 5/7) - *fun flows fast and free*
MAR 27/34 - *LDS Hall*	LDS - MIA Drama Club/Mrs. Arthur N. Green; Assisting Artists: Audrey Leonard & Warren Russell	3 Act Comedy-Drama, Happy Go Lucky: Lorena Jones, Mae Heninger, Cora Green, B.C. Poulson, Bill Sykes, Clifford Peterson, Tom Green (Mar 28/9) - *proved delightful entertainment*
APR 12/34 - *St. Augustine's*	St. Augustine's Men's Club/Percy Morris/K.A. Maclure [mus dir]; E.V. Rose [unit dir]	Minstrel Show: H.W. Church [Interlocutor], Charles Dawson, P. Morris, Ted Lawrence, Howard Bambrick, Jack Westbrook, Jack Dawson, G. Chiswick, G.W. O'Meara, Norman Ritchie, Norman Fox, G. White, Bill Raby, Gordon Hales & chorus (Apr 13/11) - *good singing & clean snappy jokes*

DATE/PLACE	GROUP/DIRECTOR(S)	PRODUCTION/CAST/REFERENCES
NOV 26,27/34 - *MT*	Lethbridge Rotary Club/Francis Stevenson [mus dir]/Harry Hutchcroft [prod mgr]/George Brown [orch leader] assisted by the Bernadette Fisher & the Mrs. F. Humby School of Dance; Eric Eisenhauer [m.c.]	Rotary Sunshine Revue, <u>Racy Daze</u>: Bob Lawrence, Percy Morris, Charles Dawson, Byron Tanner, Janet McIlvena, Lola Strand, Ross Robinson, Lou McGuire, Katherine Stevenson, Jean Gibson, Beth Scott, Marjorie Raby, Harvey Greenway, Harry Baalim, Max Hoffman, Dorothy Frier, Ronald Hick, Josephine Hughes, Lawrence Edwards, Alex Johnston, Bruce Anderson, George Lakie, Frank Pratt, Jim Wood, Ted Faunch, George Parson, Bernadette Fisher, Dorothy Craddock & others (Nov 27/6) - *snappiest ever*
JAN 21/35 - *MT* (auspices of Playgoers)	Lethbridge Playgoers present: Cardston Players Playgoers of Lethbridge Stirling Drama Society/Solon E. Low - Medicine Hat/J. M. Gilmour -	Evening of One Act Plays, <u>The Conflict</u>: Mildred Stutz, Winnifred Newton, Le Maughan Burton, Beth Burt <u>Good Theatre</u>: <u>The Dregs</u>: Theodora Brandley Nelson, E.R. Paulsen, Jessie Ellen Low, S. E. Low <u>The Tangled Web</u>: Peter McQueen, Emmeline Conrad, M.L. Moore, Mrs. R.B. Davidson (Jan 4/8; 19/7; 22/7) - *well contrasted bill pleases audience* [Assist. Artist: George Brown's Orchestra]
FEB 13,14/35 - *Knox Ch.*	Knox United Church Ladies; Assisting Artists: Sunday School Orchestra/George Brown	3 Act Comedy, <u>Fickle Fortune</u>: Mrs. Farstad, Mrs. F.N. Hewer, Mrs. R.C. Niven, Mrs. Thornhill, Mae Barrowman, Mrs. Dawson, Mrs. Wallace, Mrs. John MacIntosh, Mrs. John Brodie, Mrs. Cruikshank, Mrs. Summerfeld, Miss McGiffen (Feb 14/11) - *please audience*
MAR 30/35 - *LDS Auditorium*	LDS-MIA/Mrs. George Laycock Lethbridge Ward Taber Ward/Ernest Bennion, (m.c.) Assisting Artists: MIA Orchestra/George Laycock	Musical and Theatrical Program: Operetta, <u>Where There's a Will</u> One Act Play, <u>Teapot on the Rock</u> (Apr 2/7) - *marked by success*
JUL 22-24/35 - *Exhibition Grandstand*	Lethbridge Exhibition Board assisted by Bernadette Fisher School of Dance directed by Eildon Brander, Lethbridge Legion Band under David Scott	Golden Jubilee Pageant, <u>Fort Whoop-Up Days</u> directed by Frank Hemingway of Toronto: Helen Lewis, Eric Johnson, Alice Thresher, Stafford Peat, A. Graham, G.W.G. O'Meara, C.P. Lambert, Irene Tanner & others (July 23/7) - *lavishly staged before about 5000 people*
MAR 5,6/36 - *MT*	Lethbridge Rotary Club/Rhyddid Williams [mus dir]/Katherine Brown [accomp]/Harry Hutchcroft [prod mgr] Assisted by the three dance schools, (Alice Murdock/Lola Strand) (Bernadette Fisher/Eildon Brander) & (Mrs. P. Humby)	2nd Sunshine Revue, <u>Grand Slam</u>: Chris Hansen [m.c.], Marjorie & Harvey Greenway, Byron Tanner, Jean Gibson, Charles Daniel, Elvina Wright, Ben Martin, Beth Scott, George Brown, Aurline Tanner, Verna Russell, Howard Bambrick, Ted Lawrence, Archie Watson, Ted Faunch, Edna Pizzey, J.R. Bailey, Eveline Meech, Norma Raney, Bernice Rose, Ruth Meads, Bea & Charlie Dawson, chorus & dancers (Feb 26/7; Mar 3/9; 4/9; 6/6) - *pleasing entertainment delights crowded theatre*
APR /36 - *Southminster (Sm Ch.)*	Southminster Players/Agnes Davidson	Religious Play, <u>The Conqueror</u>
APR /37 - *Sm Ch.*	Southminster Players/Agnes Davidson	Religious Play, <u>The Alabaster Box</u>
APR 22,23/37 - *MT*	YMCA/Ralph Johnson/George Etherington [orch]/Tom Ferguson [stage mgr]/J.M. Samson & Reg T. Rose [prods]/H. Frey & W. Royer [lights]/Hilda Church & Mrs. K. E. MacDonald [makeup]/C. Humphries, M. Hoffman, T. Middleton, S. Peat, Bob Brander [crew]	Spring Variety Show, <u>Eight Bells</u>: George Brown, Jr., William Stott, Kay Frey, Roberta Needs, Crin Evans, Minnie Thrall, Harold S. Baker, Leo Singer & others (Apr 14/7; 16/14; 23/7; 27/7) - *cast of 65 makes hit*
MAR 10,11/38 - *MT*	Lethbridge YMCA/Ralph Johnson [mus dir]/George Etherington [orch leader]/Tom Ferguson [stage mgr]/Hector Frey & W. Royer [lighting]/William Murray & Reg Rose [prods]/Playgoers [make-up]/Jean Campbell & Allan Cullen [accomps]	<u>Eight Bells of 1938</u>: George Swedish, Elva Easterbrook, George Castles, Larry Rogers, Doug Williams, Jim Johnson, Minnie Thrall, Carlisle Peck, W. Pineau, Jean Gibson & others (Mar 5/7; 11/6) - *cast of 254 with 12 piece concert orchestra - scores hit*
APR 24/38 - *Sm Ch.*	Southminster Players/Agnes Davidson	Religious Play, <u>For He Had Great Possessions</u> by Dorothy Clark Wilson: Mrs. C. Jackson, Margaret Davidson, Effie Reid, Miss G. Roberts, E. Faunch, R. Bailey, S. Vallance, Billy Jackson (Apr 11/7)
JUN 3/38 - *Arena*	Rotary Club/Reg Rose & Max Hoffman/George Etherington [leader, Lethbridge Concert Orchestra]/Lola Strand & Mrs. Yuell [chors]	<u>Sunset Revue</u> [and Jitney Dance]: 280 participants including Slovak Choir of St. Peter's & St. Paul's Church, Hungarian Girls' Club, YMCA Leaders Corps, School groups, 20th Field Battery (Jun 1/9; 2/7; 4/13) - *enthusiastic reception by crowd of 2500*
FEB 27/39 - *MT*	MIA Drama Club of LDS Church/Maydell Palmer (presented in conjuction with Playgoers)	<u>Romance is a Racket</u>: Ila Green, Carol Stead, Dora Walburger, Mabel Johansen, Harold Harris, Tom Green, Wayne Matkin (Feb 28/6)

DATE/PLACE	GROUP/DIRECTOR(S)	PRODUCTION/CAST/REFERENCES
APR 2/39 - Sm Ch. APR 9 - Claresholm United Ch.	Southminster Players/Agnes Davidson	Sacred Drama, Simon the Leper: Blakely Pritchard, Sydney Vallance, J.R. Bailey, E.J. Faunch, Mrs. C. Jackson, Effie Reid, Margaret Davidson, Gwyneth Roberts (Apr 6/6) - impressive drama
FEB 28,29; MAR 1/40 - LDS Ch.	LDS Little Theatre Group/Maydell C. Palmer assisted by Josie Knowlton/Caroline Pitcher & Anne Green [costumes]/Ila Green [make-up]/Verena Ur-senbach [music]/George W. Green [props]	3 Act Biblical Play, A Man's House by John Drinkwater: L.B. Knowlton, George Green, Owen Steed, Kay Llewellyn, Mabel Johansen, Gerald Snow, Elmo Fletcher, Fred Smith, Melvin Sherwood, Forest Sherwood, Leo Spackman, Helen Merrill (Feb 28/7; Mar 4/6) - beautifully presented
DEC 26/40 - MT	IODE assisted by Playgoers; Central School students under direction of Agnes Davidson also presented the operetta Pirate King	Boxing Day Concert including The Happy Journey by Thornton Wilder, dir. by Maybelle Bryans: Minnie Thrall, George Frayne, Margaret Davidson, Robert Armstrong, Barbara Baalim, Alden Green (Dec 17/10; 21/11; 27/8)
FEB 9/41 - Sm Ch.	Southminster Players/Agnes Davidson accompanied by singers Gladys and Annie Pizzey with W.M. Mawer at the organ	Religious Drama, The King's Son by Dorothy Clarke Wilson: J.R. Bailey, Lawrie Fisher, Margaret Davidson, Jimmie Linn, Betty Cull, Dora Mileson (Feb 10/8) - extremely well presented
APR 6/41 - Capitol (Cap)	Medicine Hat Concert Party, Melody Maids/Robert Bullen (auspices of Kiwanis Club in aid of War Service Fund)	Patriotic Concert & Musical Revue (Mar 29/7; Apr 5/7; 7/6) - one of finest performance heard here in a long time
MAR 8/42 - Sm Ch.	Southminster Drama Group/Agnes David-son; Assisting Artists: LAC A. White, George Brown, Jr., Mrs. C. Geiger and Mrs. J. Thomson	Religious Drama, A Good Soldier: Sydney Vallance, J.R. Bailey, E.J. Faunch, Robert Ranson, Effie Reid (Mar 9/8) - fine dramatic worship service
MAR 15/42 - LDS Ch.	LDS Drama Society/Jessie R. Ursenbach	Sacred Pageant written by Jessie R. Ursenbach to commemorate the centennial of the National Women's Relief Society (Mar 11/8; 14/9)
APR 12/42 - Sm Ch.	Southminster Drama Society/Agnes David-son	Biblical Drama, Magda (Apr 11/11)
APR 16-18/42 - MT	YMCA War Services Committee assisted by Playgoers of Lethbridge & other local performers with participants from Air Force schools at Pearce, Macleod, Claresholm & Lethbridge/Produced by P.O. Ronald Morton & A. G. Clarke/Orchestra dir. by George Brown/Ernest McFarland [m.c.]	War Time Spring Revue: One Act Farce, Goodnight Please dir. by Maybelle Bryans: LAC George Fay, George Frayne, Dora Mileson, Lena Connor, Sgt. Ratcliff, Jim Worthington, Margaret Brenton Various acts & musical numbers: Sgt. H.A. Bradley, LAC J.A. Phelphs, AC2 D. Prior, LAC M. MacKenzie, LAC D.J. Sinden, Cpl. Chas. Homer, Cpl. Norman Chapman, PO. Jack Parkinson, Margaret Le Brink, Mrs. Jack Bryans, Miss M. Davies, Miss W. Long, Miss M. Buchanan, Miss G. Cameron, Miss G. Baalim, Miss N. Rice, Flt. Sgt. Salt, Sgt. McLean (RCMP), Sgt. Ross, Hilda Morgan, FO. T. Knight, Ivy Pink, Marion Tuff, George Brown, Jr., Betty Cull, Mary Needs, Mavis Moffatt & the following members of RCAF Women's Division No. 7SFTS (#7 Service Flying Training School) Macleod: D.L. Reed, M.L. Wiley, L.L. Holmes, M.E. Corder, J.H. Thibedeau, M. Yuill, G.M. Thomas, D.M. Smithson, M.A. Brett, D. Timberlake, R.M. Schwindt, V.M. Lafoy, M.E. Robinson, E.M. Holmes, G.I. Pybus (Apr 6/8; 11/5,8; 16/6; 17/6) - delights
MAY 7,8/43 - New LDS Auditorium	MIA Drama Club of LDS Church/Marian Bradley, Irene Elton [mus dir]/Hilda Rus-sell, M. Moskovich, G. Henderson, George Brown [musicians]	Two Act Operetta, Erminie by Jacobowski: Aurline Tanner, Tom Green, B.W. Stringham, Milton Strong, Ila Green, Marjorie Steele, Colleen Peterson, Anne Tanner, Ruel Gilchrist, Walter Webster, Milton Hansen, Clifford Peterson, Hugh Laycock, William Fawns, Dehlin Bennett & chorus (May 8/7; 10/8) - charming presentation
JAN 21/44 - LDS Auditorium	MIA Drama Group/Arline Gilchrist, with assisting artists: Byron Palmer [piano], Miss N. Newby [piano], Alberta Nielsen [vocal]; Delbert Palmer [m.c.]	Evening of One Act Plays, When Shakespeare's Ladies Meet directed by Hazel Hyde & Marie Johnson: June Larsen, Lila Le Baron, Irene Rowley, DaNaze Spencer, Arline Gilchrist The First Dressed Suit directed by Allan Fowler: Owen Asplund; Gwen Storie, Georgia Lou Green, Reed Zemp Dark Wind directed by Milton Hansen - Marian Brandley, De Veda Reagh, Jean Nelson, Clifford Peterson, Jr. (Jan 25/6) - presented with sustained dramatic interest; unusually good acting
MAR 28; APR 7,8 et.al./44 - #8 B & G LDS Auditorium Various Southern Alta. communities	#8 Bombing & Gunnery School assisted by Dixie Botterill [piano], Cliff Palmer [violin] & his Kinsmen Orchestra (auspices of Lethbridge Kinsmen Club) in aid of milk for Br. Fund; Jim MacDonald [m.c.]	Victory Revue: L.A.W. Leone Marshall [vocal] Jean Gauld's dancers, Helen McKenzie [piano], Elsie Persson [violin], LAC Bernie Bray [harmonica], Dixie Botterill [piano], Sgt. George Claxton [vocal], Sgt. John Blair [vocal], Ft. Sgt. Jim MacDonald [vocal], LAC "Moe" Feinstein [saxaphone] (Mar 21/7; 29/8; Apr 4/6; 5/7) - scores hit
JUN 12,13/44 - LDS Auditorium	LDS/Milton Strong/Maydell Palmer [narrator]/Colleen Peterson & Irene Harris [accomps]/12 piece orchestra	Concertized version of Opera, Martha: chorus of 50 voices (Jun 13/6) - delights audience
JAN 26,27/45 - LDS Auditorium	MIA of Lethbridge LDS Church/Maydell Palmer	Shubert Alley [all girl cast] (Jan 30/6,9)

DATE/PLACE	GROUP/DIRECTOR(S)	PRODUCTION/CAST/REFERENCES
APR 19,21/45 - *LDS Auditorium; Numerous engagements in various southern Alberta communities*	YMCA/Ken Howard/Clifford Palmer [orchestra leader & violinist] with Walter Hay [piano], LAC "Moe" Feinstein [sax & clarinet], Eddie Burton [drums], Stan Warren [trombone], Bill Nelson [trumpet], Walter Hay [accomp]	<u>Springtime Revue</u>: Joyce Smith, LAC Victor Klassen, LAC Gil Preston, Bryce Spencer, Henry Vogt, DaNaze Spencer, & Jean Gauld dancers: Jean Robinson, Helen McLeod, Doreen Johnson, Betty Demers, Ivy Knibbs (Apr 18/7; 19/7; 20/6) - *delightful stage show*
MAY 2-4/46 - *YMCA*	YMCA So-Ed Club/Mrs. Percy Cull & Mr. Morton Brown [mus dirs]/Accompanying Artists: Leo Banks "Canada's Boy Wonder"	<u>Minstrel Show</u>: George Brown, Jr., Elva Easterbrook, Gwen Daniels, Pearl Routh, Muriel Gentleman, Morton Brown [Interlocutor], William Burrows, William Murdock, & chorus, Ballroom Dance Club/Joyce Bateman Hill (May 1/7; 3/6; 6/7)
FEB 21/47 - *LDS Auditorium*	Taber MIA	3 Act Play, <u>It Shall Keep Thee</u> (Feb 20/70)
MAR 24/47 - *YMCA*	YMCA Little Theatre Group/Maybelle Bryans, P.H. Henson, Kaye Horsman	One Act Plays: <u>Permanent</u> by James Reach: Betty McKay, Marjorie Rannard, Margaret McColl, Joyce Thomkins, Kay Ervine, Wilma Wismer, Helen Robbins <u>Dust of the Road</u> by Kenneth S. Goodman: Ab Chervinski, Lois Cunning, George Patey, Norma Fisher <u>Sugar & Spice</u> by Florence & Colin Clements: Yvonne Turner, Jack Craine, Janet Davies, Vicky Sendesky, Walter Aherns (Mar 25/6) - *convincingly presented*
APR 25/47 - *LDS Auditorium*	Lethbridge MIA/Ila Green	Unidentified One Act Comedy: Mrs. T. Pratt, Jack Regher, Frank Johansen, Renee Newby, Geraldine and Malcolm Asplund (Apr 28/8)
MAY 8,10/47 - *YMCA* JUN 13 - *Raymond*	So-Ed Club/Bill Cross [prod.]/Remo Baceda [mus dir]/Lois Dannatt [accomp] with the Joyce Hill School of Dance	<u>Minstrel Show</u> written by Ab Chervinski: Walter Lewis [Interlocutor], Jean Robinson, George Patey, Toni Biron, Pat Tompkins, Dixie Perry, Fred Leitch, Marvin Qually, Yvonne Turner, Davey Howell, Davy Davidson, Janet Davies, Muriel Gentleman, Lois, Cunning, Vicki Sendesky (May 8/7, 9/6; 10/7) - *makes big hit - a great show*
MAY 15/47 - *Barnwell*	Lethbridge Stake MIA/Mrs. A.E. Palmer	<u>The Hickory Stick</u>: Viola Johansen, Audrey Leonard, Alice Zemp, Allan Fowler, Kenneth Anderson, Reed Zemp, Roy Riley, Don Steele, Wanda Beaumont, Jackie Newby, Ernest Pankhurst, Leah Pankhurst, Jack Regher, Jerry Brown (May 15/5)
DEC 15/47 - *YMCA*	YMCA Little Theatre Group/P.H. Henson, Kay Horsman, Margaret Rodinyak/Bob Reed [lighting]/E. Aubert [set]/Eloise Olson [make-up]	<u>Christmas Carol</u>: Ab Chervinski, Bill Rasmussen, Mike Skaronski, Ed Aubert, Ed Swailes, Erma Bikman, Beth Orosz, Rita Malbert, Vicki Sendesky, Pat Dimock, George Patey, Val Toronto, Bob Blount, Al MacDonald, Sharon Howe, Ken MacDonald, Ray Whittick, Morven Gentleman, Lydia Turbirz, Rita Bertiotti, Edna Nelson, Frances MacDonald, Valerie Hoefer, Betty Smerek, Ernie Lourme, Joyce Hansen, Joe Kunigiskis, Marguerite Cook <u>Christmas at Home</u>: Helen Robbins, Edward Swailes, Dorothy Kulpas, Yvonne Turner, Muriel Gentleman, Bill Rasmussen, Bob Blount (Nov 22/7; Dec 15/7; 16/8)
MAR 22,23/48 - *YMCA*	YMCA Little Theatre/Yvonne Turner, Mr. Crawford, Mary Rodinyak; Accompanying Artists: Jackie Boyle & Frances Cullen [vocals], Frances Sainsbury [piano]	Comedy, <u>The Bride</u> by Gertrude Jennings: Muriel Gentleman, Pearl Routh, Esther Hill, Helen Miron, Beth Orosz <u>Airman's Forty-Eight</u>: Bill Rasmussen, Helen Robbins, Dick Cottingham, Vickey Sendesky, Ann Strick, Ed Aubert <u>The Valiant</u> by Holloway Hall: Ab Chervinski, Ted Turnbull, Rita Malvert, Ed Swailes, Curly Kettler, Bill Rasmussen (Mar 16/8; 23/8)
APR 1/48 - *LDS Auditorium*	LDS Little Theatre/Eleanor Matkin	<u>What Doth it Profit</u> by Nathan & Ruth Hale: Donnene Merrill, John Campbell, Wayne Anderson, Arlene Green, Nora Bullock, Carol Steed, Don Steele, Joyce Johansen, Fred Smith, John Gibbons, R. Riley (Apr 1/9) - *play of early Mormon pioneer life*
MAY 12,13/48 - *Cap*	YMCA So-Ed Club/Bill Cross [prod]/Bob Reed [lights]/Ted Fairies & Ed Aubert [sets]/Maude Crawford & Betty Culler [costumes]/Irma Bikman [makeup]	Minstrel Show written by Bill Rasmussen & Ab Chervinski - Remo Baceda, Boyd Anderson, Jackie Boyle, Ted Turnbull [Interlocutor], Dick Cottingham, Fred Leitch, Laverne Cunning, Toni Biron, Pat Tomkins, Gwen & Lloyd Daniels, David Howell & chorus (May 8/6; 13/7) - *pleases large audience*
OCT 4,5/48 - *Cap*	Lethbridge Lion's Club/Dorothy Griffith of Fort Worth, Texas	Mock Radio Stage Show, <u>Fun For You</u>: Remo Baceda & others (Sept 28/6; Oct 1/7; 5/7)
DEC 13/48 - *YMCA*	YMCA Little Theatre Group/Yvonne Turner, P.H. Henson, Margaret Rodinyak; Accompanying Artists: Carol Singers/Mrs. P. Cull	Comedy, <u>Guest House, Very Exclusive</u> by Reby Edmond: Dorothy Kulpas, Dale Boddard, Greig Farstad, Lynn Anderson, Morven Gentleman, Keith De Armond, Lydia Turbirz, Helen May White, Vicky Sendesky, Bob Blount <u>Christmas Carol</u>: Ab Chervinski, Bill Rasmussen, Paul Deschamps, Ed Aubert & others (Dec 9/7; 10/6; 11/6; 13/6; 14/7) - *impress audience*

DATE/PLACE	GROUP/DIRECTOR(S)	PRODUCTION/CAST/REFERENCES
FEB 14,15/49 - *YMCA (Preliminary elimination for Provincial Regional Festival*	YMCA Little Theatre Group/Maybelle Bryans, P.H. Henson, Helen Robbins	The Happy Journey: Lydia Turbirz, Ed Aubert, Lorraine Lewis, John Cashore, Glenda Gentleman The Black Sheep: Yvonne Turner, Bob Edwards The Gallant Lady: Vicky Sendesky, Helen May White, Paul Deschamps, Keith De Armond (Feb 15/7) - *local talent shows up well*
APR 22,23/49 - *LDS Auditorium*	MIA Drama Group/Julia Asplund & Ila Green/Hazel Wooley [costumes and props]/Collette Green [make-up]/Junior McCue [lighting]/A.D. Palmer, L. Heppler, W.F. Le Baron [sets]	3 Act Comedy, Ever Since Eve by Florence Ryerson & Colin Clementas: Mary Stringham, Ron Peterson, Milton Hansen, Ted Knowlton, Geraldine Asplund, Joan Storie, Verlin Jarvis, Tom Pratt, Stan Van Orman, Arlene Green, Royden Shurtz, Rulon Peterson, Junior McCue, George Fletcher, Frank Johansen (Apr 26/8) - *smartly staged*
MAY 30,31/49 - *Cap*	YMCA, So-Ed Club/Bill Rasmussen assisted by Alex Harper/Joe Montgomery [prod]/Effie Reid & Lois Donnat [mus dirs]/Phyl Trca [chor]/Bob Reed [lighting]/Syd Holberton [set]/Jackie Boyle & Frances Sainsbury [casting]	Variety Show, The Gay Nineties Show written by Ab Chervinski: Bill Rasmussen, Jackie Boyle, Ed Firth, Arthur Woitte, Maureen Kirby, Anne Tompkins, Del McCorkle, Don Jackson, Phyl Gow, Bert Stretton, Bill Murphy, Rod Stafford & chorus (May 27/2,8; 28/5,9; 31/2,9) - *delights capacity audience*
DEC 3/49 - *LDS Auditorium*	LDS 1st Ward MIA/Dr. Wayne Matkin	Operetta, Belle of Barcelona: Ron Watmough, Eloise Olson, DeCon Pitcher, Mrs. John Mitchell & chorus of 25 (Nov 30/8)
DEC 19/49 - *YMCA*	YMCA Little Theatre Group/Miss Vye Ulasovetz, Mr. Henson/Vicky Sendesky/Bob Reed [lights]	The Boor by Anton Chekov: Paul Bourret, Peter Stewart, Violet Ulasovetz; Dust on the Road by Kenneth Sawyer Goodman: Ab Chervinski, Victoria Sendesky, Lydia Turirz, P.H. Henson (Dec 9/8; 16/9; 20/6) - *receive enthusiastic reception*
FEB 9,10/50 - *Cap*	Rotary Club/R.S. "Bob" Lawrence Assisting Artists: Lithuanian Folk Dancing Group/Vladas Zankaitis; Rotary Girls' Chorus/Mrs. P. Cull; YMCA Theatre Group/P.H. Henson; soloists - George Brown, Jr., & Frances Cullen; Accompanists: Nell Lawrence & Mrs. George Brown, Sr.	Rotary Minstrel Show of 1950: Bill Dawson [Interlocutor], R.S. Lawrence, Harry Stewart, C.W. Farstad, Charles Daniel, Frank Calder, R.C. Tennant [end men], G.O. Gowlland, T.J. O'Grady, George Gillis, D.S. O'Connell, E.A. Lawrence, O. Williams & chorus (Feb 10/7) - *revived after many years; a lot of fun*
MAY 1,2/50 - *Cap*	YMCA So-Ed Club/Joe Montgomery/Effie Reid [mus dir]	Musical Revue, Chinook Tales: Bill Rasmussen, Ed Firth, Don Jackson, Arthur Woitte, Lloyd Daniel, Jean Miers, Sadie Dykes, Phyl Trca [dancer] (Apr 28/12; May 2/15) - *fourth annual musical show produced by the So-Ed Club*
NOV 22,23/50 - *Sm Ch. Youth Centre*	Southminster Choir/A.K. Putland & Southminster Teenage Players/Agnes Davidson/piano accompaniment provided by Joan Rylands	Gilbert & Sullivan Operetta, Trial By Jury: H.M. [Bert] Turner, Effie Reid, Jim Cousins, V.M. [Buck] Rogers, E.J. Faunch & other members of Southminster Church Choir (Nov 16/8; 23/8) - *scores hit, well cast and expertly staged* Comedy, House Guest by Helen Miller
FEB 7-9/51 - *Cap*	Rotary Club/"Bob" Lawrence/George Brown and Orchestra	Rotary Minstrels: Dennis O'Connell, Charles Daniels, Harry Hargrave [Interlocutor] & other Rotary members (Jan 30/2; Feb 8/7; 10/7) - *proves enjoyable to 2700 patrons*
MAR 29-31; APR 1/51 *LDS Auditorium*	Lethbridge Stake MIA of the LDS Church/Wayne Matkin	The Vigil by Ladislas Fodor: Irene Harris, Wes Orr, B. Wayne Matkin, Ron Watmough, Cliff Peterson, Ernest Jensen, Jack Stevens, Willard Anderson, Ross Munroe, Reg Peters, Vivian Griffin, Ray Williams, Howard Fletcher, Octave W. Ursenbach, Ida Clark, Allan Fowler, Ernest Poulson, Della Paxman, Calvin Johnson, Joyce Peters, Eleanor Matkin, Decon Pitcher (Apr 2/51/5) - *an outstanding stage presentation; ably staged*
MAY 3,4/51 - *Sm Ch. Youth Centre*	Southminster Men's Club	Musical variety show, Going Places: Reg Bailey, Bill Murdock, Cleve Hill, Mrs. George McKillop, Vic Rogers, Dianne Lyon, Jerry Martin, Pat Garrett, Ralph Erdman, Betty Dalton, & others (May 3/6; 5/7) - *sprightly production*
MAY 7-12/51 - *Civic Center (Recreation Week)*	Lethbridge Recreation Department/R. Robinson, Harry Baalim, Phillip Godsell, Adam [Ab] Chervinski, Lefty Eshpelter, Jim Brook, Melva Smith, George Talbot, Freddi Morris	Historical Musical Revue pageants, Indian Era; Gay Nineties; The Roaring Twenties, Atomic Era, Circus Extravaganza (Feb 21/6; May 8/7; 9/6; 10/7; 11/6,7 12/6) - *thrill large crowds*
MAY 21/51 - *LDS Auditorium*	Raymond Operatic Group/W.C. Stone	Naughty Marietta: Nora Stone, Frank Clawson and chorus (May 22/5) - *skillfully done*
DEC 4,5/51 - *St Andrews Ch.*	William Tell Club Mrs. E.G. Sinclair, Mrs. T.M. Allen	One Act Plays 1. Thursdays At Home 2. She Was Only a Farmer's Daughter (Dec 3/7)

DATE/PLACE	GROUP/DIRECTOR(S)	PRODUCTION/CAST/REFERENCES
FEB 6,7/52 - *Sm Ch. Hall*	Southminster Choir/A.K. Putland/Tom Ferguson [sets]	Comic Opera, <u>My Lady Jennifer</u>: E.J. Faunch, Betty Martindale, Yvonne Turner, Effie Reid, Jim Cousins, V.M. Rodgers, G. Linc Coward, H.M. Turner, O. Williams, Mary Thomson, Ed Firth, William Rasmussen, Doris Lewis, A. Woitte, E. Stouffer (Feb 7/7) - *receives fine reception*
FEB 13,14/52 - *Cap*	Rotary Club/R.S. "Bob" Lawrence Assisting Artists: Bette & Al Dickson [dancers], Ron Ronenburg [magician, Medicine Hat], George Brown & Orchestra	<u>Rotary Musical Revue & Variety Show</u>: Chuck Daniel, Terry Justice, George Gillis, Bob Lawrence, Dennis O'Connell, Doreen Justice, Harry Hargrave, John Thompson, Ralph Tennant, Duke Simpson, Stan Peszat, Con Miller & others (Feb 14/6) - *enjoyed by capacity house*
MAR 17,18/52 - *Civic Center*	Produced by Maybelle Bryans with Harry Baalim [stage mgr] & Hazel Long [make-up] **1.** LDS Players/B. Wayne Matkin **2.** Playgoers/Hugh Buchanan **3.** Coaldale Players/Murray Robison	Evening of one act plays sponsored by Playgoers **1.** <u>Grandma Pulls the Strings</u> by E.B. Delano & D. Card: Mary Deeb, William Gibb, Da Veda Reagh, Pamela Russell, Evelyn Burr, Irene Francis **2.** <u>Fumed Oak</u> **3.** <u>Eldorado</u> by Bernard Gilbert - D. Baldwin, Yvonne Robison, Charles Bryant, Ivy Manuel (Mar 18/7) - *a good bit of well contrasted comedies*
MAR /52 - *LDS Auditorium*	Lethbridge and East Lethbridge Stake LDS Church/Wayne Matkin, Mrs. A.W. Stringham, Mrs. Robert Reagh	<u>Road Show Festival</u>: 8 twenty minute original musical comedy acts (Mar 1/8) - *marked by success*
APR 4,5/52 - *St. Andrew's Ch.*	St. Andrew's Choir/Mrs. L.A. Wylie/Janet McLeod [mus dir]/Mrs. A. Stafford [make-up]	Operetta, <u>Miss Polly's Patchwork Quilt</u> (Apr 4/7) - *pleases large crowd*
DEC 5,6/52 - *LDS Auditorium*	MIA/Wayne Matkin/E.E. Reithman [sets]/Nora Bullock [costumes]	<u>Comedy of Errors</u>: A. Delbert Palmer, Howard Fletcher, Lemaun Webster, John Campbell, Lowell Olsen, Glen Russell, Dennis Price, Byron Palmer, Eldon Edwards, Ron Watmough, Reg Peters, La Veda Sherwood, Carol Steed, Afton Van Orman, Joyce Peters, Ruby Pierson, Betty Asplund (Dec 1/10; 5/9; 6/10,21) - *full house was pleased*
FEB 4,5/53 - *Sm Ch.*	Southminster Church Choir/A.K. Putland [mus dir]/Buck Rodgers [stage dir]	Three Act Musical Comedy, <u>The Fountain of Youth</u>: Effie Reid, E.J. Faunch, G.L. Coward, Lois MacEachern, W.J. Cousins, V.M. Rodgers, W. Rasmussen, H.M. Turner, Anne Campbell, Mac Evanoff, Jean Robinson & chorus (Jan 24/9; 31/8; Feb 5/9; 6/10) - *good sized audience; highly enjoyable*
APR 27,28; MAY 7/53 - *Civic Centre* JUN 10 - *(Claresholm)*	Lethbridge Recreation Department/Hardy Diemert/Lefty Eshpeter [prod]/Hazel Cook & Ian Pollock [piano accomp]	**1.** <u>Junior Minstrel Show</u>: Reg Arnold [Interlocutor] Betty Asplund, Glenda Moore, Joanne White, Delano Luciani, Frances Gow, Vivian Dong, Karen Dunn **2.** <u>Senior Minstrel Show</u>: Charles Virtue [Interlocutor], Don Slade, Don MacLean [end men], Walter Jordan, Ella Findlay, Art Hunt, Dawn Bowers, Howard Richie, Vaughn Hembroff and chorus (Feb 23/10; Apr 27/10; 28/9; May 6/3; 8/14) - *two shows in one*
OCT 8,9/53 - *Civic Centre*	United Church men from 10 city and district congregations	8 Act Pageant, <u>Triumphs of Faith</u> [The United Church of Canada from its earliest foundation until the present] (Oct 6/10; 7/13; 8/9,10; 9/14) - *witnessed by 1300*
DEC 9/53 - *LDS Auditorium*	Stirling Drama Society/Elodia Christensen	3 Act Play, <u>Snow White and The Seven Dwarfs</u> (Dec 8/3,10)
JAN 29/54 - *Cap*	Howard Richie with Barbara Simpson, Jewel Smith/Lefty Eshpeter [prod-dir]	<u>One Man Show</u>: dancing, pantomime, magic (Jan 28/3; 29/9; 30/9) - *scores in stage debut*
FEB 10,11/54 - *Cap*	Lethbridge Rotary Club/R.S. "Bob" Lawrence/Tom Ferguson [stage mgr]/Harold Clark [props]/George Brown & Orchestra	Variety Show, <u>Rotary Roundup</u> [vaudeville & western show]: Mary Miller, George Brown, William Harvie, Bob Lawrence, Harry Hargrave, "Chuck" Daniels, Dennis O'Connell, George Gowlland, Jr., Arthur Haig, Doreen Justice, Wuotila Sisters (Feb 10/13; 11/10; 12/10) - *rousing entertainment*
NOV 24,25/54 - *Sm Ch. Hall*	Southminster Choir/A.K. Putland/V.M. "Buck Rodgers [stage mgr]/Katherine Brown [accomp]/W. Royer & Bob Reed [lights]	<u>H.M.S. Pinafore</u> by Gilbert & Sullivan: Effie Reid, Jim Cousins, Anne Campbell, L. Wright, Mary Thomson, E. [Ted] Faunch, Buck Rodgers, A.V. Walker & others (Nov 23/9; 24/9; 25/9) - *standing room only; audience kept entertained throughout*
DEC 4/54 - *LDS Auditorium*	Lethbridge MIA/Ila Green assisted by Lillian Snow, Nellie Harker, Carol Steed, Thomas Green, Myrna Davies, Ethel Randreth, Bessie Pratt, Fred Reagh, Carl Sommerfeldt, Eugene Wasserman	Melodrama, <u>Craig's Wife</u> (Nov 10/10; 12/3; 25/9; 27/9; 29/2)- *well presented*
MAR 16,17/55 - *Cap*	Rotary Club/R.S. "Bob" Lawrence, Dennis O'Connell	<u>Minstrel Show</u>: Delores O'Connell; Barbershop Quartet/"Buck" Rodgers (Mar 16/9; 17/3,9; 18/9)
SEPT 6-8/55 - *Exhibition Grandstand*	Lethbridge Jubilee Committee/Dean Goodman/Wayne Matkin [mus supervisor]/Bob Reed [lights]/Doug Card [sound]	Pageant, <u>Saga of a Prairie Town</u> by Harry Baalim, [Lethbridge history in review] (Sept 7/9; 8/9; 9/9; 13/9) - *small crowds, cast of over 300*

DATE/PLACE	GROUP/DIRECTOR(S)	PRODUCTION/CAST/REFERENCES
MAR 24/56 - *Wilson Jr. H.S.*	Southminster United Church & Playgoers of Lethbridge present an evening of festival plays/Mary Waters; Kaye Watson & Elsie Biddell; Phyl Ellerbeck, Bill Lazaruk	The Happy Journey; Bathsheba of Saaremaa; Jane Wogan; Cajun (Mar 26/10) - *provide good entertainment*
JUL 31/56 - *Civic Centre*	Chinook Theatre Guild/Elsie Biddell	Children's Theatre Productions 1. The Elves and the Shoemaker: Audrey Baines, Marilyn Simon, Elsie Biddell, Vi Brandley, Ann Leggett, Phyl & Paddy Ellerbeck, Sharon Boyle, Karen Sneddon, Kaye Watson, Leslie Hunt, Alfred Pratte, Kirstie & Morvin Gentleman, Mary Leigh, Leslee Watson 2. Playlet, Widget: Kirstie Gentleman, Leslee Watson, Leslie Hunt, Kaye Watson (Jul 28/10; Aug 1/14) - *successful debut of Lethbridge's first Children's Theatre Group*
MAR 13/57 - *Moose Hall*	Lethbridge Branch of the Rehabilitation Society of Alberta	One Act Comedy, The Mrs. Savage directed by Margaret O'Neil with Mrs. A. Ashmead, Betty Gol, Claire Allen, Mrs. M. Powell, Mrs. E. Jardine and Lillian Scott
MAR 19/57 - *Civic Centre* APR 1-3/57 - *Taber*	Chinook Theatre Guild Evening of One Act Plays: Regional One Act Festival Entries/1. Bessie McCully/2. Elsie Biddell/3. Elsie Biddell; Stan McCrea [scenery]; Fred Weiler [lights]	1. The Duchess Says Her Prayers: Don Eccleston, Jean Ede, Donna Bishop 2. Riders To The Sea: Phyl Lilly, Yvonne Kennedy, Marilyn Simons 3. The Boor: Fred Vervoort, Jean Block, Guy Vervoort (Mar 12/10; 20/10) - *The Boor stole the show*
APR 6/57 - *LCI*	Medicine Hat Civic Theatre/Harry Allergoth (auspices of Playgoers)	Stalag 17 (Apr 8/10) - *a brilliant success*
FEB 16/58 - *LDS Auditorium*	Lethbridge Stake MIA/and The Choralaires/Wayne Matkin	Pageant, Preludes to Eternity by Eva R. Ellison (Feb 19/16) - *depicted the various ages & development of moral life*
DEC 16/58 - *YMCA*	YMCA Members	Nativity Play, Unto Us a Child is Born (Dec 17/20)
MAY 8/59 - *Cap*	Medicine Hat Civic Theatre	Diary of Anne Frank (Apr 28/3; May 1/9; 7/14; 8/13; 9/12) ($1.00 - $2.00) - *it was a triumph*
FEB 24/61 - *LDS Auditorium*	Lethbridge Stake MIA/Marie Smith	All My Sons: Stewart Hatch, Theodore Nelson, Lorin Mendenhall, Viola Brandley, Bill Ericksen, Bill Thompson, Georgie Fooks, Harold Tanner, Marilyn Bagshaw, Gordon Milne (Feb 8/14; 23/10; 27/10) - *difficult task, well done*
OCT 26-30/61 - *LDS Auditorium*	Lethbridge Stake MIA/Eleanor Matkin, Marie Smith, Grant Erickson	Musical Historical Play, Promised Valley: Hugh Allred, Gwen Legge, Thomas Green, Nellie Harker, Carl Young, Anthony Blake, Clinton Pierson, Alexander Allison and cast of 100 singers & dancers (Oct 21/14; 24/10)
MAR 25; APR 1/62 - *McKillop Un. Ch., Sm Un. Ch.*	McKillop United Church Players/Joy Pritchard	Christ in the Concrete City by P.W. Turner: Gwen Bell, Kay Horvath, John Dutton, Fred Pritchard, Bill Matheson, Sandy McCallum (Mar 26/9) - *powerful & dramatic*
JUL 29-30/63 - *LDS Stake Center*	Lethbridge Stake MIA	5 One Act Road Shows (Jul 31/18) - *well received*
MAR 28/64 - *Civic Centre*	Calgary Workshop 14	The Robe with Gordon Ross, Beven Patterson (Mar 12/12; 26/17; 30/13) - *cast of 22 - plays to small audience of 150*
DEC 3/64 - *Civic Center*	SPEBQSA Production/V.M. "Buck" Rodgers director & quartet bass with Earl Colpitts (tenor), Max Baines (lead), Bert Stretton (baritone)	Minstrel Show & Harmony Night: Fred Pritchard [Interlocutor], Bill Matheson, Bud Iverson, Cliff Black, Bruce Branston [end men] (Dec 1/10; 7/10) - *loudly applauded*
MAR 22,23/67 - *Yates*	Salvation Army presents The Bridge Players/Gordon Lowe	The Robe: Don Hagen, Lynn Lowe Brent Robertson, Helen Barnaby, Ted Dawson, Ed Sloboda, John Heynan, Major C. Smith, Erica Robertson, Margaret Just, Dale Benningfield & others (Mar 21/12; 23/12) - *scenery & costumes were highlights*
APR 14/67 - *Yates*	Home & School Association of Christian Immanuel School	Talent night with one act play, The Bishop's Candlesticks: Harry Earkes (Apr 4/10; 12/15)
MAY 20/67 - *Yates*	Medicine Hat Centennial Committee/Dorothy Jones/David Peterkin [mus dir]	Original musical comedy, Medicine Hat by Jack McCreath: Don Jackson, Ann Lonson, Lois Dongworth, Eva Weiller, John Dunlop (Mar 16/3; 23/10) - *show has spirit but played to 200 only*
DEC 22,23/67 - *Yates*	The Choralaires/Wayne Matkin (accompanied by orchestra & guest soloists)	Christmas Opera, Amahl & the Night Visitor: Don Hagen, Jim Cousins, Edwin Palmer, Dawn Higgins, Sherri McNair, Jim Moyer, Gwen (Legge) Dell, Courtney Loose & others (Dec 18/12; 23/14) - *refreshing statement on the meaning of Christmas*
JAN 21/68 - *McKillop Ch.*	McKillop Players	One Act Play, It Should Happen to a Dog by Wolf Mankiewicz: Bill Matheson, Fred Pritchard (Jan 19/10) - *aim is to provoke discussion on man's contemporary condition*

DATE/PLACE	GROUP/DIRECTOR(S)	PRODUCTION/CAST/REFERENCES 356
APR 17-22/68 - *Yates*	Western Canada Arts Festival - White Rock Players Club/Franklin Johnson Coaldale Little Theatre/Murray Robison Regina Little Theatre/Margaret Woodward Edmonton All Saint's Friendship Guild	Drama Festival [non-competitive] Adjudicator: Firman Brown [University of Montana] <u>Barefoot in the Park</u> - *incomplete characterization and slow* <u>Playboy of the Western World</u> - *smooth performance* <u>Lo and Behold</u> -*fairly bland presentation* <u>The Hollow Crown</u> (Apr 18/12; 19/12)
DEC 20,21/68 - *Yates*	The Choralaires/Wayne Matkin	Christmas Opera, <u>Amahl & the Night Visitors</u>: soloists: Gwen Dell, James Moyer, Don Hagen, Jim Cousins, Edwin Palmer, Courtney Loose, Dawn Higgins, Sherri McNair (Dec 6/3; 20/14; 21/21) - *free admission*
MAR 13/69 - *Yates*	Lethbridge Musical Theatre/Dick Mells	<u>Bus Stop</u>: Don Runquist, Cliff Black, Mark Lowrie, Ellyn Ford, Melanie Harker, Laverne Ankers, Al Greenway, Ed Bayly (Mar 19/7; 14/14) - *well worth seeing*
MAR 15/69 - *Yates*	Western Canada Arts Festival Grande Prairie Little Theatre Playgoers of Lethbridge Jean McIntyre (Edmonton)	One Act Plays and Dramatic Readings: <u>The Bespoke Overcoat</u> <u>Red Peppers</u> Dramatic Readings (Mar 17/12) - *well planned evening*
DEC 19,20/69 - *Yates*	Allied Arts Council (AAC) presents a Malcolm MacDonald production/Malcolm Gimse [set design], Joan Waterfield [drama coach]	One Act Opera: <u>Sister Angelica</u> by Puccini: Donna MacDonald, Mary Thomson, Evelyn Mills, Sheila Pisko, Mary Martin, Ruth Strate, Jean Boon, Sandi Balcovske, Lynne O'Brien, Donna Coulter (Oct 17/14; 22/18; 25/14; Dec 16/8; 17/18; 19/16) - *more rehearsal needed*
MAR 23,24/70 - *Yates*	Lethbridge LDS Church MIA/Georgia Fooks	Musical Comedy, <u>Blue Ribbon Affair</u> (Mar 24/12) - *100 participants*
NOV 13/71 - *Bowman*	Lethbridge Youth Theatre & Mini Theatre/Joan Waterfield	**1.** <u>Hullabaloo</u>; **2.** <u>The Princess & The Woodcutter</u>; **3.** <u>Five Chinese Brothers</u> (Oct 20/12)
MAY 7/72 - *St. Andrew's Ch.*	Folk Rock Musical	<u>Natural High</u> (May 6/2)
MAY 27/72 - *Yates*	Salvation Army presents the Calgary Inter-denominational Production	Musical Play, <u>Hosea</u> (May 24/17; 27/15) - *cast & crew of 70*
MAY, JUN /72 - *Various Lethbridge schools*	Sunshine Players (Lethbridge Opps. for Youth Project)	Plays written, directed & acted by the group: Doug Smith, Sandra Balcovske, Lois Dongworth, Kirk Jensen, Bob Bainborough & Patricia Parks (May 27/15)
JULY 6,7/72 - *Bowman*	Shoestring Players (Lethbridge Youth Theatre)/Joan Waterfield	**1.** <u>Hullabaloo</u>; **2.** <u>The Five Chinese Brothers</u>; **3.** <u>The Magic Echo</u> (Jun 15/17; 7/15)
JUL 26,27/72 - *Bowman*	Shoestring Players and Sunshine Players	Children's Theatre - **1.** <u>How Big is a Foot</u>; **2.** <u>The Lion That Lost Its Roar</u>; **3.** <u>The Man Who Stole Laughter</u> (Jul 25/9; 27/13; 28/13,14)
MAY 9/73 - *Yates*	LDS, MIA/Georgia Fooks	<u>Pirates of Penzance</u>: Ian Mandin, Doug Castleton, Kathleen Thompson, Courtney Loose, Betty Sorenson, Dick Humphries (May 11/17) - *entertained an appreciative capacity audience*
MAY 21,22/73 - *Yates (Playgoers 50th Anniversary)*	Jolliffe Academy of Dance/Muriel Jolliffe in conjunction with Playgoers' <u>Black Comedy</u>	Comedy Ballet, <u>Pineapple Poll</u> (May 16/18; 22/14) - *took itself too seriously* (Lynne Van Luven)
MAY 23/73 - *Yates (Playgoers 50th)*	Coaldale High School/Frank Featherstone	An Evening of One Act Plays - **1.** <u>For Love of a House</u>; **2.** <u>Nero Fiddles</u>; **3.** <u>The Unseen</u>; **4.** <u>Fanny of Funny Brook Farm</u> (May 24/13)
MAY 25/73 - *Yates (Playgoers 50th)*	Lethbridge Youth Theatre/Joan Waterfield with Youth directors: Laurin Mann, David Mann, Jim Veenstra, Annette Green	Theatre for Children (May 18/11) - *special guest Frank Featherstone as Dame Alice*
JUN /73 - *Lakeview Sch.*	Sunshine Players (a Lethbridge opportunity for Youth Project)	**1.** <u>The Treatment</u>; **2.** <u>The Cantina</u> David Mann, Bob Bainborough, Sandi Balcovske, Scott Dobbie, Jain Kurany, David Diamond, Jane Wilson, James Rae (Jun 14/22)
JUL 26/73 - *Bowman Arts*	Lethbridge Youth Theatre & The Sunshine Players	Three plays for children (Jul 25/21)
JUL /73 - *Leth. & District Communities*	Sunshine Players/Sandi Balcovske & Bob Bainborough (both plays designed by Scott Dobbie)	**1.** <u>A Message From Cougar</u>: David Mann, Bob Bainborough, Jain Kurany **2.** <u>Six Cold Cans and a Coffee</u>: David Diamond, James Rae, Jain Kurany, Jane Wilson (Jun 14/22; Jul 4/22) - *Canada's Secretary of State, Hugh Falkner, will be in attendance*
JUL 16-21/73 - *Youtharama Bldg.*	Young Street Coffee House	Talent show (Jul 19/13) - *at the Exhibition Grounds*

DATE/PLACE	GROUP/DIRECTOR(S)	PRODUCTION/CAST/REFERENCES
JUL 16-21/73 - *Local Playgrounds*	Pocket Lane Players (Calgary)	Children's theatre production & puppet workshops (Jul 21/18)
AUG 10/73 - *Civic Centre*	Lethbridge Summer Youth Festival including new theatre group New Dawn	Children's theatre presentation (Aug 7/11)
SEPT 3,4/73 - *Leth. Correctional Inst., Yates*	Firehouse Theatre (Grande Prairie) [sponsored by Lethbridge Kiwanis Club]	Original one act plays (Aug 31/14) - *Opportunities for Youth Project*
SEPT 30/73 - *Norbridge Comm. Ch.*	Hillcrest Evangelical Church (Medicine Hat)	60 minute drama on the rapture of the saints (Sept 29/10)
MAY 15,16; 22-23; 30-31; JUN 7,14,15/74 - *Holiday Inn*	Dick Mells presents The Inn Crowd	Musical Farce, Canterbury Tales based on writings by Chaucer: Sheila Pisko, Ray Mercer, Sheri McFadden, David Mann, Jim McHugh, A. Azzara, Linda Johnson, Kirk Jensen (May 16/6; 24/6)
MAY 28-JUN 1/74 - *Yates*	LDS/Georgia Fooks/Grant Erickson [mus dir]	Musical Drama, The Promised Valley by Crawford Gates: Kathleen Thompson, Nelson Maxfield, Ian Mandin, Thomas Green, Helen Hartley & cast of 40 (May 17/7; 24/7; 25/8; 27/14; 29/14) - *several moving moments*
AUG 15,16/74 - *Public Library Th.*	AAC presents Bowman Centre Summer Drama class & Lethbridge Youth Theatre	Children's Theatre & dance drama - **1.** The Seven Silly Wisemen; **2.** Unnamed short play; **3.** Dance of Death (dance drama) (Aug 10/15; 14/14)
MAR 17/75 - *Public Library Th.*	AA Council and Lethbridge Public Library present Ken Feit	A Fool & His Vision [clowning, mime, puppetry, music ritual making, story telling, sound poetry] (Mar 15/17; 19/13) - *seeks to show wonder, mystery of life*
MAR 22/75 - *Library*	Ken Roberts (children's librarian) presents local children	acrobatics, card tricks, etc. (Mar 25/30) - *entertainment at its best*
APR 22/75 - *Stan Siwik Pool*	Lethbridge Synchronized Swim Club instructed by Linda Stephens, Jackie Hall, Val Patterson, Penny O'Brien	Water show, Themes From the Movies: Judy Wren, Melanie Ellis & others (Apr 17/10; 23/13) - *played to 400*
APR 26/75 - *Library*	LDS Players (3rd ward)	Winnie the Pooh (Apr 5/6)
MAY 21-24/75 - *Yates*	LDS East Stake/Betty Sorenson/Grant Erickson [mus dir]	HMS Pinafore, Carla Young, Courtney Loose, Bill Erickson, Ken Hicken & others (May 9, L&TV Week/11; 22/16) ($2.00 - $2.50) - *no three cheers and one cheer more here (Lynn Van Luven)*
AUG 20-23/75 - *Public Library*	Allied Arts Council presents a Dick Mells production	Of Mice & Men by John Steinbeck: A. Azzara, David Mann, Dick Mells, Sheri McFadden, Jack Warburton, Al Greenway, Greg Martin, Randy Rae, Dave Cunningham, Kirk Jensen (Aug 21/16) - *an experience in fine drama*
NOV 1/75 - *Yates*	Salvation Army presents Calgary Glenmore Temple Musicians	Musical drama, Jesus Folk by John Larsson & John Gowan (Oct 25/22; Oct 31 L&TV Week/15) ($2.00) - *written by two English Salvation Army officers*
NOV 29/75 - *Public Library*	Gerry Bell (Edmonton)	One woman children's show Charlotte of Charlotte's Web (Dec 1/16)
MAR 11,12/76 - *Stan Siwik Pool*	Lethbridge Synchronized Swim Club directed by Lydia Stevens, Penny O'Brien, Ursula Kasting with Melanie Ellis	Water Show (Mar 10/39) - *cast of 40*
JUN 8-13/76 - *420 - 6 St. So.*	Dick Mells Production	Dinner Theatre, South Pacific [at Sherlock's Den]
JULY /76 - *Leth. Exhibition*	Children's Theatre production/Bryan Frances	The Clam Made a Face/Doug McMullen, David Mann, Ivan Morgado, Anne Goodall, Lou Ludwig (Jul 22/17) - *delightful*
APR 27-30/77 - *Yates*	Top Twenty Production/Dick Mells	Musical Review, Bye, Bye Elsie High (featuring highlights from the Broadway musical, Grease) Mike Day, Mark Campbell, Mark Russell, Greg Martin (Apr 18/8; 28/12) - ($2.50) - *disappointing evening (Richard Epp)*
MAY 3-6/77 - *Yates*	Paterson Community School/Ione Dergousoff, Lea Blaquiere, Don Hagen/Dawn Davis & Blanch Rother [chors]/Gwen West & Joyce Felner [chorus dirs]/Melody Hagen [set design]/Nora Hawn [costumes]/Kirk Ramsay [orch dir]	Musical Comedy, The Music Man by Meredith Wilson: Jack Hunter, Lea Blaquiere & others (Apr 29/12; Mar 4/14) - *was a winner (J. Waterfield)*
JUN 2,3/77 - *Stan Siwik Pool*	Lethbridge Synchronized Swim Club	20 Swim Routines, Music Through the Years/with Melanie Andres, Toby Lees, Kim Creighton, Barb Costanzo, Brenda Olesky, Sandra Filuk, Barb Wilson & Diane Yucytus (Jun 3/10)
AUG 25,27,31; SEPT 2/77 - *Yates*	AAC presents a Dick Mells production/Jean-Pierre Fournier [sword fight dir]	Romeo & Juliet/Michael Hoyt, Deb Grey, Mike Day, Phil Kunst, Dick Mells, Laurin Mann, Joan Waterfield, Greg Martin, Kelly Fiddick, Albert Azzara, Al Greenway, Karen Kay, David Mann, Michael Nowlin, Mark Russell, Wes Stefan, Les Smolnicky (Jul 20/16; Aug 23/18)

DATE/PLACE	GROUP/DIRECTOR(S)	PRODUCTION/CAST/REFERENCES
DEC 9/77 - *Leth. Library*	Lethbridge Public Library/Joan Waterfield	One Act Play, <u>Lemonade</u> by James Prideaux with Winnifred Smith & Kate Connolly (Dec 9/37)
MAR 17/78 - *Public Library*	Lethbridge Shoestring Theatre presents Playgoers of Lethbridge/Cathy Evins	<u>The Rehearsal</u> by Mike Rogers (Mar 13/18)
JUL 27-30; AUG 3-6; 10-13/78 - *Catholic Central H.S. Drama Centre*	Stage 3/Peter Mueller [art dir]/Hugh Spencer [prod designer]/Larry Erdos & Pat Slemko [mus dirs]	<u>Spoon River Anthology</u> by Edgar Lee Masters/Larry Erdos, Michael Melling, Shelley Irvine, Pat Slemko, Les Smolnicky, Janice Tilley (Jul 13/10; 28/18) - *a success*
FEB 24/79 - *Yates*	Kintown Players/Doug Hinds and Jim Hamilton	<u>Thursday's Child Has Far to Go</u> by Doug Hinds/Doug Hinds, Ron Christensen, Jim Hamilton, Jack Warburton, Lin McRae (Feb 26/5) - *Everything was right (Arthur McDougall)*
MAR 24/79 - *Public Library*	Raymond McCleary and Ken Roberts (Lethbridge)	Magic show for youngsters & adults (Mar 23/11)
APR 6,7/79 - *Stan Siwik Pool*	Lethbridge Synchronized Swim Club	Two acts & numbers based on musical, <u>Grease</u> (Apr 5/11)
JUL 25/79 - *Yates*	Community Services Drama Mobile Co. dir. by Shelley Irvine	Family Western, <u>Simon Pure Sam</u> (Jul 21/8)
AUG 1-4/79 - *CCHS Drama Centre, 3rd Ave. & 18th St. So.*	Stage Three dir by Larry Erdos with 5 Lethbridge student actors	One Act Plays: **1.**<u>Line of Enquiry</u> by Brian Tyson; **2.** <u>Companion Piece</u> by Brian Tyson (Jul 28/22) - *both plays were 2nd prize winners in Alberta Adult One Act Play writing competition*
FEB 29/80 - *Public Library*	Shoestring Theatre/Jane McCoy	A Tribute to Love, <u>Amor, Amas, Amat</u> poetry, music & an excerpt from <u>The Importance of Being Ernest</u> (Feb 16/A6)
MAR 20/80 - *CFCN T.V.*	CFCN Production (locally produced, starring local performers)	<u>The Day Belongs to Me</u> (30 minutes of action, comedy, romance) (Mar 19/D6)
APR 18/80 - *Public Library*	Shoestring Theatre produced & directed by Jane McCoy and Joan Waterfield	<u>A Celebration of Spring</u> (poetry prose & music) William Latta, Cherie Baunton, Elizabeth Hall (Apr 21/B7) - *so deep & so touching (Arthur McDougall)*
APR 30-MAY 3/80 - *Yates*	Cardston Community Theatre/Terry Petrie	Musical, <u>The Sound of Music</u> (Apr 26/B10)
MAY 1/80 - *Public Library*	Shoestring Theatre presents the LCI Student Players/Michael Nowlin	<u>No Exit</u> by Sartre (Apr 26/B10)
MAY 15/80 - *Public Library*	Shoestring Theatre presents High School Drama Societies	Recent High School festival productions: **1.** <u>Krapp's Last Tape</u> by Samuel Beckett **2.** <u>Loveliest Afternoon of the Year</u> by John Guare (Mar 16/A5) - *stage presence riveting (A. McDougall)*
MAY 30; JUN 1/80 - *PLib; Yates*	The Young Generation Singers (St. Andrew's Presbyterian Church)/Martin James	Musical, <u>I'm Here, God's Here, Now We Can Start</u> (May 30/B2)
JUN 14/80 - *Public Library*	Dawn McCaugherty, Ray McCleary, Tom Ripley, Derek Scott & Pat Doyle	Revue of stories, mime & magic, <u>Fruit Salad</u> [(Jun 7/C8) Waterfield's Column)]
AUG 6-9; 13-16/80 - *Drama Centre (333 - 18 St. So.*	Stage 3/Larry Erdos & Brian Solberg	<u>One Night Stand</u> by Carol Bolt: Deb Waterfield, Larry Erdos and Christine Kenwood (Jul 29/B3; Aug 7/A7) - *impressive work (A. McDougall)*
AUG 16-22; 24-30/80 - *Indian Battle Park*	Historama Society of Lethbridge/Peter Mueller/Ken Hicken [mus dir]/Ed Bayly [tech dir]	Historical Pageant, <u>Who We Were</u> by Paddy Campbell: Jeremy Davis, Keith Harris, Tweela Houtekamer, Shelley Irvine, Ray Martens, Jane Paterson, John Tyreman, (Apr 16/A9; 18/A6) - *suffers from flawed script (A. McDougall)* [in commemoration of Alberta's 75th Anniversary]
JAN 23/81 - *Public Library*	Lethbridge Senior Citizen's Organization/Mary Heinitz (auspices of Lethbridge Shoestring Theatre)	<u>Joint Owners in Spain</u>: Mary Skelton, Mary Heinitz, Ethel Underdall, Mildred Byrne (Jan 21/B3)
JAN 29/81 - *Public Library*	Lethbridge Shoestring Theatre production	<u>A Joy Forever</u>: An evening of prose, poetry & music with Ken Roberts, David Spinks, Joan Waterfield, Martin James (Jan 24/B11)
FEB 17-21/81 - *R.I. Baker Sch.* MAR 27,28/82 - *Yates*	A Neil Boyden production dir by Fran Rude/Brian Parkinson [designer], Murray Robison [props]	<u>How the Other Half Loves</u> by Alan Ayckbourn/Ed Bayly, Bob & Cherie Baunton, Frank Featherstone, Kate Connolly, Jane McCoy (Feb 6/B4; 18/B6) - *well done - most enjoyable (Arthur McDougall)*
APR 13/81 - *Public Library*	Shoestring Theatre presents Lethbridge Community College Speech Arts Department/Yvonne Holm (auspices AAC & Lethbridge Library)	Readers' Theatre, <u>Canadian Seasons</u> (Apr 13/C13)

DATE/PLACE	GROUP/DIRECTOR(S)	PRODUCTION/CAST/REFERENCES
AUG 4/81 - *Public Library*	Shoestring Theatre presents Lethbridge Sr. Citizens/Mary Heinitz	<u>Save Me a Place at Forest Lawn</u>: M. Heinitz and Mildred Byrne (Aug 1/B11)
AUG 8/81 - *U of L*	Alberta Summer Games presents	Theatre Sports (Aug 1/B11; 10/B1)
DEC 11/81 - *Public Library*	Shoestring Theatre presents Playgoers of Lethbridge/Pat Hammond	<u>Optimism</u> by John Patrick (Dec 8/A1)
APR 16,17/82 - *U of L Th.*	Psycle Theatre/Larry Erdos	<u>How to Beat a Computer While Stoned on Acid</u> by Larry Erdos: Larry Erdos (Apr 17/C11) - *Innovative play becomes tedious (Peter Mueller)*
JUL 30/82 - *Leth. Theatre Gallery*	Shoestring Theatre/Arthur McDougall	<u>Counting the Ways</u> by Edward Albee; <u>Endgame</u> by Samuel Beckett Judy Ann McCarthy, Tim Nowlin, Ron Christensen, Rae Ann Sparks, Michael Nowlin, Raymond McCleary (Jul 30/B7) - *a most exciting & challenging evening (Sara Stanley)*
AUG 21/82 - *PLib*	Shoestring Theatre/Deb Waterfield	Improvised production, <u>Hanging In</u> (Aug 21/B10)
AUG 26,28/82 - *Yates*	Lethbridge County Opera/Ted Wilson/Mike Richey [mus dir]; Allan Bevins [vocal dir]; Richard Coombs [vocal coach]	<u>Madame Butterfly</u> [shortened version]: Janice Ohno, Kazue Nagasawa, Mardene Francis, Peggy Evans, Grace Mathis, Michael Kaufman (Jul 27/B2; Aug 27/B2) - *appreciative audience of 350*
DEC 29-31/82 - *New Hope Christian Centre*	New Hope Christian Centre	<u>King of Kings</u> by John Syratt [local pastor]: Rudy Zalesak, David Erdman (Dec 29/A11)
MAY 24/83 - *Yates*	Chinook Christian Academy of New Hope Christian Centre	Young People's Musical, <u>What's the Difference</u> (Mar 19/A12)
NOV 25-27/83 - *4101 - 2 Ave. S.*	New Hope Christian Centre	Musical Drama, <u>King of Kings</u>
DEC 6/83 - *Public Library*	Brown Bag Theatre presents Lethbridge Sr. Citizens' Organization/Mary Heinitz	Concert of Songs & Skits (Dec 2/83/TV Week/10)
JAN 24/84 - *Sportsplex*	Gyro Club	3rd Annual Variety Show [Clowns, acrobats, magicians] (Jan 26/A13) - *usually held in conjunction with Fall circus*
APR 20-21/84 - *NHCC*	New Hope Christian Centre	Musical, <u>Is It True</u> written by Christian Centre members/Deb Crossland, Henry Klok & others
AUG 3O-31/84 - *2710 College Dr.*	College Drive Community Church	A Music Drama Production <u>Dreamer</u> (Aug 30/A10)
OCT 20,21/84 - *Leth. Centre Mall & NHCC*	New Hope Christian Centre	Dance, drama and mime production, <u>Toymaker & Son</u> (Oct 17/C4)
AUG 17/85 - *NHCC*	The Acting Faith Drama Co.	Christian Dinner Theatre (Aug 13/A3)
JAN 24/87 - *4H Bldg. Exhibition Grounds*	Gyro Club	Variety Show (Jan 26/A5)
APR 4/87 - *U of L Exp. Th.*	U of L Students/Lynn Hunter Johnston with original music by Wendy Grant Wolfe	<u>Tyrne</u> by Lynn Hunter-Johnston: Roger Hamm, Clark Wilson, Linda Jacquot, Samantha Archibald, Wendy Grant Wolfe, Mari-Jane Getkate, Don Lomas (Apr 6/A9) - *different but enjoyable*
APR 12/87 - *U of L*	Joan Waterfield & Ed Bayly accompanied by Lethbridge Symphony Wind Quintet playing original music by Stewart Grant	<u>A Band of Storytellers</u> Folk tales from around the world (Apr 3/B8; 13/A9) - *delicious fare*
MAY 22-23/87 - *Lethbridge East Stake Centre*	MIA of LDS Church/Rita Peterson	<u>The Mousetrap</u> by Agatha Christie/Sherry Van Buskirk, Jon Kelly, Brent Hamilton (May 22/B6)
AUG 12-16/87 - *NHCC*	Acting Faith Drama Co.	multimedia presentation, <u>Oh Canada</u>/Chris Davidson, Ian Byrd, Ruth Ballinger, Danielle Smith, Cindy Weiss, Dale Greeno (Aug 13/C6) - *moral and spiritual future of Canada is topic*
MAR 30-APR/2/89 - *El Rancho Motor Inn*	Back Door Theatre Workshop/Mark Russell/Roger Schultz [set design]	Dinner Theatre: One Act Plays by James McClure 1. <u>Laundry and Bourbon</u> with Narda McCarroll, Lorraine McFadden Bellikka, Neana Meeks 2. <u>Lone Star</u> with Mark Russell, Roman Pfob, Jerry Bellikka (Mar 15/89; 31/C6) - *promising start for BDT Workshop (Dave Mabell)*

Playgoers of Lethbridge
Lethbridge Productions (April 9, 1923–December 31, 1989)

DATE/LOCATION	PRODUCTION/ TECHNICAL PERSONNEL	DIRECTOR/CAST/REFERENCE(S)/COMMENTS
APR 9,10/23 - *Majestic*	Musical Going Up by Otto Harbash and James Montgomery; A. McAlpin, E. Hicks, Capt. Palmer, Louise A. Hirsch, P. Sangster, J. & R. Wellington/C.J. Ferguson [mus dir]/H. Church [chor]	E.G. Sterndale Bennett/Hilda Church, Chris Gibson, E.C. Guilbault, Minnie Hazell, Eric Ings, G. Roy Keivill, Avril Little, A.H.L. Mellor, G.W. Parsons, A.C. Raworth, Louise (Louie) Ritchie, Fred Rose (Apr 10/10) - *Playgoers' Club strikes very high standard*
JUN 5/23 - *St. Augustine's Hall*	Little Theatre Evening **1.** Thursday Evening **2.** Suppressed Desires	E.B. Sterndale Bennett Maybelle Bryans, Mary Higginbotham, George Holman, Jeanette Leech L. Ritchie, E.B. & E.G. Sterndale Bennett (Jun 6/14) - *proved a great success*
SEPT 27/23 - *St. Augustine's Hall*	Little Theatre **1.** No Questions Asked - **2.** Catesby **3.** The Man in the Stalls	E.B. Sterndale Bennett Charles Hiscocks, A. Little, P. Sangster, E.G. Sterndale Bennett, Fred G. Teague Jennie Bixby, Carl Sandquist Echo Becker, Richard Hincks, Eric Ings (Sept 28/14) - *a distinctly commendable showing*
DEC 3,4/23 - *Majestic*	Drama, Raffles by Eugene Presbery (based on stories by E.W. Horning)/A. McAlpin	E.G. Sterndale Bennett/E. Becker, C. Gibson, E. Hicks, C. Hiscocks, G.A. Holman, E. Ings, Aileen Jones, R. Keivill, Florence MacKenzie, A.C. Raworth, Blanche Roy, E.B. & E.G. Sterndale Bennett, F.G. Teague (Dec 4/4) - *very creditable performance*
FEB 6,7/24 - *St. Augustine's Hall*	Little Theatre **1.** The Twelve Pound Look by J.M. Barrie **2.** Variety Program	E.B. Sterndale Bennett Rose Pomeroy, F.M. Rose, C. Sandquist, Katherine Sick, Betty Church, Ernest & & Mrs. Layton, Janet McIlvena, Nan Thomas, Charles Whitfield (Feb 7/7; 8/15) - *a splendid attendance*
APR 24-26/24 - *Majestic*	Musical: Oh, Lady! Lady!! by Guy Bolton & D.G. Wodehouse; music by Jerome Kern/A. McAlpin, Arthur Wade, P. Sangster/Charles Whitfield [mus dir]/Maisie Vivyan & Hilda Church [chor]	E.G. Sterndale Bennett/H. Church, P.J. Collins, E. Ings, G.R. Keivill, F.M. Rose, B. Roy, Margaret Stafford, E.N. Sturrock, Isobel Teague, N. Thomas (Apr 25/7) - *a very fine & artistic performance*
OCT 1,2/24 - *St. Augustine's Hall*	Little Theatre **1.** Op 'O Me Thumb by Frederick Feen and Richard Pryce **2.** Cin 'M Buns **3.** Dawn, Dawn by Percival Wilde	E.B. Sterndale Bennett P.J. Collins, Mrs. Schweitzer, N. Thomas, Millie Wakelen, Maisie Vivyan, Isobel Teague Arthur H. Baines, Vinnie Burritt, Ethel Jones, C. Sandquist K. Mackenzie, F. Rose, E.B. and E.G. Sterndale Bennett (Oct 3/14) - *proved quite a success*
NOV 27-29/24 - *Majestic*	Musical, The Prince of Pilsen by Frank Pixley/music by Gustav Luders/A. McAlpin, P. Sangster/C.H. Whitfield [mus dir]/Maisie Vivyan & Hilda Church [chor]	E.G. Sterndale Bennett/H. Church, Fay Davies, G.A. Holman, P.M. de Jourdan, G.R. Keivill, Art McIlvena, F.M. Rose, E.N. Sturrock, F.G. Teague, N. Thomas, Minnie Thrall, Maisie Vivyan (Nov 28/11) - *scores great triumph*
MAR 13,14/25 - *St. Augustine's Hall*	Sketch (in association with YMCA Minstrel Show)	Lyn Fairbairn, R. Keivill, Bob Lawrence, F. Rose, C. Sandquist, P. Sangster, Hod Seamans (Mar 14/7)
MAR 18,19/25 - *St. Augustine's Hall*	Little Theatre **1.** When Its Spring by Phoebe Hoffman **2.** Her Country by Euphemia Van Rensselaer Wyatt **3.** Thank You Doctor by Gilbert Emery	E.B. Sterndale Bennett Ethel Jones, R. Keivill C. Gibson, Aileen Jones, F. Teague Vinnie Burritt, G.A. Holman, E. Ings, C.R. Matthews, H.C. Moore, Mary Simpson (Mar 19/7) - *cleverly rendered*
APR 17,18/25 - *Majestic*	Farce, The Whole Town's Talking by John Emerson & Anita Loos/A. McAlpin, P. Sangster	E.G. Sterndale Bennett/Ethel Brander, Natalie Bletcher, L. Fairbairn, G.A. Holman, Ethel Jones, R. Keivill, Myrtle Leech, Percy Morris, E.B. and E.G. Sterndale Bennett, N. Thomas, M. Thrall (Apr 18/12) - *splendid acting*
OCT 8/25 - *Majestic*	Little Theatre **1.** The Mayor and the Manicure - **2.** Moonshine **3.** The Ghost of Jerry Bundler -	E.B. Sterndale Bennett Robert Hume, Marguerite Matthews, A.C. Raworth, Mildred Seamans Chas. King, F.M. Rose P.J. Collins, G.A. Holman, C.R. Matthews, H.L. Seamans, E.G. Sterndale Bennett, Reverend C. Swanson, F. Teague (Oct 9/25) - *excellent program*

DATE/LOCATION	PRODUCTION/ TECHNICAL PERSONNEL	DIRECTOR/CAST/REFERENCE(S)/COMMENTS
MAY 3,4/26 - *Majestic*	Operetta, <u>HMS Pinafore</u> by William Gilbert & A. Sullivan/A. McAlpin, P. Sangster/George E. Bower [mus dir]	E.G. Sterndale Bennett/Elsie Aitken, Isabel Allen, E. Ings, Eleanor Lindsay, Robert S. Rannard, F.M. Rose, E.G. Sterndale Bennett, F.G. Teague, M. M. Thrall, J.T. Vallance & chorus (May 4/10) - *commendably played*
SEPT 29/26 - *Majestic*	Little Theatre 1.<u>The School for Scandal</u> (screen scene) by R.B. Sheridan 2.<u>Letters</u> by Florence Ryerson 3.<u>Unexpected Youth</u> by Roland Pertwee 4.<u>Action</u> by Holland Hudson	E.B. Sterndale Bennett V. Burritt, C.R. Matthews, A.C. Raworth, F. Rose, E.G. Sterndale Bennett M. Bryans, H. Church, F. Teague Kathleen Lindsay, C.R. Matthews, Dorothy Marrs, Mr. Pearson, Isa Shearer Reverend Walter Cripps, Thomas Evans, Lyn Fairbairn, W.E. Huckvale, Robert Hume, Arthur McIlvena, Fred Rose, Phil Sangster, Harriett Stoakley, E.G. Sterndale Bennett, J.E. Thompson (Sept 30/14) - *highly pleasing performance*
MAR 25,26,28/27 - *Majestic*	Drama, <u>The Green Goddess</u> by William Archer/A. McAlpin, P. Sangster, C.R. Matthews, A.I. Brander	E.G. Sterndale Bennett/Ethel Brander, P.J. Collins, P.M. de Jourdan, T.H. Fleetwood, Art McIlvena, H.C. Moore, F. Rose, E.B. & E.G. Sterndale Bennett & others (Mar 26/11) - *a real triumph*
SEPT 26/27 - *Majestic*	Little Theatre 1. <u>The Romance of the Willow Pattern</u> by Ethel Beekman Van Der Veer 2. <u>The Master Salesman</u> by William Hazlett Upson 3. <u>The Valiant</u> by Holworthy Hall & Robert Middlemass	E.B. Sterndale Bennett Cecily Baalim, Joyce Davis, Edith Gibson, Marjorie Shepherd, Muriel Sterndale Bennett (juvenile participants) L. Fairbairn, E. Ings, Georgina Reardon - Eric Lingard, M. Matthews, P. Morris, A.C. Raworth, E.G. Sterndale Bennett (Sept 27/12) - *score another triumph - splendidly enacted*
JAN 30,31/28 - *Majestic*	Musical, <u>The Toreador</u> by Arden Ross, Percy Greenbank with music by Ivan Caryll & Lionel Monckton/A. McAlpin, P. Sangster, C.R. Matthews, A.I. Brander/Percy T. Moseley [mus dir]/Hilda Church [chor] (costumes by Malabar's, Winnipeg, Toronto)	E.G. Sterndale Bennett with assistance from E.B. Sterndale Bennett & C.R. Matthews/A.C. Ahrens, Ruth Becker, J.W. Berry, H. Church, Margaret Clark, Nancy Farris, Ted Faunch, Tom Ferguson, G. N. Frost, Percy H. Gaynor, C. Hiscocks, R. Hume, D.R. Innis, K. Lindsay, H. McKenna, H.C. Moore, Norman D. Smith, Isobel Teague (Jan 31/7) - *outstanding achievement*
OCT 8/28 - *Majestic*	Little Theatre 1. <u>Growing Wings</u> by Harriet Ford - 2. <u>Jazz and Minuet</u> by Ruth Giorloff - 3. <u>The Maker of Dreams</u> by Oliphant Downs 4. <u>Uptown Woman</u> by Vina Delmar	E.B. Sterndale Bennett Myrtle Delay, David H. Elton, Ronald Hick, Ethel Jackson, Alfred Morris M. Bryans, Dixie Daniel, Gerry Gaetz, Edith Gibson, Tom Green, Helen Maynard, Yvonne Schweitzer, M. Sterndale Bennett Edith Gibson, Yvonne Schweitzer, M. Sterndale Bennett George Frost, B. Roy, E.G. Sterndale Bennett (Oct 9/14) - *appreciative audience*
FEB 11,12/29 - *Majestic*	Musical, <u>The Earl & The Girl</u> by Seymour Hicks & Ivan Caryll/A.I. Brander, C.R. Matthews, Percy Morris, William Watson/Mrs. Ethel Brander [mus dir]/Hilda Church [chor] (costumes by Malabar's)	E.G. Sterndale Bennett/J.H. Berry, S.J. Burridge, Lena Connor, D.H. Elton, G. Frost, Pearl Gaynor, R.M. Hume, Kay Jenks, A. Jones, H.C. Moore, A. Morris, Max Peters, F.M. Rose, B. Roy, J. Skeith, E.B. Sterndale Bennett, F. Teague & chorus (Feb 12/14) - *very credibly presented on the whole*
OCT 24/29 - *St. Augustine's Basement*	Little Theatre 1. <u>The Drums of Oude</u> by Austin Strong - 2. <u>Evarannie</u> by Horace Vachiel 3. <u>Little Red Shoes</u> by Harold Brighouse 4. <u>On the Park Bench</u> by Essex Dane	E.B. Sterndale Bennett T. Faunch, R. Hume, C.R. Matthews, I.J. McKinnon, C.H. Rhodes, Louie Ritchie, E.G. Sterndale Bennett T. Faunch, Mildred Seamans, Mary Sydal Eildon Brander, P.J. Collins, C.R. Matthews, Margery Round, N.D. Smith Camille Connor, Gerry Gaetz, Olive Haw, Ronald Hick, Muriel Sterndale Bennett (Oct 25/8) - *well staged & well acted*
FEB 15/30 - *Grand Theatre Calgary (no local performance)*	Alberta Drama League Festival <u>The School for Scandal</u> [screen scene]	E.G. Sterndale Bennett/A.C. Raworth, F. Rose, E.B. & E.G. Sterndale Bennett, C.R. Matthews (Feb 19/1; *C.H.*, Feb 17/15) - *appearance of Mr. Sterndale Bennett was one of the outstanding successes of the evening*
MAY 19,20/30 - *Majestic*	Comedy-Mystery, <u>Cock Robin</u> by Elmer Rice & Philip Barry/William Watson	E.G. Sterndale Bennett/E. Becker, M. Bryans, D. Doorbar, F. Duncanson, T. Ferguson, Edith Gibson, Ian Hendry, Hazel Kelly, Ted Lawrence, P. Morris, H. Poole, A.J.M. Round (May 20/7) - *delights audience*
NOV 12,13/30 - *St. Augustine's Basement*	Little Theatre 1. <u>The Eligible Mr. Bangs</u> 2. <u>The 'Ole in the Road</u> 3. <u>So's Your Old Antique</u>	E.B. Sterndale Bennett T. Ferguson, R. Hick, A. Jones, Kathleen Martin E.G. Sterndale Bennett, C. Swanson Jean Forbes, I. Hendry, H. Poole, T. Lawrence, M. Sydal (Nov 13/7) - *a pleasing performance*

DATE/LOCATION	PRODUCTION/ TECHNICAL PERSONNEL	DIRECTOR/CAST/REFERENCE(S)/COMMENTS
FEB 16/31 - *Majestic*	Little Theatre **1.** Back of the Yards by Kenneth Sawyer Goodman (1931 festival entry) **2.** Confessional by Percival Wilde - **3.** The Fourth Mrs. Phillips by Carl Glick - **4.** Red Carnations by Glen Hughes	E.B. Sterndale Bennett E.G. Sterndale Bennett, Arthur Beaumont, I. Hendry, H. Poole, T. Lawrence, M. Sydal Norman D. Smith/N. Farris, R. Hick, C.R. Matthews, Vinnie (Burritt) Martin, H. Poole, Phyllis Raworth Maybelle Bryans/Lena Connor, Edith Gibson, Marguerite Lightbound, C.R. Matthews, Reid Stoakley, M. Sydal, F. Teague N.D. Smith/T. Ferguson, K. Martin, A.J.M. Round (Feb 17/5) - *large audience...favorably impressed*
FEB 17/32 - *Majestic*	Little Theatre **1.** And So To Bed by J.B. Fagan - (1932 festival entry) **2.** Dad Meet My Girl by C.R. Matthews **3.** The Perfect Crime by C.R. Matthews **4.** Second Fiddle by E.G. Sterndale Bennett	E.B. Sterndale Bennett/Ernest J. Atherton, L. Connor, H. Church, N. Farris, C.R. Matthews, E.G. Sterndale Bennett M. Bryans/E. Becker, Laura Brown, R. Hick, S.J. Shepherd N.D. Smith/E.J. Atherton, Baxter Ridley, James Rosewarn E.B. Sterndale Bennett/N. Bletcher, I. Hendry, L. Jordan, W.D. Lowe, C.R. Matthews, P. Raworth (Feb 18/7) - *original one-act plays create great interest*
APR 20/32 - *Majestic*	Comedy, The Servant in the House by Charles Rann Kennedy/Percy Morris, Arthur Wade	James Rosewarn/Bertha Ford, C. Hiscocks, C.R. Matthews, A.C. Raworth, L. Ritchie, J. Rosewarn, F. Teague (Apr 21/7) - *effectively staged*
OCT 12/32 - *Majestic*	Little Theatre **1.** Believe It Or Not - **2.** The Goal **3.** Unarmed **4.** Novelty Interlude	E.B. Sterndale Bennett/Douglas Cameron, H. Church, Rosalind Goodman, L. & Madge Jordan, E. Vincent Rose, F. Teague, Jack Westbrook, George Young E.B. Sterndale Bennett/Camille Connor, T. Ferguson, C.R. Matthews, J.D. Pierce, A.C. Raworth, M. Sydal Percy Gaynor/F.R. Duncanson, L. Fairbairn, Cliff Mitchell, J. Rosewarn Ethel Brander, P. Gaynor, A. Jones, L. Jordan, B. Roy, E.G. Sterndale Bennett (Oct 13/6) - *pleasing variety*
DEC 16,17; 26/32 - *Majestic*	Musical, The Country Girl/Percy Morris, C.R. Matthews, Dennis Pierce, L. Jordan, Hilda Church [chor] (costumes & wigs by Malabar's, Winnipeg) (auspices of BPO Elks)	Lyn Jordan/Kathleen (Lindsay) Barnhill, William Bond, Ethel Brander, T. Ferguson, Elaine & Bernadette Fisher, Percy Gaynor, C. Gibson, Lin & Madge Jordan, Madge Lightbound, Hazel Long, D. Pierce, E.V. Rose, J. Rosewarn, B. Roy, Tom Smith, E.G. Sterndale Bennett, F. Teague, Art Westley, Jean Wilcocks (Dec 17/7) - *clever presentation*
MAR 11/33 - *Majestic*	Becky Sharpe by Olive Conway	Maybelle Bryans/Kathleen Barnhill, Douglas Cameron, C.R. Matthews, V. Martin, J. Rosewarn (Mar 11/7; 13/7)
NOV 16,17/33 - *Majestic*	3 Act Farce, A Little Bit of Fluff/Lyn Jordan [stage mgr]/George Meech [props]/A.W. Shackleford [bus mgr]/J.P. Alexander [orch]	James Rosewarn/Betty Buchanan, Susan Chiswick, T. Ferguson, Madge Jordan, Hazel Kelly, M. Lightbound, C.R. Matthews, A.C. Raworth, Frank Steele (Nov 18/6) - *replete with fun*
FEB 16,17/34 - *Majestic*	**1.** Musical Revue, Musical Pie by Lyn Jordan/L. Jordan [set design & scenic artist]/Bernadette Fisher [chor]/J.P. Alexander [orch]/Ralph Johnson [choral dir] Ralph Cooper [producer]/Mrs. E. McMillan [costumes] M. Bryans, S. Chiswick, T. Ferguson, Elaine Fisher, Madge Jordan, Mrs. Kain, Mrs. P.V. Lewis, Mrs. Ellis McMillan, Ed Richards, L. Ritchie, J. Rosewarn, B. Roy, Will Russell **2.** Road of Poplars by Vernon Sylvaine	Lyn Jordan/H. Church, L. Connor, "Brownie" & Charles Daniel, B. Fisher, Jean Gibson, L. Jordan, Audrey Rea Leonard, M. Lightbound, C.R. Matthews, Douglas McElgunn, Tom Pizzey, A.C. Raworth, B. Roy, Warren Russell, Dora Walburger, Dorothy Westley & dancers from B. Fisher School (Feb 17/7) - *pleasing variety, superb staging* M. Bryans/P.M. de Jourdan, L. Fairbairn, Louis Gaetz, L. Jordan, Andree Houlton* , J. Rosewarn, B. Roy* (*double cast) (Feb 17/7) - *a beautiful interlude*
APR 27,28/34 - *Majestic*	**1.** Mystery, The Thirteenth Chair by Bayard Veiller **2.** Variety Program (orchestra under direction of George Brown)	C.R. Matthews/H. Baalim, Arthur Beaumont, W. Bond, H. Greenway, R. Hick, Josephine Hughes, Helen James, A. Jones, Jean Kelly, C.R. Matthews, H. Ostlund, Ronald H. Preston, Norman Ritchie, Jean Scott, Marjorie Wallis, Phyllis Wray (Apr 28/7) ($0.35 - $0.50 [children, $0.15]) - *provides thrills*
OCT 29/34 - *Majestic*	Little Theatre **1.** The Dear Departed by Stanley Houghton **2.** The Inner Urge by Irene Beecher - **3.** The House With Twisty Windows by Mary Packington **4.** The Man in the Stalls by Alfred Sutro	- Florence Mackenzie/T. Faunch, Eveline Meech, F. Steele, Daphne Summerfield, M. Sydal, J.T. Vallance Bertha Karp/Harry Baalim, Leona Freng, Josephine Hughes, Kay Jenks, Ralph Johnson Louie Ritchie/I. Hendry, C.F. Hiscocks, Marion Johnson, Alathea Mellor Langdale, George O'Meara, Stan Peszat, Jean Scott H. Church/Percy Cranston, Lois McGuire, William Rea (Oct 30/6) - *action good throughout*

DATE/LOCATION	PRODUCTION/ TECHNICAL PERSONNEL	DIRECTOR/CAST/REFERENCE(S)/COMMENTS
DEC 10/34 - *Majestic*	Little Theatre 1. The Miracle (in pantomime) - 2. Quimby Comes Back by Stewart Blanchard - - 3. The Rehearsal by Christopher Morley	- M. Bryans/Eildon Brander, Margaret Davidson, R. Hick, V. Martin, B. Roy (soloist) J. Rosewarn/J.A. Anderson, Mrs. J. Barr, B. Church, D.H. Elton, (Kitchener Elton/Allan Lewis**), T. Ferguson, Harvey Greenway, W.L. Jacobson, A. Jones, H. Poole, M. Raby, A.W. Shackleford, H.G. Stretton, Alice Thresher, J.T. Vallance, Marjorie Wallis Madge Jordan/Ethel Brander, Mary Clarke, Camille Connor, Jean MacBeth, Marjorie Shepherd, Dora Walburger (Dec 11/7) - *presentations of distinction* (**Lewis replaced K. Elton)
JAN 21/35 - *Majestic*	Little Theatre Good Theatre by Christopher Morley [presented in conjunction with plays from Cardston, Medicine Hat, Stirling]	Florence Mackenzie/L. Connor, Thomas Evans, H. Greenway, A.C. Raworth, J. Rosewarn (Jan 22/7) - *not very appealing to a general audience*
MAR 4/35 - *Majestic*	Little Theatre 1. Thank You Doctor by Gilbert Emery - 2. Thirst by Freda Graham Bundy - 3. Thursday Evening by Christopher Morley 4. Where But In America by Oscar M. Wolfe	- L. Jordan/Walter Adnitt, Stan Faulkner, B. Karp (Hal Lindsay/L. Jordan**), Gladys Talbot N. Bletcher/Bob Bletcher, Josephine & Donald Clark, (Horace Poole/A. Lewis**), H. Maynard, Stafford Peat H. Church/Marge Farstad, Fred Holmes, Mildred Seamans, Ethel Shepherd Lloyd Elliott/Kathleen Collins, L. Elliott, May G. Fawcett [Coaldale Members of Playgoers] (Mar 5/7) - *Four short plays nicely portrayed* (**Jordan replaced Lindsay; Lewis replaced Poole)
NOV 7,8/35 - *Majestic*	Musical, The Gingham Girl, Book by Daniel Kussell; Music by Albert Von Tilzer; Lyrics by Neville Fleesom/Tom Ferguson, Mrs. A.E. Heninger, M. Bryans, H. Long, J. Hawkins, E. Armstrong, E. Atherton, Don Carpenter, Mrs. J. Craig, Mrs. W.E. Everson, E. Fisher, Hector Frey, Walter Hay, Max Hoffman, Cliff Humphries, Margaret Jackson, Eric Johnson, Mrs. MacDonald, Tom Middleton, L. Ritchie/Aileen Jones [mus dir]/Bernadette Fisher [chor]	H. Church/Olga Anderson, Reg Bailey, J. Clark, Chas. Dawson, Cleve Hill, F. Holmes, B. Lawrence, H. Maynard, E. Meech, Hulda Pack, Edna Pizzey, Gladys Talbot, Byron Tanner, Violet Wilks [Lead Dancers: Bernadette Fisher, Stafford Peat, Allan Lewis, Crawford Fisher, Vivian Buffet, Charles Dawson] (Nov 8/6) - *clever staging & costuming*
DEC 2/35 - *Majestic*	Little Theatre 1. Black Knight by John Bourne - 2. The Devil Among the Skins by Ernest Goodwin 3. In Port by Harold Simpson	- N. Bletcher/Bernice Burnard, Mary Clarke, F. Nowell Johnson, William Kergan, Robert Meldrum, Loretta Niven, Elizabeth Wilcox Maybelle Bryans/T. Faunch, Carl P. & Villa Lambert, J.T. Vallance Harvey Greenway/Geoffrey Blake, C. Gibson, H. Poole (Dec 3/7) - *well merited applause*
FEB 3/36 - *Majestic*	Little Theatre 1. Folly of Faith by Michael Rayne 2. A Man of Ideas by Miles Maleson 3. The Man Who Thought of Everything by E.N. Taylor 4. The Recoil by Eric Logan	- J. Rosewarn/F. Holmes, Marie Lange, Jean Rose, Helen Rivers F. Nowell Johnson/F. Humby, Mary Hoar, F.N. Johnson, A. Lewis Elizabeth Wilcox/H. Baalim, M. Greenway, H. Rivers M. Bryans/Geoffrey Blake, T. Faunch, H. Greenway, Eric Johnson (Feb 4/7) - *Recoil is Highlight*
MAY 27/36 - *Majestic*	Romance Comedy, The Middle Watch by Ian Hay & Stephen King Hall/T. Ferguson, Jim Hawkins, H. Church, Don Carpenter, Crawford Fisher, H. Frey, W. Hay, M. Hoffman, Cliff Humphries, Tom Middleton	Maybelle Bryans/Ernest Armstrong, G. Blake, B. Church, T. Evans, George Frayne, Josephine Hughes, Eric Johnson, F.N. Johnson, H. Long, S. Peat, J. Rosewarn, Jean Scott, Joan Shepherd, M. Sydal, J.T. Vallance (Mar 28/7) - *humorous situations effectively handled*
OCT 16/36 - *Majestic*	Little Theatre 1. Courage Mr. Greene by James P. Ferguson 2. November Afternoon by Anthony Pelissier 3. Perfect Ending by Florence Ryerson & Colin Clements 4. Twenty-Five Cents by W. Eric Harris	- Robin Ritchie/S. Faulkner, Margaret Hoyt, G. Rice, Fred Robins, M. Sydal - Mrs. D.H. Elton/Ralph Johnson, Dorothy Palmer Hilda Church/Ethel Brander, H. Church, Frances Stoltze - Eric Johnson/Jessie Doe, E. Fisher, C. & V. Lambert, T. Lawrence, Bill Raby (Oct 17/6) ($0.25 members; $0.50 guests) - *pleasing variety* - *Perfect Ending was offered at Little Theatre Evening, Medicine Hat Nov 13/56*

DATE/LOCATION	PRODUCTION/ TECHNICAL PERSONNEL	DIRECTOR/CAST/REFERENCE(S)/COMMENTS
NOV 16,17/36 - *Majestic*	Melodrama, Ruth Ripley or The Orphan's Sacrifice/T. Ferguson, C. Humphries, H. Frey, H. Church, Ada Hogg, Winnie Helseth, Floss Armstrong (sponsored by Lethbridge Kiwanis Club)	C.R. Matthews with M. Bryans/R. Bailey, L. Connor, D.H. Elton, T. Faunch, G. Frayne, H. & M. Greenway, F. Holmes, A. Lewis, G. Rice, Beth Wilcox; specialty singers: George Brown Jr., B. & T. Lawrence, M. Thrall (Nov 17/6) - *great attention to detail*
JAN 8/37 - *Majestic*	Little Theatre 1. Heaven on Earth by Philip Johnson 2. Highness 3. Miss Marlowe at Play by A.A. Milne	- Hilda Church/M. Bryans, P. Clarke, K. Jenks, Robin Ritchie, Herbert G. Stretton Ralph Johnson/M. Davidson, J. Galbraith, Warren Johnson, S. Vallance J.E. Ayres/G. O'Meara, B. Roy, Helen Ruthven, F. Steele (Jan 9/6) - *delightful evening*
FEB 15/37 - *Majestic*	Comedy, Children to Bless You by Sheila Donisthorpe/T. Ferguson, C. Humphries	M. Bryans/Eildon Brander, Marion Clarke, L. Connor, (Betty Garissere/M. Davidson**), E. Fisher, A. Lewis, A. Mellor Langdale, Josephine Lucas, Agnes McKerrow, C. Parker, Frank Tilley (Feb 16/8) - *a good show, thoroughly well presented*
MAR 8/37 - *Majestic*	Little Theatre 1. Four Into Seven Won't Go by Stephen King-Hall & Val Gielgud 2. They Refuse to be Resurrected by H.K. Smith 3. World Without Men By Philip Johnson 4. Dance Frolic by Brander-Fisher School of Dance	M. Bryans/H. Church, M. Clarke, C. Lambert, C.R. Matthews, Robin Ritchie - Robin Ritchie/George Brown, Jr., Ann Kostiuk, A. Lewis, Robin L. Ritchie - L. Ritchie/S. Chiswick, Chang Fletcher, Helen James, Marie Lange, Marie Louise Loescher, V. Martin, Effie Reid, M. Sydal - (Mar 9/8)
NOV 15/37 - *Majestic*	Little Theatre 1. Created by Lol Norris 2. The Princes & The Swineherd (adapted from Hans Christian Anderson) 3. Tickets, Please 4. Villa For Sale -	J.T. Wallace/Ted Faunch, Olive Pauling, H.G. Stretton, S. Vallance Pauline E. Watkins/Ten children - Elizabeth Crowe/Ada Hogg, Mrs. C. Jackson, Annie Kergan, Roderick Paterson E. Becker/Ethel Humby, Martha Karp, A. Mellor Langdale, Hester Murray, W. P. Pineau (Nov 16/7) - *new players & new directors featured*
DEC 13/37 - *Majestic*	Little Theatre 1. Star Fantasy by Elizabeth Lewis 2. The Miracle [Revival (in pantomime)] 3. The Murder Scream by Mikhail Aklom 4. You Can't Joke With a Woman by Helen T. Torrence 5. Dance Revue under direction of Lola Strand	- Agnes Davidson/Seven children including: Betty Cull, Jimmie Linn, Blakely Pritchard, Mavis Moffat, Bobby Steele, Willis Tanner, Alden Green M. Bryans/Eildon Brander, M. Davidson, F. Holmes, Helen McMahon, V. Martin [Musicians: R. Johnson (organ), Cliff Palmer (violin), B. Roy (vocal)] H. Greenway/J. Galbraith, Fred Gibson, K. Jenks, B. Raby, James Worthington Camille (Connor) Hay & Jean Galbraith/Paddy Bowman, Bernice Burnard, Ruth Hughes, Bernard Simmons (Dec 14/7) - *effective staging*
FEB 1/38 - *Majestic*	Little Theatre 1. Russian Salad by Philip Johnson 2. The Breaking of the Calm 3. She Was No Lady 4. Dance Interlude by Eildon Brander School of Dance	- W.P. Pineau/G. Frayne, W.P. Pineau, Alice Sather, Doug & Margaret Sutherland, Nora Williamson H. Greenway, & C.R. Matthews/R. Bailey, Perry Duffy, Afton Elton, Eric Farris, C.R. Matthews, Victor Meech Eric Johnson/Ethel Brander, Nancy Farris, T. Faunch, J.T. Vallance (Feb 2/8) - *pleases majority of audience*
MAR 14/38 - *Majestic*	Farce, Squaring the Circle by Valentine Kaytayev/T. Ferguson	M. Bryans/George Anderson, Ralph Baines, T. Ferguson, G. Frayne, Irene Faunch, Helen Maynard, O. Pauling, Bobby Ranson, T.E. Rodie, S. Vallance, J. Worthington (Mar 15/8) - *enthusiastic laughter & applause but small audience*
NOV 21/38 - *Majestic*	Comedy, Counsel For the Defence by Eugene G. Hafer/T. Ferguson	W.P. Pineau/Eildon Brander, M. Davidson, T. Faunch, Helen Hill, Ann Kostiuk, Lloyd Murray, W. P. Pineau, H.G. Stretton, S. Vallance, J. Worthington (Nov 22/8) - *club scores success*
FEB 6/39 - *Majestic*	Little Theatre 1. On Dartmoor 2. One Hundred Dollars 3. The Paragon	M. Bryans/T. Ferguson, H. Frey, A.W. King, Jean Scott, M. Thrall Doris Hester/M. Davidson, J. Galbraith, D. Hester, A. Murray, O. Pauling, B. Simmons Agnes Davidson/children (Feb 7/8) - *well contrasted program. Macleod Players also presented Relief*

DATE/LOCATION	PRODUCTION/ TECHNICAL PERSONNEL	DIRECTOR/CAST/REFERENCE(S)/COMMENTS
FEB 27/39 - *Majestic*	Little Theatre **1.** The Beginning of the End by Sean O'Casey **2.** Poppin the Question (Scottish comedy) **3.** Dance Revue, Toy Shop by Brander School of Dance	- L. Ritchie/William Dormier, G. Frayne, Margaret Savage - Elizabeth Crowe/E. Crowe, Mary Hogg, Roderick Paterson, Tommy Walker - (Feb 28/6) - *another delightful evening - Little Theatre Club of the LDS Church also presented Romance is a Racket dir by M. Palmer*
MAR 29/39 - *Macleod Th., Macleod, Alta.*	Little Theatre Its Autumn Now by Philip Johnson	Florence Mackenzie/Eveline Meech, W.P. Pineau, M. Seamans, M. Sydal, Georgie Thomas, J.T. Vallance (Mar 30/7) - *presented in conjunction with Little Theatre groups from Macleod & Granum*
APR 3/39 - *Majestic*	Little Theatre **1.** The Royal Touch by Elsie Park Gowan - **2.** The Week of Weeks by Elva Cooper Magnusson **3.** It's Autumn Now	- N. Bletcher/Jimmy Linn, H. Maynard, O. Pauling, D. Sutherland, S. Vallance [with Ralph Johnson at the organ] Echo Becker/Stuart Bodard, Camille Hay, A. Lewis, F. Stoltz - (see Mar 29/39) (Apr 4/6) - *three artistically presented plays*
DEC 20/39 - *Rec. Hut, Lethbridge Garrison*	Entertainment including two short plays	Echo Becker, W.E. Blair, S. Bodard, M. Davidson, Gordon Hamilton, Mrs. W. Hay, T. Lawrence, A. Lewis, T. Ferguson (m.c.), T. Faunch (piano) (Dec 21/6) - *first of a series*
JAN 28/40 - *Rec. Hut, Lethbridge Garrison*	Entertainment including two short plays/Tom Ferguson [stage mgr]	Doris Hester/Dalton Elton, Irene Faunch, Helen Maynard, Dorothy Raby, J. Worthington; Maybelle Bryans/T. Faunch, G. Frayne, O. Pauling, J.T. Vallance (Jan 29/7) - *enlisted men enjoys plays*
DEC 26/40 - *Majestic*	One act comedy, Happy Journey by Thornton Wilder [presented as part of IODE Boxing Day Concert]	Maybelle Bryans/Robert Armstrong, Barbara Baalim, M. Davidson, G. Frayne, Alden Green, M. Thrall (Dec 27/8) - *unusual & interesting presentation*
NOV 17/41 - *RAF School, Medicine Hat*	Skit (in cooperation with YMCA War Services Entertainment Committee - arranged by Mrs. C.A. Long)	Doris Hester/Tom Ferguson, Sydney Vallance (Nov 18/7) - *a warm reception was accorded the visitors*
APR 16-18/42 - *Majestic*	One act farce, Goodnight Please (presented as part of the Spring Wartime Revue)	M. Bryans/Margaret Brenton, L. Connor, L.A.C. George Fay, G. Frayne, Dora Mileson, Sgt. Radcliffe, J. Worthington (Apr 17/6) - *entire cast gave a smooth performance*
1943-1950	**NIL**	
NOV 26,27/51 - *Civic Center*	Arsenic & Old Lace by Joseph Kesselring/Harry Baalim [tech dir] & stage mgr]	Wayne Matkin/Gordon Appell, Charles Beasley, Cecil H. Biddell, Elsie Biddell, Denise Black, Jim Brooke, Ed Francis, Ted Faunch, Jack Haberman, Doris Halifax, John Mackie, Ed Rossetti, Stan Sawicki (Nov 27/7) - *marks revival of Playgoers*
JAN 7,8/52 - *Civic Center* JAN 22 - *(Edmonton)*	Suspense Drama, Angel Street by Patrick Hamilton/Harry Baalim [tech dir stage mgr]	Maybelle Bryans/Harry Baalim, Hugh Buchanan, Lena Connor, Eric Hohm, Eleanor Matkin, C.R. Matthews, Yvonne Turner (Jan 8/7) - *very satisfying & well produced show*
MAR 17,18/52 - *Civic Center*	Little Theatre Fumed Oak by Noel Coward	Hugh Buchanan/Ed Francis, Joy Meek, Mary Waters, Shirley Wilson (Mar 18/7) - *Maintained a sparkling pace. Accompanied by production from Coaldale (Murray Robison) & LDS Players (Wayne Matkin)*
FEB 19/53 - *L.C.I.* MAR 3 - *Capitol*	Suspense Drama, Night Must Fall by Emlyn Williams/Harry Knowles, Mike Pisko, Joan Waterfield, Jessie Baalim, Doug Card, Elsie Biddell, John Campbell, Bill Hay, Fred Holmes, Ron Johnson, Milt Moffatt, Tom Waterfield	Hugh Buchanan/Molly Barron, C.H. Biddell, Elsie Biddell, Bill Fruet Jr., Lois Head, Bill Lazaruk, Anita Susman, Pat Wagner, Mary Waters (Feb 20/9; Mar 4/9) - *1500 observe spirited production - a hit*
APR 1/53 - *Cardston Soc. Center*	One Act Festival entry The Twelve Pound Look by J.M. Barrie	G.H. Knowles/Brian & Doris Halifax, Harry Knowles, Joan Mackwood (Apr 2/13) - *under-rehearsed*
APR 13,14/53 - *Capitol*	Comedy, You Can't Take It With You by George S. Kaufman & Moss Hart/Harry Knowles, Bill Hay, George Wilson, Lois Head, Joan Waterfield	Elsie Biddell/Gordon Appell, Reg Bailey, Cecil Biddell, Jean Block, Bill Ede, Ella Findlay, Jack Gibson, Ethel Halyung, Ron Johnson, Ann Leggett, Peter McGilvray, Evelyn Robinson, Ralph Robinson, Richard Stonehocker, Daphne Sweda, Gay Wensveen, George Wilson, Kathleen Wilson (Apr 14/10) - *funny all the way through*

DATE/LOCATION	PRODUCTION/ TECHNICAL PERSONNEL	DIRECTOR/CAST/REFERENCE(S)/COMMENTS
NOV 24,25/53 - *Canadian Legion Memorial Hall (Lethbridge)*	Little Theatre: 1. Demitasse - 2. Mail Order Bride by Effie Reid 3. Eros at Breakfast by Effie Reid 4. The Unseen [Coaldale Little Theatre] by Alice Gerstenburg	- Denise Black with Pat Wagner/Gordon Appell, Shirley Blackwell, Denise Black, Margaret Huszar Agnes Davidson/Ron Calhoun, Jack Gibson, C.R. Matthews, Evelyn Robinson, Daphne Sweda Ron Johnson/Bob Best, John Dafoe, Bart McCulloch, Daphne Sweda, John Wilton (Nov 25/14) - *warmly received*
JAN 21,22/54 - *L.C.I.* FEB 16 - *Calgary*	Drama, The Silver Cord by Sydney Howard/Harry & Jessie Baalim, Harry Knowles, Maybelle Bryans, Doris Balcovske, Bruce Busby, Nancy Heron, Ron Johnson, Ralph Robinson	Hugh Buchanan/Shirley Blackwell & Jean Block (alternating), Bruce Busby, Daphne Manson, Jack Maynard, Mary Waters (Jan 22/9) - *well handled* production
APR 1/54 - *Coaldale*	One Act Festival Entry Mail Order Bride by Effie Reid	Agnes Davidson/for cast see Nov 24,25/53 (Apr 2/10) - *a great deal of teamwork & sparkle*
APR 7-9/54 - *Wilson Jr. H.S. & L.C.I.*	Farce Comedy, The Man Who Came To Dinner by George S. Kaufman & Moss Hart/Bruce Busby, Doris Balcovske, Maybelle Bryans	Hugh Buchanan/Harry Baalim, Doris Balcovske, Bob Best, Cliff Black, Denise Black, Bruce Busby, Kent Duncan, Helen James, Ron Johnson, Harry Knowles, Pat Maggs, Daphne Manson, C.R. Matthews, Jack Maynard, Maureen Parker, Evelyn Robinson, Ralph Robinson, Amy Stevens, Colin Turner, Mary Waters (Apr 8/10) - *kept a fair crowd in a cheerful mood - a hit*
NOV 22,23/54 - *Lethbridge Legion Hall*	Little Theatre: 1. The Stepmother by A.A. Milne 2. Lonesome Like by Harold Brighouse 3. The Rehearsal by Christopher Morley	Denise Black/B. Busby, H. Knowles, C.R. Matthews, Joan Perkinson Mary Waters/Muriel Gentlemen, H. Knowles, Leo Lancaster, Anita Susman Cam Hay & Daphne Manson/Marian Bolokoski, Louise Bishop, Vonda Chmelauskas, M. Huszar, M. McElgunn, Inga Kromand (Nov 23/10) - *all 3 plays came off in first rate style*
MAR 8/55 - *L.C.I.* APR 23 - *Red Deer*	One Act Festival Entry Lonesome Like by Harold Brighouse	Mary Waters/Muriel Gentleman (replaced by Daphne Manson in Red Deer Festival) Harry Knowles (replaced by Jack Maynard in Red Deer), Leo Lancaster, Anita Susman (Mar 9/14) - *adjudicators were very pleased with the overall production (Apr 25/10) actors praised*
MAR 7,8/56 - *Wilson Jr. H.S.*	Comedy, Harvey by Mary Chase/Bill Lazaruk, Cecil H. Biddell, Phyl Ellerbeck, Bob Reed & W. Royer, Doris Balcovske, C.R. Matthews, Cliff Black, Ward Ingoldsby, Daphne Manson, Jack Pickering, Colin Turner, Mary Waters	Elsie Biddell with Bill Lazaruk/Reg Bailey, Audrey Baines, Alan de Jardin, Sandy McCallum, Bessie McCully, Joan Perkinson, Stan Sawicki (Mar 8/9) - *proves hilarious*
MAR 24/56 - *Wilson Jr. H.S.* MAR 26-28/56 - *Taber H.S.*	1. The Cajun by Ada Jack Carver - 2. Jane Wogan by Florence Howell 3. Bathsheba of Saaremaa by Aino Kallas (translated by Alex Martin) 4. The Happy Journey by Thornton Wilder presented by Southminster Y.P.	Bill Lazaruk/Bill Lazaruk, Stan Sawicki, Colin Turner, Adrian & Metta Vaselenak, Mary Waters Phyl Ellerbeck/Audry Baines, Bruce Busby, P. Ellerbeck, Joan Perkinson, Kaye Watson Elsie Biddell with Kaye Watson/Elsie Biddell, Jean Ede, Sandy McCallum Mary Waters - (Mar 26/10) - *provide good entertainment* (Mar 29/1) - *Bathsheba sweeps festival honors*
JAN 30-FEB 1/57 - *Wilson Jr. H.S.*	Drama, The Heiress by Ruth Augustus Goetz based on Washington Square by Henry James/Percy Morris, Bill Lazaruk, Joan Waterfield, Metta Vaselenak, Audrey Baines, Dale Blair, Doris Balcovske, P.J. Collins, Brenda Cordwell, Ella Findlay, Bill Goldie, Ralph & Susan Kuipers	Daphne Manson with Percy Morris/Bernard Baxter, B. Cordwell, Mary Gallagher, Helen James, C.R. Matthews, Rita MacCauley, Joan Perkinson, Colin Turner, M. Waters (Jan 31/10) - *best drama in years* (Feb 7/1,2) - *an extremely good show says British adjudicator, Cecil Bellamy*
APR 1-3/57 - *Taber Community Centre* APR 24/57 - *Red Deer Memorial Centre* APR 25/87 - *Wilson Jr. H.S.*	Little Theatre: 1. Drought by M.S. Armstrong 2. Hello, Out There by William Saroyan 3. After Many Years by C.R. Matthews 4. From Paradise to Butte by Robert Finch	- Bruce Busby/Bill Bagshaw, J. Perkinson Harry Baalim/Denise Black, Ralph "Lefty" Eshpeter, Theresa King, Bill Matheson, Sandy McCallum Mary Waters/Ella Findlay, H. James, R. & S. Kuipers, C.R. Matthews, C. Turner Harry Baalim/R. Eshpeter, S. McCallum, B. Matheson, Howard Palmer (Apr 4/1,2; 26/10; 29/1) - *an interesting evening of good amateur theatre*
MAY 1/57 - *S.A. Jubilee Aud., Calgary*	1. Hello Out There 2. From Paradise To Butte	Harry Baalim/H. Baalim, A. Baines, T. King, B. Matheson, S. McCallum Harry Baalim (same cast as performed on Apr 25) (May 2/2) - *mixed reaction*

DATE/LOCATION	PRODUCTION/ TECHNICAL PERSONNEL	DIRECTOR/CAST/REFERENCE(S)/COMMENTS
MAR 7,10/58 - *Civic Centre; Wilson Jr. H.S.* MAR 15 - *S.A. Jubilee Aud., Calgary*	Comedy, White Sheep of the Family by L. du Garde Peach & Ian Hay/Percy Morris, Margaret Willis, Doreen Morita, Phyl Ellerbeck, Jean Ede, M. Waters, Doris Halifax, Connie & Ward Ingoldsby, R. Kuipers, C.R. Matthews	Wayne Matkin/Audrey Baines, D. Black, Marjorie Burdon, B. Cordwell, George Hall, Wilfred (Bill) Halifax, B. Matheson, John Thackray, C. Turner (Mar 17/1,2) - *fine teamwork* (Mar 8/11) - *proves most entertaining*
MAY 12,13/58 - *Civic Center*	Little Theatre 1. How He Lied to Her Husband by G.B. Shaw 2. The Invisible Worm by Elda Cadogan 3. The Monkey's Paw by W. Jacobs	- Mary Waters/Jack Gibson, H. James, B. Matheson - Connie Ingoldsby/B. Bagshaw, D. Black, Angus Paton Joan Perkinson/Bill Ede, Pete Nadeau, Brander Parsons, Frank Vervoort, Kaye Watson (May 13/10) - *small audience treated to a thoroughly enjoyable evening*
MAY 4/59 - *Wilson Jr. H.S.*	Little Theatre: 1. The Valiant by Holworthy Hall & Richard Middlemass 2. From Five to Five Thirty 3. Variety skits	- Jean Ede/Paul Ciesla, Peter Hornsby, Yvonne Kennedy, S. Sawicki, Kent Simpson, C. Turner Phyl Ellerbeck/D. Black, J. Ede, E. Findlay, H. James, Kaye Watson Phyl Ellerbeck, Grant Kennedy, Jean Loetscher, S. McCallum, J. Perkinson, K. Watson (May 5/10) - *score limited success*
OCT 18/59 - *CJLH T.V.*	For Old Time's Sake	Babs Pitt/B. Cordwell, C. Turner
OCT 24; 28/59 - *Vauxhall; Hamilton Jr. H.S.* NOV 5,6 - *Stirling*	Little Theatre: 1. Overlaid by Robertson Davies - 2. To The Lovely Margaret by Pearl & Thatcher Allred	- Mary Waters/D. Black, J.A. Hornsby, Mellisa Matkin, Margaret Nimmons, Tony Pybee, Syd Salter Jean Ede/J.A. & Peter Hornsby, M. Matkin, Bonnie Perry, Jan Wilton
JAN 18,19/60 - *Hamilton Jr. H.S.*	Comedy, The Curious Savage by John Patrick/Doryanne Robertson, Kay Haworth, B. Ede, P. Hornsby, A. Plant, Joy Meek, T. Pydee, Bill Bale, J. Ede, Peter Lofts, M. Waters, Leslee Watson	Phyl Ellerbeck/P. Ciesla, Hazel Evans, C. Ingoldsby, H. James, B. Lazaruk, Phyllis Lilly, R. MacCauley, B. Parsons, Allan Sackman, Ted Scheurkogel, K. Watson (Jan 19/10) - *enjoyable but lacks polish, lustre*
MAR 19/60 - *Hamilton Jr. H.S.* MAR 24/60 - *Towne Th., Medicine Hat*	Thriller, Gently Does It by Janet Green/Cornelius Martens, P. Ellerbeck, Betty Old, Bruce MacKenzie, Marvin Haynes, Jean Ede, Hazel Evans, H. James, Babs Pitt, B. Bale, P. Ciesla, B. Ede, C. & W. Ingoldsby, T. Pydee, L. Watson	Sam Pitt/D. Black, Russell Fairhurst, S. McCallum, J. Perkinson, J. Waterfield, K. Watson (Mar 21/14) (*MIIDN*, Mar 25/3) - *scores hit with adjudicator, Robert Gill, who exclaimed, "WOW"!*
FEB, MAR/60 - *CJLH T.V.*	1. Overlaid 2. To The Lovely Margaret	See OCT 24/59 for directors and casts
NOV 28,29/60 - *Hamilton Jr. H.S.*	Little Theatre: 1. Still Life by Noel Coward 2. A scene from Anastasia 3. Rise & Shine by Elda Cadogan	- Bill Lazaruk/B. Bale, H. Evans, P. Hornsby, B. Old Daphne Manson/D. Black, Cam Cathcart, Susan Lancaster Kaye Watson/P. Ciesla, C. & W. Ingoldsby, Leslee Watson (Nov 29/10) - *theatrical fare of excellence*
MAR 6,7/61 - *Civic Centre* MAR 17 - *S.A. Jubilee Aud., Calgary*	Drama, Anastasia by Marcelle Maurette (English adaptation by Guy Bolton)/Craig Montgomery, P. Ciesla, Elaine Harrison, H. Evans, K. Watson, C. Ingoldsby, Al Candy, Bobby Reed, Brian Manson, M. Waters, B. Bale, Chris Cathcart, B. & J. Ede, Norville Getty, H. Hones, C.R. Matthews, D. Morita, K. Watson	Daphne Manson/D. Black, Cam Cathcart, Chris Cathcart, P. Ciesla, J. Ede, Bob Hendricks, P. Hornsby, W. Ingoldsby, Susan Lancaster, B. Lazaruk, T. Scheurkogel, Joe Shannon, J. Waterfield (Mar 18/17) - *a most delightful production* (Mar 7/10) - *Individual portrayals by Black & Lancaster presentation*
OCT 24/61 - *Capitol*	Comedy, Blithe Spirit by Noel Coward/J. Pritchard, K. Watson, Fay Brosgard, George Nuttall, Doris Colpitts, K. Haworth, Frank Bennett, D. Black, Bill Ede, Norville Getty, T. Scheurkogel, Joe Shannon	Phyl Ellerbeck/J. Ede, P. Ellerbeck, H. Evans, B. Matheson, B. Old, Fred Pritchard, K. Watson (Oct 25/16) - *warm, humorous production attended by about 350*

DATE/LOCATION	PRODUCTION/ TECHNICAL PERSONNEL	DIRECTOR/CAST/REFERENCE(S)/COMMENTS
MAR 19,/62 - *Capitol* MAR 20 - *Stirling Sch.* MAR 24 - *Red Deer* APR 4 - *Capitol* MAY 5 - *Taber* MAY 15 - *Playhouse Th., Winnipeg*	Drama, The Dark at the Top of the Stairs by William Inge/N. Getty, Faye Olsen, Wally Nishida, F. Bennett, L. Connor, Kaz Ayukawa, B. Manson, J. Shannon, B. Bagshaw, Virginia Black, B. Ede, R. Kemp, Stan Jenkins, Jack Ralleson, Hans Winckler	Denise Black/Helen (James) Bennett, Norville Getty, (Kaz Ayukawa in DDF festival presentation), Jack Ralleson, (Frank Bennett - DDF festival presentation), Cliff Black, Sharon Bolen, Audrey Corcoran, Jean Ede, Kirk Patterson, Bonnie Perry, J. Shannon, Con Van Der Lee (Mar 26/1,2) - *Playgoers clean up in Drama Festival*
DEC 3,4/62 - *Capitol*	Comedy, The Cradle Song by Gregorio Martinez Sierra/N. Getty, K. Ayukawa, P. Ellerbeck, M. (Waters) Heinitz, C.R. Matthews, C.W. Chichester, Tina Olt Shoorn	Phyllis Lilly/H. & F. Bennett, Sharon Bolen, Iris Duban, J. Ede, Lewis Kelly, Susan Molnar, Pat Phillips, Martha Rae, Ted Scheurkogel, Joe Shannon, Leona Thorpe, J. Waterfield, K. Watson (Dec 4/10) - *hardly a dry eye in the house*
MAR 27/63 - *Capitol*	Thriller, Rebecca by Daphne du Maurier/N. Getty, Winona Anderson, B. Ede, Sharon Gostola, Truus Baird, Frank Bennett, M. Rae	Cliff Black with Denise Black/Frank Bennett, Sharon Bolen, Derek Charnley, Syd Clarke, Jim Elliott, Mary Heinitz, George Mann, John Massakers, D. Morita, J. Perkinson, Ted Scheurkogel (Apr 1/1,2) - *capture 3 festival awards*
NOV 4/63 - *Capitol*	Drama, Dark of the Moon by Howard Richardson & William Berney/N. Getty, Joan Abbott, Truus Baird, Denise Black, Winona Anderson, Sharon Gostola, Bill Ede, Cliff Black, Frank Bennett, Martha Rae	Mary (Waters) Heinitz/Joan Abbott, Bob Befus, F. Bennett, C. Black, Sharon Bolen, D. Charnley, Syd Clarke, J. Ede, F. Gostola, C. Ingoldsby, Dennis Jones, P. Lilly, G. Mann, D. Manson, C.R. Matthews, Lee Mells, D. Morita, Kirk Patterson, C. Turner, J. Waterfield, K. Watson (Nov 5/10) - *contentious play a success*
FEB 14/64 - *Capitol*	Fortieth Anniversary Reunion Presentation; Excerpts from: 1. Going Up - - - 2. various productions from the 1950s & 60s/Frank Gostola, D. Jones, D. Charnley, W. Ingoldsby, C. Turner, J. Ede, George Mann	Mary Heinitz/Cliff Black (Chairman), Mrs. W.A. Nelson (accompanist) - 1. Maybelle Bryans, P.J. Collins, Lena Connor, Tom Ferguson, Chris & Mamie Gibson, Charles Dawson, Mrs. Harold Jelfs, Marguerite Lightbound, Marie Louise Loescher, Bob Lawrence, C. R. Matthews, Kitty Reber, Gladys Talbot, Minnie Thrall, Phyllis Walker, Violet Wilks 2. W. & E. Matkin, Yvonne Hohm, Jean Block, Mary Heinitz, D. Manson, S. McCallum, J. Waterfield, K. Watson, D. Block, T. Baird, F. Pritchard, H. (Evans) Skaronski, H. & F. Bennett, J. Ede., J. Shannon, P. Ellerbeck, S. Gostola, C. Ingoldsby, M. Rae (Feb 17/1,14) - *Playgoers of the past are honored*
MAR 18/64 - *Capitol* MAR 21 - *Allied Arts Centre, Calgary*	Mystery, Therese by Thomas Job based on Emile Zola's Therese Raquin/David Thompson, C. Black, F. Gostola, D. Charnley, B. Ede, J. Abbott, W. Anderson, Pat Bland, B. Ede, S. Gostola	Denise Black/C. Black, S. Clarke, J. Ede, D. Jones, P. Lilly, S. (Bolen) Magee, G. Mann, J. Waterfield (Mar 19/10) - *enthusiastic & appreciative audience of 425* (Mar 22/1,2) - *wins 5 trophies*
MAR 10/65 - *Capitol*	Comedy, Born Yesterday by Garson Kanin/Frank Gostola, Jean Ede, W. Anderson, F. Bennett, Dick Mells, Jon Redfern, Brian Coutts, L. Mells, C. Black, Angela Baird, Jim Cousins, M. Heinitz, C. Turner, K. Watson	Denise Black/W. Anderson, T. Baird, F. & H. Bennett, C. Black, Philip Black, Jim Cousins, Brian Coutts, F. & S. Gostola, Ian Mandin, G. Mann, C.R. Matthews, Jon Redfern, C. Turner (Mar 11/10; 12/18) - *lots of laughs*
MAR 29,30/66 - *Capitol* APR 1/66 - *Medicine Hat*	Comedy, You Can't Take It With You by Moss Hart & George Kaufman/Ed Bayly, Ray Jolliffe, Marilyn Mossey, Al Candy, Bob Reed, Wendy Carson, K. Watson, L. Mells, W. Anderson, Len Ankers, F. & S. Gostola, Al Greenway, Martha Rae, H. Skaronski	Dick Mells/Laverne Ankers, Len Ankers, E. Bayly, B. Befus, D. Black, J. Ede, Howard & Marilyn Ellison, Frank Featherstone, F. Gostola, Peter Grantham, Al Greenway, Bruce Haig, Muriel & Ray Jolliffe, G. Mann, L. Mells, Frank Murphy, K. Watson (Mar 30/17) - *gets good laugh* (Apr 2/2) - *Lethbridge play meets criticism by adjudicator Boretski*
SEPT 23,24/66 - *Yates*	Drama, The Children's Hour by Lillian Hellman/Al Greenway, F. Gostola, C. Ingoldsby, Leslee (Watson) Nuttall, Wendy Carson, L. Mells, Ed Bayly, Marilyn Ellison, S. Gostola, Marion Greenway, G. Mann, M. Rae, K. Watson	Lee Mells/Jean Block, Eva Jane Bruce, Verna Cannady, J. Ede, P. Grantham, A. Greenway, S. Gostola, Pam Hutchison, Peggy Matthews, Debbie McCulloch, Joanne Morgan, H. Skaronski, J. Waterfield, K. Watson (Sept 24/14) - *beautifully acted but play lacks conviction*

DATE/LOCATION	PRODUCTION/ TECHNICAL PERSONNEL	DIRECTOR/CAST/REFERENCE(S)/COMMENTS
FEB 15-17/67 - *Yates* (*Playgoers/Our Town Workshop joint production*)	Comedy, <u>Madwoman of Chaillot</u> by Jean Giraudox adapted by Maurice Valency/Cathy Evins, Vaughn Hembroff, H. Ellison, Ern, Fran & Ed Bayly, Doug Card, Wayne Matkin, Judy White, Elaine Liebelt, Freda Walton, Ross Whitmore, Linda Albertson, Bery Allan, J.R. Brown, John Carter, Mike Cleaver, Doris Crawford, P. Ellerbeck, A. & Marion Greenway, Angela Gunstone, Irene Hacker, Betty Hamilton, Anne Hominuke, Bob Ives, Weste Jensen, Jim & Myrtle Jones, Brenda Knight, Marg Kokott, Donna Koziak, Lily Larter, Claire Malmberg, Andrew Marshall, Paulette Robertson, John Smith, Phil Story, Carol Watkinson, Jim Wright	Ron Hartmann (professional dir)/Bery Allan, Kathryn Ankers, Laverne Ankers, T. Baird, Wayne Barry, Ed Bayly, B. Befus, C. Black, D. Black, J. Block, Bill Bushell, Barry Corenblum, H. Ellison, Russell Fairhurst, Angela Gunstone, Bruce Haig, Weste Jensen, Marland Larter, Gordon Lowe, Norma MacInnis, Bob McHardy, L. & D. Mells, Ted Orchard, Gary Orr, Claudia Peterson, Sheila Pisko, F. & J. Pritchard, Gordon Schmaus, Glen Seeman, Doug Smith, C. Turner, Robert Waldren, Jack & Jean Warburton, J. Waterfield, John Wecels, Shirley Wilson (Feb 16/12) - *did not achieve its potential*
MAR 10,31/67 - *Yates*	Comedy, <u>Chinook</u> by Bill Matheson, with additional material by Dick Mells/D. Mells, J. Ede, A. Greenway, B. Reed, S. Gostola, H. Skaronski, M. Jolliffe, M. Rae, W. Anderson, Ern Bayly, H. & M. Ellison, F. Gostola, Wayne Sende, Jean Warburton	Denise Black with Dick Mells/C. Black, Wendy Carson, J. Ede, F. Gostola, A. Greenway, G. Mann, B. & Muriel Matheson, Deb McCulloch, D. & L. Mells, Joanne Morgan, C. Turner, J. Waterfield (Mar 11/13) - *well received; Paxton Whitehead praises cast*
MAR 15/69 - *Yates* MAR 26 - *Leth. Prov. Jail*	Little Theatre Comedy, <u>Red Peppers</u> by Noel Coward/produced for Western Canada Arts Festival	Denise Black/E. Bayly, D. Black, F. Featherstone, Kirk Jensen, Jack Warburton, J. Waterfield (Mar 17/12) - *fast-paced, hammy & delightful*
MAR 10/70 - *Yates* MAY 18/70 - *Playhouse Th., Winnipeg*	Drama, <u>The Hostage</u> by Brendan Behan/Ed, Ern & Fran Bayly, Bob Johnston, Garry Kohn, Linda (Albertson) Bayly, Chris Burgess, Hazel Durrans, Maureen Henchel, Albina Barry, Jim Jones, Charlie Scott	Dick Mells/Wayne Barry, Ed Bayly, Lois Dongworth, Hazel Durrans, Jim Elliott, Al Greenway, Bill & Muriel Matheson, Willie Mathis, Ellyn Mells, Sheila Pisko, Chip Schott, Clare Scott, H. Skaronski, Phil Story, Jack & Jean Warburton (Mar 11/18) - *superb production*
MAY 12-15/71 - *Yates*	Musical Comedy, <u>Fings Ain't Wot They Used T'</u> Be by Lionel Bart/Ed, Ern & Linda Bayly, Chris Burgess, Shirli Gonzy, M. Jolliffe, B. Reed, M. Matheson, Peter Durrans, Marion Greenway, Ray Mercer, Charlie Scott, Phil Story	Dick Mells/Ed Bayly, L. Dongworth, H. Durrans, J. Elliott, A. Greenway, B. Matheson, W. Mathis, Grant & Sheila Pisko, Diane Pokarney, Don Runquist, Clare Scott, Wes Stefan, Michael Sutherland, Jack & Jean Warburton (May 15/15) - *lightweight*
MAY 11-13/72 - *Yates*	Comedy, <u>A Midsummer Night's Dream</u> by William Shakespeare/Cathy Evins, Ellyn Mells, Muriel Matheson	Dick Mells/Ed Bayly, L. Dongworth, F. Featherstone, A. Greenway, Faith Harms, Frank & Wanda Huszar, K. Jensen, Linda Johnson, Winstan Jones, Katie Lee, B.Matheson, W. Mathis, Jane McCoy, Val McIntyre, E. Mells, Ray Mercer, Doug Smith, Jack Warburton, Liz Waterfield (May 11/14) - *commendable job*
FEB 24/73 - *Yates* (*L&D/AF*)	A scene from <u>A Midsummer Night's Dream</u>, "Pyramus & Thisbe"/E. Mells, L. Bayly, M. Jolliffe	Jean Warburton with choreography by Muriel Jolliffe/Ed Bayly, F. Featherstone, A. Greenway, F. Huszar, B. Matheson, W. Mathis, E. Mells, R. Mercer, Jack Warburton (Feb 26/12)
MAY 20-26/73 - *Yates* (*Playgoers Golden Jubilee Festival*)	**MAY 21, 22:** Farce, <u>Black Comedy</u> by Peter Shaffer/Ed & L. Bayly, Bob Baunton, Sheila Pisko, David Mann **MAY 25, 26:** Musical, <u>Oh, What a Lovely War</u> by Joan Littlewood/C. Evins, Ed Bayly, Ailsa Chalmers, B. Reed, Denise Dobek, Garry Kohn, Doris Balcovske, F. Huszar, Karen Kay, Marg McKay, D. Pokarney, Anne Reid, Neil Reid, Shirley Ann Walkey, Muriel Matheson	Dick Mells/B. & Cherie Baunton, Ed Bayly, K. Jensen, B. Matheson, Sheri McFadden, Ray Mercer, Sheila Pisko (May 22/14) - *hilarious* Dick Mells with Muriel Jolliffe (choreo)/Sandi Balcovske, B. Baunton, Ed Bayly, Wendy Burrows, A. Greenway, Wanda Huszar, Tim Johnson, L. Larter, B. Matheson, S. McFadden, Tom Melling, D. & E. Mells, R. Mercer, Ted Orchard, S. Pisko, Fran Rude, Jack & Jean Warburton, Pat Waterfield, Jane Wilson **ORCHESTRA:** Ellyn Mells, Ken Duce, Bryan Pritchard, Sara Francis, Willie Mathis, Bryan Francis (May 26/18) - *200 attend first performance*
FEB 7,8/74 - *Yates*	1. <u>The Rising of the Moon</u> by Lady Gregory 2. <u>Hello Out There</u> by Thornton Wilder/Ann Reid, Linda Bayly, Jim Veenstra, David Mann	Ed Bayly/B. Baunton, Ed Bayly, F. Huszar, David Lynagh Jim Veenstra/Albert Azzara, Laurie Mann, B. Matheson, D. Pokarney, Len Robison (Feb 9/16)

DATE/LOCATION	PRODUCTION/ TECHNICAL PERSONNEL	DIRECTOR/CAST/REFERENCE(S)/COMMENTS
APR 25-27/74 - *Yates*	Comedy, <u>Breath of Spring</u> by Peter Coke/C. Evins, B. Baunton, F. Huszar, Ed Bayly, A. Reid, Betty Sorenson, W. Anderson, D. &. S. Balcovske, L. Bayly, Eileen Cashmore, Marg Kokott, G. Mann, M. Matheson, Fred, Marg & Vicki McKay, Murray Robison, Vic Rude, Eleanor Thompson, S.A. Walkey	Joan Waterfield/A. Azzara, C. Baunton, Ed Bayly (stood in for Bill Matheson), F. Featherstone, Kaye Robison, F. Rude, H. Skaronski, Winifred Smith (Apr 26/18) - *myrthful, entertaining and comical*
JUL 15-20/74 - *Leth. Exhibition Pavilion (Whoop-Up Days)*	Melodrama, <u>Priscilla Pringle's Predicament</u> or <u>All's Swell That Ends Swell</u> by Ed Bayly	Ed Bayly/Various casts: A. Azzara, D. Balcovske, Ed & L. Bayly, Doug Borcoman, Bob Baunton, Linda Benz, Pat Hammond, Ed Henley, F. Huszar, Garry Johnson, B. & M. Matheson, Nora Rose, F. Rude, H. Skaronski (Jul 23/4) - *Playgoers complimented*
OCT 17,19,20/74 - *Yates*	Comedy, <u>Arsenic & Old Lace</u> by Joseph Kesselring/Elizabeth Blair, L. Bayly, Bob Rose, K. & M. Robison, S. Balcovske, M. Matheson, Alice Gordon, A. Reid, D. Balcovske, B. Baunton, Ern Bayly, W. Carson, E. Cashmore, Jean Danyluk, Barb Day, Bob Hawn, Jerry Harker, K. Kay, D. Mann, Marg & Vicki McKay, V. Rude, H. Skaronski, S.A. Walkey	Joan Waterfield/B. Baunton, Ed Bayly, Buryl Clark, Michael Day, C. Evins, F. Featherstone, G. Mann, B. Matheson, Mardi Renyk, N. Rose, P. Story, C. Turner, Jack Warburton (Oct 18/16) - *worth savoring*
FEB 18/75 - *Yates (also viewed on CJOC T.V.)*	<u>Priscilla Pringle's Predicament</u> by Ed Bayly - non-competitive entry in Lethbridge & District One Act Festival	Ed Bayly/D. Balcovske, Ed & L. Bayly, F. Huszar, Garry Johnson, M. Matheson (Feb 7/11) - *CJOC T.V. has come up with a winner*
APR 3-5/75 - *Yates*	Drama, <u>The Crucible</u> by Arthur Miller/B. Baunton, A. Reid, C. Evins, Ed Bayly, B. Francis, F. Rude, D. Balcovske, K. Kay, L. Bayly, Eric Low, Darlaine Mahoney, H. Skaronski, Jacquie Shockley, R. Jolliffe, Bill Swenson, B. Rose, N. Gregg, Helen Many Fingers, Linda Nagy, Bill Goldale, G. Mann, S. Balcovske, M., F. & V. McKay, S.A. Walkey	Terry Theodore with Susan Murguly/Laurie Anderson, A. Azzara, Ed Bayly (stood in for Chet Wayne), Diane Byrne, Buryl Clark, Jim Cummings, B. Day, J. Elliott, C. Evins, F. Featherstone, Janine Folkins, Ed Henley, F. Huszar, S. Murguly, Debbie Rakos, M. Renyk, F. Rude, P. Story, J. Waterfield, Bill Wright (Apr 4/18) - *well cast and well acted*
JUL 17-22/75 - *Leth. Exhibition Pavilion*	Melodrama, <u>She Was Only a Farmer's Daughter</u> by Millard Crosby	George Mann/L. Bayly, M. Day, K. Kay, G., Laurin & Nellie Mann, N. Rose, P. Story, Bert Timmermans, C. & B. Baunton, F. Rude, C. Evins, M. Renyk, Sandi Balcovske (Jul 18/24) - *wows whoop-up spectators*
OCT 29-31/75 - *Yates*	Comedy, <u>Come Blow Your Horn</u> by Neil Simon/B. Rose, F. Huszar, C. Evins, A. Reid, Ed & L. Bayly, F. Rude, Jodi Snow, V. McKay, K. Kay, S.A. Walkey, Buryl Clark, J. Waterfield, G. & L. Johnson, M. Robison, Dave Robin, Win Smith, Darlaine Mahoney, V. Rude, W. Anderson	George Mann/C. Baunton, Martin Hoyt, Eric Low, L. Mann, Jim Robinson, K. Robison (Oct 30/10) - *enjoyable*
FEB 21/76 - *Yates*	1. <u>Birdbath</u> by Leonard Melfi 2. <u>The New Play</u> by William Saroyan 3. <u>The Dirty Old Man</u> by Lewis John Carlino/Jodi Snow [stage mgr], David Mann [lighting]	Nora Rose/A. Azzara, Wynne Royer Eric Low/Diane Byrne, Nancy Grigg, E. Low, J. Robinson, M. Renyk, Bill Wright Terry Theodore/Ed Bayly, A. Azzara, Janine Folkins - (Feb 23/15) - *Birdbath was selected to be presented at AIAF in Medicine Hat*
APR 20-23/76 - *Yates*	Comedy, <u>The Time of Your Life</u> by William Saroyan/L. & Ed Bayly, F. McKay, G. Holland, C. Evins, F. Rude, E. Low, K. Kay, S.A. Walkey, B. Clark, D. Cunningham, Ern Bayly, Greg Royer, Gary & Darlaine Mahoney, Neil Boyden, A. Reid, V. McKay Lil Ramage, Dawn De Vito, Heather Joyce, Bob & N. Hawn, K. Robison, C. Baunton	Wes Stefan/Ed & L. Bayly, B. Baunton, John Scott Black, David Cunningham, B. & Jamie Day, Pat and Todd Hammond, Gail Holland, F. Huszar, G. & Linda Johnson, Bill Mallalieu, D. Mann, M. McKay, Gil Poirier, A. Reid, Len Robinson, N. Rose, W. Royer, Chip Seibert, W. Stefan, P. Story, Gary Terlesky, Janice Tilley, John Van Egland (Apr 22/14) - *a gallant attempt*
JUL 19-24/76 - *Leth. Exhibition Pavilion*	Melodramas: 1. <u>Ten Barrooms in One Night</u> (a spoof) 2. <u>Set a Thief to Catch a Thief</u>	Ed Bayly/Ed Bayly, C. Evins, E. & Jody (Snow) Low, D. Mann, P. Story Ed Bayly/Garry Johnson, L. Bayly, D. Cunningham, P. Story (Jul 21/33) - *Playgoers antics entertaining*

DATE/LOCATION	PRODUCTION/ TECHNICAL PERSONNEL	DIRECTOR/CAST/REFERENCE(S)/COMMENTS
OCT 20-23/76 - *Yates*	Mystery, Night Must Fall by Emlyn Williams/L. Bayly, G. & L. Johnson, G. Holland, J. Snow, Al Candy, E. Low, F. Rude, K. Kay, S.A. Walkey, F. & M. McKay, Rod Flexhaug, M. Robison, Ron Nagel, M. Wright, B. Rose, A. Reid, Flor Groenen, Win Smith, L. Mann, M. Renyk, B. Day, H. Joyce, Rene Brown, Dawn (McKay) Flexhaug, Lynn Franklin	Joan Waterfield/B. & C. Baunton, Ed Bayly, E. Cashmore, C. Evins, F. Featherstone, Anne Hay, H. Skaronski (Oct 22/16) - *performance was nothing short of remarkable*
FEB 26/77 - *Yates* MAR 5 - *Grande Prairie*	1. The Crickets Sing By Beverley Cross 2. Ernie's Incredible Illucination by Alan Ayckbourne 3. Steinway Grand by Ference Karenthy	Joan Waterfield/Ed & L. Bayly, Kelly Fiddick, Bryan Francis, F. Huszar, G. Johnson, E. Low, H. Skaronski, Chris Tobin Michael Wright/C. Evins, G. & L. Johnson, Michael Nowlin, Chip Seibert, H. Skaronski Joan Waterfield/Ed Bayly, N. Rose (Feb 25/7) - *entries in the One Act Play Festival*
MAR 24-26/77 - *Leth. Public Library*	Comedy, A Comedy of Errors by William Shakespeare/C. Evins, L. Bayly, Jody Snow, Ed Bayly, G. Johnson, C. Baunton, Win Smith, F. Huszar, B. Francis, F. Rude, E. Cashmore, Larry Fekete, L. Johnson, A. Reid, M. Renyk, S.A. Walkey	Eric Low/B. Day, K. Fiddick, B. & Leon Francis P. Hammond, Janet Ing, K. Kay, E. Low, Annelise Machielse, Glen Piper, C. Seibert, Gary Terleski, C. Tobin, Debbie Waterfield, M. Wright (Mar 25/6) - *no review*
JUL 18-23/77 - *Ex. Pavilion*	Western Melodrama, Polly Pardon Gets Her Own Back, or Kitty Litter Strikes Again by Ed Bayly	Ed Bayly/C. Evins, L. Johnson, F. Huszar, L. Bayly, A. Azzara, P. Story & others (Jul 13/14)
OCT 20-22/77 - *Yates*	Comedy, Life With Father by Clarence Day/C. Evins, H. Skaronski, F. McKay, B. Rose, G. Holland, E. Cashmore, F. Rude, Ed Bayly, Rosemary Allen, A. Azzara, B. & C. Baunton, L. Bayly, L. Fekete, Brian Fromme, H. Joyce, Roy Godstyn, F. Huszar, Christine Kenwood, Les Krushnel, Andrew & Jon Madill, Bill Mallalieu, F. McKay, Carla Millar, Dave Nash, K. & M. Robison, Win Smith, Ken Rodzinyak, S.A. Walkey, C. Watkinson, Susan Wishaw	Joan Waterfield/Russell Baunton, Doug Campbell, Kate Connolly, B. Day, C. Evins, F. Featherstone, G. Mann, Michael Nowlin, Anne Penton, David Plaxton, M. Renyk, N. Rose, H. Skaronski, P. Story, Deb Waterfield (Oct 21/6) - *once the cast loosens up LWF should be hilarious*
FEB 17,18/78 - *Yates*	1. Canadian Gothic by Joanna M. Glass/L. Bayly, M. Wright, Steve Alexander, E. Cashmore, G. Johnson, G. Mann, Michael Skaronski, John Carlson, Doug Campbell 2. The Rehearsal by Michael F. Rogers/M.F. Rogers, M. Wright, E. Cashmore, M. Renyk	Fran Rude/Ed Bayly, Keith Chief Moon, A. Reid, D. Waterfield - - - Cathy Evins/Rose Marie Bothi, Doug Campbell, Mark Campbell, Paul Cohen, Larry Ettling, Sheila Horon, Greg Martin, Bill McCann, Brian Woodcock (Feb 20/10) - *Canadian Gothic took top honors among eight productions at regional festival in the city*
MAR 3/78 - *Yates*	Canadian Gothic	Fran Rude/(Mar 6/78/18) - *Drama Achievement Award to Fran Rude for "sensitive direction"*
MAY 5,6/78 - *Public Library*	Reader's Theatre: 1. The Journals of Susanna Moodie by Margaret Atwood 2. Under Milkwood by Dylan Thomas - CREW: A. Azzara, M. Wright, L. Blaquiere, F. Rude, A. Reid, Bill Main, P. Story, E. Bayly, M. Day, H. Skaronski	- Martin Oordt/L. Bayly, Kate Connolly, B. Day, C. Evins - M. Oordt/Ed Bayly/Lea Blaquiere, M. Campbell, E. Cashmore, A. & M. Day, L. Etling, Don Goerzen, K. Kay, J. Tilley, D. Waterfield (May 4/7)
JUL 16-21/78 - *Ex. Pavilion (Whoop-Up Days)*	Melodrama, A Trucker is a Girl's Best Friend by Albert Azzara	Albert Azzara/A. Azzara, Annelise Machielse, Deb Waterfield & others (Jul 19/13) - *popular*

DATE/LOCATION	PRODUCTION/ TECHNICAL PERSONNEL	DIRECTOR/CAST/REFERENCE(S)/COMMENTS
OCT 23-28/78 - *Yates*	Comedy, <u>No Sex Please, We're British</u> by Anthony Marriott & Alistair Foot/C. Evins, F. Rude, L. Bayly, H. Joyce, A. Reid, M. Day, L. Etling, J. & D. Waterfield, Ed Bayly, B. Baunton, Dave Best, John Carlson, E. Cashmore, L. Fekete, Michael Gibbs, G. Holland, F. Huszar, G. & L. Johnson, B. Mains, M. McKay, Lynn Poole, M. Renyk, Dave Robin, H. Skaronski, P. Story, Jean Warburton, Merle Waterfield	<u>David Poole</u>/B. & C. Baunton, Ed Bayly, Geoff Calvert, M. Campbell, A. Day, C. Evins, Jane McCoy, Doug Petherbridge, Keith Robin, Keith Western (Oct 24/25) - *stuff of good farce*
FEB 24/79 - *Yates*	<u>Another Midsummer Night's Dream</u> by Eilonwy Morgan	<u>Eilonwy Morgan</u>/B. Day, L. Johnson, J. McCoy, D. Poole, Jean Warburton, Candy Williams (Feb 26/5) - *a play of voices - not action*
OCT 16-20/79 - *Yates*	Drama, <u>Walsh</u> by Sharon Pollock/Ed Bayly, K. Kay, M. Day, A. Reid, C. Evins, E. & Jody (Snow) Low, F. Rude, B. Mains, K. Sinclair, C. Baunton, L. Blaquiere, B. Baunton, Peter Brown, Geoff Calvert, E. Cashmore, A., B., J. & M. Day, Ron Maack, Greg Martin, A. Reid, M. Renyk, Tom Ripley, H. Skaronski, Marilyn Soop	<u>Fran Rude</u>/A. Azzara, Ed Bayly, Jim Coates, Patrick Doyle, Camelia Dumont, Simon Gladeau, Al Greenway, P. Hammond, Danny & Steven Healy, M. Renyk, Ken Sinclair, Louis M. Soop, P. Story, Pat Twigg, Jean Warburton, Bryan Yel-lowhorn (Oct 13/6) - *a theatrical event*
MAY 14-17/80 - *Yates*	Musical Comedy, <u>The Fantasticks</u> by Tom Jones & Harvey Schmidt/C. Evins, A. Reid, F. McKay, B. Day, Ed Bayly, H. Joyce, M. McKay, K. & Joyce Western, E. Cashmore, C. Baunton, L. Bayly, Bob & Pat Bunn, Karen Dobek, Amy Day, Dawn & Rod Flexhaug, Sharon Hagel, G. Holland, F. Huszar, K. Kay, Jane Paterson, M. Renyk, K. & M. Robison, Johanna Rocco, F. Rude, H. Skaronski, P. Story, Jean Warburton	<u>Keith Harris</u> & Wes Stefan/Arla Burbank, M. Day, R. Gordon, K. Harris, Lesley Palmer, K. Sinclair, W. Stefan, Candy Williams **MUSICIANS:** Eleanor Lawson, Randy Paskuski, Neil Sheets **CHORAL DIR:** Arla Burbank (May 15/B10) - *a credit to the group*
DEC 6/80 - *Public Library*	Little Theatre: 1. <u>Alexander's Horse</u> or <u>Catherine Parr</u> 2. Historical Readings	- <u>Murray Robison</u>/G. Mann, K. Robison, H. Skaronski B. Baunton, F. Featherstone, J. McCoy, M. Renyk (Dec 8/C6; 10/A4)
1981	No major Playgoers Productions but the club sponsored a Lethbridge run of <u>How the Other Half Loves</u> by Alan Ayckbourne	dir. by Fran Rude & produced by Neil Boyden (Feb 18/B6)
DEC 11/81 - *Public Library*	<u>Optimism</u> by John Patrick (auspices of Shoestring Theatre)	<u>Pat Hammond</u>/ (Dec 8/A1)
FEB 25-27/82 - *Yates*	Comedy, <u>Never Too Late</u> by Arthur Long/C. Evins, L. & Ed Bayly, Laurie Meyers, Barry Hegland, Bert Timmermans, Brian Tedder, G. Holland, L. & G. Johnson, K. Robison, Bryce Walton, Marcie Adler, B. & C. Baunton, N. Boyden, E. Cashmore, Ed Finley, Dale Haigh, Luella Lee, Carla Mil-lar, Chet Mook, F. Rude, H. Skaronski, J. Waterfield	<u>George Mann</u>/B. Baunton, Lawrence Kotkas, E. Low, Jesse Martin, Ross Miller, K. Robison, Charles Schott, Kathy Sharp, Barbara Warren (Feb 26/B8) - *enjoyed by Yates audience*
JUN 11/82 - *Public Library*	Playgoers sponsors	An Evening of One Act Plays from the recent High School Drama Festival (Jun 5/B10)
FEB /83 - *Local Con-vention Centres*	Convention Productions 1. <u>Priscilla Pringle's Predicament</u> by Ed Bayly 2. <u>Chinook</u> by Bill Matheson	- <u>Ed Bayly</u>/Ed Bayly, G. & L. Johnson, Brenda Laycock, G. Mann, L. Mann, Nellie Mann (piano) <u>Joan Waterfield</u>/G. Johnson, Jesse Martin, C. Mook, K. Sinclair, H. Skaronski, C. Williams
FEB 26/83 - *Yates*	<u>A Bench at the Edge</u> by Luigi Jannuzzi	<u>Kathy Sharp</u>/Todd Hammond, Jeffrey Haslam, Barbara Wilson (Feb 26/C4) - *Katherine Sharp is having her first directoral fling*

DATE/LOCATION	PRODUCTION/ TECHNICAL PERSONNEL	DIRECTOR/CAST/REFERENCE(S)/COMMENTS
MAY 5-8/83 - *Yates* (*60th Anniversary Production*)	Comedy Drama, <u>Da</u> by Hugh Leonard/Roger Schultz, L. & G. Johnson, W. Wiebe, K. Sharp, G. & L. Mann, L. Lee, C. Evins, B. Day, C. Williams, J. Waterfield, L. Bayly, C. Baunton, N. Boyden, E. Cashmore, Marj Dalke, Dawn Flexhaug, G. Holland, Brenda Laycock, E. Low, F. McKay, C. Mook, Cina Opel, Duncan Rand, A. Reid, M. Renyk, M. Robison, K. Sinclair, P. Story, Bryce Walton, Christine Warren, Bev Webber	Fran Rude/Ed Bayly, Jeff Haslam, Winstan Jones, Sally Moore, H. Skaronski, Pat Sullivan, John Warren, Barbara Wilson (May 6/A12) - *bold & arresting* produc-tion
APR 11-14/84 - *Yates*	Mystery, <u>Suddenly at Home</u> by Frances Durbridge/R. Schultz, M. Day, C. Evins, B. Tedder, Donna Kampen, Sandra Mandzuk, F. Rude, L. Bayly, Bery Allan, Lyndon & Susan Bray, Marj Dalke, Amy & Barb Day, F. Huszar, Fred Lewis, Clare Malmberg, A. Reid, Nancy Seefeldt, P. Story	Joan Waterfield/B. & C. Baunton, Ed Bayly, John Duddy, Kate Johnstone, Doug Petherbridge, Mardi, Renyk, Candy Williams (Apr 12/C4) - *another job well done*
MAY 17/84 - *Public Library*	Little Theatre <u>The Flattering Word</u> by George Kelly	Annette Martin/B. Day, Lawrence Kotkas, Sheila Martin, Sally Moore, P. Story
SEPT 12; OCT 10/84 - *Public Library*	Dramatic Readings	1. Cherie Baunton/B. & C. Baunton, Kate Johnstone, G. Mann, J. Waterfield, Nellie Mann (piano) 2. Joan Waterfield/C. Baunton, Ed Bayly, J. Waterfield
FEB 6-9/85 - *Yates*	Drama, <u>The Miracle Worker</u> by William Gibson/Ed Bayly, J. Snow, C. Williams, H. Skaronski, Herb Matis, B. Tedder, Kathy Erickson, David Hignell, K. Johnstone, E. Cashmore, Jean Warburton, L. Dongworth, B. & C. Baunton, Ed Bayly, Laurie Cargo, A. & Mike Day, L. Dongworth, John Duell, Donna Gallant, Elton Henry, G. Johnson, Carol Johnson, Donna Kampen, Kathy Koshman, L. Lee, Paul Liska, Judith Mowat, Joan Norris, M. Renyk, Joyce Sloboda, P. Story, Bob Thompson, J. Waterfield, Emma Wayne	Fran Rude/L. Bayly, Winstan Jones, Lawrence Kotkas, Jesse Martin, Tsuaki Marule, Judy Melnyk, Junior Oliver, Carla Serkin, Cindy Turner, Deb Waterfield, Analea Wayne, W. Chet Wayne (Feb 7A3) - *powerful, yet tender production*
MAR 4/85 - *Public Library* MAR 15,16/85 - *Yates*	Little Theatre: 1. <u>Spreading the News</u> by Lady Gregory - 2. <u>Mother Figure</u> by Alan Ayckbourne	- Ed Bayly/B. Baunton, Kenn Blom, Mark Connellan, L. Dongworth, Bridget Duddy, C. Evins, G. Johnson, G. Mann, D. Petherbridge, H. Skaronski (replaced L. Dongworth for festival presentation), P. Story Cherie Baunton/Libby & Mike Day, Kate Johnstone (Mar 18/A3) - *Honorable mention for <u>Spreading the News</u>*
JUN 15/85 - *Public Library*	Little Theatre: 1. <u>Funeral Tea</u> 2. <u>Yes Dear</u> by Warren Graves 3. <u>Shatterproof</u> (presented by Windmill Players of High River)	- Neil Boyden/Lucy Bohac, Janice (Tilley) Brown, B. Day, C. Evins, K. Johnstone Joan Waterfield/C. Baunton, Ed Bayly, Janice Brown (Jun 15/A11, A12)
OCT 26/85 - *Public Library*	Little Theatre Evening 1. <u>The Happy Journey</u> by Thornton Wilder - 2. <u>Yes Dear</u> by Warren Graves 3. <u>Priscilla Pringle's Predicament</u> by Ed Bayly	- Chet Wayne/L. Kotkas, Richard Mack, G. Mann, Michelle Mills, Sheila Pisko, Analea Wayne Joan Waterfield/C. Baunton, E. Bayly, J. Brown Ed Bayly/E. & L. Bayly, Marie Caveny, G. & L. Johnson, G. Mann, N. Mann (piano) (Oct 25/9)
OCT 30/85 - *Yates*	Computer Promotion in conjunction with CFCN T.V. <u>Focus on the Future</u>	Neil Boyden/Bery Allan, L. Bayly & the voices of: E. Bayly, N. Boyden, M. Day, M. Mills, M. Renyk (Oct 31/A11)
NOV 7/85 - *Convention Centre*	Convention Entertainment, <u>Yes Dear</u> by W. Graves	J. Waterfield/C. Baunton, E. Bayly, J. Brown

DATE/LOCATION	PRODUCTION/ TECHNICAL PERSONNEL	DIRECTOR/CAST/REFERENCE(S)/COMMENTS
FEB 5-8/86 - *Yates*	Drama Comedy, On Golden Pond by Ernest Thompson/Dawn McCaugherty, John A. Johnston, Bruce Sekella, K. Johnstone, B. Day, Ruth Liska, B. Tedder, C. Evins, M. Renyk, Ginny Hofarth, Khym Goslin, L. Johnson, J. Waterfield, L. Bayly, J. Low, Janet Snow, Laurie Cargo, M. Dalke, Sandra Fullerman, Sheena Lawson, Kathy Walburger, Don Ryane, E. Bayly, A. & M. Day, John Duell, L. Fekete, Y. Fredrick, Paul Liska, Rick Mrazek, Ruth Nelson, Greg Rohovie, Iris Sedore, P. Story	Neil Boyden/Gavin Crawford, Julie Ellis, G. Johnson, G. Mann, Lee Prindle, K. Robison (Feb 6/A11) - *meaningful production, enjoyed by audience*
MAR /86 - *Medicine Hat*	Yes Dear by W. Graves	*Selected to represent Lethbridge Regional at A1AF but did not participate in Grande Prairie (Mar 10/A2)*
APR 25-26/86 - *Yates*	Little Theatre Evening **1.** Dirty Old Man by Lewis John Carlino **2.** Seeds by Gordon Pengilly **3.** Run to the Roundhouse Nellie He Can't Corner You There by Shubert Fredrick **CREW:** Gordon Barthel, Bob Prysiazny, B. Tedder, G. Holland. L. C. Johnson	- Ed Bayly/E. Bayly, Bill Lawson, Kari Matchett Dawn McCaugherty/D. McCaugherty, Don Ryane Neil Boyden/Jane Holmes, L. Johnson, Lee Prindle, Jeanette Reid, John Sauve - (Apr 23/B7) - *no review*
JUN 12/86 - *Public Library*	An Evening of Readings	E. & L. Bayly, G. & N. Mann
AUG /86 - *1. Coaldale (Settler's Day) 2. Lethbridge Extendicare 3. PNR Convention*	Melodrama, Run to the Roundhouse Nellie	Neil Boyden/N. Boyden, Jane Holmes, G. & L. Johnson, Lee Prindle, Jeannette Reid (Jul 30/A3; Aug 11/A5)
DEC 29,30/86 - *Public Library*	Readings: "A Celebration of Christmas" **1.** The Woman at the Inn by Carolyn Jerome **2.** A Child's Christmas in Wales by Dylan Thomas **3.** A Christmas Carol by C. Dickens (adapted by Richard Epp)	Ed Bayly/Joan Waterfield (m.c.), E. Bayly, M. Day, K. Kay, Simon Cashmore, G. Holland, Kaaren Kotkas, Bill Lawson, F. Huszar, K. Sinclair, Lee Van Andel SOLOISTS: Sandra McFarlane, Neana Meeks, Lawrence Kotkas (piano) (Dec 30/A2) - *one more Christmas treasure*
FEB 4/87 - *Yates*	Comedy, The Odd Couple (female version) by Neil Simon/G. Johnson, J.A. Johnston, John Malcolm, B. Tedder, E. Bayly, G. Holland, Y. Fredrick, K. Goslin, M. Renyk, S. Cashmore, Gordon Levy, Shane Sillitto, P. Story, M. Day, G. Mann, H. Matis, Rose Rossi, L. Meyers, Duncan & John Rand, M. & H. Skaronski, L. Van Andel, W. Wiebe, L. Lee, Anne Leong, Jane DeCoste, S. Pisko	Neil Boyden/L. Bayly, L. Dongworth, F. Huszar, G. Holland, L. Johnson, Sandra McFarlane, Neana Meeks, Lee Prindle (Feb 5/A11) - *all good performances*
FEB 3-6/88 - *Yates*	Comedy, The Teahouse of the August Moon by John Patrick/L. Johnson, J. Johnston, Jonathan White, Bill Lawson, B. Tedder, M. Day, Dave Gibson, H. Matis, E. Bayly, L. & Kim Van Andel, G. Holland, M. Renyk, Donna Kampen, Linda, Bob, Rob & Steve Thomsen, Rita Zaugg, Kim Onofrychuk, Sandra (McFarlane) Robin, P. Story, L. Bayly, D. & J. Rand, Bradley Nicholas, Bob Brunelle, Stan Shimozawa, Paul Liska, Kevin Matis, Lloyd Pollock, Doug Kampen, Jeremy Erb, Denise Von Chorus, Mike Dolezal, Sylvia Babin, J. Brown, Lee Ann Koenen, Diane Peters, Ranae Rasmussen, Y. Fredrick, A. Leong, Collette Willetts, Monica Hricise, Jackie Mark	Neil Boyden/Sanae Maeda (musician & speech coach)/Ihoko Asakuma, Carolyn Brocca, Jane DeCoste, Khym Goslin, Stevie Hall-Thomsen, Patti Ikeda, Garry Johnson, Yoshie Kaneda, Nancy Katakami, Ruth & Susanne Liska, Eric Low, John Malcolm, Lee Prindle, Brian Sakamoto, Mel Sameshima, Carla Serkin, Stan & Tate Shimozawa, Hisako Takahashi, Florence, Gerry & Tom Tomiyama, Katsuko & Yukie Uchimura, Gene & Jim Yamada (Feb 4/C9) - *a rich, rare comedy*
JUN 25/88 - *Public Library Th.*	Readers' Theatre, The Hollow Crown devised by John Barton/Brian Tedder (lighting)	Linda Bayly/Ed Bayly, Eric Low, Brian Tyson, Joan Waterfield (readers); Michael Day, Ruston Harker, Ian Mandin (singers); Marie Woodrow (accompanist)

DATE/LOCATION	PRODUCTION/ TECHNICAL PERSONNEL	DIRECTOR/CAST/REFERENCE(S)/COMMENTS
FEB 1-4/89 - *Yates*	Comedy Drama, <u>Steel Magnolias</u>/ by Robert Harling/J.A. Johnston, G. Johnson, Ed Bayly, Herb Matis, Jonathan White, Gerry Tomiyama, Toni Dyck, Gail Holland, Mardi Renyk, Sue Koshman, Khym Goslin, Frank Huszar, David Green, Anne Reid, George Mann, Linda Johnson, Brian Sakamoto, Jackie Mark, Lauri Meyers, Phil Story	<u>Neil Boyden</u> with John Malcolm (A.D.)/Linda Bayly, Jane De Coste, Tammi Pretty, Sheri (McFadden) Thomson, Cathie Thys, Joan Waterfield (Feb 2/89/A11) - *warms hearts with a powerful real life story (Dave Mabell)*
FEB 28/89 - *Yates*	One Act Plays: **1.** <u>Tell Me Another Story, Sing Me a Song</u> by Jean Lenox Toddie **2.** <u>The Exhibition</u> by Thomas Gibbons **3.** <u>Black & Silver</u> by Michael Frayne **CREWS:** Ed Bayly, Brian Tedder, Scarlette Downey, Gail Holland, Herb Matis, Dave Gibson, Joanne Bayly, Mardi Renyk, Simon Cashmore	- <u>Ed Bayly</u>/Marcie Main, Ginger Ames - <u>Ed Bayly</u>/Wes Stefan, Ed Bayly <u>John Malcolm</u>/Mike Smith, Laurie Meyers (Mar 1/C6) - *Playgoers' entries open drama festival*

Playgoers of Lethbridge: Onstage Participants
April 9, 1923–June 30, 1989

<table>
<tr><td colspan="7">A. MEMBERS WHO PARTICIPATED IN PLAYGOERS
BOTH BEFORE 1942 AND AFTER 1950</td></tr>
<tr><td rowspan="2">PARTICIPANT</td><td colspan="3">1923-42</td><td colspan="2">1951-70</td><td rowspan="2"></td></tr>
<tr><td>M</td><td>L</td><td>C*</td><td>M</td><td>L</td></tr>
<tr><td></td><td>M</td><td>L</td><td>C*</td><td>M</td><td>L</td><td>TOTAL</td></tr>
<tr><td>Baalim, Harry</td><td>1</td><td>2</td><td>2</td><td>2</td><td>1</td><td>8</td></tr>
<tr><td>Bailey, Reg</td><td>2</td><td>1</td><td>1</td><td>2</td><td>-</td><td>6</td></tr>
<tr><td>Baines, Audrey (Chiswick)</td><td>-</td><td>-</td><td>1</td><td>2</td><td>2</td><td>5</td></tr>
<tr><td>Bennett, Helen (James)</td><td>1</td><td>1</td><td>-</td><td>7</td><td>3</td><td>12</td></tr>
<tr><td>Bryans, Maybelle</td><td>1</td><td>4</td><td>-</td><td>-</td><td>-</td><td>5**</td></tr>
<tr><td>Connor, Lena</td><td>4</td><td>4</td><td>-</td><td>2</td><td>-</td><td>10</td></tr>
<tr><td>Faunch, Ted</td><td>3</td><td>9</td><td>4</td><td>1</td><td>-</td><td>17</td></tr>
<tr><td>Gibson, Chris</td><td>2</td><td>3</td><td>-</td><td>-</td><td>-</td><td>5**</td></tr>
<tr><td>Matthews, C.R.</td><td>4</td><td>15</td><td>1</td><td>5</td><td>4</td><td>29</td></tr>
<tr><td colspan="7">*M = Major Production; L = Little Theatre Production;</td></tr>
<tr><td colspan="7">C = Chorus</td></tr>
<tr><td colspan="7">**Active members but no stage participation during the later era.</td></tr>
</table>

<table>
<tr><td colspan="9">B. MEMBERS DURING THE PERIOD 1923 - 1942 ONLY</td></tr>
<tr><td>Participant in:
I. 10 or more productions</td><td>M</td><td>L</td><td>C</td><td>T</td><td></td><td>M</td><td>L</td><td>C</td><td>T</td></tr>
<tr><td>Church, Hilda</td><td>5</td><td>5</td><td>2</td><td>12</td><td>Rose, Fred</td><td>6</td><td>7</td><td>-</td><td>13</td></tr>
<tr><td>Ferguson, Tom</td><td>5</td><td>8</td><td>4</td><td>17</td><td>Roy, Blanche</td><td>4</td><td>6</td><td>-</td><td>10</td></tr>
<tr><td>Jones, Aileen</td><td>3</td><td>5</td><td>5</td><td>13</td><td>Sterndale Bennett, E.G.</td><td>5</td><td>13</td><td>-</td><td>18</td></tr>
<tr><td>Martin, Vinnie (Burritt)</td><td>-</td><td>9</td><td>2</td><td>11</td><td>Sydal, Mary</td><td>1</td><td>9</td><td>-</td><td>10</td></tr>
<tr><td>Raworth, Arnold</td><td>5</td><td>5</td><td>-</td><td>10</td><td>Teague, Fred</td><td>6</td><td>6</td><td>-</td><td>12</td></tr>
<tr><td>II. 7-9 Productions</td><td>M</td><td>L</td><td>C</td><td>T</td><td></td><td>M</td><td>L</td><td>C</td><td>T</td></tr>
<tr><td>Brander, Ethel</td><td>2</td><td>3</td><td>2</td><td>7</td><td>Keivill, Roy</td><td>5</td><td>2</td><td>-</td><td>7</td></tr>
<tr><td>Davidson, Margaret</td><td>2</td><td>6</td><td>-</td><td>8</td><td>Lawrence, Ted</td><td>2</td><td>5</td><td>-</td><td>7</td></tr>
<tr><td>Frayne, George</td><td>3</td><td>5</td><td>-</td><td>8</td><td>Lewis, Allan</td><td>3</td><td>6</td><td>-</td><td>9</td></tr>
<tr><td>Hick, Ronald</td><td>1</td><td>6</td><td>2</td><td>9</td><td>Poole, Horace</td><td>1</td><td>6</td><td>-</td><td>7</td></tr>
<tr><td>Holman, George</td><td>3</td><td>4</td><td>2</td><td>9</td><td>Rosewarn, James</td><td>3</td><td>5</td><td>1</td><td>9</td></tr>
<tr><td>Ings, Eric</td><td>4</td><td>3</td><td>-</td><td>7</td><td>Sterndale Bennett, E.B.</td><td>4</td><td>3</td><td>1</td><td>8</td></tr>
<tr><td>Jones, Ethel</td><td>1</td><td>2</td><td>4</td><td>7</td><td>Thrall, Minnie</td><td>5</td><td>2</td><td>1</td><td>8</td></tr>
<tr><td>Jordan, Lyn</td><td>2</td><td>5</td><td>-</td><td>7</td><td>Vallance, J.T.</td><td>2</td><td>6</td><td>-</td><td>8</td></tr>
<tr><td>III. 5-6 Productions</td><td>M</td><td>L</td><td>C</td><td>T</td><td></td><td>M</td><td>L</td><td>C</td><td>T</td></tr>
<tr><td>Barnhill, Kathleen (Lindsay)</td><td>2</td><td>2</td><td>1</td><td>5</td><td>Martin, Kathleen</td><td>-</td><td>4</td><td>1</td><td>5</td></tr>
<tr><td>Becker, Echo</td><td>2</td><td>3</td><td>-</td><td>5</td><td>Matthews, Marguerite</td><td>-</td><td>2</td><td>4</td><td>6</td></tr>
<tr><td>Bletcher, Natalie (Betty)</td><td>1</td><td>1</td><td>3</td><td>5</td><td>Maynard, Helen</td><td>1</td><td>4</td><td>1</td><td>6</td></tr>
<tr><td>Brander, Eildon</td><td>2</td><td>3</td><td>1</td><td>6</td><td>Moore, Hazelton C.</td><td>3</td><td>1</td><td>1</td><td>5</td></tr>
<tr><td>Collins, Philip J.</td><td>2</td><td>3</td><td>-</td><td>5</td><td>Morris, Alfred</td><td>1</td><td>1</td><td>3</td><td>5</td></tr>
<tr><td>Fairbairn, Lyn</td><td>1</td><td>5</td><td>-</td><td>6</td><td>Morris, Percy</td><td>2</td><td>1</td><td>3</td><td>6</td></tr>
<tr><td>Farris, Nancy</td><td>1</td><td>3</td><td>1</td><td>5</td><td>Pauling, Olive</td><td>1</td><td>4</td><td>-</td><td>5</td></tr>
</table>

Gibson, Edith	1	4	-	5	Sandquist, Carl	-	4	2	6
Greenway, Harvey	2	3	-	5	Seamans, Mildred	-	4	1	5
Hendry, Ian	1	4	-	5	Sterndale Bennett, Muriel	-	4	1	5
Hiscocks, Charles	3	2	-	5	Stretton, Herbert	1	4	-	5
Holmes, Fred	2	3	1	6	Thomas, Nan	3	2	-	5
Hume, Robert	2	3	1	6	Vallance, Syd	2	4	-	6
Jenks, Kay	1	3	1	5	Worthington, James	2	3	-	5
Lightbound, Marguerite	3	1	1	5					
IV. 3-4 Productions	**M**	**L**	**C**	**T**		**M**	**L**	**C**	**T**
Blake, Geoffrey	1	2	-	3	McElgunn, Douglas	1	-	2	3
Church, Betty	1	2	1	4	McIlvena, Art	2	1	-	3
Clarke, Mary	-	4	-	4	Meech, Eveline	1	2	1	4
Coffay, Jack	-	-	3	3	Mellor Langdale, Alathea	1	2	-	3
de Jourdan, P.M.	2	1	-	3	Pineau, W.P.	1	3	-	4
Elton, David H.	2	2	-	4	Pizzey, Tom	2	1	-	3
Evans, Tom	1	2	1	4	Proctor, Hilda	1	-	2	3
Fisher, Bernadette	3	-	-	3	Rannard, Robert S.	1	-	2	3
Fisher, Elaine	2	1	-	3	Raworth, Phyllis	1	2	-	3
Frost, George	3	1	-	4	Reardon, Georgina	-	1	2	3
Galbraith, Jean	-	3	-	3	Ritchie, Louise	2	2	-	4
Gaynor, Percy	3	1	-	4	Ritchie, Robin	-	3	-	3
Hay, Camille (Connor)	-	4	-	4	Russell, Warren	1	-	2	3
Hughes, Josephine	2	1	-	3	Sangster, Phil	-	4	-	4
Johnson, F. Nowell	1	2	-	3	Scott, Jean	2	2	-	4
Jordan, Madge	2	1	-	3	Seamans, Hod	-	2	1	3
Kelly, Hazel	2	1	-	3	Shepherd, Marjorie	-	2	1	3
Lambert, Carl	-	3	-	3	Steele, C. Frank	1	2	1	4
Lingard, Eric	-	1	3	4	Teague, Isobel	2	1	1	4
Long, Hazel	2	1	-	3	Westley, Dorothy	1	-	3	4
Marrs, Dorothy	-	1	3	4					

V. 1-2 Productions With at Least One Speaking Role

Walter Adnitt, A.C. Aherns, Elsie Aitken, Isobel Allen, George, J.A. & Olga Anderson, Ernest & Robert Armstrong, Ernest Atherton, Barbara & Cecily Baalim, Ralph Baines, Margaret Barr, J.H. Barry, Arthur Beaumont, Ruth Becker, J.W. Berry, Jennie Bixby, Shirley Blackwell, W.E. Blair, Bob Bletcher, Stuart Bodard, William Bond, Paddy Bowman, Margaret Brenton, George Brown, Jr., Laura Brown, Betty Buchanan, Vivien Buffet, Bernice Burnard, S.G. Burridge, Douglas Cameron, Susan Chiswick, Josephine, Donald & Margaret Clark, Marion & Pauline Clarke, Kathleen Collins, Percy Cranston, Elizabeth Crowe, Brownie, Charles & Dixie Daniel, Fay Davies, Joyce Davis, Charles Dawson, Myrtle Delay, Jessie Doe, P. Doorbar, William Dormier, Perry Duffy, F.R. Duncanson, Lloyd Elliott, Afton, Dalton & Kitchner Elton, Eric Farris, Marge Farstad, Stan Faulkner, Irene Faunch, May Fawcett, George Fay, Crawford Fisher, T.H. Fleetwood, George E. Fleming, Berta Ford, Jean Forbes, Leona Freng, Hector Frey, Gerry & Louise Gaetz, Betty Garissere, Fred & Jean Gibson, Pearl Gaynor, Rosalind Goodman, Alden & Tom Green, M. Greenway, E.C. Guilbault, Gordon Hamilton, Olive Haw, Mrs. Walter Hay, E. Hicks, Mary Higginbotham, Cleve & Helen Hill, Richard Hincks, Mary Hoar, Ada & Mary Hogg, Andree Houlton, Margaret Hoyt, J. & Ruth Hughes, Ethel & F. Humby, D.R. Innis, W.L. Jacobson, Ethel & Mrs. C. Jackson, Eric, Marion & Ralph Johnson, Bertha & Martha Karp, J. Kelly, Annie & William Kergan, A.W. & Charles King, Ann Kostiuk, Villa Lambert, Marie Lange, Bob Lawrence, Ernest & Mrs. Layton, Jeannette & Myrtle Leech, Audrey Rea Leonard, Eleanor & Hal Lindsay, Jimmie Linn, Avril Little, Marie Louise Loescher, B. Long, W.D. Lowe, Josephine Lucas, Jean MacBeth, Florence & K. Mackenzie, Lois McGuire, Janet McIlvena, Agnes McKerrow, H. McKenna, I.J. McKinnon, Helen McMahon, Victor Meech, D. Morris, Robert Meldrum, A.H.L. Mellor, Dora Mileson, Cliff Mitchell, Hester & Lloyd Murray, Loretta Niven, George O'Meara, H. Ostlund, Hulda Pack, Dorothy Palmer, C. Parker, Roderick Paterson, Mr. Pearson, Stan Peszat, Max Peters, Dennis & J.D. Pierce, Edna Pizzey, Rose Pomeroy, Ronald H. Preston, Bill, Dorothy & M. Raby, William Rae, Sgt. Radcliffe, Bob Ranson, Effie Reid, C.H. Rhodes, George Rice, Baxter Ridley, Norman Ritchie, Helen Rivers, Fred Robins, T.E. Rodel, Jean & E. Vincent Rose, Margery & A.J.M. Round, Helen Ruthven, Alice Sather, Margaret Savage, Yvonne Schweitzer, A.W. Shackleford, Iza Shearer, Ethel, Joan & S.J. Shepherd, Katherine Sick, Bernard Simmons, Mary Simpson, Jack Skeith, Norma & Tom Smith, Margaret Stafford, Reid Stoakley, Frances Stoltz, Daphne Summerfield, E.N. Sturrock, Doug & Margaret Sutherland, Reverend C. Swanson, Gladys Talbot, Byron Tanner, Georgie Thomas, Alice Thresher, Frank Tilley, Maisie Vivyans, Millie Wakelen, Dora Walmburger, Tommie Walker, Marjorie Wallis, Jack Westbrook, Art Westley, Jane & Jean Wilcocks, Elizabeth Wilcox, Violet Wilks, Nora Williamson, Phyllis Wray, George Young

VI. 1-2 Productions: Chorus Role(s) Only

Rita Aird, Allen & Marian Alford, Bernice Anderson, G. Baalim, Ann, Lucille & Marie Barber, John & Mabel Barr, Loraine & Marjorie Barton, Dorothy Barry, Angela & Edith Bawden, Lillian Bennett, Natalie Blite, Alma Bourgett, Ruth Bower, Gwen Bowman, Norma Brooks, Laura Brownlee, E.V. Butler, Agnes Cameron, Billie Chaplin, Jack P. Church, Dick Clark, L. Cochrane, Jean Coffay, William Cowan, Dorothy Craddock, Edith & Marjorie Craig, A. Crawford, S. Crerar, Reverend Walter Cripps, Pearl Cross, Kathleen Cull, Dorothy Daniel, James Davidson, George & May Davies, Helena Davis, Sydney Dinning, Katherine & Kathleen Donaldson, M.E. Dutton, Eleanor & F.S. Dyke, Rowley Evans, C. Fairbanks, Evelyn Faunch, Ethel Felger, Eleanor Fleming, Chang Fletcher, Margaret Flinn, Catherine Freeman, Dorothy Frier, Betty Frost, Ruth Galbraith, M. Gibson, Jean Gillies, Margaret Gogan, John Grant, Ethel Haimes, Virginia Harris, S. & W. Harrison, Blanche Helling, Betty Hewer, Ila Hicks, L. & Marguerite Hill, Martha Houston, W.E. Huckvale, F., James & Olive Jackson, Mary James, J.W. Jamieson, Daisy Jelfs, Warren Johnson, Hazel Keith, S.D. Kennedy, Peggy Kerr, Meri Knight, Patricia Lacey, J. Lackenby, Loraine Lee, Kathleen Levitt, Helen Lewis, Avis Lillie, Jessie Lindley, Olga Lloyd, Marie Lomas, Aileen & Hettie Long, Dennis & Nora Macleod, Margaret McKie, Bob MacMillan, Margaret Malahill, Queenie Maltby, Martha Matthews, Ben Martin, Martin Maughan, Margaret McKay, Edith McKillop, Avis & Don McNabb, Birdie, Ethel & Gertie Metcalf, Pearl Moir, Nellie Moore, A. Murray, Erminie & F. Neumarch, Teddy Nobles, Frank Nuttall, Freda Oliver, Louise & Winnifred Osborne, Camille Palmer, Florence Parkes, G.W. Parsons, Dwight Patterson, Flora Pike, Annie, Bill & J. Pizzey, F. Pratt, Jack Randle, E. Rannard, Dorothy Rasmussen, Alfred Raue, Kitty Reber, Maurine Redd, J. Redman, L. & Marjorie Rhodes, S. Rivers, Marion, Marvel & R. Rogers, Bessie Rose, E.J. Rossiter, Jean Routledge, Austin & Beth Russell, Agnes Rylands, Annie Schweitzer, Beth, Gordon & John Scott, Lenore Sehl, E. Sellens, Marie Shearer, Evelyn Shillington, Adaire Simpson, Louise & Robert Smith, Carolyn Stauffer, John Stavert, Harriet Stoakley, Norris Stolz, Esther Strole, D. Strother, Grace Strutton, Betty Sutherland, Denise Sydal, Norman Taylor, J.E. Thompson, Eric & Hazel Thornhill, Ralph Thrall, Frances Virtue, Arthur Wade, Clara Walburger, Molly Walton, M.J. Ward, Nora Wellington, Charles Whitfield, Phyllis Whitton, Dora & Vincent Williams, Arthur Witham, Jim & Rose Marie Wood, H. Woolsey, Helen & S. Wright, Mr. Yeomans

C. MEMBERS DURING THE PERIOD 1951 - 1989 ONLY							
I. Participant in 10 or more productions	**M**	**L**	**T**		**M**	**L**	**T**
Baunton, Bob	8	5	13	Johnson, Garry	3	7	10
Bayly, Ed	15	18	33	Mann, George	9	7	16
Bayly, Linda	4	8	12	Matheson, Bill	11	5	16
Black, Denise	8	5	13	Robison, Kaye (Watson)	11	5	16
Ede, Jean	10	2	12	Skaronski, Hazel (Evans)	8	6	14
Evins, Cathy	5	5	10	Turner, Colin	8	4	12
Featherstone, Frank	8	2	10	Waterfield, Joan	11	5	16
Huszar, Frank	5	5	10				
II. 7-9 Productions	**M**	**L**	**T**		**M**	**L**	**T**
Azzara, Albert	4	4	8	Johnson, Linda	3	4	7
Baunton, Cherie	6	3	9	Low, Eric	4	4	8
Black, Cliff	8	-	8	Perkinson, Joan	4	4	8
Day, Barbara	4	4	8	Renyk, Mardi	5	2	7
Day, Michael	2	5	7	Story, Phil	5	4	9
Greenway, Al	9	-	9	Warburton, Jack	7	1	8
Heinitz, Mary (Waters)	5	2	7				
III. 5-6 Productions	**M**	**L**	**T**		**M**	**L**	**T**
Bennett, Frank	5	1	6	McCallum, Sandy	2	4	6
Dongworth, Lois	4	1	5	Pisko, Sheila	5	1	6
Knowles, Harry	1	4	5	Rose, Nora	3	3	6
Magee, Sharon (Bolen)	5	-	5	Warburton, Jean	5	1	6
Manson, Daphne	3	2	5	Waterfield, Deb	5	1	6
IV. 3-4 Productions	**M**	**L**	**T**		**M**	**L**	**T**
Appell, Gordon	2	1	3	Lazaruk, Bill	3	1	4
Balcovske, Doris	1	2	3	Lilly, Phyllis	3	-	3
Befus, Bob	3	-	3	Mann, Laurin	1	2	3
Biddell, Cecil	3	-	3	Mann, Nellie	-	4	4
Biddell, Elsie	2	1	3	Mathis, Willie	4	-	4
Block, Jean	4	-	4	Maynard, Jack	2	1	3
Busby, Bruce	2	2	4	McCoy, Jane	2	2	4
Campbell, Mark	1	2	3	Mells, Dick	2	1	3
Ciesla, Paul	2	2	4	Mells, Ellyn (Ford)	1	3	4
Clarke, Syd	3	-	3	Mells, Lee	4	-	4
Cordwell, Brenda	2	1	3	Mercer, Ray	4	-	4
Ede, Bill	2	1	3	Peat, Stafford	2	1	3
Ellerbeck, Phyl	1	2	3	Petherbridge, Doug	2	1	3
Elliott, Jim	4	-	4	Prindle, Lee	3	1	4
Findlay, Helen "Ella"	2	2	4	Robinson, Evelyn	2	2	4
Gibson, Jack	1	3	4	Rude, Fran	3	1	4
Gostola, Frank	4	-	4	Sawicki, Stan	2	2	4
Hammond, Patrick	3	1	4	Scheurkogel, Ted	4	-	4
Holland, Gail	2	1	3	Shannon, Joe	3	-	3
Hornsby, Peter	1	3	4	Seibert, Chip	2	1	3

Name				Name			
Ingoldsby, Connie	2	1	3	Sinclair, Ken	2	1	3
Jensen, Kirk	1	2	3	Stefan, Wes	3	1	4
Johnstone, Kate	1	3	4	Susman, Anita	1	3	4
Jones, Winstan	3	-	3	Sweda, Daphne	1	2	3
Kay, Karen	1	3	4	Thomson, Sheri (McFadden)	2	1	3
Kotkas, Lawrence	2	2	4	Williams, Candy	2	1	3
Lancaster, Leo	-	3	3				

V. 1-2 Productions

Joan Abbott, Bery Allan, Ginger Ames, Laurie Anderson, Winona Anderson, Kathryn Ankers, Laverne Ankers, Len Ankers, Ihoko Asakuma, Kaz Ayukawa, Bill Bagshaw, Truus Baird, Sandi Balcovske, Bill Bale, Shirley Blackwell, Doug Barcoman, Molly Barron, Wayne Barry, Russell Baunton, Bernard Baxter, Charles Beasley, Linda Benz, Rob Best, Louise Bishop, John Scott Black, Philip Black, Lea Blaquiere (Switzer), Kenn Blom, Lucy Bohac, Marion Bolokoski, Rose Marie Bothi, Carolyn Brocca, Jim Brooke, Janice (Tilly) Brown, Eva Jane Bruce, Hugh Buchanan, Arla Burbank, Marjorie Burton, Wendy Burrows, Bill Bushell, Diane Byrne, Ronald Calhoun, Geoff Calvert, Doug Campbell, Verna Cannaby, Wendy Carson, Eileen Cashmore, Simon Cashmore, Cam Cathcart, Chris Cathcart, Marie Caveny, Derek Charnley, Keith Chief Moon, Vonda Chvmelauskas, Buryl Clark, Jim Coates, Paul Cohen, Mark Connellan, Kate Connolly, Audrey Corcoran, Barry Corenblum, Jim Cousins, Jr., Brian Coutts, Gavin Crawford, Jim Cumming, David Cunningham, John Dafoe, Amy Day, Jamie Day, Libbie Day, Jane DeCoste, Alan deJardin, Patrick Doyle, Iris Duban, Bridget Duddy, John Duddy, Camelia Dumont, Hazel Durrans, Julie Ellis, Howard Ellison, Marilyn Ellison, Ralph Eshpeter, Larry Etling, Russell Fairhurst, Kelly Fiddick, Bryan Francis, Edward Francis, Leon Francis, Bill Fruet, Janine Folkins, Mary Gallagher, Muriel Gentleman, Norville Getty, Simon Gladeau, Don Goerzen, Shirli Gonzy, Rik Gordon, Khym Goslin, Sharon Gostola, Nancy Grigg, Peter Grantham, Angela Gunstone, Jack Haberman, Bruce Haig, Brian Halifax, Doris Halifax, Wilfred Halifax, George Hall, Stevie Hall-Thomson, Ethel Halyung, Todd Hammond, Ruston Harker, Keith Harris, Jeffrey Haslam, Faith Harms, Anne Hay, Lois Head, Danny Healy, Steven Healy, Bob Hendricks, Ed Henley, Eric Holm, Jane Holmes, J.A. Hornsby, Sheila Horon, Martin Hoyt, Margaret Huszar, Wanda Huszar, Pam Hutchison, Patti Ikeda, Janet Ing, Ward Ingoldsby, Weste Jensen, Ron Johnston, Tim Johnson, Muriel Jolliffe, Ray Jolliffe, Dennis Jones, Yoshie Kaneda, Nancy Katakami, Lewis Kelly, Grant Kennedy, Yvonne Kennedy, Theresa King, Kaaren Kotkas, Inga Kromond, Susan Kuipers, Ralph Kuipers, Susan Lancaster, Lily Larter, Bill Lawson, Brenda Laycock, Katie Lee, Ann Leggett, Ruth Liska, Susanne Liska, Jean Loetscher, Jody Low, Gordon Lowe, David Lynagh, Analise Machielse, Sandra McFarlane, Norma MacInnis, Richard Mack, John Mackie, Joan Mackwood, Sanae Made, Pat Maggs, Marcie Main, John Malcolm, Bill Mallalieu, Ian Mandin, David Mann, John Massakers, Greg Martin, Jesse Martin, Sheila Martin, Tsuaki Marule, Kari Matchett, Muriel Matheson, Mellisa Matkin, Wayne Matkin, Peggy Matthews, Rita McCauley, Dawn McCaugherty, Bart McCulloch, Debbie McCulloch, Bessie McCully, Marg McElgunn, Peter McGilvray, Bob McHardy, Val McIntyre, Marg McKay, Joy Meek, Neana Meeks, Tom Melling, Judy Melnick, Laurie Meyers, Ross Miller, Michelle Mills, Susan Molnar, Chester Mook, Sally Moore, Joanna Morgan, Doreen Morita, Frank Murphy, Susan Murgully, Pete Nadeau, Margaret Nimmonds, Michael Nowlan, Betty Old, Junior Oliver, Ted Orchard, Garry Orr, Howard Palmer, Lesley Palmer, Maureen Parker, Brander Parsons, Angus Paton, Kirk Patterson, Anne Penton, Bonnie Perry, Claudia Peterson, Pat Phillips, Glen Piper, Grant Pisko, David Plaxton, Diane Pokarney, David Poole, Gil Poirier, Tammi Pretty, Fred Pritchard, Jay Pritchard, Tony Pybee, Martha Rae, Debbie Rakos, Jack Ralleson, Jon Redfern, Anne Reid, Jeannette Reid, Keith Robin, Jim Robinson, Len Robinson, Ralph Robinson, Ed Rossetti, Wynne Royer, Don Runquist, Don Ryane, Allan Sackman, Brian Sakamoto, Syd Salter, Mel Sameshima, John Sauve, Gordon Schmaus, Charlie Schott, Charles Schott, Jr., Clare Scott, Glenn Seeman, Carla Serkin, Kathy Sharp, Stan Shimozawa, Tate Shimozawa, Kent (Duncan) Simpson, Mike Skaronski, Doug Smith, Mike Smith, Winnifred Smith, Louis Soop, Amy Stevens, Richard Stonehocker, Pat Sullivan, Michael Sutherland, Hisaki Takahashi, Gary Terlesky, John Thackray, Cathy Thys, Bert Timmerman, Leona Thorpe, Chris Tobin, Florence Tomiyama, Gerry Tomiyama, Tom Tomiyama, Cindy Turner, Yvonne Turner, Pat Twigg, Katsuko Uchimura, Yukie Uchimura, Lee Van Andel, Con VanDerLee, John Van Egland, Adrian Vaselenak, Mette Vaselenak, Frank Vervoort, Pat Patt Wagner, Robert Waldren, Barbara Warren, Liz Waterfield, Pat Waterfield, Leslee Watson, Analea Wayne, Chet Wayne, John Wecels, Gay Wensueen, Keith Western, Barbara Wilson, George Wilson, Jane Wilson, Kathleen Wilson, Shirley Wilson, John Wilton, Jan Wilton, Brian Woodcock, Bill Wright, Michael Wright, Gene Yamada, Jim Yamada, Bryan Yellowhorn

Playgoers of Lethbridge: Executive Members (1923–1989)

TERM	PRESIDENT/ HON. PRESIDENT	VICE-PRESIDENT	SECRETARY/ TREASURER	GENERAL DIR.\ MUSICAL DIR.	BUSINESS MANAGER	TECHNICAL DIRECTOR	DIRECTORS AT LARGE
JAN-JUN/23	H.W. Church	L. Ritchie	R. Thrall/L. Smith	E.G. Sterndale Bennett/C. Ferguson	-	A. McAlpin	H. Church, A.C. Raworth, G. Davies
1923-24	H.W. Church	L. Ritchie	G.A. Holman/ A. Raworth	E.G. Sterndale Bennett/C. Whitfield	-	A. McAlpin	E.B. Sterndale Bernett, R. Keivill, R. Hincks
1924-25	H.W. Church	L. Ritchie	Mrs. W.J. Armstrong/ G. Davies	E.G. Sterndale Bennett/C. Whitfield	R.V. Gibbons	A. McAlpin	N. Thomas, R. Keivill, F. Rose
1925-26	H.W. Church	L. Ritchie	C. Matthews/ G. Davies	E.G. Sterndale Bennett/G.E. Bower	E. Sharman	A. McAlpin	F. Rose, G.A. Holman, A.C. Raworth
1926-27	F.M. Rose	L. Ritchie	W.E. Huckvale/G. Davies	E.G.S.B.	E. Sharman	A. McAlpin	H. Church, E.B. Sterndale Bennett, F. Teague
1927-28	A.C. Raworth	E. Brander	W.E. Huckvale/ H. Moore	E.G.S.B./P.T. Moseley	F. Teague	A. McAlpin	E. Ings, F. Rose, C Matthews, E.B. Sterndale Bennett (dir., L. Th.)
1928-29	A. McAlpin	L. Connor	R.M. Hume/Miss Glayzer & T. Fleetwood	E.G.S.B./Ethel Brander	N.D. Smith	C. Matthews/ A. Brander	A. Raworth, F. Rose, E. B. Sterndale Bennett (dir., L. Th.)
1929-30	C.R. Matthews	L. Connor	N.D. Smith/J. Jones & A. Round	E.G.S.B./E.F. Layton & Aileen Jones	R.M. Hume	W. Watson	C. Hiscocks, A. Raworth, Mrs. C. Peters, D. Elton, E.B. Sterndale Bennett (dir., L. Th.)
1930-31	H.W. Church	M. Bryans	N. Smith/A.J.M. Round	E.G.S.B./H. Mellor Langdale & R. Williams	F. Teague	W. Watson	A. Raworth, F. Duncanson, A. McAlpin, H. Poole, A. Jones, E.B. Sterndale Bennett (dir., L. Th.)
1931-32	H.W. Church	M. Bryans	I. Hendry/ A.J.M. Round	E.G.S.B./A. Jones	F. Teague	P. Morris	L. Connor, C. Matthews, A. McAlpin, N. Smith, Mrs. Kelly, E.B. Sterndale Bennett (dir. L. Th.)
1932-33	S.J. Shepherd	E. Becker	C. Matthews/ A. Round	E.G.S.B./A. Jones	F. Teague	P. Morris	M. Bryans, N. Smith, L. Connor, E. Atherton, J. Rosewarn, E.B. Sterndale Bennett (dir., L. Th.)
1933-34	C. Matthews	L. Connor	J. Rosewarn/F. Duncanson		J.E. Muir	P. Morris	M. Bryans, A. Raworth, L. Ritchie, L. Jordan, P. Gaynor
1934-35	A.B. Hogg	H. Long	Hilda Church/ H. Church		J. Sutton	L. Jordan	O. Williams, C.F. Steele, M. Bryans, W. Rea, F. MacKenzie, H. Jordan, E. Brancer, M. Clarke, H. Greenway, R. Davidson, T. Ferguson
1935-36	A. Hogg/Senator W.A. Buchanan	H. Long	H. Church/H. Church		J. Sutton		Davidson, T. Ferguson, H. Greenway, M. Bryans, J. Sutton, J.Hawkins, J. Rosewarn

TERM	PRESIDENT/ HON. PRESIDENT	VICE-PRESIDENT	SECRETARY/ TREASURER	GENERAL DIR.\ MUSICAL DIR.	BUSINESS MANAGER	TECHNICAL DIRECTOR	DIRECTORS AT LARGE
1936-37	G. Blake/Senator Buchanan	H. Long	H. Church	-	Mrs. W.J. Armstrong	T. Ferguson	M. Bryans, H. Greenway, F. Johnson, A. Hogg
1937-38	C. Mathews/Sen. Buchanan	H. Long	J. MacBeth/R. Ritchie	-	Mrs. W. Armstrong	-	N. (Betty) Bletcher, M. Bryans, C. Connor, H. Greenway, Mrs. W. Hay, E. Johnson, Mrs. H. Meech, T. Ferguson
1938-39	H. Long/Senator Buchanan	A. Hogg	J. MacBeth	M. Bryans/N.A.	M. Hoffman	T. Ferguson	M. Sutherland, E. Becker, D. Sutherland
1939-40	H. Long/Senator Buchanan	A. Hogg	J. MacBeth	M. Bryans/N.A.	Mrs. C.R. Matthews	T. Ferguson	W. Pineau, J. Vallance, Mrs. L. Hester, C. Matthews, Mrs. W. Hay, Mrs. N. Stoltze
1950	RE-ESTABLISHMENT COMMITTEE: M. Bryans (Chairman), Mrs. Jack Malbert, Wayne Matkin, Hugh Buchanan, Lena Connor, Don Oates, Tom Ferguson, Don Frey						
JAN.-MAY/51	C. Matthews	W. Matkin	M. Dobbs/W. Halifax	M. Bryans/N.A.	G. Robins		D. Frey, H. Buchanan, M. Whalen
1951-52	M. Whalen	H. Buchanan	M.J. Miten/W. Halifax	M. Bryans	W. Halifax		W. Martindale, C. Matthews, L. Connor, H. Long
1952-53	W. Halifax	E. Reid	D. Meek/B. Skeith	M. Bryans			C. Matthews, H. Baalim, W. Matkin, H. Buchanan
1953-54	H. Knowles	J. Waterfield	B. Skeith/L. Head	M. Bryans	R. Johnson		R. Robinson, Mrs. W. Hay, C. Black
1954-55	C. Gibson	D. Manson	H. James/R. Best				E. Rossetti, P. Wagner, B. Busby
1955-56	M. Waters	E. Biddell	J. Perkinson/D. Balcovske	E. Biddell	J. Maynard	L. Lancaster	H. Knowles, H. Baalim, D. Manson
1956-57	M. Waters	M. Vaselenak	D. Balcovske/C. Gibson	H. Buchanan		B. Lazaruk	D. Manson, H. Baalim, K. Watson, W. Matkin
1957-58	C. Matthews	H. James	Mrs. R. Kuipers/R. Kuipers	W. Matkin	W. Ingoldsby	B. Lazaruk	M. Waters, D. Black, B. Cordwell
1958-59	W. Ingoldsby	D. Black	P. Ellerbeck/W. Ede	B. Parsons			M. Bryans, D. Manson, P. Morris
1959-60	D. Black	B. Bagshaw	B. Ede/P. Ellerbeck	S. Pitt	K. Watson		C. Matthews, J. Ede, C. Turner
1960-61	K. Watson	J. Ede	B. Old/C. Matthews	S. Pitt	M. Waters		B. Lazaruk, J. Waterfield, C. Ingoldsby
1961-62	C. Montgomery	T. Scheurkogel	D. Moria/B. Old/J. Shannon		B. Lazaruk		C. Cathcart, D. Black, B. Heindricks

TERM	PRESIDENT/ HON. PRESIDENT	VICE-PRESIDENT	SECRETARY/ TREASURER	GENERAL DIR.\ MUSICAL DIR.	BUSINESS MANAGER	TECHNICAL DIRECTOR	DIRECTORS AT LARGE
MAY-NOV/62	T. Scheurkogel		D. Morita				
1962-63	T. Scheurkogel	J. Waterfield	P. Phillips & P. Lilly/ J. Heinitz		D. Black		J. Ede, K. Watson, C. Black
NOV/63 - MAY/64	C. Black	P. Lilly	M. Rae & P. Lilly/ J. Heinitz		D. Black		J. Ede, K. Watson, J. Abbott
1964-65	C. Black	C. Turner	W. Anderson & L. Nuttall/ C. Gibson	D. Black	K. Watson		L. Mells, M. Rae, J. Ede
1965-66	C. Black	C. Turner	T. Baird & L. Nuttall/ W. Baird	D. Black	K. Watson		J. Ede, F. Gostola, L. Mells, M. Rae
1966-67	G. Mann	A. Greenway	N. Mann & L. Nuttall/ W. Baird		K. Watson		J. Ede, L. Mells, D. Black
1967-68	A. Greenway	L. Mells	D. Black & N. Jacobson/ W. Baird				
MAY/68 - NOV/69	L. Mells	J. Warburton	L. Albertson/R. Fairhurst				J. Block, L. Ankers G. Lowe, Jean Warburton, W Berry
NOV/69 - JAN/71	Jack Warburton	C. Black	L. (Albertson) Bayly				J. Waterfield, F. Burrows, C. Burgess, H. Skaronski, Jean Warburton, W. Berry
1971-72	J. Warburton	C. Black	L. Bayly/Chas. Scott				C. Burgess, Claire Scott, J. Pokarney, J. Waterfield, Jean Warburton, W. Berry
1972-73	B. Matheson	E. Bayly	L. Bayly/Chas. Scott	D. Mells			W. Huszar, Jim Elliott, F. Bayly
1973 FEB-SEPT	B. Matheson	C. Baunton					
1973-74	F. Rude	D. Lynagh	J. Cherniawsky/K. Kay		B. Baunton		Bill Matheson
1974-75	F. Rude	A. Reid	V. McKay/M. Renyk	Ed Bayly	F. Huszar		L. Bayly, S. Balcovske, L. Baines
1975-76	A. Reid	P. Story	V. McKay/M. Renyk	E. Bayly	L. Bayly		B. Clark, E. Cashmore, S. Walkey, F. Rude
1976-77	A. Reid	P. Story	G. Holland/M. Renyk	E. Bayly	L. Bayly		J. Snow, L. Johnson, K. (Watson) Robison, F. Rude
1977-78	F. Rude	A. Azzara	G. Holland/M. Renyk	C. Evins	H. Skaronski		P. Cowan, B. Day, F. Rude
SEPT/78 - JAN/80	F. Rude	A. Azzara	L. Johnson/M. McKay & H. Skaronski	C. Evins			
1980-81	C. Evins & (C. Baunton)	C. Baunton	A. Reid/L. Johnson	J. Waterfield			M. Robison, P. Story, E. Cashmore, G. Holland, K. Watson, B. Day
1981-82	C. Baunton	K. Weston & (M. Renyk)	R. Tompkins/H. Skaronski	J. Waterfield			M. Robison, P. Story, E. Cashmore
1982-83	C. Baunton	E. Bayly	L. Johnson/H. Skaronski	J. Waterfield			F. Rude, M. Renyk, M. Robison
1983-84	Ed Bayly	E. Low	H. Joyce/H. Skaronski	J. Waterfield			B. Day, N. Boyden, C. Mook

TERM	PRESIDENT/ HON. PRESIDENT	VICE-PRESIDENT	SECRETARY/ TREASURER	GENERAL DIR.\ MUSICAL DIR.	BUSINESS MANAGER	TECHNICAL DIRECTOR	DIRECTORS AT LARGE
1984-85	E. Bayly	E. Low	A. Martin/H. Skaronski	J. Waterfield			B. Day, J. Martin, S. Moore
1985-86	N. Boyden	G. Mann	L. Bayly/S. Moore & L. Bayly	J. Waterfield			K. (Erickson) Walburger, M. Renyk, B. Day, M. Day
1986-87	N. Boyden	G. Mann	L. Bayly/G. Holland	M. Robison			K. Walburger, M. Day, B. Day, M. Renyk
1987-88	N. Boyden	G. Mann	L.Bayly/G. Holland	E. Bayly			K. Walburger, M.Day, M. Renyk, G. Johnson
1988-89	G. Mann	L. Johnson	L. Bayly/G. Holland	E. Bayly			J. Malcolm, S. MacFarlane, G. Johnson, B. Tedder
1989-90	G. Mann	L. Johnson	L. Bayly/G. Holland	E. Bayly			J. Malcolm, G. Johnson, S. Downey, H. Matis

Coaldale Little Theatre (1953–1975)
Attic Theatre (1975–1978)
Productions

TIME/PLACE	PRODUCTION/PLAYWRIGHT/ TECHNICAL PERSONNEL	DIRECTOR/CAST/REFERENCES/COMMENTS
FEB 4,6/53 - *Coaldale East Sch., Coaldale*	Blithe Spirit by Noel Coward/Esther Nelson [consultant & tech advisor]/Charles Connor, Peter Slemko, Diana Cote, Ethel Korth, Peggy McCann, Pauline Archer, Jintie Graham, Dorothy Hughes, Yvonne Robison, Dorothy Smith, Donna Kenny, Anna Huber	Murray Robison assisted by Carrole Eaves & Tom Hughes/Theresa King, Jennie Emery, Russell Fairhurst, Gwen Meroniuk, Tom Hughes, Betty Smith, Jean Mannington (Feb 10/53/5) - *screamingly funny play worth driving 100 miles to see*
MAR/53 - *Coaldale* APR 2/53 - *Cardston* APR 17/53 - *Red Deer*	The Case of the Crushed Petunias by Tennessee Williams/R. Fairhurst, P. Archer, C. Connors, M. Robison	Murray Robison/Y. Robison, P. Slemko, C. Bryant, P. McCann (Apr 4/53/13) - *named best play - the characterization was good*
NOV 24,25/53 - *Legion Memorial Hall (Lethbridge)*	Evening of One Act Plays produced by Ralph Robinson of Lethbridge Playgoers, including The Unseen by Alice Gerstenburg/Peggy McCann [props]	Betty Smith/M. Robison, Y. Robison, Esther Corey (Nov 25/14) - *interesting, nicely presented*
DEC 2/53 - *R.I. Baker Sch.*	Little Theatre Evening: 1. The Unseen 2. To What Purpose by Lorette Boissonneault & Bernice Chapman/Marvin Pickering [sound]/Joan Emery [book holder]	- Betty Smith/M. Robison, Y. Robison, Esther Corey Y. Robison/Dorothy Hughes, A. Huber, P. Mallalieu, Donna Kenny, J. Emery
MAR 24/54 - *R.I. Baker Sch.* APR 1,2/54 - *Lethbridge* MAY /54 - *Red Deer*	Riders by the Sea by John Millington Synge/Ida Wiens, Edward Mantler, D. Smith, D. Hughes, G. Meroniuk	Murray Robison/Y. Robison, T. King, P. Mallalieu, R. Fairhurst, P. McCann, B. Smith, Eugene Gregorash, Bill Knibs, Jennie Emery, Esther Corey, Ray Birch (Apr 3/54/10) - *praised for detailed work in staging and characterization*
FEB 17,18/55 - *R.I. Baker Sch.*	Ladies in Retirement by Edward Percy & Reginald Denham/R. Fairhurst, Ray Birch, I. Wiens, T. King, D. Hughes, Susan Roberts, Y. Robison, J. Emery, Marienne Sisko, Irene Leigh, Tom Hughes, George Peck	Murray Robison assisted by Helen Nikkel/J. Emery, P. McCann, B. Smith, J. Mannington, Fred Bodie, D. Hughes, P. Mallalieu (Feb 18/10) - *a good show, well worth seeing*
MAR 8/55 - *L.C.I.*	Catherine Parr Costumes by Malabar's	Murray Robison/Helen Nikkel, R. Fairhurst, T. King (Mar 9/14) - *praised for its fine interpretation & direction*
JAN 12,13/56 - *R.I. Baker Sch.* JAN 17/56 - *Subsequent performance in Coaldale & Medicine Hat*	Papa is All by Patterson Greene/Walter Wiebe, D. Hughes, E. Corey, P. McCann, J. Graham, D. Smith, Y. Robison	Murray Robison/J. Emery, T. King, P. Mallalieu, R. Fairhurst, Al Blakie, F. Bodie (Jan 18/15) - *A beautiful well thought out production. The details were remarkable.*
DEC 11/56 - *R.I. Baker Sch.* FEB 6-9/57 - *Capitol Theatre (Lethbridge)*	Ladies in Retirement/Walter Wiebe, J. Graham, Betty McLennan, Y. Robison, Dorothy & Betty Smith, Elizabeth MacIntyre, Lorene Harrison, M. Robison, T. Hughes, R. Fairhurst	M. Robison assisted by Tom Hughes/J. Emery, P. McCann, Irene Leigh, J. Mannington, R. Fairhurst, D. Hughes, P. Mallalieu (Dec 10/5) - *pre-festival adjudication by Jack McCreath* (Feb 8/1,2) - *congratulations to cast - a creditable job with a difficult play*
MAR 6,7/58 - *R.I. Baker Sch.* MAR 12-15/58 - *Calgary* MAY 12-17/58 - *Halifax DDF*	All Summer Long by Robert Anderson/Ivan Meyers, Percy Wiebe, Bob Skiba, J. Graham, P. McCann, G. Meroniuk, B. McLennan, L. Harrison, Y. Robison, M. Robison, T. & D. Hughes, Fred Pritchard	Murray Robison assisted by T. Hughes/David Mannington, R. Fairhurst, J. Emery, Sandy McCallum, J. Mannington, Phil Story, Wendy Robison (Mar 17/1; May 20/10) - *Coaldale captures coveted Calvert trophy - praised for fine effort*
JAN 14,15/59 - *R.I. Baker Sch.*	Liliom by Ferenc Molnar/Ivan Meyers, F. Pritchard, G. Meroniuk, J. Graham, E. McIntyre, P. Mallalieu	Jennie Emery assisted by Murray Robison/Gordon Johns, Y. Robison, S. McCallum, P. Story, J. Emery, Joy & F. Pritchard, Derek & Hazel Charnley, Harold Pankratz, Aldo Bianchini, G. Meroniuk, P. McCann, Bruce McKenzie, R. Fairhurst, Chester Kovak, T. Hughes, L. Harrison, Carrole Eaves (Jan 10/11; 12/3)
NOV 5,6/59 - *Stirling* NOV 21 - *Red Deer also televised by CJLH T.V.*	The Jack and The Joker by Gwen Pharis Ringwood/set construction and painting by Cornelius Martens	Peggy Mallalieu/S. McCallum, Fred Pritchard, J. Mannington, P. McCann, Hazel Charnley (Nov 4/14; 6/12; 7/13) - *delightful costuming & effective simple staging (Mrs. David Cormack)* (Nov 23/1) - *Fred Pritchard wins final festival award*

TIME/PLACE	PRODUCTION/PLAYWRIGHT/ TECHNICAL PERSONNEL	DIRECTOR/CAST/REFERENCES/COMMENTS 386
NOV 18,19/60 - *Red Deer*	The Devil Among the Skins/Ivan Meyers Y. Nicol, Y. Robison, J. Emery	Murray Robison/J. & F. Pritchard, P. Story, Edwin Davidson (Nov 22/3) - *Coaldale & Hat Players get awards*
MAR 10,11/61 - *R.I. Baker Sch.* MAR 15-18/61 - *S.A. Jubilee Auditorium* APR 11/61 - *Capitol Th. (Lethbridge)* MAY 15-20/61 - *Montreal DDF*	The Beautiful People by William Saroyan/I. Meyers, J. Graham, Y. Robison, Y. Nicol, P. McCann	Murray Robison assisted by Joy Pritchard/Russell Wiber, J. Emery, T. King, S. McCallum, F. Pritchard, Bill Matheson, P. Story, Vince Ditrich, B. McIntyre (Mar 20/1; 24/4; May 22/1,2) [Sunny South News - Mar 24] - *a beautiful and moving presentation*
MAR 27-30/63 - *Capitol Th. (Lethbridge)* APR 19,25,26/63 - *Pincher Creek, Coaldale, Cardston, Taber* MAY 10/63 - *Kitchener, Ont. DDF*	The Well of the Saints by John Synge/I. Meyers, Katherine & Elizabeth Brauer, Audrey Davidson, Y. Robison, Jacquie Backman, P. McCann, Betty Meyers	Murray Robison assisted by J. Emery/S.McCallum, P. Mallalieu, Ed Bayly, Y. Robison, T. King, B. Matheson, P. Story, E. Davidson, Ingrid Lucas (Mar 29/11; Apr 1/1,2; May 3/3, 14/12} - *the outstanding direction was made even better by the first-class teamwork of the actors (Esse Ljungh)*
OCT 29/64 - *Lethbridge Jr. College* NOV 14/64 - *Banff*	The Tinker's Wedding by John Synge/I. Meyers, A. Davidson	Murray Robison assisted by E. Davidson/Ed Bayly, Y. Robison, R. Fairhurst, J. Emery (C.H. Nov 16) - *magnificent work*
APR 3-5,6/65 - *R.I. Baker Sch.* APR 5-10/65 - *U of A, Edmonton*	The Red Shoes by Robin Short/I. Meyers, Ray Jolliffe, Fran & Ed Bayly, A. Davidson, Y. Robison, Arthur Nishimura, B. Meyers	Murray Robison assisted by J. Emery, with Muriel Jolliffe (chor)/Frank Featherstone, Wendy Robison, E. Davidson, Carol Davidson, Ed Bayly, P. McCann (Apr 2/5; 5/10; 12/1) - *the best entertainment of the week (adjudicator, Walter Massey)*
NOV 12,13/65 - *Banff* DEC 4/65 - *R.I. Baker Sch. & additional performance in Medicine Hat Library Th.*	Winner of the Alberta Drama League One Act Playwriting Competition: The Golden Goose by Joyce Doolittle/I. Meyers, R. Jolliffe, B. Meyers, A. Davidson, F. Bayly, Dorothy Tilley, Jane MacDonald, Ed Bayly	Murray Robison assisted by J. Emery/Wendy Robison, Sigfried Schmold, Linda McIntosh, Ed Bayly, P. Mallalieu, L. Harrison, Marsha Wood, E. Davidson, F. Featherstone, P. Story, Mary Jane Meyers (Nov 6/6; 22/5; Dec 1/3,5) - *excellent characterizations; a great deal of charm, care and simplicity*
MAR 8-11/67 - *Yates Centre, Lethbridge* APR 7,8/67 - *R.I. Baker Sch.*	Teach Me How to Cry by Patricia Joudry/I. Meyers, R. Jolliffe, Audrey Davidson, Fran & Ern Bayly, Phil Story	Murray Robison assisted by P. Story/J. Emery, Kaye Robison, Adele Stephens, Linda Zgurski, Frank Huszar, Beverly Venechuck, Eileen Nishimura, Ed Bayly, E. Davidson, P. Mallalieu (Apr 3/9; 6/10; 10/9) - *the whole thing gave pleasure, a very good choice*
APR 18/68 - *Yates Centre, Lethbridge Western Canada Arts Festival*	Playboy of the Western World by John M. Synge/R. Jolliffe, I. Meyers, A. Davidson, Pat Oshiro, F. and Ern Bayly, K. Robison, J. Emery, Wanda Huszar, Carol Watkinson	Murray Robison assisted by P. Mallalieu & J. Pritchard/Kaye Robison, P. Story, F. Huszar, Terry O'Donnell, E. Davidson, E. Bayly, J. Emery, L. Harrison, Fred Fitzpatrick, Wendy Carson, Bill Matheson, Ray Jolliffe (Apr 18/12; May 2/3) - *rich, lively & attractive*
DEC 26-28/68 - *Yates*	Produced the English Pantomime Mother Goose	*(see Appendix M)*
APR 24,25/73 - *Yates*	Butterflies Are Free by Leonard Gershe/I. Meyers, P. & Bill Mallalieu, Elizabeth Robison, Ed & Linda Bayly, M. Matheson, K. Robison, P. McCann	Murray Robison assisted by Frank Huszar/David Mann, Jean Graham, Kaye Robison, F. Huszar (Apr 21/6) [No Review]
FEB 17/75 - *Yates* FEB /75 - *Attic Th.*	The Case of the Crushed Petunias by Tennessee Williams/K. Robison, P. Mallalieu, F. Huszar	Murray Robison/Fran Rude, P. Story, B. Matheson, L. Bayly (Feb 18/16)

TIME/PLACE	PRODUCTION/PLAYWRIGHT/ TECHNICAL PERSONNEL	DIRECTOR/CAST/REFERENCES/COMMENTS
FEB /75 - *Attic Th.* FEB 18/75 - *Yates* MAR 8/75 - *Banff*	Mooney's Kid Don't Cry by Tennessee Williams/Murray & Kaye Robison	Murray Robison/David Mann, Patricia Matheson
WINTER/76 - *Attic Th.*	Attic Youth Theatre: Rise and Shine by Elda Cadogan	Murray Robison/Elizabeth Robison, Pam Rose, Margo Graham
MAY /76 - *Attic Th.*	The Rainmaker by N. Richard Nash/Murray & Kaye Robison	Murray Robison assisted by Fran Rude/Laurin Mann, Albert Azzara, George Mann, Bob Baunton, Pat Hammond, Phil Story, Neil Boyden
MAR /77 - *Attic Th.*	My Three Angels by Sam & Bella Spewack/Murray & Kaye Robison	Murray Robison assisted by Elizabeth Robison/George Mann, Albert Azzara, Neil Boyden, Renee Brown, Peter Mueller, Phil Story, Bob Baunton, Kaye Robison, Peggy Mallalieu, Les Smolnicky
FEB 17,18/78 - *Yates*	Where Have All the Lightning Bugs Gone by Louis E. Caton/Murray & Kaye Robison	Murray Robison/Laurin Mann, Albert Azzara
APR 10-12; 14-15; 17-21/78 - *Attic Th.*	Papa is All by Patterson Greene/Murray & Kaye Robison	Murray Robison assisted by Heather Joyce/George, Nellie & Laurin Mann, Michael Nowlin, Kaye Robison, Terry Moore

Our Town Workshop (Lethbridge) Productions
(1963–1968)

DATE/PLACE	PRODUCTION/DIRECTOR/ TECHNICAL PERSONNEL	CAST/REFERENCES/COMMENTS
MAR 9/63 - *Taber* MAR 11,12/63 - *Hamilton Jr. H.S. (auditorium)*	Our Town by Thornton Wilder/Joy Pritchard/Al Candy [lighting]/Ed Sloboda, Earl & Doris Colpitts, Joan Haig, Lorraine Moore, Pat Lancaster, Ila O'Brien, Betty Chapman, M.V. Rodgers, P. Ellerbeck, Kay Haworth, Kathleen Montgomery, Thelma Parker [organist]	Stu Chapman, Nina Sejersen, Mel Spackman, Bruce Haig, Ed Sloboda, Fred Pritchard, Earl Colpitts, Doris Colpitts, Diane Matisz, Gordon Moir, Pat Phillips, Don Chapman, Jack O'Brien, Jay Pritchard, Donna Bishop, Martha Rae, Cliff Black, V.M. Rodgers & "Townspeople" (Mar 2/14; 11/3,10; 12/9; 13/16) - *250 at 1st Lethbridge performance; directed with skill & feeling; Stu Chapman steals the show*
APR 6/63 - *Stirling* MAY 9/63 - *St. Francis Sch.*	Chinook (one act) by Bill Matheson/Joy Pritchard/Earl & Doris Colpitts, Betty Chapman	Sandy McCallum, Joan Waterfield, Nina Sejersen, Larry Sherwood, Fred Pritchard, Bill McCann (Apr 18/10; May 1/17; 9/12; 10/12) - *City players major (festival) winners at Red Deer, May 11.*
NOV 2/63 - *Lethbridge Junior College* NOV 16/53 - *Banff School of Fine Arts Auditorium*	1. Red Peppers/Joy Pritchard assisted by Gloria Albritton/Orchestra: Nellie Mann (Jack McCreath), Bruce Haig, Blayne Bastedo, Frank Duff 2. Fool's Errand by Margery Wood/Joy Pritchard assisted by Vera Ferguson; Fred Pritchard [stage mgr]; Fran Bayly [costumes]; Bruce McKenzie [lights]; Earl Colpitts, Fred Pritchard [sets]	Joan Waterfield, Fred Pritchard, Gary McNair, Sandy McCallum, Stewart Little, Doris Colpitts - Muriel Matheson, Bruce Haig, Kirk Patterson, Dianna Turner, Lois Duff, Jack Horn, Leslie Ker - (Nov 1/12; 4/10; 5/10; 16/14; 18/1) - *Delightful evening of drama; Lethbridge tops One Act Festival (Fool's Errand)*
NOV 13,14/63 - *Lethbridge Jr. College*	Romanoff & Juliet by Peter Ustinov/Sandy McCallum/Fran Bayly [costumes]; Bruce McKenzie [lights]; Gerald Litchfield [sound]; Hans Winckler, Jr. [stage mgr]; Helen McKenzie, Ed Sloboda, Camillia Pilling [props]; Earl Colpitts, Fred Pritchard [sets]	George Mann, Fred Pritchard, Bill Matheson, Ed Bayly, Sheila (Hawn) Pisko, Earl Colpitts, Bill Berg, Stewart Little, Kathleen Montgomerie, Velma Litchfield, Joan Haig, Gary McNair, Bruce Haig (Aug 3/14; Nov 8/10; 12/9; 14/12) - *proves popular*
FEB 25/64 - *Lethbridge Jr. College* FEB 28/54 - *Taber*	I Remember Mama by John Van Druten/Joy Pritchard/Fred Pritchard [stage mgr]; Bruce McKenzie [lights]; Fran Bayly & Marie Rokas [costumes]; Helen McKenzie, Gloria Trapp, Joan Haig [props]; Doris Colpitts [bus mgr]	Fay Olson, Camillia Pilling, Earl Colpitts, Diane Matisz, Dianna Turner, Ed Bayly, Gary McNair, Muriel Matheson, Leslie Ker, Doris Colpitts, Bud Iverson, Gloria Albritton, Bill Berg, Jack Horn, Dennis Colpitts, Sheila Hawn, Helen McKenzie, Jay Pritchard, JoAnne Ondus, Velma Litchfield (Dec 16/9; Jan 7/10; 15/14; 22/9; 24/14; 26/18) - *friendly, fun filled warm performance*
OCT 28/64 - *Lethbridge Jr. College*	1. Riders to the Sea/Joy Pritchard - 2. A Phoenix Too Frequent/Joy Pritchard 3. The Dumbwaiter/Fred Pritchard	Doris Colpitts, Joan Haig, Leslie Ker, Bruce McKenzie, Helen McKenzie and village folk Muriel Matheson, Dianna Turner, Jim Elliott Bud Iverson, Peter Grantham (Oct 19/10; 23/18; 27/10; 29/11; 30/11) - *praised by adjudicator, Mary G. Cairns of Calgary*
JAN 29/65 - *Pincher Creek H.S.* FEB 4-6/65 - *Lethbridge Jr. College*	The Glass Menagerie by Tennessee Williams/Joy Pritchard/Bud Iverson, Gloria Albritton, Marie Rokas, Earl Bruce McKenzie, Bill Matheson	Jim Elliott, Joan Haig, Doris Colpitts, Bruce Branston (Jan 29/10; Feb 3/14; 4/3; 5/9) - *captured the mood*
MAR 31/65 - *Capitol* APR /65 - *Edmonton (ARDF)*	The Queen and The Rebels by Ugo Betti/Joy Pritchard/Doris Colpitts [stage mgr]; Leslie Ker, Gloria Albritton [props]; Keith Driver and Marilyn Duaire [set design]; Bruce McKenzie [lights]; Jack Innes [make-up]; Earl Colpitts [sound]	Bruce Haig, Bruce Branston, Earl Colpitts, Bill Matheson, Fred Pritchard, Muriel Matheson, Joan Waterfield, Bud Iverson, Hart Kirch, Jay Pritchard, Murray Pritchard & others (Mar 31/14; Apr 1/12) - *generally everyone had a roaring good time*
NOV 13/65 - *Banff School of Fine Arts*	The Dock Brief by John Mortimer/Joy Pritchard	Bruce Haig, Fred Pritchard (Oct 18/12; Nov 12/14) - *performed at One Act Festival, Banff*
MAR 5,6,13/66 - *Various Lethbridge & S.A. United Churches*	The Coffee House/Joy Pritchard	Dianna Turner, Frances Anderson, Joan Haig, Ed Bayly, Phil Story, Fred Pritchard (Mar 3/15) - *a one act play about social problems of society*
MAR 27/66 - *Lethbridge Jr. College* MAR 30/66 - *Medicine Hat (ARDF)*	The Caretaker by Harold Pinter/Fred Pritchard/Bruce McKenzie, Joan Haig, Judy White, Dianna Turner, Francis Anderson, Joy Pritchard	Bill Matheson, Bud Iverson, Jim Elliott (Mar 23/17; 28/16; 31/2) - *considerable plaudits from adjudicator, Peter Boretski; Iverson gives a truly professional performance*

DATE/PLACE	PRODUCTION/DIRECTOR/ TECHNICAL PERSONNEL	CAST/REFERENCES/COMMENTS
MAY 9-12/66 - *Yates*	The Teahouse of the August Moon by John Patrick/Dick Mells assisted by Muriel Jolliffe/(in conjunction with the Lethbridge Japanese Canadian Citizens' Association)	Margaret Trockstad, Graham Allen, Marjorie Higa, Bud Iverson, Al Greenway, Kevin Simpson, John Charnetsky and others (May 7/14; 9/10; 10/10) - *lacked polish but made up for it in enthusiasm*
MAY 6,7/66 - *Yates*	The Three Little Pigs/Joy Pritchard/Ray Jolliffe, Bruce McKenzie, Judy White, Leslie Ker, Camillia Pilling, Marie Rokas, Effie & Bill Langmead, Joan Haig	Bud Iverson, Phil Story, Joan Haig, Fred Pritchard, Jim Elliott, Frances Anderson, Jim Cousins, Dianna Turner, Esther Goorevitch, Jolliffe School of Dance, McKillop AOTS Boys' Choir (May 7/13) - *theatre for children - tickles the palate*
SPRING/66 - *Yates*	Sketch, Here We Are (in conjunction with Bridge City Chorus program Spring Fever	Dianna Turner, Ed Bayly
DEC 2,3,9,10/66 - *Yates*	Little Red Riding Hood/Joy Pritchard/Phil Story, Bruce McKenzie, Elaine Liebelt, Pheona Sloboda, Wendy Chamber, Dorothy Carnine, Joan Haig, Marie Rokas, Esther Goorevitch	Bud Iverson, Glen Seeman, Bonnie Ingoldsby, Fred Pritchard, Ed Sloboda, Esther Goorevitch, Bill Matheson, Dorothy Carnine, Jack Hopman (Dec 2/14; 3/14; 7/17; 9/14) - *an amusing show*
MAR 8/67 - *Yates (ARDF)*	The Wheel/by Mac Reilley/Joy Pritchard/Ed Sloboda, Elaine Liebelt, Judy White, Marie Rokas, Kay Londsdale, Pheona Sloboda, Bruce McKenzie	Fred Pritchard, Dianna Turner, Jack Hamilton, Bud Iverson (Mar 9/9) - *cast praised but Wheel fails to enthuse adjudicator, Paxton Whitehead*
NOV 15,30/67 - *Wilson Jr. H.S., Assumption R.C. Ch., other venues & times in Leth. & S. Alberta*	Tomorrow Is Another Day/Joy Pritchard/(in association with the National Council of Jewish Women)	Jean Block, Judy White, Frances Anderson, Glen Seeman, Bonnie Ingoldsby, Martha Rae, Elaine Liebelt (Nov 15/15) - *well received mental health education play*
FEB 15-17/68 - *Yates*	The Madwoman of Chaillot/by Jean Giraudox/Ron Hartmann (Toronto professional director [under auspices of Canada Council & the DDF])/Muriel Jolliffe [chor]; Fran Bayly [costumes]; Cathy Evins [set designer]; Vaughn Hembroff [prod mgr]; Garry Kohn [musical background]	Joan Waterfield & cast of 32 (Feb 6/10) [in association with Playgoers of Lethbridge] - *[See Appendix I]*
OCT 15,16/68 - *Yates*	A Taste of Honey/by Sheilagh Delaney/Joy Pritchard (assisted by Jennifer Butterfield)/Fred Pritchard, Cathy Evins, Jim Green, Phil Story, Pete Rokas, Bruce McKenzie, Bob Emery, Garry Kohn, Marie Rokas, Bonnie Ingoldsby, Judy White, Stan McDonald, Leslie Ker	Angela Gunstone, Joan Waterfield, Erwin Adderley, John Bowman, Glen Seeman, Garry Kohn (Oct 12/3,13; 15/17,16) - *lost its tempo too often*
FALL/68	1. High Pressure Area/Joy Pritchard 2. Room Upstairs/Joy Pritchard (in association with National Council of Jewish Women & the Mental Health Association of Canada)	

Centre Stage Productions Society: Productions
Lethbridge, Alberta (September 1985–May 1989)

DATE/PLACE	PRODUCTION/DIRECTOR/ PRODUCTION PERSONNEL	CAST/REFERENCES/COMMENTS
SEPT 3/85 - *U of L Th.*	Musical, <u>A Chorus Line</u> by Nicholas Dante (book) & Marvin Hamlich (mus)/<u>Fran Rude</u>/Candy Williams [chor]/Don Robb [mus dir]/Arla Burbank [voc dir]/Jody Low [lights]/Hazel Skaronski [cost]/Orchestra: Tanya Arnold, Barb Darby, Lori Porkka, Bruce Redstone, Tracy Lowe, Chris Lee, Jerry & Ken Rogers, Randy Selnes, Neil Sheets, Richard Ericksen, Brenda Shaw	Rhonda Ruston, Narda McCarroll, Kathleen Simmons, Mark Litchfield, Kim & Terri-Jo Ully, Thom Heggie, Randy Bennett, Deb Waterfield, Bill Lawson, George Gallant, Marcel Khan, Tim Jones, Bob Akroyd, Candice Elzinga, Keith O'Sullivan, Rita Petersen, Elizabeth Day, George Szilagyi, Trenton McQuarrie, Jeff Carlson, Megan Sullivan, Leah Kelly, Brian Solberg (Aug 3/A8; 19/B9; 31/D1; Sept 4/B1,B8) - *$8.50 - a hit...pleases full house*
APR 1-4/86 - *Yates (auspices of the General Stewart Branch, Royal Canadian Legion*	A Musical Reminiscence, in celebration of the Royal Canadian Legion Diamond Jubilee, <u>We'll Meet Again</u> by Paul Gaffney & Nancy Turner (additional musical arrangements by John S. Reid)/<u>Fran Rude</u>/Candy Williams [chor]/John S. Reid [mus dir]/Morris MacFarlane [prod] assisted by Doris Balcovske/Fred McKay[stage mgr]/Herb Matis [set]/John Duell, Brian Tedder [sound]/Eileen Cashmore [props]/Jody Low [lights]/Hazel Skaronski [cost]/Orchestra: R. Ericksen, Paul Walker, Dale Ketcheson, Don Robb, B. Redstone, J.S. Reid	John S. Reid, Rhonda Ruston, Roger Schultz, Pat Sullivan, Jean Warburton, Wilma Wiebe, George Gallant, Jesse Martin, Ray Mercer, Dawn Flexhaug, Al Greenway, Mark Litchfield, Neana Meeks, Sandra McFarlane, Marg McKay, Lloyd Pollock (Jan 25/A10; Mar 19/B12; Apr 1/A9; 2/B5) - *excellent (Carol Laycock)*
SEPT 8-14/86 - *Yates*	Musical, <u>Evita</u> by Andrew Lloyd Webber/<u>Fran Rude</u>/Candy Williams [chor]/John S. Reid [mus dir]/David Hignell [tech dir] with assistance from: Herb Matis, Blair Amundsen, Winstan Jones, Paul Liska, Dale Martin, Jesse Martin, Kevin Matis, Gil Poirier, Mike Skaronski, Bob Thomsen, Ian Amundsen, Val Cooke, Margaret Roberts, Peter Toop, Kelly Mezerecky, Sandra Fellner, Sue Koshman, Linda Going, Annette Nieukerk, Nancy Amundsen, Hazel Skaronski, Lil Erdos, Leanne Kading, Fran Lee, Ruth Liska, Rita Peterson, Cathy Pollock, Peter Brown, Patti Merrick & others	Rhonda Ruston, Doug Castleton, Mark Campbell, George Gallant, Kaaren Kotkas, Bill Baker, Al Greenway, Lawrence Kotkas, Max Martin, Tony Bowman, John Duell, Stephen Graham, Mark Litchfield, Roger Schultz, Mark Ward & others (Sept 8/B7; 9/B7) - *cast rises to the demands (Carol Laycock)*
APR 18,20-25/87 - *U of L Th.*	Musical, <u>Jesus Christ Superstar</u> by Andrew Lloyd Webber/<u>Fran Rude</u>/Candy Williams [chor]/John S. Reid [mus dir]/Kenneth Rogers [vocal dir]/Roger Schultz [set designer]/Leslie Robison [cost]/Jody Low [lights]	George Gallant, Lyndon Bray, Becky Davidson, Martin Madge, David Mikuliak, Bill Lawson, Al Greenway, Cliff Stoakley, Patrick Hankey, Lorrie Willets, Tony Bowman, Karen Kay, Laurie Meyers, Kaaren Kotkas, Tim Jones, Mark Campbell, Shane Wagg, Yvonne Fredrick, Rhonda Nugent, Arlie Langager, Dawn Flexhaug, Shauna Stuckert, Peter Brown & others (Apr 18/B9; 20/A7; 21/A8) - *theatrically excellent (Carol Laycock)*
SEPT 10-13,15-19/87 - *U of L Th.*	Musical, <u>Guys & Dolls</u> by Jo Swerling, Abe Burrows (book) & Frank Loesser (music & lyrics)/<u>Fran Rude</u>/Candy Williams [chor]/Don Robb [mus dir]/Ken Rogers [voc dir]/Janel Snow [stage mgr]/Jody Low [prod mgr]/Roger Schultz [set design]/David Hignell [tech dir & lights]/Neil Sheets [sound]/Leslie Robison [cost]/Amy Day [art dir]/Kaaren Kotkas & Tony Bowman [props] & others	Mark Litchfield, Yvonne Frederick, George Gallant, Rhonda Ruston, Mark Ward, Tom Melling, Chris Davidson, Lee Prindle, Al Greenway, Joy Jones, Martin Madge, Joe Weststeijn, Phil Story, Bill Lawson, Max Martin, Geoff Wallins & chorus (Sept 11/A12) - *another winner (Dave Mabell)*
MAR 14,15/88 - *U of L Th. (in association with the Leth. Symphony Assoc.)*	Musical (in concert) <u>Follies</u> by James Goldman (book) & Stephen Sondheim (music & lyrics)/<u>Fran Rude</u>/Candy Williams [chor]/John S. Reid [mus dir]/Kenneth Rogers [voc asst]/David Hignell [lights & tech dir]/Jody Low [stage mgr]/H. Skaronski [cost]/Eric Low [sound]/Chris Kadijk & Rosemarie Gattiker [prod man]/Lethbridge Symphony Orchestra dir by John S. Reid	Michael Kaufmann, Sheila Pisko, George Evelyn, George Gallant, Roger Schultz, Mark Campbell, Rhonda Ruston, Karen Hudson, Winstan Jones, Lisa Webber, Margaret McKay, Al Greenway, Yvonne Fredrick, Lois Dongworth, Dawn Flexhaug, Jean Warburton, Colleen Kaufmann, Neana Meeks, Karen Kay, Sheena Lawson, Rhonda Nugent, Christopher Davidson, Stephen Graham, David Mikuliak, Lloyd Pollock, Sarah Nowlin, Wendy Spoulos (Mar 15/B9) - *a unique showcase (Dave Mabell)*
APR 25-30/88 - *U of L Experimental Th.*	Drama, 'Night, Mother by Marsha Norman/<u>Eric Low</u>/Amy Day [set design]/Jody Low [lights]/Carolyn Walker [stage mgr]/Yvonne Fredrick [prod mgr]/Stephen Graham, Ardith E. Stone, David Green, Angela Luck, Lynne Richardson, Tom Lindl, David Lee, Mark Campbell, Cliff Stoakley & others	Lois Dongworth, Janice Brown (Apr 16/B4; 26/B7) - *provocative, disturbing...abruptly forces us to consider our feelings & values (Dave Mabell)*

DATE/PLACE	PRODUCTION/DIRECTOR/ PRODUCTION PERSONNEL	CAST/REFERENCES/COMMENTS
MAY 9-14/88 - *CCH Drama Centre*	Musical, I'm Getting My Act Together & Taking It On The Road/Fran Rude/Candy Williams [chor]/Kathy Gurney [prod mgr]/Edward Johnson & Tracey Lowe [mus dirs]/Neil Sheets [sound]/Jody Low [stage mgr]/Mark Baldwin	Rhonda Ruston, Martin Madge, Sheena Lawson, Rhonda Nugent, Edward Johnson, Bill Lawson, Roger Schutlz, Scott Baldwin, Keith Landry (May 9/B5) - *strong performances... enthusiastic audience (Dave Mabell)*
SEPT 12-17/88 - *U of L Th.*	Comedy, Noises Off by Michael Frayn/Fran Rude/David Hignell [set & light design]/Jody Low [stage mgr & tech dir]/Lynette Collin [cost]/J.A. Johnston [scenic art]/Neil Sheets [sound]/Doug Ross, Walter Clarke, Barbara Lacey, Bob Thomsen, Denise Plett, Rebecca Low, Karen Goertz, Sue Koshman, Cliff Stoakley & others	Candy Chiselle Williams, Eric Low, Wade Scott Pierson, Tammi Pretty, Lorraine McFadden Bellikka, Mel Fletcher, Kate Connolly, Lloyd Pollock, Winstan Jones, Sean Low (Sept 13/A11) - *another smash hit (Dave Mabell)*
JAN 6-14/89 - *U of L Th.*	Musical, Annie by Thomas Meehan (book), Charles Strouse (music), Martin Charnin (lyrics)/Fran Rude/Candy Williams [chor]/Kenneth Rogers [mus dir]/Tracey Lowe [vocal asst]/Robert Hirano [set design]/ Leslie Robison-Greene [cost]/Jody Low [lights & tech dir]/Eric Low [sound]/Karen Hudson [prod mgr]/Nancy Thibert, Ardith Stone, James McDowell, David Hignell, Neil Sheets, Rosemarie Gattiker, Sue Koshman, Cliff Stoakley & others	Michelle Williams, Lois Dongworth, Mark Russell, Patrick Hankey, Lee Prindle, Stephen Graham, Al Greenway, John Duell, Roger Schutlz, Rhonda Nugent, Mel Fletcher, Yvonne Fredrick, Michael Smith, Carol Laycock, Jerry Bellikka, Susan Koshman, Erin Demers, Neana Meeks, Sheena Lawson, Heather Lawson, Gerald DeBow, Diane Plantinga, Jordanna Kohn, Carla Serkin, Lorrie Willets, Krysa (Sandy) & others (Jan 9/A11) - *heart-warming (Dave Mabell)*
MAY 18-21; 23-27/89 - *U of L Th.*	Musical, Sweeney Todd: The Demon Barber of Fleet Street by Hugh Wheeler (book), Stephen Sondheim (music & lyrics) from an adaptation by Christopher Bond/Fran Rude/Candy Chiselle-Williams/Tom Staples [mus dir]/Kenneth Rogers [vocal]/J.A. Johnston [set design]/Don Acaster [lights]/Leslie Robison-Greene [cos]/David Hignell [sound] & others	Michael Richey, Sheila Pisko, Karen Rees, David Mikuliuk, Juran Greene, Darrilyn Penton, Mark Ward, Eric Low, George Gallant, Scott Carpenter, Gavin Crawford, Stephen Graham, Patrick Hankey, Karen Hudson, Karen Kay, Jordanna Kohn, Barbara Lacey, Gordon Lowe, Sally Pittman, Doug Shepherd, Michael Smith, Heather Shepherd, Geoffrey Wallins, Lisa Webber, Maria Zappone (May 19/C4) - *big & bold; another musical triumph (Dave Mabell)*

Major Alberta Drama Festivals
Alberta Drama League (1930–32)
DDF: Alberta Regional Drama Festival (1933–39; 46–70)

TIME/PLACE CRITIC OR ADJUDICATOR	A*	GROUP/DIRECTOR	PRODUCTION/AWARDS
FEB 15/30 - *Grand Th., Calgary (non-competitive)* *L.W. Brockington, K.C., Calgary*		Calgary Green Room Club/Betty Mitchell Lethbridge Playgoers/E.G. Sterndale Bennett Medicine Hat Dramatic Society/H.N. Davis U of A Players/Elizabeth S. Haynes	Punch and Go The School for Scandal (screen scene) The Monkey's Paw Shall We Join the Ladies
FEB 20,21/31 - *Grand Th., Calgary (non-competitive)* *L. W. Brockington, Calgary*		Banff Literary & Drama Club/Margaret E. Greenham Calgary Little Theatre/Mrs. Roland Winter Calgary Green Room Club/E.J. Thorlakson Drumheller Dramateurs/Alice Edwards Edmonton Little Theatre/Ethel Hyndman Lethbridge Playgoers/E.B. Sterndale Bennett Medicine Hat Players/N. Davis	Trifles The Maid of France The Bishop's Candlesticks Romance of the Willow Pattern Campbell of Kilmohr Back of the Yards Half an Hour
FEB 20,21/32 - *Convocation Hall, U of A (non-competitive)* *No critique*		Calgary Little Theatre/Mrs. W. Roland Winter Calgary Green Room Club/Betty Mitchell Drumheller Dramateurs/Alice Edwards Edmonton Little Theatre/Theodore Cohen Lethbridge Playgoers/E.B. Sterndale Bennett Medicine Hat Players/N. Davis SunAlta Drama Club (Calgary)/Mrs. Ward H. Patterson	The Valiant A Wonder Hat The Medicine Show The Dark Lady of the Sonnets And So To Bed (Act II) The Second Lie The Patchwork Quilt
MAR 10,11/33 - *Majestic Th., Lethbridge* *L.W. Brockington*	- **2nd - **1st -	Banff Literary & Drama Club/Aileen Harmon Edmonton Little Theatre/Theodore Cohen Lethbridge Playgoers/Maybelle Bryans Medicine Hat Little Theatre/N. Davis Calgary Theatre Guild/Betty Mitchell	An Evening on Dartmoor Riders to the Sea Becky Sharpe The Twelve Pound Look The First & the Last
FEB 23,24/34 - *Grand Th., Calgary* *Rupert Harvey (London, Eng.)*	- 3rd - - - 2nd **1st	Banff Literary & Drama Club/Mrs.W.H. Greenham Calgary Theatre Guild/Mrs. E.J. Thorlakson Coleman Players/Arthur Graham Drumheller Amateurs/Jack Smith Edmonton Little Theatre/Theodore Cohen Lethbridge Playgoers/Maybelle Bryans Medicine Hat Little Theatre/Norman Davis U of A Dramatic Club/Larry Davis	Coercion by Capt. Alexander Ramsay (Banff) The Undercurrent Seven Women Where Did They Meet Again The Well The Road of Poplars Suppressed Desires Derelict by E.J. Thorlakson (Calgary)
FEB 7-9/35 - *Grand Th., Calgary* *Malcolm Morley (London, Eng.)*	- 3rd - - - **1st - 2nd - - -	Banff Literary & Drama Club/Mrs. W.H. Greenham Calgary Theatre Guild/Betty Mitchell Cardston Drama Club/J.S. Smith Drumheller Dramateurs/Elsie Edwards Edmonton Little Theatre/R.V. Clark Joachim Drama Club (Edmonton)/Alphonse Hervieux Lethbridge Playgoers/Florence Mackenzie Medicine Hat Little Theatre/C.S. Bullard Mount Royal College Players/Inger Rasmussen, Beth Lockerbie U of A Drama Club/Elsie Park Gowan Innisfail Drama Club/Mrs. C.F. Dorsey	Garafelia's Husband Sicilian Limes Vindication The Camberley Triangle The Artist Bon Sang Ne Ment Pas by Emma Morrier (Edmonton) Good Theatre The Wasp The Second Visit God Made the Country Pygmalian
FEB 6-8/36 - *Grand Th., Calgary* *Allan Wade (London, Eng.)*	- - 2nd - **1st 3rd - - - - -	Banff Drama Club/N. Vernon Wood Calgary Light Opera Society/C. Max Bishop Calgary Theatre Guild/Frank Holroyd Cardston Players/J.S. Smith Edmonton Little Theatre/Aubrey Proctor Innisfail Players/Mrs. C.F. Dorsey Lethbridge Playgoers/Maybelle Bryans Medicine Hat Little Theatre/Norman Davis Mount Royal College/Inger Rasmussen Red Deer Drama Club/Eva Beattie U of A Drama Club/Mary Sutherland	Destiny by N. Vernon Wood Barbara's Wedding They Refuse to be Resurrected To Die With a Smile by Madeline Blackmore Literature What Never Dies Recoil Thirst The Lovely Miracle A Fool of a Man Boccaccio's Untold Tale

TIME/PLACE CRITIC OR ADJUDICATOR	A*	GROUP/DIRECTOR	PRODUCTION/AWARDS
MAR 18-20/37 - *Grand Th., Calgary* *George de Warfaz (London, Eng.)*	-	Alliance Française de Calgary/Doris Hunt	L'Ete de la St. Martin
	-	Banff Literary & Drama Club/Mrs. Marg Greenham	Judas by Rev. T. Londsdale (Banff)
	-	Calgary Theatre Guild/Frank Holroyd	Twentieth Century Lullaby
	-	-	Best Actress - *Muriel Langfield*
	3rd	Cardston Drama Club/J.S. Smith	The Proposal
	2nd	Clive Dramatic Club/V.G. Duffy	Ali the Cobbler
	-	-	Best Actor - *Robert Haskins*
	-	Drumheller Dramateurs/E.F. Key	The Lord's Will
	-	Edmonton Little Theatre/Eva Howard	The Clod
	-	Jr. College Players of Calgary/Beth Lockerbie	Mansions
	-	Le Cercle St. Joachim D'Edmonton/Laurier Pickard	Le Coeur Decide
	-	Le Cercle Dramatique Molière Edmonton/Alphonse Hervieux	Les Rantzau (Act II)
	-	Lethbridge Playgoers/Maybelle Bryans, CDA	Four Into Seven Won't Go
	**1st	Medicine Hat Little Theatre/C.S. Blanchard	Heaven on Earth
	-	Strathmore Drama Club/Margaret Gordon	The Knife
	-	U of A Drama Society/Gwen Pharis & Jeff Bullock	The Dreamy Kid
FEB 17-19/38 - *Grand Th., Calgary* *Malcolm Morley (London)*	-	Banff Literary & Drama Club/A.B. Hodges	One Evening at Nero's
	2nd	Calgary Elks Players/James Jack	The Hand of Siva
	-	Calgary Theatre Guild/Frank Holroyd	Birds of Paradise
	-	Drumheller Dramateurs/	The Lord's Will
	-	Innisfail Players/Edith Dorsey	Joint Owners in Spain
	-	Lethbridge Playgoers/Eric Johnson	She Was No Lady
	-	Medicine Hat Little Theatre/Mrs. W.M. Currie	Highness
	3rd	Red Deer Players/Eva Beattie	The Valiant
	-	-	Best Actor - *Wesley Oke*
	**1st	U of A Drama Society/George England	The Happy Journey
			Best Actress - *Sheila Morrison*
FEB 24,28/39 - *Empire Th., Edmonton* *George Skillan (London, Eng.)*	-	Banff Literary & Drama Society/	Russian Salad
	**1st	Clive Dramatic Club/V.G. Duffy	The Bear
	-	-	Best Actor - *Robert Haskins*
	2nd	Innisfail Amateur Players/	Kate Larsen
	3rd	Le Cercle Molière Edmonton/	Les Trois Masques
	-	Medicine Hat Little Theatre/Mrs. L.N. Laidlaw	Still Stands the House by Gwen Pharis
			Best Actress - *Ethel Finley*
		U of A Drama Society/	Helena's Husband
1940-45		**NO ALBERTA REGIONAL FESTIVALS**	
MAY 4/46 - *Western Canada H.S. (Calgary)* *Elizabeth S. Haynes (Edm.)*	***	Calgary Workshop 14/Conrad Bain	John Doe;
	-	-	Best Actor - *Ron Rosvold*
	-	Cardston Drama Club/Norma Peterson(Calgary)	Funeral Flowers for the Bride
	-	Cardston Players/Alice Dowdle	To Die With a Smile;
	-	-	Best Actress - *Alice Dowdle* (shared)
	-	Coleman Players/Arthur Graham	The Giants' Stair;
			Best Actress - *Polly Purvis* (shared)
MAR 22/47 - *Edmonton* *R.G.H. Orchard (U of A)*	-	Calgary Theatre Players/Evelyn Hambly MacLauchlan	Bathsheba of Saaremaa
	-	-	Best Actress - *Florence Thorpe*
	-	Cardston Players/	The Women in the Freight Car
	**	Edmonton Community Theatre Players/Eva O. Howard	My Heart's in the Highlands (excerpts);
	-	-	Best Actor - *Frank Holroyd*
	-	Medicine Hat Little Theatre/Edwin McKenzie	The Wind on the Heather
MAR 5,6/48 - *Empress Th., (Medicine Hat)* *Robert Stuart (London, Eng.)*	-	Banff Literary & Drama Club/Marg Greenham, CDA	The Shadow of the Glen
	**1st	Calgary Workshop 14/Gordon Atkinson	Maistre Pierre Patelin;
	-	-	B. Actor - *Jack Phillips*
	-	-	B. Dir.- *G. Atkinson*
	-	Coleman Players/Arthur Graham	The Monkey's Paw
	**2nd	Edmonton Community Theatre Players/E.S. Haynes, CDA	Victoria Regina (excerpts);
	-	-	B. Actress- *Milwyn Davies*
	-	Medicine Hat Little Theatre/Edwin McKenzie	Intermezzo
	-	Fairview Drama Group/Mrs. M.E. Grimshaw	The Valiant

TIME/PLACE CRITIC OR ADJUDICATOR	A*	GROUP/DIRECTOR	PRODUCTION/AWARDS
MAR 7-9/49 - Central H.S. (Calgary) Robert Speaight (London, Eng.)	- - ** - -	Calgary Civic Theatre/Douglas Doherty - Calgary Workshop 14/Betty Mitchell University Dramatic Society/Robert Stuart University Provincial Players/Robert Orchard	Gaslight; B. Actor - *Clarence Newcombe* Hedda Gabbler; B. Actress - *Doreen Richardson* The Sordid Story (one act) 3 One-Act Plays: Box and Cox by J.M. Morton Breeches from Bond Street by Elsie Park Gowan The White Man & the Mountain by Robert Orchard
JAN 26-28/50 - (Edm.), Maxwell Wray (London, Eng.)	- ** - -	Calgary Civic Theatre/R. Gibb assisted by Nora Snelgrove Calgary Workshop 14/Betty Mitchell U of A Studio Players/Robert Orchard	Laura; B. Actress - *Evelyn Lawson* The Rivals; B. Actor - *Ed Holmes* Henry IV (Pirandello)
APR 2-4/51 - Western Canada H.S. (Calgary) Robert Newton (London, Eng.)	- - - **	Arts & Letters Club (Calgary)/Doug Doherty Calgary Civic Theatre/R. Gibb Calgary Workshop 14/Betty Mitchell -	Harvey Shop at Sly Corner; B. Actor - *Michael Burton* The Gioconda Smile; B. Actress - *Pat Laidlaw*
JAN 21-23/52 - Edmonton Pierre La Fevre (Eng.)	** - - -	Calgary Workshop 14/Betty Mitchell Civic Service Playhouse (Edmonton)/Marjorie Buckley Lethbridge Playgoers/Maybelle Bryans	Pygmalion; B. Actress - *Nana Canning* The Barretts of Wimpole Street B. Actor - *Tim Byrne* Angel Street
FEB 19-21/53 - LCI Aud., Lethbridge John Allen (Eng.)	- - - **	Civil Service Playhouse (Edmonton)/Marjorie Buckley Playgoers of Lethbridge/Hugh Buchanan - Studio Theatre (U of A)/Elizabeth Sterling Haynes	The Emperor Jones Night Must Fall; B. Sup. Actress - *Mary Waters (Heinitz)* Othello; B. Actor - *Robert Orchard* B. Actress - *Rosemary Hood*
FEB 15-18/54 - Calgary (Western Canada H.S.) Graham Suter (Eng.)	- - - **	Calgary Civic Theatre/T.E. Snelgrove Pirikapo Players (Edm.)/Walter Kaasa Playgoers of Lethbridge/Hugh Buchanan Workshop 14 Associated (Calgary)/Betty Mitchell	The Hasty Heart The Blue Bird The Silver Cord; B. Actress - *Mary Waters* The Lady's Not For Burning; B. Actor - *Ron Poffenroth* B. Dir./Prod. - *Betty Mitchell*
MAR 9-12/55 - Edmonton Andre Van Gyseghem (Eng.)	- - - - - **	Brooks Little Theatre/ Buskins (Calgary)/ Circle 8 (Edmonton)/ Medicine Hat Civic Theatre/Ronald Thompson Pirikapo Players (Edmonton) David Cormack Workshop 14 (Calgary)/Betty Mitchell	The Internal Machine The Glass Menagerie The Heiress Born Yesterday; B. Actress - *Evanthia Evangelos* The Yellow Jacket The Applecart; B. Actor - *Chris Wiggins (also best actor in DDF)*
JAN 16-19/56 - Medicine Hat H.S. Pamela Stirling (Eng.)	- ** - - - - - - -	Brooks Little Theatre/Lorin Mair Calgary Buskins/Allan McLennan Calgary Workshop 14/Betty Mitchell - Coaldale Little Theatre/Murray Robison - - Medicine Hat Civic Theatre/Ronald Thompson U of A Alumni Studio A/Don Pimm	Antigone The Innocents The River Line; B. Sup. Actor - *Robert Cruse* Papa is All; B. Actress - *Jennie Emery* B. Dir. - *Murray Robison* B. Sup. Actress - *Theresa King* Best Char. Actress - *Peggy Mallalieu* Of Mice and Men Dr. Arcularis; B. Actor - *Walter Kaasa* B. Visual Presentation

TIME/PLACE CRITIC OR ADJUDICATOR	A*	GROUP/DIRECTOR	PRODUCTION/AWARDS
FEB 6-9/57 - *Capitol Th., Lethbridge* *Cecil Bellamy (Eng.)*	- - - ** - - - - - -	Calgary Workshop 14/Betty Mitchell Coaldale Little Theatre/Murray Robison Medicine Hat Civic Theatre/Henry Allergoth - - - - Playgoers of Lethbridge/Daphne Manson U of A Studio A (Edmonton)/Joan Rivet	Anne of the Thousand Days Ladies in Retirement; B. Sup. Actress - *Jennie Emery* Stalag 17; B. Actor - *Garry Mitchell* B. Sup. Actor - *John Komanchuk* B. Dir. - *H. Allergoth* B. Visual - *Fred Kirkpatrick* The Heiress The Country Girl; B. Actress - *Shirley Higginson*
MAR 12-15/58 - *S.A. Jubilee Aud. (Calgary)* *Richard West (Eng.)*	** - - - - - - - - -	Coaldale Little Theatre/Murray Robison - - Workshop 14 (Calgary)/Betty Mitchell - - Cothburn of Red Deer/Allen B. Gibb Playgoers of Lethbridge/Wayne Matkin - Medicine Hat Civic Theatre/John Komanchuk	All Summer Long; B. Dir. - *Murray Robison* B. Sup. Actor - *Sandy McCallum* Arms and the Man; B. Visual - B. Actress - *Violet Powlan* My Three Angels White Sheep of the Family B. Actor: *George Hall* B. Char. Actress - *Brenda Cordwell* Angel Street
MAR 19-23/59 - *N.A. Jubilee Aud. (Edmonton)* *Richard Ainley (Eng.)*	- - - - ** - - -	Buskins of Calgary/Jo Cormack - Calgary Players Society/Harold Patton - Court Players (Edm.)/Michael Porosz Medicine Hat Civic Theatre/Henry Allergoth - - U of A Alumni Players/Gordon Peacock	The Caine Mutiny Court Martial; B. Actor - *Allen Kerr* Ring Around the Moon; B. Visual - Ghosts Diary of Anne Franke; B. Dir. - *H. Allergoth* Male Char. - *Russell Stone* Female Char. - *Jennifer Kerr* The Lark; B. Actress - *Irene Powlan*
MAR 22-26/60 - *Towne Th., Medicine Hat* *Robert Gill (Toronto)*	** - - - - - - - - -	Medicine Hat Civic Theatre/Dorothy Jones - - Medicine Hat Civic Theatre/Henry Allergoth Medicine Hat Civic Theatre/Patrick Stiles Playgoers of Lethbridge/Sam Pitt - - - RCAF Cold Lake Drama Group/Mary MacDonald	Come Back Little Sheba; B. Actress - *June Ferguson* B. Sup. Actor - *Wayne Chesley* The Happy Time Janus Gently Does It; B. Actor - *Sandy McCallum* B. Dir. - *Sam Pitt* B. Sup. Actress - *Kaye Watson* B. Char. Actress - *Joan Waterfield* B. Visual - *Cornelius Martens* The Mousetrap; B. Char. Actor - *Andre Hughes*
MAR 15-18/61 - *S.A. Jubilee Aud., Calgary* *Norma Springford*	** - - - - - - - - -	Coaldale Little Theatre/Murray Robison - - - - - Cothburn of Red Deer/Joseph Rutten Medicine Hat Civic Theatre/Henry Allergoth Parkland Players (Red Deer)/Doris Oliver - Playgoers of Lethbridge/Daphne Manson	The Beautiful People; B. Dir. - *Murray Robison* B. Actor - *Russell Wiber* B. Sup. Actor - *Sandy McCallum* B. Char. Actor - *Fred Pritchard* B. Sup. Actress - *Theresa King* B. Stage Mgt. - *Ivan Meyers* Rashomon The Rainmaker The Heiress B. Actress: - *Gloria Bubb* Anastasia; B. Char. Actress - *Denise Black*

TIME/PLACE CRITIC OR ADJUDICATOR	A*	GROUP/DIRECTOR	PRODUCTION/AWARDS
MAR 21-24/62 - *Memorial Centre (Red Deer)* *David Gardner (Toronto)*	- - - - - - **	Cothburn of Red Deer/Marion F. Taylor - - Medicine Hat Civic Theatre/Dorothy Jones Medicine Hat High School/Henry Allergoth Parkland Players of Red Deer/Mary Trueman Playgoers of Lethbridge/Denise Black	An Inspector Calls; B. Sup. Actor - *Gary Wilson* B. Sup. Actress - *Jane MacQuarrie* Time Remembered Teach Me How to Cry The Importance of Being Ernest The Dark at the Top of the Stairs B. Dir. - *Denise Black* B. Actor - *Cliff Black* B. Actress - *Helen Bennett* B. Stage Mgt.-*Norville Getty* B. Visual -
MAR 27-30/63 - *Capitol Th., Lethbridge* *E.W. Ljungh (Toronto)*	** - - - - - - -	Coaldale Little Theatre/Murray Robison - - - - Cothburn of Red Deer/Mary Lou Armstrong Medicine Hat Civic Theatre/Richard Mells Playgoers of Lethbridge/Cliff Black	The Well of the Saints; B. Dir. - *Murray Robison* B. Actor - *Sandy McCallum* B. Actress - *Peggy Mallalieu* B. Visual - *Katherine & Elizabeth Brauer* B. Stage Mgt. - *Ivan Meyers* All for Mary Summer of the Seventeenth Doll B. Char. Actress - *Lois Dongworth* Rebecca; B. Sup. Actress - *Joan Perkinson* B. Sup. Actor - *Derek Charnley* B. Char. Actor - *George Mann*
MAR 19-21/64 - *Allied Arts Centre (Calgary)* *Herbert Whittaker (Toronto)*	- - - - - - - - **	Medicine Hat Civic Theatre/Dorothy Jones - Playgoers of Lethbridge/Denise Black - - - - - Theatre '64 of Calgary/Joyce Doolittle	Teahouse of the August Moon B. Char. Actor - *Richard Wray* B. Stage Mgt. - Therese; B. Actor - *Syd Clarke* B. Sup. Actor - *George Mann* B. Sup. Actress - *Sharon Bolen* B. Char. Actress - *Jean Ede* B. Visual - Happy Days; B. Dir. - *J. Doolittle* B. Actress - *Ruth Frost*
APR 5-10/65 - *Arts & Letters Club (Edm.)* *Walter Massey (Montreal)* No Alberta play selected for DDF	- - 1st - - - - - - - - - - -	Arts & Letters Club (Calgary)/Bert Cairns - Buskins of Calgary/Joyce Doolittle - Coaldale Little Theatre/Murray Robison - - - Edmonton Group Theatre/Mickey MacDonald - Medicine Hat Civic Theatre/Anthony Pydee Our Town Workshop (Leth.)/Joy Pritchard - - - St. Paul's United Drama Club Grande Prairie/	The Pleasure of His Company; B. Char. Actor - *Jack Johnston* The Birthday Party; B. Sup. Actor - *Bill Romance* B. Sup. Actress - *Agatha Mercer* The Red Shoes; B. Visual - *Ed Bayly* B. Stage Mgt. - *Ivan Meyers* Special Award: Wendy Robison Two for the Sea Saw; B. Dir. - *M. MacDonald* End Game The Queen & the Rebels; B. Actor - *Bill Matheson* B. Actress - *Joan Waterfield* B. Char. Actress - *Muriel Matheson* Grubstake For the Eye-Opener Man

TIME/PLACE CRITIC OR ADJUDICATOR	A*	GROUP/DIRECTOR	PRODUCTION/AWARDS
MAR 29 - APR 2/66 - *Vocational Sch.,* *(Medicine Hat)* *Peter Boretski (Winnipeg-* *Toronto-Hollywood)*	** - - - - - - - - - - -	MAC Theatre Society (Calgary)/Joyce Doolittle [Also judged best play in DDF with individual awards: B. Actor - Michael Ball; B. Actress - Sharon Pollock; B. Actor Under 25 - James Eberle] Medicine Hat Civic Theatre/Dorothy Jones - - Our Town Workshop (Leth.)/Fred Pritchard - - - - Playgoers of Lethbridge/Dick Mells The Swan City Players (Grande Prairie/Len Milne	The Knack; B. Actor - *Robert Haley* - - Billy Liar; B. Char. Actress - *Margaret Phillips* B. Sup. Actress - *Sandra Brown* The Caretaker; B. Sup. Actor - *Bud Iverson* B. Char. Actor - *Bill Matheson* B. Visual - B. Dir. - *Fred Pritchard* You Can't Take It With You Anne of Green Gables; B. Stage Mgt. - *Rod Burton*
MAR 8-11/67 - *Yates (Lethbridge)* *Paxton Whitehead* *(England & Shaw Festival,* *Niagara-on-the-Lake) No* *Alberta play selected for* *DDF*	1st - - - - - - - - - - -	Coaldale Little Theatre/Murray Robison - - - - - Medicine Hat Civic Theatre/Henry Allergoth - Playgoers of Lethbridge/Denise Black - - - Our Town Workshop (Leth.)/Joy Pritchard	Teach Me How to Cry by Patricia Joudry B. Dir. - *Murray Robison* B. Visual -*M. Robison* B. Actor - *Ed Bayly* B. Char. Actress - *Peggy Mallalieu* B. Stage Mgt. - *Ivan Meyers* Flight Into Danger by Arthur Hailey; B. Sup. Actress - *Jean Van Wert* B. Lighting - *Ron McAffey* Chinook by Bill Matheson in collaboration with Dick Mells; B. New Canadian Play: B. Actress - *Joan Waterfield* B. Sup. Actor - *George Mann* The Wheel by Mac Reilley
1968		**NO ALBERTA REGIONAL FESTIVAL**	
MAR 10-15/69 - *Yates (Lethbridge)* *Dennis Sweeting (Toronto)*		Lethbridge Musical Theatre (Actors' Studio)/Dick Mells (only Alberta entry)	Bus Stop; no individual awards given in 1969
MAR 9-11/70 - *Yates (Lethbridge)* *Roberta Dolby*	- ** - - - - - - -	Medicine Hat Civic Theatre/Palmer Huckle Playgoers of Lethbridge/Dick Mells (At DDF, Sheila Pisko was awarded Best Actress under the age of 25) - - - - - University of Lethbridge Drama Society/Brian Tyson	Luv The Hostage; B. Dir. - *Dick Mells* B. Actress - *Lois Dongworth & Sheila Pisko* B. Sup. Actor - *Charles Schott, Jr.* B. Char. Actress - *Hazel Skaronski* B. Char. Actor - *Bill Matheson* B. Visual - *Ed Bayly* The Miser; B. Actor - *Charlie Schott* B. Sup. Actress - *Nora Needham* B. Stage Mgt. - *Weste Jensen* B. Sup. Actor - *Charles Schott, Jr.*

*Adjudicator's decision [1st, 2nd, 3rd - ranked according to overall presentation]
**Selected to represent Alberta Regional Festival at DDF
***Selected to represent Alberta at the Western Drama Festival in Winnipeg [May 25]

Lethbridge and District One Act Festivals (1953–1989)
and Alberta One Act Festivals Staged in Lethbridge

DATE/LOCATION ADJUDICATOR(S)	ADJ	GROUP/DIRECTOR	PRODUCTION/AWARDS
APR 1-2/53 - *CARDSTON SOCIAL CENTRE* Sue Laycock, Esther Nelson (Edmonton) ****A1AF - Red Deer* *Apr 17,18*	- - - - - **	1. Alberta Stake MIA, LDS Church of Cardston/Janet Baker 2. Playgoers of Lethbridge/G.H. Knowles 3. Taylor Stake MIA, LDS Church, Raymond/Myron Holmes 4. Lethbridge Stake MIA, LDS Church, Lethbridge/Wayne Matkin 5. Coaldale East School/Murray Robison 6. Coaldale Little Theatre/Murray Robison	Michael The Twelve Pound Look The Maker of Dreams Dr. Faustus - The Romances The Case of the Crushed Petunias (Apr 1/13, 2/13, 4/13)
APR 1,2/54 - *COALDALE* Jack Medhurst (Coaldale) ****A1AF - Red Deer* *May 1,2*	- ** - - -	1. Cardston High School Studio Theatre/Thomas Hughes 2. Coaldale Little Theatre/Murray Robison 3. Coutts Amateur Drama Society/Victor Brosz 4. Playgoers of Lethbridge/Agnes Davidson 5. Taber CYO/Adam (Ab) Chervinski	The Valiant Riders to the Sea Dark Brown Mail Order Bride by Effie Reid Dust of the Road
MAR 8/55 - *LCI - LETHBRIDGE* Agnes Davidson, Bruce Busby, Joan Waterfield (Lethbridge) ****A1AF - Red Deer* *April 1955*	1st - - ** - -	1. Coaldale Little Theatre/Murray Robison 2. Garbutt Business College/Helen R. Matkin 3. Playgoers of Lethbridge/Mary Waters 4. Southminster United Church YPS/Mary Waters	Catherine Parr (opted out of the Alberta One Act Festival) The Dragon Lonesome Like B. Actress - *Anita Susman* Rise and Shine B. Actor - *Wally Kemp*
MAR 26-28/56 - *TABER* Walter Kaasa (Edm.) ****A1AF - Red Deer* *Apr 21, 22*	- ** - - - - - - - - -	1. McKillop YPA/Bruce Busby 2. Playgoers of Lethbridge/Kaye Watson, Elsie Biddell 3. Playgoers of Lethbridge/Phyl Ellerbeck 4. Playgoers of Lethbridge/Bill Lazaruk 5. Taber Little Theatre/Winnifred Barr 6. Taber High School/H.B. Myers 7. Taber Stake MIA, Raymond/Shirley W. King 8. Southminster YPA/Mary Waters	The Poacher Bathsheba of Saaremaa B. Actress - *Elsie Biddell* Jane Wogan B. Actor - *Bruce Busby* B. Sup. Actress - *Kaye Watson* The Cajun B. Sup. Actor - *Colin Turner* Ali The Cobbler A Phoenix Too Frequent The Man Who Came To Gettysburg The Happy Journey
APR 1-3/57 - *TABER* Walter Kaasa (Edm.) ****A1AF - Red Deer* *Apr 26, 27*	- - - - - - - ** - -	1. Chinook Theatre Guild/Elsie Biddell, Jean Block 2. Chinook Theatre Guild/Bessy McCully, Elsie Biddell 3. Chinook Theatre Guild/Elsie Biddell, Stan McCrae 4. Garden City Players, Magrath/Franklin H. Smith 5. Playgoers of Lethbridge/Bruce Busby 6. Playgoers of Lethbridge/Harry Baalim 7. Playgoers of Lethbridge/Mary Waters 8. Playgoers of Lethbridge/Harry Baalim 9. Taber First Ward, MIA/Thelma Barton 10. Taber Little Theatre/Winnifred Barr	The Boor The Duchess Says Her Prayers B. Sup. Actor - *Don Eccleston* Riders to the Sea; B. Sup. Actress - *Yvonne Kennedy* The Court Scene From the Merchant of Venice Drought Hello Out There; B. Actress - *Theresa King* After Many Years by C.R. Matthews From Paradise to Butte; B. Actor - *Bill Matheson* Boy Friend For Dinner The Devil Among The Skins
NOV 5,6/59 - *STIRLING* Mrs. David Cormack (Cal.) ****A1AF - Red Deer* *Nov 21, 22*	** - - - - - - -	1. Coaldale Little Theatre/Peggy Mallalieu 2. Playgoers of Lethbridge/Mary Waters 3. Playgoers of Lethbridge/Jean Ede 4. Raymond MIA/Eleanor Hudson 5. Stirling MIA/Dorothy Hirsche	The Jack & The Joker by Gwen Pharis B. Actor - *Sandy McCallum* B. Actress - *Jean Mannington* B. Sup. Actress - *Peggy McCann* Overlaid To the Lovely Margaret; B. Sup. Actor - *Peter Hornsby* This Night Shall Pass The Fog in the Valley

**Represented Lethbridge & District at the Alberta One Act Drama Festival

DATE/LOCATION ADJUDICATOR(S)	ADJ	GROUP/DIRECTOR	PRODUCTION/AWARDS
1960 **NO LETHBRIDGE & DISTRICT ONE ACT FESTIVAL**		Lethbridge & District represented at A1AF in Red Deer by: Coaldale Little Theatre/M.Robison (Nov 18,19)	The Devil Among the Skins
APR 20/63 *- STIRLING* *Irene McPhail (Med. Hat)* ***A1AF - Red Deer* *May 20,11*	- - ** - -	1. Lethbridge Stake MIA/Milton Hansen 2. Lethbridge United Church Young People's Drama Group 3. Our Town Workshop (Lethbridge)/Joy Pritchard - - 4. Vulcan Little Theatre/Jessie Sharpe	Opened By Mistake The Unseen Chinook by Bill Matheson; B. Actor - *Fred Pritchard* B. Actress: *Joan Waterfield* For The Love of a Horse B. Sup. Actress - *Margaret Shaw* B. Sup. Actor - *Louis Shaw*
NOV 2/63 *- LETHBRIDGE JR. COL-LEGE Commentary by Murray Robison **A1AF - Banff* *Nov 15,16/63*	** **	1. Our Town Workshop/Joy Pritchard 2. Our Town Workshop/Joy Pritchard	Red Peppers (non-competitive) Fool's Errand
OCT 28,29/64 *- LETHBRIDGE JR. COL-LEGE* *Mary Cairns (Calgary)* ***A1AF - Banff* *Nov 13,14/64*	** - - - - - - - -	1. Coaldale Little Theatre/Murray Robison - - - 2. Our Town Workshop/Joy Pritchard 3. Our Town Workshop/Joy Pritchard - - 4. Our Town Workshop/Fred Pritchard	The Tinker's Wedding B. Dir. - *M. Robison* B. Actress - *Y. Robison* (shared) B. Sup. Actress - *J. Emery* B. Visual - *Ed Bayly* Riders to the Sea A Phoenix Too Frequent B. Actress - *M. Matheson* (shared) B. Actor - *J. Elliott* The Dumbwaiter B. Sup. Actor - *B. Iverson*
FALL/65 *- **A1AF - Banff* *Nov 12,13*	- - - -	No Lethbridge & District Regional Festival but the following were invited to participate in the A1AF, Banff. 1. Our Town Workshop/Joy Pritchard 2. Coaldale Little Theatre/Murray Robison	- The Dock Brief The Golden Goose by Joyce Doolittle (non-competitive)
1966 - 1970		**No Lethbridge & District One Act Festivals - Alberta Drama League disbanded in 1967**	
MAY 25,27/71 *- YATES CENTRE* *(A Festival of Community Theatre)* *Written evaluations by Dick Mells, Ed Bayly, Joan Bowman, Muriel Jolliffe*	- - - - - - - - -	Auspices of Lethbridge Allied Arts Council: 1. Coaldale Teen Players/Murray Robison 2. Coaldale Teen Players/Murray Robison 3. Jolliffe Academy/Muriel Jolliffe 4. Kate Andrews High School/Lily Larter 5. Lethbridge Youth Theatre/Christine Puhl 6. Rachel Luca, Laurin Mann & Sheri McFadden 7. R.I. Baker School/Murray Robison 8. The Shoestring Players/Joan Waterfield 9. Wilson Jr. High School/David Lynagh	- Catherine Parr Macbeth (Act V, Scene 1) Mime The Man in The Bowler Hat Ah-Tush Mit by E. Joan Marshall (Calgary) The Spoken Word (Speech Arts Performance) Johnny Dunn The In Group She Walks in Beauty
FEB 24/73 *- YATES (Auspices of Allied Arts Council)* *Dr. Brian Tyson (U of L)* ***A1AF - Banff,* *Mar 3/73*	- ** - -	1. The Archers (Lethbridge Youth Theatre/Jim Veenstra 2. Bowman Players/Jim Veenstra 3. Harlequin Players of LCC/Betty Sorenson 4. Playgoers of Lethbridge/Jean Warburton with Muriel Jolliffe (choreography)	The Stronger by A. Strindberg Babel Rap by Lazarus The Black Box Pyramus & Thisbe (non-competitive)
FEB 7,8/74 *- YATES (Auspices of Lethbridge AAC in cooperation Alberta Drama Festival Association* *Bryan Tyson* ***A1AF - Banff,* *Mar 3*	- - - - - ** -	1. LCC Harlequin Players/Betty Sorenson - 2. Playgoers of Lethbridge/Jim Veenstra 3. Playgoers of Lethbridge/Ed Bayly 4. The Theatre Troupe on Tour/Mike Wright 5. Lethbridge Youth Theatre/Joan Waterfield 6. The Windy Hollow Players (Pincher Creek)/Henry Hammond	Where Have All the Lightning Bugs Gone by Louis E. Catron Hello Out There by William Saroyan The Rising of the Moon by Lady Gregory The Happy Journey by Thornton Wilder Eliza & the Lexicon by Robert Green Ladies of Camelot by Robert Macleod

DATE/LOCATION ADJUDICATOR(S)	ADJ	GROUP/DIRECTOR	PRODUCTION/AWARDS
FEB 18/75 - *YATES (Auspices of AAC in cooperation with ADFA)* *Bryan Tyson* ***A1AF - Banff* *Mar 7,8*	****1st** - - - - - - - - - - - ******	1. Attic Theatre/Murray Robison - 2. Coaldale Little Theatre/Murray Robison - 3. LCC Harlequin Players/Scott Mitchell, Betty Sorenson - - - 4. Playgoers of Lethbridge/Ed Bayly - 5. Quarter Theatre/Eric Low, Bryan Francis - - 6. Westside Players/Richard Epp 7. U of L Drama Department/Terry Theodore	Mooney's Kid Don't Cry by Tennessee Williams The Case of the Crushed Petunias (non-competitive) by T. Williams a) A Sound and Light Presentation b) When Shakespeare's Ladies Meet by Charles George c) Cobbler, Stick To Thy Last by Kay Hill Priscilla Pringle's Predicament by E. Bayly (non-competitive) a) A Marriage Proposal by A. Chekov b) Holed Up (non-competitive) by Betty Keller The First Plateau by Richard Epp A Swan Song by Anton Chekhov
FEB 21/76 - *YATES (AAC & BDFA)* *Dick Mells* ***A1AF - Med. Hat* *Mar 12,13*	****** - -	1. Playgoers of Lethbridge/Nora Rose 2. Playgoers/Terry Theodore 3. Playgoers/Eric Low	The Birdbath by Leonard Melfi The Dirty Old Man by Lewis John Carlino The New Play by William Saroyan
FEB 26/77 - *YATES (AAC & ADFA)* *Dick Mells* ***A1AF - Grande Prairie,* *Mar*	****** ****1st** ******	1. Playgoers/Joan Waterfield 2. Playgoers/Michael Wright 3. Playgoers/J. Waterfield	The Crickets Sing by Beverly Cross Ernie's Incredible Illucination by Alan Ayckbourn Steinway Grand
FEB 17,18/78 - *YATES (AAC & ADFA)* *Robert Block (Med. Hat)* ***A1AF - Lethbridge* *Mar 3,4*	- - - - ****1st** - ****** - -	1. Attic Theatre/Murray Robison assisted by K. Robison 2. Lethbridge Musical Theatre/Dick Mells 3. Marquis Players/Ivan Morgado 4. Playgoers of Lethbridge/Fran Rude 5. Playgoers of Lethbridge/Cathy Evins 6. Stage Three/Pat Slemko 7. Windmill Players (High River)/A. Wally Geres - 8. Windmill Players/Wally Geres	Where Have All the Lightning Bugs Gone by Louis E. Catron Two Gentlemen of Soho by A.P. Herbert 7-4-2 by Benjamin Morgado Canadian Gothic by Joanna M. Glass The Rehearsal by Michael F. Rogers The Zoo Story by Edward Albee Smoking is Bad For Your Health by A. Chekhov The Station by Rod Langley
MAR 3,4/78 - *YATES (A1AF)* *Alice Polley (Edm.)*	- - - - - - - -	1. Firehall Theatre (Medicine Hat)/Greg Moroz - 2. Drumheller Drama Society/ 3. Grande Prairie Little Theatre/Conrad Boyce - 4. Playgoers of Lethbridge/Fran Rude 5. Selkirk & Co. (Red Deer)/Mark Wilson 6. M and M (Red Deer) 7. Stage Three/Pat Slemko	a) Electric Gunfighters by Bryan Wade b) The Feast The Marriage Proposal by A. Chekhov Miss Julie by A. Strindberg I'm Herbert by Robert Anderson Canadian Gothic Parts by John Selkirk Cowboys Number Two by Sam Shephard The Zoo Story
FEB 24/79 - *YATES (AAC & ADFA)* *Dick Mells* ***A1AF - Red Deer* *Mar 8-10*	****** - -	1. Kintown Players/Doug Hinds assisted by Jim Hamilton 2. Playgoers of Lethbridge/Cathy Evins 3. Windmill Theatre Players (High River)/Jim Goodwin	Thursday's Child Has Far To Go by Doug Hinds Another Midsummer Night's Dream by Eilonwy Morgan Pause by Frank Moher
1980		**CANCELLED**	
1981		**CANCELLED**	
MAR 13/82 - *YATES (AAC & ADFA)* *Richard Epp (U of L)* ***A1AF - Red Deer* *Mar 26-28*	- ****** -	1. Lethbridge Senior Citizens' Organization/Mary Heinitz 2. U of L Drama Club/Arthur McDougall 3. One & Two Company (U of L Students)/Larry Erdos	Save Me a Place at Forest Lawn Seeds by Gordon Pengilly The Observer by Larry Erdo
FEB 26/83 - *YATES (AAC & ADFA)* *Sara Stanley* ***A1AF - Medicine Hat,* *Mar 10-12*	- - - ******	1. Blue Light Players/Robert Chomiak & Barbara Wilson 2. Lethbridge Senior Citizens' Organization/Mary Heinitz 3. Playgoers of Lethbridge/Kathy Sharp 4. Quarter Theatre Troupe/Eric Low, Rebecca Dwyer	Honeymoon by Robert Chomiak Lemonade by James Prideaux A Bench at the Edge by Luigi Jannuzzi The Golden Fleece by A.R. Gurney, Jr.
1984		**CANCELLED**	

DATE/LOCATION ADJUDICATOR(S)	ADJ	GROUP/DIRECTOR	PRODUCTION/AWARDS
MAR 15,16/85 - YATES (A1AF) (Auspices of AAC in cooperation with Alberta Culture & ADFA) Dick Mells & Rick McNair	- - - - - 1st - - - - - -	1. Central Alberta Players (Red Deer)/Glynis Wilson Boultbe 2. College Players (Grande Prairie)/Kathy Harper 3. Firehall Players (Medicine Hat)/Peggy Bengert 4. Keyano Players (Ft. McMurray)/Keith Benford 5. Paragon Players (Camrose)/Bob Moore - 6. Ploeg Street Players (Drumheller)/Wesley Miller 7. Playgoers of Lethbridge/Cherie Baunton 8. Playgoers of Lethbridge/Ed Bayly 9. Workshop Theatre Society (Calgary)/Reginald Graves 10. Windmill Theatre Players (High River)/Mark Aitcheson	Dr. Kheal by Maria Irene Farnes The Art of Self Defense by Trish Johnson The Footsteps of Doves by Robert Anderson The Insanity of Mary Girard by Lanie Robertson The Loveliest Afternoon of the Year by John Guare Seeds by Gordon Pengilly Mother Figure by Alan Ayckbourne Spreading the News by Lady Gregory Crush by David Foxton Sundance by M.Z. Ribalow
MAR 7/86 - MEDICINE HAT Richard Epp	- - -	Playgoers of Lethbridge/Joan Waterfield (only entry in Lethbridge & District Festival, therefore, adjudicated during Medicine Hat & District Festival)	Yes Dear selected to participate in A1AF (Grande Prairie) but unable to take part
1987 & 1988		CANCELLED	
FEB 28, MAR 1/89 - YATES Stephen Hair (Auspices of AAC, Playgoers of Lethbridge, ADFA, Alberta Culture) **A1AF - Whitecourt Mar 10,11	- - 2nd - **	1. Playgoers of Lethbridge/Ed Bayly - 2. Playgoers of Lethbridge/Ed Bayly 3. Playgoers of Lethbridge/John Malcolm 4. U of L Students/Tom Gillespie 5. U of L Students/Mark Russell	Tell Me Another Story, Sing Me a Song by Jean Lenox Toddie The Exhibition by Thomas Gibbons Black & Sliver by Michael Frayn Anniversary Waltz by Tom Gillespie PVT Wars by James McLure

Lethbridge Musical Theatre: Executive Officers
(1964–1988)

PRESIDENT	YRS	VICE-PRESIDENT\or BUSINESS MANAGER	YRS	SECRETARY	YRS	TREASURER	YRS	PRODUCTION MANAGER	YRS
Gordon Moir	1	Ross Whitmore	17	Louise Hammel	3	R. Wildeman	1	Vaughn Hembroff	2
Horace Barrett	2	George Varzari	6	Ian Kinnell	1	Ev Nowlin	4	Len Ankers	2
Vaughn Hembroff	8	Bob Fenton	2	Linda Bayly	7	Ernie Lawson	12	Pat Webb	2
George Varzari	2	Al Greenway	2	Lenore Beyer	2	Lenore Beyer	9	Charlie Scott	1
Bob Fenton	12	Ernie Lawson	2	Dawn Flexhaug	2			Ed Bayly	1+
				Jo Trockstad	2			Fred McKay	4+
				Gloria Silsbe	2			Rick Braund	1
								Marg McKay	2
								Mike Brooks	2
								Cathy Evins	4+

PUBLICITY	YRS	HOUSE MANAGER	YRS	LIAISON/ PERSONNEL	YRS	DIRECTOR/ OTHERS	YRS	CAST REPS	YRS
Pat Rodnunsky	1	Rita Berlando	1	R.K. Whitmore	1	R.W. Ward		Al Greenway	
Bill Matheson	1	Len Ankers	3	Shirley Ann Walkey	6+	Dave Gillis		Albert Azzara	
Howard Ellison	1	Stan McDonald	1	Heather Joyce	2	Margaret Kokott		Mark Russell	
Joan Waterfield	3	Bob Fenton	6	Linda Thomsen	2	Jack Price		Sandra McFarlane	
Stan McDonald	2	Larry Higa	2			Anne Reid		Karen Kay	
Jack Warburton	4	Ross Whitmore	2			Ed Bayly		Mike Brooks	
Ken Lewis	2	Ken Mills	9			Mike Brooks		Donna Jorgensen	
Linda Bayly	2	Karen Kay	1			Joan Waterfield		Lee Anne Tedder	
Marg McKay	5	Dick Varley	6						
Mike Brooks	4								
Duncan Rand	2+								

Lethbridge Musical Theatre: Production Directors
(1964–1988)

STAGE DIRECTOR	NO.	ORCHESTRA DIRECTOR	NO.	VOCAL DIRECTOR	NO.	CHOREOGRAPHER	NO.
Dick Mells	16	A. Rodnunsky	3	A. Rodnunsky	3	Muriel Jolliffe	20
Harold Baldridge	1*	Cliff Palmer	1	B. Wayne Matkin	1	Kim Ully	2
Wes Stefan	2**	Malcolm MacDonald	1	Malcolm MacDonald	1	Joy Ackerman	4****
Fran Rude	4	David Peterkin	2	David Peterkin	2	Theresa Dee	1
Jack McCreath	2	Willie Mathis	1	Willie Mathis	1	Wendy Spoulos	2***
Joan Waterfield	1	Jerry Pokarney	3	Ellyn Mells	7	Patricia Livingstone	1*****
Ed Bayly	2	Ellyn Mells	2	Shelagh Stefan	2		
		Stewart Grant	1	Arla Burbank	4		
		Larry Yelland	1	Larry Yelland	1		
		Bob Brunelle	10	Mark Ward	1		
		Tanya Arnold	2	Bonnie Jean (Brown)			
				Pokarney	4		

*Advisor to Dick Mells for Man of La Mancha
**Also Assistant Director for Brigadoon
***Co-Choreographer (Sound of Music, 1987) (South Pacific, 1988)
****Co-Choreographer (Sound of Music) & Advisor to Theresa Dee (Hello Dolly, 1986)
*****Co-choreographer (South Pacific, 1988)

Lethbridge Musical Theatre: Productions and Lead Cast Members
(1964–1988)

YEAR & PRODUCTION	CAST (MAJOR CHARACTERS)
SPRING 1964 *FINIAN'S RAINBOW*	Bill Matheson, Gwen Legge, Allan James Monk, Sandra Niedermier, Peter Grantham, Cliff Black, Phyllis Kristiansen, Bud Iverson, Bill Berg, Norman Thomas
FALL 1964 *OKLAHOMA!*	Doug Crosley, Kathleen Stringam, Kaye Watson, Dick Mells, Lee Mells, George Mann, Herb Bishop, Marilyn Ellison, Norm Thomas, Linda Bauman, Horst Mueller, Ike Lanier, Bud Iverson, Earl Colpitts
FALL 1965 *LI'L ABNER*	Ron Nelson, Marilyn Ellison, Cliff Black, Kaye Watson, Muriel Jolliffe, Frank Murphy, Ed Bayly, Geri Young, Frank Ward, Marilyn Lamb, Colin Turner, Peter Grantham, Joyce Cann
FALL 1966 *SOUTH PACIFIC*	Jan Rubes, Gwen (Legge) Dell, Ruth Strate, Bob Befus, Howard Ellison, Peter Dell, Frank Ward, Ed Bayly, Margaret Trockstad, Jack Hamilton, Cliff Black, Ted Dawson, Ike Lanier, Kim Hall, Jim Moyer, Terri Ann Illingsworth, Rhoda C. Hall
FALL 1967 *SHOW BOAT*	Robert McFerrin, Darryl Sherwood, Kathleen Stringam, Bobbi Sherron, Ed Bayly, Kaye (Watson) Robison, Lee Mells, Howard Ellison, Jean Warburton, Jack Warburton, Bob Befus, Frank Gostola, Al Greenway, Cliff Black, Lee Mells
FALL 1968 *GUYS AND DOLLS*	Doug Crosley, Norma MacInnis, Wayne Barry, Ellyn Ford, Jack Warburton, Mark Lowrie, Tom Melling, Al Greenway, George Mann, Jean Warburton, Bill Matheson, Michael Sutherland, Jim Green, Marilyn Ellison, Wendy Anderson, David Nattress, Pat Thompson, Chip Schott
FALL 1969 *DESTRY RIDES AGAIN*	Don Runquist, Ellyn (Ford) Mells, Mike Sutherland, Ed Bayly, Jean Warburton, Dunc Gillespie, Jack Warburton, Wayne Barry, Lois Dongworth, Chris Burgess, Garry Kohn, Cliff Black, Muriel Matheson, Dick Humphries, Paul Lowrie, Vaughan Hembroff
FALL 1970 *MY FAIR LADY*	Sheila (Hawn) Pisko, Bill Matheson, Frank Featherstone, Chet Wayne, Peggy Mallalieu, Brian Walker, Joan Waterfield, Kaye Robison, Jack Warburton, Edward Henley, George Mann, Shirley Wilson, Phyllis Kristiansen, Wendy Grigg (Burrows)
FALL 1971 *FIDDLER ON THE ROOF*	Jack Warburton, Joan Waterfield, Lois Dongworth, Frank Featherstone, Sheila Pisko, Brian Walker, Don Runquist, Lily Larter, Linda Johnson, David Mann, Albert Azzara, Linda Zgurski, Barbara Gorko, George Mann, Ellyn Mells
FALL 1972 *MAN OF LA MANCHA*	Dick Mells, Jack Warburton, Maura K. Wedge, George Mann, Phil Kristiansen, Tom Melling, Ellyn Mells, Bob Baunton, Joan Waterfield, Frank Huszar, Jean Warburton, Jim Gray, Wendy Burrows, Bill Matheson
FALL 1973 *MAME*	Nora Rose, Jean Warburton, Ray Mercer, Shirley Wilson, Albert Azzara, Jack Warburton, Mardi Renyk, Al Greenway, Sheri McFadden, Denise Black, Charles Schott, Jim Veenstra, Fay Dzeidic, Michael Melling
FALL 1974 *ZORBA*	Jack Warburton, Sheila Pisko, Wes Stefan, Ellyn Mells, Kathleen (Stringam) Thompson, Albert Azzara, Al Greenway, Chip Seibert, Pat Hammond, Jean Warburton, Charles Schott, Frank Huszar, Neil Boyden, Michael Hoyt
FALL 1975 *OLIVER*	Frank Featherstone, Jean Warburton, Michael Nowlin, Greg Martin, Jack Warburton, Wes Stefan, Phyllis Kristiansen, Judy Rapuano, Ray Mercer, Fran Rude, Charles Bell, Cathy Evins, Shirli Gonzy, Charles Schott
FALL 1976 *NO, NO, NANETTE*	Ray Mercer, Carol Virtue, Judy Rapuano, Jim Robinson, Laurin Mann, Kirk Jensen, Fran Rude, Lilian Kolodziej, Debbie Waterfield, Janice Gross
FALL 1977 *ANNIE GET YOUR GUN*	Wes Stefan, Lilian Kolodziej, Jack Warburton, Jean Warburton, Ray Mercer, Mark Campbell, Karen Dobek, Marlin Howg, Mark Russell, Lea Blaquiere, Michael Hoyt, Patti Henderson, Freddy Kotch, Julie Miller, Sheri Rae
FALL 1978 *CAMELOT*	Wes Stefan, Kathleen Thompson, Neil Millar, Frank Featherstone, Chester Mook, Duncan Rand, Allen Gunderson, Ray Mercer, Mark Russell, Greg Martin, Jack Warburton, Jack Tyreman, Tim Pittman, Michael Plouf
FALL 1979 *THE PAJAMA GAME*	Sheri McFadden, Mark Campbell, Jane McCoy, Linda Connors, Keith Harris, Blaine Goodridge, John Tyreman, Keith Western, Rik Gordon, Candy Williams, Romola Ully, Barb Tate, Milton Chambers, Cory Chomiak, Larry Fekete

YEAR & PRODUCTION	CAST (MAJOR CHARACTERS)
FALL 1980 *ONCE UPON A MATTRESS*	Laurae Tomashewski, Delani Kye Kela, Dawn Flexhaug, Frank Wilson, Mark Campbell, John Tyreman, Lorne Gullage, Ken Sinclair, Wes Stefan, Roger Schultz, Nola Dahl, Allyson Kenney, Ken Firth, Sheri Rae
FALL 1981 *THE KING AND I*	Wes Stefan, Lea Blaquiere, Jack Warburton, Jean Warburton, Sandra McFarlane, Lyndon Bray, Shaun Sakamoto, David Plaxton, Mark Switzer, Ray Mercer, Ken Sinclair, Sasha Sakamoto, Joy Ackerman, Roger Schultz, Wendy Spoulos, Andrea Jasiukiewicz
FALL 1982 *THE MUSIC MAN*	Lyndon Bray, Neana Meeks, George Mann, Joan Waterfield, Jack Warburton, Lois Dongworth, Gavin Crawford, Carla Serkin, Jeff Haslam, Jill Carlson, Linda Bayly, Jordanna Kohn, Tom Melling
FALL 1983 *KISS ME KATE*	Wes Stefan, Lea (Blaquiere) Switzer, Lyndon Bray, Debra Spackman, Mark Campbell, Al Greenway, Chet Wayne, Roger Schultz, George Mann, Lloyd Pollock, Lawrence Kotkas, Candy Williams, Marg McKay
SPRING 1984 *DOWN MEMORY LANE*	Ed Bayly, Dawn Flexhaug, Sandra McFarlane, George Mann, Neana Meeks, Lloyd Pollock, Rhonda Ruston, Roger Schultz, Mark Switzer, Jack Warburton, Jean Warburton, Mark Ward, Wilma Wiebe, Candy Williams
FALL 1984 *BRIGADOON*	Lyndon Bray, Sandra McFarlane, Mark Campbell, Roger Schultz, Brenda Laycock, George Gallant, Wendy Spoulos, Duncan Rand, George Mann, Al Greenway, Shantelle Kirkvold, Mardi Renyk, Ken Sinclair, Lee Prindle
FALL 1985 *CABARET*	Sheri (McFadden) Thomson, George Gallant, Wes Stefan, Linda Sprinkle, Roger Schultz, Kaye Robison, Peter Brown, Al Greenway, Larry Kotkas, Narda McCarroll, Sandra McFarlane, John Duell
FALL 1986 *HELLO DOLLY*	Sheila Pisko, Douglas Castleton, Sandra McFarlane, George Gallant, Neana Meeks, Jeff Carlson, George Mann, Yvonne Fredrick, Cliff Stoakley, Martin Hoyt, Dana Elzinga, Brian Tedder, Cathy Evins
FALL 1987 *THE SOUND OF MUSIC*	Elizabeth Martin-Jong, Wes Stefan, Hildie Kornelsen, Deanne May, Cara Leslie, Judith Melnyk, Vaughn Atkinson, Karen Hudson, Trish Jensen, Carol Laycock, Darryl Konynenbelt, Chet Wayne, Mel Fletcher, Bery Allan
FALL 1988 *SOUTH PACIFIC*	Vicki Gibson, Christopher Lyle, Jean Warburton, Ian Mandin, George Gallant, Al Greenway, Lee Prindle, Analea Wayne, Moira & Michael Munton, Chet Wayne, Mike Day, Bob Brunelle, Eric Dyck, Frank Huszar

Lethbridge Musical Theatre: Onstage Participants (1964–1988)

I. PARTICIPANTS (10 or More Productions)						
	S	C	T*		S	C	T
Al Greenway	8	8	16	Jack Warburton	13	1	14
Marg McKay	1	15	16	George Mann	9	1	10
Jean Warburton	10	4	14	Karen Kay	-	10	10

II. (6-9 ROLES)						
	S	C	T		S	C	T
Ray Mercer	6	3	9	Linda Bayly	1	5	6
Wes Stefan	8	1	9	Cliff Black	5	1	6
Kaye (Watson) Robison	5	4	9	Mark Campbell	5	1	6
Phil Kristiansen	4	4	8	Marilyn Ellison	3	3	6
Shirley Wilson	2	6	8	Sandra McFarlane	5	1	6
Dawn (McKay) Flexhaug	2	5	7	Sheila Pisko	4	2	6
Frank Huszar	2	5	7	Fran Rude	2	4	6
Roger Schultz	6	1	7	Jack Tyreman	4	2	6
Candy Williams	3	4	7				

III. (3-5 ROLES)						
	S	C	T		S	C	T
Albert Azzara	3	2	5	Gwen (Legge) Dell	2	1	3
Ed Bayly	5	-	5	Craig Baceda	-	3	3
Jeff Carlson	1	4	5	Truus Baird	-	3	3
Howard Ellison	2	3	5	Jean Ede	-	3	3
Cathy Hawn	-	5	5	Candice Elzinga	-	3	3
Ike Lanier	2	3	5	Dana Elzinga	1	2	3
Norma MacInnes	1	4	5	Yvonne Fredrick	1	2	3
Tom Melling	3	2	5	Dunc Gillespie	1	2	3
Ellyn (Ford) Mells	4	1	5	Peter Grantham	2	1	3
Julie Miller	1	4	5	Bill Hacker	-	3	3
Sheri Rae	1	4	5	Wanda Huszar	-	3	3
Wendy Spoulos	1	4	5	Bud Iverson	2	1	3
Joan Waterfield	4	1	5	Kirk Jensen	1	2	3
Lyndon Bray	4	-	4	Donna Jorgensen	-	3	3
Mike Day	-	4	4	Garry Kohn	1	2	3
Karen Dobek	1	3	4	Lilian Kolodziej	2	1	3
Lois Dongworth	4	-	4	Lily Larter	1	2	3
Frank Featherstone	4	-	4	Bill Lawson	-	3	3
George Gallant	4	-	4	Brenda Laycock	1	2	3
Narda McCarroll	1	3	4	Cara Leslie	1	2	3
Sheri (McFadden) Thomson	3	1	4	Muriel Matheson	1	2	3
Bill Matheson	4	-	4	Deanne May	1	2	3
Neana Meeks	3	1	4	Claire Marie Pacard	-	3	3
Lee Mells	2	2	4	Rita Peterson	-	3	3

Name	S	C	T	Name	S	C	T
Laurie Meyers	-	4	4	Diane Pokarney	-	3	3
Horst Mueller	1	3	4	Lloyd Pollock	2	1	3
Ken Sinclair	3	1	4	Don Runquist	2	1	3
Mike Sutherland	2	2	4	Charles Schott	3	-	3
Lea (Blaquiere) Switzer	3	1	4	Chip Seibert	1	2	3
Kathleen (Stringam) Thompson	4	-	4	Cliff Stoakley	1	2	3
Maurice Trockstad	-	4	4	Mark Switzer	2	1	3
Chet Wayne	4	-	4	Kim Walburger	-	3	3
Bery Allan	-	3	3	Frank Ward	2	1	3
Lavern Ankers	-	3	3				

*S = Speaking role; C = Chorus; T = Total number of productions

IV. 2 ROLES: (LEADING AND/OR SPEAKING ONLY)

Bob Befus, Wayne Barry, Doug Crosley, Cathy Evins, Michael Hoyt, Lawrence Kotkas, Dick Mells, Judy Rapuano, Duncan Rand, Mardi Renyk, Mark Russell, Norman Thomas, Brian Walker

V. 2 ROLES MIXED (SPEAKING AND CHORUS)

Joy Ackerman, Bob Baunton, Charles Bell, Neil Boyden, Peter Brown, Jill Carlson, Milton Chambers, John Duell, Faye Dziedzic, Shirli Gonzy, Janice Gross, Lorne Gullage, Allen Gunderson, Jack Hamilton, Pat Hammond, Jeff Haslam, Patti Henderson, Edward Henley, Shantelle Kirkvold, Jordanna Kohn, Marilyn Lamb, David Mann, Greg Martin, Judith Melnyk, Chester Mook, Lee Prindle, Margaret Trockstad, Colin Turner, Carol Virtue, Debbie Waterfield

VI. 2 ROLES: (CHORUS ONLY)

Laurel Anderson, Kenn Blom, Marion Bolokoski, Mike Brooks, Sandra Brunelle, David Cunningham, Larry Dye, Ron Francis, Gay Gray, Marion Greenway, Merry Jo Hahn, Lorene Harrison, Audrey Harper, Jack Horn, Terri Anne Illingworth, Luella Lee, David Lynagh, Melanie Mah, Jane Paterson, Laimus Rimkus, Margaret Roseboom, Keith Sanford, Chip Schott, Roy Schow, George Szilagyi, Terri Jo Ully, Gerry Vander Linden, Carina Van Leuken, Florence Ward

VII. 1 ROLE (SPEAKING PART)

Vaughn Atkinson, Linda Bauman, Bill Berg, Herb Bishop, Denise Black, Chris Burgess, Wendy Burrows, Doug Castleton, Cory Chomiak, Earl Colpitts, Linda Connors, Gwen Crawford, Nola Dahl, Ted Dawson, Peter Dell, Ken Firth, Mel Fletcher, Vicky Gibson, Blaine Goodridge, Rik Gordon, Barba Garko, Frank Gostola, Jim Gray, Jim Green, Wendy Grigg, Keith Harris, Marlin Howg, Martin Hoyt, Karen Hudson, Dick Humphries, Trish Jensen, Muriel Jolliffe, Elizabeth Martin-Jong, Linda Johnson, Delaine Kye Kela, Allyson Kenney, Hilda Kornelsen, Freddy Kotch, Darryl Konynenbelt, Carol Laycock, Mark Lowrie, Christopher Lyle, Jane McCoy, Robert McFerron, Peggy Mallalieu, Ian Mandin, Laurin Mann, Michael Melling, Neil Miller, Allan J. Monk, Michael Munton, Moria Munton, Frank Murphy, Ron Nelson, Sandra Niedermier, Michael Nowlin, Tim Pittman, David Plaxton, Michael Plouf, Jim Robinson, Nora Rose, Jan Rubes, Rhonda Ruston, Sasha Sakamoto, Shaun Sakamoto, Carla Serkin, Bobbi Sherron, Darryl Sherwood, Debra Spackman, Linda Sprinkle, Ruth Strate, Barb Tate, Brian Tedder, Laurae Tomashewski, Romola Ully, Jim Veenstra, Mark Ward, Analea Wayne, Maura K. Wedge, Keith Western, Wilma Wiebe, Frank Wilson, Geri Young, Linda Zgurski

VIII. ONE ROLE (CHORUS ONLY)

Pat Abbott, Allison Aldridge, David Ames, Linda Ames, Wendy Anderson, Rhonda Andre, Andrew Arcand, Karen Baldry, Aldena Baranyi, Debbi Barnard, Deb Bauming, Ern Bayly, Mic Bate, Simon Beach, Barbara Bell, Roxanne Bender, Leith Birch, Dawn Bishop, Phil Blakeley, Linda Blakenship, Margaret Boardman, Phil Boon, Lyle Boswall, Tony Bowman, Doreen Brooks, Marlene Brown, Bob Brunelle, Stephanie Bulva, Arla Burbank, Albi Colman, Delanie Campbell, Lori B. Campbell, Joyce Cann, Scott Carpenter, Wendy Carson, Cathy Chirka, Bruce Chretian, Brad Churchill, Curtiss Closson, Beverly Corrigan, Beverly Cousins, Fred Cummins, Carolyn Cunningham, Karen Cunningham, Lyn Davidson, Susan Davis, Cliff Daw, Morgan Day, Tony Dimnik, Brian Dobek, Barry Doe, Joyce Dong, Mickey Dorogdi, Carol Lee Doughty, Susan Draffin, John Duddy, Jamie Dudley, Yvette Dudley, Hazel Durrans, John Duvan, Erich Dyck, Bob Elliot, Jim Elliott, Mar-Jane Ellison, Flora Erdos, Pauline Erno, Natasha Evdokimof, John Farrington, Larry Fekete, Treva Fellendorf, Heidi Felner, Tara Fenton, Heidi Fisher, John Fisher, Melanie Fisher, Brandon Fletcher, Janine Folkins, Georgia Fooks, Marjorie Frame, Bryan Francis, David Francis, Connie Friesen, Hilda Friesen, William Gelowitz, Bob George, Carol Godlonton, Ann Gordon, Krissy Gordon, Roger Goshinmon, Jamie Graham, Jean Gregory, Nancy Grigg, Myrna Guay, Harry Hahn, Kim Hall, Rhonda C. Hall, Todd Hammond, Kendra Harding, Linda Hardy, Gary L. Harker, Melanie Harker, Ruston Harker, Liana Harper, Sheila Harrison, David Head, Vaughn Hembroff, Maureen Henchel, Kelly Henderson, Dianna Henke, Charlie Hepler, John Heymen, Sue Hicken, Alaysha Hickman, Dianne Hicks, Pat Hill, Connie Hirsche, Debbie Houghton, Cheryl Houtekamer, Dean Hovey, Mark Huxley, J. Norah Jacobsen, Andrea Jasiukiewicz, Weste Jensen, Arlan Johnson, Murray Johnson, Ray Jolliffe, Tim Jones, Terrah Jong, Dale Ketcheson, Elaine Klassen, Diana Kolpak, Linda Kohn, Susanah Konrad, Linda Kotak, Kaaren Kotkas, Ramona Kotke, Debbie Krampl, Simon Lacey, Geoff Lacey, Pamela Lacusta, Darcy Larson, Tom Lavers, Christine Laycock, Terra Leavens, Julie Leishman, Catherine Leon, Christopher Leong, Kar Kong Leung, Lorraine Linquist, Brian, Chris & Suzanne Liska, Mark Litchfield, Paul Lowrie, Tracy Lukacs, Fran Lutz, Cathy Mack, Carol Macleod, Rudy Magnesen, Rhett Mandin, Thad Mandin, Darin Mann, Barry Marquardson, Lori Marquardson, Andrew Marshall, Cindy Marthienson, Annette Martin, Jesse Martin, Kay Martin, Max Martin, Sheila Martin, Lisa Matthews, Erik Mason, Dawn McCaugherty, Gailene McKague, Margaret Mells, Loralee Merkley, Carie Meyers, Dave Moline, Jim Moyer, Esther Murillo, Laurie Musgrove, Alyssa Myshok, David Nattress, Ron Nease, Diane Nelson, Brad Nicholas, James Nicholas, Dan Niehaus, Charlene Nikiforuk, Dawn Nilsson, Sarah Nowlin, Amy Olsen, Lee Onofrechuk, Cina Opel, Gary Orr, Lawrence Orr, Keith O'Sullivan, Wolfgang Otto, Jody & Wesley Owen, Warren Pacard, Howard, Leslie & Vicky Palmer, Camille Palsky, Claudia Peterson, Danny Pigat, Joy Pizzingrilli, Linda Plomp, Dora Pocza, Karen Porkka, Nancy Porter, June Powlesland, Tammy Pretty, Rose Primachuk, Fred Pritchard, Jack Qually, Leslie Quilty, Bill Rasmussen, Maureen Reimer, Lee Reinhardt, Brent Robertson, Len Robinson, Murray Robison, Pat Rodnunsky, Ken Rodzinyak, Kenneth Rogers, Fred Roycroft, Karren Runquist, Wayne Saende, Kelly, Kim & Tracy Sawa, Ingrid Scheffer, Ron Scheurkogel, Eric Schill, Tom Schuler, Charlie, Claire & Shelly Scott, Carolyn Sera, Shauna Selk, Janet Sheets, Tate Shimozawa, Doug Shorthouse, Zina Simighan, Myra Skaronski, Allan Skretting, Doug Smith, Les Smolnicky, Cheryl Snider, Janet Southern, Lindzi Spackman, Sonia Spohn, Debbie Steed, Adele Stephens, Barb Sterenberg, Hans Stierwalt, Phil Story, Greg Strang, Rachel Stefan, Gail & Sarah Stringam, Tracy Takahashi, Sheri Tamura, Victoria Tanne, Lee-Anne Tedder, Trent Terakita, Pat Thompson, Janice Toomer, Geri Tomiyama, Gloria Torrance, Colin, Dave & Dianne Turner, Kim Ully, Nancy Uren, Roy Uttley, Fred Uwazny, Trevor Uyesugi, Lee Van Andel, Randy Van Zwal, Barbara Varley, Louise Vaura, Beverly Venechuk, Charles & Jane Virtue, Elaine Vogel, Henry Waack, Robert Waldren, Jean & Randolph Wall, Bryce & Freda Walton, Pat Waterfield, Tim Waters, Clarence Watson, Shauna Wellman, Margret Welsh, Jonathan White, Lorrie Willets, Barbara, Bill, David, Foster & Iris Wilson, Barbara Wish, Elizabeth Zalys, Nerida Zaugg, Sheila Zieffle

Lethbridge Musical Theatre: Production Personnel
(1964–1988)

	PRODUCTION PERSONNEL
1. SET DESIGNER	Ed Bayly, Lazlo Funtek, John A. (Jay) Johnston, John Charnetski, Cathy Evins, Cornelius Martens, John Madill, Roger Schultz, David Thomson, Brent Seeley, Herb Matis
2. STAGE MANAGER	Ray Jolliffe, Fred McKay, Ern Bayly, Mike Day, Al Greenway, Bob Baunton, Ralph Martin, Duncan Rand, Wes Stefan, Wilma Wiebe, Johnathan White
3. PROPERTIES DESIGNER AND/OR SUPERVISOR	Cathy Evins, Kathy Kirkham, Ann Reid, Joy Pritchard, Nancy Seefeldt, Eileen Cashmore, Marj Dalke, Dianna Henke, Heather Joyce, Martha Rae, Dianna Turner, Bery Allan, Phil Story
4. LIGHTING DESIGNER AND/OR SUPERVISOR	Ed Bayly, Bob Reed, Al Candy, Bob Johnson, Barry Hegland, Ron Chambers, Dave Gibson
5. MAKE-UP ARTIST AND/OR HAIR DESIGNER	Mardi Renyk, Fran Rude, Eleanor Matkin, Freda Walton, Ed Bayly, David Francis, Muriel Matheson, Nora Hawn, Sue Koshman, Eva Zacharias, Terry Pitt, Ron Stubert
6. SOUND DESIGNER AND/OR SUPERVISOR	Doug Card, Ed Bayly, Brian Tedder, Rob Morrison
7. COSTUME MISTRESS AND/OR WARDROBE COORDINATOR	Gail Holland, Fran Bayly, Cathy Evins, Shirley Ann Walkey, Cherie Baunton, Mrs. J. Carson, Ailsa Chalmers, Jean Ede, Audrey Harper, Nora Hawn, Dawn Howes, Connie Ingoldsby, Donna Kampen, Anne Reid, Pat Rodnunsky, Hazel Skaronski, Barb Stefan
8. MASTER CARPENTER AND/OR SUPERVISOR OF SET CONSTRUCTION	Ed Bayly, Herb Matis, Don Ryane, Fred McKay, Bob Rose, Ray Jolliffe
9. CONSTRUCTION CREW	**A. Very Active Participants:** Bery Allan, Ed Bayly, Ern Bayly, Rod Flexhaug, Bob Hawn, Ray Jolliffe, Herb Matis, Fred McKay, Phil Story, Rob Thomsen, Duncan Rand **B. Moderately Active Participants:** Bob Baunton, Ann Beaty, David Best, Peter Brown, Lynn Carlson, Jack Carson, Bruce Chambers, Mary Coombs, Frank Featherstone, Ed Finlay, Al Greenway, Tom Gross, Ted Hazard, Vaughn Hembroff, Jim Jones, Gary Jackson, Paul Liska, George Mann, Dana Martin, Scott Mitchell, Bradley Nicholas, Nick Patson, Bob Rose, Vic Rude, Eric Schill, Shane Sillito, Mike Wright **C. Others:** Erwin Adderly, Daryl Aolinski, Angela Areshenko, Bob Avery, Judith & Rachel Bain, Donald & Marilyn Bakos, Debbie Biesbrock, Arlene Bolokoski, Neil Boyden, Pamela Brand, Richard Burke, Joan Carmichael, Barry Close, Tracy Cook, Kathy Erickson, Stephen Evins, Dave Fehr, Larry Fekete, Bob Fiorico, Norma, David & Bob Fournier, Leon Francis, George Gallant, Dennis Gaudet, Mike Gibbs, Jim Green, Bill Hacker, Sue Hall, Gary Harker, Murray & Ray Harper, Pat Henderson, Diane & Larry Hicks, Sharon Hudson, Harold Hughes, Cliff Irvine, Weste Jensen, Michael Jolliffe, Heather Joyce, Douglas & Walter Kampen, Pat Kerber, Adolph & Betty Kolodziej, Anne Leong, Bill Main, Bert Marquardson, Andrew Marshall, Greg Martin, Ken McKeen, Tom Melling, Ray Mercer, Elaine Molyneux, Chester Mook, Horst Mueller, Don Mumford, Dave Nash, Leonard Newton, Noel Patson, Allison Pavan, Lee Prindle, Tom Rand, Kathy Redfern, Anne Reid, Murray Robison, Ken Rodzinyac, Bill Russell, Don Runquist, Harold Schwant, Roger Schultz, Gary Shilliday, Mike Skaronski, Alan Skretting, Les Smolnicky, Deb Stallenberg, Wes Stefan, Bob Stephens, Ken Tennant, Nicole Titsing, Maurice Trockstad, Trent Tucker, Shelagh Tyreman, Len Ully, Valarie Vold, Lee Van Andel, George Varzari, Carol Watkinson, Dick Wells, Cliff Wentworth, Ron Willis, Johnathan White

	PRODUCTION PERSONNEL
10. SEWING CREW	**A. Most Active Participants:** Fran Bayly, Cherie Baunton, Eileen Cashmore, Doris Crawford, Barbara Day, Cathy Evins, Eleanor Fenton, Nora Hawn, Gail Holland, Anne Hominuke, Wanda Huszar, Shirley Ivison, Ruth Liska, Dawn (McKay) Flexhaug, Mardi Renyk, Kaye Robison, Hazel Skaronski, Barb Stefan, Gloria Torrance, Mary Varzari, Shirley Ann Walkey, Jean Warburton, Joan Waterfield **B. Moderately Active Participants:** Linda Bayly, Pam Bailey, Sara Burke, Mrs. J. Carson, Wendy Carson, Rita Cemuline, Diana Crawford, Lois Dongworth, Jean Ede, Marion Greenway, Holly Green, Irene Hacker, Betty Hamilton, Linda Harmon, Marilyn Hembroff, Dawn Howes, Janet Illingsworth, Melanie Jackson, Irene Jesson, Myrtle Jones, Heather Joyce, Donna Kampen, Linda Kohn, Lee Mells, Mary Peachey, Sheila Pisko, Diane Pokarney, Robert Powers, Martha Rae, Anne Reid, Pat Rodnunsky, Hazel Schwass, Janet Vucurevich, Carol Watkinson, Emma Wayne, Jane Wilson **C. Others:** Joy Ackerman, Enid Afsteder, Grace Allen, Linda Ames, Doris Balcovske, Christine Birch, Denise Black, Annette Bolduc, Ruth-Ann Brewster, Chris Burgess, Lillian Carrico, Wendy Chalmers, Carol Clifford, Fran Cofell, Doris Colpitts, Edith Cook, Carolyn & Jane Cunningham, Jeanne Danyluk, Linda Dobbin, Martha Draffin, Mrs. G. Duff, Yoni Dyck, Phyllis Edwards, Lil Erdos, Larry Fekete, Ione Forbes, Yvonne Fredricks, Donna Gallant, Shirli Gonzy, Stella Grismer, Myrtle Hamilton, Darlene Harker, Jackie Hawrelak, Nettie Hayman, Sheila Hedley, Maureen Henchel, Gerry Herbert, Ruth Horn, Theresa Ichino, Ruth James, Tanya Jesson, Betty & Cora Jones, Ruth Kemp, Phil Kristiansen, Daisy Kosaka, Bev Kowalko, Lea Ledbetter, Luella Lee, Cecilia Loetscher, Sandra Mandzuk, Ann Martin, Louise Marshall, Ingrid McCarroll, Irene Miller, Mrs. J. Morton, Marilyn Mossey, Judy Mowat, Lyn Newman, Mrs. Orr, Claire Pacaud, Terry Prince, Lillian Pruitt, Elisha Rasmussen, Lynn Richardson, Marg Roberts, Nancy Seefeldt, Carol Sefton, Beulah Sinclair, Danielle Smith, Lorena Smith, June Swanson, Debbie Thompson, Mary Thomson, Dorothy Trotter, Lee Van Andel, Mrs. Vipond, Mrs. R. Whitmore, Lana Winkler, Diedre Wyrostak (masks), Florence Zimmer
11. LIGHTING CREW	Art Baldry, Shannon Bastedo, Allen Block, Pamela Branch, Jean & Stan Charles, Tracy Cook, Kurt Ellison, Anne Leong, Lawrence McDougall, Chester Mook, Dave Robin, Johanna Rocco, Johnathan White
12. MAKE-UP & HAIR DRESSING CREW	**A. Very Active Participants:** Donna Kampen, Karen Kay, Sandra Mandzuk, Linda Thomsen, Cherie Baunton, Eileen Cashmore, Laurel Webser, Myrtle & Donna Thackray, Karla Millar, Jean Block, Marilyn Ellison **B. Others:** Ingrid Ander, Lucille Bennett, Jean Block, Rick Bounds, Sara Burke, Monte Byam, Lillian Carrico, Linda Cemulini, Marilyn Crighton, Mrs. D. Crosley, Feather Dienner, Joy Francis, Vinnie Fromm, Marion Grey, Janice Gross, Trish Gunderson, Nora Hawn, Anne Hay, Ginny Hoffarth, Barbara Hoyt, Wanda Huszar, Kathy Jeggo, Carol Jensen, Louis Livingstone, Virginia Korth, Marg McKay, Gwen Merriman, Sally Moore, Joanne Munroe, Lyn Murphy, Marina Newby, Lee Onofrechuk, Leanne Passey, Jane Paterson, Margo Ritchie, Vivian Ruttan, Barbara Sherrey, Heather Smithdorf, Connie Steed, Shelagh Stefan, Mary & Sharon Stringam, Arlene Tokitsu, Ellen Zubach

	PRODUCTION PERSONNEL
13. OTHER BACKSTAGE PERSONNEL (Props, Set Decoration, Painting, Stage Hands, etc.)]	Rick Albrecht, Bery Allan, Frances, Gail & Winona Anderson, Roland Argyle, Truus Baird, Keith Banfield, Ed, Ern & Linda Bayly, Shirley Bedard, Joanne & Mike Brooks, Eva Jane Bruce, Jean Brunneu, Mark Bunning, Ronnie Calman, Eileen Cashmore, Paul Ciesla, Kate Connolly, Val Cooke, Josee Couture, Lynn Crawford, Megan Crighton, Marj Dalke, Kent Davidson, Barbara & Mike Day, Dawn DiVito, Denise Dobek, Mike Doran, Bob & Vaughn Driscoll, Fern & Pierre Dubeau, Jerry Dunne, Phil Ellerbeck, Cathy & Stephen Evins, Larry Fekete, Maxine Fettig, David Francis, Ana Fuentas, Dennis Gaudet, Scott Glum, Kevin Goldie, Shirli Gonzy, Jamie Graham, Al & Marion Greenway, Tom Gross, Julian & Landon Guay, Angela Gunstone, Pat Hammond, Ted Haszard, Alaysha Hickman, Diane & Larry Hicks, Gail Hunt, Andy Isbister, Bob Ives, Garry & Linda Johnson, Jim Jones, Heather Joyce, Karen Kay, Denise Kenny, Leslie Ker, Pat Kerber, Kathy Kirkham, Margaret Kokott, Adolphe & Betty Kolodziej, Tammy Kovacs, Bev Kowalko, Andrew Kulpa, Fran Lamane, Lily Larter, Allison Lavers, Gordon Levy, Rick Lichuk, Paul Liska, Darlene Mahoney, Bill Mallalieu, Muriel & Sam Matheson, Laurieanne Matisz, Dawn, Fred, Marg & Vicki McKay, Trenton McQuarrie, Eilowny & Susan Morgan, Judy (Melnyk) Munier, Linda Nagy, Barbara Nault, Peter Oliver, Deanna Overn, Florence Pastoor, Alison Paterson, Ellen Pearson, Tammy Plett, Diane Pokarney, Lloyd Pollock, Sandy Ponech, Joy Pritchard, Chris Puhl, Duncan & Tom Rand, Elisha Rasmussen, Anne Reid, Bruce Robin, Murray Robison, Nora Rose, Eric Schill, Jack Schwass, Rhonda Sincennes, Ken Sinclair, Dave Skelton, Gwyneth Staddon, Wes Stefan, Phil Story, Brian Thomas, Rob Thomsen, Lap Truong, Dianna Turner, Bill Uhryn, Cory Varzari, Kathy (Erickson) Walburger, Kim Walburger, Shirley Ann Walkey, Jean Warburton, Joan, Liz & Pat Waterfield, Carol & Gillian Watkinson, Pat Webb, Judy White, Paul Wiens, Lorrie Willets, Lana Winkler, Lena Wipf

Locally Produced Summer Musicals
Lethbridge, Alberta (1966–1979)

DATE/PLACE SPONSOR	PRODUCTION/ PRODUCTION PERSONNEL	CAST/REFERENCES
AUG 19,20; 26,27/66 - YATES (Leth. Allied Arts Council [AAC])	Babes in Arms/Dick Mells [prod dir]/Muriel Jolliffe [chor]/Henry Waack [mus dir]/Henry Waack [piano] & Ernie Block [drums] (pit musicians)/Ray Jolliffe [crew dir]	Adele Stephens, Marilyn Lamb, Michael Sutherland, Susan Young, Brian Walker, Kathryn Keate, Cliff Black, Lee Mells, Bruce Ferguson, Carol Lee Dougherty, Shirley Wilson, Ed Bayly, Linda Hardie, Margaret Trockstad, Sandra Snowden, Bill Hacker, Greg Strong and chorus (Aug 20/14) - a rollicking hit
AUG 29-SEPT 2/67 - Yates (AAC)	The Pajama Game/Dick Mells [prod dir]/Muriel Jolliffe [chor]/Cathy Evins [designer]/Henry Waack [mus dir]/Henry Waack and Ernie Block [musicians]	Spencer McMullen, Janice Miller, Kathleen Stringam, Bob Befus, Jean Warburton, Mike Sutherland, Dick Mells, Bill Hacker, Bryan Francis, Stewart Campbell, Tom Hardie, Jo Anne Munroe, Linda Hardie, Dawn Nilsson, Cliff Black & others [cast of 45] (Aug 30/16) - a winner
AUG 27-31/68 - Yates (AAC)	The Boy Friend/Dick Mells [prod dir]/Muriel Jolliffe [chor]/Cathy Evins [designer]/Henry Waack [mus dir]/Ernie Block & Henry Waack [musicians]/Margaret Kokott [crew dir]	Sheila Pisko, Ed Bayly, Nora Needham, Jack & Jean Warburton, Mark Lowrie, Grace Baines, Melanie Harker, Lynn Johnston, John Bowman, Marg Welsh, Jim Green, Weste Jensen, Jack Qually, Wayne Barry, Ray Harding, Mark Boh, Bruce Seely, Vicky Palmer, Joy Tustian, Pat Johnston (Aug 29/14; 30/14) - playful, rollicking good humor
AUG 18-23/69 - Yates Leth. Musical Th. (LMT)	Little Mary Sunshine/Dick Mells [prod dir]/Muriel Jolliffe [chor]/Henry Waack & Ellyn Ford [mus dirs]/Ellyn Ford (Mells) [piano]/Henry Waack [piano]/Ernie Block [drums]/Chris Puhl [flute]/Bob Johnson [crew dir]	David Hunt, Doug Smith, Lily Larter, Jamie Graham, Dianne Palmer, Wendy Grigg, Linda Johnson, Paul Lowrie, Ray Bick, Al Janzen, Jack Warburton, Al Greenway, Sue Helen Hunt, Dale Filkowski, Garry Orr, Karl Ksaizek, Raynham Harding, Anne Green, Susan Matthews, Suzanne Brooke, Debra Baldry, Elizabeth Zalys (Aug 15/7; 16/14; 19/11; 21/12) - first two nights - student performances; opening night done to perfection
AUG 21,22; 29,30/70 - Yates (LMT)	Your Own Thing/Lee Drew [dir]/Dick Mells [prod]/Darlene Snyder [chor]/Lily Larter [mus dir]/Kaye Dick [piano], Glenn Diener [guitar], Don Runquist [drums]/Les Omotani [crew dir]	Kim Drew, Al Janzen, Lee Drew, Ellyn Mells, Doug Smith, Cliff Black, Bob Bainborough, Kirk Jensen, Ian Noble, Virginia Reid and chorus: Darlene Snyder, Barb Jameson, Marilyn Blakey, Lily Larter, Lora Braun, Florence Cameron (Aug 11/16; 13/12; 15/17; 21/12; 22/14; 27/14; 28/13; 29/14) - not up to potential of the play
AUG 21-25/73 - Yates (AAC)	West Side Story/Dick Mells [prod dir]/Muriel Jolliffe [chor]/Ellyn Mells [mus dir]/Ellyn Mells [piano], Bruce Robin [drums]/Bruce Ives [crew dir]	A. Azzara, Mark Burrows, Mike Hoyt, Mike Wright, Rick Blair, Jim Veenstra, Mike Day, Kirk Jensen, Bryan Francis, Randy Van Zwal, Chip Seibert, Dave Moline, Pat Hammond, Debbie Anderson, Deb Grey, Jeanne Comstock, Marlene Francis, Gaye Williams, Liz Waterfield, Linda Johnson, Wendy Burrows, Sheri McFadden, Marg Marus, Amy Day, Barb Brown, Ray Mercer, Lilian Kolodziej, Al Greenway, Lee Reinhardt (Jul 21/6; AUG 15/18; 17/17; 27/18) - entertaining and enjoyable - exuberant & talented
AUG 20-24/74 - Yates (AAC)	Damn Yankees/Dick Mells [prod dir]/Muriel Jolliffe [chor]/Ellyn Mells [mus dir]/Joe Cryszchuk & Bob Baunton [crew dirs]/Susan (Young) Garrie [piano]/Bruce Robin [drums]	David Mann, Sheri McFadden, Tony Dimnik, Rhonda Ruston, Chip Schott, Faye Dzeidzic, Lee Reinhardt, Noel Paton, Louis Ouellette, Marlin Howg, John Duban, Mark Campbell, Mike Day, Tricia Matheson, Karen Kay, Randy Rae, Jim Hepler, Hedy Dimnik, Lori Finnerty, Deb Grey, Judy Modrzejewski, Carol Moore, Ingrid Schefter (Aug 10/8; 21/14) - a winner
AUG 12-16/75 - Yates (AAC)	L'il Abner/Dick Mells [prod dir]/Muriel Jolliffe [chor]/Ellyn Mells [mus dir]/Kirk Jensen [crew dir]/Ellyn Mells [piano], Bruce Robin [drums], Jim Hepler [banjo]	Brian King, Carol Virtue, Shelly Irvine, Chip Seibert, Marlin Howg, Mike Day, Kirk Jensen, Dave Mann, Sheri McFadden, Al Azzara, Rick Blair, Rhonda Ruston, Carol Jolliffe, Randy Rae, Greg Martin, Laurin Mann, Dawn McCaugherty, Debbie Mann, Marg Marus, Jim Hepler, Dave Cunningham, Tony Seberg, Deb Grey, Pat Burchak, Cathy Chirka, Lilian Kolodziej, Sandra Carnine, Karen Cunningham, Carol Moore, Cathy Murray, Jane Ward, Dale Ward, Craig Baceda (Aug 1/L&TVWK/18; 6/10; 8/L&TVWK/4,20; 13/10,22) - cast carries play despite script
AUG 24-28/76 - Yates (AAC)	Paint Your Wagon/Dick Mells [prod dir]/Carol Jolliffe [chors]/Ellyn Mells, Cathy Chirka & Shelagh Stefan [mus dirs]/Mike Day & Chuck McDougall [crew dirs]/Ellyn Mells & Cathy Chirka [piano], Norbert Boehm [violin]	Al Greenway, Karen Cunningham, Greg Martin, Deb Grey, Tom Melling, Marlin Howg, A. Azzara, Blake Hendley, Rick Drew, Lilian Kolodziej, Jack Tyreman, Dave Cunningham, Randy Rae, Chip Seibert, Barry Doe, Brad Harper, Holt Zaugg, Harold Hahn, Will Lanier, Jane Ward, Connie Matisz, Lori Finnerty, Sandi Carnine, Loretta Bailey (Aug 20/L&TVWk/8,9; 25/14) - a bit of a let down
AUG 24,26; SEPT 1,3/77 - Yates (AAC) (presented in Tandem with Romeo & Juliet)	West Side Story/Dick Mells [prod dir] assisted by David Mann & Mike Wright/Muriel Jolliffe [chor]/Ellyn Mells [mus dir]/Ellyn Mells [piano]/Bruce Robin [drums]	David Mann, Michael Hoyt, Mark Switzer, Greg Martin, A. Azzara, Michael Nowlin, Kelly Fiddick, Doug Campbell, Mark Johnson, Rae Ann Sparks, Judy Poile, Janice Tilley, Janice Gross, Mark Russell, Al Greenway, Michael Day, Valerie O'Toole, Brenda Laycock, Bruce Chretian, Rick Credico, Murray Redman, Larry Fekete, Holt Zaugg, Michael Wright, Laurin Mann, Kendra Harding, Debbie Mann, Karen Kay, Loretta Bailey, Barb Erickson (Jul 28/16)

DATE/PLACE SPONSOR	PRODUCTION/ PRODUCTION PERSONNEL	CAST/REFERENCES
AUG 30-SEPT 2/78 - *Yates (AAC)*	Fiddler on the Roof/Dick Mells/Norbert Boehm [violin], Cathy Bullock [piano], Dwaine Prosk [bass]/Arla Bach [mus dir]/Carol Godlonton [chor]/Christine Kenwood, Lori Anderson, Ed Bayly, Arlene Shwetz, Mardi Renyk, Mary Ann Schaarschmidt, Tammy Racz, Janice Gross	Mark Russell, Linda Connors, Loretta Bailey, Al Greenway, Dick Mells, Barbara Sterenberg, Greg Martin, Catherine Hawn, Arla Bach, Aldena Paranyi, Sheila Zeiffle, Sandra McFarlane, Don Goerzen, Al Greenway, Allen Gunderson, Tim Pitman, Lorne Gullage, Larry Fekete, Julie Miller, Elsa Dravland, Brenda Galts, Mark Switzer, Tom Gerencser, Ed Bayly & others (Aug 26/16; 31/10; Sept 2/8) - *some sparkling highlights*
AUG 21-25/79 - *Yates (AAC)*	Godspell/Dick Mells/Bruce Mackay [mus dir]/Ron Byer [guitar]/Carol (Jolliffe) Godlonton [chor]	Mike Day, Pat Hammond, Karen Dobek, Joanne Rocco, Deb Waterfield, Thomas Ripley, Mark Switzer & others (Jun 23/8; Aug 18/22; 22/38) - *most entertaining summer musical in long time (Lynne Van Luven)*

Locally Produced Christmas Pantomimes*
Lethbridge, Alberta (1966–1985)

DATE/PLACE	PRODUCTION/SPONSOR/PRODUCTION CREW	CAST/REFERENCE/COMMENTS
DEC 28-30/66; JAN 5-7/67 - *Yates*	Aladdin (AAC)/Ray Jolliffe, Cliff Black, Cathy Evins, Carol Watkinson, Gladys Carson, Bob Reed, Al Candy, Marion Greenway, Diane Turner, Lee Mells, Muriel Matheson, Jean Block, Catherine Leon, Shirley Wilson, Leslie Hall and others with Ernie Block [drums] & Henry Waack [piano]	Frank Featherstone, Norma MacInnes, D. Mells, Peter Grantham, Carol Lee Dougherty, Margaret Trockstad, Allan Skretting, Bill Hacker, Darlene Snyder, Bob Befus, Paula Carroll, Al Greenway & the Jolliffe School of Dance (Dec 24/14; 2910) - *a feast of sound, sight & laughter*
DEC 28-30/67; JAN 5,6/68 - *Yates*	Cinderella (AAC)/Cathy Evins [designer]/Muriel Matheson [makeup]/Ernie Block and Henry Waack [musicians]	F. Featherstone, Gay Gray, Norma MacInnes, Peter Grantham, Jack Warburton, Ed Davidson, Wendy Carson & the Jolliffe Academy of Dance (Dec 26/9; 29/10) - *excellent cast*
DEC 26-28/68 - *Yates*	Mother Goose/(Coaldale Little Theatre)/Ray Jolliffe, Carol Watkinson, Murray Robison, Ivan Meyers [sets]; Gladys Carson [costumes]; Bob Johnson [lights]; Muriel Matheson [makeup]; Peggy Mallalieu [props]; Shirley Wilson [rehearsal pianist]; Ernie Block and Henry Waack [musicians]	F. Featherstone, Bill Matheson, Adele Stephens, F. Huszar, Kathy Wilson, Kaye Robison, Wendy Carson, Jack Qually, Kirk Jensen, Jim Green, Leah Brown, Kathy Wilson and the Jolliffe Academy of Dance (Dec 11/18; 27/14) - *the usual blarney mixture of dancing, razzle-dazzle costumes, gags & farce. . . is fun*
DEC 26-27/69 - *Yates*	Queen of Hearts/(AAC)/Ray Jolliffe, Carol Watkinson [set design & construction]; Gladys Carson [costumes]; Bob Johnson [lights]	F. Featherstone, Kirk Jensen, Phil Boon, F. Huszar, Linda Johnson, Norma MacInnes, Joan Waterfield, Margaret Welsh and the Jolliffe Academy of Dance (Nov 28/10; Dec 27/16) - *jolly holiday fun*
DEC 26;28,29/70 - *Yates*	Babes in the Woods (AAC)/Ray Jolliffe, Charles Lanier, Ed and Peter Davidson, Gil Poirier, Bob Johnson, Carol Watkinson, Laurin Mann, Muriel Matheson with Ellyn Mells and Willie Mathis [musicians]	F. Featherstone, F. Huszar, George Mann, Kirk Jensen, David Mann, Ron Duda, Carol Jolliffe, Kim Ully, Anne Lanier, Nola Dahl, Leah Brown with Wendy Carson & Mark Litchfield (Henry the Horse) & the Jolliffe School of Dance (Dec 8/10; 23/9; 28/9) - *audience enjoys hiss & boo session*
DEC 26-28/71 - *Yates*	Old King Cole/(AAC)/Ed Bayly, Ray Jolliffe, Doreen Pizzey, Gladys Carson, Allyn Greenway, Sheri McFadden, Ed Davidson, Ivan Meyers, David Francis, Charlie Scott, Gil Poirier, Doug Smith, Dorothy Beckel & others with Susan Young and Willie Mathis [musicians]	Laurin Mann, David Mann, Mark Litchfield, Paul Featherstone, Albert Azzara, Winstan Jones, Linda Johnson, Kirk Jensen, Ron Duda, Jim Robinson, Carol Jolliffe & the Jolliffe School of Dance (Dec 2/6,18; 3/17; 15/6; 18/6; 23/10; 28/9; 29/11)
DEC 26-29/72 - *Yates*	Old Woman in the Shoe (AAC)/Ray Jolliffe, Ed Bayly, Lance Willis, Gladys Carson, Kathleen Mills, Karen Kay, E. Davidson, I. Meyers, G. Poirier, D. Francis, Jim Veenstra, Bill McIntyre, Audrey Davidson, Diana Lanier, Tricia Matheson, Kathy Sawicki, Masda Pahulje, Ricki Poirier with Susan Young & Willie Mathis [musicians]	F. Featherstone, L. Johnson, K. Jensen, A. Azzara, Brian Walker, C. Jolliffe, M. Litchfield, Brian King, D. Mann and the Jolliffe School of Dance (Dec 14/17; 23/14; 26/12; 26/17; 29/22) - *merry mix up of fairytale nursery rhyme & slapstick*
DEC 26-29/73 - *Yates*	Sinbad (AAC)/R. Jolliffe, E. Bayly, G. Carson, E. Davidson, George Gowlland, Ike Lanier, Randy Van Zwol, Bob Rose, I. Meyers, B. McIntyre, D. Mann, Jody Snow, Liz Waterfield, Brent Puttle with Susan (Young) Garrie & Willie Mathis (musicians)	F. Featherstone, L. Johnson, K. Jensen, F. Huszar, Randy Van Zwol, A. Azzara, Dawn McCaugherty, Mike Day, Pat Hammond, Bryan Francis, D. Mann, Ed Henley, Carol Jolliffe & the Jolliffe School of Dance (Dec 8/6; 28/14) - *enjoyed by sold out audiences*
DEC 26-28/74 - *Yates*	Cinderella (AAC)/R. Jolliffe with Susan Garrie [piano] & Bruce Robin [drums]	Tony Dinnik, F. Huszar, Linda Johnson, Charles Schott, Al Azzara, Bryan Francis, Neil Boyden, Brian Walker, Carol Jolliffe, John Duban, Michael Hoyt, Bill Wilson & the Jolliffe Academy of Dance (Dec 21/18; 23/13; 28/16)
DEC 26,27,29,30/75 - *Yates*	Aladdin (AAC)/R. Jolliffe, G. Carson	Eric Low, Chip Seibert, F. Huszar, Lilian Kolodziej, Carol Jolliffe, Gerry Tomiyama, Mike Day & Jolliffe School of Dance (Dec 5 Leisure & TV Week/8, 12; 27/13)
DEC 26-29/76 - *Yates*	The Queen of Hearts (AAC)/Ray Jolliffe, Ed Bayly, Carol Jolliffe, Gladys Carson, George Spoulos, George Mann, Fred McKay, Lee Byane, Gil Poirier, Tom Nosal, Bob Rose, Rachel Layng, Ricky Poirier, Carol Blom, Karen Kay, Carol Gemer with Ellyn Mells [piano] and Bruce Robin [drums]	Eric Low, A. Azzara, Randy Rae, F. Huszar, Lilian Kolodziej, Karen Kay, Kathleen Mills, Chip Seibert, Carol Jolliffe, Pat Hammond, Mark Litchfield, Les Smolnicky, Barry Doe, Michael Melling, Margaret Mills and the Jolliffe Academy of Dance (Dec 22/17)
DEC 26-29/77 - *Yates*	Mother Goose (AAC)/R. Jolliffe, Ed Bayly, Gladys Carson, Karen Kay, Michael Wright, Ricki Poirier and others with Debra Mann [piano] & Bruce Robin [drums]	Albert Azzara, Laurin Mann, Karen Kay, Michael Day, Les Smolnicky, Ken Rodzinyak, Chip Seibert, Carol (Jolliffe) Godlonton, F. Huszar, Wendy Carson & the Jolliffe School of Dance (Dec 16/L&TVWk/11; 22/27; 27/13)

*Written, directed and choreographed by Muriel Jolliffe

DATE/PLACE	PRODUCTION/SPONSOR/PRODUCTION CREW	CAST/REFERENCE/COMMENTS
DEC 26-29/78 - *Yates*	Sinbad (AAC)/Ray Jolliffe, Ed Bayly, Gladys Carson	Albert Azzara, Chip Seibert, Carol Godlonton, F. Huszar, Dawn McCaugherty, Neil Millar, Jolliffe Academy (Dec 19/26; 23/36)
DEC 26-29/79 - *Yates*	Dick Whittington & His Cat (AAC)/Ray Jolliffe, Ed Bayly, Gladys Carson, Fran Lee, Amy Day, Karen Kay, Jane Paterson, Tammy Isaacson, Carina van Leuken, Jan Moore, Barbara Simmons, Barb Day, Simon Cashmore, Nick Myshok, Terry Moore, Miles Godlonton, Brian Moore with Margaret Dean [piano] & Bruce Robin [drums]	Eric Low, Chip Seibert, Carol Godlonton, Jody Low, Karen Kay, Michael Day, F. Huszar, Greg Martin, Flora Erdos, Michael Henchcliffe, Mark Huxley, A. Azzara & the Jolliffe Academy of Dance (Dec 22/9; 24/1)
DEC 26-28/85 - *Yates*	The Queen of Hearts/(Centre Stage)/Muriel Jolliffe/Herb Matis [prod mgr & set designer]/David Hignell [lights]/Gladys Carson [costumes]/Mavis Matis [props]/Gloria Serkin [publicity]/Kate Johnstone [house mgr]/Val Cooke [art dir]/with Susan Sametz [piano], Ernie Block [drums]	Eric Low, Narda McCarroll, Bill Nelson, Jeff Carlson, Carol Godlonton, Mark Litchfield, Candy Williams, Iris Sedore, Brian Solberg, Rick Braund, Jolliffe Academy Dancers (Dec 11/C6; 20/B8; 27/A4) - *Centre Stage renews Christmas tradition; a real treat (John Farrington)*

Major University of Lethbridge Productions
Lethbridge, Alberta (1969–1988)

TIME/PLACE	DIRECTOR	PRODUCTION/CAST/REFERENCES
MAR 27-29/69 - *Yates*	Brian Tyson	School for Scandal - Morgan Gadd, Charles Schott, Caran Larson, Winstan Jones, Nora Needham, Ted Orchard, Tony Blake, Gerry Grimes, George Mann & others (Mar 26/17; 27/14; 28/14) - *deserves to be seen; fine theatre fare although not always true to the genre*
MAR 5-7/70 - *Yates (Alberta Regional Drama Festival)*	Brian Tyson	The Miser - Charles Schott, Charlie (Chip) Schott, Jr., Nora Needham, Gerry Grimes, Morgan Gadd, Marsha Grey, Dan Bratton, Caran Larson, Ted Orchard, Winstan Jones, Brent Sabey, Rick Schott, Les Forczek, Rich Skauge (Feb 27/7; Mar 6/11; 7/13) - *hilarity & bon vivante*
MAR 19-21/71 - *Yates*	Brian Tyson	A Man For All Seasons by Robert Bolt/Winstan Jones, Richard Finlay, Charles Schott, George Mann, Ted Orchard, Nora (Needham) Rose, Robert Tarleck, Dan Bratton, Gerry Grimes, Awny Cassis (Mar 15/10; 19/16; 20/18) - *falls well short of its aspirations*
DEC 5,6,8,9/72 - *U of L Dramatic Th.*	U of L Drama 2000 students/David Spinks with student directors: Eric Low, Kirk Jensen, Randy Mercer, Wes Miller	1. Riders to the Sea by Synge/Patricia Parks, Brian Atkinson, Janet Patterson, Sylvia Chik 2. The Glass Menagerie by Williams/Sandi Balcovske, David Mann, Patti Robison, Eric Low, Kirk Jensen 3. In the Shadow of the Glen by Synge/Janice Nelson, Tom Snee, Daryll Nelson, Randy Mercer 4. No Exit by J.P. Sartre/Alan Matisz, Mike Wright, Lea Pohjakos, Marilyn Selk (Dec 9/14) - *learn their lesson well & take their tasks seriously*
NOV 1-3/74 - *U of L; PLib*	Richard Epp	Reader's Theatre Everyman, Dawn McCaugherty, Eric Low, Laurin Mann, Shirley Boswell, Debbie Rakos, D. Mann, Bert Timmerman, Bill Wright, Bryan Francis, Kim Campbell, Doria Stark, Vance Bellerose, Ardith Oseen, Jim McDowell (Nov 1/18; 2/20) - *closely knit & moving rendition appealing to the cerebral*
NOV 29, DEC 1,6/74 - *U of L Drama Studio; PLib*	Richard Epp	Reader's Theatre A Christmas Carol/D. McCaugherty, K. Campbell, D. Mann, B. Timmerman, B. Francis, S. Buswell, L. Mann, D. Rakos, B. Wright, D. Stark, V. Bellerose, D. Bellerose, E. Low, A. Oseen, J. McDowell (Nov 22/11; Dec 6/13)
APR 3-5/75 - *Yates*	Terry Theodore	The Crucible (Mar 17/7) - *in cooperation with Playgoers of Lethbridge*
MAR /76 - *U of L Drama Studio*	Richard Epp	Don Juan by Moliere (translated by John Wood)/Jim Robinson, Sam Montoya, Albert Azzara, Liz Waterfield, Rhonda Ruston, Bill Wright, Carol Jolliffe, Pat Slemko, Phil Kuntz, Carol Virtue, Wynne Royer
NOV 29,30/76 - *PLib*	Richard Epp	Reader's Theatre, Right You Are If You Think You Are by L. Pirandello adapted by Richard Epp (Nov 28/L&TV Week/5)
MAR 10-12; 17-19/77 - *U of L New Th. Lab*	Richard Epp with Patty Trautman	J.B. (a play in verse) by Archibald Macleish/James Robinson, Philip Kuntz, Carol Virtue, Dawn King-Hunter, Janice Tilley, Janet Ing, Garfield Trautman, Chip Seibert & others
NOV 2-5; 9-12/77 - *U of L Th. Lab*	Richard Epp & Brian Parkinson	Equus by Peter Shaffer/Michael Melling, Michael Hoyt, Richard Epp, Linda Hurd, Rhonda Ruston, Garfield Trautman, Janet Ing, Albert Azzara, Deborah Grey, Sharon Hamilton, Rhonda Holmen, Denny Sumara, Liz Waterfield (Nov 1/6,14)
MAR 8-11; 15-18/78 - *U of L Th. Lab*	Brian Parkinson	Tartuffe by Moliere (English version translated by Richard Wilbur)/Patrick Hammond, Debbie Wells, Brenda Laycock, C. Virtue, Vladas Zajancauskas, Rhonda Holmer, A. Goodall, A. Azzara, Blake Richardson, Dave Jorgensen, Phillip Christou, Larry Erdos, Richard MacKenzie (Mar 9/7) - *a lark of an evening, staged with zest & spirited performances - thoroughly delightful (Joan Waterfield)*
APR 5-8/78 - *U of L Th. Lab*	Ches Skinner	Vanities by Jack Heifner/Cindy Gleb, Deb Grey, Sheryl Keith (Apr 4/10; 5/6)
NOV 1-4; 8-11/78 - *U of L Th. Lab*	Ches Skinner	The Shadow Box by Michael Cristofer/A. Azzara, Deb (Anderson) Waterfield, Larry Erdos, Deb Grey, Paul Doucette, Barbara Warren, Arlene Wagner, Brian Solberg (Nov 1/32; 2/6) - *ensnares audience; taut, sensitive direction*
MAR 14-17; 21-24/79 - *U of L Th. Lab*	Brian Parkinson	Twelfth Night/D. Waterfield, L. Keet, P. Hammond, A. Azzara, L. Erdos, Mark Russell, Amy Day, K. Bernstein, Denny Sumara (Mar 10/16; 15/16) - *commended for sense of pace and timing*

TIME/PLACE	DIRECTOR	PRODUCTION/CAST/REFERENCES	417
NOV 24/79 - *U of L Th. Lab*	David Spinks/Dean Blair, Carl Granzow [mus & art creations]/Neil Little [chor]	The Caucasian Chalk Circle by Bertold Brecht/L. Erdos, L. Keet, Deborah (Grey) Rae, K. Bernstein, L. Smolnicky, J. Melnyk, R. MacKenzie, M. Russell, Winstan Jones, A. Azzara & others (Nov 10/6; 20/15; 24/21) - *actors have covered themselves with glory (Arthur McDougall)*	
FEB 27-30/80 - *U of L Th. Lab*	Richard Epp	Les Canadiens by Rick Salutin & Ken Dryden/Larry Erdos, Don Flaig, Al Fritz, Tweela Houtekamer, Larry Keet, Randy Langhofer, Richard MacKenzie, Judith Melnyk, Scott Pierson, Les Smolnicky, Brian Solberg, Janice Tilley, Mike Warner, David Young, Vladas Zajancauskas (Feb 28/A10) - *magnificent*	
NOV 3-8/80 - *U of L Th. Lab*	Brian Parkinson/Aristedes Gazetas [designer]	The Birthday Party by Harold Pinter/Monty Hughes, Barbara Warren, Linda Sprinkle, Mark Russell, Winstan Jones, David Young (Nov 4/C9) - *brilliant third act saves day*	
MAR 18-21/81 - *U of L Performing Arts Th. (official opening)*	Richard Epp	The Cherry Orchard by Anton Chekhov/Joan Waterfield, Brian Tyson, George Mann, Winstan Jones, Deborah Rae, Dawn McCaugherty, Larry Keet, Lindzi Spackman, Don Flaig, Brenda Brinker, Brian Solberg, Pat Hammond, Eric Low, James Bell (Mar 19/B2) - *cast perfectly by director (Arthur McDougall)*	
MAR /81 - *U of L*	U of L Arts' Departments	1st Annual Festival of the Arts	
APR 7-11/81 - *U of L Experimental Th.*	Ches Skinner/Robert Hirano [set designer]	Cat on a Hot Tin Roof by T. Williams/K. Bernstein, Richard MacKenzie, Janice Tilley, Judith Melnyk, Charles Schott, Myron Deardon, Les Smolnicky, David Young, Lyle Jones, Trevor Smythe, Sophie Gazetas, Karen Smythe, Jenny Kaleta, David McCarthy (Mar 28/B3; Apr 1/C9, 8/B9) - *boasts some fine acting, but too soft an edge put on a hard play (Arthur McDougall)*	
NOV 4-7/81 - *U of L Th.*	R. Epp/John A. Johnston [set designer]	Rosencrantz & Guildenstern Are Dead by Tom Stoppard/Brian Solberg, Larry Erdos, Monty Hughes, Mike Warner, Kirk Easthope, Otto Rapp, Tim McCashim, Richard Hamilton, Eric Low, Delanie Kye Kela, Les Smolnicky, Arthur McDougall, Rebecca Dwyer, Jess R. Anderson, Winstan Jones, Kyby McFarlane (Nov 5/B2) - *witty worthy production (Peter Mueller)*	
DEC 15-19/81 - *U of L Th.*	David Spinks with Sara Stanley/ J. Johnston [set design]	Toad of Toad Hall by A.A. Milne/Brenda Brinker, W. Jones, Wade Scott Pierson, L. Jones, Bill Ross, Mark O'Reilly, H. Squires, Teresa Ham, Shirley Bertrand, Donna-Lee Ost, Andrea Black, Josina Davis, Anne Penton, Mike Warner, David Young, Sheri Thompson, Kathy Wiley, Kathleen Pawlowski, Cori-Jo Petrunik & others (Nov 26/B2; Dec 17/C5) - *beset with flaws (Peter Mueller)*	
FEB 9-13/82 - *U of L Experimental Th.*	Ches Skinner/Robert Hirano [set design]	The Madwoman of Chaillot/W.S. Pierson, William J. Ross, Allison Stott, L. Jones, H. Squire, M. Hughes, R. Epp, D.K. Kela, John Malcolm, Sandy Roberts, Michael Campbell, David Foster, Kirk Easthope, Ron Christensen, J. Melnyk, M. Warner, M. O'Riley, Willis Lowe, Jeff Oviatt, Ted Wilson, K. Bernstein, J.A. McCarthy, A. Penton, Glenda Cooke, L. Spackman & others (Feb 10/D8) - *second act saves production*	
MAR 30-APR 3/82 - *U of L Experimental Th.*	Sara Stanley/J.A. Johnston [set designer]	Waiting For the Parade by John Murrell/Carrie Gursendorf, H. Squires, Deb Waterfield, D. McCaugherty, Lorraine Dowell	
OCT 26-30/82 - *U of L Th.*	David Spinks with Sara Stanley/J.A. Johnston [set design]	A Midsummer Night's Dream by William Shakespeare/D. Falbo, L. Spackman, W.J. Ross, R. Dwyer, Robert Chomiak, L. Jones, J.A. McCarthy, Tim Nowlin, Pat Fry, K. Connolly, M. Hughes, W. S. Pierson, Kevin Notter, J. Malcolm, R. Chambers, Glen Prusky and others	
DEC 8-11/82 - *U of L Experimental Th.*	Ches Skinner/J.A. Johnston [set design]	The Gayden Chronicles by Michael Cook/Ron Chambers, Ron Skolrood, Robert Skoye, Michael Campbell, Judy Ann McCarthy (Dec 4/D4) - *lacks focus & intensity*	
FEB 15-19/83 - *U of L Th.*	Brian Parkinson/Charlotte Burke [set design]	A Flea in Her Ear by George Feydeau translated by John Mortimer/Max T. Wilson, J. Martin, Greg Jarvie, T. Nowlin, J.A. McCarthy, H. Squires, J. Robinson, R. Skolrood, L.E. Jones, Amanda Forbis, M. Hughes, D. Kye-Kela, W. Lowe, L. Elford, R. Chambers, B. Brinker, Sandi Nichol, Juanita Williams, Kevin Notter (Feb 5/A3; 16/D7) - *cast...believable, brilliant (Peter Mueller)*	
APR 6-7/83 - *U of L Experimental Th.*	Adv. Directing Project/Monty Hughes/J.A. Johnston [sets]/Lynne Hunter-Johnston [costumes]/Barry Hegland [lights]/H. Squires, Jennifer Parker, J.A. Johnston, William G. Tice, Janice Sauverwald, Mary Ann Passey, Siona Gunn-Graham, Randy Paskuski, Max Wilson, Carolyn Patton, A. Harper, K. Libbert, Jim Coates, D. Hignell, J. Low, Les Sanderson, J.A. McCarthy	The Birds by Aristophanes, translated by William Kerr/Luigi Esposito, Shelley Scott, A. Black, B. Brinker, A. Penton, W. Lowe, Kevin Notter, Kyle McFarlane, Christine Kurina, H. Erick, James Kendrick, Cordula Quint, Jo-Ann Zaborowski	

TIME/PLACE	DIRECTOR	PRODUCTION/CAST/REFERENCES	418
SUMMER /83 - *U of L Experimental Th.*	TheatreXtra (Summer Repertoire Co.)/1. Brian Parkinson; 2. Sara Stanley; 3. Ron Skolrood/J.A. Johnston [designer]/Janice Sauverwald, Cheryl Harrison, Chris Shaskin, William G. Tice, Cordula Quint, Ron Chambers, Christine Kurina, Audrey Harper, Terry Schwengler, Mark O'Riley, Andrea Black, Jennifer Pavka, Randy Paskuski, Bruce MacKay	1. <u>Table Manners</u> by Alan Aykbourne 2. <u>Jitters</u> by David French 3. <u>Poli-SciPie-In-The-Sky</u> (Revue created by the Company)	
OCT 10-15/83 - *U of L Experimental Th.*	Brian Parkinson/Terry Bennett [designer], Alan Friesen [costumes]	<u>Hedda Gabbler</u> adapted by Christopher Hampton/Audrey Harper, Shelley Scott, Robert C. Chomiak, Judy Ann McCarthy, Raine Dowell, Greg Jarvie, Maxwell T. Wilson	
NOV 22-26/83 - *U of L*	Richard Epp/T. Bennett [designer], Clinton Rothwell [chor], Lynne Hunter-Johnston [costumes]	<u>Antigone</u> adapted from the translation by R.C. Jebb/Erin Graham, Cathie Thys, Delani Kye Kela, Wade Scott Pierson, Terry Schwengler, Ron Christensen, Randy Kuryvial, Amanda Forbis, Barry Hegland, Brad Miskulin, with chorus and dancers (Nov 17/C9)	
FEB 6-11/84 - *U of L Experimental Th.*	Ches Skinner/Terry Bennett [designer]	<u>Buried Child</u> by Sam Shepard/Sara Stanley, Monty Hughes, David Gibson, Randy Paskuski, Ron Chambers, Sheila Hillis, Michael MacLean (Jan 26/A13)	
MAR 26-31/84 - *U of L*	David Spinks with George Evelyn [mus dir]	<u>Oh What a Lovely War</u> (Mar 15/B8) - *cast of 35*	
SUMMER/84 - *U of L*	TheatreXtra (Student Summer Stock) Heather Squires, Andrea Black, Willis Lowe, Ron Chambers, Raine Dowell, Shelley Scott, Lynne Richardson, Dave Gibson, Mark O'Reilly, Robert Chomiak	1. <u>The Imaginary Invalid</u> by Moliere directed by Sara Stanley 2. <u>Nurse Jane Goes to Hawaii</u> by Allan Stratton directed by Brian Parkinson 3. <u>Saying Something (But Not Too Much)</u> written, designed & directed by the cast (May 26/A3; Jun 12/A9; Jun 29/A13) - *good summer evening of drama*	
OCT 14-20/84 - *U of L Experimental Th.*	Sara Stanley/Terry Bennett [designer]	<u>Les Belles Soeurs</u> by Michael Tremblay/Brenda Brinker, Erin Graham, Shelley Scott, Maureen Herman, Colette Brown, Andrea Black, Cordula Quint, Cheryl Harrison & others (Oct 17/C12) - *entertainment value was high (Eric Low)*	
NOV 20-24/84 - *U of L Experimental Th.*	Brian Parkinson/John A. Johnston [designer], Leslie R. Robison [costumes]	<u>The School for Scandal</u> by R.B. Sheridan/Raine Dowell, Clark Wilson, Brenda Brinker, Karl Meintzer, Lyle Jones, Shawna Cunningham, Shelley Scott, Andrew J. Arcand, Wade S. Pierson, Robert Chomiak, Mike MacLean, Les Smolnicky, Don Philpott, Maxwell T. Wilson and others (Nov 17/A12)	
FEB 3-9/85 - *U of L Experimental Th.*	Ches Skinner/Terry A. Bennett [designer], Leslie R. Robison [costumes]	<u>Oedipus Rex</u> by Sophocles/Greg Jarvie, Maxwell T. Wilson, Ron Chambers, Michael MacLean, Kate Connolly, David Gibson, Willis Lowe, Astasia Lloyd-Campbell, Darilyn McCaffrey, Sean Low and chorus (Feb 2/A8, A10)	
MAR 25-30/85 - *U of L Th.*	Richard Epp/Robert Dick, J.A. Johnston, David Hignell [sets]	<u>Easter</u> by A. Strindberg/Eric Low, Michael McLean, Shawna Hogensen, Ingrid McCarroll, Maureen Lowe, Martin Williams (Mar 27/C7) - *performed remarkably well*	
SUMMER/85 - *U of L Th.* AUG 1/Cardston AUG 2/Waterton	TheatreXtra/U of L Students Summer Stock/Ches Skinner, Sara Stanley, J.A. Johnston/with Mark Falkenberg, Janice Sauverwald, Andrew Arcand, Delai Kye Kela, Tammy McClung, Michael MacLean, Neil Sheets, Maureen Niwa, Lynne Richardson, David Gibson, Ron Chambers, Shelley Scott & Kaaren Kotkas [company mgr] (funded by Federal government Summer Experience Employment Development [Seed] Grant)	1. <u>Love Among the Coulees</u> by the Company 2. <u>Seascape</u> by Edward Albee 3. <u>A Very Modest Orgy</u> by Patricia Joudry (Jun 12/C7; 27/A10; Jul 17/A3; 18/B4; Aug 3/A9) - *1. well worth seeing (John Farrington)* *2. Orgy is funniest production so far*	
JUN 24/85	**U of L Board of Governors approved BFA in drama with concentration in performance and/or design - 1st possible grads in 1986**		
OCT 2-5; 9-12/85 - *U of L Experimental Th.*	Richard Epp/J.A. Johnston [designer]	<u>Kristallnacht</u> by Richard Epp (world premiere)/Hal Weaver, Maureen Lowe, David Loney, Michael MacLean, Wade Scott Pierson, Richard Gibson (Oct 4/B9) - *everything it promised to be and a whole lot more (John Farrington)*	
NOV 11-16/85 - *U of L Th.*	Brian Parkinson/Terry Bennett [designer]	French farce, <u>Hotel Paradiso</u> by Georges Feydeau/Daniel Heaton, Candice Elzinga, Bob Arnett, Greg Jarvie, Shelley Scott, Marselle Jobs, Harold Braun, Kelly Roberts (Nov 5/B7; 13/B12) - *laughter plentiful... (John Farrington)*	
FEB 6-8; 12-15/86 - *U of L Experimental Th.*	Ches Skinner	<u>Crimes of the Heart</u> by Beth Henley/Marselle Jobs, Shelley Scott, Shauna Cunningham (Feb 7/B8) - *to miss [it] would be a crime (Carol Laycock)*	

TIME/PLACE	DIRECTOR	PRODUCTION/CAST/REFERENCES
MAR 10-15/86 - *U of L Th.*	Sara Stanley/Richard McRae [set design]	The Firebugs by Max Frisch and translated by Michael Bullock/Michael MacLean, Willis Lowe, Michael Campbell, Linda Sprinkle, Babbette Biedermann, Bob Arnett, Teresa Sawchuk, Michael Bellinger, Cathy Ann Glockner (Mar 10/A13)
JUN 18-AUG 6/86 - *U of L Experimental Th.*	TheatreXtra/Robert Chomiak, Sara Stanley, David Barnett	4th Summer Repertoire 1. Going Ape by Nick Hall 2. True West 3. Two Beers Without Asking by the Company (Jul 25/A9)
OCT 9-11; 15-18/86 - *U of L Experimental Th.*	Richard Epp	The Importance of Being Ernest by Oscar Wilde/Deborah Solberg, Narda McCarroll, Shawna Cunningham, Andrew Sheridan, David Loney, Andrew Arcand, Eric Low, David Connors, Daniel Lomas
NOV 18-22/86 - *U of L Th.*	Sara Stanley/Terry Bennett [designer], Leslie Robison [costume designs]	The Children's Hour by Lillian Hellman/Dena Haynes, S.J. Millar, Andrea Gerencser, Heather Jackson, Christine Ramotowski, Lorna Braun, Marie Anderson, Miriam McKenna, Teresa Sawchuk, Robin Yeast, Roger Hamm, Myrna Dembicki, Kirsten Patey, Gordon Barthel
FEB 5-7; 11-14/87 - *U of L Experimental Th.*	David Spinks	Pinocchio adapted by Brian Way/Denyse Harrison, Roman Pfob, Robin Yeast, Dena Haynes, Roger Hamm, Harold Barum, Gail Walker, Mark Nading (Feb 6/B6; 9/B7) - *wonderful*
MAR 10-14/87 - *U of L Th.*	Brian Parkinson	Who's Afraid of Virginia Woolf by Edward Albee Mark Russell, Judith Melnyk, Jeff Carlson, Narda McCarroll (Mar 12/B6) - *acting is first rate and the technical artistry is inventive (C. Laycock)*
MAR 25-28/87 - *Exp. Th.*	Richard Epp	Othello/David Loney, Robin Yeast, Robin Pfob, Roger Hamm (Mar 21/B6) - *1st production within the newly created BFA performance program*
SUMMER/87 - *Exp. Th.*	TheatreXtra assisted by John A. Johnston, David Hignell, George Evelyn, Randy Paskuski, Keith Dudly/with Michelle Adler, Rae Alexander, Marie Anderson, Florence Lott-Campbell, Loretta Coleman, David Connors, Barbara Darby, Tom Gillespie, David Lomas, Miriam McKenna, S.J. Millar, Lorri Porkka, Christina Ramotowski, Lynne Richardson, Neil Sheets, Brad Snowden, George Szilagyi, Robin Yeast	1. You're a Good Man, Charlie Brown by Clark Gesner (Based on the comic book characters of Charles M. Schultz) directed by Sara Stanley Sara Stanley 2. Sleuth by Anthony Shaffer directed by Eric Low 3. Night of the Naughty Nineties created and directed by Leslie Robison (May 15/B6; 30/B10; Jun 12/B6)
OCT 7-10; 14-17/87 - *Exp. Th.*	Terry Bennett	Mother Courage & Her Children/Bertolt Brecht/Tom Gillespie, Roger Hamm, David Connors, Vickie Gibson, Jaybo Russell, Michelle Adler, Deb (Waterfield) Solberg, Kate Connolly, Brian Solberg (Oct 2/C6; 8/A11) - *heavy stuff (C. Laycock)*
NOV 24-28/87 - *U of L Th.*	David Spinks/J.A. Johnston (set design)	Nativity adapted by David Spinks/Charles Schott, Jeff Reynold, Roger Hamm, Tom Gillespie, Mark Harding, Narda McCarroll, Marlin Howg, Beverley Bayer, Miriam McKenna, Kelly Roberts, Lyle Jones (Nov 21/B4; 25/B6) - *could be highlight of the year*
FEB 9-13/88 - *U of L Th.*	Ron Chambers (sessional instructor)/Roger Schultz (set design)	Rhinoceros by Eugene Ionesco/Wade Scott Pierson, Roger Hamm, David Loney, Roman Pfob, Narda McCarroll, Brian Solberg, David Connors, Marie Anderson, Brad Snowden, S.J. Millar, Robin Yeast (Feb 9/A11; 10B7) - *effectively asks probing questions*
MAR 4,5; 8-12/88 - *Exp. Th.*	Ches Skinner/Dave Gibson (set design)	The Marriage of Bette and Boo by Christopher Durang/Michelle Adler, Scott Moffatt, Marie Anderson, Carol Skelton, Kelly Roberts (Mar 1/B7; 7/B9) - *takes jab at society's values*
SUMMER/88 - *Exp. Th.* Jun 10-Jul 9; Jul 27-Aug 20	TheatreXtra/Sara Stanley, Eric Low/with David Connors, Robin Yeast, Christine Ramotowski, Marie Anderson, Michelle Adler, George Szilagyi, Brad Snowden, Terry Sherwood, Scott Moffatt CREW: Rae Alexander, Connie Bowes, James McDowell, Ken Lowenberg, Jake de Peuter, Roly Peter (s.m.)	1. The Mousetrap by Agatha Christie directed by Eric Low 2. What the Butler Saw by Joe Orton directed by Brian Parkinson assisted by Gerrard Morrison (Apr 29/C6; Jun 13/A11)

Touring College, University, & Drama School Troupes
Lethbridge (1946–1986)

DATE/HALL	COMPANY/DIRECTOR(S)/CAST	PRODUCTION/REFERENCES
JUN 14/46 - *LDS Auditorium*	U of A Provincial Players/Sydney Risk	One Act Plays: The Boor; Raising the Devil; To Meet the Chinooks (Jun 11/7) - *auspices of Lethbridge MIA*
JUL 7/47 - *LDS Auditorium*	U of A Provincial Players/Robert Orchard with Violet Ulasovetz, Edith Cardiff, Richmond Olson, Gordon Peacock, Jim Scott	Johnny Dunn; The Happiest Man on Earth; Peter Patelin (Jul 7/6; 8/7) - *well received by small but appreciative audience*
JUL 4/50 - *Civic Center*	U of A Provincial Players/Gordon W. Atkinson (of Pasadena Playhouse) with Joe Pitcher, Eric Harvey Grant Reddick, Ted Kemp, June Richards, Dick Davies	Three plays by Roberson Davies: Eros at Breakfast, Overlaid; The Voice of the People (Jul 3/2,7; 5/21) - *$0.50 - $0.75 - gave fine performance*
MAY 28/54 - *Civic Center*	U of A Puppet Troupe/Carl Hare	(May 28/10)
AUG 14/58 - *Capitol*	Banff School of Fine Arts [BSFA (Opera Division)]	The Barber of Seville (Aug 7/3, 15/9) ($1.00 - $2.00) - *acclaimed by packed house*
AUG 13/59 - *Capitol*	BSFA (Opera Division)/Andrew MacMillan	Madame Butterfly (Aug 13/10; 14/11) - *Sylvia Grant gives thrilling performance (Brander Parsons)*
AUG 11/60 - *Capitol*	BSFA (Opera Division)	Die Fliedermaus (Jul 30/12; Aug 10/3; 12/10) - *first rate show*
MAR 2/61 - *LDS Auditorium*	BYU Players (Logan, Utah)	Blithe Spirit (Mar 1/18)
AUG 10/61 - *Capitol*	BSFA (Opera Division)	La Traviata (Aug 5/12; 8/10; 11/9) - *enchants capacity audience*
JUN 9/62 - *LCI*	Mount Royal College Opera Workshop/Harold Ramsey	The Gondoliers by Gilbert & Sullivan (Jun 2/14; 9/14) - *special guest soloist: George Brown*
AUG 9/62 - *Capitol (AAC)*	BSFA (Opera Division)/James Craig [mus dir]; Ernesto Vinci [art dir]	Marriage of Figaro by Mozart (Aug 8/13; 10/9) - *Banff School triumphs*
JAN 9/63 - *LDS Auditorium*	Rick's College (Rexburg, Idaho)	The Miracle Worker (Jan 10/10) - *youngster steals the show*
AUG 8/63 - *Capitol (AAC)*	BSFA (Opera Division).E. Vinci [art dir]/James Craig [mus dir]	Tosca by Verdi (Aug 9/10) - *well received here; Marvene Cox outstanding*
AUG 13/64 - *Capitol (AAC)*	BSFA (Opera Division)	Falstaff by Verdi (Aug 8/14; 10/11; 12/18; 13/9; 14/11) - *full house enjoys this musical scream*
AUG 12/65 - *Capitol (AAC)*	BSFA (Opera Division)	L'Elisir D'Amore by Donezetti (Aug 9/10; 10/10; 11/14; 13/11) - *masterful, merry madcap performance*
AUG 4/66 - *Capitol*	BSFA (Opera Division)	Orpheus in the Underworld by Offenbach (Jul 25/10; Aug 1/9; 3/10; 5/10) - *a real howler*
AUG 11/66 - *Yates*	BSFA (Musical Theatre Division) John Stanzel/Gladys Forrester [chor]	Original musical, Come North, Come North by Bill Soly (Aug 12/12) - *near professional but more polish needed*
APR 5/67 - *Bethel Baptist Ch.*	The Royal Players (Bethel College, St. Paul, Minnesota)/Dale Rott	Drama, Sacrifice (Mar 29/18)
APR 5/67 - *McKillop United Ch.*	Student and Staff of United Church Lay Training Centre (Naramata, B.C.)	Musical Drama Life at the Centre (Apr 3/9)
FEB 23/68 - *Yates*	Alberta Colleges & Universities **1.** Olds Agricultural & Vocational College **2.** Medicine Hat College **3.** S.A.I.T. **4.** Red Deer Jr. College	Festival - Adjudicator, Donald Pimm (Edm) The Bore Hello Out There Why Am I a Bachelor The Lesson (Feb 24/14; 26/13) - *best production award to S.A.I.T.*
MAY 2/68 - *Yates*	U of Calgary Drama Dept/Victor Mitchell	The Recruiting Officer by George Farquhar (May 1/3; 2/11; 4/14) - *discouraged by slim crowd of 40*
JUL 30/69 - *Yates*	BSFA (Opera Division)	Così fan Tutte by Mozart (Jul 31/12) - *captivated large audience*
AUG 28/69 - *Yates*	Many Glaciers (Montana) Hotel Theatre Co. (summer staff)	The Three Penny Opera by Kurt Weill (Jul 25/13; 31/12; Aug 21/11)

DATE/HALL	COMPANY/DIRECTOR(S)/CAST	PRODUCTION/REFERENCES
SEPT 25/71 - *Yates*	University of Calgary/Department of Drama/with David R. Allen, Jan Nickleson, Brian Torpe, Hamish Thoms, Ken Rayner (Sp. by LAAC)	You Never Can Tell by G.B. Shaw (Sept 17/14; 23/14; 27/9) - *an enjoyable evening*
AUG 25/72 - *LDS Stake Centre*	Lamanite Generation (4 international students from BYU)	Variety Show - International dances, etc. (Aug 24/12)
SEPT 21/74 - *Yates*	University of Calgary, Polish Youth Club of Calgary	Balladyna by Juliusz Slowacki (Sept 2/20) - *presented in Polish with printed English synopsis*
OCT 15/78 - *LCC*	Montana State University Summer Language Camp for the Deaf	90 minutes of mime, sign language and music (Oct 6/18; 14/11) - *students organized drama group to entertain the deaf and educate the public*
NOV 13/79 - *Public Library*	Montana State University Language Camp for Deaf	Theatre of Silence (Nov 10/6; 14/10)
FEB 9/80 - *Immanuel Christian Sch.*	The King's Servants of King's College, Edmonton	A Man for All Seasons by Robert Bolt (Feb 9/A6)
OCT /80 - *St. Mary's Sch.*	Missoula Children's Theatre	Snow White and the Seven Dwarfs (Oct 7/80/B3)
NOV 9/80 - *LCC*	University of Montana (program for the deaf)	Mime theatre, Theatre of Silence (Nov 10/B1) - *popular*
FEB 5/82 - *Various schools in Lethbridge & District*	Missoula Children's Theatre (University of Montana) [This troupe made numerous successive tours to southern Alberta]	The Wizard of Oz (Feb 3/B2)

Index

McAlpine, Alan, 40, 44, 45, 82, 83, 113
McCallum, Neil, 156
McCallum, Sandy, 155-159, 164, 165, 167, 169, 175, 180
McAffer, Mrs. M.E., 175
McCann, Alan, 164
McCann, Peggy, 159, 162, 164
McCarroll, Narda, 221, 232, 257, 258
McCaugherty, Dawn, 219, 221, 224, 229, 249
McCaul, Charles, 7
McCreath, Jack, 157, 158, 161, 183, 185, 251
McCurdy, Brian, 213
McCurdy, Grace, 34, 68
MacDonald, Malcolm, 190,
MacDonald, Ron, 198
Macdonald, W.H., 12
Macdonnell, A.R., 3
McDougall, Arthur, 247
McDowell, Charlotte, 201
McFadden, Sheri (see Thomson)
McFarlane, Sandra, 257, 258, 259
McFarland, E.R., 126
McFarland, John I., 64
McFerrin, Robert, 191
MacInnes, Norma, 170, 191, 195, 259
MacIntosh, Ella, 47
MacIntyre, Jean, 183
MacKay, Fred, 243, 259, 261
MacKay, Marg, 243, 256, 259
McKenzie, Bruce, 147, 174
Mackenzie, Florence, 118
MacKenzie, Muffy McHugh, 127, 140
MacKenzie, W'm., 14, 15, 277
McKenzie, Helen, 123, 174
Mackie, Ian, 127, 140
McKendry, Marion, 199
McKillop, Mrs. K.G., 85
McKillop United Church, 168, 171
McKinnon, Catherine, 202
McLean, Gerald, 89, 90
MacLeod, Bruce, 200
MacLeod, Colonel James F., 11
MacLeod, Norris, T., 7, 10, 11, 14
McLaughlin, Murray, 267
MacLure, K.A., 115
McNabb, Tom, 16
McNair, Garry, 240
McNaughton, Charles, 52, 55
McNulty, Grace, 47
McPhee, Andrew & Co., 18, 47
McPhillip, A.E., 111
McRaye, Walt, 21, 22

Madge, Martin, 262, 263
Magee, Sharon, (Bolen), 153
Magrath Amateur Comedy Co., 18
Magrath, Charles A., 1, 7, 10, 11
Magrath-Cardston Marching Band, 267
Majestic Players, 87
Majestic Theatre, 26, 31, 33-37, 39, 44, 46, 47, 50, 54-56, 58, 60, 67, 68, 77, 87, 96, 103, 104, 108, 114, 128, 271, 282
Malabar Ltd., 47, 116, 270
Malacord, Mr., 16
Malick, Terence, 267
Malbert, Mrs. Jack, 140
Mallalieu, Peggy, 159, 163, 180, 185, 248
Malone, Edna, 38
Mandrake The Magician, 204
Manitoba Theatre Centre, 134
Mann, David, 216, 219, 221, 224, 247, 249, 264, 287
Mann, Debra, 221
Mann, George, 152, 153, 156, 180, 195, 214, 219, 224, 239, 240, 248, 257
Mann, Laurin, 219, 221, 224, 234, 240, 243, 247, 248, 249, 259, 287
Mann, Nelle, 185, 189, 248
Mannahan, Margaret, 128
Manning Ernest, 99
Mannington, Jean, 163
Mannington, David, 163
Manson, Brian Jr., 200
Manson, Daphne, 145, 146, 152, 200
Manz, Linda, 267
Maple Leafs, The, 37, 58, 90, 91, 94
Margaret Eaton Hall, 78
Margolin, Stuart, 267
Maridor-Goulding Co., 22
Marie, Eva, 153
Marks, Arlie Co., 89
Marks, Bob & Ernie, 50
Marks, Tom Co., 29, 30, 48, 50
Marquis Hotel, 63, 64, 113, 127
Marshall, Leona, 124, 125
Martens, Cornelius, 145-147, 167
Martin, Ben B., 281
Martin, Enid, 14
Martin, Greg, 216, 217
Martin, H. Milton, 109
Martin, Shirley, 40
Martin, Sidney, 109
Martin-Harvey, Sir John, 37, 57, 80, 89
Martin-Harvey, Muriel, 57
Marx Brothers, 60

Massey, Vincent, 65, 78, 111
Massey, Walter, 160
Mathes, Clara (Theatre Co.), 19
Matheson, Bill, 155, 164, 165, 169, 174, 180, 189, 195, 242, 248, 256
Matheson, Mrs., 85
Matheson, Muriel, 174
Matheson, Patricia, 249
Mathis, Willie, 190, 221, 252
Matis, Herb, 243, 244, 261, 262
Matkin, B. Wayne, 137-139, 140, 141, 146, 177, 190, 286
Matkin, Eleanor, 137, 138, 140, 142
Matthews, Cameron, 89
Matthews, Charles R., 44, 83, 85, 86, 117, 118, 141, 142, 150, 154, 155, 158, 175
Matthews, Mary, 198, 199
Max Bell Theatre, 207, 210
May, Dawson, 30, 39
Mayeska, Irena, 79
Maynard, Jack, 200
Medhurst, Jack, 79, 199
Medicine Hat Civic Theatre, 144, 179, 183
Medicine Hat Drama Club, 18
Medicine Hat Little Theatre, 111, 112, 157, 177, 180
Medicine Hat Opera Society, 47, 74
Medicine Hat Stroller's Dramatic Society, 71
Meeks, Neana, 258
Meier, Joseph, 201
Mells, Dick, 146, 169, 183, 184, 188-191, 194, 195, 215, 216, 218, 220, 221, 233, 240, 249, 250, 252, 260, 266
Mells, Ellyn (Ford), 241, 252
Mells, Lee, 146, 150, 169
Melling, Tom, 261
Mercer, Ray, 241, 257, 259
Mermaid Puppet Theatre, 265
Merrytime Clown Puppet Co., 265
Metropolitan Opera Co., 21
Mewburn, Dr. Frank H., 12, 16, 277
Mews, Peter, 202
Meyerhoff, Rosemarie, 200
Meyers, Betty, 162, 165, 166
Meyers, Ivan, 162, 165, 166, 180
Middleton, Tom, 114
Mikhail, Edward, 227
Mikuliak, David, 263, 288
Military, Shows, 58, 92, 102, 124-126
Millar, Lee, 50
Miller, Gilbert, 88
Miller, Irving C., 126
Mills, Ken, 250